Time Out

Madrid Guide

Penguin Books

PENGUIN BOOKS

Published by the Penguin Group
Penguin Books Ltd, 27 Wright's Lane, London W8 5TZ, England
Penguin Books USA Inc., 375 Hudson Street, New York, New York 10014, USA
Penguin Books Australia Ltd, Ringwood, Victoria, Australia
Penguin Books Canada Ltd, 10 Alcorn Avenue, Toronto, Ontario, Canada M4V 3B2
Penguin Books (NZ) Ltd, 182-190 Wairau Road, Auckland 10, New Zealand

Penguin Books Ltd, Registered Offices: Harmondsworth, Middlesex, England

First published 1995
10 9 8 7 6 5 4 3 2 1

Copyright © Time Out Group Ltd, 1995
All rights reserved

Colour reprographics by Argent, 32 Paul Street, London EC2A 4LB
Mono reprographics, printed and bound by William Clowes Ltd, Beccles, Suffolk NR34 9QE

Edited and designed by
Time Out Magazine Limited
Universal House
251 Tottenham Court Road
London W1P OAB
Tel: 0171 813 3000
Fax: 0171 813 6001

Editorial
Managing Editor
Peter Fiennes
Editor
Nick Rider
Consultant Editor
Nick Lyne
Researcher
Lola Delgado
Listings Assistant
Ethel Rimmer

Design
Art Director
Warren Beeby
Art Editor
John Oakey
Designers
Paul Tansley, Elroy Toney
Ad Make-up
Carrie Lambe
Picture Editor
Fiona Seres

Advertising
Group Advertisement Director
Lesley Gill
Sales Director
Mark Phillips
Advertisement Sales Coordinator (Madrid)
Christopher Seth

Administration
Publisher
Tony Elliott
Managing Director
Mike Hardwick
Financial Director
Kevin Ellis
Marketing Director
Gillian Auld
Production Manager
Mark Lamond

Features in this guide were written and researched by:
Introduction Nick Lyne. **Essential Information** Nick Rider. **Getting Around** Nick Rider.
Accommodation Anne Salmerón. **Madrid by Season** Sarah Podro; *How to be a Castizo* Nick
Rider. **Sightseeing** Anne Salmerón. **History** Nick Rider; *Dictatorship & Rebirth* Grant Bracey.
Madrid Today Nick Lyne; *New Madrileños* Sarah Podro. **Madrid by Area** Robert Latona; *Life's
a Lottery* Nick Lyne. **Restaurants** Vicky Hayward. **Tapas** Vicky Hayward. **Cafés & Bars**
Nick Lyne. **Nightlife** Howell Llewellyn. **Shopping** Harvey Holtom; *Rastro* Lawrence Crimmins.
Services Harvey McGavin. **Art Galleries** Dos Rios. **Museums** Anna Marie de la Fuente.
Media Harvey McGavin. **Bullfighting** Ciaran Giles. **Dance** Susan Crow. **Film** Anna Marie de
la Fuente. **Music: Classical & Opera** Stephen Mackey. **Music: Rock, Roots & Jazz**
Harvey McGavin. **Flamenco** Larry Lilue. **Sport & Fitness** Harvey Holtom. **Theatre** Paul
Freeman. **Business** Paul Isbell. **Children** Susan Crow. **Gay Madrid** Javier R Polanco.
Students Christine Monteleone. **Women's Madrid** Christine Monteleone. **Trips Out of Town**
Getting Started, El Escorial, Avila, Segovia, La Granja, Cuenca, Salamanca Robert Latona; *Alcalá
de Henares, Toledo, Aranjuez, Guadalajara, The AVE* Grant Bracey; *The Sierras, Sierra de
Guadarrama, Out & About* Nicholas Law, Maria Victoria Bocos; *Sierra de Gredos, Sepúlveda,
Sigüenza* Vicky Hayward. **Survival** Harvey Holtom. **Further Reading** Nick Rider.

The Editors would like to thank the following people and institutions for their help: Carlos
Cristóbal and Javier Aldecoa of the Consorcio de Transportes de Madrid; Luisa de la Cruz of the
Patronato Municipal de Turismo de Madrid; Pilar de la Cuerda; Sarah Guy; Tom Jago; Kei
Kikuchi; Natalia Marshall; Caroline Roux.

Maps on pages 277-279, 282 supplied by the Consorcio de Transportes de Madrid.

Photography by John Perugia except for: **Bridgeman A.L.** page 165
Courtesy of the Museo Nacional Centro de Arte Reina Sofía pages 166-7
Courtesy of the Museo Thyssen-Bornemisza pages 32, 168-9

Contents

About the Guide

This is the first edition of the *Time Out Madrid Guide*, one in a series of city guides that includes London, Amsterdam, Paris, New York, Berlin, Prague, and Rome. It gives you a complete picture of Madrid – flamenco bars in cellars, high-fashion shopping streets, backstreet *tabernas*, architectural eccentricities, all-night clubs and five-star restaurants as well as the city's fabulous art museums and well-known monuments. We've laboured to make it as useful as possible. Addresses, telephone numbers, transport details, opening times, admission prices and credit card details are all included in our listings.

Although it covers all the major sights and attractions, the *Madrid Guide* is much more than a book solely for tourists and casual visitors. It reflects both the city's past and its frenetic present. We point you towards hundreds of the city's more obscure and hidden-away shops, events and venues, and explain how much you should pay to see a football match and how, if you are staying for a while, you can arrange residency. We tell you both what to see and what to avoid. Written and researched by people who live in the city, this *Guide* offers an informed, insider's view: Madrid as the Madrileños know it.

CHECKED & CORRECT

All information was checked and correct at the time of writing. However, please bear in mind that, as in any city, things can change and places can close unpredictably. In addition, in Madrid small shops and neighbourhood bars in particular often keep to approximate rather than precise opening hours, and may decide to close earlier or later according to the level of trade. Similarly, the programmes of

arts festivals and similar events are often finalised very late, and their dates can fluctuate considerably from year to year. Before going anywhere out of your way it may be as well to phone first to check opening times, dates and other important details.

PRICES

The prices listed throughout this *Guide* should be used as guidelines. Fluctuating exchange rates and inflation can cause prices, in shops and restaurants especially, to change rapidly. If prices and services somewhere vary wildly from those we've quoted, ask if there's a good reason. If there's not, take your custom elsewhere and, then, please let us know. We try to give the best and most up-to-date advice, so we always want to hear if you've been overcharged or badly treated.

TELEPHONES

Telephone numbers in Spain are sometimes changed at relatively short notice for technical and other reasons. In Madrid, in particular, most numbers beginning with a *2* have been changed to begin with a *5*. If you have to call a number beginning in *2* and can't get through, try again substituting a *5* as the first digit. Other changes are less predictable.

CREDIT CARDS

The following abbreviations have been used for credit cards throughout this guide: **AmEx** – American Express; **DC** – Diners Club; **EC** – Eurocard; **JCB** – Japanese credit bank card; **MC** – Mastercard/Access; **TC** – travellers' cheques in any currency; **$TC**, **£TC** – travellers' cheques in US dollars or pounds sterling; **V** – Visa.

RIGHT TO REPLY

It should be stressed that the information we give is impartial. No organisation or enterprise has been included in this guide because its owner or manager has advertised in our publications. Impartiality is the reason our guides are so successful and well respected. We trust you will enjoy the *Time Out Madrid Guide* and that it helps you make the most of your stay. But if you disagree with any of our assessments, let us know; your comments on places you have visited are always welcome. You'll find a reader's reply card included with this book.

Introduction

For what was once no more than a scruffy market town in the middle of an arid plain, 350 kilometres from the nearest sea, Madrid has since the beginning of this century boasted the best fish and seafood in Europe. Sixty years ago, Laurie Lee noted the ice-packed wagons hurtling down from Galicia or up from the Mediterranean, brimful of squid, oysters and hake, while passenger and goods carriages sat waiting in sidings for hours at a time. And all this so that the capital's population could sip cold sherry and nibble on a prawn, the way civilised people do....

Madrid offers the whole of Spanish cuisine. The paella matches any in Valencia, while the *bacalao al pil-pil* rivals the best that San Sebastian can muster. Long unable to provide its own fruit and vegetables, Madrid demands and pays for the choicest on offer, wherever in the country it might come from and at whatever time of the year.

In the euphoria of newly-democratic Spain at the beginning of the eighties, when anything and everything seemed possible, Madrid was suddenly full of artists, actors, musicians, film-makers, writers and dancers, the much-lauded *Movida*. This outpouring of street-level creativity was encouraged by a city council policy of pro-viding heavy funding for popular arts, with festi-vals running back-to-back throughout the year. Madrileño-in-chief Pedro Almodóvar (originally from Ciudad Real in La Mancha) declared that one of his early movies, the 1982 *Labyrinth of Passions*, was based on the obvious fact that Madrid was now the centre of the world. The joke was all the greater because people were immediately set to thinking, well, why the hell shouldn't it be.

Madrid is an invention. A quimera, to be made of and into whatever you wish. The moment you try to define it, it contradicts you. Like Spain itself, a ragbag of distinct realities producing a whole greater than the sum of its parts, Madrid is at once Spain, while remaining something unique.

Very few of its residents can seriously call them-selves *Madrileño*. At best they are likely to be second generation, and with strong links to the *pueblo* or town somewhere else in Spain where many of the family still live. Yet the presence of migrants from all over Spain makes the capital what it is. In short, Madrid offers the best of Spain.

Andalusia may be the birthplace of flamenco, but no other city can match the capital for top class venues, and sooner or later, the best artists make their way here, often to stay. Equally, much of the new lease of life injected into flamenco over the last couple of years has come from musicians living in the capital. The country's premier bull-ring, too, is in Madrid, and any aspiring *torero* must make his debut in Las Ventas if he is to establish a name for himself.

Since then, the recession which had to come, drugs, and the restrictive policies of a conservative city administration have all taken their toll on this early, bouncy optimism. And yet, the vital bar, café and club society which emerged through the *Movida* is still with us, and Madrid today offers a greater variety of nightlife than any other European city.

Meanwhile, the city is changing. Prices have risen, accommodation is tight, and jobs tighter. Madrid seems unsure where it is going, perhaps just waiting for that next historic opportunity, that next imaginative generation. In the meantime, make the best of it, or better still, make it your own. *Nick Lyne*

Wish they were here?

Call home.

No matter how exciting the places you visit on your travels, chances are you're still going to miss relatives and friends back home. So dial some smiles with the AT&T access number below. An AT&T Operator (or simple English-language voice prompts) will help connect you to the States quickly and easily. Between over 75 other countries, too. With convenient billing either on your AT&T Card or U.S. Local Telephone Company calling card, or by calling collect.*

So don't miss a thing while you're here. Catch up back home with AT&T.

From Spain dial 900 99 00 11

Essential
Information

When to go and where to change money, how to queue and what to tip – the basics you'll need before taking your first steps.

Visas

Visas are not needed by European Union nationals, or by US, Canadian and New Zealand citizens for stays of up to three months. All non-EU citizens must have full passports. For British citizens a one-year Visitors Passport is sufficient at time of writing, but it will almost certainly no longer be accepted from autumn 1995. Citizens of Australia, South Africa and several other countries must have visas to enter Spain. They can be obtained from Spanish Consulates in other European countries as well as in the home country.

EU citizens intending to work, study or live permanently in Spain officially should register with the police within 15 days of arrival to obtain a Residence Card (*carta de residencia*). They must have a full passport to do so. Non-EU nationals who wish to work or study in Spain for more than three months should, again officially, have the relevant visa before entering the country. For more information on working in Spain and dealing with its bureaucracy *see chapter* **Survival**.

Customs

Under European Union rules EU residents do not have to declare goods imported into Spain for their personal use. Spanish Customs, however, unlike those of most other EU countries, still theoretically have set limits as to what they take this to mean. Random checks are also made for drugs. Some of the quantities accepted as being for personal use are:
• up to 800 cigarettes, 400 small cigars, 200 cigars or 1kg of loose tobacco
• 10 litres of spirits (over 22% alcohol), 90 litres of wine (under 22% alcohol) or 110 litres of beer.

For non-EU residents the following limits apply:
• 200 cigarettes or 100 small cigars or 50 cigars or 250 grams (8.82 ounces) of tobacco
• 1 litre of spirits (over 22% alcohol) or 2 litres of fortified wine (under 22% alcohol)
• 50 grams (1.76 ounces) of perfume

There are no restrictions on the import of cameras, watches or electrical goods, within reasonable limits. Visitors can also carry up to 1 million pesetas in cash.

Insurance

EU nationals are entitled to medical care through the Spanish state health service, provided they have an E111 form, which in Britain is available from Health Centres, Department of Social Security (DSS) offices and post offices. This will cover you for emergencies, but using an E111 will inevitably involve dealing with some of the complexities of Spanish health bureaucracy. For short-term visitors the simplest thing to do is to take out private travel insurance before departure, particularly as this will normally cover you for stolen or lost cash or valuables, as well as medical costs.

Non-EU citizens should take out private medical and travel insurance for all eventualities before arriving in Spain. For more information *see chapter* **Survival: Health**.

Money

The Spanish currency is the *peseta*, the usual abbreviation of which is ptas. There are coins for 1, 5, 10, 25, 50, 100, 200 and 500 pesetas. Confusingly, there are three different kinds of 1-peseta coin (one so small they inevitably get lost), two varieties of 5ptas, two of 25ptas, including the commemorative 1992 edition with a hole in the middle, and two each of 50 and 200ptas. A 5-peseta coin is called a *duro*, and people often talk about larger amounts as multiples of them, so that 25ptas is *cinco duros*, 100ptas is *veinte duros*, and so on. Notes begin with the green 1,000ptas, sporting a picture of Madrid's great nineteenth-century novelist Benito Pérez Galdós, and continue through 2,000 (red), 5,000 (purple) and 10,000ptas (blue).

Banks & Foreign Exchange

Banks and savings banks (*cajas de ahorros*) generally offer better exchange rates than private bureaux de change (*cambio*). Commission rates vary greatly, so it's worth shopping around before changing money. Banks and savings banks are normally open from 9am to 2pm, Monday to Friday. Between 1 October and 31 May many branches also open from 9am to 1pm on Saturdays. Some bank branches may also be open slightly earlier or later. All banks are closed on public holidays. Outside normal hours you can change money at the airport, at the main train stations (**Atocha**, 9am to 9pm, **Chamartín**, 8am to 10pm, daily), in **El Corte Inglés** (*see chapter* **Shopping**), in large hotels, and at private *cambio*, most of which are around the Gran Vía. The airport exchange desk and the Plaza Callao branch of **Chequepoint** are the only offices open 24 hours daily.

Banks and savings banks readily accept travellers' cheques, provided you have your passport with you, but are often less willing to take personal cheques with the Eurocheque guarantee card. It is always quicker and more trouble-free to change money at major bank offices rather than at local branches. Holders of major credit cards can also get money from the automatic cash machines at most banks (*see below*). At the Airport, Chamartín station and several banks in the Gran Vía and Puerta del Sol there are automatic cash exchange machines which accept notes in most major currencies, so long as they are in good condition.

If you need to have money sent over to you, the most convenient method is through American Express or Western Union.

American Express

Plaza de las Cortes 2 (572 03 03). Metro Banco de España/bus 9, 14, 27, 37, 45. **Open** 8.30am-4.30pm Mon-Fri.

The standard American Express services such as bureau de change, poste restante, card replacement and a travellers' cheque refund service are available here, as well as a cash machine usable with AmEx cards. Money can be transferred from American Express offices anywhere in the world within 24 hours. Charges must be paid by the sender.
Branch: Francisco Gervás 10 (572 03 03).

Caja de Madrid

Plaza de Celenque 2 (379 20 00). Metro Sol/bus all routes to Puerta del Sol. **Open** 8.15am-2.30pm Mon-Wed, Fri; 8.15am-2.30pm, 5-7.30pm, Thur.

The central office of the Madrid savings bank, a short distance from the Puerta del Sol along the Calle Tetuán, opens in the afternoon one day a week. The many other Cajamadrid offices in the city operate normal hours.

Chequepoint

Plaza de Callao 4 (532 29 22). Metro Callao/bus all routes to Plaza de Callao. **Open** *Oct-May* 9am-3am daily; *June-Sept* 24 hours daily.

An international money-exchange company.
Branches: Calle Preciados 7 (531 02 60); Puerta del Sol 8 (521 67 02); Gran Vía 56 (559 03 06). **Open** 9am-midnight daily.

Western Union Money Transfer

Change Express *Gran Vía 16 (523 45 31). Metro Gran Vía/bus all routes to Gran Vía.* **Open** 8am-midnight daily.

As well as a *cambio* office, Change Express is also the local agent for Western Union. This is the quickest, if not the cheapest, way to have money sent from abroad, which should arrive within an hour. Commission is paid by the sender on a sliding scale.
Branches: Gran Vía 48; Gran Vía 36; C/de Postas 7.

Credit Cards

Most shops, restaurants above budget level and hotels of more than two stars take major credit and charge cards. Note that Visa is more widely accepted in Spain than other international cards. You can also use the major cards to withdraw cash from bank automatic cash machines carrying the *Telebanco* logo (the majority), which provide instructions in different languages at the push of a button. However, they often run out of cash over weekends and holidays. Banks will advance cash against a credit card, although they prefer you to withdraw the money directly from a cashpoint.

If you lose a credit or charge card, phone one of the emergency numbers listed below. All lines have English-speaking staff and are open 24 hours daily.
American Express *(card emergencies 572 03 03/travellers' cheques freephone 900 99 44 26).*
Diner's Club *(547 40 00).*
MasterCard/Access/Carta Sí/Eurocard *(519 21 00).*
Visa *(519 21 00).*

Tourist Information

The office of the city tourist board, the *Patronato Municipal de Turismo*, and the four offices run by the regional authority, the *Comunidad de Madrid*, all provide similar basic information on sights, attractions and events in the city and the region, and free street maps (for more on maps, *see chapter* **Getting Around**). They do not have an accommodation service, but will advise on vacancies, and bookings can be made through the **Brújula** agency (*see chapter* **Accommodation**).

Two useful free publications available at all tourist

offices are the Patronato's *En Madrid*, a monthly
guide to events in Spanish and English, and the bi-
monthly *Enjoy Madrid*, in English. The best information on what's on at any time, though, will be
found in local listings magazines (*see chapter* **Media**).

Oficina Municipal de Turismo
*Plaza Mayor 3 (588 16 36). Metro Sol/bus 3, 18, 23, 31,
50.* **Open** 10am-8pm Mon-Fri; 10am-2pm Sat.

Oficinas de Información Turística de la Comunidad de Madrid
Main Office *Duque de Medinaceli 2 (429 49 51). Metro
Banco de España/bus 9, 14, 27, 37, 45.* **Open** 9am-7pm
Mon-Fri; 9am-1pm Sat.
Barajas Airport *International Arrivals Hall (305 86
56).* **Open** 8am-8pm Mon-Fri; 9am-1pm Sat.
Plaza de España *Torre Madrid, C/Princesa 1 (541 23
25). Metro Plaza de España/bus all routes to Plaza de
España.* **Open** 9am-7pm Mon-Fri; 9.30am-1.30pm Sat.
Chamartín Station *near Platform 14, Estación de
Chamartín (315 99 76). Metro Chamartín/bus 5, 47,
147.* **Open** 8am-8pm Mon-Fri; 9am-1pm Sat.

Phonelines

010
Open 8.30am-9.30pm Mon–Fri.
This city-run information line, primarily directed at local citizens, will answer inquiries of any and every kind on Madrid,
and particularly on cultural and other events promoted by the
city council. Calls are accepted in French and English, although
you may have to wait for an English-speaking operator. To call
the service from outside Madrid-city ring Madrid 366 66 05.

Help Line
(559 13 93). **Open** 7-11pm Mon-Fri.
This independent English-language phoneline mainly offers
a listening service, but can also provide a wide range of general information on different aspects of life in the city (*see
also chapter* **Survival: Helplines**).

Tourist Information Telephone
(901 300 600). **Open** 10am-8pm daily.
If you are thinking of travelling on from Madrid this free
phoneline will connect you directly with the tourist office in
the province you want to go to.

Public Holidays

On public holidays (*fiestas*) virtually all shops,
banks and offices, and a number of bars and restaurants, are closed. There is, though, a near-normal
public transport service, except on Christmas Day
and New Year's Day, and many museums are also
open, although for shorter-than-usual hours.

Madrileños now take slightly fewer days off
than in the past, but when a holiday falls on a
Tuesday or Thursday many people still take the
intervening day before or after the weekend off as
well. The resulting long weekend is called a *puente*
(bridge). Many offices and businesses are also
closed for the whole of Easter Week. For a calendar of the city's traditional and modern festivals,
see chapter **Madrid by Season**.

The city's usual official holidays are:
New Year's Day (Año Nuevo) 1 January; **Three
Kings (Reyes Magos)** 6 January; **Good Friday**
(Viernes Santo); **May (Labour) Day (Fiesta del
Trabajo)** 1 May; **Madrid Day (Día de la
Comunidad de Madrid)** 2 May; **San Isidro** 15 May;
Saint James (Santiago) 25 July; **Virgin of the
Paloma (Virgen de la Paloma)** 15 August;
Discovery of America (Día de la Hispanidad) 12
October; **All Saints' Day (Todos los Santos)** 1
November; **Virgin of the Almudena (Virgen de la
Almudena)** 9 November; **Constitution Day (Día de
la Constitución)** 6 December; **Immaculate
Conception (La Inmaculada)** 8 December;
Christmas (Navidad) 25 December.

Time & the Seasons

Spanish time is one hour ahead of British time,
except at the beginning and end of summer. Clocks
are changed earlier than in the UK, so that for a
while the two coincide. Hence, for most of the year,
when it's 6pm in Madrid, it's 5pm in London, and
midday in New York.

Madrid's dry, mountain climate has been melo-
dramatically described as 'six months of winter
(*invierno*) and three months of hell (*infierno*)',
which is a gross exaggeration. However, it does
tend to extremes and, as a result, the city's atmosphere changes greatly with the seasons.
Spring *Average temperatures 6.5-18.5°C (43.7-65.3°F).*
One of the most pleasant times of year, with moderate sun-
shine and clear skies, though there are occasional bursts of
rain. Pavement cafés begin to fill up the streets from around
Eastertime, and late spring and early summer is one of the
liveliest times to be in Madrid, with a wide range of open-air
events on offer. May is dominated by Madrid's biggest fiesta, San Isidro.
Summer *Average temperatures 15.5-30.5°C (59.9-86.9°F).*
June and early July are another time when Madrid is at its
best, but also its most crowded. From mid-July to mid-
August temperatures regularly get close to 40°C (104°F), and
activity steadily winds down. Traditionally, anyone who can
leaves the city for the whole of August. For the visitor, this
means it's less crowded, but many places are closed and it's
hard to do much in such heat. One thing that is worth doing
is getting up early (or seeing the night through), as the early
morning air is often so fresh you could drink it. In the last
few years more staggered holidays have become fashionable;
the August exodus has been noticeably smaller and more
places are staying open. After mid-August the peak of the
heat has passed and the atmosphere is much more pleasant.
Autumn *Average temperatures 7.5°-20.5°C (45.5-
68.9°F).*
The weather is lovely, particularly in September. The return
from the summer holidays is usually greeted by a burst of
new cultural programmes, and the start of the football season. When the summer finally finishes in October, there is
often heavy rain. Most cafés take in their pavement tables
by late October.
Winter *Average temperatures 0.5-10.5°C (32.9-50.9°F).*
January is the coldest month: temperatures can drop down
to freezing point and snow is not unknown, although the air
is usually more crisp than wet. This is one of the busiest
times culturally, and Madrileños still go out, but rather less
than at other times of year.

Street Crime

Street crime is no more of a problem in Madrid
than in other major cities, but naturally there are
parts of the city where you should be extra care-

ful. The area around the junction of the Gran Vía and the Calle Montera is one of the main centres of street prostitution, and can be heavy at night. You should, of course, avoid empty, unlit streets at night, particularly in the old city. On weekend nights in the main nightlife areas such as Huertas and the Calle Fernando VI, on the other hand, the sheer number of people in the street creates a sense of security that's often hard to find late-night in northern European cities.

Pickpocketing is more likely than mugging here. Places where you should be especially on your guard are the Puerta del Sol, the Plaza Santa Ana and its bars, and, above all, the Rastro. The usual rules apply: don't leave bags and coats where you can't see them, especially at pavement cafés; don't carry shoulder bags around at your back, and keep a hand on your bag; don't pull out large notes if you can help it (ask for smaller ones when you change money); and if someone hassles you for money or to buy something, just keep walking.

For details of what to do if you are a victim of crime or lose your passport, *see chapter* **Survival: Police & Security**.

Reference Points

Electricity

The standard current in Spain is now 220v, although a few old buildings still have 125v circuits, so it's advisable to check before using electrical equipment in hotels, particularly in older, cheaper places. Plugs are all of the two-round-pin type. The 220v current works fine with British-bought 240v products, with a plug adaptor. If you do not have a travel plug with you they are usually available at **El Corte Inglés** department store (*see chapter* **Shopping**). If you have US 110v appliances you will also need a current transformer.

Estancos (Tobacco Shops)

Although no longer as ubiquitous as a few years ago, the tobacco shop or *estanco* (identified by a brown-and-yellow sign with the word *Tabacos*) is still a very important Spanish institution. Their principal role is, naturally enough, to supply the needs of a nation of smokers for cigarettes and every other tobacco-related product, but they are also the main places to buy postage stamps, and sell multi-journey and season tickets for buses and the Metro, phonecards, and such things as sweets and postcards. The *estanco* is also the only place where you can obtain the official stamps (*polizas*) and money vouchers (*papel de estado*) which you will need if you have many dealings with Spanish bureaucracy.

Opening Times

Shop hours are flexible, but most shops open from 9.30-10am to 2pm, and 5-5.30 to 8-8.30pm, Monday to Saturday, although many may stay closed on Saturday afternoons. Food markets open earlier in the day, at 9pm. Major stores and shopping centres are open from 10am to 9pm, Monday to Saturday. After much controversy (over people's right to a day off, not religion), the big stores are now also allowed to open on two Sundays in each month except August, and every Sunday in the month before Christmas. This situation may change again in the future. Traditionally the only type of shop to open regularly on Sundays has been the *pastelerías* (cake shops). There are now also several modern, multipurpose shops that open late-night and on Sundays, such as the **Vips** chain (*see chapter* **Shopping**).

Madrileños famously eat, drink and go out later than their neighbours in virtually every other European country. Most restaurants are open from 1 to 4pm, and 9pm to midnight, and you will find it hard to get a full evening meal before 9pm. Many restaurants, particularly in the centre, are closed on Sundays. Many restaurants and shops also close for the whole of August

Queuing

Not many people in Madrid will wait in an orderly line for a bus, but in other situations Spaniards have a very highly developed queuing culture. Lining up resignedly if irritatedly at official counters has been one of the constants of local life since Madrileño bureaucracy was first invented. In busy small shops and at market stalls people may not necessarily be standing in line, but they generally have a very clear idea of when it is their turn. One common practice is to ask when you first arrive, to no one in particular, *¿Quién es el último/la última?* ('Who's last?'); see who nods back at you, and follow on after them. Remember to say *yo* ('me') to the next person who asks the same question.

Smoking

Despite some rather belated and half-hearted official health campaigns, the majority of adult Spaniards still smoke (a lot). Tobacco prices are much lower than in other European countries, and it's quite common for people to ask strangers for a cigarette as well as a light on the street. It's very unusual to find non-smoking areas in restaurants or bars, although smoking bans in cinemas, theatres and on main-line trains are generally respected. Smoking is also officially banned throughout the Metro, but many people take this to mean on the trains only, and not the station platforms. For more information on buying cigarettes and tobacco, *see chapter* **Shopping**.

Tipping

Rapid economic change has meant that tipping is now less generalised than it once was in Spain. There are no fixed rules, nor any expectation of a set 10% or more, and many Spaniards tip very little. It is still customary to leave around 5-10% for the waiter in a restaurant, though, and many people will also leave something in a bar, maybe part or all of the small change, according to the level of service. It's also usual to tip hotel porters, toilet attendants, in places that have them, and the ushers in the more traditional cinemas. In taxis, the usual tip is around 5%, but more is given for longer journeys, or if the driver has helped with luggage.

Water

Madrid's water no longer comes from the fast-flowing streams that earned the city its name, but nevertheless the local tap water is good and safe to drink, with none of the chlorine taste found in some Spanish cities. There are occasional water shortages in summer, and signs are posted in most hotels urging guests to avoid wasting water.

Essential Vocabulary

Like other Latin languages, Spanish has different familiar and polite forms of the second person (you). Many young people now use the familiar *tú* form most of the time. For foreigners, though, it's always advisable to use the more polite *usted* with people you do not know, and certainly with anyone over thirty. In the phrases listed here all verbs are given in the *usted* form.

See also chapters **Restaurants** *and* **Tapas** *for help in making your way through menus.*

Pronunciation Peculiarities

c, before an i or an e, and **z** are like **th** in **th**in
c in all other cases is as in **c**at
g, before an i or an e, and **j** are pronounced with a guttural h-sound that does not exist in English – like **ch** in Scottish lo**ch**, but much harder
g in all other cases is pronounced as in **g**et
h at the beginning of a word is normally silent
ll is pronounced almost like a **y**
ñ is like **ny** in ca**ny**on
A single **r** at the beginning of a word and **rr** elsewhere are heavily rolled

General Expressions

hello *hola*
hello (when answering the phone) *hola, diga*
good morning, good day *buenos días;* **good afternoon, good evening** *buenas tardes;* **good evening** (after dark), **good night** *buenas noches*
goodbye/see you later *adios/hasta luego*
please *por favor*
thank you (very much) *(muchas) gracias*
you're welcome *de nada*
Do you speak English? *¿habla inglés?*
I don't speak Spanish *no hablo español*
I don't understand *no entiendo*
speak more slowly, please *hable más despacio, por favor*
wait a moment *espere un momento*
Sir/Mr *señor (sr.);* **Madam/Mrs** *señora (sra);* **Miss** *señorita (srta.)*
excuse me/sorry *perdón*
excuse me please *oiga* (the standard way to attract someone's attention; literally 'hear me')
OK/fine/(or to a waiter) **that's enough** *vale*
how much is it? *¿cuánto es?*
where is... *¿dónde está...?*
why? *¿porqué?;* **when?** *¿cuándo?;* **who?** *¿quién?;* **what?** *¿qué?;* **where?** *¿dónde?;* **how?** *¿cómo?*
is/are there any... *¿hay...?*
very *muy;* **and** *y;* **or** *o;* **with** *con*
open *abierto;* **closed** *cerrado*
what time does it open/close? *¿a qué hora abre/cierra?*
I would like... *quiero...* (literally, 'I want...')
how many would you like? *¿cuántos quiere?*
good *bueno/a;* **bad** *malo/a;* **well/badly** *bien/mal;* **small** *pequeño/a;* **big** *gran, grande;* **expensive** *caro/a;* **cheap** *barato/a*
do you have any change? *¿tiene cambio?*
price *precio;* **free** *gratis;* **discount** *descuento*
toilet *los servicios*
bank *banco;* **post office** *correos*
stamp *sello;* **postcard** *postal*

Getting Around

airport *aeropuerto;* **railway station** *estación de ferrocarril/estación de RENFE* (Spanish railways);
Metro station *estación de Metro*
car *coche;* **bus** *autobus;* **train** *tren*
a ticket *un billete;* **bus stop** *parada de autobus;* **the next stop** *la próxima parada*
excuse me, do you know the way to...? *¿oiga, señor/señora/etc., sabe como llegar a...?*
left *izquierda;* **right** *derecha;* **here** *aquí;* **there** *allí*
straight on *recto;* **to the end of the street** *al final de la calle;* **as far as** *hasta;* **towards** *hacia*
near *cerca;* **far** *lejos*

Accommodation

do you have a double/single room for tonight/one week? *¿tiene una habitación doble/para una persona para esta noche/una semana?*
we have a reservation *tenemos reserva*
an inside/outside room *una habitación interior/exterior*
with/without bathroom *con/sin baño;* **shower** *ducha;* **double bed** *cama de matrimonio;* **with twin beds** *con dos camas*
breakfast included *desayuno incluido*
lift *ascensor;* **air-conditioning** *aire acondicionado*

Time

morning *la mañana;* **midday** *. mediodía;* **afternoon/evening** *la tarde;* **night** *la noche;* **late night** (roughly 1-6am) *la madrugada.*
yesterday *ayer;* **today** *hoy;* **tomorrow** *mañana;* **tomorrow morning** *mañana por la mañana.*
at what time...? *¿a qué hora...?*
in an hour *en una hora;* **it will take 2 hours (to get there)** *tardará dos horas (en llegar).*
at 2 *a las dos;* **at 8pm** *a las ocho de la tarde;* **at 1.30** *a la una y media;* **at 5.15** *a las cinco y cuarto;* **at 22.30** *a veintidos treinta.*

Numbers

0 *zero;* 1 *un, uno, una;* 2 *dos;* 3 *tres;* 4 *cuatro;* 5 *cinco;* 6 *seis;* 7 *siete;* 8 *ocho;* 9 *nueve;* 10 *diez;* 11 *once;* 12 *doce;* 13 *trece;* 14 *catorce;* 15 *quince;* 16 *dieciséis;* 17 *diecisiete;* 18 *dieciocho;* 19 *diecinueve;* 20 *veinte;* 21 *veintiuno;* 22 *veintidós;* 30 *treinta;* 40 *cuarenta;* 50 *cincuenta;* 60 *sesenta;* 70 *setenta;* 80 *ochenta;* 90 *noventa;* 100 *cien;* 1,000 *mil;* 1,000,000 *un millón.*

Days, Months & Seasons

Monday *lunes;* **Tuesday** *martes;* **Wednesday** *miércoles;* **Thursday** *jueves;* **Friday** *viernes;* **Saturday** *sábado;* **Sunday** *domingo.*
January *enero;* **February** *febrero;* **March** *marzo;* **April** *abril;* **May** *mayo;* **June** *junio;* **July** *julio;* **August** *agosto;* **September** *septiembre;* **October** *octubre;* **November** *noviembre;* **December** *diciembre.*
Spring *primavera;* **Summer** *verano;* **Autumn/Fall** *otoño;* **Winter** *invierno.*

Getting Around

Madrid is best explored on foot, but an excellent public transport system is on hand for when the heat is on and time is short.

Madrid is an easy city to explore on foot, so long as you have a map. Until the last century the city was confined to the area bounded by the Palacio Real, Glorieta de Bilbao, the Retiro park and Puerta de Toledo, and most of its main attractions are within comfortable walking distance of the main axes of the Puerta del Sol, Plaza Mayor, Plaza de Oriente, Gran Via and the Paseo del Prado. The best-known restaurant, nightlife and bar-hopping districts are within this area too. The Puerta del Sol is the undisputed centre of the city, the main hub of the bus and Metro systems, and the site of *kilometro cero*, the point from which all distances in Spain are officially measured. All street numbers in Madrid run outwards from the Puerta del Sol.

The Paseo del Prado, along the east side of the old city, continues into the Paseo de Recoletos and the Castellana, the great, endless avenue that stretches north into the more modern city and the new business areas. Madrid also has a considerable suburban sprawl, acquired above all in the last forty years. Drivers will become very familiar with the M-30, the motorway ring road that skirts the city centre in a loop to the south and along the River Manzanares.

For when you don't feel like walking, or need to get somewhere outside the centre, Madrid has a comprehensive and very efficient public transport system. The Metro (underground/subway) is the quickest means of travel, but there is also a good bus network, and taxis are easy to find and relatively cheap. Given Madrid's traffic and parking problems a car is more of a burden than an asset within the city, but is useful for trips to the sur-

rounding towns and countryside (*see chapter* **Trips Out of Town**). More handy for those prepared to face the traffic flow would be a hired bike or scooter. For information on bike and car hire and travel agencies, *see chapter* **Services**. For further information on driving, *see chapter* **Survival: Driving in Madrid**. For organised tours, walks and rides, *see chapter* **Sightseeing**.
Please note that all transport and taxi fares are subject to revision each year.

Arriving in Madrid

By Air

Barajas airport is 16km (10 miles) to the east of Madrid along the Barcelona motorway (A2). In the International Arrivals building there are 24-hour exchange facilities, a tourist information office (*see chapter* **Essential Information**) and a Railway reservations office. There are two ways to get from there into town: by bus or taxi. Phone numbers for some major airlines at Barajas and in Madrid are listed below.

Aeropuerto de Barajas
General Information (305 83 43). **Open** 24 hours daily.

Airport Bus
City Terminal *Plaza de Colón (431 61 92). Metro Colón/bus all routes to Plaza Colón.* **Open** 4.45am-2am daily.
The special airport bus runs between all the Barajas terminals and the Plaza Colón, on the Castellana in the centre of the city. There are six stops en route. At Colón the bus terminal is underground, beneath the main plaza, and connects with the Colón Metro station. Buses run in either direction about every 10-20 minutes between 4.45am and 1.30am, daily, and the journey should take between 45 minutes and one hour, depending on the traffic. A single ticket costs 325ptas. The buses are not accessible to wheelchair users. At the Plaza Colón terminal there is an office of the **Brújula** accommodation agency (*see chapter* **Accommodation**).

Taxis from the airport
A taxi to central Madrid from the airport should cost about 2,000ptas, including a 300ptas special airport supplement. There are also additional supplements at night, on Sundays and for each item of luggage placed in the car boot. Taxis are abundant at Barajas – in fact too much so. Some drivers specialise in hanging round the airport, and may try a variety of scams, such as taking you to your destination by the longest possible route. To avoid them, use only taxis from the official ranks signposted outside each terminal, and ignore drivers who approach you inside the building. Check that the meter is set at zero when you get in and that it begins the journey at the official minimum fare (160ptas). It's also

ALL MADRID'S LEISURE
WITHIN YOUR REACH

WITH MADRID'S *GUIA DEL OCIO* MAGAZINE

A weekly magazine sold each week in all of Madrid's kiosks, for a mere 100 pesetas. More than 120 pages with a complete leisure guide to all that's happening in Madrid. From the most classic of pastimes: museums, expositions giving the artists' names, performers and performances of classical music and ballet... To the most contemporary entertainment: film and theatre premiers, listing reservations numbers, tapa bars, pubs, discotheques, nightclubs. Not to mention the live pop, rock, heavy, and jazz concerts... And, of course, the bullfights! Besides any other sporting or touristic event to be held that week. With *Guía del Ocio* you will know everything that's going on in Madrid - morning, afternoon, and night - without missing out on anything. In order to choose all the leisure activities you desire most

LEISURE
ONLY LEISURE
ALL THE LEISURE
IN MADRID

a good idea, in order to avoid unwanted 'tours', to check the map first, and have in mind a recognisable landmark in the area to which you should be going. *See also below* **Taxis**.

Aer Lingus
Edificio España, Gran Via 88, planta 10 (541 41 16).
Metro Plaza de España/bus all routes to Plaza de España.
Open 9am-5pm Mon-Fri. **No credit cards.**

American Airlines
Pedro Teixeira 8, 5° (597 20 68/900 10 05 56). Metro Lima/bus 5, 14, 43, 120, 150. **Open** 9am-5.30pm Mon-Fri; 9am-3pm Sat. **Credit** AmEx, DC, EC, JCB, MC, TC, V. **Barajas** (305 83 48). **Open** 8.30am-12.30am daily.

British Airways
C/Serrano 60, 5a (431 75 75). Metro Serrano/bus 1, 9, 53, 74. **Open** 9am-5pm Mon-Fri. **Credit** AmEx, DC, EC, JCB, MC, TC, V.

Iberia
Aeropuerto de Barajas (587 47 47/Information 329 57 67/International reservations 329 43 53/Domestic reservations 411 10 11). **Open** 9.30am-2pm, 4-7pm, Mon-Fri. **Credit** AmEx, DC, EC, MC, TC, V.
Main sales office *C/Velázquez 130 (587 75 92). Metro Avda de América/bus 9, 12, 19, 51.* **Open** 9.30am-2pm, 4-7pm, Mon-Fri.

TWA
Plaza de Colón 2, 2a (310 30 94). Metro Colón/bus all routes to Plaza Colón. **Open** 9am-5.30pm Mon-Fri. **Credit** AmEx, DC, MC, $TC, V.
Barajas (305 42 90). **Open** 6.30am-4pm daily.

By Bus

All international and long-distance coach services to Madrid terminate at the **Estación Sur de Autobuses**, C/Canarias 17 (general information 468 42 00; individual companies have their own phone lines), a short way south of the central area and next to Palos de la Frontera Metro station, on line 3. Segovia, Toledo and some other destinations near Madrid are served by companies that have their own depots (for details, *see chapter* **Trips Out of Town: Getting Started**). Taxi fares from the bus station will include a 125ptas supplement.

By Train

All trains from France, Catalonia and northern Spain, and most of those from Portugal, arrive in Madrid at **Chamartín** station, on the north side of the city some distance from the centre. The high-speed AVE trains from Seville, express services from Lisbon and trains from southern and eastern Spain arrive at the lavishly-renovated station of **Atocha**, on the south side of the city centre and close to the Paseo del Prado. There are exchange facilities and accommodation agencies at both stations, and a tourist information office at Chamartín (*see chapter* **Essential Information**). Atocha is also the main hub of the extensive network of local (*Cercanías*) lines that Spanish national railways (RENFE) operates in the Madrid area, though local services also operate from Chamartín and the

small **Príncipe Pío/Estación del Norte** (*see below* **Local Trains**). For more information on all rail services *see chapter* **Trips Out of Town: Getting Started**.

Both Chamartín and Atocha are on the Metro. To get to the centre from Chamartín take line 8 to Plaza Castilla, then change onto line 1. Alternately, take the RENFE local line connecting Chamartín with Atocha, and get off at Recoletos station, which is also centrally placed, particularly for the Salamanca and Chueca/Malasaña areas. Atocha is three Metro stops from Puerta del Sol on line 1.

The taxi fare from Chamartín to the centre should be about 1,200ptas, in normal conditions. This includes the 125ptas station supplement. There are further supplements at night, on Sundays and for luggage. The same need for caution regarding taxi drivers at the airport (*see above*) applies here – drivers who tout for fares at the main rail stations are best avoided.

RENFE Information
(563 02 02/telephone reservations 562 33 33). **Open** *Information* 24 hours daily.

Estación de Chamartín
C/Agustín de Foxá (323 21 21). Metro Chamartín/bus 5.

Estación de Atocha
Glorieta del Emperador Carlos V (527 31 60/AVE 534 05 05). Metro Atocha Renfe/bus 6, 14, 19, 26, 32, 37, 45, 57, C.

Left Luggage

Luggage lockers are available at the following locations:

Barajas Airport
International Arrivals Terminal. **Open** 7am-midnight daily. **Rates** 400ptas first 24 hours; 500ptas per day thereafter.

Estación Sur de Autobuses
C/Canarias 17. Metro Palos de Frontera/bus 6, 19, 45. **Open** 6.35am-11.45pm Mon-Fri. **Rates** 80ptas per day.

Train Stations
Open *Chamartín* 7.30am-11.30pm daily; *Atocha* 6.30am-12.30am daily. **Rates** 300, 400 or 600ptas per 24-hour period, according to size of locker; maximum 15 days.

Maps

City centre and Metro maps are included at the back of this guide. Metro maps are available at all Metro stations: ask for *un plano del Metro*. The best free maps available are the ones produced by the *Consorcio de Transportes*, particularly the *Plano de los Transportes del Centro de Madrid*, from which the central-area map given in this guide is taken. This gives both a very clear street map and full information on buses and the Metro. It should be available at tourist offices, some Metro stations and the bus information and ticket booths at Sol, Callao and Cibeles, but they often run out.

If you wish to buy a map, the most detailed are those published by the *Almax* company, available from most bookshops (*see chapter* **Shopping**).

Public Transport

The Metro and city bus network are run by the *Empresa Municipal de Transportes* (EMT). Transport services throughout the Madrid region, including suburban and out-of-town buses and local RENFE trains are co-ordinated by the *Consorcio Regional de Transportes* (information 580 19 80).

For information on lost property offices, *see* chapter **Survival**.

Season Tickets

Anyone spending more than a week or so in Madrid might be interested in acquiring a monthly season ticket (*Abono Transportes*) instead of using the separate ticket systems detailed below. The *Abono* gives unlimited travel on the Metro, buses and local trains, within a specified area. A one-month ticket for zone A, which covers virtually the whole of Madrid-city, costs 3,750ptas, and there are substantial reductions for people under 21 or over 65. *Abonos* are sold at *estancos* (tobacconists) – to get one, you will need two passport-size photos, and will have to fill in a brief form. Note, though, that an *Abono* is always valid from the first to the end of a calendar month, regardless of when during the month you buy it. If your stay runs across two months it may not be particularly economical, unless you qualify for a discount.

Metro

The Madrid Metro is safe and clean, and the simplest way of getting around the city. There are ten lines, each of them identified by a number and a different colour on maps and station platforms. The network is still being extended, and during 1995 the stretch of line 6 between Laguna and Ciudad Universitaria is due to be completed, making the line a complete circle.

The Metro is open from 6am to 1.30am daily. Tickets are available at all stations from automatic machines and staffed ticket booths. A single ticket costs 125ptas, but a much better option is the 10-journey ticket, for 600ptas. To get one, ask for *un bono* or *un billete de diez*. You then insert the ticket into the machine at the gate through to the platform, which automatically cancels one unit for each trip, and will reject expired tickets. There is no checking or collection of tickets at station exits.

Trains run on each line every 3-5 minutes during the day, and about every 10 minutes after 11pm. The Metro gets very crowded during rush hours (7.30-9.30am, 1-2.30pm, 7.30-9pm), and can also be very hot in summer, despite air-conditioning in the trains. At the major station interchanges, such as Avenida de América, there are often very long tunnels between lines which are particularly stuffy. There is little crime on the Metro, although

as elsewhere you should be wary of pickpockets. The most common form of harassment is begging, but it's rarely very oppressive. Smoking is officially banned throughout the network, but you will still often see people lighting up on the platform.

Metro Information

C/Cavanilles 58 (552 59 09). Metro Conde de Casal/bus 10, 56, C. **Open** 8.30am-2.30pm Mon-Fri.

Buses

The EMT operates 150 local bus routes, running throughout the city. Stops are easy to find, and clearly marked with the numbers of the routes that stop there and the other stops on each route. Due to the many one-way systems buses do not necessarily follow the same route in both directions, so a bus map is often useful. All routes run from 6am to midnight daily, with buses about every 10-15 minutes on each route.

Outside these times special night buses operate. There are also extra routes to the University area, identified by letters, that only run in termtime, and there is a special service on Sundays and public holidays only to the Zoo in the Casa de Campo.

You board buses at the front, and get off through the doors at the middle or rear of the bus. The fare is the same for each journey, however far you travel. A single ticket, bought from the driver, costs 125ptas. Drivers do not usually have much change. More economical is the 10-journey ticket or *Bonobus*, for 600ptas. Each time you get on a bus you insert the *Bonobus* into a machine behind the driver, which clips off one unit. These tickets can be bought from tobacconists, newsstands and the EMT sales and information kiosks that are distributed around the city. There are EMT kiosks in the Puerta del Sol, the Plaza de Cibeles, the Plaza de Callao and many other locations. They are all open from 7.30am to 7.30pm, Monday to Friday, and those in the main squares are also open on Saturdays.

Most buses are air-conditioned, and are quite comfortable when not too crowded. They are useful for getting to places a little away from the city centre, but within the old centre they can often be delayed by traffic.

EMT Information

Phoneline *(401 99 00).* **Open** 24 hours daily.
Offices *C/Alcántara 24-26 (401 31 00). Metro Lista/bus 1, 74.* **Open** 8am-2pm Mon-Fri.

Useful routes

2 From the Avda Reina Victoria, in the Moncloa/University area, to the Plaza de España, then along the Gran Via to the Plaza de Cibeles and past the Retiro park to Plaza Manuel Becerra.
3 From Puerta de Toledo up the Gran Via de San Francisco and the Calle Mayor to the Puerta del Sol, then up C/Hortaleza and C/Santa Engracia to Cuatro Caminos and Plaza San Amaro, near the Estadio Bernabéu.

5 From the Puerta del Sol via the Plaza de Cibeles, Plaza de Colón and the Castellana to Chamartín station.
14 From Avda del Mediterráneo along Paseo Reina Cristina to Atocha station, then along the Paseo del Prado, Recoletos and the Castellana to Chamartín station.
C The 'Circular' route runs in a wide circuit around the city centre, passing Atocha, Embajadores, Campo del Moro, Plaza de España, Moncloa, Cuatro Caminos, Plaza Manuel Becerra and the Retiro.

Night Buses

Between midnight and 6am there are 20 routes in operation nightly numbered N1 to N20 and called *Búho* ('owl') buses. All routes begin from the Plaza de Cibeles and run out from there to the suburbs, and are numbered in a clockwise sequence; thus, N1 runs north to Manoteras, N2 a little further east to Hortaleza, and so on. The N18 runs along the Gran Via to Moncloa and Tetuán; the N20 runs along the length of the Castellana to Fuencarral. Night buses run every half hour between midnight and 3am, and every hour after that. Tickets and fares are the same as for daytime services.

Local Trains

The *Cercanías* or local network of Spanish national railways (RENFE) for the Madrid area consists of eight lines, radiating out from Atocha. Several stations have connections with Metro lines. They are most useful for trips to the outer suburbs, or to the Guadarrama and towns around Madrid such as El Escorial or Alcalá de Henares. Particularly convenient is the RENFE line (on lines C-1, C-7 and C-8) between Chamartín and Atocha which provides a more direct connection between the main rail stations than the Metro.

Cercanías lines run between 5-6am and midnight-1am daily. Fares vary according to distance and whether you have a return, but the lines are included in the monthly season ticket (*see above*). Leaflets showing the full *Cercanías* network are available at any RENFE station. For more information on all rail services, *see chapter* **Trips Out of Town: Getting Started**.

Taxis

Madrid taxis are white, with a diagonal red stripe on the front doors. The city has over 15,000 taxis, so they are rarely ever hard to find, except perhaps late at night when it's raining heavily. They're also relatively cheap.

When a taxi is free a green light will be showing on the roof, and there will be a sign saying *Libre* ('Free') behind the windscreen. If there is also a sign showing the name of a Madrid district in red this means that the driver is on his way home, and is not obliged to take you to anywhere that isn't near that route. There are taxi ranks, indicated by a blue sign with a white T, at several places in the central area. However, taxi drivers who spend all their time waiting for fares at ranks in the city have a bad reputation for scams, and those in the know prefer to flag a cab down in the street (*see above* **Arriving in Madrid**).

Fares

The official fare rates and supplements are shown inside each cab, on the right hand sunvisor and/or the rear windows. Currently the minimum fare is 160ptas, and that is what the meter should show when you first set off. The fare will then increase at a rate of 75ptas per kilometre, or on a time rate if you are travelling at under 21kph. These basic rates on the meter are the same at all times, but extra supplements are added between 11pm and 6am and on Sundays and public holidays (150ptas), for trips to and from the bus and train stations (125ptas), to and from the trade fair complex (150ptas), to and from the airport (300ptas), and for each item of luggage (50ptas). Also, the basic fare will increase for journeys outside the city limits, except to the airport.

Receipts & Complaints

Taxi drivers will provide receipts on request. Ask for *un recibo, por favor*. If you think you have been overcharged or have any other complaint you should insist that the receipt is made out in full, with the time, beginning and end of the journey, a breakdown of the fare and the driver's signature. Make a note too of the taxi number, shown inside and on the rear doors of the cab. Take or send the receipt, keeping a copy yourself, with a complaints form to the City Hall at the address shown below. A copy of the complaints form is included in the Taxi Information leaflet, available from Tourist Offices.
Taxi complaints *Area de Circulación y Transportes, Ayuntamiento de Madrid, Plaza de la Villa 4, 28005 Madrid (447 07 15).*

Phone Cabs

You can call for a cab from any of the following companies. The operators will not usually speak much English, but as a direction to the driver try giving the name of the street and of a bar or restaurant where you want to wait, or position yourself near a street corner and say, for example, *Sagasta, esquina Larra* ('Sagasta, corner [of] Larra'). You'll also be asked your name. Radio cabs will start the meter from the point when the call is answered.
Radio Taxi *(447 51 80).* **No credit cards**.
Radio Taxi Independiente *(405 12 13).* **No credit cards**.
Radioteléfono Taxi *(547 82 00/547 85 00/547 86 00).* **Credit** AmEx, V.
Tele-Taxi *(445 90 08).* **Credit** V.

Disabled Travellers

There are only limited transport facilities for the disabled (*minusvalidos*) in Madrid. The Metro stations have a lot of steps and no lifts, but there are seats reserved for people with mobility problems, slightly lower than the other seats, behind the driver on all buses.

There are some fully-accessible buses, with low entry points, ramps, no steps on board and points for wheelchairs, which alternate with standard buses on some routes, currently **3**, **10** and the **C** route (*see above* **Buses**). Special taxis adapted for wheelchairs can also be called through **Radioteléfono Taxi** on 547 82 00/547 85 00/547 86 00. Since this is also a general phone cab service when calling you must make clear you want a *Eurotaxi* to get an adapted model. There are currently only 15 such taxis in Madrid, and the waiting time could be up to half an hour. Fares are the same as for standard cabs. *See also chapter* **Survival**.

Accommodation

Five-star serenity, rococo kitsch or shared bathrooms: the best beds for weary heads.

Madrid is not a city overflowing with quaint hotels and charming rooms, and time spent trying to track down something cute and cosy down a little side street is likely to be wasted. There are, however, plenty of perfectly acceptable places to stay – so many, in fact, that only in exceptional circumstances can finding a bed become a problem.

Neither is it difficult to find accommodation near the city centre, the **Puerta del Sol**, or Madrid's artistic 'Golden Triangle', the great museums of the Prado, the Thyssen and the Reina Sofía. There is any number of hotels in all price ranges within a brief walk of all these points, but far fewer places to stay away from the heart of town, although there are quite a few mid-range, business hotels around the Castellana and in the Salamanca district.

Other factors are as important as location. Given the Madrid summer, when temperatures hover around the 40° mark, air-conditioning is pretty desirable (don't believe hotel staff who try to insist their rooms are naturally cool in July or August) and swimming pools are not to be sniffed at. And if you're driving, try to find a hotel with garage parking. This will be both safer and easier, as parking in central Madrid is severely restricted (*see chapter* **Survival: Driving in Madrid**).

Ritz vs Palace

Like Oxford and Cambridge, the Mets and the Yankees and Tom and Jerry, Madrid's most famous hotels, the **Ritz** and the **Palace**, have enjoyed a fierce rivalry ever since they first opened for business, earlier this century. While some might claim that it's nonsense to pit one against the other (after all, the Palace dwarfs the Ritz in its number of rooms by roughly 3 to 1), for many it's difficult not to mention both institutions in the same breath.

The fact that the two hotels are so closely situated, on opposite sides of the Castellana, only encourages comparisons. The Ritz sits on a square adjacent to the Prado and a moment's walk from the Retiro; the Palace is across the street from the Cortes (Parliament building) and the Thyssen museum, and just down the hill from the Puerta del Sol.

If you had to choose one over the other, there are a few other matters to consider, too. The Madrid Ritz, placed by several polls among the ten best hotels in the world, has just 156 rooms, all superbly renovated over the last ten years in the hotel's original *belle-époque* style. Every guest finds a basket of fruit, fresh flowers and chocolates to welcome them, and the garden terrace, a fashionable Madrid meeting-point, is truly lovely.

The Palace, by contrast, is something of a frumpy monster. Its 475 bedrooms are currently being refurbished, only nine years after the previous attempt, and for the time being worn carpets and dull furnishings remain. Not that this matters so much. The Palace, with an enormous entrance floor centred on a stunning lobby, has public areas that really are outstandingly grand.

Indeed, the Palace has not lost its spark, and spark is what it's all about. It has a reputation around town as a spot for kicking up your heels, and shamelessly went down a star (from five to four) in 1993 to curry up more business. The crowd that gathers there isn't remotely subdued about its desire to hobnob, and the hotel is proud of its popularity with rock stars and big Hollywood names.

The more intimate Ritz, on the other hand, built with royal patronage, continues to lure a more formal and polished clientèle to its plush lounges, although this is beginning to change. The tour groups and celebs that it once shunned are now appearing on the register.

As for service, both places do whatever they can to treat guests with the utmost courtesy and satisfy their every whim. You might not like the prices, but you can't help loving these grand hotels (for details of both, *see* **reviews**).

STARS & PRICES

Hotel prices in Madrid are generally a little lower than the European norm. All prices include IVA (Value-Added Tax) at 6%, except for five-star hotels, where the rate is 15%. Apart from this, the local star ratings (from one to five) are not the best guide to a hotel's facilities, particularly at the top end of the range. Indeed, several luxury hotels, including the very swish **Hotel Palace** (*see below* **Grand Luxury**), actually contrived to drop a star during 1993 in order to qualify for the lower-rate IVA, so they could lower their prices and increase turnover. At the other end of the scale, the distinction between hotels, *hostales* and *pensiones* is now quite blurred, although in general anywhere called a *hostal* or a *pensión* may not have bathrooms in every room and will have only very limited facilities in terms of bars, lounges and so on.

At certain times in the year many hotels reduce their prices. De luxe hotels which are geared towards business clients frequently offer discounts at weekends, Christmas, during Easter Week and in August. As such, they can sometimes provide a better deal all-in-all than more moderate establishments.

The hotels and *hostales* listed here, apart from **Apartment Hotels** and **Youth Hostels**, are divided roughly according to the basic price of a double room at standard rates. 'Grand Luxury' means over 28,000ptas per night; 'Expensive' over 18,000ptas; 'Moderate' over 6,000ptas; and 'Budget', 6,000ptas and below. All prices quoted are per room, not per person, and do not include breakfast. Most hotels will offer coffee and a roll as breakfast, but it's rarely included in the price of the room and is often unreasonably expensive. Unless you insist on breakfast in bed, it's a better bet to go to a local bar, where breakfast will be better and cheaper.

If you arrive in Madrid without a room and don't feel like looking around yourself, the **Brújula** agency will make bookings for you for a small fee. If you are staying in Madrid for some time, and need information on flats and renting a room longer-term, *see chapters* **Students** and **Survival**.

Brújula

C/Princesa 1, 6° (559 97 05). Metro Plaza de España/bus all routes to Plaza de España. **Open** *Apr-Sept* 9am-7pm Mon-Fri; 9am-1pm Sat. *Oct-Mar* 9am-2pm, 4-7pm, Mon-Fri; 9am-2pm Sat.

This private accommodation agency (the name means 'Compass') will book rooms in hotels of all categories in Madrid and the surrounding region, and provide a map and directions on how to get there, for a fee of under 300ptas. You can phone the head office, but it's often difficult to get through and easier to go in person to one of the branches. The main office is in the same building as the Plaza de España tourist office, six floors up.

Branches: **Airport Bus terminal** Plaza de Colón (575 96 80). **Open** 8am-10pm daily.

Opposite: *the very plush* **Hotel Ritz***. See page 18.*

Hotel Palace. See page 18.

Atocha station (539 11 73). **Open** 8am-midnight daily.
Chamartín station (315 78 94). **Open** 7.30am-11pm daily.

Grand Luxury

Hotel Castellana Inter-Continental

Paseo de la Castellana 49, 28046 (310 02 00/fax 319 58 53/telex 27686). Metro Rubén Darío/bus all routes to Castellana. **Rates** *single* from 23,800ptas; *double* from 29,700ptas. **Credit** AmEx, DC, EC, JCB, MC, TC, V.

Walk into this four-star hotel and the staff may actually smile. With an attractive flower-decked lobby, the 308-room hotel is right on the Castellana near the Glorieta de Castelar. Its best rooms are modern, with bright colours and furnishings, and balconies overlooking the garden. Others, however, are in need of some work, and the rooms facing the main road are noisy despite double-glazed windows. Also on offer is a hip roof-top gym with roof terrace, and the private garden is a wonderfully peaceful spot for an afternoon drink.
Hotel services *Air-conditioning. Bar. Babysitting. Boutiques. Car park. Conference facilities. Currency exchange. Fax. Garden. Gym with sauna, massage. Hairdressers & beauty salon. Interpreting service for conferences. Laundry. Lifts. Multi-lingual staff. Non-smoking floor. Restaurant. Wheelchair access.* **Room services** *Hairdryer. Minibar. Room service (24-hours). Rooms adapted for the disabled. Safe (in most rooms). Telephone. TV (satellite).*

Hotel Palace

Plaza de las Cortes 7, 28014 (429 13 02/fax 420 00 56/telex 22272). Metro Banco de España/bus 9, 14, 27, 37, 45. **Rates** *single* from 25,000ptas; *double* from 32,000ptas. **Credit** AmEx, DC, EC, JCB, MC, TC, V.

This colossal hotel opened in 1913. Renovation work is overdue in some rooms, but the lobby and lounge areas have maintained an air of sumptuousness, and this and its bubbling, moving-and-shaking atmosphere are undoubtedly why the crowds keep coming back. *See box* **Ritz vs Palace**.
Hotel services *Air-conditioning. Bar. Car park.*

Conference facilities. Currency exchange. Fax. Hairdressers & beauty salon. Interpreting service on request. Laundry. Lifts. Multi-lingual staff. Non-smoking rooms. Restaurant. Wheelchair access. **Room services** Minibar. Radio. Room service (24-hours). Rooms adapted for the disabled. Safe. Telephone. TV (satellite). VCR on request.

Hotel Ritz
Plaza de la Lealtad 5, 28014 (521 28 57/fax 523 87 76/telex 43986 RITZ-E). Metro Banco de España/bus 9, 14, 27, 37, 45. **Rates** single from 42,000ptas; double from 49,500ptas. **Credit** AmEx, DC, JCB, MC, TC, V.
Madrid's most élite hotel was built in 1910 thanks to a personal intervention by King Alfonso XIII, who had been embarassed during his wedding in 1906 because his official guests had not been able to find any hotel in the city of the standard they expected. The hotel is still gorgeous, right down to the hand-made carpets and fine linen sheets; the service is matchless; and the restaurant, serving Spanish and French cuisine, is also superb. See box **Ritz vs Palace**. **Hotel services** Air-conditioning. Bar. Car park. Conference facilities. Currency exchange. Fax. Garden. Hairdressers & beauty salon. Laundry. Lifts. Multi-lingual staff. Non-smoking rooms. Restaurant. Safe in reception. **Room services** Fax on request. Hairdryer. Minibar. Radio. Room service (24 hours). Telephone. TV (satellite). VCR on request.

Hotel Santo Mauro
C/Zurbano 36, 28010 (319 69 00/fax 308 54 77). Metro Rubén Darío/bus 7, 40, 147. **Rates** single from 27,000ptas; double from 52,000ptas. **Credit** AmEx, DC, EC, MC, TC, V.
Built in the late nineteenth century as an aristocratic palace, this recently renovated hotel has just 36 rooms, all of them different. While the lounges, restaurant and bar have retained their original flavour, with high ceilings and marble fireplaces, the bedrooms have been slickly decorated in contemporary colours. The hotel sits in a quiet, tree-filled part of the city, with gracious gardens and an austere courtyard. Open just three years – previously it housed various embassies – it has already welcomed Catherine Denueve, Duran Duran, Don Johnson and other celebrities seeking luxury and privacy. The duplex rooms are fabulous. **Hotel services** Air-conditioning. Babysitting on request. Bar. Car park. Conference facilities. Currency exchange. Fax. Garden. Interpreting services. Laundry. Lifts. Restaurant. Swimming pool. Wheelchair access. **Room services** Hairdryer. Minibar. Radio. Room service (24-hours). Rooms adapted for the disabled. Safe. Telephone. TV (satellite).

Hotel Villa Magna
Paseo de la Castellana 22, 28046 (576 75 00 & 578 20 00/fax 575 95 04 & 575 31 58 /telex 22914 & 7738 VIMA-E). Metro Rubén Darío/bus all routes to Castellana. **Rates** single from 34,000ptas; double from 40,000ptas. **Credit** AmEx, DC, EC, JCB, MC,TC, V.
You get what you pay for, and here you pay for service: there isn't a single request you could dream up that the staff wouldn't rally round to fulfil. Business people and affluent tourists flock to this modern 182-room hotel, as well as the stars – U2, Jane Fonda, Naomi Campbell and Madonna have stayed here. The rooms are not remarkable, but they are comfortable. The glitzy main floor is reminiscent of seventies Miami Beach chic. It's conveniently located for the stylish Salamanca shopping area and, of course, the Castellana. **Hotel services** Access to nearby gym. Air-conditioning. Babysitting on request. Bar. Boutiques. Car park. Conference facilities. Currency exchange. Fax. Garden. Hairdressers & beauty salon. Interpreting services on request. Laundry. Lifts. Limousine service. Multi-lingual staff. Non-smoking floor. Restaurant. Wheelchair access. **Room services** Hairdryer. Minibar. Radio. Room service (24-hours). Rooms adapted for the disabled. Safe. Telephone. TV (satellite). VCR.

Hotel Villa Real
Plaza de las Cortes 10, 28014 (420 37 67/fax 420 25 47/telex 44600). Metro Sevilla, Banco de España/bus 9, 14, 27, 37, 45. **Rates** single from 24,800ptas; double from 31,000ptas. **Credit** AmEx, DC, EC, MC, TC, V.
When architects Fernando Chueca Goitia and José Ramos designed this intimate four-star hotel of 115 rooms at the end of 1989 they evidently set out to capture the feeling of its neighbouring competitors-to-be, the **Palace** and the **Ritz**. Though brand new it has a flavour of the past, with neo-classical embellishments in the lobby and doormen in top hats and tails. The rooms are less elegant, but still very comfortable. But what marks out the Villa Real is personal service, which has been enough to attract Julio Iglesias and other famous names. It's ideally situated for the main museums, the Puerta del Sol and Atocha railway station.
Hotel services Air-conditioning. Babysitting on request. Bar. Car park. Conference facilities. Currency exchange. Fax. Hairdressers & beauty salon. Laundry. Lifts. Multi-lingual staff. Non-smoking floor. Restaurant. Sauna/massage. **Room services** Hairdryer. Minibar. Radio. Room service (24-hours). Safe. Telephone. TV (satellite).

Hotel Wellington
C/Velázquez 8, 28001 (575 44 00/fax 576. 41 64/telex 22700). Metro Príncipe de Vergara/bus 1, 9, 19, 51, 74. **Rates** single from 19,520ptas; double from 30,500ptas. **Credit** AmEx, DC, EC, MC, TC, V.
Within spitting distance of the Retiro and a moment's walk from the chicest shopping area around the Calle Goya, this 298-room five-star hotel is absolutely swish. It's graced with a handsome entrance and a surprisingly intimate lobby, and a faithful clientele of British and American executives. During San Isidro in May many bullfighters stay here, as it's the best-situated luxury hotel in Madrid for the **Las Ventas** bullring (see chapter **Bullfighting**). The basement also houses one of the city's most prestigious flamenco dance venues, **Zambra** (see chapter **Dance**).
Hotel services Air-conditioning. Bars. Car park. Conference facilities. Currency exchange. Fax. Garden. Gym. Hairdressers & beauty salon. Interpreting services. Laundry. Lifts. Multi-lingual staff. Non-smoking floor. Swimming pool. Restaurants. Wheelchair access. **Room services** Hairdryer. Minibar. Radio. Room service (24-hours). Rooms adapted for the disabled. Safe. Telephone. TV (satellite).

Expensive

Gran Hotel Conde Duque
Plaza Conde del Valle Suchil 5, 28015 (447 70 00/fax 448 35 69). Metro San Bernardo/bus 21. **Rates** single from 15,250ptas; double from 22,850ptas. **Credit** AmEx, DC, EC, MC, TC, V.
The 143 rooms of this 40-year-old hotel were thoroughly gutted and tastefully redesigned in 1992. The lobby is adequate, but less attractive, and service is smooth. Tourists who are not too bothered about being close to the major museums will find the location refreshing, as the hotel is right on a small square on the fringes of Chamberí that's regularly full of local families with children and students socialising. **Hotel services** Air-conditioning. Bar. Car park. Conference facilities. Currency exchange. Fax. Laundry. Lifts. Multi-lingual staff. Wheelchair access. **Room services** Hairdryer. Minibar. Radio. Room service (24-hours). Rooms adapted for the disabled. Safe. Telephone. TV (satellite).

Gran Hotel Reina Victoria
Plaza Santa Ana 14, 28012 (531 45 00/fax 522 03 07). Metro Sol/bus all routes to Puerta del Sol. **Rates** single from 16,000ptas; double from 20,000ptas. **Credit** AmEx, DC, MC, TC. V.
Overlooking a square that's a magnet for foreigners, tapas-seekers and the local night-time crowd (see chapters **Madrid**

The **Hotel Zurbano**: off the tourist trail, but it's not always this soporific.

by **Area, Cafés & Bars** *and* **Nightlife**), this enormous hotel has a great history, having been a favourite put-up of bullfighters and their number-one fan Ernest Hemingway in bygone days. Today, though, it's nothing special, and seems to rely heavily on its reputation.

Hotel services *Air-conditioning. Bar. Car park. Conference facilities. Currency exchange. Fax. Laundry. Lifts. Wheelchair access.* **Room services** *Minibar. Radio. Room service (7am-11pm). Rooms adapted for the disabled. Safe. Telephone. TV (satellite).*

Hotel Cuzco

Paseo de la Castellana 133, 28046 (556 06 00/fax 556 03 72/telex 22464 CUZCO E). Metro Cuzco/bus all routes to Castellana. **Rates** *single* from 16,200ptas; *double* from 20,550ptas. **Credit** AmEx, DC, EC, MC, TC, V.

Sixties glitz might best describe this 330-room hotel complete with muzak-filled lobby. It's mostly used by business people, mainly Spanish, for obvious reasons – a government ministry is across the road, and it's minutes away from the **AZCA** financial centre and the **Palacio de Exposiciones** conference centre (*see chapter* **Business**). Non-business visitors would probably feel out of the way here.

Hotel services *Air-conditioning. Bar. Car park. Conference facilities. Currency exchange. Fax. Gym. Interpreting services. Laundry. Lifts. Multi-lingual staff. Restaurant. Wheelchair access.* **Room services** *Hairdryer. Minibar. Room service(24-hours). Rooms adapted for the disabled. Safe. Telephone. TV (satellite).*

Hotel Eurobuilding

C/Padre Damián 23, 28036 (345 45 00/fax 345 45 76/telex 22548 EUBIL-E). Metro Cuzco/bus 150. **Rates** *single* from 23,200ptas; *double* from 26,900ptas. **Credit** AmEx, DC, JCB, MC, TC, V.

The very name conjures up large, modern, glossy blankness, and this twin tower 500-room giant does not disappoint. It does, however, offer almost every service and facility imaginable, and as such is a haven for business people. The hotel

used to have five stars but, like the **Palace** (*see above* **Grand Luxury**), discarded one in order to lower its prices. Apartment-size suites are available for any length of time. The hotel also has a great pool which is open to non residents (*see chapter* **Sport & Fitness**). It's in a residential and business neighbourhood with few tourists in sight.

Hotel services *Air-conditioning. Bars. Boutiques. Car park. Conference facilities. Currency exchange. Fax. Garden. Gym. Hairdressers & beauty salon. Interpreting services. Laundry. Lifts. Multi-lingual staff. Non-smoking floor. Swimming pool. Wheelchair access.* **Room Services** *Hairdryer. Minibar. Radio. Room service (24-hours). Rooms adapted for the disabled. Safe. Telephone. TV (satellite). VCR.*

Hotel Los Galgos Sol

C/Claudio Coello 139, 28006 (562 66 00/fax 561 76 62). Metro Núñez de Balboa/bus 9, 19, 51, 61. **Rates** *single* from 18,000ptas; *double* from 22,500ptas. **Credit** AmEx, DC, EC, JCB, MC, TC, V.

Fountains, mirrors, plants... only the piped music is missing from the lobby of this 350-room hotel on the north side of Salamanca. The rooms are tamer, and the bathrooms have recently been renovated. It's owned by the Spanish hotel chain, Sol, and service is professional. Although it's outside the main sightseeing area, it is well-placed on one of Salamanca's most fashionable thoroughfares, Claudio Coello, and has easy access to public transport.

Hotel Services *Air-conditioning. Bar. Car park. Conference facilities. Currency exchange. Fax. Laundry. Lifts. Multi-lingual staff. Non-smoking floors. Restaurant. Safe.* **Room services** *Hairdryer. Minibar. Radio. Room service (24-hours). Telephone. TV (satellite).*

Hotel Zurbano

C/Zurbano 79-81, 28003 (441 55 00/fax 441 32 24/telex 27578). Metro Ríos Rosas/bus 7, 12, 40, 147. **Rates** *single* from 17,400ptas; *double* from 21,750ptas. **Credit** AmEx, DC, EC, MC, TC, V.

In a quiet area just west of the Castellana near the **Nuevos Ministerios** (*see chapter* **Sightseeing**), this 270-room hotel is divided between two buildings. Contemporary, bright and decorated with bleached wood and modern Spanish art, this is a good choice for anyone who'd prefer to be slightly off the tourist trail. The restaurant and bars are great, and Metro and bus connections are only a short walk away.
Hotel services *Access to nearby gym. Air-conditioning. Bars. Car park. Conference facilities. Currency exchange. Fax. Laundry. Lifts. Multi-lingual staff. Restaurant. Safe. Wheelchair access.* **Room services** *Hairdryer. Minibar. Radio. Room service (7am-midnight). Rooms adapted for the disabled. Telephone. TV (satellite).*

Moderate

Galiano Residencia

C/Alcalá Galiano 6, 28010 (319 20 00/fax 319 99 14). Metro Colón/bus all routes to Plaza de Colón. **Rates** *single* from 10,000ptas; *double* from 14,000ptas. **Credit** EC, MC, TC, V.
This 29-room hotel is considered one of Madrid's best-kept secrets, one that the many regulars are keen to guard. Tucked away on a quiet street just off the Castellana, the sixteenth-century building was formerly the palace of the family of the Marqués de Perija and Conde de Atares. The same family still lives on the top floor, while their antique furniture and works of art decorate the hotel entrance. The spacious, airy rooms have an almost English feel. The bar has now been closed to maintain the private, low-key image. The director is so charming that guests often lunch with him, but the reception staff could use some coaching.
Hotel services *Air-conditioning. Car park. Conference facilities. Fax. Laundry. Lifts.* **Room services** *Hairdryer. Minibar. Radio. Room service (24-hours). Safe (outside of the room, but individual). Telephone. TV (satellite).*

Hostal-Residencia Senegal

Plaza Santa Bárbara 8, 1° dcha, 28004 (319 07 71). Metro Alonso Martinez/bus 3, 7, 21. **Rates** *single* from 5,000ptas; *double* from 6,800ptas. **No credit cards.**
A hostal – not a hotel, and so with only limited facilities – that's directly above one of Madrid's best-known beer emporia, the **Cervecería Santa Bárbara** (*see chapter* **Cafés & Bars**). It has just seven rooms, all with private baths, which justifies the higher than usual hostal prices. The rooms are well-kept and reasonably comfortable, but not outstanding, and the nervous owner can be hard to deal with.

Hotel Alcalá

C/Alcalá 66, 28009 (435 10 60/fax 435 11 05). Metro Príncipe de Vergara/bus all routes to C/Alcalá. **Rates** *single* from 12,200ptas; *double* from 17,900ptas. **Credit** AmEx, DC, EC, MC, TC, V.
Close to the Retiro, this could be the friendliest hotel in town. Many of the staff have worked here for years, and know what good service is all about. This is one reason why the hotel has a good many regular clients, mostly Spanish. The 153 rooms have recently been refurbished, and the inside rooms overlook an attractive garden.
Hotel services *Air-conditioning. Bar. Car park. Conference facilities. Currency exchange. Fax. Garden. Laundry. Lifts. Multi-lingual staff.* **Room services.** *Hairdryer. Minibar. Radio. Room service (24-hours). Safe. Telephone. TV (satellite).*

Hotel Arosa

C/de La Salud 21, 28013 (532 16 00/fax 531 31 27/telex 43618 HARO-E). Metro Sol/bus all routes to Puerta del Sol. **Rates** *single* 11,000ptas; *double* 17,000ptas. **Credit** AmEx, DC, JCB, MC, TC, V.
With the Puerta del Sol and Gran Via at opposite ends of the street, this 138-room hotel could hardly be more central. The

immediate area can be a bit sleazy, but the street itself is quiet and the hotel entrance is clean and sensibly guarded. The reception area is on the second floor. The rooms are clean, families are welcome, and the hotel has long been popular with British and American guests.
Hotel services *Access to nearby gym. Air-conditioning. Bar. Car park. Conference facilities. Currency exhange. Fax. Hairdressers & beauty salon. Laundry. Lifts. Multi-lingual staff. Non-smoking floor.* **Room services** *Hairdryer. Minibar. Radio. Room service (8am-11pm). Safe. Telephone. TV (satellite).*

Hotel Asturias

C/Sevilla 2, 28014 (429 66 76/fax 429 40 36). Metro Sevilla/bus all routes to C/Alcalá. **Rates** *single* from 8,2.60ptas; *double* from 10,350ptas. **Credit** MC, TC, V.
Two hundred metres from the Puerta del Sol, this 170-room hotel, first opened in 1875, has been extensively renovated in the last five years. It's nothing great, but decent value, and the location is ideal for anyone keen to have the city's sights and nightlife on their doorstep. Ask for an inside room, as the streets on either side are noisy. Lots of foreigners stay here, and service is attentive.
Hotel services *Bar. Currency exchange. Fax. Laundry. Lifts. Multi-lingual staff. Restaurant.* **Room services** *Safe. Telephone. TV (satellite).*

Hotel Carlos V

C/Maestro Vitoria 5, 28013 (531 41 00/fax 531 37 61). Metro Sol/bus all routes to Puerta del Sol. **Rates** *single* from 8,900ptas; *double* from 11,200ptas. **Credit** AmEx, DC, EC, JCB, MC, TC, V.
With 67 unexceptional rooms, this hotel is in the pedestrian-only shopping area just north of the Puerta del Sol. The entrance is clean and bright and there is an attractive second-floor lounge and restaurant area. Go for the fifth-floor rooms with private balconies.
Hotel Services *Air-conditioning. Currency exchange. Fax. Laundry. Lift. Multi-lingual staff.* **Room services** *Radio. Room service (7.30am-11pm). Safe. Telephone. TV (satellite).*

Hotel Emperador

Gran Via 53, 28013 (547 28 00/fax 547 28 17). Metro Gran Via/bus all routes to Gran Via. **Rates** *single* from 13,400ptas; *double* from 16,800ptas. **Credit** DC, MC, V.
An immaculately maintained 50-year-old hotel that is ideally placed for the centre of town. The rooms are spacious, with original furnishings in impeccable shape, and surprisingly quiet, despite the traffic below. Bathrooms are brand new. The staff are gracious, and a superb rooftop pool is a great plus for summer visitors (*see chapter* **Sport & Fitness**). Even though it has 232 rooms, you may need to book in early. The area is okay, but be careful with your bags, particularly at night.
Hotel services *Access to nearby gym. Air-conditioning. Bar. Beauty salon. Conference facilities. Currency exchange. Fax. Garden. Laundry. Lifts. Swimming pool.* **Room services** *Hairdryer. Minibar. Radio. Room service (7am-midnight). Safe. Telephone. TV (satellite).*

Hotel Inglés

C/Echegaray 8, 28014 (429 65 51/fax 420 24 23). Metro Sevilla/bus all routes to Puerta del Sol. **Rates** *single* from 6,500ptas; *double* from 9,500ptas. **Credit** AmEx, DC, MC, EC, TC, V.
This 58-room hotel dating from 1853 is so clean and bright you might be tempted to grab for your sunglasses as you walk inside. It's been family owned for some 30 years, has more character than many hotels. The rooms overlooking the sometimes hectic street are pleasant and have lovely morning light; those on the inside are quieter. Good value.
Hotel services *Bar/cafeteria. Car park. Currency exchange. Fax. Lifts. Multi-lingual staff.* **Room Services** *Room service (24-hours). Safe. Telephone. TV (satellite).*

The Hotel Monaco

Anyone with a sense of humour and an appreciation of kitsch that borders on the honky-tonk will get a kick out of the Hotel Monaco. This one-star hotel has just 32 rooms, and each one is unique. It also has a formidable past, and its history explains, in part, the mood of the place.

The building, in Chueca not far from the Gran Vía, was originally designed as apartments. But in 1919, a year after its construction, a French engineer acquired it and had it completely redone as a home for his lover. Within twelve months, it had become a thriving brothel.

Right through to the late fifties, this was quite the most fashionable house of ill repute in town. Mussolini's son-in-law is said to have rented the whole place for three days in 1941, and famous bullfighters hung up their capes here. So prominent did it become that two entrances were needed, so that well-known clients didn't meet as they came and went.

In 1959 the building became the Hotel Monaco, but all was not lost. The ambience is still intact and the décor is fabulous. The intimate lobby of faux marble, peacock prints and worn leather furniture has remained, as have the pink neon signs that direct you to the cafeteria – a tiny room with original leather booths. Best of all, though, are the rooms and the staff. Everyone, right down to the kitchen help, chats about the Monaco's history, almost as if they were reliving it. And they'll also direct you anywhere in, or out of, Madrid that suits your fancy.

If it's fame you're after, try room 20, on the first floor. The bathtub is in the middle of the room on a raised platform; ceiling mouldings, dramatic paintings and a wall of mirrors behind the bed complete the scene. Models have been snapped here for international fashion magazines, and the Spanish band Los Ronaldos shot a video here. Numbers 127 and 123 are equally celebrated. The first, with its salmon-coloured fabric-look ceiling, has been the backdrop for several films. The second has an enormous mirrored canopy above the bed, a stunning marble bathroom and moulded doors. But even rooms with less illustrious pasts have equally dramatic furnishings and quirkily tiled bathrooms (although if you can't stand the sight of a chipped tile, look elsewhere).

Despite its reputation, the Monaco isn't expensive, and what's more, it's honest. When you ask about rates, they may well inquire if you want the official prices, or what they're currently offering. For details, *see* **Moderate**.

Hotel Monaco

C/Barbieri 5, 28004 (522 46 30/fax 521 16 01). Metro Chueca, Gran Vía/bus all routes to Gran Vía. **Rates** *single* from 5,000ptas; *double* from 7,000 pts. **Credit** AmEx, DC, EC, MC, V.

A star among Madrid's many hotels. *See box* **The Hotel Monaco**.

Hotel services *Air-conditioning. Bar. Fax. Lifts. Multilingual staff.* **Room services** *Telephone.*

Hotel Mora

Paseo del Prado 32, 28014 (420 15 69/fax 420 05 64). Metro Atocha/bus 14, 27, 37, 45. **Rates** *single* from 4,950ptas; *double* from 7,550ptas. **Credit** AmEx, DC, MC, V.

Built in the thirties, this 62-room hotel has recently been renovated and is fresh, clean and bright. The entrance is attractive, everything else is functional. Even so, the place is often buzzing, and it can be hard to get a room. Not only is the Mora considered to be exceptional value but it's opposite the Prado and not far from Atocha station.

Hotel services *Air-conditioning. Bar. Fax. Laundry. Lift. Multi-lingual staff.* **Room Services** *Telephone. TV (satellite).*

Hotel Pintor

C/Goya 79, 28001 (435 75 45/fax 576 81 57/telex 23281). Metro Goya/bus 15, 21, 29, 52, 53. **Rates** *single* from 11,000ptas; *double* from 12,880ptas. **Credit** AmEx, EC, JCB, MC, TC, V.

The mock-Hawaiian lobby of this hotel wins hands down the prize for being the tackiest in town. The 176 recently redecorated rooms are less absurd and quite pleasant. The surrounding streets are full of shops; the hotel itself is on top of a mini-shopping mall. A ten-minute stroll from the Retiro.

Hotel Santander

C/Echegaray 1, 28014 (429 95 51). Metro Sevilla/bus all routes to Puerta del Sol. **Rates** *single* from 5,600ptas; *double* from 7,000ptas. **No credit cards**.

An antique but well-maintained and cosy entrance lobby welcomes you into this charming old hotel of just 35 rooms, perfectly located between the Puerta del Sol and the Prado. With lots of high ceilings, generous bathrooms and individual furniture, this is something of a gem. Some rooms face onto the Carrera de San Jerónimo and can be noisy, and the hallways are a bit dark, but the staff are friendly, and the place is far more likeable than a great many Madrid hotels.

Hotel services *Laundry. Lift. Multi-lingual staff. Safe.* **Room services** *Room service (8am-10pm). Telephone. TV on request.*

Hotel Serrano

C/Marqués de Villamejor 8, 28006 (435 52 00/fax 435 48 49). Metro Núñez de Balboa/bus all routes to Castellana. **Rates** *single* from 11,500ptas; *double* from 14,770ptas. **Credit** AmEx, DC, EC, MC, TC, V.

Just off the chic Calle Serrano, one of Salamanca's busiest thoroughfares, this is one of the area's better business hotels. It's small, with only 34 rooms, some of them suites. Such a compact hotel could be a real find, and the newly-redone lounge and reception area are headed in the right direction, but the rooms are pretty stark and need better lighting.

The **Hotel Pintor**: *is this the tackiest lobby in town?*

Hotel services *Air-conditioning. Bar. Currency exchange. Fax. Laundry. Lift. Multi-lingual staff.* **Room services** *Hairdryer. Minibar. Room service (8am-11pm). Safe. Telephone. TV.*

Hotel Suecia

C/Marqués de Casa Riera 4, 28014 (531 69 00/fax 521 71 41/telex 22313). Metro Sevilla, Banco de España/bus all routes to C/Alcalá. **Rates** *single* from 17,900ptas; *double* from 21,000ptas. **Credit** AmEx, DC, JCB, MC, TC, V.

This one gets the location award. In a peaceful section of the old city centre with good restaurants nearby, the Suecia ('Sweden') is just minutes away from the Puerta del Sol and the Golden Triangle. The rooms, 128 in all, are on the small side, but there is a comfortable lobby and a seventh-floor terrace that, while not huge, is still a relaxing place for a nap and sunbathing. The restaurant, the **Bellman**, is famous for its lavish smörgåsbord, served on Thursdays, Fridays and Saturdays. **Hotel services** *Air-conditioning. Bar. Car park. Conference facilities. Currency exchange. Fax. Laundry. Lifts. Multi-lingual staff. Non-smoking floors. Restaurant.* **Room services** *Minibar. Room Service (7am-1am). Safe. Telephone. TV (satellite).*

Hotel Tirol

C/Marqués de Urquijo 4, 28008 (548 19 00/fax 541 39 58). Metro Argüelles/bus 1, 21, 44, 133, C. **Rates** *single* from 7,830ptas; *double* from 9,600ptas. **Credit** MC, TC, V.

Reasonably priced, this 97-room hotel is convenient for the Plaza de España, the university area and the studenty Argüelles district. It's not the brightest or most characterful hotel you might find, but the rooms are spacious and clean, and it's good value.

Hotel services *Air-conditioning. Bar/cafeteria. Car park. Fax. Laundry. Lifts. Multi-lingual staff.* **Room services** *Room service (8am-1am). Safe. Telephone.*

Hotel Trafalgar

C/Trafalgar 35, 28010 (445 62 00/fax 446 64 56). Metro Iglesia/bus 3, 16, 37, 61, 149. **Rates** *single* from 7,900ptas; *double* from 13,200ptas. **Credit** AmEx, DC, EC, MC, TC, V.

In the middle of Chamberí, one of the older residential barrios of Madrid, this 48-room hotel has plain, simply-furnished rooms that are pleasant, if a bit overpriced. The hotel is popular, though, with guests who prefer something away from the heavily tourist-ridden areas of Madrid.

Hotel services *Air-conditioning. Bar. Conference facilities. Currency exchange. Fax. Laundry. Lifts. Multi-lingual staff. Restaurant. Safe.* **Room services** *Hairdryer on request. Room service (8am-11pm). Telephone. TV.*

Budget

Like other Spanish cities, Madrid has certain areas where cheap hotels are bunched together. The most important is around the Plaza Santa Ana and streets to the east such as the Calle Cervantes, in the heart of the Huertas bar-and-nightlife area. There is another big cluster further north in Malasaña and Chueca, near the Calle Fuencarral. The hotels around the main train stations are generally not as good as those further into town. Many basic hotels are in apartment blocks, the addresses of which may be identified as *izq* (*izquierda*, left) or *dcha* (*derecha*, right) after the floor number.

Hostal Armesto

C/San Agustín 6, 1° dcha, 28014 (429 90 31). Metro Antón Martín/bus 9, 14, 27, 37, 45. **Rates** *single* from 4,500ptas; *double* from 5,500ptas. **No credit cards.**

A six-room hostal, with baths in each room, that's owned by a wonderfully friendly woman and her husband. It's right in the centre, handy for the Prado and Atocha train station, and especially well-placed for taking in the Huertas bars. A special treat for those with inside rooms is a view over the garden of a nearby old palace, which makes it easy to forget you're in the middle of Madrid.

Hostal Cervantes

C/Cervantes 34, 2°, 28014 (429 83 65/429 27 45). Metro Antón Martín/bus 9, 14, 27, 37, 45. **Rates** *single* from 5,000ptas; *double* from 6,000ptas. **No credit cards.**

Just round the corner from the **Armesto** (*above*), and equally close to the Huertas and Santa Ana bar scene. The 12-room hostal is tidy, with new furniture, and has a relaxed atmosphere kept up by friendly, helpful owners. All rooms have private baths, and firm beds.

Hostal Delvi

Plaza Santa Ana 15, 3° dcha, 28012 (522 59 98). Metro Sol/bus 6, 26, 32, 50, 57. **Rates** *single* from 1,800ptas; *double* from 3,000ptas; *triple* from 4,500ptas. **No credit cards.**

Anyone who wants to be in the middle of things couldn't do better than stay on the Plaza Santa Ana itself. This pleasant and very cheap third-floor hostal has eight rooms, all different in size. Five rooms have showers, and one its own toilet. If you prefer more quiet, ask for a room that faces the side street, away from the main square. The owner is obliging.

Hostal Filo

Plaza Santa Ana 15, 2° izq, 28012 (522 40 56). Metro Sol/bus 6, 26, 32, 50, 57. **Rates** *single* from 2,000ptas; *double* from 4,500ptas; *triple* from 5,200ptas. **No credit cards.**

Another hostal on Santa Ana; 20 high-ceilinged rooms have great furniture and lots of light. The owner seems grumpy, but is no dummy, and over the years has acquired just enough English to deal with his guests. Only four rooms actually face the plaza. Each room has its own shower, but four toilets are shared by all guests.

Hostal Olga

C/Zorrilla 13, 28015 (429 78 87). Metro Sevilla/bus 9. **Rates** *single* from 3,800ptas; *double* from 4,800ptas. **Credit** EC, MC, TC, V.

With warmly-decorated sitting rooms that are inviting after a day of sightseeing, this 20-room, family-owned hostal offers slightly more sophisticated service than many in this price range, although the rooms themselves are spartan. It's well-located on a side street behind the **Cortes** (*see chapter* **Sightseeing**) and midway between the Puerta del Sol and the Golden Triangle. **Hotel services** *Safe.* **Room services** *Telephone.*

Hostal-Residencia Coruña

Paseo del Prado 12, 3° dcha, 28014 (429 25 43). Metro Banco de España/9, 14, 27, 37, 45. **Rates** *single* from 2,000ptas; *double* from 3,800ptas. **No credit cards.**

You'd love to camp inside the Prado – or put up at the Ritz – to get closer to the Goyas. The six clean rooms, with two shared bathrooms, have high ceilings, pretty chandeliers and plain furniture, and the friendly owners are clearly delighted to have guests. It's also an easy walk from Santa Ana and Atocha station. One of the best-value budget hotels.

Hostal-Residencia Gloria

C/Conde de Xiquena 4, 28004 (522 04 42). Metro Chueca/bus 37. **Rates** *single* from 2,000ptas; *double* from 3,500ptas. **No credit cards.**

A tidy, decent 14-room hostal located some way away from the main budget-hotel cluster, on a quiet street in Chueca,

*The bucolic charms of **Albergue Juvenil Casa de Campo**. See page 25.*

another fashionable, sometimes grungy, nightlife area. Some rooms have bathrooms, but the very low prices are the same as for those without. Some guests have been staying permanently here for years.

Hostal-Residencia Sud Americana

Paseo del Prado 12, 6° izq, 28014 (429 25 64). Metro Banco de España/9, 14, 27, 37, 45. **Rates** *single* from 2,100ptas; *double* from 4,000ptas. **No credit cards.**
In the same building as the **Coruña** (*see above*) and sharing its great advantages as far as location is concerned. This charming hostal has eight rooms with some fantastic features: tasteful, vintage furniture; priceless chandeliers; high ceilings; and creaky wooden floors.

Hostal Retiro/Hostal Narváez

C/O'Donnell 27, 4° & 5° dcha, 28009 (576 00 37/575 01 07). Metro Príncipe de Vergara/bus 2, 15, 63, C. **Rates** *single* from 3,000ptas; *double* from 4,500ptas. **No credit cards.**
You can practically roll out of bed and into the Retiro from these two hostals, one above the other, both run by the same family, and in a particularly untouristy area. The 27 rooms all have private showers, and are bright and recently painted with new furniture.

Hostal Riesco

C/Correo 2, 3°, 28012 (522 26 92). Metro Sol/bus all routes to Puerta del Sol. **Rates** *single* from 3,000ptas; *double* from 4,000ptas. **No credit cards.**
Heavy on the decoration, but clean just the same, this 26-room hostal just off the Puerta del Sol is for those who really want to stay in the absolute centre of the city. All rooms have bathrooms, and several have balconies decorated with flowers. It's been run by the same family for 24 years, and the lady of the house can be severe, but is efficient.
Room services. *Telephone.*

Hostal Valencia

Plaza de Oriente 2, 3°, 28013 (559 84 50). Metro Opera/bus 3, 25, 33, 39, 148. **Rates** *double* from 6,000ptas. **No credit cards.**

If you're interested in having a view of the **Palacio Real** (*see chapter* **Sightseeing**) this seven-room, third-floor walk-up right on the lush Plaza de Oriente is a must. Only some of the rooms have balconies with a view of the palace – and they're the most noisy – but all have their own bathrooms, and one has TV.

Hostal Villamáñez

C/San Agustín 6, 2° dcha, 28014 (429 90 33). Metro Antón Martín/bus 9, 14, 27, 37, 45. **Rates** *single* from 4,000ptas; *double* from 5,500ptas. **No credit cards.**
This hostal is on the floor above the **Armesto** (*see above*), bang in the centre of town. The 14 rooms all have private bathrooms and plenty of plain, cheap furniture. As one of very few budget hotels to have air-conditioning, it's a particularly good choice in summer.
Hotel services *Air-conditioning. Safe.* **Room services** *Telephone. TV.*

Pensión Jaén

C/Cervantes 5, 3° dcha, 28014 (429 48 58). Metro Antón Martín/bus 9, 14, 27, 37, 45. **Rates** *single* from 2,600ptas; *double* from 3,800ptas. **No credit cards.**
The genial owners are the main plus at this tiny, basic hostal of seven rooms in a safe building on the Calle Cervantes, very close to the Plaza Santa Ana. Some rooms have their own toilets, but showers are shared.

Posada del Dragón

C/Cava Baja 14, 28005 (365 32 25). Metro La Latina/bus 17, 18, 23, 35, 60. **Rates** 800ptas per person. **No credit cards.**
Males travellers on a super-shoestring budget might just appreciate this dusty, 26-room spot dating back to the last century – about the only survivor of the innumerable rough-and-ready *posadas* that over the last 400 years have catered to the many who arrived in Madrid seeking fame and fortune. Women, as is traditional, are not allowed. The rooms are either individual or shared, and there is one shared bathroom on each floor. There is no TV or telephone for residents' use, nor is any food served. Many of the long-term residents (at weekly rates) are elderly,

down-at-heel and sometimes shady men. There are few foreigners staying here.

Apartment Hotels

Apartamentos Juan Bravo
*C/Juan Bravo 58-60, 28006 (402 98 00/fax 309 32 28).
Metro Diego de León/bus 29, 52, 61.* **Rates** *studios*
31,000-39,000ptas per week, 94,000-120,000ptas per
month; *one-bedroom apartments* 41,000-45,000ptas per
week, 128,000-142,000ptas per month. **No credit cards.**
In a comfortable residential area on the edge of Salamanca
that's inconvenient for tourist attractions, these 150 apartments are in need of some refurbishment, even though
they're barely a decade old. The hallways are dark, the fittings and furniture shoddy. None of that matters too much,
though, come summer, as there's a great swimming pool at
the back. It's popular with German guests.
Hotel services *Air-conditioning. Car park. Fax.
Laundry. Multi-lingual staff. Swimming pool.* **Room
services** *Telephone. TV on request at additional cost.*

Apartamentos Plaza Basílica
*C/Comandante Zorita 27 & 31, 28020 (535 36 42/fax
535 14 97). Metro Lima/bus 3, 5, 43, 149.* **Rates**
studios 14,880ptas per single night, 77,000ptas per week,
225,000ptas per month; *suites* 19,600ptas per single night,
105,000pts per week, 330,000ptas per month; *luxury
apartments* 24,000ptas per single night, 140,000ptas per
week, 450,000ptas per month. **Credit** AmEx, DC, EC,
JCB, MC, TC, V.
Built in 1989, this 80-apartment complex is professionally
run and well-appointed, although the prices are bewilderingly high. It's conveniently located for anyone with business in the financial district, or attending an event at the
Palacio de Exposiciones (*see chapter* **Business**).
Hotel services *Air-conditioning. Cafeteria. Car park.
Currency exchange. Fax. Laundry. Lifts. Multi-lingual
staff.* **Room services** *Minibar. Radio. Room service
(8am-11pm). Safe. Telephone. TV (satellite).*

Youth Hostels

To get a bed in one of Madrid's two official youth
hostels it's usually necessary to reserve well
ahead, although if you feel like trying your luck
you can turn up on the door to see what they
have left for that night. Reservations must be
made in writing at least 15 days in advance, and
should be sent to the hostels themselves or to the
Instituto de Albergues Juveniles, Central
de Reservas, C/Alcalá 31, 28014 Madrid (580 42
16/fax 580 42 15). Reservations by fax are also
accepted at the C/Alcalá office. IYHF cards are
required, and you can stay a maximum of three
nights consecutively, and six nights in total during a two-month period. There is a 1.30am curfew at both hostels, although if you tell the
administration you really want to stay out later
they are often prepared to be flexible and provide
a means of getting back in. Doors re-open at 8am.
Note that in summer Spanish youth hostels are
often booked by school parties, who tend to set
the atmosphere.

Albergue Juvenil Casa de Campo
Casa de Campo, 28011 (463 56 99). Metro Lago/bus 33.

Rates (inc breakfast) 800ptas per person; 650ptas under-
26s. **No credit cards.**
Groups of ten or more should reserve at this hostel, but individuals are welcome to turn up at the door. Its attraction is
its location, in the middle of Madrid's largest park, the
Casa de Campo (*see chapter* **Sightseeing**). It's a long
way from the centre, but a great setting if you're into
nature. The hostel has its own bar, and is quite comfortable and well maintained. All rooms have four beds, and
each bathroom is shared by two rooms. It's quite a walk
from the Lago Metro station, where prostitutes and kerb-
crawlers congregate at night. Ask at the hostel about the
best way of getting back after dark, as it's not advisable to
walk around alone.

Albergue Juvenil Santa Cruz de Marcenado
*C/Santa Cruz de Marcenado 28, 28015 (547 45 32).
Metro Argüelles/bus 2, 21.* **Rates** (inc breakfast) 800ptas
per person; 650ptas under-26s. **No credit cards.**
Individuals or groups of less than ten should write to reserve
at this hostel, which is in a quiet street in the studenty
Argüelles area, and near the **Centro Cultural Conde
Duque** (*see chapters* **Madrid by Area** and **Art Galleries**).
The hostel is modern and quite well fitted-out, with 72 beds
split between rooms for four to eight people. Some English
is spoken at the reception.

Campsites

There are several more campsites around the
Madrid region, and towards the Guadarrama and
Gredos mountains (*see chapter* **Trips Out of
Town: The Sierras**). A full list is available from
tourist offices.

Aterpe Alai
*Carretera de Burgos (N1), km. 25, 28700 San
Sebastián de los Reyes, Madrid (657 01 00). Bus
Interbus 161, 166 from Plaza de Castilla/by car
Carretera de Burgos to Fuente del Fresno.* **Rates**
550ptas per person per night; 500ptas under-10s. **No
credit cards.**
This long-established campsite is quite a long way outside
Madrid, north of the suburban town of San Sebastián de
los Reyes and near the **Jarama** motor-racing circuit (*see
chapter* **Sport & Fitness**). Open all year, it has shower
facilities, small shops and a bar, but no swimming pool,
which in the Madrid summer can be an insufferable omission.

Camping Madrid
*Carretera de Burgos (N1), km. 11, 28050 (302 28 35).
Bus 129 from Plaza de Castilla/by car exit 12 from the
Carretera de Burgos.* **Rates** 500ptas per person per
night; 400ptas under-10s. **Credit** EC, TC.
Recently renovated, this site is in the northern outskirts of
Madrid, but reasonably well-connected by bus and road with
the centre. It's quite peaceful and nicely-situated, and has a
swimming pool, a supermarket and modern showers.

Camping Osuna
*Avda de Logroño s/n, 28042 (741 05 10). Metro
Canillejas, then bus 105, 115.* **Rates** 500ptas per person
per night; 425ptas under-10s. **Credit** EC, TC.
The closest campsite to central Madrid, and the only one
within reasonable distance of a Metro station. The site, open
all year, is pleasantly located amid pines, and has a
bar/restaurant, shop, playground, and 17 rooms available to
rent in case you've forgotten your tent. However, it's also
near the airport, and can be noisy.

Madrid by Season

Local tradition, raucous fun and avant-garde arts are all to be found in Madrid's yearly round of celebrations.

Madrid has festivals, fairs and traditional *fiestas* almost back-to-back throughout the year. And, since Madrid is still a relatively small city with a very definite centre, they're hard to miss. Another feature of the city's celebrations is the importance given to keeping up popular traditions, not as museum pieces but as a living part of the city, and the way in which old and new are integrated in *fiesta* programmes to involve people from all age groups.

The most traditional Madrid celebrations are the down-to-earth local street fiestas or *Verbenas*, the centres of the city's own *castizo* sub-culture (*see* **How to be a Castizo**), which reach a peak with **La Paloma** in August. **Carnaval** and **Semana Santa** are less spectacular here than in other parts of Spain, but Madrid's major festivals, particularly the largest of them all, **San Isidro**, more than make up for this with a whole range of performances, parties and events. Also on the calendar is a string of arts festivals, such as the summerlong programme **Veranos de la Villa**, not to mention the many arts and craft fairs, political *fiestas* and exhibitions that go on through the year.

Getting information on festival programmes much in advance is often not easy, as they are often finalised late. Tourist offices and the 010 information line (*see chapter* **Essential Information**) have details of current events, and programmes are also advertised in the local press and the *Guía del Ocio* (*see chapter* **Media**). In the listings below all public holidays are marked *. For more information on trade fairs, *see chapter* **Business**. For sports events, *see chapter* **Sport & Fitness**.

Spring

Día de la Mujer/Semana de la Mujer
Information Dirección General de la Mujer (580 47 00).
Dates 8 Mar and surrounding week.
International Women's Day, 8 March, is marked in Madrid with a march through the centre of the city during the day, and then *fiestas* organised by women's groups in bars and clubs at night. The Comunidad de Madrid's official *Direccion General de la Mujer* also organises a week of events, cinema, theatre and concerts by women artists and performers in various venues around the city.

EXPO-OCIO
Feria de Madrid/IFEMA, Parque Ferial Juan Carlos I (722 50 00/722 51 80). Metro Arturo Soria, then bus 122. **Dates** Mar.
At this huge leisure fair, held at the **Feria de Madrid** complex (*see chapter* **Business**), you can buy sports gear, adventure holidays, beds, cars, boats and even houses. If you don't have that kind of money or are worried that a water-bed won't fit into your suitcase you can try a virtual reality machine, go indoor rock climbing or have a ride on a life-size scalextric.

Semana Santa
Information City information line (010) and Tourist Offices. **Dates** Easter Week, Mar-April.
Holy Week is a less impressive event in Madrid than in southern Spain but nevertheless there are a number of religious processions in the city during the week with the traditional hooded figures of the *Penitentes* (Penitents) and huge images of Christ and the Virgin carried on the shoulders of troops of sturdy bearers. The most striking in Madrid is that of the brotherhood of *Jesus Nazareno el Pobre*, which winds its way round La Latina. There are also organ concerts in churches and chapels throughout the city. Easter is a more important in the towns around Madrid than in the city itself. The procession in **Toledo**, held in silence, is particularly solemn and ceremonious, and the one in **La Granja** offers the eerie spectacle of the hooded penitents bearing huge crucifixes on their backs. In **Chinchón** there is a performance of a medieval Passion Play in the Plaza Mayor, on Good Friday. For all these towns, *see chapter* **Around Madrid**.

Festival Internacional de Teatro
Information Comunidad de Madrid (580 26 77).
Dates April-May.
Madrid's international theatre festival mainly features young and less-known writers, directors and companies from around Spain and the rest of the world, and covers an enormous range of international theatre, good, not so good, and sometimes marvellous. Many of the theatres around the city host performances. *See also chapter* **Theatre**.

Dia de los Trabajadores* (May Day)
City centre and Casa de Campo. Metro Lago, Batán/bus 33, 41, 75. **Date** 1 May.
May Day in Madrid is marked by a march through the centre of the city, while the three main labour unions, CCOO, CNT and UGT, stage music and other events, mainly during the day, in the **Casa de Campo** (*see chapter* **Sightseeing**). The different *Casas Regionales*, the social clubs for migrants from different regions of Spain, set up temporary 'patios' and bars in the park for the occasion where they serve their various traditional dishes, and there are many other *chiringuitos* (makeshift bars) offering the usual beers, spirits and grilled *bocadillos* (rolls). With another official holiday the next day, May Day is a suitable beginning to Madrid's major month of *fiestas*.

All kinds of everything are featured in the **Veranos de la Villa.** *See page 28.*

Dos de Mayo*

Malasaña. Metro Tribunal, Bilbao, Noviciado/bus 3, 40, 147, 149. **Date** 2 May.

The 2 May 1808, when the people of Madrid rose up in an attempt to expel Napoleon's invading army (*see chapter* **History: Revolutions & Railways**), is a day hallowed in local legend. Today it is the official holiday of the Madrid region, the Comunidad de Madrid. Resistance was strongest in the Malasaña area around the Monteleón artillery barracks, which stood where the Plaza Dos de Mayo is today, and the district takes its modern name from the teenage heroine of the struggle Manuela Malasaña (*see chapter* **Madrid by Area**). The modern *fiesta*, the beginning of the summer *verbena* season, is also centred in Malasaña, with live bands playing traditional and other dance music in the Plaza Dos de Mayo, and a more mixed crowd in the streets than the young rockerish bunch that most frequently frequent the *barrio*'s bars. The Comunidad de Madrid also organises other concerts and dance stages in venues around the city, particularly in the Parque de las Vistillas.

San Isidro

Plaza Mayor and all over Madrid. **Information** City information line (010) and Tourist Offices.

Dates 8-15 May.

San Isidro, the humble local twelfth-century labourer famed for his many miracles in aid of the needy (*see chapter* **History: A Small Frontier Fortress**), is Madrid's patron saint, and the week leading up to his day, 15 May, is the whole city's *fiesta mayor*, its biggest wing-ding. In the Plaza Mayor there is dance music each night and performances by local bands playing traditional music, modern folk or flamenco, and a giant *cocido* (*see chapter* **Restaurants**), available to anyone who wants some, is cooked up on the Sunday

preceding 15 May. This is the most traditional part of the fiesta, with the old and the very young dressing up in traditional *castizo* attire. Many other events are included under the San Isidro umbrella, some of them going on beyond the week itself. In Las Vistillas, the park next to the Palacio Real with a view out over the sierra, there is a dance stage with salsa from Latin American groups and Spanish bands playing the traditional Madrileño *chotis*. The largest music venue, though, is in the **Casa de Campo**, where there are rock concerts with international and Spanish groups. At the **Colegio San Juan Evangelista** (*see chapter* **Music: Rock, Roots & Jazz**) there is a small jazz festival and a one-day flamenco festival. San Isidro is also Madrid's (and so the world's) most important bullfighting *feria*, with *corridas* every day for a whole month at Las Ventas (*see chapter* **Bullfighting**). In addition, San Isidro also includes a separate children's programme, and many more exhibitions, demonstrations of local gastronomy, local events and craft and book fairs, some of which are listed below.

Feria de la Cerámica *Plaza de Dalí. Metro Goya, Príncipe de Vergara/bus 29, 30, 43, 63, C.*

A high-quality ceramics fair which now includes other crafts, and runs through the week of San Isidro.

Feria de la Cerámica y Cacharrería *Plaza de las Comendadoras. Metro Noviciado, San Bernardo/bus 21, 147.*

More of a 'household crockery' fair, and so cheaper, but still featuring a variety of traditional Spanish ceramics.

Feria del Libro Antiguo y de Ocasión *Paseo de Recoletos. Metro Colón, Banco de España/bus all routes to Plaza Colón.*

An old and second-hand book fair held usually on weekends only during the San Isidro period, and where you might find rare treasures or recent remaindered editions.

La Feria del Libro (Madrid Book Fair)

Parque del Retiro. Metro Retiro, Ibiza, Atocha/bus all routes to Retiro. **Information** Asociación de Libreros (562 98 54). **Dates** end May-June.

The Book Fair began as a local show 55 years ago, but is now an important international event, with personal appearances by major writers from throughout the Hispanic world, and usually from further afield too. It gets bigger every year, and the different sections of the booktrade – distributors, publishers and bookshops – are all represented in the hundreds of stands set up in the Retiro. Public attendance is massive throughout the two weeks of the fair. It is one of the few events to take place in the Retiro, and there has been some opposition to it recently on environmental grounds. However, for the moment, the fair looks set to continue amongst the trees, lakes and statues of Madrid's best park.

Summer

San Antonio de la Florida

Ermita de San Antonio de la Florida, Paseo de la Florida 5 (547 07 22). Metro Norte/bus 46, 75. **Date** 12 June.

The hermitage of San Antonio de la Florida, with its Goya frescoes (*see chapter* **Sightseeing**), is also the place where single women looking to find a suitable chap have traditionally gone on the Saint's day, 12 June, to leave a needle in the hope that this might get him to intervene and send one along. The occasion (not necessarily taken seriously) was in the past a big day out for Madrid's traditional seamstresses. Today, there's a big street party outside.

Festival Mozart

Information Teatro de la Zarzuela (429 82 25). **Dates** June-July.

Initiated in 1988, and held mainly in the **Teatro de la Zarzuela** and the **Auditorio Nacional**, although performances are also staged at other venues (*see chapter* **Music: Classical & Opera**). Though the centrepiece is opera, the programmes cover the full range of Mozart's work, performed by internationally-renowned artists. The dates of the festival are variable, and in some years it has begun in May.

Veranos de la Villa

Information City information line (010) and Tourist Offices. **Dates** July-mid-Sept.

Through the summer Madrid offers one of the most varied cultural menus of anywhere in Europe with this city-run arts season, featuring opera, flamenco, modern dance, ballet, pop, folk, jazz, rock cinema and many other things. Classical music, opera and flamenco are performed in the open air in the beautiful patios of the **Centro Cultural Conde Duque** (*see chapters* **Madrid by Area** *and* **Art Galleries**). The season of nightly *zarzuela* performances in **La Corrala** (*see chapter* **Music: Classical & Opera**) also comes within the festival umbrella. The park in front of Madrid's Moorish Wall, the **Muralla Arabe** (*see chapter* **Sightseeing**) is the venue for a festival of world music and arts that has featured musicians such as Caetano Veloso, Milton Nascimento, Salif Keita and Bobby McFerrin and traditional Japanese ballet, and most recently there has also been a Celtic music festival at **Celtibaria** in the Parque Tierno Galván, in the south of the city. Other regulars include open-air cinema (*see chapter* **Film**) and a wide variety of drama in the city's theatres. For kids, there's an international puppet festival in the Retiro, and many other events (*see chapter* **Children**).

Verbenas de San Cayetano, San Lorenzo & La Paloma

La Latina & Lavapiés. Metro La Latina, Lavapiés, Puerta de Toledo/bus 3, 17, 18, 23, 35, 60, 148. **Information** City information line (010) and Tourist Offices. **Dates** 6-15 Aug.

In August those who have not quit Madrid for the beach or the mountains gather in what seems to be their entirety at these street *fiestas*, the most traditional and *castizo* in Madrid. San Cayetano (7 August), San Lorenzo (10 August) and La Paloma (15 August) follow each other in quick succession, and all blend into the one event. The action takes place all around the archetypically Madrileño districts of La Latina and Lavapiés, where just about every street and square is dressed out with flowers and bunting, and many people appear in all their *castizo* finery. During the day, there are parades and lots of events for kids. The main *fiesta* really gets going after the sun goes down, and from ten until the early hours the drink is flowing freely, and there are stalls selling nuts, coconut, rolls, sangría and lemonade, and live bands and competing sound systems provide music from pop and salsa to Madrid's very own *chotis*. To take it all in, it's best just to walk around the district from about 9pm onwards, going down as many side streets as you find.

Autumn

Fiestas del Partido Communista

Casa de Campo. Metro Lago, Batán/bus 33, 41, 75. **Dates** Sept.

The Spanish Communist Party organises this three-day jamboree on the last weekend in September in the **Casa de Campo** (*see chapter* **Sightseeing**). As on May Day the *Casas Regionales* provide local delicacies, and there are live bands, theatre performances and stalls set up by campaigning and community groups.

Música en Las Ventas

Plaza de Toros de Las Ventas. C/Alcalá 237 (726 48 00/356 22 00). Metro Ventas/bus 21, 38, 53, 201, 106. **Dates** Sept-Oct.

Come September and Madrid's giant bullring begins to double up as a music venue. There are concerts almost nightly during the short season, featuring as well as Spanish acts some major international names such as Sting or Peter Gabriel. With a capacity of over 22,000 but terraced in a way that means you're never far from the centre, Las Ventas makes a wonderful concert venue.

Festival de Otoño (Autumn Festival)

Information Comunidad de Madrid (580 25 75). **Dates** mid-Sept-mid-Nov.

This festival, a little over ten years old, was initially devoted above all to theatre, but it now provides a wide artistic umbrella as a celebration of all the *artes escénicas* (performing arts). Each year a specific country (or sometimes countries) is chosen as the focus of the festival, with a wide selection of its music, theatre and dance. The countries chosen generally alternate between Europe and Latin America. In addition, there are also many other groups, ensembles and performers from other countries all around the world, all performing in their original languages. Included in the theatre strand of the festival is the *Muestra Internacional de Teatro Alternativa*, centred on the **Sala Triángulo**, a gathering of avant-garde theatre groups that recently has featured around 80 groups or performers in over 100 productions. The music programme, similarly, takes in every type of musical performance. At the end of the Festival in November comes Madrid's **Festival de Jazz** (*see chapter* **Music: Rock, Roots & Jazz**). The centre of the mainstream festival is the **Teatro Albéniz**, although performances are also presented in the **Teatro Alcalá Palace** and many other venues around the city and in the surrounding towns of the Comunidad de Madrid. *See also chapter* **Theatre**.

Teatro Alcalá Palace *C/Alcalá 90 (435 46 08). Metro Retiro/bus all routes to Plaza de la Independencia.*

This theatre does not have a normal programme but is regularly used as a festival venue.

How to be a Castizo

London has cockneys, and Madrid has *Castizos*. The word *castizo* itself, roughly meaning pure or authentic, was once used to describe things considered distinctly Spanish, but around the end of the last century Madrid appropriated it to refer only to anything of *its* own. It can be applied to anything, from architecture to food. More specifically, though, it became attached to a particular working-class street type that appeared during the rapid growth of Madrid from the 1880s onwards, and which is now enshrined as the classic Madrileño character.

Castizos, the descendants of the *Majos* and *Majas* painted by Goya (*see chapter* **History: Bourbon Madrid**), had a cocky, street-smart style of their own, always putting on a show of flash even if they only had two coppers to rub together. Their slang and humour were celebrated in many *Zarzuelas*, the archetypal *castizo* art form. Known for their sharp, sarcastic wit, they were full of an attitude known as *chulería*, a combination of aggression, humour and self-sufficiency. Try flicking your head back and clicking your tongue at somebody and you'll get the idea.

Much of this may all be in the past, but in a city where most people are from somewhere else those who can trace their origins here back more than a generation or so are proud to celebrate the fact. Different districts dispute the status of being the heart of *castizo*-dom, the main contenders being Chamberí and, above all, La Latina and Lavapiés. People turn out in full *castizo* regalia for the most traditional Madrid fiestas, **San Isidro** and, particularly, the August *Verbenas* leading up to **La Paloma** – men as *chulos* in dogtooth-check jackets and flat caps, women as *chulapas* in long skirts, lots of petticoats, flowered shawls and headscarfs, with an obligatory carnation in the hair.

It's then you have a chance to gather round the barrel-organ and dance the *chotis*, a bouncy, short stepped dance in which you cling very tightly to your partner in a kind of wobble, and hear fifty times a day the local anthem *Madrid, Madrid, Madrid* (actually written by a Mexican, Agustín Lara). The open-air *Zarzuela* season at **La Corrala** is another major *castizo* event (*see chapter* **Music: Classical & Opera**). It's not necessary to show that your granma was born in Madrid to go along, and even people who've not been here five years dress their kids up in *castizo* rig-out and join in.

There ain't no fiesta without food.

Winter

Navidad* (Christmas)
Date 25 Dec.
The Christmas period still only starts in December in Madrid. Festivities centre around 24 and 31 December and 6 January, the Feast of the Three Kings, or Epiphany. Traditionally, the main Spanish Christmas decoration is a crib, not a tree, and children receive their presents from the Three Kings, not on Christmas itself, but in the last few decades Father Christmas and all the other international trappings of the season have become increasingly visible, while kids sometimes expect to get presents on *both* days. In the weeks preceding Christmas the Plaza Mayor is filled with stalls selling Christmas trees, traditional cribs and other festive trinkets, department stores put on lavish seasonal displays, and Recoletos is packed for the annual crafts fair, ideal for present-buyers. The main Christmas celebrations take place not on Christmas Day but on the night of Christmas Eve, which is when Spanish families have their traditional Christmas meal at home. The streets are consequently empty, although things liven up a little after midnight, and many of the clubs are open all night. Christmas Day itself is more a day for recovering.

Feria de Artesanía
Paseo de Recoletos. Metro Colón, Banco de España/bus all routes to Plaza Colón.
Madrid's biggest craft fair takes over the Paseo de Recoletos in the weeks before Christmas and continues until the end of the festive season, 6 January. The official covered stalls run from the Plaza de Cibeles to the Plaza Colón, but unlicensed traders, *piratas*, stretch away as far again on each side, selling a mixture of original work, cheap tack and ethnic knick-knacks. There is plenty worth buying, but it's best to go early as the last few days are frantic.

Noche Vieja (New Year's Eve)
Puerta del Sol. Metro Sol/bus all routes to Puerta del Sol.
Date 31 Dec.
As on Christmas Eve, many people start the evening with a traditional meal with family or friends. The thing to do for those who don't stay in is to head down to the Puerta del Sol,

where thousands gather beneath the clock for a communal countdown, fireworks and the traditional grape-stuffing session that is the centre of a Spanish New Year's Eve – you're supposed to eat one grape for each chime of midnight to get good luck for the rest of the year. Then, it's off to the bars for the rest of the night, although be warned that drinks are a lot more expensive than during the rest of the year.

Reyes* (Three Kings)
Date 6 Jan.
On 5 January, the eve of the arrival of the Three Kings, there is an evening *Cabalgata* (parade) around the city, with hundreds of elaborate floats, from where the costumed riders throw sweets to the children in the crowd. Thousands of people gather to watch the parade, which is also televised. Afterwards, adults, as on these 'eves', have another big dinner, while kids are tucked up in bed preparing for their big day on the sixth, when they get their presents.

ARCO
Feria de Madrid/IFEMA, Parque Ferial Juan Carlos I (722 50 00/722 51 80). Metro Arturo Soria, then bus 122. **Dates** Feb.
The scale of Madrid's international contemporary art fair, which attracts galleries from all over the world, is mind-boggling, and it provides a great opportunity to see a huge range of works all under one roof. *See also chapter* **Art Galleries**.

Carnaval
Date the week before Lent (usually late Feb/Mar).
The Carnival celebrations are opened with a speech by a famous artist or writer, followed by a Carnival parade, the route of which varies from year to year. In clubs and other venues there are Latin music gigs to dance to, and ribaldry, a fair amount of drinking and a lot of dressing up goes on around the town, especially in the gay clubs in Chueca (*see chapter* **Gay Madrid**). There is also a famous masked ball in the **Círculo de Bellas Artes** (*see chapters* **Sightseeing** *and* **Music: Classical & Opera**), although tickets are pricey and hard to come by. The end of the Carnival on Ash Wednesday is marked by the hilarious procession of the *Entierro de la Sardina* (Burial of the Sardine), a bizarre and ancient ritual in which the said fish is escorted around town in its tiny coffin, nowadays with a jazz band, before its interment on the Paseo de la Florida.

Sightseeing

A walk around Madrid will take you past expansive plazas, grand monuments, architectural eccentricities and some wonderful parks.

Even for those on a tight schedule, Madrid is an easy city to explore. The city's most internationally-famous attraction, the Prado, as well as the two other museums in Madrid's artistic 'Golden Triangle', are all on the same avenue. Indeed, most of the city's other major sights are also found within 'Old Madrid' (until the last century the entire city), which can be covered on foot without great difficulty. A map is handy, but even visitors who prefer to wander without a specific destination in mind shouldn't lose out, for wherever they are in the city centre some of Madrid's eclectic sights will be comfortably within reach.

For more on Madrid's very individual districts, *see chapter* **Madrid by Area**. For a list of sights, restaurants, cafés and other facilities by area, *see page 264* **Area Index**.

Plazas & Paseos

Paseo del Prado

Metro Atocha, Banco de España/bus 9, 14, 27, 37, 45.
Visitors to the major art museums soon become familiar with this tree-lined boulevard between the Plaza de Cibeles and Atocha rail station, with the **Museo del Prado** and the **Museo Thyssen** on either side of its central plaza. The Paseo itself, chiefly designed by José de Hermosilla, was laid out in 1775-82 for King Charles III, as part of his plan to dignify his capital with a grand avenue lined by centres of learning and science (*see chapter* **Bourbon Madrid**). Its form was modelled on the Piazza Navona in Rome, with a line of fountains designed by Ventura Rodriguez, from Cibeles at the most northern point followed by Apolo, Neptune and finally the Four Seasons, in front of the Museo del Prado. Traffic is often heavy on the Paseo today, but in the last century this was the great promenade of Madrid. Virtually the whole population took a turn along it each evening, to see and be seen, and show off their clothes and carriages.

Built for carnivals, bullfights and buying and selling, the **Plaza Mayor***. See page 33.*

The mistreated Goddess **Cibeles**.

Plaza de Cibeles

Metro Banco de España/bus all routes to Cibeles.
Midway between the **Puerta del Sol** and the **Parque del Retiro**, this four-way intersection and its statue and fountain signify Madrid to Spaniards as much as Nelson's Column, the Eiffel Tower or the Empire State Building identify their particular cities. It's surrounded by some of the city's most prominent buildings. Clockwise from the most imposing of the four, the **Palacio de Comunicaciones**, they are the **Banco de España**, the Palacio Buenavista (now the army headquarters) and the Palacio de Linares, which now houses the **Casa de América** (*see chapter* **Art Galleries**). The Ventura Rodriguez statue in the middle is of *Cybele*, a Graeco-Roman goddess of fertility and symbol of natural abundance, on a chariot drawn by lions. The goddess has lately been in a rather sorry state, having been robbed of one of her arms by rejoicing football fans following a Spanish victory during the 1994 World Cup. However, the limb was tracked down and repair work was begun immediately. North of Cibeles the Paseo changes name to the Paseo de Recoletos, which shortly becomes the Paseo de la Castellana, Madrid's endless north-south artery.

Plaza de España

Metro Plaza de España/bus all routes to Plaza de España.
This expanse at the end of the Gran Via could be called the Franco regime's very own plaza, as it was mainly laid out in the forties and is flanked by two classic buildings of the type sponsored by the regime when out to impress, the fifties-modern Torre Madrid (1957) and the humungous mass of the Edificio España, of 1948-53. The three statutes in the middle – of Cervantes, Don Quixote and Sancho Panza – are by Teodoro Ana Sagasti and Mateo Iniria, from 1928. The plaza around them is so large it can be a relaxing place to sit.

Plaza Mayor

Metro Sol/bus all routes to Puerta del Sol.
Madrid's grand main plaza was the city's hub for centuries. It was first built in the fifteenth century as a humble market square, then called the Plaza del Arrabal (Square outside the Walls). After Madrid was made capital of Spain by Philip II Juan de Herrera drew up plans for it to be completely rebuilt, but the only part built immediately was the **Casa de la**

Carpaccio's Young Knight in a Landscape
(**Museo Thyssen-Bornemisza**). *See pages 35, 168-9.*

Panadería (The Bakery). Dominating the square, with two pinnacle towers, it was completed under the direction of Diego Sillero in 1590. Within the last ten years, in a move that would not even be contemplated in most countries, this historic edifice has been decorated with some eye-catching, vaguely hippy-ish frescoes. The rest of the Plaza was built by Juan Gómez de Mora under Philip III and completed in 1619. Large sections had to be rebuilt after a disastrous fire in 1790. Bullfights, carnivals and all the great festivals and ceremonies of imperial Madrid were held here (*see chapter* **History: Capital of a Golden Age**). At its centre today is a 1616 statue of Philip III on horseback by Giambologna and Pietro Tacca, originally in the Casa de Campo and moved here in the last century. The ample expanse of the plaza can be enjoyed in different ways at different times. Weekday mornings are calm, a perfect time to study the architecture or enjoy breakfast in one of the attractive-but-expensive cafés. Jewellery, hats, fans and other souvenirs can be bought in the plaza's shops, many of which retain their traditional façades. On Sunday mornings the plaza bustles with a stamp and coin market (*see chapter* **Shopping**); other weekend activities include the serving of World-Record breaking paellas and the **San Isidro** *cocido* to long lines of Madrileños. For Christmas, it houses a traditional fair with stalls offering trees, nativity scenes, decorations and jokes and toys for kids (*see chapter* **Madrid by Season**).

Plaza de Oriente

Metro Opera/bus 3, 25, 33, 39, 148.
Oddly enough, Madrid owes this stately square that seems ideally to complement the Palacio Real to Spain's 'non-King', Joseph Bonaparte. After he had initiated its clearing it was left as a dusty space for many years, and then laid out in formal style in 1844. At the centre is a fine equestrian statue of King Philip IV that originally stood in the main courtyard of the Buen Retiro (*see chapter* **Madrid by Area**). It was designed by Velázquez and the sculptor Pietro Tacca, and engineered in Italy supposedly with the aid of Galileo. On the opposite side from the palace is Madrid's ill-starred opera house, the **Teatro Real** (*see chapter* **Music: Classical & Opera**). It took over 30 years to build, between 1817 and 1850, and was again closed for renovation in 1987. A smart vantage point on the plaza is the terrace of the **Café de Oriente** (*see chapters* **Tapas** *and* **Cafés & Bars**). Now fading into memory are the mass rallies Franco used to address here from the palace balcony, for which devotees were bussed in from all over the country.

Puerta del Sol

Metro Sol/bus all routes to Puerta del Sol.
It's nearly impossible to visit Madrid and not pass through this semi-circular space, if only because it is very much the hub of the public transport system. From here, too, the Calles Arenal and Mayor lead away to the Plaza Mayor and the Palacio Real, while to the west Calle Alcalá and the Carrera de San Jerónimo run to the Huertas area, the Paseo del Prado and the main museums. It is called a *Puerta* (gate) because this was indeed the main, easternmost gate of fifteenth-century Madrid. Under the Habsburg Kings it was surrounded by churches and monasteries, and the space between them supplanted the Plaza Mayor as the city's main meeting place. It was rebuilt in its present form in 1854-62. It still is Madrid's most popular meeting point, particularly by the monument with the symbols of Madrid, a bear and a *madroño* or strawberry tree, at the junction with Calle Carmen. Across from there is the square's most important building, the **Casa de Correos**, built in 1766 by Jaime Marquet as a post office for Charles III. Today it houses the Madrid regional government, the *Comunidad de Madrid*. It was altered significantly in 1866 when the large clock tower was added. Some find it architecturally objectionable, but this clock is the best-known feature of the building today, because it's the one that the entire country looks to on New Year's Eve. Indeed, thousands of Madrileños crowd into the

MUSEO

THYSSEN –
BORNEMISZA

Pº DEL PRADO, 8 - MADRID
SPAIN

**EIGHT CENTURIES
OF ART**

OPEN EVERY DAY EXCEPT MONDAY
10 AM - 7 PM

Madrid's bear, **Puerta del Sol.** *See page 33.*

square to await the twelve chimes (*see chapter* **Madrid by Season**). In front of the building is *kilometro cero*, the mark from which all distances in Spain are measured.

The Golden Triangle

For full details of the 'Big Three' and Madrid's other art museums, *see chapter* **Museums**.

Museo Nacional
Centro de Arte Reina Sofía

C/Santa Isabel 52 (467 50 62). Metro Atocha/bus all routes to Atocha. **Open** 10am-9pm Mon, Wed-Sat; 10am-2.30pm Sun. **Admission** *Mon, Wed-Fri, 10am-2.30pm Sat* 400ptas; 200ptas students; free under-18s, over 65s. *2.30-9pm Sat, Sun* free.

This giant slab-sided building was originally the Hospital de San Carlos, yet another project commissioned by Charles III, and designed by Francesco Sabatini. Built in 1776-81, it remained a hospital until 1965. It lay idle until 1977, when work began on its conversion into a multi-purpose museum, exhibition space and cultural centre. It first opened as an exhibition space in 1986, but the project was not completed until 1990, with the installation of a permanent collection of contemporary art and the addition of the striking glass lifts either side of the entrance. In 1992 it controversially acquired its greatest attraction, Picasso's *Guernica*. It is also one of the best venues in Europe for temporary art exhibitions, and hosts a comprehensive range of other cultural activities. There's a fine bookshop too. *See also chapter* **Art Galleries**.

Museo del Prado

Paseo del Prado (429 07 70/420 28 36/420 37 68). Metro Atocha, Banco de España/bus 9, 14, 27, 37, 45. **Open** 9am-7pm Tue-Sat; 9am-2pm Sun, public holidays.

Admission *Tue-Fri, 9am-2.30pm Sat* 400ptas; 200ptas students; free under-18s, over 65s. *2.30-7pm Sat, Sun* free.

This neo-classical structure was designed by Juan de Villanueva in 1785 for King Charles III, who died before it was finished. The King had intended it to be a Museum of Natural Sciences (*see chapter* **History: Bourbon Madrid**). However, the massive building, of three distinct sections linked by galleries with an elegant Doric façade at the centre, eventually opened in 1819 as an art museum in which to display the Spanish royal picture collection. Today few visitors to Madrid dare miss this, one of the world's greatest galleries, with, many say, a higher concentration of masterpieces than any other. Apart from Spanish painters such as Goya, El Greco and Velázquez (80 per cent of his entire output), there are celebrated works by Bosch, Botticelli and Rubens, to mention but a few. It is so full of treasures that it is only possible to display a small part, around 1,500 works, of its 9,000-piece collection at any one time.

Museo Thyssen-Bornemisza

Palacio de Villahermosa, Paseo del Prado 8 (369 01 51/420 39 44). Metro Banco de España/bus 9, 14, 27, 37, 45. **Open** 10am-7pm Tue-Sun. **Admission** 600ptas; 350ptas students, under-18s, over 65s.

Spain's landing of the art hoard of Baron Hans-Heinrich Thyssen-Bornemisza could easily be the country's greatest coup, however much they had to pay out in the process. It really breaks all the norms, with works from just about every major figure in the history of western art – Ghirlandaio, Goya, Degas, Picasso or Andy Warhol – and it might be easier to list the artists not featured than those present. The building, the Palacio de Villahermosa, was an aristocratic residence completed in 1805 by Silvestre Pérez and Antonio López Aguado, and previously had stood empty for several years. For it to house the Thyssen, architect Rafael Moneo gave it an entirely new interior, with salmon-coloured walls, marble floors, and superb, elegant lighting, making the museum stunning even without the works of art. Curiously enough, from the outside it is easy to overlook, as the building is quite plain and the entrance is through a courtyard that could be mistaken for a private garden.

Medieval Madrid

Only a few relics of the humble medieval town of Madrid survive, mostly in the narrow streets around the Plaza de la Paja and Calle San Nicolás.

Muralla Arabe (Arab Wall)

Cuesta de la Vega. Metro Opera/bus 3, 31, 50, 65, 148. Until recently this crumbling stretch of ninth-century rampart, the only remaining relic of Madrid's Moslem founders, was virtually ignored by the city. As some recompense the

The grand **Puerta de Alcalá.** *See page 43.*

ZOO

**DE LA CASA DE CAMPO
MADRID**

MORE THAN 3,000 ANIMALS FROM 5 CONTINENTS.
DOLPHINARIUM AND PARROT CLUB. WONDERS OF NATURE:
GREAT SNAKES, GIANT PANDA, RED PANDA, MALAYAN TAPIR ...
NEW IN APRIL 1995: 1,800,000 LITRE TROPICAL AQUARIUM.

METRO BATAN OR DAILY 33 BUS FROM OPERA.
SUNDAYS AND PUBLIC HOLIDAYS:
BUSES FROM BATAN, ESTRECHO, VALLECAS AND VENTAS.

Now mostly vacated for the tourists, the vast **Palacio Real**. *See page 39.*

area around it has now been renamed the Parque Emir Mohammed I. It's used as a venue in the summer arts festival (*see chapter* **Madrid by Season**). A good starting point if you're keen to see things in chronological order.

San Jerónimo el Real

C/Moreto 4 (420 30 78). Metro Banco de España, Retiro/bus 9, 14, 27, 37, 45. **Open** *Sept-May* 8am-1.30pm, 5-8pm, Mon-Fri; 9-1.30pm, 5.30-8pm, Sat, Sun. *May-Sept* 8am-1.30pm, 6-8pm, Mon-Fri; 9-1.30pm, 6.30-8pm, Sat, Sun.
Founded in 1464 and then rebuilt for Queen Isabella in 1503, this church near the Retiro was particularly favoured by the Spanish monarchs, and even today is still used for state ceremonies. Most of the original building was destroyed in the Napoleonic wars, however, and the present church is largely a reconstruction carried out between 1848 and 1883.

San Nicolás de los Servitas

C/San Nicolás (559 40 64). Metro Opera/bus 3, 25, 33, 39, 148. **Open** 9am-1.30pm,5.30-8.30pm Mon; 9-10am, 6.30-8.30pm Tue-Sat; 10am-1.30pm, 6.30-8.30pm Sun.
The oldest surviving church in Madrid, only a few minutes from the Plaza de Oriente. The twelfth-century tower is one of only two *Mudéjar* towers, built by Moslem craftsmen living under Christian rule, in the city. Most of the rest of the church was rebuilt in the fifteenth and sixteenth centuries.

San Pedro el Viejo

Costanilla de San Pedro (365 12 84). Metro La Latina, Sol/bus 31, 35, 50, 65. **Open** 6-8pm daily.
The other *Mudéjar* brick tower in Madrid, from the fourteenth century. Again, the rest of the church is much later.

San Andrés & Capilla de San Isidro

Plaza de San Andrés 1 (365 48 71). Metro La Latina/bus 3, 17, 18, 23, 35, 60, 148. **Open** 8.15-11.30am Mon-Sat; 8am-2pm Sun.
The fifteenth-century **Capilla del Obispo** (Bishop's Chapel) on one side of this church in the heart of old Madrid, is the best-preserved Gothic building in the city, with finely-carved

tombs of local aristocrats of the period. As with most of Madrid's medieval churches, other sections were rebuilt and made grander in later centuries. Most important is the baroque **Capilla de San Isidro**, built in 1657-69 by Pedro de la Torre to house the remains of the saint, although they were later transferred to the Cathedral (*see below*). The rest of this refined church is sixteenth-century.

The Habsburgs

Most of the major buildings erected for Spain's most powerful dynasty in Madrid – including the **Plaza Mayor** – were in the distinctive, Flemish-influenced style, with grey-slate, pinnacle towers, developed by Philip II's favourite architect Juan de Herrera, and known as 'Castilian Baroque'.

Catedral de San Isidro

C/Toledo 37-39 (369 23 10). Metro La Latina/bus 17, 18, 23, 35, 65. **Open** 8.30am-12.30pm, 6.30-8.30pm, Mon-Sat; 9am-2pm, 5.30-8.30pm, Sun, public holidays.
This giant church was originally built as part of the *Colegio Imperial*, the centre of the Jesuit order in Spain, in 1622-33. The design was by Pedro Sánchez, himself a member of the order, who took his inspiration from the mother church of the Jesuits, the Gesù in Rome. The façade was completed by Francisco Bautista in 1664. In 1767, after Charles III's dispute with the Jesuits (*see chapter* **Bourbon Madrid**), the church was dedicated to San Isidro and the remains of the saint and his spouse were brought here. It was made Madrid's provisional cathedral in 1885.

Plaza de la Villa

Metro Sol/bus all routes to Puerta del Sol.
This historic square, the market square of Moslem and early medieval Madrid, contains three distinguished buildings all in different styles. Dominating it is the **Casa de la Villa** or City Hall, designed in Castilian-baroque style by Juan Gómez

de Mora in 1630, although financial problems prevented it being completed until 1695. The façade was also altered by Juan de Villanueva in the 1780s. It contrasts nicely with the **Casa de Cisneros**, built as a palace by a relative of the great Cardinal Cisneros in 1537. It was restored in 1910, and now also houses municipal offices. Opposite the Casa de la Villa is the simple **Torre de los Lujanes**, once the residence of one of Madrid's aristocratic families, from the 1460s. It is believed that King Francis I of France was kept prisoner here by Charles V after the Battle of Pavia, in 1525.

Puente de Segovia
C/Segovia. Bus 25, 31, 33, 39, 138, C.
When travelling over this stone bridge by car it's hard to imagine that it was commissioned by Philip II from Juan de Herrera and completed in 1584. Below the Palacio Real, it's best appreciated from a distance, along the river's edge. As people have often noted, its elegant multiple arches make it much grander than the sorry Manzanares beneath it.

Real Monasterio de las Descalzas Reales
Plaza de las Descalzas 3 (522 06 97). Metro Callao, Sol/bus all routes to Puerta del Sol. **Open** *guided tours only* 9am-6pm Tue-Sat; 9am-3pm Sun, public holidays. **Admission** 800ptas; 300ptas students, under-18s, over-65s.
This atypical monastery was first built as a palace for Alonso Gutiérrez, treasurer of Charles V, and made into a convent by Charles' daughter Joanna of Austria when she herself became a nun. Rebuilt in 1556-1564 by Antonio Sillero and Juan Bautista de Toledo, it is the most complete sixteenth-century building in Madrid. Lavishly decorated, it is most known for its grand painted staircase, seventeenth-century tapestries and a remarkable, and long-forgotten, collection of art. It can be visited only with the official guides. *See also chapter* **Museums**.

Palacio de Comunicaciones. *See page 43.*

Real Monasterio de La Encarnación
Plaza de La Encarnación 1 (547 05 10). Metro Opera, Santo Domingo/bus 25, 33, 39, 148. **Open** 10.30am-12.30pm, 4-5.30pm, Wed, Sat; 10.30am-12.30pm Sun. **Admission** *Sat, Sun* 350ptas; *Wed* free.
This understated monastery was built in 1611-16 for Margaret of Austria, wife of Philip III. Initially designed by Juan Gómez de Mora, it was severely damaged by fire in 1734, and rebuilt in a classical-baroque style in the 1760s by Ventura Rodríguez. It was opened to the public in the 1960s, but still houses a small community of nuns, and is also famous for its extraordinary relics room. *See also chapter* **Museums**.

Bourbon Madrid

The Bourbon dynasty arrived in Spain with a new broom and different tastes, and in the 1760s King Charles III set out on a lightning campaign to make his capital a monumental city on a par with any in Europe.

Basilica de San Francisco el Grande
Plaza de San Francisco (365 38 00). Metro Puerta de Toledo/bus 3, 60, 148. **Open** *Oct-May* 11am-1pm, 4-7pm, *June-Sept* 11am-1pm, 5-8pm,Tue-Sat. **Admission** 50ptas.
This huge, multi-tiered church between the Puerta de Toledo and the Palacio Real is difficult to miss. A monastery on the site, reputedly founded by Saint Francis of Assisi himself, was knocked down in 1760. In its place Francisco Cabezas and later Francesco Sabatini built this neo-classical church between 1761 and 1784. Especially challenging was the construction of the dome, which has a diameter of 33 metres. So unusual (and potentially unstable) was it that it has since needed extensive restoration work, some of which is still going on. Inside there is an early painting by Goya, *The Sermon of San Bernardino of Siena* of 1781, as well as several frescoes by other artists.

Ermita de San Antonio de la Florida
Paseo de la Florida, 5 (542 07 22). Metro Norte/bus 46, 75. **Open** *Oct-14 July* 10am-2pm, 4-8pm, Tue-Fri; 10am-2pm Sat, Sun. *15 July-Sept* 9.30am-2pm Tue-Fri; 10am-2pm Sat, Sun. Closed public holidays. **Admission** *Mon, Tue, Thur-Sun* 200ptas, 100ptas students, under-18s, over 65s; *Wed* free.
This plain neo-classical chapel was built by Felipe Fontana for King Charles IV between 1792 and 1798. It is, however, most famous for the burial-place of Goya, and for the unique frescoes based on scenes of ordinary life in Madrid he painted there in 1798. In contrast to the rather staid exterior, the colour and use of light in Goya's images are stunning. Many consider them among his finest work, and they can be appreciated all the better since a four-year restoration programme was completed in 1993. Work is still continuing on some parts of the building.

Palacio Real (Palacio de Oriente)
Plaza de Oriente & C/Bailén (542 00 59). Metro Opera/bus 3, 25, 33, 39, 148. **Open** 9am-6pm Mon-Sat; 9am-3pm Sun, public holidays. **Admission** 800ptas; 300ptas students, under-18s, over 65s.
You are unlikely to catch sight of Spain's royal family here, as this 3,000-room official residence is only visited by them for occasional state functions requiring additional grandeur. The rest of the time the palace, commissioned by Philip V after the earlier Alcázar was lost to a fire in 1734, is open to view. The architects chiefly responsible for the final design were the Italians Gianbattista Sacchetti and Francesco Sabatini and the Spaniard Ventura Rodríguez. Filippo Juvara, Philip V's first choice, had planned for a palace four times as large, but after his death the project became a little

The Retiro

The Retiro is a jewel among parks. Covering nearly 300 acres in all, the gardens date from the 1630s, when they were laid out as part of the Buen Retiro palace of Philip IV (*see chapter* **Madrid by Area**). Most of the palace was destroyed during the Napoleonic Wars. Charles III first opened part of the gardens to the public in 1767, but it was only after the fall of Isabel II in 1868 that it became entirely free to the citizens of Madrid. After it became a park it acquired most of its many statues, particularly the giant 1902 monument to King Alfonso XII that presides over the lake.

Since becoming open to all, the Retiro has established a very special place in the hearts and habits of the people of Madrid. A Sunday morning stroll, especially before lunch, will reveal just how much it is made use of. You will see multi-generational families watching puppet shows and magic acts, dog owners letting free their hounds, children playing on swings and climbing frames, vendors hawking everything from traditional wafers (*barquillos*) to etchings, palm and tarot readers, buskers from around the globe, couples on the lake in hired boats, kids playing football, elderly men in leisurely games of *petanca* (boules), cyclists, runners and a good many bench-sitters who want nothing more than to read the paper. During the week it's much emptier, and it's easier then to take a look at some of its 15,000 trees, the rose garden, or the exhibition spaces. Once inside the Retiro, you can always forget the city beyond the gates and relish the lushness of this well-kept treasure.

The Retiro also contains several interesting buildings. At the very south end of the park is the **Observatorio Astronómico**, another of Charles III's scientific institutions, completed after his death in 1790. Beautifully proportioned, it is the finest neo-classical building in Madrid, designed by Juan de Villanueva. It still contains a working telescope, but this can only be seen and used by prior request. One room is also open to the public. Also an important part of the Retiro are its fine exhibition spaces, the **Palacio de Cristal**, the **Palacio de Velázquez** and the **Casa de Vacas**. Built for international exhibitions in the last century, they were all extensively renovated during the 1980s (*see chapter* **Art Galleries**).

Parque del Retiro

Main entrance *Plaza de la Independencia. Metro Retiro, Ibiza, Atocha/bus all routes to Retiro.* **Open** *Oct-April* 6.30am-10.30pm, *May-Sept* 6.30am-11pm, daily.

Observatorio Astronómico

C/Alfonso XII 3 (527 01 07). Metro Atocha/bus all routes to Atocha. **Open** 9am-2pm Mon-Fri.

FEBRERO 9 - 1

95

U.S.A. EN ARCO 9

A R

PARQUE FERIAL JUAN CARLOS
MADRID

C O

FEBRERO 8 - 1

96

ALEMANIA EN ARCO 9

FERIA INTERNACIONAL DE ARTE
CONTEMPORANEO
INTERNATIONAL CONTEMPORARY ART FAIR
Apdo. de Correos 67067. 28067 MADRID
Tels.: 722 50 00/17. Fax: 722 57 98/99

IFEMA
Feria de
Madrid

less ambitious. Completed in 1764, the late-baroque style palace is built almost entirely of granite and white Colmenar stone, and, surrounded by majestic gardens, undoubtedly contributes to the splendour of the city. Inside, the palace is a bit of a rambling mess, and impresses more by its size than anything else. However, there are clocks, porcelain, tapestries, medals and paintings by Tiepolo, Goya and Velázquez on display in separate museums within the building, and you can also tour a few of the former royal apartments.

Puente de Toledo
Glorieta de las Pirámides. Metro Pirámides/
bus 18, 23, 35.
The second of Madrid's major bridges, designed by Pedro de Ribera for Philip V and built in 1718-32. If you want to see the bridge and get in a good walk after exploring the Rastro, follow the Calle Toledo south until it ends.

Puerta de Alcalá
Plaza de la Independencia. Metro Retiro/
bus all routes to Plaza de la Independencia.
A short distance along Calle Alcalá from Cibeles, in the middle of another hectic traffic junction, stands this monumental neo-classical gate built for Charles III by his favourite Italian architect Francesco Sabatini to provide a grand entrance to the city. It was built in 1769-1778, using granite and stone from nearby Colmenar. Like Cibeles, it is often used as a symbol of Madrid. Possible to miss in the daytime traffic, it is certainly impressive when floodlit at night.

Puerta de Toledo
Glorieta de la Puerta de Toledo. Metro Puerta de
Toledo/bus all routes to Puerta de Toledo.
Not really a part of Bourbon Madrid, as this fairly simple gate was commissioned by Napoleon's brother Joseph, briefly King of Spain. After his departure it was quickly rejigged to honour the return of the delegates from the Cortes in Cádiz, and then the Bourbon King Fernando VII instead.

1814-1939

As monarchical rule crumbled, Madrid welcomed a remarkable hodgepodge of architectural styles.

Banco de España
Plaza de Cibeles. Metro Banco de España/
bus all routes to Cibeles.
A grandiose pile designed in 1882 by Eduardo Adaro and Severiano Sainz de la Lastra to house the recently-created Bank of Spain. The style is highly eclectic, but most influenced by French Second-Empire designs. The decorative arched window and elaborate clock above the main entrance are best seen from a distance.

Bolsa de Comercio de Madrid
Plaza de la Lealtad 1 (589 26 00). Metro Banco de
España/bus 9, 14, 27, 37, 45. **Open** *exhibition space*
10am-2pm Mon-Fri. **Admission** free.
In the same plaza as the Hotel Ritz, Madrid's stock market is a distinguished landmark as well as a business centre. Enrique María Repullés won the competition to design the building in 1884, with a neo-classical style chosen to match and reflect that of the nearby Prado. Today the building consists of two distinct areas. One, where trading is done, and the pace is unsurprisingly hectic. The second, open to the public, houses an exhibition on the market's history. *See also* chapter **Business**.

Catedral de Nuestra Señora de la Almudena
Plaza de la Armería (542 22 00). Metro Opera/bus 3, 25,
33, 39, 148. **Open** 10am-1.30pm, 6-8.30pm, Mon-Sat; 6-
8pm Sun. **Admission** free.

If ever a project looked like it would last forever, this was it. For centuries, church and state could not agree on whether Madrid should have a cathedral. When they did, in the 1880s, the project took 110 years to complete. In 1883 work began on a neo-Gothic design by the Marqués de Cubas, but this scheme gradually went off course. Another architect, Fernando Chueca Goitia, took over in 1944, and introduced a neo-classical style. Consequently, it has failed to attract any popular affection, but it was finally finished in 1993 – such an achievement that it was marked by a visit from the Pope. Until 1870, when it was knocked down by liberal urban reformers, the site contained the church of Santa María de la Almudena, formerly the main Mosque of Moslem Madrid.

Círculo de Bellas Artes
C/Marqués de Casa Riera 2 & C/Alcalá 42 (531 77 00).
Metro Banco de España, Sevilla/bus all routes to C/Alcalá.
Open *café* 8am-2am daily; *exhibitions* 5-9pm Tue-Fri;
11am-2pm, 5-9pm, Sat; 11am-2pm Sun.
Admission 100ptas.
Enormous windows giving onto the Calle Alcalá allow passers-by a look into what is certainly one of Madrid's most stunning clubs, built in 1919-26 by Antonio Palacios. Fortunately, entry nowadays isn't restricted to members, provided you pay the very modest fee. As well as the spacious main floor café, which spreads onto a gracious pavement café with enormous awnings in summer, this artistic society offers a plethora of art classes, exhibitions, lectures and concerts, as well as an annual Carnival Ball. Also, there is a cosy, dark library. *See also chapters* **Cafés & Bars**, **Art Galleries** *and* **Music: Classical & Opera**.

Congreso de los Diputados
Plaza de las Cortes (390 60 00). Metro Sevilla, Banco de
España/bus 9, 14, 27, 37, 45. **Open** *guided tours only*
10.30am-12.30pm Sat. Closed public holidays and Aug.
Many visitors to Madrid find themselves walking past this building uncertain of what it could be. It is in fact Spain's *Cortes*, the parliament, built in 1843-50 by Narciso Pascual y Colomer on the site of a recently-demolished monastery. A classical portico gives it a suitably dignified air, but the building is best distinguished by the handsome bronze lions that guard the entrance. Tourists are welcome on the free weekly guided tours, which in '93-94 attracted 60,000 people. Given this demand, it's best to phone ahead.

Nuevos Ministerios
Paseo de la Castellana 67. Metro Nuevos Ministerios/
bus 7, 14, 27, 40, 147, 150.
A seemingly endless, bunkerish building on the Castellana that is in fact a complex of government ministries, begun in 1932 and one of the largest projects bequeathed by the Spanish Republic to Madrid. It was designed by a team led by Secundino Zuazo, the principal architect of the *Gran Madrid* plan (*see chapter* **History: Republic & Civil War**). Aggressively monolithic in style, it was completed under the Franco regime. Through archways at the front it's just possible to see a park-like garden, open to the public, that's often frequented by Madrileños taking a break from the city along with the civil servants.

Palacio de Comunicaciones
Plaza de Cibeles (521 65 00). Metro Banco de España/bus
all routes to Cibeles. **Open** 8am-9pm Mon-Fri;
8am-3pm Sat.
Recent arrivals in Madrid often refuse to believe that this extraordinary construction, dwarfing the Plaza de Cibeles on which it stands and regularly compared to a sand castle or a wedding cake, can be just a post office. However, that's what it is. Madrid's main post office was designed in 1904 by Antonio Palacios and Joaquín Otamendi and completed in 1918, and is the best example of the extravagant style favoured by Madrid's élite at their most expansive. The design was influenced by Viennese art nouveau, but also fea-

tures all kinds of traditional Spanish touches. Customers who come in to buy a simple stamp or post a parcel are treated to a grand entrance (modernised with an over-sized revolving door), a Hollywood film-set staircase, soaring ceilings, stunning columns and grand marble floors. For details of postal services, *see chapter* **Survival**.

Plaza de Toros de Las Ventas

C/Alcalá 237 (356 22 00). Metro Ventas/bus 21, 53, 74, 146. **Open** 10am-2pm, 5-8pm, daily.
More than 22,000 spectators can catch a bullfight in this, Spain's largest arena and a mecca for all *aficionados*. It was completed in 1929. Like most turn-of-the-century bullrings it is in neo-*Mudéjar* style, with much use of ceramic tiles in a design that could almost be called playful. Around it there is ample open space to accommodate the crowds and food vendors, so it's easy to get a good look at the exterior. It's not necessary to go to a *corrida* to see the ring from within, too, for when the bulls are back on the ranch concerts are held here (*see chapter* **Madrid by Season**). The bullring makes a great music venue. Anyone interested in the history of bullfighting should visit the **Museo Taurino**, alongside the ring (*see chapter* **Museums**). The bullfight season itself runs from May to October. *See also chapter* **Bullfighting**.

Sociedad General de Autores (Palacio Longoria)

C/Fernando VI 6 (349 95 14). Metro Alonso Martínez/bus 3, 37, 40, 149.
Given the extraordinary output of Catalan Modernist architects – and Gaudí in particular – in Barcelona around the turn of the century, it is remarkable, to non-Spaniards at least, that there is not a single example of their work in Madrid. The only thing at all like it is this unusual building in Chueca, constructed by José Grasés Riera in 1902 as a residence and social setting for banker Javier González Longoria. The façade looks like it was formed out of wet sand, moulded by an expert in giant cake decoration. If a building could be considered voluptuous, this would be it. It was once thought that Catalan architecture had influenced the design, but Héctor Guimard and other French architects seem to have been a much more direct source of inspiration. It's now owned by the Spanish writers' and artists' association. Until very recently it had kept its original character, but early-nineties renovation has included some unattractive changes, particularly the green paint used for trim. Still, this is a treasure.

Modern Madrid

Three emblematic edifices of the last fifty years.

Estación de Atocha

Glorieta de Emperador Carlos V. Metro Atocha/ bus all routes to Atocha.
Madrid's classic wrought-iron and glass main rail station was built in 1888-92, to a design by Alberto del Palacio. It remained much the same, gathering a fair coating of soot, until the 1980s, when Rafael Moneo – he of the Museo Thyssen – began completely renovating the station in preparation for Spain's golden year of 1992. Entirely new sections were added to accommodate the AVE, the high-speed train to Seville (*see chapter* **Trips Out of Town**) and Madrid's expanded local rail network. Also, as well as the original building being thoroughly cleaned up, a 2,000-square metre indoor tropical garden was installed. Even if you've no plans to catch a train, a visit to Atocha is worthwhile to see this very imaginative, elegant blend of old and new.

Estadio Santiago Bernabéu

C/Concha Espina (350 06 00). Metro Lima/bus 7, 14, 43, 120, 150.
The temple of Real Madrid football club, designed by Manuel Muñoz Monasterio and Luis Alemany in the forties, and

named after the club's founder and long-time Chairman. A colossal grey structure alongside the Castellana, it resembles a stack of cans each one larger than the next, with swirling stairwells at each corner. It was renovated for the 1982 World Cup and again in the last few years, giving it a capacity for 105,000 fans. *See also chapter* **Sport & Fitness**.

Urbanización AZCA

Paseo de la Castellana & Avda General Perón. Metro Lima, Nuevos Ministerios/bus 7, 14, 27, 40, 147, 150.
Known to some as 'Little Manhattan', this glitzy skyscraper development was first projected during the Franco regime's industrial heyday in the sixties, but picked up with extra vigour in democratic Spain's eighties' boom to become a symbol of Madrid yuppiedom. The most striking of the several giant blocks are the circular Torre Europa and the Torre Picasso, designed by Japanese architect Minori Yamasaki in 1988 and, at 157 metres, Madrid's tallest building. Between them is the Plaza Picasso, a well-maintained park. Originally built to lure businesses to a less traffic-ridden area of the city, the development has grown so much that it now generates more than its share of traffic itself. Apart from office buildings, a chic shopping centre, *Moda*, restaurants and several other facilities have popped up, allowing business people to spend their entire day without having to venture outside the confines of the complex. As to the name, don't waste time trying to figure out what AZCA stands for, as the letters apparently don't mean anything.

Parks

Madrileños are very attached to their parks, many of which were once royal gardens, and recent city authorities have also created fine new open spaces.

Campo del Moro

Paseo Virgen del Puerto (542 00 59). Metro Norte/bus 25, 33, 39, 46, 75, 138, C. **Open** *Oct-April* 10am-6pm Mon-Sat; 9am-6pm Sun, public holidays. *May-Sept* 10am-8pm Mon-Sat; 9am-8pm Sun, public holidays.
Before or after a visit to the Palacio Real it's worth visiting this off-the-beaten track formal garden with a slightly British flavour. Two monumental fountains are likely to catch your eye. The first, nearer the palace, is *Los Tritones*, originally made in 1657 for the palace in Aranjuez (*see chapter* **Trips Out of Town**). The second, *Las Conchas*, is from the eighteenth century and was designed by the architect Ventura Rodríguez. Both were installed here in the 1890s.

Capricho de la Alameda de Osuna

Paseo de la Alameda de Osuna. Metro Canillejas/bus 101, 105. **Open** 9am-9pm Sat, Sun, public holidays.
One of Madrid's most unusual parks, a formal garden designed by Marie-Antoinette's gardener J-B Mulot for the Duchess of Osuna, a great hostess of her day and friend of Goya, in the 1790s. Wonderfully cool and peaceful, the gardens are something of a romantic fantasy, with an artificial lake with islands in the middle. In this century they fell into decay, while all around them spread the semi-industrial suburban sprawl between Madrid and the airport. Work on restoration began in 1974. *See also* **Madrid by Area: Outer Limits**.

Casa de Campo

Metro Lago, Batán/bus 33, 41, 75.
Covering nearly 4,500 acres, this is by some way the largest park in Madrid. It was the last of the royal estates to be opened to the public, by the Republic in 1931. The park is huge, and it's possible to have a real country walk across it. It also houses sports facilities including public tennis courts, swimming pools and a sizeable lake, where boats can be hired. Cyclists criss-cross the park, savouring the more traffic-free areas, and it also contains a youth hostel (*see chap-*

The pinewoods of the **Casa de Campo**.

ter **Accommodation**). Many visitors also head directly for the **Zoo** or the **Parque de Atracciones** funfair (for both, *see chapter* **Children**). Another attraction is the **Teleférico** cable car between the park and the **Parque del Oeste** (*see below*). For the moment the park is open to traffic, a controversial matter. At night the atmosphere changes, and prostitutes line many of the park roads, particularly near the Lago Metro station, waiting for kerb-crawling drivers. Traffic restrictions have been proposed as a means of obstructing them, raising loud protests from the prostitutes. Ecologists, meanwhile, also support the measure out of concern for the state of the park. For information on sports facilities in the Casa de Campo, *see chapter* **Sports & Fitness**.

Jardín Botánico

Plaza de Murillo (585 47 00) Metro Atocha/bus 14, 27, 37, 45. **Open** *Nov-Feb* 10am-6pm; *Oct, Mar* 10am-7pm; *April, Sept* 10am-8pm; *May-Aug* 10am-9pm. **Admission** 200ptas; 100ptas students, under-18s, over 65s.

Madrid's luscious botanical gardens were created for Charles III by Juan de Villanueva and the botanist Gómez Ortega in 1781. They are between the Paseo del Prado and the Retiro, just south of the Prado museum, but inside it's easy to feel that the city has been put on hold. There are more than 30,000 plants from around the globe, arranged in formal style. It's an ideal place for a stroll or a moment's peace in spring, early summer or autumn.

Jardines de las Vistillas

C/Beatriz Galindo. Metro La Latina/ bus 3, 31, 50, 65, 148.

The biggest reason to head for these gardens is the view. Easily seen from this high open spot are the Almudena, the whole of the Casa de Campo and even the Guadarrama. There's also a great terrace bar nearby, and the park is often used for neighbourhood events during *fiestas* and in summer (*see chapters* **Madrid by Season** *and* **Cafés & Bars**).

Museo de Escultura al Aire Libre

Paseo de la Castellana 41. Metro Rubén Darío/ bus 5, 14, 27, 45, 150.

A very untraditional museum, this creatively-arranged space, inaugurated in the 1970s, was the brainchild of engineers José Antonio Fernández Ordóñez and Julio Martínez Calzón. While designing a bridge across the Castellana, they decided that the space underneath would be a good art venue. Sculptor Eusebio Sempere convinced 15 fellow sculptors or their families to donate their work, the most imposing of which is the six-ton cube *The Meeting* by Eduardo Chillida. Suspended by a cable, it's one piece that's difficult to miss. What could have been a dreary space has thus been made much more intriguing. Skateboarders use it a lot too.

Parque Juan Carlos I

Avda de Logroño & Avda de los Andes (722 50 00). Metro Canillejas/bus 101, 105, 122. **Open** *Oct-April* 10am-8pm, *May-Sept* 10am-10pm, daily.

Madrid's newest park, between the airport and the Feria de Madrid trade fair centre (*see chapter* **Business**), and still in its infant stages. With time, it could become one of Madrid's more attractive places. A state-of-the-art park, it's very large, with different gardens within a circle of olive trees, and an artificial river and other water features. For the moment, it's little used as it's so awkward to get there by public transport. It would also be more popular if it had more shade.

Parque del Oeste

Metro Moncloa, Norte/bus 21, 46, 74, 82, 132, 133.

A special method to reach this park could be the **Teleférico** (*see below*) from the Casa de Campo. Once you've landed, it's easy to understand why this park, designed by landscape gardener Cecilio Rodríguez in the 1900s, is considered one of the city's most attractive open spaces. Particularly beautiful is *La Rosaleda*, the rose garden, which is magnificent in spring. The park was virtually destroyed during the Civil War, and then relaid. The Montaña del Príncipe Pío, at the south end of the park, is one of the highest points in Madrid, with wonderful views of the Palacio Real and the Casa de Campo. It was the site of the Montaña barracks, where the Nationalists had their stronghold at the start of the Civil War in 1936 (*see chapter* **History: Republic & Civil War**). This was later demolished, and the hill incorporated into the park. Bizarrely, it is now home to the **Templo de Debod**, a genuine Egyptian temple from the fourth century BC that was presented to Spain by the government of Egypt after it had been removed from its original site because of the Aswan Dam. Alongside the Parque del Oeste is the Paseo del Pintor Rosales, one of the most popular places in Madrid for pavement cafés (*see chapter* **Cafés & Bars**).

Viewpoints & Rides

Faro de Madrid

Avda de los Reyes Católicos (544 81 04). Metro Moncloa/bus 46, 82, 132, 133. **Open** *Sept-May* 10.30am-2pm, 5.30-8pm, *June-Aug* 11am-1.45pm, 5.30-8.45pm, Tue-Sun. **Admission** 200ptas; 100ptas 2-12s, over-65s.

If heights aren't a problem, the best way to get a good overview of Madrid and its surroundings is from this tower, opened as part of the 1992 celebrations. It's even exactly 92 metres high. Squeeze into the 12-person glass lift and before

*For a leisurely overview of things, take the **Teleférico**.*

you know it you're atop the city with nearly a 360° view. A huge success, the tower attracts a million visitors each year.

Teleférico de Madrid

Paseo del Pintor Rosales (541 74 50). Metro Argüelles/bus 21, 74.
Casa de Campo. Metro Lago/bus 33.
Open *Oct-April* noon-8pm Sat, Sun, public holidays.
May-Sept 11am-2.30pm, 5pm-9.30pm, daily. **Tickets** 445ptas return; 315ptas one-way; under 5s free.

If you have only ten minutes and 42 seconds to see Madrid, consider a ride in these modern, six-person cable-cars that connect the Casa de Campo and the Parque del Oeste. The trip takes you right over the Casa de Campo, with great views of the Palacio Real, the Almudena and the Manzanares. It can carry 1,200 passengers each hour, so don't panic if there's a long queue at the ticket office. Note that closing times often vary with the sunset rather than follow fixed times.

Tours

Bus Tours

For a quick overview of the city a bus tour may be a good bet, although most available in Madrid are fairly predictable. All are in Spanish, English, and sometimes other languages. **Madrid Vision** provides a cheaper and more flexible service. Most of these tours can also be booked through hotels.

Juliá Tours

Gran Via 68 (559 96 05). Metro Santo Domingo/bus all routes to Gran Via. **Open** 8am-8pm Mon-Sat; 8am-noon Sun. **Tours** 9.45am, 3pm, daily. **No credit cards.**

A well-known company offering a standard range of tours including bullfights, evening tours with flamenco shows and so on. Prices are from 4,315ptas-6,610 ptas. They also operate tours to towns near Madrid, for 5,000-10,000ptas.

Madrid Vision/Trapsatur

C/San Bernardo 23 (542 66 66). Metro Noviciado/bus 147. **Open** 7.30am-8.30pm daily. **Credit** V.

Two divisions of the same company. **Madrid Vision** is a special tourist bus service that runs six buses per day on a set route around all the major sights, with 16 stops en route. With a full ticket you can get on and off the buses as many times as you wish during that day. On the buses there are hostesses and a multi-lingual commentary through headsets. A full ticket costs 1,000ptas; a 500ptas ticket entitles you to stay on the bus for the whole trip, or to get off at one stop, but not to re-board. Tickets can be bought on the bus or at the main office. **Trapsatur** offers more conventional tours within Madrid, one of two hours and one of four hours, focussing on the Prado and the Palacio Real. Tours cost 2,615ptas and 4,310ptas.

Pullmantur

Plaza de Oriente 8 (541 18 07). Metro Opera/bus 3, 25, 33, 39, 148. **Open** 8am-8.30pm daily. **Tours** 9.30am, 3pm Tue-Sun. **Credit** MC, V.

Tours of the traditional sights run during the day, while night-time packages that include dinner and dancing, tours of fountains and plazas and so on are also available. Prices start at 3,720ptas. There are also tours of towns near Madrid, Toledo, Segovia, Aranjuez and others, for which prices vary from 5,000-10,000ptas.

Walking Tours

Descubre Madrid

C/Mayor 69 (588 29 06/07). Metro Sol/bus all routes to Puerta del Sol. **Open** *bookings* 9am-2pm Mon-Fri.

Run by the city tourist board, this service offers walking and bus tours covering nearly every nook and cranny of Madrid, its architecture, literary life, little-known figures and so on. Unfortunately, most are available only in Spanish. However, even if you don't speak much of the language, they might be worth it just to see the sights. Prices are very reasonable, with most tours including those by bus at under 1,000ptas.

History

Key Events

Frontier Outpost

c860 Madrid founded during the reign of Emir Mohammed I of Córdoba.
1085-86 Alfonso VI of Castile conquers Emirate of Toledo, including Madrid
1109 Madrid besieged by Moorish army
1202 Madrid given *Fuero* (Statutes); population c3,000
1212 Battle of Navas de Tolosa: decisive defeat of Moslems in Spain
1309 First *Cortes* held in Madrid
c1360 King Pedro the Cruel rebuilds Alcázar of Madrid
1476 Isabella becomes unchallenged Queen of Castile after battle of Toro
1492 Conquest of Granada; Expulsion of Jews from Spain; Discovery of America
1520-21 Madrid joins *Comuneros* revolt
1547 Birth of Cervantes in Alcalá de Henares

Capital of a Golden Age

1561 Philip II moves Court to Madrid from Toledo; population then c20,000
1562 Lope de Vega born in Madrid
1563-84 Building of El Escorial
1566 Beginning of Dutch Revolt
1574 First theatre in Madrid, the *Corral de la Pacheca*
1588 Defeat of the Armada against England
1599-1600 Plague and famine throughout Castile
1601-6 Court moved to Valladolid
1605, 1615 Don Quijote published, in two parts
1609 Expulsion of the *Moriscos*, the former Moslems
1617-1619 Completion of Plaza Mayor
1630-33 Buen Retiro palace built; population of Madrid c.150-170,000
1640 Revolts begin in Portugal and Catalonia
1643 Battle of Rocroi: Spanish army in Flanders decisively defeated by the French.
1660 Death of Velázquez
1665 Philip IV succeeded by Charles II, then aged four
1700 Charles II dies without an heir

Bourbon Madrid

1702-14 War of the Spanish Succession: Philip V, first Bourbon King of Spain. Population of Madrid c.100,000
1715 Decree of *Nova Planta*; Spain created as one state
1734 Alcázar of Madrid destroyed by fire
1761 Charles III bans waste dumping in Madrid streets
1775-82 Paseo del Prado created
1778 Goya moves to Madrid from Aragon
1795 In wars following French Revolution Spain changes sides to form alliance with France
1800 Population of Madrid c180,000

Revolutions & Railways

1808-13 French Occupation: Joseph Bonaparte made King of Spain
1812 *Cortes* in Cádiz agrees first Spanish Constitution
1814 Fernando VII abrogates Constitution
1810-24 Latin American Wars of Independence

1820-23 Military coup begins three years of liberal rule
1823 French army restores Fernando VII to full power
1833 Carlist Wars begin on death of Fernando VII
1836 Main decree on Disentailment of Monasteries; University of Alcalá de Henares moved to Madrid
1851 Railway line to Aranjuez inaugurated
1854-62 Puerta del Sol rebuilt
1858 Canal de Isabel II, bringing water from the Guadarrama, inaugurated
1860 Plan for *Ensanche* of Madrid approved
1868 Revolution overthrows Isabel II
1871 Amadeo of Savoy becomes King of Spain. First trams in Madrid, drawn by mules
1872 Population of Madrid 334,000
1873 February: Amadeo abdicates; Republic declared

The Restoration

1874 January: Republic becomes military dictatorship after coup; December: Alfonso XII declared King
1879 Spanish Socialist Party (PSOE) founded
1898 Spanish-American War: disaster for Spain. Madrid's tramlines electrified
1900 Population of Madrid 539,835
1907 First registration of motor vehicles in Madrid
1910 Building of Gran Via initiated
1917 General Strike in the whole of Spain
1919 First Madrid Metro line opened
1923 General Primo de Rivera establishes Dictatorship
1929-31 Barajas airport opened
1930 Fall of Primo de Rivera; Madrid's population 952,832

Republic & Civil War

1931 14 April: Proclamation of Second Republic
1931-33 *Gran Madrid* plan approved
1934 October: General Strike against entry of right-wing ministers into government; in Asturias, bloodily suppressed by General Franco
1936 February: elections won by Popular Front; 18 July: military uprising against left-wing government; 9 November: Francoist forces launch assault on Madrid
1939 1 April: Franco declares war over

Dictatorship & Rebirth

1946-50 UN imposes sanctions on Spain
1953 Cooperation treaty with USA
1950-60 Population of Madrid passes two million
1959 Stabilisation Plan opens up Spanish economy
1961 First violent attack by Basque nationalists of ETA
1970 Juan Carlos declared Franco's successor; population of Madrid 3,146,000
1975 20 November: Death of Franco
1977 15 June: First democratic general election
1979 April: Enrique Tierno Galván, Mayor of Madrid
1980 Pedro Almodóvar makes his first feature, *Pepi, Luci, Bom...*
1982 Socialist Party under Felipe González wins national elections
1986 1 January: Spain joins European Community
1991 Popular Party wins power in Madrid city council

Frontier Outpost

Founded by a Moorish Emir, Madrid was only a footnote in history for its first 700 years.

In the seventeenth century, after Madrid had become the capital of the Spanish Empire, an attempt was made to give it an ancient past. Several writers developed the story of its descent from a Roman city called *Mantua Carpetana*.

These accounts, however, were almost entirely the product of wishful thinking. The area around Madrid has one of the longest histories of continuous settlement of anywhere in Europe, and is extraordinarily rich in prehistoric relics, many of which are now in the **Museo Arqueológico Nacional** (*see chapter* **Museums**). Later, there were Roman towns nearby at Alcalá de Henares (*Complutum*) and Toledo (*Toletum*), and several Roman villas along the valley of the Manzanares. There is, though, no real evidence that there was ever a local Mantua, or that any of these settlements was the origin of modern Madrid.

The story of *Mantua Carpetana*, however, served to obscure the insignificance of Madrid before Philip II moved his Court here in 1561, and particularly the embarassing fact that it had been founded by Moslems. Specifically, in the reign of Mohammed I, fifth Emir of Córdoba, in about 860.

Following their irruption into the Iberian peninsula in 711 the Moslems did not occupy the inhospitable lands to the north of the Sierra de Guadarrama, but instead established a frontier more or less along the old Roman road linking Mérida, Toledo and Saragossa. The original *Al-Kasr* (a word absorbed into Spanish as *Alcázar*) or fortress of Madrid was one of a string of watch-towers built north of this line in the ninth century as Christian raids into *Al-Andalus* became increasingly frequent. The rocky crag on which it stood, where the Palacio Real is today, was particularly suited to the purpose, since it had a view of most of the main tracks south from the Guadarrama. It also had excellent water, from underground streams within the rock. Madrid's original Arabic name, *Maŷrit*, means 'place of many springs'.

The most important of the outposts protecting Toledo, *Maŷrit* was more than just a fortress, with an outer citadel or *Al-Mudaina* (later hispanicised as Almudena), the eastern wall of which ran along the modern Calle Factor, and a wider town or *Medina* bounded by the modern Plaza de la Villa and Calle Segovia. The section of wall along the Cuesta de la Vega (*see chapter* **Sightseeing**) is the only remnant of Moslem Madrid visible today.

Citadel and *Medina* consisted mainly of a mass of narrow alleys, like the old quarters of North African cities. They did, though, have a sophisticated system for channeling the underground springs, which, much extended, would continue to serve Christian Madrid for centuries.

Maŷrit was attacked by Christian armies in 932 and 1047, and in the 970s was used by the great minister of Córdoba, Al-Mansur, as a launching-point in his celebrated hundred campaigns against the north. By the eleventh century it had a population of about 7,000, among them Abul-Qasim Maslama, mathematician, astronomer, translator of Greek literature and experimenter in magic.

CHRISTIAN CONQUEST

In the early eleventh century the Caliphate of Córdoba disintegrated into a mass of petty princedoms called *Taifas*, and *Maŷrit* became part of the Emirate of Toledo. In 1086 Alfonso VI of Castile was able to take advantage of this situation to conquer Toledo, and with it Madrid. The main mosque became the church of Santa María de la Almudena, which stood until the nineteenth century.

For many years, though, Madrid continued to be in the front line. In 1109 it was again besieged, by a Moorish army camped below the Alcázar in the place ever since known as the *Campo del Moro* ('Field of the Moor'). A new wall was built, enclosing an area between the Alcázar and Plaza Isabel II, Plaza San Miguel and the Plaza Humilladero.

Nevertheless, by 1270 the Castilians had taken Córdoba and Seville. Christian Madrid, however, was a humble place that grew only very slowly. Its population was probably no more than 3,000. Only in 1202 was Madrid given its *Fuero*, or Royal Statutes. It was a decidedly rural town, and most of the population who worked did so on the land. Madrid did acquire some large religious houses, notably the Friary of San Francisco, where San Francisco el Grande now stands, supposedly founded by Saint Francis of Assisi himself in 1217.

Madrid was still not entirely Christian. Many Moslems, known as *Mudéjares*, had stayed in the conquered areas, retaining their own laws and religion. They were particularly prized by the Castilian monarchs for their skills as builders and masons. In Madrid they moved into the area known as the *Morería* (*see chapter* **Madrid by Area: Villa y Corte**). Medieval Madrid also had a smaller Jewish population, believed to have been concentrated outside the walls in Lavapiés.

Very little of medieval Madrid is still visible today precisely because it was so undistinguished, and was for the most part discarded in the last four centuries. The most important remaining buildings are the towers of **San Nicolás de los Servitas** and **San Pedro el Viejo**, built by *Mudéjar* craftsmen in their distinctive Hispano-Moorish style. Most of the local notables had their residences around the Plaza de la Villa, where the fifteenth-century **Torre de los Lujanes** still stands today (*see chapter* **Sightseeing**).

During the Middle Ages Madrid did, however, acquire its future patron saint, San Isidro. He was a local farm labourer, believed to have died in 1172, who with his wife Santa María de la Cabeza was known for extreme piety and a series of miraculous and saintly acts, among them that of never failing to give food to another member of the poor. The cult of Isidro, remarkable for the very lowly status of its central figure, became extremely popular locally. Once Madrid had become the Spanish capital the couple would both be canonised, as the only husband-and-wife saints in history.

ROYAL FAVOUR

Madrid did finally begin to play a slightly larger role in the affairs of Castile in the fourteenth century. In 1309 the *Cortes* or Parliament met here for the first time. Medieval Castile did not have a fixed capital, but instead the Court followed the King around the country, and similarly the *Cortes* met in several different towns.

Fourteenth- and fifteenth-century Castile was dogged by a series of social revolts and civil wars, between the monarchs, the nobility, and rival claimants within the royal family itself. Against this backdrop Madrid began to gain popularity as a royal residence, more as a retreat than as a centre of power. King Pedro 'the Cruel' (1350-69) first began to turn the old Alcázar into something more habitable. That it was not a very prized royal possession, however, was shown when it briefly became Armenian territory. In 1383 Leo V of Armenia lost his kingdom to the Turks, and as consolation Juan I of Castile gave him three of his own estates, among them Madrid. Later it reverted to Castilian sovereignty. Madrid was most favoured by Juan II (1407-54) and above all Enrique IV (1454-1474), who gave it the title of *muy noble y muy leal* ('very noble and very loyal').

In addition, political instability did not prevent there being substantial economic progress in fifteenth-century Castile, which enabled Madrid to become for the first time a reasonably thriving trading centre. The old market in the Plaza de la Villa became inadequate, and in the 1460s an area east of the twelfth-century wall was built up as a ramshackle market square, the origin of the later

Plaza Mayor. Around 1450 a new town wall was also built, not for defence but so that taxes might be levied in the new parts of the city. Its main eastern entrance was a new gate, the Puerta del Sol.

At the end of the fifteenth century a new era was opening up in Castilian and Spanish history. In 1476 Enrique IV's sister Isabel and her husband Fernando of Aragon – Ferdinand and Isabella – succeeded in bringing the civil wars to an end. Through their marriage they united the different Spanish kingdoms, although each retained its own institutions for another two centuries. Within Castile they imposed their authority upon the aristocracy, establishing an absolute monarchy and a powerful professional army that enabled them to intervene in the wars of Renaissance Italy. The earnestly devout Isabella was also one of the initiators of the militant sense of religious mission that would be a mark of Imperial Spain. Detesting the religious coexistence that had characterised medieval Spain, she ordered the expulsion of the Jews in 1492 and the forcible conversion of the remaining *Mudéjar* Moslems in 1502, and established the Inquisition to police these measures. Also in 1492 came the conquest of Moslem Granada, which won Ferdinand and Isabella the title 'Most Catholic Kings' from the Pope. It was also, of course, in this same year that they sponsored Columbus' first voyage to America.

Madrid retained a degree of royal favour, partly because of its connections with some key figures at Isabella's Court. Most important was Cardinal Cisneros, the austere Franciscan, born just north of Madrid at Torrelaguna, who she made Archbishop of Toledo and head of the church in Spain in 1495. Consequently, it continued its modest growth, and at the end of the Middle Ages had a population of around 10–15,000.

The **Torre de los Lujanes**.

Capital
of a Golden Age

Brought out of obscurity by royal whim, Madrid became the centre of Spain's brief but dazzling Golden Age.

On 11 May 1561 the small-time aristocrats who ran the town of Madrid received a letter from their king, Philip II, informing them that he, the entire royal household and all their hundreds of hangers-on would shortly be coming to stay. They immediately set about panic buying of food stocks from surrounding towns, using the money set aside for the *fiesta* of Corpus Christi, much to the irritation of the local population. No-one quite realised, though, that this transformation was intended to be permanent.

In the previous fifty years the Spanish monarchy had been transformed. Ferdinand and Isabella were succeeded by their grandson Charles of Habsburg (1516-1556), who through his father Philip, Duke of Burgundy, also inherited Burgundy (the Netherlands and large parts of eastern France) and the Habsburg lands in central Europe, and would in 1519 receive the title of Holy Roman Emperor, as Charles V. He would also, of course, acquire ever-larger territories in America. Spain thus became part, and increasingly the centre, of a European and world-wide empire.

When he first visited Spain in 1517 Charles appointed French-speakers to many state offices. This led in 1520 to the revolt of the *Comuneros*, in which the historic towns of Castile, Madrid among them, rose up in opposition to foreign influence and the encroachment of royal power on their traditional freedoms. However, after this uprising had been suppressed in 1521, Charles came to value Spain – above all Castile – more and more, as the most loyal part of his empire.

Charles and his successors had an immense sense of the dignity of their dynasty and their imperial mission, believing that their vast territories had come to them through Providence and that it was their right and duty to defend both them and the Catholic faith. This would involve continual and ever more costly wars, against the French, the Moslem Turks and, increasingly, the northern Protestants. This idea of mission combined perfectly with the crusading spirit already imbued in the Castilian church and aristocracy. Castile also had a regular army that was establishing a repu-

tation for invincibility, and was a ready source of money, thanks to American metals and to the fact that after the crushing of the *Comuneros* it was incapable of refusing any royal request for funds.

Charles V made no attempt to give Castile a capital. However, on his visits to Spain he did spend considerable time at Madrid, hunting at El Pardo and giving the town another title, *Imperial y Coronada* ('Imperial and Crowned'). In 1525, after his victory at Pavia, he had his great enemy Francis I of France brought to Madrid and imprisoned in the Torre de los Lujanes.

In 1555 Charles abdicated and retired to the Monastery of Yuste, in the Sierra de Gredos (*see chapter* **The Sierras**). Austria and the title of Holy Roman Emperor went to his brother Ferdinand, but Spain and Burgundy were passed on to Charles' son, Philip II (1556-1598).

The fundamental figure in Madrid's history, Philip was a deeply pious, shy, austere man. Factors personal and political led him to feel a need for a permanent capital. His father had travelled incessantly about his many dominions, and led his armies into battle. Philip, in contrast, sought to rule his inheritance from behind a desk as a kind of 'King-Bureaucrat', sometimes dealing with 400 documents a day. This extraordinary administrative exercise naturally required a permanent base.

Moreover, in the 1540s Charles V had introduced Burgundian state ritual into the previously relatively informal court of Castile. Every appearance of the monarch – such as meals, in which food could only be served to the royal family by gentlemen-in-waiting, exalted Dukes and Marquises, on their knees – followed a set ceremonial order, in an etiquette that became ever more elaborate as the Habsburgs expanded their idea of their own grandeur. The number of court attendants mushroomed, also making an itinerant court impractical.

Precisely why Philip chose Madrid as his capital, a town without a single printing press, let alone a cathedral, remains unclear. In the 1540s, as Crown Prince, he had already ordered the extension of Madrid's Alcázar into a large, rambling, palace. The fact that Madrid was almost at the dead centre of the Iberian peninsula may have appealed to Philip, who was fascinated by geometric patterns, but it made no economic sense at all, as it would give Spain the only major European capital not on a navigable river.

Valladolid and Toledo were both more obvious candidates, but their historic importance seems itself to have been a disadvantage. In contrast Madrid – which for centuries would normally be referred to in Spain as *la Corte*, the Court, never as a city in its own right, which indeed it wasn't – would be a capital of the monarchy's own creation, a pure expression of royal power.

BOOM TOWN

Having established his ideal capital, Philip strangely did very little to build or plan it. After the completion of the Alcázar his attention shifted to his palace-monastery of **El Escorial** (*see chapter* **Around Madrid**), where he would increasingly spend his time. Royal piety was demonstrated by the endowment of lavish new houses for religious orders, such as the **Descalzas Reales** (*see chapters* **Sightseeing** *and* **Museums**). Philip II founded 17 convents and monasteries in Madrid, Philip III 14 and Philip IV another 17, and they would cover a third of the city until the nineteenth century. A wider city wall was put up in 1566, and the Puente de Segovia built in the 1580s. Philip's favourite architect, Juan de Herrera, planned the rebuilding of the **Plaza Mayor**, but the only part built during his reign was the Casa de la Panadería in 1590. Philip's idea of a capital seemed more a collection of royal establishments than a living city.

Reality, however, was more powerful than this rudimentary concept. The establishment of the Court and aristocracy in Madrid, the great centres of consumption and patronage, made it a magnet for people from all over Spain and abroad. The population went from around 16-20,000 in 1561 to 55,000 in 1584 and close to 85,000 by 1600. Building did not keep up with the influx, and a law decreed that in any house of more than one storey the upper floor could be requisitioned to house members of the Court. In response people simply put up houses with only one floor, and much of the new Madrid grew as a mass of shabby, low buildings slapped together out of mud.

This improvised capital did not impress foreign visitors. Lambert Wyts, a Flemish aristocrat who arrived in 1571, said that it was 'the foulest and filthiest town in Spain'. Thick mud made it impossible to ride a horse down the main streets in winter until some cobbles were put down in the 1580s, and even then they were grossly inadequate. There were no drains of any kind, and the streets were full of waste thrown out of the houses every night, producing an 'unbearable stench'.

From the start Madrid would take on a characteristic that would stay with it to this day – that it was a city of outsiders, in which at least 50 per cent of the population, and often much more than that, were from elsewhere, sustained by a steady flow of new arrivals. Another trait for which Madrid would often be condemned was that it was a city that consumed but did not produce anything. The trades that did develop in Madrid – carpenters,

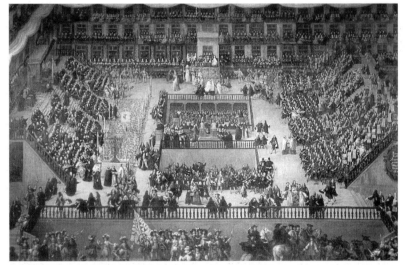

A packed house for an Auto de Fe *in the Plaza Mayor in 1680.*

shoemakers, jewellers, fan-makers, workers in fine lace – were overwhelmingly oriented to servicing the Court and aristocracy.

The economic frailty of Madrid reflected that of Castile as a whole. The gold and silver of Mexico and Peru seemed to give the Habsburg kings limitless potential wealth. The demands of their wars, however, were immediate, and could only be met by loans from German and Italian bankers. The result was spiralling, uncontrollable debts that not even American gold could match. Also, the country's political hierarchy had been built on the basis of giving the aristocracy, the *hidalgos* or lesser gentry and the church immense privileges, among them exemption from taxation. This meant that the always-increasing war taxes hit precisely and only the few productive sectors of the population. Young men of working age were also continually being drawn off for the army. For a country with the social system of Castile, constant imperialism was near suicidal; in time, it would lead to the eradication of the growth visible under Ferdinand and Isabella, and a catastrophic decline in the rural population.

One aspect of Spain during its 'Golden Century' was certainly its intense Christian faith. This was also, though, the golden age of the *pícaro*, the chancer, the figure living on his wits portrayed in the *picaresque* novels of the period. In a society that valued aristocracy, status and military or state service over any productive activity, and in which the real economy was rapidly dwindling, their numbers naturally multiplied.

The mecca for all *pícaros* was Madrid, the place where discharged soldiers, landless peasants and other drifters would be most likely to find a niche, as servants or bodyguards, or by gambling, prostitution, simple thieving or many other means. The great poet and satirist Quevedo wrote a whole book cataloguing the different varieties of Madrid's low life and how they acquired cash. It also contained a great many of the very poor, for whom the huge number of religious houses in the city, all sources of charity, was a major attraction.

Pícaros were not only found among the poor. Madrid also drew in thousands at the other end of society, often *hidalgos* but with estates run to nothing, who came hoping to attach themselves to some lordly patron and so break into the circles of the Court. For them, appearance, the image of aristocracy, was everything. In 1620 Madrid acquired its first guide book, the 'Guide and Advice to Strangers who Come to the Court, in which They are Taught to Flee the Dangers that there are in Court Life', by Antonio Liñán y Verdugo, a lawyer from Cuenca. He warned other provincials who might come to do business in Madrid that in 'this Babylon', 'of every four things one sees, one cannot believe even two', for everything was just 'fabulous appearances, dreamed-up marvels, fairy-tale treasures, and figures like actors on a stage'.

This volatile mass naturally needed entertainment. One source was the theatre, in the permanent *corral* theatres that began to be built in Madrid in the 1570s (*see chapter* **Theatre**), the focus of the extraordinary literary vitality of the city at this time. There were also the major *fiestas* and royal ceremonies, many of them also occasions for mass revelry. And, even foreigners who complained about the mud and the stink were impressed by the variety of luxuries that could be had in Madrid, from Italian lace to 'fresh' fish, brought caked in ice on a five-day journey from the Basque coast.

NO LONGER CAPITAL

In 1571 came the greatest single success of Philip II's reign with the defeat of the Turkish fleet off Lepanto in Greece. In 1580, after the Portuguese throne had fallen vacant, Philip also became King of Portugal. He appeared to be at the height of his strength. However, suspensions of payments on his debts were becoming frequent occurrences, and in the 1560s a rebellion had broken out in the Protestant northern Netherlands that would develop into a morass into which Spanish armies and wealth would disappear without trace. His dispute with England, also, not only resulted in the catastrophe of the Armada but also gave the Dutch a vital ally. Interventions in the religious wars in France were equally costly.

As problems mounted without any ever being resolved, a gnawing frustration spread through Castilian society. The response of the leaders of Court and church to this multiplication of external threats was to turn in on themselves. The former Moslems (*Moriscos*), nominally converted to Catholicism, were subjected to increasing pressure that culminated in their expulsion from Spain in 1609, and the Inquisition – if never the all-pervading force it became in Protestant caricatures – was given great powers to investigate deviations from Catholic orthodoxy.

Philip II died in 1598 at El Escorial, aged 71. His son Philip III (1598-1621) and grandson Philip IV (1621-65) had neither the intelligence, confidence or normally the motivation to carry on with the awesome burden of work he had set as an example. Philip III began the practice of ruling through a favourite or *valido*, for most of his reign the Duke of Lerma. The country's impoverished state, aggravated by a devastating plague in 1599, was impossible to ignore, and Lerma responded by making peace with England and the Dutch.

Lerma also committed the ultimate injury to Madrid by moving the Court to Valladolid, in 1601. His main stated reason was that this would serve to revive the prostrate economy of northern Castile, although he also stood to benefit from the move personally. He also argued that Madrid, in any case, was so overrun with undesirables that it had become intolerable. The monarchy's purpose-built capital had run out of control, and it would be best to write it off and start again, in a city where controls could be imposed on all those with no good reason to be there.

Within a few months Madrid was so deserted that 'it appeared as if the Moors or the English had sacked and burnt it'. By 1605 the population had fallen back to just 26,000, little more than it had been before Philip II's arrival in 1561. However, the Valladolid experiment did not work, and it became evident that in forty years Madrid had acquired a momentum that it was difficult to disregard. In 1606 the Court returned to Madrid, amid huge rejoicing, and only a year later the population was already back to 70,000.

BAROQUE THEATRE

It was after the definitive establishment of Madrid as capital, with Philip III's brief declaration *'Sólo Madrid es Corte'* ('Only Madrid is the Court'), that more was at last done to give it the look of a grand city. The Plaza Mayor was finally completed in 1619, followed within a few years by the Ayuntamiento or City Hall and, grandest of all, the Buen Retiro Palace. The aristocracy also built palaces around the city once they were assured they would not have to move on again. Madrid still did not have a cathedral, but it did acquire several more elaborate church buildings, such as the Jesuit church of San Isidro, completed in 1633.

The Plaza Mayor was the great arena of Habsburg Madrid. Able to hold a third of the city's

Philip IV, by Velázquez.

population at that time, it was the venue for state ceremonies, bullfights, public executions, *autos de fe* (the ritual condemnation of heretics), mock battles, circus acts and carnival fiestas, as well as still being a market. Particularly lavish entertainments were staged in 1623 for the Prince of Wales, the future King Charles I, who arrived under the bizarre alias of 'Tom Smith' in an attempt to negotiate a marriage with the sister of Philip IV.

Habsburg Madrid functioned rather like a giant theatre, a great backdrop against which the monarchy could display itself to its subjects and to the world. On either side were royal estates, which would determine the shape of the city left in the middle and its peculiar north-south pattern of growth. Several times a year royal processions were held through the city, nearly always along a similar route: from the Retiro along the Calle Alcalá to the Puerta del Sol, Calle Mayor and the Alcázar, then back again via the Calle Arenal and Carrera de San Jerónimo, with stops for ceremonies in the Plaza Mayor and High Masses in various churches. For the occasion, buildings were covered in garlands, and temporary arches erected all along the route with extravagant decoration covered in texts and images extolling the virtues of the monarchy. As the Spanish monarchy slid towards economic collapse the lavishness of these ceremonies only increased, maintaining an illusion of continuing power and opulence.

Away from this ceremonial route, the Habsburgs built few squares and no grand avenues, and old Madrid continued to develop along the disorderly, tangled street plan it retains today, as a shabby amalgam of little, low houses, packed in between the looming walls of aristocratic palaces and religious houses. Even so, the opulence of the court – and the poverty outside the capital – still served to attract more and more people into the city's floating population, and in about 1630 Madrid reached its maximum size under the Habsburgs, with possibly as many as 170,000 inhabitants. In 1656, Madrid was given its fifth and final wall, roughly surrounding the area now considered 'old Madrid', and which would set the limits of the city for the next two hundred years.

The centre of all the Court pomp was for many years King Philip IV, whose gloom-laden face is familiar from many a Velázquez portrait. His *valido* was the Count of Olivares, who he gave the unique title of Count-Duke, *el Conde-Duque*. Philip IV was a great lover of theatre and painting, and in 1623 appointed Velázquez, then only 23 himself, as Court Painter. Like his father, though, Philip would feel overwhelmed and exhausted by the responsibilities of his office.

Philip IV combined devout Catholicism with an active if guilt-ridden sex life, and is believed to have fathered 30 illegitimate children. The Habsburg court was not, though, like that of Louis

XIV of France, where royal mistresses were installed with semi-queenly status; it was far too formal and decorous for that, and the King's affairs had to be carried on very much below stairs. More prominent were the royal dwarfs and clowns, of whom Philip IV was particularly fond. As their difficulties mounted, the Habsburgs and their court retreated more and more into rigid ritual. 'The King of Spain', a Dutch visitor wrote in 1655, 'adopts such a degree of gravity that he walks and behaves with the air of a statue'.

Olivares, meanwhile, was struggling to maintain the Spanish empire, by then embroiled in the Thirty Years' War. In the 1620s Spain won a series of victories, and for a time it seemed as if the rot had been stopped. In 1639, though, a Spanish fleet was destroyed by the Dutch, and in 1643 the French crushed the Spanish army at Rocroi in Flanders, ending abruptly the legend of Spanish invincibility. Naval defeats made it ever more difficult for Spain to control the imports of gold and silver from America. Olivares attempted to extend taxation in the non-Castilian dominions of the crown, which led in 1640 to revolts in Portugal and Catalonia. Portugal regained its independence, and the Catalan revolt was only suppressed after a twelve-year war.

By mid-century the effects of endless wars on Castile were visible to all, in the shape of abandoned villages and social decay throughout the country. The fall in population was such that even Madrid went into decline, so that by 1700 the city's population had fallen back to about 100,000. In the 1660s, the total collapse of the Spanish empire seemed an immediate possibility. Characteristic of seventeenth-century Spain was the mood of *desengaño*, or disillusion. The heroic efforts, all the posturing at greatness had come to nothing, and left Castile, the first world power, poorer than any of the countries it had tried to dominate.

DECADENCE

In the Court, meanwhile, life became ever more of a baroque melodrama. Of Philip IV's 12 legitimate children by his two wives, only two girls had survived to adulthood – the youngest the Infanta Margarita, the little princess at the centre of Velázquez' *Las Meninas*. In 1661, however, when Philip was already prematurely aged, the Queen, Mariana of Austria, gave birth to a son, conceived, the King confided, 'in the last copulation achieved with Doña Mariana'.

The new heir, the future King Charles II, provided the dynasty with scant consolation. The Habsburgs' marked tendency to ill-health had been accentuated by their habit of marrying cousins or nieces. The formidable Habsburg jaw, the growth of which can be followed through the family portraits, had in Charles become a serious disability. He was unable to eat solid food. Because of this –

or more likely, due to the endless cures he was subjected to for his innumerable ailments – he suffered from uncontrollable diarrhoea, which detracted from the stately dignity of Court ceremonies.

In 1665 Philip IV died, leaving as regent his widow Mariana. Born in Vienna, she chose as her adviser her confessor, a Tyrolean Jesuit called Father Nithard, who was the first of many foreigners to attempt to ban bullfighting. She was forced to dismiss him by Juan José de Austria, one of Philip IV's healthier, illegitimate children, who himself had ambitions on the throne. Mariana then took a different tack by promoting a good-looking and totally corrupt groom, Fernando Valenzuela, before being obliged to get rid of him too.

In the meantime, the economy and administration of the country continued to slide. Concern centred again on the need for an heir, and Charles was married off twice, despite a general belief that he was both impotent and sterile. As it became evident that the throne of the Spanish empire would soon become vacant, the Court was overrun with bizarre intrigues, with different factions and the agents of European powers jockeying to capture the prize, all waiting on Charles' final demise. In 1695 the French Ambassador reported that the King 'appeared to be decomposing', and could not walk more than fifteen paces without assistance. Even so, Charles resisted everything his 'healers' threw at him until the age of 38. In 1700, though, with the pathetic last words *'Me duele todo'* ('It hurts everywhere'), he finally died, and the Spanish Habsburg dynasty came to an end.

Sad Charles II.

Bourbon Madrid

In the Age of Reason, Madrid had Enlightenment thrust upon it.

Philip V (1700-46), first Bourbon King of Spain, secured his throne in 1714, after the 12-year War of the Spanish Succession. He was the grandson of Louis XIV of France and María Teresa, the daughter of Philip IV of Spain. Castile, abandoning its more usual francophobia, gave him complete support. The alternative candidate, Archduke Charles of Austria, was supported by Catalonia and the other Aragonese territories, to whom he had promised a restoration of their traditional rights. Twice, in 1706 and 1710, Charles and a mixed British, Dutch, Portuguese and Catalan army took Madrid, but were unable to hold it.

Once victorious, Philip reformed his new kingdom along lines laid down by his illustrious grandfather in France. In 1715 the remaining rights of the former Aragonese territories were abolished, so that it is from this date that 'Spain' can formally be said to exist. Spain was also given a set of academies on the French model, beginning with the Royal Academy of the Language, in 1713.

A French king brought with him other foreign innovations. Philip V, raised at Versailles, and his Italian second wife Isabella Farnese were not taken with Madrid or the gloomy Habsburg palaces of the Alcázar and the Escorial. As consolation they built their own Franco-Italian villa at **La Granja** (*see chapter* **Trips Out of Town**). They were not overly upset when the entire Alcázar burnt down in 1734, and a new **Palacio Real** was commissioned from Italian architects (*see chapter* **Sightseeing**). Philip V and his administrator in Madrid the Marqués de Vadillo also sponsored other new public buildings, such as the Hospice – now the **Museo Municipal** – the **Cuartel Conde-Duque** and the **Puente de Toledo**, all by their favoured local architect Pedro de Ribera.

Reform led to economic recuperation and a recovery in Spain's population. Madrid once again had 150,000 inhabitants by 1760, and 180,000 by 1800. People still came and went continually, but it had also acquired a more stable resident population, with a merchant community building fortunes in the transport and distribution trade, and a testy artisan and working class (*see* **Majos y Majas**).

Even so, in many ways Madrid had changed little. Its main function was still to serve the Court, whose ceremonies continued to set the city's calendar. They were as lavish as ever, particularly the processions by night with candles along every balcony lining the ceremonial route and the Plaza

Mayor, creating an impression of 'indescribable grandeur'. Until the 1770s the amount spent annually by the Crown in Madrid was always greater than the entire budget of the Spanish navy.

Within the Court itself the Bourbons introduced a much lighter style. Isabella Farnese was highly educated, and particularly interested in the arts and music. One Italian musician at the Court was Domenico Scarlatti, who arrived in 1729 as music teacher to Bárbara de Braganza, the Portuguese princess who married the future King Fernando VI. Scarlatti spent the last 28 years of his life here, and wrote most of his 555 harpsichord sonatas for Bárbara and her Court – and only for them, since they were never performed in public in his lifetime.

THE KING-MAYOR

Fernando VI (1746-59) was a shy but popular King who avoided wars, and so gave Spain its longest period of peace for over two hundred years. However, he died childless. He was succeeded by his half-brother Charles III (1759-88). Previously King of Naples for twenty years, he too was unimpressed by Madrid. However, more than any of his predecessors he set out to improve it, becoming known as Madrid's *Rey-Alcalde* or 'King-Mayor'.

Charles was fascinated by the Enlightenment ideas of progress, science and the applied use of reason. No democrat, he sought to bring about rational improvement from the top, as the very model of an enlightened despot. Further centralising reforms were undertaken in the bureaucracy and armed forces, and to improve trade with Spanish America. He challenged the privileges of the religious orders, and expelled the Jesuits from Spain in 1767 for their refusal to cooperate.

In Madrid, Charles first undertook to do something about the mud in winter, suffocating dust in summer and foul smells at all times noted by every visitor to the city. A 1761 decree banned the dumping of waste in the streets, and the Italian engineer Francesco Sabatini began the building of sewers and street lighting. A series of major public buildings was erected, of which the Post Office in the **Puerta del Sol** and Sabatini's **Puerta de Alcalá** are only the best-known. A later Queen of Spain remarked that it sometimes seemed that *all* the monuments of Madrid had been built by Charles III.

Charles III's grandest project, though, was the **Paseo del Prado**, completed in 1782. Along his Paseo Charles intended to place educative institutions archetypically of the Enlightenment era. He had sent scientific expeditions to every corner of his empire, and his plan was that the fruits of their researches should be exhibited in a Museum of Natural Sciences – now the **Museo del Prado** – the **Jardín Botánico** and the **Observatorio** (*see chapter* **Sightseeing**).

Popular reaction to the King's improvements was highly ambiguous, some being resented as foreign impositions. A decree of Charles III's Italian Minister the Marqués de Squillace provoked one of history's first fashion revolts. In 1766 he banned the traditional long cape and wide-brimmed hat and ordered the use of the international three-cornered hat, with the justification that the capes were used by criminals to conceal weapons. In what became known as the *Motín de Esquilache* (Squillace Riot), a mob marched on the Palacio Real and forced the repeal of the decree.

Similar ambiguity was also found among the educated classes. This was the time that saw the emergence of the debate over whether in order to catch up with the world Spaniards had to become something they're not, which has recurred frequently ever since. Circles of 'enlightened' aristocrats were keen to admit new ideas from wherever they could find them, but others stressed a belief in Spain's distinctiveness and the need for it to be true to its roots. One strongly-maintained tradition was bullfighting. Madrid was given its first purpose-built bullring in 1754, just north of the Retiro, roughly where the Calle Velázquez runs today.

Reform and improved trade did create a feeling of well-being in late-eighteenth-century Madrid. The aristocracy engaged in a new round of palace-building and hedonistic entertaining. Balls went on from eight at night to ten the next morning, the most renowned in the Duchess of Alba's Palacio de Buenavista in Cibeles, now the Army Headquarters. This is the world seen in the early Madrid paintings of Goya, who lived in the city from 1778.

Nevertheless, Spain was still a very feudal society, and the real economy remained backward and frail. And, since this was an absolute monarchy, a great deal depended on the character of each monarch. Charles IV (1788-1808), whose rather dozy face was captured forever by Goya, had none of his father's energy or intelligence. Moreover, he chose as his minister the incompetent, corrupt Manuel Godoy. After the French Revolution, Spain joined the other monarchies of Europe in attacking the new régime; in 1795, however, Godoy made peace and then an alliance with France. This was highly unpopular, and in March 1808, when Godoy was vacillating over changing sides once again, he was forestalled by an anti-French riot in Madrid that proclaimed Charles IV's son Fernando as King in his place. Napoleon sent troops to Madrid, assuming this decrepit state would be as easy to conquer as any other.

Majos y Majas

In the eighteenth century, the appearance of ordinary people in European cities became increasingly similar, with more or less the same three-cornered hats, breeches and mop-caps appearing everywhere. Not so in Madrid, where this era saw the appearance of the *Majos* and *Majas* – the word itself means 'fine' or 'pretty' – also known as *Manolos* and *Manolas*. A *Majo* wore embroidered shirts, a short jacket with a swathe of buttons, their hair held in a net, and always carried a knife. *Majas* wore short, mid-calf skirts with a mass of petticoats, pearl-white stockings, embroidered bodices, an intricately braided hairstyle and, on top, a dramatic lace mantilla. They were drawn from trades such as coachmen, seamstresses, cigarette makers or market traders, and most often from Lavapiés. *Majas* especially were known for their wit, grace and verbal ferocity. In a capital that was still to a great extent a city of servants, but whose servants were renowned for talking back, they were not deferential to anybody.

They were most seen in all their finery at *fiestas* such as the Romería de San Isidro. Goya depicted them often. Also, their cocky elegance led to them being taken up by the upper classes, so that even *Grandes Dames* like the Duchess of Alba would dress up as *Majas*, which is what probably gave rise to the story that Goya's nude and clothed *Majas* are portraits of the Duchess herself. It also became quite fashionable for ladies to have a *Majo* somewhere in attendance. *Majos* and *Majas* survived the Napoleonic Wars but had disappeared by the 1850s, although many of their characteristics would reappear in the later *Castizo* (*see chapter* **Madrid by Season**).

Revolutions & Railways

In fits and starts, and often behind barricades, Madrid stumbled towards the modern world.

The Second of May 1808, when the people of Madrid rose up against the French army in hand-to-hand fighting through the streets, has traditionally been seen as the beginning of modern Spanish history. Left to themselves the authorities in the city would certainly have capitulated. The ferocity of popular resistance astonished the French, who could not understand why a people never included in the deliberations of government should care so much about who ruled them.

Napoleon made his brother, Joseph Bonaparte, King of Spain. In Madrid he tried in a well-meaning way to make improvements, among them some squares for which the city has since been very grateful, notably the Plaza de Oriente and the Plaza Santa Ana. However, this did nothing to overcome the animosity around him. In 1812 the Duke of Wellington and his army arrived to take the city, in a battle that destroyed much of the Retiro palace. The French were finally driven out of Spain in 1813.

The suffering and devastation this war caused in Spain is seen with matchless vividness in Goya's *The Disasters of War*. As well as the fighting itself, the year 1812 also brought a catastrophic famine, which in Madrid killed over 30,000 people.

The shock of this upheaval initiated a period of constant instability that continued until 1874, although it could be said that it only really ended with the death of Franco. Taking little part in international affairs, Spain withdrew into its own problems, with one conflict after another between conservatives, reformists, revolutionaries and other factions. Each attempted, unsuccessfully, to impose their model on the state and create a political system that could accommodate, or hold back, the pressures for modernisation and some form of democracy.

During the war a *Cortes* had met in Cádiz in 1812 that had given Spain its first-ever Constitution. This assembly also first gave the world the word 'Liberal'. However, when Fernando VII (1808-1833) returned from French captivity in 1814 his only thought was to cancel the Constitution and attempt to return to the methods of his ancestors. His absolute rule, though, was incapable of responding to the bankruptcy of the country. The régime was also trapped in the futile but immensely costly struggle to hold on to its American colonies, by then in complete revolt.

In 1820 an army revolt forced Fernando to reinstate the Constitution. He was saved three years later, ironically by a French army, sent to restore monarchical rule. Meanwhile, defeat at Ayacucho in Peru (1824) left Spain with only Cuba, Santo Domingo and Puerto Rico of its former American territories, for three centuries an essential last resort for the state's budget.

In 1830, however, Fernando VII's wife María Cristina gave birth to a daughter, soon to be Queen Isabel II (1833-68). Previously, the most reactionary sectors of the aristocracy, the church and other groups deeply suspicious of economic liberalism had aligned themselves behind his brother Don Carlos. When Fernando died in 1833, Carlos demanded the throne, launching what became known as the Carlist Wars. The Regent María Cristina, to defend her daughter's rights, had no choice but to look for support to the liberals, and so promised some form of constitutional rule.

For the next forty years Spanish politics was a see-saw, as conservative or liberal factions vied for power, while the Carlists, considered off the political spectrum by most sections in Madrid, occasionally threatened at the gates. Madrid was the great centre for aspiring politicians, and the problems of Spain were discussed endlessly in its salons and the new cafés, which multiplied rapidly at this time. This was the era of Romanticism, and Romantic writers such as the journalist Larra and the poet José Espronceda were heavily involved in political projects. Similarly, many politicians were also writers.

Much of the time, however, these reformers tended to be shepherds in search of a flock, for there were no real political parties. The only way a faction could really hope to gain power was with the support of a General with troops at his back. The army had become inextricably involved in politics. The *Pronunciamiento* or coup was the main form of changing government, and the soldiers identified with particular sides – Espartero, Serrano and

The old Jesuit Novitiate on Calle San Bernardo, Madrid's University from 1836.

Prim for the progressives, Narváez and O'Donnell, descended from Irish soldiers in the Spanish army, for the conservatives – were the heroes of their followers. Later most were given monuments or streets named after them in Madrid, together with civilian politicians such as Bravo Murillo, Argüelles, Cea Bermúdez and Martínez de la Rosa.

The people of Madrid – an indeterminate group that stretched from lawyers to labourers – played an important part in these ebbs and flows. In crisis after crisis they would form a *Milicia Nacional* and march on Charles III's Post Office in the Puerta del Sol, by then the Interior Ministry. They were not for a long time anti-monarchist, but instead demanded changes in the Constitution, or the replacement of some ministers. These clashes were never decisive, and it was later said that Spain had gone through 70 years of agitation without ever experiencing a revolution.

MADRID IN MID-CENTURY

This political instability did not mean that life in Madrid was chaotic. Visitors to Madrid at the beginning of the 1830s found a small, sleepy, shabby city, seemingly sunk in the past. Convents and palaces still occupied nearly half its area.

It was around this time that Spain acquired its romantic aura. An increasing number of foreigners visited the country, drawn above all by its timeless, vaguely exotic qualities. The English traveller George Borrow, who visited in 1836, described Madrid's population as 'the most extraordinary vital mass in the entire world'. Another visitor in 1830 was the French romantic writer Prosper Merimée, who in 1845 would write his novel *Carmen*, which would fix the image of Spain forever, above all when given music by Bizet, who himself never visited Spain at all.

The 1830s, however, also saw the single most important change in old Madrid during the nineteenth century. In 1836 the liberal minister Juan Alvarez Mendizábal was able to take advantage of the church's sympathy for Carlism to introduce his law of *Desamortización* or Disentailment, which dissolved most of the country's monasteries. In Madrid, the church lost over 1,000 properties. Most were demolished remarkably quickly, to the horror of later art historians. An enormous area thus became available for sale and new building.

Some urban reformers saw this as an opportunity to give Madrid broad, airy avenues, following the always-cited example of Paris. Some major projects were undertaken, the most important the rebuilding of the Puerta del Sol, in 1854-62. The seat of the new régime, the **Cortes**, was built on the former site of the Convent of the Holy Spirit, in 1843-50. However, most of the local traders who benefited from *Desamortización* lacked the capital to contemplate any grand projects, and built individual blocks on individual plots, without challenging the established, disorderly street plan.

As a result the districts of old Madrid took on the appearance they have kept more or less until today, with great numbers of *Corrala*-type tenement blocks appearing in areas like Lavapiés (*see chapter* **Madrid by Area**). They allowed Madrid to grow considerably in population, without actually going outside its still-standing wall of 1656.

A few factories had appeared in Madrid, but for the most part the industrial revolution seemed to be ignoring the city. Its overriding business was still that of government, and it had many more lawyers than industrialists. The constitutional governments steadily expanded the State administration, and the ambitions of the middle class were focussed more on obtaining official posts than on entrepreneurial ventures. They employed a great many servants, for labour was very cheap. Most other manual work still went on in small workshops, producing consumer goods that were too expensive ever to sell outside Madrid.

BEYOND THE WALLS

Two more major changes both arrived in the 1850s. In 1851 Madrid got its first railway, to Aranjuez, followed a few years later by a line to the Mediterranean coast. Railways would transform Madrid's relationship with the rest of the country, for the first time opening up a realistic possibility of its fulfilling an economic function. Equally important was the completion of the *Canal de Isabel II*, bringing water to the city from the Guadarrama, in 1858. Madrid's water supply, still partly based on Moorish water-courses, had been wholly inadequate for years. The Canal, inaugurated with a giant spurt of water in Calle San Bernardo, removed a crippling obstruction to the city's growth.

Madrid's population was by this time over 300,000. Consequently, steps were finally taken for it to break out of its old walls and in 1860 a plan by Carlos María de Castro was approved for the *Ensanche* ('Extension') of Madrid. It proposed the building of an orderly arc of grid-pattern streets within the line of the street now called at different points Joaquín Costa, Francisco Silvela and Doctor Esquerdo. However, as with earlier rebuilding, the plan came up against the chronic lack of large-scale local investors. Some areas, such as the new working-class district of Chamberí, were built up in reasonable time, but others remained empty for decades. The only major development undertaken immediately was in the section along the Calle Serrano bought up by the flamboyant speculator the Marqués de Salamanca, whose name was later attached to the whole district (*see chapter* **Madrid by Area**). Moreover, even he was unable to sell them to Madrid's conservative-minded upper classes at a viable price, and he went bankrupt in 1867.

Meanwhile, the political situation was deteriorating once again, after a long period of conservative rule initiated in 1856. Isabel II had become deeply unpopular, and was discredited by the sleaze and scandal surrounding her Court. In September 1868 yet another military revolt overthrew the government and, this time, dethroned the Queen too.

There followed six years of turmoil. The provisional government invited an Italian prince, Amadeo of Savoy, to be King of a truly constitutional monarchy. However, in December 1870 General Prim, the strongman of the new régime, was assassinated. Carlist revolts broke out in some areas, while on the left new, more radical groups appeared. At the end of 1868 a meeting in Madrid addressed by Giuseppe Fanelli, an Italian associate of the Russian anarchist Bakunin, led to the founding of the first anarchist group in Spain. The Cortes itself was riven by factions, and Amadeo decided to give up the struggle and go back to Italy.

On 12 February 1873 Spain became a Republic. Rightist resistance became stronger than ever, while many towns were taken over by left-wing *Juntas* who declared them autonomous 'cantons', horrifying conservative opinion. To keep control, Republican governments relied increasingly on the army. This proved fatal, and on 3 January 1874 the commander in Madrid General Pavía marched into the Cortes, sent its members home, and installed a military dictatorship.

Come Back Tomorrow

In 1833 Mariano José de Larra, the great satirist considered the founder of Spanish journalism, wrote a piece called *Vuelva Usted Mañana* ('Come Back Tomorrow'). He describes how he has met a foreigner, *M. Sans-Delai*, who has arrived in Madrid in order to sort out a family inheritance and to propose a project of great mutual benefit to the Spanish government. He expects to do all this in 15 days. Larra promises to buy him lunch in 15 months, as he'll assuredly still be here. The man finally gives up and leaves six months later, having achieved nothing he wanted to do. Wherever he goes, he's told it's not quite the right time to see the right person, and that he should come back tomorrow; his grand scheme is passed round between various Ministries, and disappears without trace when one Ministry declares it has sent it on while another denies ever having received it.

Spain's bureaucracy was first established by the Habsburgs, but became much larger and more professional under the Bourbons, who, inspired by Louis XIV, created Spain as a centralised state. The constitutional governments of the nineteenth century expanded the administration much further, and established its system of hierarchies and the examinations for entrance to public service which, once passed, guaranteed a job for life. Irrespective of the surface instability of governments, the bureaucracy's procedures, routines and rituals remained in place; and in Madrid, the city whose whole purpose was government, they long set the tone of much of middle-class life.

The Restoration

With the twentieth century, Madrid entered one of the richest, and most turbulent, periods in its history.

At the end of 1874 the army decided to restore the Bourbon dynasty, in the shape of Alfonso XII (1874-85), son of Isabel II. The architect of the Restoration regime, however, was a civilian politician, Antonio Cánovas del Castillo. He established the system of *turno pacífico* or peaceful alternation in power between a Conservative Party, led by himself, and a Liberal Party made up of former progressives. Their readiness to cooperate with each other was based in a shared fear of the social tensions visible during the previous six years.

The dominance of these 'dynastic parties' over the political system was ensured by election-rigging and occasional repression. Backing up the new regime was the army, in which conservative and progressive wings had similarly buried their differences, making it a pillar of the social order. The years after 1874 saw the culmination of a process already visible in the 1840s, in which old aristocratic families fused with those who had done well out the acquisition of church lands to form a new dominant class in the country. Again, they were united by a common desire to protect what they had – and to display it, as seen in the glittering life of Madrid 'society' during the 1880s.

In the late 1870s the wealthy of Madrid, in confident mood, set out on a ten-year building boom. They overcame their reluctance to leave the old city, and the Salamanca area became the new centre of fashionable life. Most of the new apartment blocks built in the district had lifts, first seen in Madrid in 1874, and which had a significant effect on the social climate. In earlier blocks the humble upper floors had been let cheaply, so that rich and poor had continued to live side by side, as they always had done in old Madrid. With lifts, however, a top floor could be as desirable as a first, and this kind of class mixing faded rapidly.

The government and official bodies, too, undertook a huge round of new building. The Bank of Spain, the *Bolsa* (Stock Exchange), the main railway stations and even the wrought-iron municipal markets are all creations of the 1880s. It was also proposed that Madrid should at last be given a cathedral, on the site of the former Mosque Santa María de la Almudena, demolished by the progressives in 1869. The building of the **Almudena** cathedral, however, would prove to be an endless saga that has only recently been concluded (for all buildings, *see chapter* **Sightseeing**).

As well as an opulent, bourgeois élite, Madrid also acquired a larger professional middle class, with many more doctors, engineers, journalists and architects. It attracted intellectuals from throughout the country, from the threadbare bohemians seen in the works of the playwright Valle-Inclán, always on the look out for something to pawn, to professors at the university, transferred to Madrid from Alcalá de Henares in 1836 and rapidly expanded after the Restoration.

At the same time, Madrid was also receiving a continual, accelerating influx of poor migrants from rural Spain, with over 200,000 new arrivals between 1874 and 1900. The main work available for them was in building, for men, and in the always-expanding area of domestic service for women. Economic expansion was reflected in the appearance of yet more small workshops rather than factories.

There were also many in Madrid with next to no work. The presence of beggars in the streets had long been cited as a symbol of the problems of Spain, but the 1880s also saw the beginning of a steadily worsening housing crisis, with the appearance around Madrid of a ring of shanty towns regarded with fear by respectable opinion. One of the many remedies put forward made Madrid the site of a curiously modern experiment in planning, the *Ciudad Lineal* or 'Linear City', proposed in the 1890s by the engineer Arturo Soria. His idea was that new housing should be organised around a means of transport, the railway line along the continuation of the Calle Alcalá. Each area would consist of small houses with gardens, of different sizes for residents of different incomes, thus recreating the inter-class ambience of old Madrid. However, few affluent residents were drawn to the *Ciudad Lineal*, which became a predominantly working-class area.

Despite this level of poverty, the established regime seemed to be in little danger during the first decades of the Restoration. The events of 1868-74 had discredited the old Romantic idea of the unity of the people in the pursuit of democracy. In 1879 the Spanish Socialist Party, the PSOE, was founded in the Casa Labra *taberna* (*see chapter* **Tapas**). Led by the printer Pablo Iglesias, it was committed to the idea that working people had to organise for themselves. Nevertheless, for a long time the level of agitation in the capital was very limited.

THE NEW CENTURY

Just before the end of the century, however, the preconceptions on which Spanish political life had been based received a shattering blow. The Restoration regime presented itself as having returned the country to stability and some prestige in the world. In the 1890s, however, Spain was involved in colonial wars against nationalists in Cuba and the Philippines. In 1898, the government allowed itself to be maneouvred into war with the United States. In a few short weeks, almost the entire Spanish navy was sunk, and Spain lost virtually all its remaining overseas territories.

Known simply as 'The Disaster', this was a devastating blow to Spain's self-confidence. The pretensions of the regime were shown to be a sham, and it was revealed as a decrepit, incompetent state based on a feeble, rustic economy. Among intellectuals, this sparked off an intense round of self-examination and discussion of Spain's relationship to the very concept of modernity. Politically, it signalled the beginning of the disintegration of the cosy political settlement of 1874.

A significant part in this process was played by the King himself, Alfonso XIII (1885-1931). Arrogant and erratic, Alfonso ultimately alienated even his right-wing allies. He was the object of several assassination attempts, the most dramatic when a Catalan anarchist, Mateo Morral, threw a bomb at his wedding procession in 1906.

Though the intellectual debates of this time were centred on Spain's apparent inability to deal with the modern world, the problems of the regime were not due to the country being backward. Rather, they spiralled out of control because after 1900 the country began to undergo an unprecedented period of change.

This sudden expansion was set off by three main factors. One, ironically, was the loss of the colonies, which led to large amounts of capital being brought back to the country. Most important of all was World War I. Spain remained neutral, and the war provided unheard-of opportunities for the Spanish economy in the supply of goods to the Allied powers. Then, during the world-wide boom of the 1920s, the country benefited greatly from foreign investment.

Within a few years the country had one of the fastest rates of urbanisation in the world. The economic upheaval caused by the World War led to runaway inflation, spurring a massive movement into the cities. Madrid did not grow as rapidly as industrial Barcelona, which had become the largest city in the country. Nevertheless, after taking four centuries to reach half a million, it doubled its population again in only thirty years, to just under a million by 1930. Only 37 per cent of its people had actually been born in the city.

The most visible manifestation of this growth in Madrid was a still-larger building boom. Bombastic creations such as the Palacio de Comunicaciones in Cibeles were symptomatic of the expansive mood. Most important was the opening of the Gran Vía in 1910, a project first discussed 25 years previously, and not completed for another 20, that would transform the interior of the old city with a new grand thoroughfare for entertainment, business and banking.

Another fundamental innovation was electricity. The city's trams were electrified in 1898, and the first Metro line, between Sol and Cuatro Caminos, was opened in 1919. Electricity allowed Madrid finally to experience an industrial take-off in the years after 1910. It was still a long way behind Barcelona as an industrial city, but was much more important as a base for major banks, which lined the Gran Vía.

The pace and tone of life in Madrid had changed greatly. Larger companies and new industries brought with them more aggressive styles of working, and a much more industrial working class. Many lived in shabby slum districts in the outskirts. Others were still in the 'misery-villes' of shanties, which mushroomed around the city as its housing crisis became steadily more acute. At the same time, the expansion in banking and administrative work also created greatly increased opportunities for white-collar workers.

Madrid was also, more than ever, the mecca for intellectuals and professionals from around the country. This was the background to the enormous vigour of the city's intellectual life at this time, the 'Silver Age' of Spanish literature. From writers of 1898 such as Antonio Machado and Baroja to the poets of the 1927 generation Rafael Alberti and García Lorca, the city welcomed an extraordinary succession of literary talent, as well as painters, scientists and historians. Its cafés were full of talk, forums for discussion and new projects multiplied, and any number of newspapers and magazines were published. The sheer range of activity was remarkable, above all by comparison with the near-silence that fell upon Madrid in the 1940s.

Morral spoils Alfonso XIII's wedding, 1906.

The crowds in the streets, 1931.

throughout the country demanded sweeping constitutional reform. In the following years the main focus of conflict was in Barcelona, where virtual urban guerrilla warfare broke out between the anarchist workers' union the CNT and employers and the state. A crisis had also developed in Spain's last colonial war in Morocco. In 1923, the Captain-General of Barcelona, General Primo de Rivera, suspended the Constitution and declared himself Dictator under the King, returning Spain to military rule.

In Madrid, this event was first greeted with relative indifference. However, by his action Primo de Rivera had discredited the old dynastic parties without leaving anything in their place, leaving the conservative forces in the country apparently paralysed. A widespread movement against the monarchy developed during the twenties, based in a complex sentiment that a society that felt itself to be increasingly mature should not have a ramshackle, discredited government imposed upon it.

In 1930 Primo de Rivera resigned, exhausted. The King appointed another soldier, General Berenguer, as new prime minister. In an attempt to move back towards some form of constitutional rule, the government decided to hold municipal elections, on 12 April 1931. They were not expected to be any kind of referendum on the monarchy. However, when the results came in two days later it was seen that republican candidates had won sweeping majorities in all of Spain's cities.

COLLAPSE OF THE REGIME

One of the first problems this urban expansion created for the 'dynastic parties' was that it made it impossible for them to control elections in the way they were able to do in small towns and rural areas. In 1910, a Republican-Socialist coalition won the elections in Madrid for the first time. Tensions came to a head in 1917, when a General Strike

The Golden Age of the *Tertulia*

A *tertulia* is an informal gathering of friends to talk, in a discussion that differs from a simple chat in that it is held roughly to a topic. It can be held anywhere, from a shop to a park bench. The true literary *tertulia*, however, began with the appearance of cafés in the early nineteenth century. Supposedly, the first open *tertulia* in Madrid met in the Café Príncipe, in the street of the same name, in the 1830s, and was attended by Romantic writers such as Larra, Espronceda and Tomás Bretón. As the century went on they acquired an ever more central role in the cultural life of the city, their popularity based in a very Spanish love of talk for its own sake. Most of the writers of Spain's 'Silver Age' had their regular *tertulia*, and equally any new arrival in the city could soon find out exactly where they had to go to hear the main figures of the day hold forth on matters sacred and profane.

Like the cafés themselves, *tertulias* tended to be male institutions, but the novelist Emilia Pardo Bazán held one in her house. With so

much talk going on, there were naturally also figures better known for their part in *tertulias* than for anything else. A legendary figure of Madrid at this time was Ramón Gómez de la Serna, who presided over the gathering at the Café Pombo in the Calle Carretas, attended by Buñuel and García Lorca and credited with the introduction of surrealism and dadaism into Spain. *Ramón*, as he was known to all and sundry, was the author of over a hundred books, but it was always known that his best ideas had gone up in the smoke and coffee fumes.

The true *tertulia* tradition failed to survive the Civil War, although a trace of it can be seen in Camilo José Cela's forties' novel *La Colmena*, with writers huddled together in the Café Gijón out of the cold. Many of the great cafés that formed the venues for these endless discussions also disappeared during the fifties and sixties, and only a few such as the **Gijón** and the **Comercial** (*see chapter* **Cafés & Bars**) survive as a reminder of former times.

Republic & Civil War

In eight brief years, Madrid went from euphoria to defeat.

On 14 April 1931, as the results of the local elections became clear, the streets of Spain's cities filled with people. In Madrid, a vast, jubilant mass converged on the Puerta del Sol. It was the presence of the exultant crowds in the streets that drove the King to abdicate and spurred republican politicians into action, for they had never expected their opportunity to arrive so soon.

The second Spanish Republic thus arrived amid enormous optimism, as the repository of the frustrated hopes of decades. Among the many schemes of the first republican government, a Republican-Socialist coalition, was a particular project for Madrid, the *Gran Madrid* or 'Greater Madrid' plan. Whereas previous plans for the growth of Madrid had been based on concentric circles spreading from the old centre, *Gran Madrid* was based on transport axes, centred on Cibeles, the extension of which it was hoped would permit the integration of the sprawling slum and shanty areas around the city's edge.

A key part of the plan was the extension of the Castellana, then blocked by a race course above the Calle Joaquín Costa. It was demolished, and the Castellana was allowed to snake endlessly northward, becoming one of the modern city's most distinctive features. Another project completed under the Republic was the last section of the Gran Vía, between Callao and the Plaza de España, site of Madrid's finest Art Deco architecture.

CRISIS

Possibilities of further change, however, were bound up in the accelerating social crisis that overtook the Republic. The new regime aroused expectations which would have been difficult to answer at the best of times. Instead, its arrival coincided with the world-wide depression. Moreover, Spain's own twenties boom had exceeded the real capacity of the economy. Activity slowed down, and unemployment spread.

At the same time, labour agitation and republican legislation had brought wage increases for those in work. This caused panic among employers, particularly in small businesses, and they became easy fodder for a belligerent, resurgent right. The optimistic harmony of April 1931 thus broke down. Tension was even more intense in the countryside, where agrarian reform was bogged down by conservative opposition.

As frustration grew among workers, tendencies grew apace that called for the end of republican compromise in a second, social revolution, most importantly the anarchist CNT and the Communist Party. Even the previously-moderate Socialist Party became radicalised. On the right, similarly, the loudest voices were those demanding authoritarian solutions as the only means of preserving social order, such as the fascist Falange, founded in Madrid in 1933 by José Antonio Primo de Rivera, son of the former dictator. The vogue for extremism was intensified by the mood of the times, in which Nazism, Italian Fascism and Soviet Communism appeared the most dynamic international models.

In 1933 the coalition between Socialists and liberal republicans broke down. With the left vote split, elections were won by conservative republi-

cans backed up by the CEDA, a parliamentary but increasingly authoritarian right wing party. For those who had assumed a Republic would be inseparable from sweeping reform, this was a profound shock. In October 1934 the CEDA demanded to have ministers in the government. A general strike was called in response. It was strongest in the mining region of Asturias, where it was savagely suppressed by army units commanded by a rising general called Francisco Franco.

Left-wing parties were subjected to a wave of repression that radicalised their supporters still further. In new elections in February 1936, however, the left, united once again in the *Frente Popular* or Popular Front, were victorious. In Madrid, the Front won 54 per cent of the vote.

A liberal-republican government returned to power, with Manuel Azaña as President. By this time, however, the level of polarisation and sheer hatred in the country was moving out of control. Right-wing politicians, having lost the elections, called virtually openly for the army to save the country. Among the military, meanwhile, plans had already been laid for a coup.

REVOLUTION AND SIEGE

On 18 July the Generals finally made their move, with risings in cities all over Spain, while German and Italian aircraft ferried Franco's colonial army from Spanish Morocco to Andalusia. In Madrid, troops barricaded themselves inside the Montaña barracks, where the Parque del Oeste is today.

The coup was the spark for an explosion of tension. The workers' parties demanded arms. On 20 July, as news came that the army had been defeated in Barcelona and many other cities, the Montaña was stormed and its defenders massacred, despite political leaders' efforts to prevent it.

With the right apparently defeated, Madrid underwent a revolution. Left-wing militants were in an ecstatic mood. Factories, schools and public services were taken over, although the banks were left alone and the government remained in place, albeit with little effective power. Old social divisions were eroded: few people wore hats, and the normal form of address became the familiar *tu*.

For right-wingers trapped in the city the atmosphere was naturally very different. The aristocrat Agustín de Foxá wrote that 'it wasn't Spain anymore. In the Gran Vía, in Alcalá, the mob had camped out.' Ad-hoc militias and patrols had become the only power on the streets. Amid the paranoia and hatred that was the other side of revolutionary excitement, summary executions of suspected rightists were common.

In the meantime, the war still had to be fought. During the summer fighting mostly consisted of skirmishes in the Guadarrama with Falangist columns from Segovia. A far more serious threat was approaching, however, in the shape of Franco's regular troops, advancing from Seville preceded by stories of reprisals more terrible than anything done by the 'red terror' in Madrid. The militias seemed powerless to stop them. General Mola, when asked which of the four Nationalist columns would take Madrid, coined a phrase that won immediate international currency; the fifth, he said, referring to the rightists already there.

Defeat for the Republic seemed inevitable. German planes bombed the city. On 6 November, Franco's advance guard were already in the outskirts, and the government left for Valencia, a move widely seen as desertion.

Without a government, however, an entirely new resolve became visible in the popular mood. In the southern industrial suburbs, the troops were resisted street by street. Women, children, the old and the unmilitary joined in building trenches and barricades, and comparisons were immediately made to 2 May 1808. On 9 November the first international volunteers, the International Brigades, arrived, doing wonders for morale. Madrid, the imperial court, had suddenly become the front line of international democracy. After a month of savage fighting, above all in the Ciudad Universitaria, Franco ordered a halt to the frontal assault on Madrid at the end of November 1936.

Madrid saw little more direct fighting. From the Casa de Campo, where the remains of trenches and bunkers are still easily visible today, the army settled in to a siege. Attempts to push them back north and south of Madrid were unsuccessful. The city was regularly bombed, and bombarded by Nationalist artillery, who took their sights from the Gran Vía, known as 'Howitzer Avenue'.

People adapted to the situation. One could go to war by tram, and combatants were taken their lunch on the line along the Gran Vía. Right-wingers were scarcely harassed after the first few months. The siege, however, ground down the determination of November 1936. Shortages were acute, and lentils often the only food available. Particularly terrible was the severe winter of 1937-38, when doors and furniture were burnt for fuel. The powerful role of the Communists, won through the Republic's dependence on the Soviet Union as its only source of arms, also alienated many who were not Party supporters.

Franco, meanwhile, was advancing on other fronts. During 1937 the Nationalists overran the Basque Country and Asturias, and in March 1938 they reached the Mediterranean near Castellón. In January 1939 they conquered Catalonia. In Madrid, fighting broke out inside Republican lines between the Communists, committed to resistance to the end, and other groups who wanted to negotiate a settlement with Franco. Those in favour of negotiation won, but found Franco with no intention to compromise. On 28 March the Nationalist army entered Madrid.

Dictatorship & Rebirth

After years of morose authoritarianism, a transformed Madrid exploded into new life.

Welcome to my world.

Madrid emerged from the Civil War physically and psychologically battered. Hundreds of buildings stood in ruins in areas near the former battlefront. Buildings, however, could soon be rebuilt; healing the damage done to the city's spirit, on the other hand, would take decades.

The Madrid of the forties was the sombre, repressed antithesis of the expansive city of ten years previously, or its current vivacious, outgoing self. Most Madrileños had lost someone close to them, either to bombs and bullets or to post-War firing squads and prison camps. The black market rather than art and literature dominated café conversation, and the figures of earlier years were mostly in exile, or keeping indoors. The military dictatorship led by the victorious *Caudillo* Franco rapidly took over all facets of life in the capital.

The existence of 'two Spains' (right-left, monarchist-republican, rich-poor) was all too apparent in this schizophrenic melting pot of the country. When the victors marched triumphantly into the city they wasted no time in rounding up members (or merely suspected sympathisers) of 'enemy' groups, anarchists, Communists, union members and liberals. Some were turned in by neighbours, which created a sordid atmosphere of bitterness and distrust. During the early forties, while the rest of the world was wrapped up in World War II, thousands were executed in Spain. Others who had supported the losing side paid the price of defeat by serving as forced labour on fascist landmarks such as the **Valle de los Caídos**, Franco's vast victory monument and eventual tomb (*see chapter* **Around Madrid: El Escorial**).

Madrid's loyalty to the Republic almost led to it losing its capital status. Voices were raised accusing it of having betrayed 'eternal Spanish values' and calling for a more 'loyal' city to represent the country. Franco actually went to Seville to look into the feasibility of moving the capital there.

Tradition and financial interests bore more weight, however, and the capital stayed put. The Falange, official party of the regime, produced extravagant plans to turn Madrid into a Spanish version of Imperial Rome, along the lines of the schemes drawn up by Albert Speer for Hitler. However, a dire lack of funding and galloping inflation doused these nouveau-Imperialist intentions. During the first years of the Franco régime the Spanish economy was in a desperate state, and the country went through a period of extreme hardship, the *años del hambre* or 'hunger years'. Many people remember not having eaten properly for over ten years after 1936. This level of poverty also led to the phenomenon that would most shape the face of Madrid during the post-War decades: massive immigration from surrounding provinces.

DEMOGRAPHIC EXPLOSION

Madrid has grown more quickly than any other European capital this century. A 'big village' of just over half a million inhabitants at the turn of the century, and 950,000 in 1930, Madrid passed the three-million mark by 1970. Rural flight during the forties and fifties, rapid industrialisation in the 1960s and the no-holds-barred 'modernisation' of the eighties have been most responsible for this metamorphosis.

Many of those who came to Madrid were poor, ill-educated peasants from Castile, Galicia, Extremadura or Andalusia, living in shacks in shanty-towns, more than ever before, surrounding the city. Until the fifties, these migrants found few real opportunities for work, in an economy that was internationally isolated and excluded from Marshall Aid and the other reconstruction packages of post-war Europe. After 1945 many in Spain and abroad assumed that the Franco regime would shortly go the way of its former friends.

Most European countries continued to shun the regime, at least in public, but in 1953, as the Cold War intensified, Franco was saved by the US government's 'our son-of-a-bitch' policy in choosing allies. A cooperation treaty provided the régime with renewed credibility and cash in exchange for air and naval bases on Spanish soil, and later President Eisenhower flew in to shake the dictator's hand. The resentment felt against the US for propping up Franco in this way can still be seen in the occasional anti-Americanism of the Spanish left.

For those not devoted to the regime, life under Franco was often a matter of keeping one's head down and getting on with things. Football and other means of escapism played an enormous part in people's lives. The late fifties were the golden years of Real Madrid, whose successes were trumpeted to boost the prestige of the regime. One quip went that Real were not an aid to government foreign policy, they *were* its foreign policy.

The national Stabilisation Plan of 1959 gave the fundamental push to Madrid's development, and brought Spain definitively back into the Western fold. Drawn up by technocrats often associated with the Catholic lay organization the *Opus Dei*, with the assistance of the IMF and World Bank, the plan revolutionised the economy of Spain, and particularly that of the Madrid region. During the sixties, too, tourism began to pump money into the Spanish economy, which had one of the highest growth rates in the world. Madrid trebled in size and became an industrial powerhouse.

The city was transformed. Formerly quiet, pedestrian-filled, tree-lined boulevards were widened to make way for cars. Many elegant turn-of-the-century palaces lining the Castellana were torn down and modern, glass-sheathed creations built in their stead. Madrid took on much more of the look, and feel, of a big city.

THE TRANSITION

In the sixties, too, opposition to the regime revived, in the shape of labour unrest in factories around Madrid, while elsewhere in Spain the Basque terrorist organisation ETA were beginning to be active. The oil-embargo induced worldwide recession of 1973 coincided with the assassination by

ETA of Franco's prime minister Admiral Carrero Blanco. A bomb planted beneath a Madrid street launched his armour-plated car straight over a five-storey building and into its interior courtyard. The regime, already weakened by student protests – universities were sometimes closed for entire years in 1965-75 – now had to deal with rising unemployment, inflation and a moribund Franco. The transition to democracy had begun.

Franco died in November 1975, closing a parenthesis of nearly 40 years in Spanish history. A new age, uncertain but exciting, had dawned. In July 1976 King Juan Carlos, chosen by Franco to succeed him, named a former Falange bureaucrat, Adolfo Suárez, as Prime Minister. Nobody, however, knew quite what was going to happen.

To the surprise of many Suárez initiated a comprehensive programme of political reform. Clandestine opposition political leaders surfaced, and well-known exiles began coming home. The Communist Party was legalised during Easter Week 1977. The first democratic elections since 1936 were held in June, and a democratic Constitution was drafted by an all-party commission and approved by referendum in late 1978. Suárez' centrist UCD (Centre-Democratic Union) had won the nationwide elections, but local elections in Madrid in 1979 were won by the Socialists, with Enrique Tierno Galván as Mayor. Democracy was rapidly being consolidated.

The 'other' Spain, however, was still around, and getting nervous. Hard-core Francoists were horrified at the thought of Socialists and/or Communists coming to power. Many were still found among the privileged armed forces, where they naturally had great potential ability to disrupt things. Small radical groups tried to destabilise the new democracy with bombs and the like, but it was the military that everyone most feared.

On 23 February 1981 democrats' worst fears appeared to come true when a Civil Guard colonel called Tejero burst into the Cortes with a squad of men, firing his pistol into the air and shouting 'Everybody on the floor'. Spaniards hurried home, pulled down their blinds and turned on their radios. Tanks were in the streets in Valencia, and there was uncertainty everywhere. In Madrid, however, troops stayed in their barracks. At a little past midnight, Juan Carlos appeared on TV and assured the country that the army had sworn him its allegiance and the coup attempt would soon fail. The next day, people poured onto the streets to demonstrate support for freedom and democracy. The wolf had shown his teeth, but they were not as sharp as had been feared.

In national elections in November 1982, Felipe González and the Socialists won a landslide victory. Not just elections, but also a real change in the ruling party was evidently possible, and democracy was seen to be here to stay.

COMING OF AGE

In the late 1970s and early 1980s, democracy and free speech, not to mention decriminalised hashish and the breakdown of conservative sexual conventions, released long-repressed creative impulses. The suit and tie-clad, staid Madrid of earlier years gave way to an anything-goes, vivacious city in the 1980s: an explosion of art, counter-culture and nightlife, creativity and frivolity known as the *Movida Madrileña*.

In their years in power the Socialists have failed to satisfy the expectations of their more radical supporters, and in the nineties have become tarnished with a degree of sleaze worthy of the parties they once condemned. In 1991, local elections in Madrid were won by the right. No-one can deny, though, that under Socialist rule in the city and the central government Madrid was rapidly modernised. The sanitation system was renovated and ducks returned to the formally polluted Manzanares River in 1982. Squares and parks were given facelifts, and the road network was greatly improved.

Most importantly, decades of international isolation officially and definitively ended with Spain's entry into the European Community in 1986. This had a near-immediate effect on the economy, and during the late eighties foreign investment poured into the country, the fastest-growing member of the EC. Membership in Europe also opened Spaniards' eyes to new ways of doing things, new ideas. The ebullient optimism and imaginative mood of the new Spain was best expressed in the effort devoted to hugely ambitious projects such as the Barcelona Olympics, or Madrid's **ARCO** arts fair (*see chapter* **Art Galleries**).

In addition, this and increased travel abroad also began changing Madrileños' somewhat romantic perceptions of the rest of the world and themselves. In recognition of the tremendous changes that had taken place here in just 15 years, Madrid was also chosen as the 1992 Cultural Capital of Europe. This 'underwhelming' event, however, overshadowed by the Olympics and the Seville Expo, left few lasting marks on the city.

EC membership has been positive on the whole, but the breakneck change of the last decade has had its drawbacks. The number of cars registered in the Madrid region has doubled in ten years, further worsening an already serious traffic problem. Prices in general have soared, and land speculation has sent property prices and rents through the roof (apartments that cost three million pesetas in 1983 were selling for nearly 20 million by 1992). And the economic downturn since 1992 has proved as sharp as the upturn that preceded it. In short, a sense of fatigue began to be felt in the city. After seven years of uninterrupted growth and twenty years of dizzying changes, Madrid, perhaps, could be forgiven for feeling a little hung over.

The Movida

With Franco's death and the advent of democracy, Madrid shook off the yoke of nearly 40 years of military censorship, church-imposed morality and general compulsory gloom. *Serenos* (whistle-carrying street wardens, ostensibly there to open doors for you at night, but also to keep an eye on things) were replaced by pairs of pot-smoking kids making out in doorways in front of incredulous grandmothers. The *Movida* – roughly translatable as the 'Shift' or 'Movement' – had begun.

The *Movida* is often associated with certain figures, who all seemed to know each other – singer Joaquin Sabina, artists like Ouka Lele, Martirio with her outrageous costumes and headgear, and, above all, Pedro Almodóvar, who began making films in 8mm in nightclubs. It was seen in particular fields, such as the enormous expansion in the city's art scene. The *Movida*, though, was much more as well. It was, and to some extent still is, the expression of a city's 'love of life and living'.

Madrid's much-loved Socialist mayor Enrique Tierno Galvan was widely hailed as the 'sponsor' of this cultural renaissance. Known as the *Viejo Profesor* ('Old Professor'), this elderly academic combined a stately manner very reminiscent of pre-Civil War Madrid with support for all kinds of progressive causes and projects. During his term in office the **San Isidro** festival was rekindled into a multi-faceted cultural event, and the **Carnaval**, the pagan fest par excellence, reanimated (*see chapter* **Madrid by Season**). Madrid's now-legendary nightlife took off on a flight from which the city, despite recession, has yet to come down.

Madrid Today

Change everywhere, yet somehow, things remain the same...

*The **AZCA** development, a symbol of post-eighties' Madrid.*

A large part of Madrid's charm lies in the still very present provinciality that has for centuries been one of its most noted – and bemoaned – characteristics, and into which it slumped back again in the 40 years after the Civil War. Indeed, even the eighties' experimentalism of the *Movida*, epitomised by the city's best-known resident Pedro Almodóvar, arguably shared the same strength and primitivism to be found in any *pueblo*.

Wandering through the city centre, one suddenly emerges into a small square or confluence of streets presided over by elderly ladies sitting in doorways, amid the quiet bustle of grocers and butchers, while the mid-morning smell of lunch being prepared wafts down to the pavement. One of Madrid's greatest assets, its wonderful, towering, thin mountain skies, seems to encourage this air of remoteness from the business of the world.

But this slumbering small town routine has been increasingly at odds with new realities since the death of Franco and the arrival of democracy allowed – or forced – Madrid to look outward to Europe and the wider world. Since 1950, the pop-

ulation of the city has grown from 1.6 million to 3 million, and that of the Madrid region as a whole has increased at an even greater rate. Madrid is constantly changing, shedding the outer vestiges of provincialism, constantly smartening up, constantly trying to convince itself and others that it can stand as an equal alongside Europe's other capital cities

Sadly, much of the infrastructure necessary for such grand designs is still lacking, or only just getting underway. At times it seems as if the already-bursting capital and its outskirts are being rebuilt: underpasses; gas pipes; ring roads; motorway widening; inner city renovation. In some places major state-of-the-art projects have been completed, such as the AVE high-speed train, but it's hard to see them as part of a complete whole.

Despite the existence of a good public transport system huge numbers of people commute by car, arguing that the journey time is the same and it's more comfortable. Consequently the city is home to some two million cars, and in much of the centre a more or less permanent rush hour reigns. Aside

The AVE high-speed train, built for 1992.

from more tunnels, no solution to the worsening traffic problem has been offered.

In the last forty years the people of Spain as a whole have probably had to deal with a greater degree of change at a greater pace than their counterparts in any other country in western Europe. Accelerating urbanisation is only one fundamental change. Patterns of work, the family, sexual behaviour, the position of religion, leisure, have all been hugely affected. A people long thought to be puritanical have been discovered to be distinctly hedonistic.

The most recent such great burst of change was the boom of the 1980s, following Spain's liberalisation and entry into the European Community. It certainly shook Madrid up, sending prices soaring. Within a very few years a cost of living that had always been low came to be comparable to those in London, Paris or any other European capital.

Today the city is coming to terms with the aftermath of the boom, and tightening its belt. Top restaurants which only a few years ago were full to overflowing despite 10,000 peseta-a-head prices now offer special deals and wonder when the next boom will come. Glitzy shops in the smart Salamanca shopping district sit out the crisis, while private art galleries barely see a customer from one day to the next. Any taxi driver will tell you – the conspicuous spending is over.

Madrid is also struggling to deal with the consequences of a decade which in a burst of liberalisation allowed private consumption of drugs, but saw both the spread of drug addiction and an alarming increase in AIDS cases. Recent studies reveal that more than 60 per cent of the city's drug addicts carry the HIV virus, and that some 300 people die each year from drug-related illnesses; more deaths than from traffic accidents. New legislation now forbids drug use, but of course does little to combat either the causes of drug abuse, or to help users kick the habit. Instead, trafficking has been pushed out of the city centre, much of it to poorer neighbourhoods to the south, and to some of the gypsy slums.

POLITICS AS USUAL

Madrid's 1980s highpoint was overseen by a Socialist local government. Indeed, it was after the Socialist veteran Enrique Tierno Galván was elected Mayor of Madrid in 1979 that this long-discredited post regained its clout and prestige. The subsequent loss of the City Hall in 1991, as Spain's wonder-decade came to a close, was a bitter blow to the party, and they have been unable to regain the local administration since.

When the Spanish Socialist party, the PSOE, were elected to national power under Felipe González in 1982 they were the people's choice, the focus of vague but great expectations among very large sections of the population. The Party centred the country's hopes for positive change on modernisation, especially associated with membership of the EC. These were not ideologues or revolutionaries, but clean, hard-headed young administrators, free of the tawdry indolence of the Franco years, who would integrate Spain into a progressive, growing, social-democratic Europe. Freed from its bottle, Spain was enormously optimistic, and much more interested in the future than in going over past social experiments. For a good while, too, it all seemed to be working like a dream, as Spain made an initial success of EC membership that a country like Britain could only envy; at one time, the economy seemed to be growing almost by the month.

Over the years, however, this pristine image of the Socialists, their project and of Spanish politics in general has become much more clouded. The loss of Madrid was the first sign of the Spanish public's discontent with the PSOE. Since then Spanish politics has been dominated by a series of financial scandals, in which, to name only two of the most spectacular, the governor of the Bank of Spain Mariano Rubio has come under investigation, making it necessary to recall bank notes bearing his signature, and the former head of the Guardia Civil, Luis Roldán, has won a place at the top of Interpol's wanted list. All of which has robbed the Party of much of its credibility. In boom times people make big money, and the eighties' boom, in which the new political élite played such a central role, saw suspiciously large amounts of this money make its way to politicians and public officials, in a continuation of practices associated with a much older style of Spanish politics.

The dream is over, and for all the benefits and positive change the PSOE introduced – women's rights, pensions, improvements in the health service, weakening the power of the military and the church, a secure place in Europe, and most important for many, lots of consumer goodies – the party is severely discredited. It has lost direction and shifted inexorably to the right, and is dependent on the neo-conservative Basque and Catalan nationalist parties for its slim hold on parliament. Felipe González, the ultimate survivor, managed

New Madrileños

You'll see them easily around central Madrid. Africans selling souvenirs or cigarettes around the Metro, Moroccans working on the roads, black Caribbean women from the Dominican Republic cleaning hotels and offices. There are also quite a few blonde, blue-eyed poor immigrants, mostly Poles, who have established a niche for themselves in the back-breaking work of delivering gas bottles up the stairs in the many old flats that still don't have piped gas. They are Madrid's new, non-Spanish migrants, the vast majority of whom have arrived in the last ten years

Until the end of the sixties, Spain was a country from which people emigrated. Apart from the many divisions among the mainstream population – Castilians, Catalans, Galicians (Gallegos) and so on – the only ethnic minority in the country was the centuries-old Gypsy community, with their own very particular place in Spanish society. The foreigners who came here were generally from more affluent countries, and did so to sample Spanish life and enjoy themselves. Things changed radically during the eighties, when a thriving economy began to attract an accelerating flow of people from the Third World and Eastern Europe.

Today, there are 550,000 fully-legal foreign immigrants in Spain, about one per cent of the population. In Madrid alone there are officially 100,000, although there are probably another 50,000 in the city who are here illegally. This represents just 3.1 per cent of the city, nothing by comparison with capitals such as Paris or London, but still a jolt to a country accustomed to its homogeneity, and with a world view that long saw the country as itself disadvantaged with regard to the wealthier countries to the north.

Most migrants find poorly-paid work in service industries, and Latin American and Filipino women work particularly in cleaning and as private maids. Many North Africans work at the cheaper end of the construction industry. For locals they were more of a curiosity during the eighties, but since recession set in attitudes

towards Third-World migrants have changed noticeably. In bar-room grumbles they can be blamed for unemployment, undercutting wages and causing a worsening of conditions at work. They are also accused of contributing to crime, prostitution, AIDS and the drugs problem – the Dominican prostitute has become one of the stereotypes of modern Madrid. Many immigrants first entered Spain as tourists and then tried to stay on, and the idea is common that virtually all of them are in the country illegally.

Politicians have pandered to the public mood, promising crackdowns on *indocumentados* (illegals), and the police discriminate blatantly against very visible groups such as Africans and Maghrebis, periodically rounding them up on the street in the hope of finding papers not in order. Given this kind of welcome, many migrants might themselves prefer to move on, now that all jobs here are tight. How the city and the country respond to those that do not will be a real test of Spain's readiness to change in the modern world.

just to hold on to power in 1993, but in the next general election the disarray of the left will almost certainly enable the right wing Partido Popular to take control – although it's not that they arouse any widespread hopes either, as most people other than their devotees are equally cynical about them.

Spanish politics is at first glance a complicated, albeit largely dull affair. On deeper investigation (for which the press is little help) it is revealed to

be less complicated and merely dull. The system of proportional representation by party lists makes grassroots participation and feedback virtually impossible; known politicians are limited to the members of the government or one or two key opposition figures, not your local representative, who are thus largely protected from voters' ire.

Working people, in particular, have had to absorb other kinds of changes, notably the restructuring of many industries, with consequent unemployment, that the Socialists accepted as necessary for modernisation. In contrast to the tumult of the late 1970s and early 1980s, however, demonstrations are now rare in Madrid, and even the general strike in January 1994 failed to close the city down or provoke disturbances. Madrid may be the seat of government, but its inhabitants are as uninterested as the rest of the country in a system which allowed all the recent scandals to simmer away. All of the participants in this system now seem equally tainted.

THE FUTURE IS AWAITED

A generation which has grown up under the socialists has now largely turned its back on politics, and interest in current affairs among teenagers is lower than it was in 1960. The last set of changes and the affluence of the last twenty years are taken for granted, and a deep-set conservatism has set in among young people, those who didn't share in the brief, heady idealism of the late seventies and early eighties. It's matched by the cynicism found among those who missed the prosperity boat during the last ten years.

Sadly, the ones who did get on board in the 1980s have not brought that much positive change since. The madcap optimism of the *Movida* years was based on an idea – or an image – that suddenly everything was possible, that in a place where for years innovative spirits had had to look abroad for inspiration they could have the party right here. However, things are not quite so flexible, and since then a new conservatism has emerged. Today, the majority of those who run the media, advertising, the political parties, business, the arts and the entertainment scene, all of which are concentrated in Madrid, may only be in their thirties and forties, but they have created a system of patronage and favours which, while not actually corrupt, still encourages a lack of initiative in underlings.

Spain is perhaps simply going through the same death throws/birth pangs that most of western culture is, and has run out of ideas. The problem here however, is exaggerated by the (perceived) intensity of the eighties outpouring of street-cred culture and the contrast with the lack of interest seen today in, say, the music, film, or television industries in encouraging new talent. The result is often a culture of mediocrity in which the new is a threat to an already established order.

Of course, Spain is no different in all this than Britain or many other countries where people complain of a decline in quality and a lack of ideas in television, music, cinema – the difference is that in most other European countries more of an infrastructure exists that can facilitate change, and there is a degree of concern over declining standards reflected in public debate. There is very little original debate here, and what new initiatives do emerge often suffer through lack of public interest. Modern Spaniards could become a byword for accepting anything, from ultra-trashy TV to sleazy politicians.

But then, given the current state of things, this conformist indifference in attitudes to drugs, sex, fashion, music and politics may be hardly surprising. Unemployment stands at 16 per cent – up from 11 per cent a decade ago, and better than the 30 per cent levels in most of the south and west – but recent legislation giving employers greater 'flexibility' has meant low wages and short-term contracts. Soaring house prices and until recently double figure interest rates, coupled with high rents, mean young people tend to look after what they've got and live at home longer, valuing clothes, cars and a steady boy/girlfriend more than independence.

But life goes on, and now that the dust has settled and the nationalist illusion of 1992 – with madcap spending on the Olympics, the Seville Expo, and Madrid's own little *fiesta* as European Capital of Culture – is over, life in Madrid is adjusting to the realities of the 1990s like everywhere else. For the moment, there is no sign of a return to the heady, innovative days of the eighties. Nightlife has established its own rituals that have become resistant to change, as its former leader Pedro Almodóvar has pointed out, and international trends often take their time in arriving. Nevertheless, the city's extraordinary vibrancy, the sharpness and sensuality of its people, the constant pleasures of good eating and drifting through packed streets at 3am remain, and those who know Madrid and then leave always say there's nowhere quite like it for having a good time.

We come back to the paradox: a capital city with a provincial heart. Madrid is one of Europe's safer capitals, where even the seediest areas are not much more than picturesque in comparison to what New York, London or Paris have to offer. Its streets are filled with people until all hours, and even in those few areas traditionally associated with prostitutes and drug addicts, they are just going about their business; leave them alone and they'll leave you alone.

Madrid continues to change, like all cities, and at times, the change seems random, chaotic, inexplicable. A lot of what makes the city a better place to live in than most other European capitals is under pressure – particularly the small neighbourhood shops and corner bars so attractive to foreigners living or staying here. In the process, Madrid becomes more European and more blandly 'modern'.

Yet the days of Madrid as a 'doughnut' capital, where the centre is a commercial centre inhabited only by the wealthy, or worse, a virtual museum, are still a long way off. In the meantime, visitors and residents alike will continue to share, celebrate, puzzle, and of course complain about, the unique qualities that make up Madrid.

Madrid by Area

Madrid by Area

A guide to Madrid's complex and multi-varied barrios, from medieval squares to lush eighties' avenues.

Propelled by royal whim into becoming the seat of Court and empire, this former Moorish town on the Manzanares was never in any hurry to alter its way of life and become like any other European capital. It wasn't until the seventeenth century that Madrid acquired its first monumental flourishes. From the time that it became Spain's capital in 1561 observers and aspiring urban planners have complained endlessly about its lack of grandeur and a suitably orderly structure. Meanwhile, the shabby walls put up in 1656 to ensure that tolls and taxes were charged on all incoming goods continued to mark its limits until well into the 1860s.

Under the eighteenth-century Bourbons new monuments, churches and convents were added. The prolific Pedro de Ribera created a string of buildings in a distinctive style – plain brick with stone inlays, topped with elaborate baroque cake icing –, that is just one of those typical of Madrid. Between the 1760s and the 1780s Charles III added *paseos*, fountains and arches, as well as some street lighting and a rudimentary sewage system. Even

so, Madrid continued to be slammed for its seediness and lack of amenities, even by visitors such as nineteenth-century Romantics who found its people utterly fascinating.

Finally change had to happen. Beginning in the 1850s the walls came down, the railway came in and the *Canal de Isabel II* brought an (almost) unlimited supply of water down from the sierra. The wealthy began, hesitantly at first, to move out to the Salamanca district, soon the new hub of fashionable society. All these transformations paved the way for a demographic upheaval as an unstaunchable flow of countryfolk began to move from rural Spain into the big cities. In this century, Madrid has sprawled out into entirely new areas miles beyond the old city, with factories and chimneys blighting the eastern and southern approaches, dire, ever-expanding dormitory suburbs and a manic radial road system.

At the same time, old Madrid, much of it rebuilt in the nineteenth century following the great clearance of the city's monasteries, remains very much the city's centre, the site of its most important attractions, cinemas, government institutions and nightlife rounds. Only the business world has really managed to move outside it, up the great spine of the Castellana.

The different *barrios* of the old centre retain very much a life of their own. They still draw in a steady flow of new population; even districts that are considered the heart of Madrid's *castizo* identity (*see chapter* **Madrid by Season**) are full of Andalusians, Galicians, or even Ghanaians. Many of the local population have managed to stay on, too, in a fairly down-at-heel, self-contained economy based on tiny shops, bars and slightly superfluous services.

Madrileños find their way easily around this unwieldy old city, where many streets didn't even have official names until the 1870s. (People made do by saying so-and-so lived on the street where old what's-his-face, the one-eyed brother of the Aragonese candlemaker, had his fish shop.) Differences between small, individual *barrios* within the old centre are made much of. For the uninitiated, however, things are less logical, as two people may give you different ideas of where one *barrio* ends and another begins, or use different names for apparently the same place.

Administrative districts such as *Centro* are of no practical use in sorting out where you are. To orient themselves people often refer to the nearest Metro stop, or a landmark such as Santa Ana. The division into areas we have followed here is a simplification of the many possibilities, based on the names and identities most commonly used. For a listing of sights, shops, restaurants and other facilities in each area, *see page 264* **Area Index**.

Villa y Corte

Between Sol, the Palacio Real and San Francisco el Grande, and containing within it the oldest part of the city, this area is often labelled rather floridly the 'Madrid of the Austrias', although Philip II and his Habsburg descendants can scarcely claim responsibility for very much of it. At its core is the greatest monument they did build, the **Plaza Mayor**, completed in 1619 in the Castilian-baroque style they most favoured. When first built up in the 1460s, however, it had actually been outside the twelfth-century walls of little Madrid.

Battered and sometimes burnt over the years, the Plaza Mayor has been expensively restored in the last fifteen years. Despite wails of indignation, we appear to be stuck with the frescoes that, since 1992, have disfigured the plaza's 1590 centrepiece, the **Casa de la Panadería**. Those responsible missed their true calling; they could have produced a really outstanding album cover for a second-string psychedelic rock group in the sixties.

Edificio Metropolis, *Gran Vía. See page 78.*

But then, the Plaza Mayor has seen it all: executions, riots, bullfights, wild Carnival revels and the nastier doings of the Inquisition. Nowadays, coin and stamp collectors turn out in force on Sundays for their market, dance bands play during San Isidro in May and at Christmas time the plaza is given over to market stalls selling figures for traditional cribs along with *turrón* (almond nougat), dates and other seasonal purveyors of tooth-decay. It's also a magnet for tourists all year long, particularly its pavement cafés and restaurants, often wildly overpriced.

In the south-west corner of the plaza, near the tourist office, is an arch, the Arco de Cuchilleros (Knifemakers' Arch), with a spectacular bank of steps leading down through the Calle Cuchilleros to the Plaza de la Puerta Cerrada, decorated with some pretty seventies' murals. South of that is the Calle Cava Baja, following the line of the twelfth-century wall. These streets are the place to go to find the most celebrated *Mesones*, temples to Madrid's powerful traditional cuisine. Of these, **Casa Botín** is the most touristy, **Casa Lucio** is the hangout of celebrities and political bigshots, the **Posada de la Villa** is the prettiest, and **Viuda de Vacas** is so funky you forget the shortcomings of the menu (*see chapter* **Restaurants**). Directly south of the Plaza Mayor in Calle Toledo you can see the twin towers of the Cathedral of **San Isidro**,

Life's a Lottery

In its annual *El Gordo* ('the fat one') Christmas lottery Spain boasts the biggest public payout in the world. In 1993, prizes amounted to a staggering 170,000 million pesetas (£850 million). Nor is this all, for every day and every week there are plenty of other smaller prizes for the punters to bid after.

Spain's national lottery has been going since 1812. Curiously, foreigners often overlook Spaniards' love of gambling. It is estimated that throughout the country about 15 per cent of family income goes in betting. Aside from the lotteries, Spaniards spend a fortune in one-armed bandits, casinos and bingo. A great deal of this cash naturally goes directly to the state in betting taxes.

It is, though, the lottery that's become as much a part of national life as olive oil. The opportunities to have a flutter are many. As well as *El Gordo*, the National Lottery runs *El Niño* in January, also with big prizes, and every month there is some special draw or other. On a more regular basis there are the twice-weekly plain *Lotería Nacional* and the daily *Bono-Loto*, naturally with smaller stakes.

Tickets for the National Lotteries can be bought from any of the *Administraciones* found throughout the city, or from licensed street vendors who add 10 per cent onto the minimum stake of 500ptas. The minimum stake in *El Gordo* is 3,000ptas, although people often club together to share the outlay.

There is also an entirely separate lottery run by the **ONCE**, the national organisation for the blind, which consequently is extremely rich, and can offer its members an ample range of services. ONCE tickets, a snip at 100ptas for the daily draw, can be bought from the distinctive telephone-booth like cabins found on street corners, or from the licensed vendors whose cries are, again, an essential feature of the country. The results of the various lotteries are listed in all local papers, and the ONCE results have passed into folklore through the five-minute TV programme on Tele 5 at 9pm each night, presented by the inimitable Carmen Sevilla.

---

summoning you to the temple which contains the coffered bones of the city's patron, and which served as Madrid's official cathedral until 1992.

To the south-east, where the Calle Atocha runs up to the Plaza Mayor in the Plaza de la Provincia, is another major work of Castilian baroque, the squatly-proportioned **Palacio de Santa Cruz** of 1629-34. The identity of the architect is not known, but it is believed to have been either Juan Bautista Crescenci or Juan Gómez de Mora. Despite its grand appearance it was originally the Court Prison, with a dungeon so deep that prisoners had to rub their rags with lard and set them alight to stop going blind, although it now has a more dignified role as the Foreign Ministry. In former times executions often took place in the **Plaza de la Cebada**, just a tumbril ride away. The best attended of them all was that of Madrid's own Robin Hood, the bandit Luis Candelas, in 1837.

The area between Cebada, Mayor and the Palacio Real really is the oldest part of Madrid, the site of the Moslem town and of most of Medieval Madrid. The **Plaza de la Paja** ('Straw Square') on Calle Segovia probably marked the southernmost point of the Moslem wall. It was a grain market then, and continued in the same function for centuries under the Christians. The surrounding streets all mainly follow their original medieval lines. The knot of streets just to the west formed the *Morería*, where during the Middle Ages Madrid's community of *Mudéjar* Moslems were confined. The little **Plaza de la Morería** (also called Plaza del Alamillo) was the site of the Mosque and the *Aljama*, the Moslem community courts. The former inhabitants are also remembered in the Plaza Puerta de los Moros, once the 'Moors' Gate'.

Getting a sense of medieval or early Habsburg Madrid requires an exercise of the imagination. Apart from the street plan and the interconnecting squares – **Plaza de la Cruz Verde**, Paja, **Plaza de los Carros** – little remains, and even the sixteenth-century exteriors that once fronted the squares were replaced in the last century. The high Baroque **Capilla del Obispo** (Bishop's Chapel) and church of **San Andrés** are partly concealed by undistinguished modern frontage, although renovation work on the area has been underway for some time. Tucked away nearby are **San Pedro el Viejo** and, across the Calle Mayor, **San Nicolás de las Servitas**, the only two Mudéjar towers in Madrid, with distinctive horseshoe arches. If you continue down the Calle Segovia beneath the viaduct you will reach Madrid's oldest relic, a forlorn fragment of the **Muralla Arabe** (Arab Wall) embedded in a rocky ridge.

The **Plaza de la Villa**, on the Calle Mayor, began life as the main Arab souk, and continued to be Madrid's main square until the creation of the Plaza Mayor. This early importance is marked by the fact that it still contains Madrid's city hall, the **Casa de la Villa**. In pre-Habsburg Madrid it was also the preferred place for residences of the local élite, one of which, the **Torre de los Lujanes**, is still there. Together with the third but again entirely different construction on the square, the 1537 **Casa de Cisneros**, they make up a compendium of the history of Madrid from provincial town to imperial capital.

The Calle Mayor was the main thoroughfare of Madrid for centuries, its smartest residential zone and the site of many (now mainly lost) splendours. Cross streets between Mayor and Arenal offer an odd mixture of bookbinders and picture framers, liturgical outfitters and Galician restaurants. The western end of Mayor, near the Almudena and the

Palacio Real, has several old palaces and one old church now reserved for the use of the army general staff. There's also **Casa Ciriaco**, one of Madrid's most famous restaurants, and possibly the least spoilt by fame (*see chapter* **Restaurants**). Back towards the Plaza Mayor, it's good to pass by the iron-framed 1915 **Mercado de San Miguel** on Plaza San Miguel, a welcome change of pace after a surfeit of sixteenth-century brickwork, and the last market of its era still up and running in central Madrid (*see chapter* **Shopping**).

Calle Mayor runs out to the west into the Calle Bailén, connected to the south by a concrete viaduct – Madrid's jumping-off point for suicide attempts – with the hill of **Las Vistillas** and the

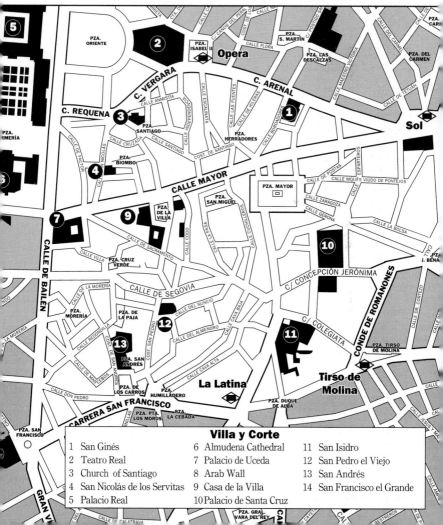

Villa y Corte

1 San Ginés	6 Almudena Cathedral	11 San Isidro
2 Teatro Real	7 Palacio de Uceda	12 San Pedro el Viejo
3 Church of Santiago	8 Arab Wall	13 San Andrés
4 San Nicolás de los Servitas	9 Casa de la Villa	14 San Francisco el Grande
5 Palacio Real	10 Palacio de Santa Cruz	

church of **San Francisco el Grande**, and which to the north runs past the **Almudena** cathedral, the hugely imposing **Palacio Real** and the **Plaza de Oriente**. It was recently decided to reroute traffic from Bailén into an underground tunnel, so that pedestrians could stroll unhindered from park to palace. This may take a while to become reality, and what they are going to do about the colony of men who sleep and hang around under the chestnut trees has not yet been announced.

To the east of Plaza de Oriente is the **Teatro Real**, Madrid's Opera, always in need of some kind of renovation or other. From here Calle Arenal, originally a stream bed, leads back to the Puerta del Sol. Off Arenal, next to the glitzy **Joy Eslava** disco, in the alleyway that snakes around the originally-medieval church of **San Ginés** are some wooden bookstalls that have been bringing in the browsers since 1850, and the **Chocolatería San Ginés**, an institution for late-night revellers in need of sustenance (*see chapter* **Nightlife**).

If instead of returning into the city you walk around the Palacio Real on either side, you will come, past the **Campo del Moro** gardens, to Madrid's often-ridiculed river, the **Manzanares**. Quevedo called it 'a ditch learning how to be a river', and a French aristocrat made the much-repeated quip, when seeing the **Puente de Segovia**, that now that they had such a fine bridge, they should get a river. Few geographical features have so consistently failed to impress.

More recently, another thing said about it was that its waters enabled you to develop films for free. Since an expensive clean-up operation under Mayor Tierno Galván in the early eighties, however, it has been much more salubrious, and a walk along the banks can be quite pleasant, so long as you don't expect to see the Mississippi.

Sol & Gran Vía

The **Puerta del Sol** is where most of the streets of Madrid converge, and where all newcomers from the rest of Spain come at least once to feel sure they've arrived. People come and go here constantly, meeting up, passing through, or maybe making for the concrete archipelago on one side where umpteen buses stop or the station where four Metro lines converge. If you stop for a couple of minutes you can check out Madrid's totemic bear-and-strawberry tree (*madroño*) symbol, at the end of Calle Carmen, and the Tio Pepe sign over the south end of the square that has been there longer than practically any other of its fixtures.

Along the Gran Vía

Fourteen streets disappeared forever when the Gran Vía was scythed out of the surrounding urban tangle in 1910 so that motor vehicles could reach Cibeles from the Calle Princesa. Intended to be a broad, modern avenue, it got grander still when World War I made neutral Madrid a clearing house for international capital. With boomtime in the economy, developers and architects set out to embrace modernity as hard as they could, and to show that, if you wanted something impressive, they could provide it. The result is quite unique.

Spanish urban reformers had often compared Madrid unfavourably to Paris, and as the first edifice on the Gran Vía they got an entire Parisian building, the **Edificio Metropolis**, designed by Jules and Raymond Février in 1905. It is handsomely off set by the lines and stacked cupolas of the newly sandblasted **Grassy** building (the one with the large Piaget sign).

As you move away from Alcalá the buildings become taller, and grander. When the **Telefónica** building by the Gran Vía Metro stop went up in 1929 everyone was thrilled by how modern (ie un-Spanish) it then seemed. At 81m (265 ft) tall, it was nothing if not conspicuous and, as Madrid's first skyscraper it had a huge impact. It was designed by Ignacio de Cárdenas, with the help of a New York engineer called Louis Weeks.

The section of the street from Callao to Plaza de España was completed under the Republic. On the corner of Calle Jacometrezo is Madrid's best art deco building, the 1932 **Edificio Carrión**, better known simply as the **Capitol**. Designed by Luis Martínez Feduchi and Vicente Eced, it is a classic of the style. The same section is also full of the Gran Vía's lavish twenties' movie palaces.

The Telefónica was finally upstaged under Franco by the **Edificio España**, at the end of the Gran Vía in the Plaza de España, built in 1948-53. A baroque skyscraper, with all sorts of curious pseudo-Habsburg details, it sums up the contradictions of the regime – obsessed with 'eternal values', but desirous to show the world that it, too, could build a skyscraper to compete with the best of them. It was designed by the brothers José María and Joaquín Otamendi, the latter of whom had worked with Antonio Palacios on the equally bizarre **Palacio de Comunicaciones** (*see chapter* **Sightseeing**).

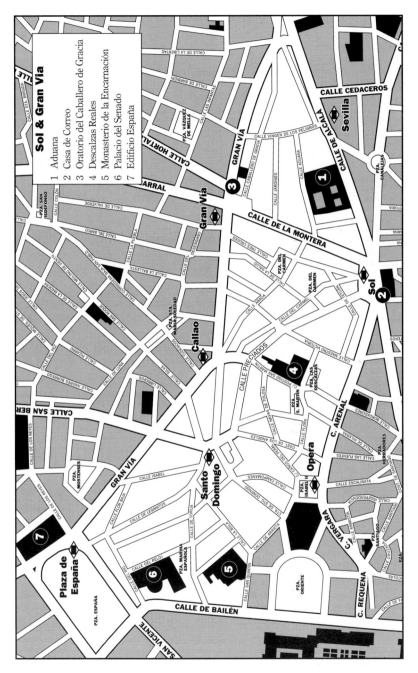

Sol & Gran Vía

1 Aduana
2 Casa de Correo
3 Oratorio del Caballero de Gracia
4 Descalzas Reales
5 Monasterio de la Encarnación
6 Palacio del Senado
7 Edificio España

The **Congreso de Diputados**, a stone's throw from the Huertas bar district. See page 82.

Famously, people have come to the Puerta del Sol to find out what's going on. Until the 1830s the block between Calle del Correo and Calle Esparteros was occupied by the monastery of San Felipe el Real, the steps and open cloister of which were, in Habsburg Madrid, one of the recognised *Mentideros* – literally, 'Pits of Lies', or gossip-mills – where people came to pick up on the latest news, anecdotes or scurrilous rumours. In a city with no newspapers, but where who was in or out of favour with the powerful was of first importance, they were a major social institution, and rare was the day when at least one of the great figures of Spanish literature such as Cervantes, Lope or Quevedo did not pass by here.

As a site for ad hoc mass rallies, too, Sol has no equal. A quarter of a million revellers turn out every New Year's Eve to douse themselves with spurting *cava* and eat their lucky grapes, one for each peal of the clock (*see chapter* **Madrid by Season**). At the climax of 1989's general strike, an even larger crowd assembled to cheer union leaders as they laid into the ruling Socialists. Ironically, just around the corner on Calle Tetúan is **Casa Labra**, famous for its zinc bar and tapas of *bacalao*, and as the place where the Spanish Socialist Party was founded in 1879 (*see chapter* **Tapas**). Sol is, too, where Napoleon's Egyptian cavalry, the Mamelukes, charged down on the Madrileño crowd on 2 May 1808, the subject of one of Goya's most famous paintings.

The 1766 **Casa de Correo**, the building with the clock, was built as Charles III's post office. It now looks harmlessly dignified, and serves as the headquarters of the Madrid regional government. For years, though, it was a place to be feared, as Franco's Interior Ministry and central police headquarters. It was here, in 1963, that Julián Grimau, a sort of Communist Scarlet Pimpernel, 'fell' from an upper window, but was patched up for his date with the firing squad.

The area between Sol, Arenal, Calle Alcalá and the Gran Via is noticeably free of residents and regular visitors most of the time. Instead, it forms central Madrid's main pedestrian axis and shopping centre, above all the **Calle Preciados**. There are banks and shoe shops, major stores such as **El Corte Inglés** and the **FNAC** and stacks of office suites, as well as plenty of bland cafeterías and fast food temples for employees on their lunch break.

Calle Montera, on the other hand, *the* shopping street of the 1950s, is now more of an urban freak show, deeply shabby, lined with tacky shops and the main area for street prostitution in the city centre. Just off Montera is Calle Caballero de Gracia, where the little nineteenth-century Oratory lays on two masses a day for the working girls, many of them from the Dominican Republic, who operate along the street. North of the Gran Via, too, behind the unmissable Telefónica building and on the south edge of Malasaña, lies Madrid's hardcore everything zone – the seediest of all the streets is called Calle Desengaño, which translates as 'disappointment'. Here purveyors of sex come second to the drug dealers, who are the stars of these mean streets. It's just seedy during the day, with grottylooking individuals of all ages coming and going in constant negotiations – maybe for drugs, maybe just arranging the delivery of a truckload of scrap – but best avoided at night.

Aside from these specific streets, the area north and east of Sol is dominated, however, by its two great avenues, the **Calle Alcalá** and the **Gran Vía**. Alcalá follows the centuries-old main route into Madrid from the east, and in the eighteenth century, when it was flanked by aristocratic palaces, it was described as the grandest street in Europe. It is still pretty grand today, for from Sol downhill to Cibeles the street is lined with a wonderful variety of early twentieth-century buildings, from the dignified **Banesto building** (No. 14) to the cautiously modernist **Círculo de Bellas Artes**. There are also some fine older constructions such as the austere neo-classical Finance Ministry, built as the **Aduana** or customs administration by Francesco Sabatini from 1761-69, and Pedro de Ribera's exuberantly Baroque church of **San José**, of 1730-42. Opposite the latter, at the point where Alcalá and Gran Via meet, there is the recent addition of a statue of **La Violetera**, the heroine of the eponymous *Zarzuela* (*see chapter* **Music: Classical & Opera**) whose theme was plagiarised by Charlie Chaplin in *City Lights*.

The Gran Vía, on the other hand, is a creation entirely of this century, sliced through the old city – albeit with a rather rusty knife, for it took over twenty years – after 1910. Although an interloper, it has a style all of its own (*see page 78*). A very symbol of modernity, it completely transformed the core of old Madrid, providing it with a new grand avenue full of bustle for banking, shopping, offices and, above all, cinemas (*see chapter* **Film**). The visitor to Madrid might love or hate it, but no one can deny it's lively. On Sundays, it's packed with people queuing under the enormous handpainted cinema posters (does this art form exist in any other country?), and Caribbean and Latin American buskers are out in force. The police are sometimes intrusive too, particularly with anyone non-white.

To the north-west the Gran Vía runs out into the sprawling space of the **Plaza de España**, completed under Franco. South of the Gran Vía, although the streets are full of shops and shoppers, there are still some corners of Habsburg Madrid tucked away, most notably nunneries such as the **Descalzas Reales** and the **Encarnación** (*see chapters* **Sightseeing** *and* **Museums**).

Just north of the Encarnación, occupying the site of another convent that was reputedly designed by El Greco, is the old, early nineteenth-century **Palacio del Senado** (Senate), now made redundant by its back-to-back counterpart in striated granite and smoked glass by Santiago Goyarre. When it opened in 1991 the new Senate was loudly criticised not so much on architectural grounds as for the shameless perk it represents (with in-house

swimming pool) for an upper house with even less of a political role than that in Britain.

Huertas & Santa Ana

Spain has the greatest number of bars and restaurants per capita in the world, and you can get the impression that all 17,729 of the ones in Madrid are crowded into the wedge-shaped swathe of streets between Alcalá and Calle Atocha. Oddly enough, this clearly-delimited area has an identity problem, for the authorities can never agree on a name, but if anyone suggests to you a pub crawl down Huertas, or a cooling jar in Santa Ana, it will always bring you – and about 15,000 others on any given weekend – to the right place.

Once this was the haunt of Madrid's seventeenth century literary set. Here were the theatres that provided them with a living, along with a fair few whorehouses and low dives. It still is Madrid's most distinctive theatre district. Close by but not too close lived the nobles who just might toss a couple of ducats your way if you buttered them up in a sonnet. Otherwise there were feuds, libellous exchanges and duels to fall back on

Reopened to the public after a long lapse, Lope de Vega's half-timbered house, with its sparse, authentic furnishings and tiny garden, is located on the street named after his bitter enemy, Cervantes (*see chapter* **Museums**). It appears the author of Don Quijote lived around the corner on the Calle León, but was probably buried in the Trinitarian convent on the Calle Lope de Vega. Which seems deliberately confusing.

A reverential nod is in order to Madrid's **Ateneo** on Calle del Prado, the cultural institution that has been a major centre of discussion and thought at many times in its history, most notably in the years running up to the Republic of 1931. It has hosted heated *tertulias* lasting from three in the afternoon till four in the morning, in which the ideas and polemics flew likes sparks from a forge. However, its strong point now is its library (*see chapter* **Students**).

In the great days of the Ateneo its members could also find nearby any number of cafés with a suitably literary atmosphere. Nowadays the Huertas-and-surrounding-streets scene comprises traditional tapas bars full of students, jazz bars, exotic cocktail emporia, bars full of yells and laughter, bars where you can't hear a thing, high-tech bars, leather bars, theme bars (movies, football, bullfights), pick-up bars, classical music bars, punk bars and others (*see chapters* **Tapas**, **Cafés & Bars** *and* **Nightlife**). There are still a few old-style cafés too.

To the south, the area is bounded by the **Calle Atocha**, terminally decadent in parts, with cheap *pensiones*, cramming academies for aspiring civil servants, and some gargantuan sex emporia such

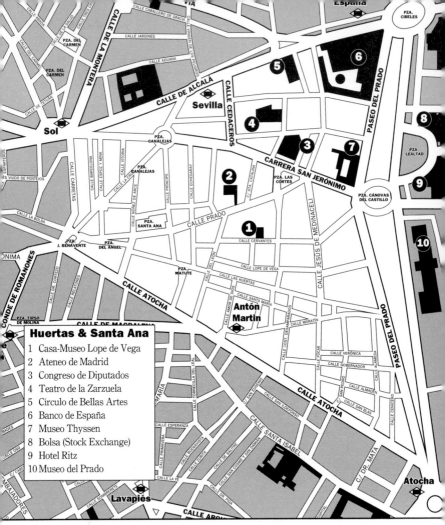

Huertas & Santa Ana

1 Casa-Museo Lope de Vega
2 Ateneo de Madrid
3 Congreso de Diputados
4 Teatro de la Zarzuela
5 Círculo de Bellas Artes
6 Banco de España
7 Museo Thyssen
8 Bolsa (Stock Exchange)
9 Hotel Ritz
10 Museo del Prado

as the **Mundo Fantástico** at no. 80. It also has a few old-fashioned revue theatres and cinemas.

Very different is the Carrera de San Jerónimo which runs through the north of the district. Part of the 'Ceremonial Route' of the Habsburg and Bourbon monarchs (*see chapter* **History: Capital of a Golden Age**), it is one of the centres of official Madrid today. On one side is the **Congreso de los Diputados**, Spain's Parliament building, with its classical portico and regal bronze lions, while opposite is the snazzy **Hotel Palace**, to which politicians can pop to relax (*see chapter* **Accommodation**).

Further up the hill on the left is **Lhardy**, the classic Franco-Spanish restaurant founded in 1839 (*see chapters* **Restaurants** *and* **Tapas**). Of its *castizo* charms, classy clientèle and *cocido madrileño* much

has been written; one need only note that a cup of consommé from its celebrated silver samovar makes an excellent restorative if the prices on the menu give you a coronary. North of San Jerónimo, behind the Congreso, is another theatre district, with the grandish 1856 **Teatro de la Zarzuela**, home of the Opera while the Teatro Real is closed (*see chapter* **Music: Classical & Opera**).

To the south of Carrera de San Jerónimo several streets run back into Huertas proper. On Calle Echegaray, among Japanese restaurants and Galician paella parlours is **Los Gabrieles**, a drinking establishment sheathed in possibly the world's most photographed wall-to-wall tiles. It's pretty expensive, and a cheaper alternative with an almost-as-good set of tiles is **Viva Madrid**, just around the corner (*see chapter* **Cafés & Bars**).

Last but in no way least is the core of the district, the **Plaza Santa Ana**. Like the Plaza de Oriente this square was created by poor, unappreciated Joseph Bonaparte, who tore down yet another superfluous convent to do so. A certain excessive quiet has descended on the plaza in the last couple of years since a certain colourful member of the conservative city administration decided to chuck out the crafts market that was held here every Saturday, and sent in the police to make sure the traders cleared off. Even so, the plaza is still a place where one can well hang out for an entire afternoon or three.

Here is the once-elegant **Hotel Reina Victoria**, the traditional bullfighters' hangout, and fine bars such as the unpretentious **Cervecería Santa Ana** and the **Cervecería Alemana**, which has got used to being known as a Hemingway favourite. In the adjoining Plaza del Angel is the **Café Central**, Madrid's best jazz club (*see chapter* **Music: Rock, Roots & Jazz**). On the eastern side of the plaza is the distinguished **Teatro Español**, on a site that has been a theatre continuously since 1583, when the Corral del Príncipe first opened its doors to the *Mosqueteros* (groundlings), whose reactions were so violent that they could force terrified playwrights to change plots in mid-play.

Lavapiés, The Rastro, Atocha

South of Sol and the Plaza Mayor, between San Francisco el Grande and Atocha, the ground slopes sharply downhill towards the rondas of Atocha, Valencia and Toledo. The districts within this area – commonly divided up by locals into La Latina, Lavapiés, Rastro and Embajadores – occupy a special place in local legend, for they are regularly cited as the *barrios* most steeped in Madrid's traditional *castizo* identity (*see chapter* **Madrid by Season**).

They used to be known as the *barrios bajos*, in the double sense of low-lying and full of low life – the closer to the river, the shabbier the surroundings. In imperial Madrid, most of the food brought to the city came in through the Puerta de Toledo, and many of the tasks that the upper classes wanted neither to see or smell, such as slaughtering and tanning, were concentrated here. Consequently, these districts became home to Madrid's first native working class. Their inhabitants also got a reputation from very early on for being uppity, and in the eighteenth century the *Majos* and *Majas* from these streets were admired by the intelligentsia for their legendary, caustic wit (*see chapter* **History: Bourbon Madrid**).

A century later, many streets in the area were rebuilt with open tenements around a central courtyard, called *Corralas*. They too created a way of life in themselves.

Today, even though most of the *Corralas* have

been replaced, these districts to a remarkable extent still convey the essence of a distinctive local way of life that has changed little since the last century. You want to buy a genuine shepherd's crook in solid walnut wood, or a litre of barley water? You've come to the right place. To argue, though, that here and only here is authentic Madrid is very ingenuous, since, surprisingly, many families do not go back more than a generation or two.

La Latina takes its name from the nickname of Beatriz Galindo, teacher of Latin and confidante to Queen Isabella, who was widely honoured for her sagacity and command of the classics. At the end of the fifteenth century she paid for a hospital to be built on the square that bears her name. Its site is now occupied by the **Teatro La Latina**, stronghold of traditional Spanish entertainment (*see chapter* **Theatre**).

The district of La Latina is relatively quiet except during its grand fiestas, around **La Paloma** in August (*see chapter* **Madrid by Season**). To the west it runs up to **San Francisco el Grande**, with its Goya frescoes, once Madrid's most fashionable place of worship.

To the east is the **Rastro**, Madrid's time-honoured flea market (*see chapter* **Shopping**). Its entrance is the **Plaza Cascorro**, with a monument honouring a young soldier raised in a nearby orphanage who volunteered for a suicide mission against Cuban rebels in the 1890s.

Apart from a cultural phenomenon, the Rastro is also a neighbourhood with a strong sense of its own identity, moulded by the centuries during which it has acted as an emporium for goods of every kind. See it on weekdays and avoid the crowds, and the pickpockets. The wicker furniture dealers will be open, and so will the junk shops and purveyors of fine antiques.

If instead of trying to make your way through the Rastro you go down Calle Embajadores, just a little to the east, you will see a truly outstanding slice of old Madrid. Embajadores and the near-parallel Calle Mesón de Paredes offer two of Madrid's most rewarding strolls. The latter has recently acquired a new touch thanks to the colourful prints worn by Africans who have settled there. On Calle Mesón de Paredes one can call in at a nineteenth-century tavern in full working order, the dark-panelled **Taberna de Antonio Sánchez**, established 1830 (*see chapter* **Cafés & Bars**).

At the end of Calle Embajadores, and abutting the busy Glorieta (roundabout) of the same name is the **Real Fábrica de Tabacos**, the Tobacco Factory, dating from 1790, and for much of the nineteenth century the largest industrial establishment in Madrid. Today, it's only a tobacco warehouse. In the past, just as in Seville, sultry Carmens used to be employed here, but when the whistle sounds today paunchy males in blue overalls come streaming out.

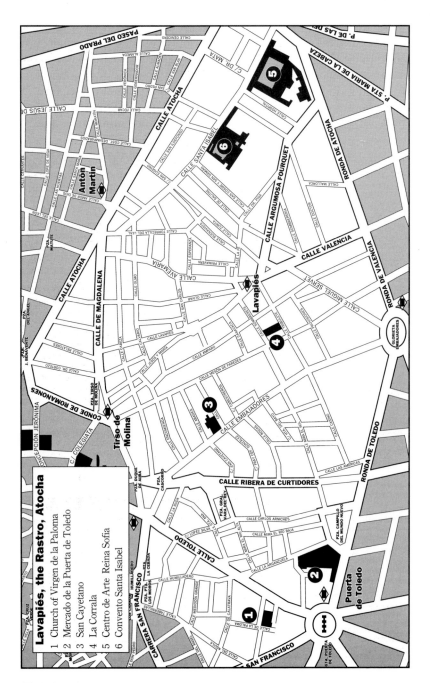

Lavapiés, the Rastro, Atocha

1 Church of Virgen de la Paloma
2 Mercado de la Puerta de Toledo
3 San Cayetano
4 La Corrala
5 Centro de Arte Reina Sofía
6 Convento Santa Isabel

The tiles of the former **Laboratorios Juanse** pharmacy, a Malasaña landmark. See page 86.

Back uphill on Mesón de Paredes is **La Corrala**, the city's best surviving example of an 1880s courtyard tenement, garnished as tradition requires with freshly washed-sheets and underwear billowing from the balconies. Restored in the eighties, it can seem so carefully fixed up and repainted that it looks more a pastiche than the real thing. Your doubts disappear, however, if you spot one of the residents in shocking pink polyester dressing-gown and curlers calling to her neighbours from her balcony. In summer the building is used to present a season of Madrileño *Zarzuela* (*see chapter* **Music: Classical & Opera**).

Corralas always faced an inner patio, multiplying the noise and lack of privacy which never have bothered Spaniards, but here the other three sides have been demolished. A somewhat later example, but enclosed on all sides and so not easily visible from the street, is at Calle Embajadores 52.

Joseph Bonaparte's **Puerta de Toledo** marks the spot where the tributaries of the Rastro empty into a torrent of traffic. Alongside it is the **Mercado de la Puerta de Toledo**, built in the 1930s as a fish market. In the 1980s it was converted into a state of the art shopping mall/urban regeneration project, but the scheme has been a dismal failure.

The **Plaza de Lavapiés** is believed to have been the centre of Madrid's medieval Jewish community, expelled like all others in her dominions by the very pious Queen Isabella in 1492. Today, it's pretty run down, but there's more to its mix than just quaintness or sleaze, since its (relatively) cheap rents have added to it a younger, more international and bohemian flavour too. This is Madrid's fringe theatre district: following the lead of the **Sala Olimpia** a number of semi-professional and fringe companies have turned older buildings, sometimes foremer stables, into new venues (*see chapter* **Theatre**). On Calle Santa Isabel there is also the **Filmoteca**, in an art-nouveau setting in the old Cine Doré, with eight daily screenings and a great café and bookshop (*see chapter* **Film**).

South-east, just before you emerge onto the Glorieta de Atocha you'll arrive at one of Madrid's major attractions, the **Centro de Arte Reina Sofía**, the opening of which has led to the appearance of a number of private galleries in the surrounding streets (*see chapter* **Art Galleries**). Close by, occupying a large stretch of the Calle Sant Isabel, is the seventeenth-century **Convento de Santa Isabel**, sponsored, like the Encarnación, by Margaret of Austria, wife of Philip III, and one of the largest religious houses in Madrid to escape the liberals' axe during the last century.

Malasaña & Chueca

At weekends massed crowds flock to these areas for loud, louche, late nights on the town, so it's easy to forget that during the day they are full of traditional charm. In most of its streets, **Malasaña**, between Calle Fuencarral and Calle San Bernardo, offers an eyeful of nineteenth-century Madrid. By day, grannies water their geraniums growing beside weather-worn wooden shutters on wrought-iron balconies. By night the streets below are where the black leather and nose-ring crowd queue up at nocturnal dives such as **La Via Lactea** and **Agapo** (*see chapter* **Nightlife**). The same streets are also the base for Madrid's community of old (and sometimes youngish) hippies.

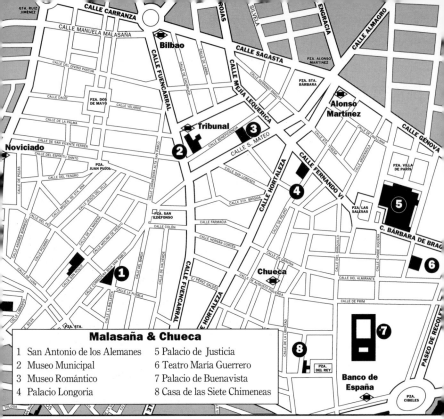

Malasaña & Chueca

1 San Antonio de los Alemanes
2 Museo Municipal
3 Museo Romántico
4 Palacio Longoria
5 Palacio de Justicia
6 Teatro María Guerrero
7 Palacio de Buenavista
8 Casa de las Siete Chimeneas

Peaceful coexistence is possible between the old and young since a lot of the time each party never actually meets. Another group – call them 'responsible' drug dealers – have tacitly agreed not to ply their trade before four in the morning. Even so, tempers have been running high in the area on the drugs issue.

In another era completely this area was the centre of resistance to the French on 2 May 1808. The name of the district comes from a 17-year old seamstress heroine, Manuela Malasaña, who was shot by the invaders for carrying concealed weapons (her scissors), or for carrying ammunition to the Spanish troops – there are various different versions of her exploits. The name of the barrio's main square, **Plaza Dos de Mayo**, also recalls that day. Where the plaza is today was then the Monteleón artillery barracks, from where the humble artillery captains Daoíz and Velarde galvanised the resistance of the people. The last remaining part of the barracks, a gate, stands with a monument to the two men in the middle of the square. It's hard to imagine the plaza as the site of such violent events today.

The cross streets between San Bernardo and Fuencarral abound with bars and restaurants, as well as indications – such as the broad arched doorways for carriages – that the nineteenth-century well-to-do were very much at home here. Among the most rewarding is **Calle San Vicente Ferrer**, with its jewellery shops and a twenties' tile display advertising the long-extinct pharmacy Laboratorios Juanse, offering all kinds of bizarre cures. Other old ceramic signs along the street feature a little boy proudly signalling that his chamber pot is full, and a dramatic reclining vamp. **Calle Espíritu Santo** also boasts some excellent tilework, and **Calle de la Palma** and **Calle Divino Pastor** are equally worth a stroll, with some unusual shops and pleasant bars.

The atmosphere gets more mobile as you approach the streets on the Fuencarral side that lead towards the Gran Vía, such as the **Corredera Baja de San Pablo** and its continuation, the **Corredera Alta**. This is an area of cheap restaurants, wholesale produce dealers in white aprons, shops selling nothing but light bulbs and working-class people who have obviously all known each other all their lives. The brick church at the corner of Corredera Baja de San Pablo and Calle Ballesta

Madrid's Great Artery

Look at any map of Madrid and you see it. A long, sometimes curving, sometimes dead-straight road, running north-south for miles right through the middle of the city, and called at different points the Paseo del Prado, de Recoletos and de la Castellana. It is as if, in a city where people had so often complained of the lack of grand avenues, somebody had suddenly decided to silence the critics with one single throughfare like they'd never seen.

Even so, this endless strip developed gradually, rather than as the result of one decision. Its oldest section, the Paseo del Prado, once an open space between the city wall and the Retiro, was given its present form as the most important of King Charles III's many attempts to give his shabby city the kind of urbane dignity he had seen in Paris, or in his youth in Italy.

As well as his creations such as the **Jardín Botánico** or the **Museo del Prado**, it contains the rest of Madrid's 'Golden Triangle' of art museums, the finely-renovated **Atocha** station and such important parts of local life as the **Hotel Ritz**, the **Bolsa** (the Stock Exchange) and the second-hand bookstalls on the **Cuesta de Moyano** (*see chapters* **Accommodation, Sightseeing** *and* **Shopping**).

The Paseo de Recoletos, north of Cibeles, was mostly added to the Prado in the 1830s and 1840s. It is as green and elegant as its predecessor, but busier, with fashionable pavement cafés such as **El Espejo** and the famous **Café Gijón** (*see chapter* **Cafés & Bars**). The curiously grand white marble palace a little further north on the right, now the **Banco Hipotecario**, is the one that was the residence of the Marqués de Salamanca, Madrid's one-time huckster-in-chief (*see page 88* **Salamanca & the Retiro**).

At the end of Recoletos on the right stands the huge building housing the **Biblioteca Nacional** and, behind it, the **Museo Arqueologico Nacional** (*see chapters* **Museums** *and* **Students**). The most ambitious project of the reign of Isabel II, it was commissioned in 1865, but was not completed until 1892. It now overlooks the **Plaza de Colón** with its **Jardines del Descubrimiento**. At Columbus' feet a cascading wall of water, beautifully cool in summer, conceals the entrance to the **Centro Cultural de la Villa** (*see chapter* **Art Galleries, Dance** *and* **Theatre**).

In 1860, when he designed the *Ensanche*, Carlos María de Castro took the significant decision, since the Paseo del Prado and Recoletos were already there, to continue along the same route with the main avenue of the new district. Thus, the Castellana was born. Until the Republic of 1931 demolished Madrid's old race-track, it reached only as far as the Calle Joaquín Costa. Today, it snakes away freely northwards, through thickets of office blocks. This is also, though, the home of the 'Costa Castellana', Madrid's 'beach' of night-time terrace bars, particularly around the junction with Calle Juan Bravo (*see chapter* **Nightlife**).

In the seventies and eighties banks and insurance companies vied with each other to commission the hot architects of the day, from Spain and abroad, to create their corporate showcases. A few of the notable constructions to see and judge in the Castellana's first stretch are the **IBM** Headquarters at the very beginning, **Bankinter** at no. 29, **Bankunión** at no. 46, and the glass-over-glass **Catalana Occidente** flagship. The next major intersection is marked, not to say dominated, by the great bulk of the 1930s **Nuevos Ministerios** government office complex (*see chapter* **Sightseeing**).

A huge branch of the **Corte Inglés** department store on the left signals your arrival at the **AZCA** complex, a monument to eighties' corporate taste. A little further up again, opposite each other, are Real Madrid's **Estadio Bernabéu** and the **Palacio de Congresos** conference centre. The plazas nearby are often staked out at night by prostitutes hoping to ply their trade in the many four-star businessmen's hotels nearby.

By this time, the view up the Castellana dominated by the giant shadow of the **Puerta de Europa**, as their promoters hope it will be called, at the Plaza Castilla. These half-finished glass blocks are embedded in the popular consciousness, however, as the **Torres KIO**, after the Kuwait Investment Office who paid for them. The Kuwaitis' Spanish agent did a bunk in mid-project, leaving the entire Spanish financial world looking extremely unreliable, and the towers literally in mid-air.

The blocks are certainly remarkable, above all for the graph-paper/smoked glass façades that loom over the plaza 15° off the perpendicular, a piece of engineering virtuosity that is said to be possible but a little risky. Work has been resumed, and the latest word is that they will finally be ready for occupancy in 1996, and a jet of pressurized water will shoot up dozens of yards into the air between them.

One of Salamanca's architectural details.

was built by Felipe III for his Portuguese subjects in Madrid. Later it was set aside for the use of German emigrés, and is still known as **San Antonio de los Alemanes**. It is difficult to see the inside of the church today, as it is rarely open.

On the eastern side of Malasaña in the Calle Fuencarral is the **Museo Municipal**, the former eighteenth-century hospice, with an entrance by Pedro de Ribera done with great Baroque brio. This is also an exceptionally fine little museum, worth visiting if only to peer at the model of old Madrid from 1830 (*see chapter* **Museums**). Just to the north, Fuencarral runs into the Glorieta de Bilbao, where you will find one of Madrid's very best cafés, the **Café Comercial** (*see chapter* **Cafés & Bars**).

Chueca, between Fuencarral and Recoletos, has seen both better days and worse. In the eighteenth century, the Calle Hortaleza was the site of the *Recogida*, a refuge for 'public sinners', where women could be confined for soliciting on the street, or merely on the say-so of a male family member, release being possible only through marriage or a lifetime tour of duty in a convent.

More recently, it had a bad reputation a few years ago as a junkie's haven, particularly the **Plaza de Chueca** itself. That it has revived has in considerable part been due to its having been colonised by the gay community, as *the* gay area in Madrid. As well as the strictly gay scene, you have trendy clubs such as **Torito**, and even some traditional bars and restaurants, such as the positively quaint *taberna* of **Angel Sierra** (*see chapters* **Cafés & Bars**, **Nightlife** *and* **Gay Madrid**).

Towards Recoletos, Chueca becomes much more commercial, and upmarket. **Calle Barquillo** is still full of electrical shops offering every stereo/video/electronic component you could think of. **Calle Almirante** meanwhile and its cross street, **Conde de Xiquena** make up one of the main high-fashion shopping zones of Madrid (*see chapter* **Shopping**). This is also one of Madrid's most exclusive residential districts.

The giant **Palacio de Justicia**, due to become the seat of the Spanish Supreme Court, is just to the north on Calle Bárbara de Braganza. It was formerly the Convento de las Salesas, built in 1750-58 under the patronage of Queen Bárbara, wife of Fernando VI. It was taken over by the state in 1870. Its refined classical baroque contrasts nicely with the frenzied art nouveau of the **Palacio Longoria**, just a few streets away.

South toward Calle Alcalá is the **Plaza del Rey**, the most venerable feature of which is the **Casa de las Siete Chimeneas**, designed by Juan de Herrera, responsible for El Escorial. Gone is the Circo Price, a covered coliseum named after its expatriate founder, impresario Thomas Price. As well a permanent three-ring circus, *Zarzuelas* were performed here from 1876 until it was torn down in 1969. Many people say the Plaza del Rey has never been the same.

Salamanca & the Retiro

In the mid-nineteenth century, as it became evident that Spanish cities needed to expand beyond their medieval walls, attempts were made to ensure that this happened in a planned and orderly way. Both Madrid and Barcelona had plans approved for their *Ensanche* ('Extension') (*see chapter* **History: Revolutions & Railways**). Carlos María de Castro's 1860 plan for Madrid envisaged the expansion of the city to the north and east in a consistent grid, with strict restrictions on building height and public open spaces at regular intervals and within each block, to ensure a healthy, harmonious urban landscape.

The problem was, however, that for a good while few of Madrid's middle classes seemed to have the money or the motivation to invest in such a scheme, and appeared to prefer to stay within the cramped, noisy old city. That Madrid's *Ensanche* got off the ground at all was due to a banker, politician and speculator notorious for his dubious business practices, the Marqués de Salamanca.

The Marqués had previously built his own vast residence, now the **Banco Hipotecario**, on the Paseo de Recoletos in 1846-50. It had the very first flush toilets in Madrid, an amenity he later offered to residents in his new housing development. He spent one of several fortunes he made and lost in his lifetime on building a first line of rectangular blocks in the *Ensanche*, along the Calle Serrano.

The Buen Retiro

In October 1632 Philip IV's great minister the Count-Duke of Olivares presented the King with the keys of a new residence in the royal park to the east of Madrid, the *Buen Retiro* or 'Good Retreat'. More than a palace it was a complex of palatial buildings, centred on a great courtyard presided over by the statue of Philip IV on horseback, designed by Velázquez, that is now in the Plaza de Oriente (*see chapter* **Sightseeing**). Olivares' aim in commissioning the palace was to make an emphatic statement of the greatness of the monarchy he served, creating a self-contained compound, with its huge formal gardens, in which the Court could be displayed at its maximum splendour. Louis XIV took the idea as his model for Versailles.

The part of the Retiro of most interest to Philip IV was the Court theatre. The King had a particular fascination for elaborate set designs and visual tricks, and an Italian designer, Cosimo Lotti, was brought in to create ever-more extravagant productions that dwarfed the human actors. Writers such as Calderón de la Barca created dramas, generally on mythological themes, to fit. All kinds of mechanical devices were used, and productions often spread out to feature the park lake, with battles between life-size ships, sea-monsters appearing from the depths, and angels flying through the air. Most performances were only for the Court, but several times a year a wider audience was allowed in to be amazed.

The full splendour of the Retiro lasted little more than a century, for the Bourbon kings had no great liking for it. Most of the palace was destroyed in 1812-13, during the Napoleonic Wars. Only two sections remain today, the **Casón del Buen Retiro** and **Museo del Ejército** (*see also chapters* **History: Capital of a Golden Age** *and* **Museums**).

However, he overstretched himself, the luxury apartments proved too expensive for local buyers, and he went terminally bankrupt in 1867. Even so, it is to him, and not the old Castilian university town, that the district owes its name.

It was only after the Restoration of 1874 that Madrid's wealthy began in large numbers to appreciate the potential benefits of wider streets and residences with more class than Madrid's musty old neighbourhoods could supply. Once the idea caught on, however, the exodus proceeded apace, and most of the core of Salamanca was built up by 1900. Castro's rather utopian regulations on building height and public amenities, however, were soon abandoned, for private investors could see little point in them.

The wealthiest families of all built individual palaces along the lower stretch of the Castellana, in a wild variety of styles – French imperial, Italian renaissance, neo-*Mudéjar*. Only a handful of these extravagances remain – the Palacio de Linares, now the **Casa de América** (*see chapter* **Art Galleries**), is perhaps the best preserved on the Castellana itself. Another good example is the palace of the Marqueses de Aboage at Calle Juan Bravo, 79, now the **Italian Embassy**.

Those who could not quite afford their own mansion moved into giant apartments in the streets behind. This has been the centre of conservative, affluent Madrid ever since. The incidence of middle-aged women in fur coats walking coiffed poodles is a fair indication that the *Barrio de Salamanca* retains its traditional status.

The affluence index is best gauged by the prices in the shop windows. Streets yield up top designers (especially Calles Jorge Juan, Ortega y Gasset, Goya and segments of Serrano), art galleries, take-out trattorias and dealers in French wines, English silver or superior leather accessories (*see chapter* **Shopping**). Salamanca has, too, its own social scene, based around Calle Juan Bravo, with several shiny smart, yuppyish bars and discos, such as **Keeper** (*see chapter* **Music: Rock, Roots & Jazz**), full of shiny, well-bred young folk discussing holidays.

Art buffs are advised to head for the marble tower with attached sculpture garden at Calle Castelló 77, where the **Fundación Juan March** possesses a no-holds-or-tendency-barred collection of first rate modern art, with a strong suit in the post-1950 Spanish avant-garde. It also underwrites concerts of contemporary music and welcomes itinerant exhibitions (*see chapters* **Art Galleries** *and* **Music: Classical & Opera**). At the northern end of Calle Serrano is the **Museo Lázaro Galdiano**, nothing much to look at from the outside, but a museum whose eclectic contents will astonish and delight (*see chapter* **Museums**).

Salamanca abuts onto Madrid's favourite green lung, the **Retiro**, originally created by the Conde-Duque de Olivares for Philip IV in order to impress the world (*see left, and chapter* **Sightseeing**). The districts around and to the south of the Retiro are in some ways similar to Salamanca, but less emphatically affluent and much more mixed, with more of a *barrio* feel.

Just south-west of the park, right on the Glorieta de Atocha, is one of the area's lesser-known sights. One cannot but marvel at the magnificent but misplaced grandeur of the **Ministry of Agriculture**, built in the 1880s by Ricardo Velázquez, the same architect who also designed the delicate exhibition

Franco's own Escorial, the **Ministerio del Aire** *in Moncloa.*

halls inside the Retiro itself. A huge pile, the Ministry is topped by a variety of giant stone beasts symbolising industry, commerce, and so on.

Further to the south-east along Paseo Reina Cristina is the dilapidated **Real Fábrica de Tapices** at Calle Fuentarrabia 2 (551 34 00), the tapestry factory for which Goya did several designs. This is no abandoned museum, but a faded but still going concern where the dyeing and weaving is done as it was when it was founded in 1721. Skilled fingers are kept busy mostly mending and darning the carpets of the Hotel Ritz, and you can also have work made to order yourself, for a very high price.

North & West
Moncloa & Argüelles

West of Malasaña lie the districts vaguely known as Argüelles and Moncloa, although it's generally hard to distinguish where either begins and ends. They run up to the university, and so form the main centre of student Madrid, with many shared flats, as well as bars and discos. So many discos, in fact, that many have been closed after complaints from local residents about noise.

Not students at all is the **Palacio de Liria**, on Calle Princesa, completed in 1783, and very much the private property of the Duchess of Alba, head of the only one of Spain's great aristocratic families to have held on to much the greater part of their wealth through all the financial ups and downs of the last 150 years. It's been under renovation for years, and until work is completed there won't be

any more Friday morning tours (by written application only) of its hidden artistic treasures.

Alongside the palace is the **Centro Cultural Conde-Duque**, Pedro de Ribera's giant barracks for King Philip V's guard, built between 1717 and 1754, and wonderfully renovated in the early eighties by the city council to become a dynamic cultural centre. Its huge courtyards make it a great venue for open-air summer concerts, and it's also a fine exhibition space (*see chapters* **Madrid by Season** *and* **Art Galleries**).

At the end of Calle Princesa, unmissable on the corner of the Paseo Moret, is one of the most significant, and most kitsch, buildings of the Franco regime, the **Ministerio del Aire**, the Air Ministry. In the first years of the regime, Spanish artists were enjoined to return to eternal values, and to take the Golden Age as a model in everything. In the Ministry, architect Luis Gutiérrez Soto did just that, and built a huge, brand-new Castilian-baroque style building, inspired by the Escorial, between 1943 and 1957. Wags referred to it as the *Monasterio del Aire*. The regime had plans for other similarly nostalgic constructions, but the state of the economy scotched them all.

In front of the ministry rises the fake Roman triumphal arch Franco built for himself as a prize for winning the Civil War, twenty years after its outbreak in 1956. More attractive is the **Faro de Madrid**, the observation tower put up in 1992, a strange construction that looks like a visored helmet stuck atop a metal maypole (*see chapter* **Sightseeing**).

Argüelles, properly speaking, is the grid of streets between Calle Princesa and Paseo del Pintor Rosales. The Paseo is famous for its *terrazas*, open-air bars where all manner of folk can take the air and shoot the breeze all through the day and night.

Chamberí

Directly north of Malasaña, just outside 'old Madrid', is the district of Chamberí. It was one of the first working-class districts outside the walls to be occupied. Consequently it became one of the few areas outside the old city on the list of those considered to have genuine *castizo* character.

As befits a *barrio* with a proper identity, Chamberí has its own bar round, with rows of good – and relatively cheap – tapas bars mostly around the Calle Cardenal Cisneros and Calle Hartzenbush (*see chapter* **Tapas**). On the north side of the district, Madrid's water system, the *Canal de Isabel II*, occupies an ample tract of land. On Calle Santa Engracia, a turn-of-the-century water tower has been converted into a unique photographic gallery, the **Sala del Canal de Isabel II** (*see chapter* **Art Galleries**).

Tetuán & the North

North of Chamberí are Cuatro Caminos and Tetuán, arranged along Calle Bravo Murillo, both modern, working areas. For the visitor Tetuán's main point of interest is probably its **Market**, the **Mercado de Maravillas** at C/Bravo Murillo 122, the largest, liveliest and most colourful in the whole city. On Sunday mornings, too, a miniature 'rastro' gets going full steam on Calle Marqués de Viana.

Vallecas

Vallecas, out beyond the M30 south east of the city, was already an industrial suburb in the 1930s, and manages still to be one of the areas of Madrid with a firmest sense of its own identity. It doesn't lay much claim to being traditionally *castizo*, even though many of its residents came here as overspill from the centre. Rather, to say Vallecas in Madrid is to suggest immediately the post-Civil War, post-fifties working class.

Vallecas is known for a strong sense of neighbourly solidarity. It has its own football team, the battling **Rayo Vallecano**, forever struggling to keep up with its money-laden neighbours (*see chapter* **Sport & Fitness**). Car window stickers defiantly proclaim 'Independence for Vallecas'. It also has an extremely pleasant tree-lined main drag where generations mingle and hang out, more than enough to mark it out from the other areas of housing blight around it, and Madrid's central wholesale market. There are also notorious problem areas near Vallecas, particularly the unemployment deserts

and drug bazaars around Entrevías, on its south side. This area contains Madrid's largest Gypsy communities, some of whom live permanently on the edge, while others are quite prosperous.

The South

Arganzuela, Usera, Carabanchel, Leganés, Getafe, Móstoles, Alcorcón – Madrid's southern industrial belt, virtually all of it built up from nothing since the sixties. Concrete flyovers and rows of near identical tower blocks make up the urban landscape. **Usera**, to name but one, is a a case study in unplanned, unrestrained urban mess. Unemployment and hard drug use are chronic problems. Yet, the district's resolutely proletarian population are a sparky bunch and almost all the best hard rock groups in the vicinity came out of Usera, where they jammed in the garages. Pedro Almodóvar says as much in one of his early films.

Central city-dwellers do sometimes come down here, too, for entertainment. **Leganés** contains a vast leisure-cum-shopping centre complex, **Parquesur**, with a water park, restaurants and a disco, **Universal Sur**, where 2,000 people can boogie at any given time. It's also one of Madrid's top rock venues. **Alcorcón**, too, contains a knot of giant rave discos on the now-not-so-fashionable 'Bakalao route' (*see chapters* **Nightlife** *and* **Music: Rock, Roots & Jazz**).

The Northern Suburbs

The thing to do for those with the cash to afford it in Madrid in the last fifteen years or more has been to adopt the Anglo-Saxon way of life and move out of their city flats to house-and-garden developments in places like **Puerta de Hierro**, north of the Casa de Campo, which takes its name from the 1753 'Iron Gate' to the royal hunting reserve of El Pardo. The posh residences in this district, however, are no match for **La Moraleja**, to the north-east on the Burgos road, which is pure Beverly Hills, an enclave for executives and diplomats.

The growing districts to the east are not nearly so posh. **Alcobendas** is home to Madrid's hands-on, child-friendly **Acciona** science museum (*see chapter* **Children**). The area along the A2 motorway between the city and the airport is intended to be Madrid's major development zone, with the huge **Feria de Madrid** trade fair complex and the all-new **Parque Juan Carlos I** (*see chapters* **Sightseeing** *and* **Business**). Oddly enough the area already contains, swallowed up in the urban spread, one of Spain's most appealing and neglected eighteenth-century gardens, the **Capricho de la Alameda de Osuna**, a delightful French garden with a river with islands and bridges, gurgling fountains, a temple to Bacchus, a neo-classical palace and endless parterre promenades (*see chapter* **Sightseeing**)

On the Town

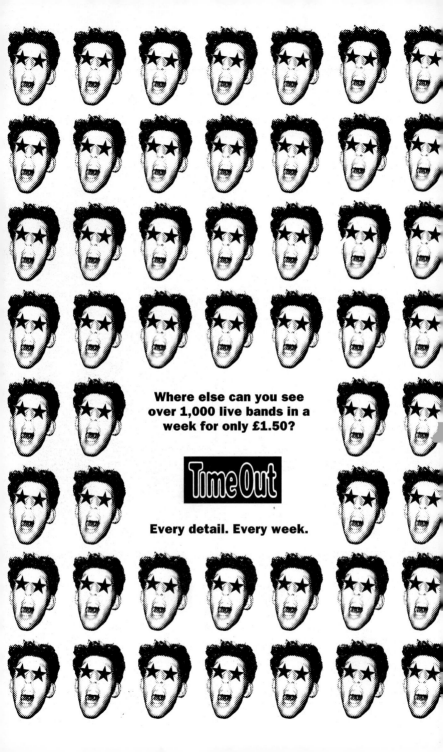

Where else can you see over 1,000 live bands in a week for only £1.50?

Every detail. Every week.

Restaurants

The finest fish, the spiciest sausage and the most robust wines: Madrid is the melting pot of Spain's culinary traditions.

Madrid has some of the most varied and unusual food in Europe, and not just from exotic or foreign cuisines. They are here, of course, but more prominent are Spain's traditional regional cuisines, with their sharply contrasting flavours from the green north, the harsh central plateau of the *meseta* and the sun-baked south. The full range of Spanish food – all of it represented in Madrid – is enormous, and often not appreciated outside the country.

The city's status as capital has meant not only that many of Spain's best cooks have gravitated here, but also that much of the finest produce from around the country is more readily available in Madrid than in its region of origin. Particularly worth looking out for – despite the distance from the sea – are fish and shellfish, which are outstandingly good here. Madrid's own traditional dishes (*see below* **Traditional Madrileño**) are humble food, with plenty of beans and lentils, and much use of offal.

Madrid is not so much a city with a restaurant culture as a place where you can eat well, since formal restaurants are only one part of a very varied whole. For more fine eating-places, *see also chapters* **Tapas** *and* **Cafés & Bars**.

Also, one consequence of Spain's post-1992 recession has been great value for money. A great many Madrileños lunch in restaurants on weekdays, and neighbourhood bars and eating-houses keep standards high to compete. Many offer *menú del día* set lunches (sometimes, also available in the evenings) for around 1,000-2,000ptas, which are often an exceptional bargain. An increasing number of gourmet restaurants are also introducing cut-price formulas.

RESTAURANT CUSTOMS

A tenet often observed in Spanish food is that, if an ingredient is good, it's best appreciated on its own, without any accompanying mush to obscure the flavours. However, a Castilian meal that consists of two pure-meat courses without a green leaf in sight can come as a shock to anyone accustomed to having vegetables provided automatically. In most restaurants, if you want greenery you should order it separately, as a first course or side salad, since main courses will normally come without vegetables (except perhaps *patatas fritas*, chips).

Virtually every Madrid restaurant has an economically-priced house wine, most commonly a

The chic **Cabo Mayor***. See page 97.*

Valdepeñas, from La Mancha – although there are now also some increasingly good-quality labels from this area. In cheap restaurants the house wine can be pretty poor, and Spaniards often mix it with lemonade (*gaseosa*), if they don't just prefer beer. Of the quality wines, the products of Spain's best-known wine-growing region, Rioja, have in recent years often been surpassed by those of other areas, notably Navarra and Ribera del Duero, two of several Spanish wine regions that have come on a great deal in the last few years. Also interesting are lesser-known wines such as the Basque Txacolí whites, Rueda from Valladolid or the Galician Ribeiro.

The Menu

For other ingredients and dishes more normally eaten as tapas (but which may also appear on restaurant menus), *see chapter* **Tapas**.

Basics

Primer plato (entrante) first-course; **Segundo plato** second or main dish; **Postre** dessert; **Plato combinado** quick, one-course meal, with several ingredients served on the same plate; **Pan** bread; **Aceite y vinagre** oil & vinegar; **Agua** water; **Con gas/sin gas** fizzy/still; **Vino** wine; **Cerveza** beer; **La cuenta** the bill; **Servicio incluído** Service included. **Propina** tip.

Cooking styles & techniques

Adobado marinated; **Al ajillo** with olive oil and garlic; **A la marinera** (fish or shellfish) cooked with garlic, onions and white wine; **A la parilla** charcoal-grilled; **A la plancha** grilled directly on a hot metal plate; **A la romana** fried in batter; **Al vapor** steamed; **Asado (al horno de lena)** roast (in a wood oven); **Crudo** raw; **En salsa** in a sauce or gravy; **Escabechado, en escabeche** marinated in vinegar with bay leaf and garlic; **Estofado** braised; **Frito** fried; **Guisado** stewed; **Hervido** boiled; **Relleno** stuffed.

Huevos (Eggs)

Huevos fritos fried eggs (sometimes served with chorizo); **Revuelto** scrambled eggs; **Tortilla asturiana** omelette with tomato, tuna and onion; **Tortilla francesa** plain omelette; **Tortilla de patatas** thick Spanish potato omelette.

Sopas y Potajes (Soups & Stews)

Caldo broth; **Gazpacho** cold soup, usually of tomatoes, red pepper and cucumber; **Sopa de ajo** garlic soup; **Sopa castellana** garlic soup with poached egg and chickpeas; **Sopa de fideos** noodle soup.

Carne, Aves, Caza y Embutidos (Meat, Poultry, Game & Charcuterie)

Bistec steak; **Buey, vacuno** (cuts **solomillo, entrecot**) beef; **Butifarra** Catalan suasage; **Callos** tripe; **Capón** capon; **Cerdo** pork, pig; **Chorizo** spicy sausage, served cooked or cold; **Choto** kid; **Chuletas, chuletones, chuletillas** chops; **Cochinillo** roast suckling pig; **Cocido** traditional Madrid stew (*see p99* **Traditional Madrileño**); **Codornices** quails; **Conejo** rabbit; **Cordero** lamb; **Costillas** ribs; **Criadillas** bulls' testicles; **Estofado de ternera** a veal stew; **Gallina** hen; **Higado** liver; **Jamón ibérico** cured ham from Iberian pigs; **Jamón serrano** cured ham; **Jamón york** cooked ham; **Lacón** gammon ham; **Lechazo, cordero lechal** milk-fed baby lamb; **Liebre** hare; **Lomo (de cerdo)** loin of pork; **Longaniza, fuet** salami-type sausages; **Morcilla** black blood sausage; **Pato** duck; **Pavo** turkey; **Perdiz** partridge; **Pepitoria** chicken casserole with wine and almonds; **Pollo** chicken; **Riñones** kidneys; **Salchichas** frying sausages; **Sesos** brains; **Ternera** veal (although in Spain it is slaughtered later than most veal, and so more similar to beef or steak).

Pescado y Mariscos (Fish & Shellfish)

Almejas clams; **Atún, bonito** tuna; **Bacalao** salt-cod; **Besugo** sea bream; **Bogavante** lobster; **Calamares** squid; **Cangrejo, Buey de mar** crab; **Cangrejo de río** freshwater crayfish; **Gambas** prawns; **Langosta** spiny lobster; **Langostinos** languostines; **Lubina** sea bass; **Mejillones** mussels; **Mero** grouper; **Merluza** hake; **Ostras** oysters; **Pescadilla** whiting; **Pescaditos** whitebait; **Pulpo** octopus; **Rape** monkfish; **Rodaballo** turbot; **Salmonete** red mullet; **Sardinas** sardines; **Sepia** cuttlefish; **Trucha** trout; **Ventresca de bonito** fillet of tuna; **Vieiras** scallops.

Verduras (Vegetables)

Acelgas Swiss chard; **Alcachofas** artichokes; **Berenjena** aubergine/eggplant; **Calabacines** courgettes/zucchini; **Cebolla** onion; **Champiñones** mushrooms; **Col** cabbage; **Ensalada mixta** basic salad of lettuce, tomato and onion; **Ensalada verde** basic lettuce salad, without tomato; **Espárragos** asparagus; **Espinacas** spinach; **Guisantes** peas; **Grelos** turnip leaves; **Habas** broad beans; **Judías verdes** green beans; **Lechuga** lettuce; **Menestra** braised mixed vegetables; **Patatas fritas** chips; **Pepino** cucumber; **Pimientos** sweet capsicum peppers; **Pimientos de piquillo** slightly hot red capsicums; **Pisto** mixture of cooked vegetables, similar to ratatouille; **Setas** wild mushrooms of different kinds; **Tomates** tomatoes; **Zanahorias** carrots.

Arroz y Legumbres (Rice & Pulses)

Alubias, judías white beans; **Arroz abanda** rice cooked in shellfish stock; **Arroz negro** black rice cooked in squids' ink; **Fríjoles** red kidney beans; **Garbanzos** chickpeas; **Judiones** large haricot beans, typical of Castile; **Lentejas** lentils; **Paella de mariscos** shellfish paella; **Pochas (caparrones)** new-season kidney beans.

Fruta (Fruit)

Cerezas cherries; **Ciruelas** plums; **Fresas** strawberries; **Higos** figs; **Macedonia** fruit salad; **Manzana** apple; **Melocotón** peach; **Melón** Melon; **Moras** blackcurrants; **Naranja** orange; **Pera** pear; **Piña** pineapple; **Plátano** banana; **Sandía** watermelon; **Uvas** grapes.

Postres (Desserts)

Arroz con leche rice pudding; **Bizcocho** sponge-cake; **Brazo de gitano** ice-cream or custard swiss roll; **Cuajada** junket (served with honey); **Flan** crême caramel; **Helado** ice-cream; **Leche frita** custard fried in breadcrumbs; **Membrillo** quince jelly (often served with cheese); **Tarta** cake; **Torrijas** sweet bread fritters.

Quesos (Cheeses)

Burgos, Requesón white, fresh cheeses; **Cabrales** strong Asturian blue-veined goats' cheese; **Manchego (tierno, anejo, semi, seco)** hard sheep's-milk cheese (young, mature, semi-soft, dry); **Tetilla** soft cow's milk cheese.

A citadel of Madrid's own classic cuisine, **La Bola**. *See page 99.*

Madrileños rarely lunch before two, and often have dinner after 11pm on hot summer nights. It's advisable to book in higher-category restaurants, although rarely essential. Children are welcome almost anywhere, if rather less so in the smarter business restaurants.

Thanks to the existence of the *menú del día* it is nearly always cheaper to eat lunch in restaurants rather than dinner. Dining can also be much cheaper, if less fun, if you stick to simple dishes rather than regional specialities. Service is occasionally included in the bill (*cuenta*), but more often tipping is at your discretion. There is never an absolute obligation to tip, but it will be welcomed, and you can certainly feel comfortable leaving ten per cent.

Averages

The average prices listed here are for a three-course meal of *primer plato*, a *segundo* and a dessert (*postre*), but do not include wine, beer or water. The set lunch *menus* given, however, do often include a drink.

Top Range

Many of Madrid's top restaurants are geared towards a business clientele and are filled by suited men at lunchtime. While jackets and ties are not necessary, except at **Zalacaín**, casual travelling clothes and especially shorts are not acceptable. There are also more first-class restaurants in some of Madrid's major hotels, above all the **Ritz** (*see chapter* **Accommodation**).

Cabo Mayor

C/Juan Ramón Jiménez 37 (350 87 76). Metro Cuzco/bus 5, 27, 40, 150. **Lunch served** 1.30-4pm, **dinner served** 9pm-midnight, Mon-Sat. Closed Easter week, Aug. **Average** 6,000ptas. **Credit** AmEx, DC, MC, V.
Of all the 1980's new-wave Spanish restaurants in the city, food impresario Pedro Larumbe's Cabo Mayor has matured most successfully. The mainly-seafood menu features modern Basque-Cantabrian dishes combining fish and vegetables together in light but luxurious offerings such as their delicate lobster salad. To follow, there are equally wonderful desserts. The nautical-themed interior is pleasantly chic, and the atmosphere much more relaxed than in many top-flight Madrid restaurants.
Air-conditioning. Tables outdoors July-Sept.

Casa Santa Cruz

C/La Bolsa 12 (521 86 23). Metro Sol/bus all routes to Puerta del Sol. **Lunch served** 1-4pm, **dinner served** 8.30pm-midnight, daily. **Average** 4,500ptas. **Credit** AmEx, DC, MC, V.
This building was originally a chapel, part of a long-demolished church, and later became Madrid's first stock exchange. Prices reflect the décor as much as the food, but it is a superb setting, and the excellent fresh salads and light, modern versions of Madrileño dishes should appeal to foreign taste-buds.
Air-conditioning. Wheelchair access.

El Cenador del Prado

C/del Prado 4 (429 15 61). Metro Sevilla/bus 6, 32, 50.
Lunch served 1-4pm Mon-Fri. **Dinner served** 9pm-midnight Mon-Sat. Closed Aug. **Average** 4,500ptas.
Credit AmEx, DC, MC, V.
The Herranz brothers produce imaginative, unfussy modern Spanish regional cuisine, with specialities such as *patatas con almejas* (potatoes with clams). With lush green conservatory décor, the restaurant has the feel of an oasis. Service is smooth, and the crowd fashionable rather than formal.
Air-conditioning. Wheelchair access.

La Gastroteca de Stéphane y Arturo

Plaza de Chueca 8 (532 25 64). Metro Chueca/bus 3, 40, 149. **Lunch served** 2-4pm Mon-Fri. **Dinner served** 9.30pm-midnight Mon-Sat. Closed Aug. **Average** 4,500ptas. **Credit** AmEx, DC, EC, MC, V.
Stéphane Guérin's cooking is characterful modern French, while her husband's front-of-house style is witty and very Spanish, making this informal place in Chueca interestingly offbeat. Favoured dishes include a black olive sorbet, *merluza* cooked six different ways, and profiteroles with honey ice-cream. The wine list is one of the most varied in town.
Air-conditioning. Wheelchair access.

Lhardy

Carrera de San Jerónimo 8 (521 33 85). Metro Sevilla, Sol/bus all routes to Puerta del Sol. **Lunch served** 1-3.30pm daily. **Dinner served** 9-11.30pm Mon-Sat. **Average** 7,000ptas. **Credit** AmEx, DC, MC, V.
This landmark restaurant, opened in 1839, is credited with having first introduced French *haute cuisine* into the culinary wilds of Madrid. Founder Emile Lhardy was supposedly enticed here by none other than *Carmen*-author Prosper Merimée, who told him there was not another decent restaurant in the city. Today it's rated as much for its history and *Belle Epoque* décor as for the (very expensive) food. The menu is as Frenchified as it has always been, although

there's also a very refined *cocido*, good game and *callos*, and an excellent, if pricey, wine list. *See also chapter* **Tapas**. *Air-conditioning.*

El Olivo

C/General Gallegos 1 (359 15 35). Metro Cuzco/bus 5, 11, 40. **Lunch served** 1-4pm, **dinner served** 9pm-midnight, Tue-Sat. Closed Aug. **Average** 6,000ptas. **Set menu** 3,750ptas. **Gourmet menu** 5,600ptas. **No credit cards.**
It took a Frenchman to show off Spain's olives and their oil to their utmost advantage, but Madrileños have taken to Jean-Pierre Vandelle's olive-green dining room, with its trolley loaded with different oils and bar stocked with over 120 different sherries. Specialities include *salmón y mero* (salmon and grouper marinated in oil), salt-cod done four different ways, and a tasty *tarta de manzana* (apple tart).
Air-conditioning. Wheelchair access.

La Taberna de Liria

C/Duque de Liria 9 (541 45 19). Metro Ventura Rodríguez/bus 1, 2, 44, 74, 133. **Lunch served** 1.15-4pm Mon-Fri. **Dinner served** 9.15pm-midnight Mon-Sat. Closed Aug. **Average** 4,500ptas.
Credit AmEx, DC, MC, V.
Excellent, sophisticated cooking is the attraction at this smart little restaurant off C/Princesa. Young chef Miguel López Castanier's menu reflects his Franco-Spanish origins and training, and might include *ceviche* (a Latin American salad of marinated fish), Provençal lamb, melon gazpacho and *estofado de oreja de cerdo* (pig's ear stew).
Air-conditioning. Wheelchair access.

Viridiana

C/Juan de Mena 14 (523 44 78). Metro Retiro/bus all routes to Puerta de Alcalá. **Lunch served** 1.30-4pm, **dinner served** 9pm-midnight, Mon-Sat. Closed Aug. **Average** 6,000ptas. **No credit cards.**

The best of Andalusian food in Madrid: **Las Cumbres**. *See page 100.*

Get gutsy at the **Freiduría de Gallinejas**. *See page 100.*

Right by the **Prado** and the **Thyssen**, and hung with stills from Buñuel films, Viridiana serves up marvellous, seasonally-changing food backed up by an outstanding wine cellar. You can enjoy inventive combinations such as *cabracho con relleno de almejas* (scorpion fish stuffed with clams and dressed with olive oil) or *solomillo de buey con trufas negras* (steak with black truffles) at one of the few of the costlier establishments that genuinely doesn't care about dress. *Air-conditioning. Wheelchair access.*

Zalacaín

C/Alvarez de Baena 4 (561 59 35). Metro Rubén Darío/bus 7, 40, 147. **Lunch served** 1.15-4pm Mon-Fri. **Dinner served** 9pm-midnight Mon-Sat. Closed Aug. **Average** 8,000ptas. **Set menu** 6,800ptas. **Credit** AmEx, DC, MC, V.
Master chef Benjamín Urdaín and proprietor Jesús María Oyarbide run the best show in Madrid, the only restaurant in the city with all of three Michelin stars. The setting is seamlessly luxurious, the seasonal, Basque-based cooking is superb, and the wine list includes a marvellous selection of vintage Riojas. It's normally as expensive as the clothing bills of most of the clientèle, but the recession has brought with it an excellent-value set menu, so these days the prime question-mark over a visit might be the rather oppressive jacket-and-tie formality.
Air-conditioning. Booking essential. Wheelchair access.

Traditional Madrileño

The city's best-known specialities – some of them hard to distinguish from Castilian food as a whole – are hearty, powerful winter food. The star dish is *Cocido*, a kind of grand stew. If you have a *Cocido Completo*, cooked slowly together all in the same pot, you will be served first the broth and noodles as a soup, then the vegetables (chickpeas, cabbage, leeks, turnips, onions and more), and

finally the meat (beef, pig's trotters, chorizo, *morcilla* blood sausage). Castilian roasts, *besugo a la madrileña* (sea-bream in a white wine and garlic sauce), garlic soup and lentil stews also feature strongly. The classic setting in which to sample such dishes is in the wood-beamed traditional inns near the Plaza Mayor – although some are now very tourist-oriented and priced accordingly.

Most distinctively Madrileño of all, though, is the range of offal dishes – *callos a la madrileña* (tripe in a peppery tomato sauce, with chorizo and *morcilla*), *orejas* (pigs' ears), *sesos* (brains) and many other things that other cultures shy away from – a long-standing local tradition. In summer, *escabeches* – marinated meat or fish, served either cold or fried – lighten the diet a little.

La Bola Taberna

C/de la Bola 5 (547 69 30). Metro Santo Domingo, Opera/bus 44, 133, 147. **dinner served** 9.15pm-midnight, Mon-Sat. **Average** 3,000ptas. **Set menu** 2,125ptas. **No credit cards.**
This home to the city's most authentic *cocido* is still run – though no longer owned – by the family who founded it in the last century. The tiled interior is almost unchanged, as is the *cocido*, served only at lunchtime, and cooked in the traditional manner over a wood fire in large earthenware pots. There is a good house wine, and the restaurant is very popular with tourists.
Air-conditioning. Wheelchair access.

Botín

C/Cuchilleros 17 (366 42 17/366 30 26). Metro Sol/bus all routes to Puerta del Sol. **Lunch served** 1-4pm, **dinner served** 8pm-midnight, daily. **Average** 4,000ptas. **Set menu** 3,645ptas. **Credit** AmEx, DC, JCB, MC, V.

The most historic of the old taverns, founded in the eighteenth century and still with its original wood-fired oven and ornamental tiling. Over the years a visit to this local institution has been obligatory for Hemingway and many other luminaries who have passed through Madrid. The great specialities are Castilian roasts, but today the kitchen often tends to rest on its laurels. It's heavily geared towards the tourist trade, including large coach parties.
Air-conditioning.

Casa Lucio

C/Cava Baja 35 (365 32 52). Metro La Latina/bus 17, 35, 60. **Lunch served** 1-4pm Mon-Fri, Sun. **Dinner served** 9-11.30pm daily. Closed Aug. **Average** 5,000ptas. **Credit** AmEx, DC, MC, V.
The most reliable of the historic inns, and the least touristy. A mixed political, artistic and business clientèle comes here for Castilian roasts, occasional inventions such as *judías con faisán* (beans with pheasant), great ham and cheese, and a sprinkling of Basque dishes. Service is brisk, but the wine list and prices are just right.
Air-conditioning. Wheelchair access.

Casa Maxi

C/Cava Alta 4 (365 12 49). Metro La Latina/bus 17, 35, 60. **Lunch served** 1.30-4pm Tue-Sun. Closed July, Aug. **Average** 2,500ptas. **Set lunch** 1,100ptas. **No credit cards.**
A mecca for offal-fans, with a sawdust-sprinkled tiled floor. A good *callos a la madrileña* has been known to convert fervent offal-haters, and Maxi's is acknowledged as the best there is. If you really can't face it, there's also cheese, good *jamón serrano* and a simple set menu.
Tables outdoors.

La Freiduría de Gallinejas

C/Embajadores 84 (517 59 33). Metro Embajadores/bus all routes to Embajadores. **Meals served** 11am-11pm Mon-Sat. **Average** 800ptas. **No credit cards.**
Another offal-haven, this tiled, bustling, spanking-clean café is one of a kind once common in the city but now increasingly difficult to find – Madrid's answer to the fish & chip shop, with traditional fry-ups of *gallinejas*, lamb's chitterlings, eaten as they come or in *bocadillos* (rolls). Also available are *entresijos* (stomach linings) and many other delights, mostly of lamb, although they do offer *criadillas* (bulls' testicles), as well as excellent home-baked apples.
Air-conditioning.

Malacatín

C/de la Ruda 5 (365 52 41). Metro La Latina/bus 17, 23, 35. **Open** 1.30-4.30pm Mon-Sat. Closed July, Aug. **Set lunch** 1,900ptas. **No credit cards.**
People wax lyrical over the *cocido* at this century-old restaurant near the Rastro. It's made to order (you must ring the day before), and served on basic wooden trestle tables with benches. There are only two sittings, at 2.30pm and 3.30pm, or you can have a tapa at the bar. If you go the whole hog, you'll probably need a siesta afterwards. The price includes wine and dessert.
Air-conditioning. Booking essential. Tables outdoors.

Posada de la Villa

C/Cava Baja 9 (366 18 60). Metro La Latina/bus 17, 23, 35. **Lunch served** 1-4pm daily. **Dinner served** 8pm-midnight Mon-Sat. Closed Aug. **Average** 4,500ptas. **Credit** AmEx, DC, MC, V.
The most picturesque of the old inns, with a domed oven and a high-beamed roof over the top floor. All the traditional Madrileño dishes are served here, plus fine wood-roast lamb and suckling pig and excellent home-made traditional puddings such as *bartolillos* (small pastries filled with custard, then fried) – old Madrid specialities that have all but disappeared from most menus.
Air-conditioning. Wheelchair access.

Salvador

C/Barbieri 12 (521 45 24). Metro Chueca/bus 1, 2,3 40. **Lunch served** 1.30-5pm, **dinner served** 9pm-midnight, Mon-Sat. Closed Aug. **Average** 4,000ptas. **Credit** AmEx, MC, V.
In former times the artistic regulars of the **Chicote** cocktail bar (*see chapter* **Cafés & Bars**) often wandered over to eat here. The clientèle is a bit less exotic these days, but the bullfighting photos on the walls are unchanged. The food is plain but well done: excellent are the *gallina en pepitoria* (chicken cooked in wine, garlic and almonds), fried *merluza* and *arroz con leche* (rice pudding).
Air-conditioning. Wheelchair access.

Taberna de Daniela

C/General Pardinas 21 (575 23 29). Metro Goya or Lista/bus 1, 29, 53, 74. **Lunch served** 11am-4.30pm, **dinner served** 8pm-midnight, daily.
Cocido menu 1,800ptas. **Credit** V.
Proof that Madrid's yuppies are traditional at heart: they pack into this nine-table dining room in Salamanca for the full *cocido* (the only other option, *besugo*, must be ordered ahead). The food is good, the service energetic, and it makes a change not to eat *cocido* in olde-worlde surroundings.
Air-conditioning. Booking essential. Wheelchair access.

Viuda de Vacas

C/Cava Alta 33 (366 58 47). Metro La Latina/bus 17, 35, 60. **Lunch served** 1.30-4.30pm, **dinner served** 9.30pm-midnight, Mon-Wed, Fri-Sun. Closed Easter week, Aug, Christmas. **Average** 2,500ptas. **Credit** AmEx, MC, V.
One of the most authentic of the old-town taverns, with its wood-oven, tiles, oak beams and spiral staircase. Their excellent-value cooking features all the traditional standards, and is easily on a level with that of much pricier rivals nearby.
Wheelchair access.

Around Spain

Andalusia

Andalusian restaurant standards are *gazpacho*, *pescadito frito* (flash-fried small fish) and *rabo de toro* (braised bull's tail). Also from this region and neighbouring Extremadura comes *jamón ibérico*, cured ham from the native Iberian breed of pig. Properly-cured ham, from pigs fed on acorns to give the meat a distinctive earthy-sweet flavour, is an increasingly-expensive luxury.

Las Cumbres

C/Alberto Alcócer 32 (458 76 92). Metro Cuzco, Colombia/bus 5, 7, 14, 40, 150. **Lunch served** noon-4pm, **dinner served** 8pm-midnight, daily. **Average** 4,500ptas. **Credit** AmEx, DC, JCB, MC, TC, $TC, V.
The most authentic of Madrid's Andalusian options, from the tile-and-whitewash interior to the distinctly southern menu. It's famous for its fried fish, but also to be recommended are the *perdiz* (partridge), *pipirrana* (a salad with ham, tuna, egg, peppers and tomatoes) and *ajo blanco* (cold garlic soup).
Air conditioning.

La Giralda

C/Claudio Coello 24 (576 40 69). Metro Serrano/bus 1, 74. **Lunch served** Sept-June 1-4pm daily; July, Aug 1-4pm Mon-Sat. **Dinner served** 9pm-midnight Mon-Sat. **Average** 5,000ptas. **Credit** AmEx, DC, MC, V.
The quaint-ish décor of tiles and wine barrels is brand new and a bit brash, but the flavours of the bull's tail, fried fish, and *salmorejo* (a thick gazpacho) are strong and good.
Branch: C/Maldonado 4 (577 77 62).

The **Casa Gallega** offers great Galician food at friendly prices. See page 103.

El Rabo de Toro (Casa Díaz)

C/Ayala 81 (402 57 50). Metro Goya/bus 29, 52, 61.
Lunch served 1-4pm, **dinner served** 9pm-midnight,
Mon-Sat. Closed Aug. **Average** 2,500ptas.
Set lunch 1,000ptas. **Credit** V.
Rough at the edges but honest, this family-owned eating
house buys bull's tail from around Spain to make its stew.
This and fried fish are the specialities, but you'll find *jamón
ibérico*, *merluza* and other choices on the menu, too.
Air-conditioning.

Asturias

The northern region of Asturias, green and cool,
is renowned for its sturdy mountain food. *Fabada*,
a rich stew of haricot beans, onions, chorizo and
black pudding (*morcilla*), is the classic dish, but
other specialities are delicious strong cheeses, rice
puddings and pastries, as well as fish soups and
stews from the coast. Cider (*sidra*) rather than wine
is the local drink, and the most traditional
Asturian cider is coarse and strong.

Casa Baltasar

*C/Ramón de la Cruz 97 (402 96 46). Metro Manuel
Becerra/bus all routes to Plaza Manuel Becerra.* **Meals
served** noon-midnight Mon-Sat; noon-6pm Sun. Closed
Aug. **Average** 2,500ptas. **Credit** AmEx, DC, MC, V.
Try the wonderful *fabada*, *fabes con almejas* (beans with
clams) or *merluza* with cider at this simple restaurant close
to Salamanca's shops. The really hungry can also take on a
plate of strong blue *Cabrales* cheese as a starter.
Air-conditioning. Wheelchair access.

Casa Mingo

*Paseo de la Florida 2 (547 79 18). Metro Norte/bus 41,
46, 75.* **Meals served** 11am-midnight daily. Closed
Aug. **Average** 1,000ptas. **No credit cards**.
Cheap, cheerful, invariably crowded and incredibly noisy,
this cavernous, much-renowned 1910 cider-house serves spit-
roasted chicken, chorizo cooked in cider, *Cabrales* cheese, salads and natural house cider. Ever-popular with students, it's
one of the cheapest places to eat outdoors in Madrid. You
can sit at one of the outside tables in fine weather, or order
a chicken to take away and eat beside the nearby river.
Tables outdoors (May-Oct). Wheelchair access.

Casa Portal

*C/Doctor Castelo 26 (574 20 26). Metro Ibiza,
O'Donnell/bus 2, 15, 26, 61, 63, C.* **Lunch served** 1.30-
4pm, **dinner served** 8-11.30pm, Mon-Sat. Closed Aug.
Average 4,000ptas. **Credit** EC, MC, V.
This traditional Asturian restaurant, with fine cheeses piled
in the window, has been serving *fabada* – including variants
with partridge and clams – fish, shellfish, soups, tortillas and
great cider for 50 years. Choose between the sawdust-strewn
bar at the front, or the more formal dining room behind it.
Air-conditioning.

Fuente la Xana

*Centro Asturiano, C/Farmacia 2 (522 42 18). Metro
Chueca/bus 3, 7, 40.* **Lunch served** 1.30-4pm daily.
Dinner served 9-11pm Mon-Sat. Closed Aug. **Average**
2,000ptas. **Credit** AmEx, DC.
There has been a restaurant on the second floor of the *Centro
Asturiano*, the official Asturian club, for many years, but
since new management in 1994 standards have risen con-
siderably. The menu offers a mix of traditional and more
innovative dishes, with particularly good fish soups.
Air-conditioning.

For light Mediterranean food in a sleek modern setting, **Balear**. See page 103.

Basque Country, Navarra & Rioja

Basque cooking has long been recognised as the most sophisticated in Spain, and many of Madrid's finest restaurants also have Basque chefs (*see above* **Top Range**). The Basque Country offers a superb, wide-ranging cuisine, with many highly original fish dishes. From inland Navarra and La Rioja come delicious vegetable dishes such as *menestra de habas* (broad beans and mixed vegetables in wine and herbs), fine meats, and fish options like *trucha a la navarra* (trout with ham).

Asador Frontón I

Plaza Tirso de Molina 7 (entry through C/Jesús y María 1) (369 16 17). Metro Tirso de Molina/bus 6, 26, 35, 57. **Lunch served** 1-3.30pm, **dinner served** 9-11pm, *Oct-May* daily, *June, July, Sept* Mon-Sat. Closed Aug. **Average** 5,000ptas. **Credit** AmEx, DC, EC, MC, V.
These grill restaurants set up by former *pelota* star Miguel Ansorena are the best known Basque grills in Madrid. Their fame is justified by first-class ingredients and grilling of meat and fish refined to perfection. Don't be put off by the giant-sized chops, as they are served cut into strips that you can share. The Pedro Muguruza branch has a broader menu.
Branch: **Asador Frontón II** C/Pedro Muguruza 8 (345 36 96/345 39 01).
Air-conditioning. Wheelchair access in Asador Frontón II.

Centro Riojano

C/Serrano 25, 1° (575 03 37). Metro Serrano/bus all routes to Plaza Colón. **Lunch served** 1.30-4pm, **dinner served** 9pm-midnight, Mon-Sat. **Average** 3,000ptas. **Credit** V.
Casual and unstuffy, this nineteenth-century dining room in the Riojan regional club serves light, modern local cooking.

The region's famed red peppers crop up in everything – roasted in a salad with anchovies and spring onions as a starter, stuffed into pullet, or dried in *patatas a la riojana*, potatoes sautéd with peppers, onions, tomatoes and chorizo. The wine list covers the Rioja's best cellars and vintages. *Air-conditioning.*

La Cocina de Rosa

C/Santiago 14 (541 70 12). Metro Opera/bus 3, 25, 33, 39. **Lunch served** *Sept-June* 2-4pm Tue-Sat. **Dinner served** *Sept-June* 8pm-midnight Tue-Sun; *July, Aug* 9pm-midnight Tue-Sat. **Average** 3,000ptas. **Set lunch** 2,400ptas. **Credit** V.
Chef-owner Rosa set up her small restaurant after a big win on the lottery, and runs it with loving care. This shows in the feminine, frayed décor, friendly service and carefully cooked dishes such as stuffed peppers and *purrusalda*, a classic Basque soup of salt-cod, leeks, potatoes and garlic. *Air-conditioning.*

Gure-Etxea

Plaza de la Paja 12 (365 61 49). Metro La Latina/bus 3, 31, 50, 65, 148. **Lunch served** 1.15-4pm, **dinner served** 8.45pm-midnight, Mon-Sat. Closed Aug. **Average** 4,500ptas. **Credit** AmEx, DC, MC, V.
For many this is where to find the best traditional Basque cooking in Madrid at the most reasonable prices. Fish is a speciality, together with *alubias de Tolosa* (braised beans), *piperada* (scrambled eggs with onion, ham, tomatoes and red peppers) and luxuries like *txangurro* (crab on a half-shell). They also have excellent Basque Txacoli wines. *Air-conditioning. Wheelchair access.*

La Taberna del Alabardero

C/Felipe V 6 (541 51 92). Metro Opera/bus 3, 25, 33, 39. **Lunch served** 1-4pm, **dinner served** 9pm-midnight, daily. **Average** 4,500ptas. **Gourmet menu** 5,500ptas. **Credit** AmEx, DC, JCB, MC, V.

Close to the **Palacio Real**, the Taberna's main claim to fame is that it's owned by a priest, although its Basque food is good too. There are two ways of eating: you can order a selection of *raciones* at the bar, or enjoy a full meal at the tables out the back. The five-course gourmet menu is good value. *Air-conditioning.*

Castile

The food of Spain's central *meseta* is, like Madrileño cooking, stout stuff. Most famous are the wood-roasts of milk-fed lamb and suckling pig, archetypically associated with Segovia (*see chapter* **Around Madrid**), and the superb Castilian lentil and bean stews. Also to be found, though, are less well-known specialities from specific areas such as Cuenca and the mountain plateau of El Bierzo in León.

Casa Ciriaco

C/Mayor 84 (548 06 20). Metro Sol/bus all routes to Puerta del Sol. **Lunch served** 1.30-4pm, **dinner served** 8.30-11.30pm, Mon, Tue, Thur-Sun. Closed Aug. **Average** 2,500ptas. **No credit cards.**
Over seventy years' worth of kitschy memorabilia and paintings donated by former clients hangs around the walls of this fine tavern, founded in 1917 and a favourite meeting-point for the intelligentsia in pre-Civil War days. From the staple Castilian fare, try the chicken *pepitoria*, trout *en escabeche*, the *cocido* on Tuesdays, and the paella served every Sunday. You can also sample fine Valdepeñas wine, with a meal or in the beautiful old tiled bar.
Air-conditioning. Booking advisable.

Mesón Prada a Tope

Cuesta de San Vicente 32 (547 80 20). Metro Norte, Plaza de España/bus 25, 33, 39, 46, 75, C. **Meals served** 10am-midnight Mon, Tue, Thur-Sun. Closed Aug. **Average** 2,500ptas. **Credit** V.
A small informal bar serving the powerful products and dishes of the tiny region of El Bierzo, just between Castile and Galicia: roasted red peppers with a spicy-hot kick, *botillo* (a heavy sausage), *cerezas en aguardiente* (cherries in grain spirit), and excellent young wines in the cask or bottle. *Air-conditioning.*

El Puchero

C/Larra 13 (445 05 77). Metro Tribunal, Bilbao/bus 3, 37, 40, 149. **Lunch served** 1.30-3.30pm, **dinner served** 9-11.30pm, Mon-Sat. Closed Aug. **Average** 3,000ptas. **Credit** V.
Check table-cloths, white-aproned waitresses and a spread of traditional meat, fish and vegetable dishes, with daily specials such as the *capón relleno* (stuffed capon) every Friday night, mark the style of this easily missed, popular basement restaurant near the Glorieta de Bilbao. It also has good Ribera del Duero house wine.
Air-conditioning.

El Tormo

Travesía de las Vistillas 13 (365 53 35). Metro La Latina/bus 3, 148. **Lunch served** 1-4pm Tue-Sun. **Dinner served** 9-11pm Tue-Sat. Closed 15 July-15 Sept. **Average** 3,000ptas. **No credit cards.**
A one-off foodie experience. Joaquín Racionero and his wife dish up food from La Mancha (especially Cuenca), as made several centuries ago: *morteruelo* (hot game pâté), *guiso de cordero* (lamb stew), *ajoarriero* (salt-cod and potato purée), or rice with honey. There's no choice; it just comes to you. There are only five tables, so booking is a must, and it's best to go in a group to share dishes.
Booking essential.

Galicia

There are hundreds of Galician bar-restaurants around the city. Most have tapas bars at the front, and many are seafood *marisquerías* (*see below* **Fish & Seafood**). As well as fine fish and shellfish, other Galician standards are *caldo gallego* (vegetable, ham and sausage broth), *lacón* (gammon ham) and *empanadas*, savoury pies with meat or fish fillings.

Casa Gallega

Plaza San Miguel 8 (547 30 55). Metro Sol/bus all routes to Puerta del Sol. **Lunch served** 1-4pm, **dinner served** 8pm-midnight, daily. **Average** 3,500ptas.
Credit AmEx, DC, MC, V.
Excellent food that doesn't burn a hole in your wallet, even the shellfish. Apart from the seafood on ice in the windows, there are the Galician standards – *caldo, lacón con grelos* (gammon with greens) and a big range of Galician wines. Great tapas are also available in the basement bar.
Air-conditioning. Wheelchair access.
Branch: C/Bordadores 11 (541 90 55).

O'Caldiño

C/Lagasca 74 (575 14 48/431 99 67). Metro Núñez de Balboa/bus 1, 9, 19, 51, 74. **Lunch served** 1.30-4.30pm, **dinner served** 8.30pm-midnight, daily. **Average** 3,500ptas. **No credit cards.**
A relaxed bar-restaurant in Salamanca. Five types of *empanada* – including *trucha* (trout) and *almejas* (clams) – and all the Galician favourites are served either informally at the front or with full service at the back.
Air-conditioning. Wheelchair access.

Mediterranean

Spain's Mediterranean coastline, from Catalonia through Valencia and the Balearic islands to Murcia, embraces sea and mountain. This area, above all Valencia, is the home of the classic paella, although it is only one of hundreds of variations and other rice dishes found along the coast. One or two Madrid restaurants are now venturing into the modern, re-invented Mediterranean cooking stemming from Catalonia.

Balear

C/Sagunto 18 (447 91 15). Metro Iglesia/bus 3, 16, 37, 61. **Lunch served** 1.30-4.30pm daily. **Dinner served** 9pm-midnight Tue-Sat. **Average** 3,500ptas.
Credit AmEx, V.
An uncluttered, emphatically modern dining room in Chamberí. The menu features a dozen Mediterranean rices, Mallorcan dishes such as *tumbet* (layers of mixed vegetables, bound with egg and baked), and a varied wine-list. There can be a long wait if several tables order at once.
Air-conditioning.

El Caldero

C/Huertas 15 (429 50 44). Metro Antón Martín/bus 6, 26, 32, 57. **Lunch served** 1-4pm Mon-Sat. **Dinner served** 9pm-midnight Tue-Sat. **Average** 3,000ptas.
Credit AmEx, DC, MC, V.
One of a handful of restaurants serving Murcian food. The star items are good: *dorado* (mullet) baked in a salt crust, and *arroz al caldero*, unadorned rice cooked in a rich fish and shellfish stock. First courses might be *judías con jamón*, or *salazones* (salt-dried tuna and roe, eaten cold).
Air-conditioning.

Can Punyetes

C/Señores de Luzón 5 (542 09 21). Metro Opera/bus 3, 25, 33, 39, 148. **Lunch served** 1-4.30pm, **dinner served** 8pm-1am, Mon-Sat. **Average** 1,500ptas. **No credit cards.**
One of the few Catalan restaurants in Madrid, and centrally-located. The menu features cheeses and pâtés – many French – and simple charcoal grills.
Air-conditioning.

Paradís Madrid

C/Marqués de Cubas 14 (429 73 03). Metro Banco de España/bus all routes to Plaza de Cibeles. **Lunch served** 1.30-4pm Mon-Fri. **Dinner served** 9pm-midnight Mon-Sat. Closed Aug. **Average** 5,000ptas. **Credit** AmEx, DC, MC, V.
New-wave, light Catalan food: fish and seafood rices, *bacallá amb gambes* (salt-cod with prawns), plus a selection of oils and infusions. There's a stylish wine bar at the front, and prices reflect the designer setting, especially on the wines.
Air-conditioning. Wheelchair access.

St James

C/Juan Bravo 26 (575 60 10). Metro Núñez de Balboa/bus 9, 19, 51. **Lunch served** 1.30-3.30pm, **dinner served** 9-11.30pm, Mon-Sat. **Average** 4,500ptas. **Credit** AmEx.
Here you'll find yourself surrounded by Madrid's rice-lovers, enjoying one of 14 expertly-made Valencian rice dishes. Prices are well justified by the skill evident in the cooking. To follow there are great home-made sorbets, too.
Air-conditioning. Booking essential. Tables outdoors June-Sept.

Comida Casera (Home Cooking)

The name given to old-fashioned – and usually cheap – Spanish food that doesn't fit into any specific regional style, but is characterised by good quality, fresh ingredients and traditional, straightforward recipes.

Las Batuecas

Avda Reina Victoria 17 (554 04 52). Metro Cuatro Caminos/bus 44, 45, C. **Lunch served** 1-4pm Mon-Sat. **Dinner served** 9-11pm Mon-Fri. Closed Aug. **Average** 1,500ptas. **Set lunch** 900ptas. **No credit cards.**
An unpretentious, much-loved *casa de comidas* serving *pepitoria*, kidneys, *tortilla de callos* (tripe omelette) and other local favourites. Go early, or late, to avoid the peak-hour crowds.
Air-conditioning. Wheelchair access.

El Buey

C/General Pardiñas 10 (431 44 92). Metro Goya/bus 21, 29, 52, 53. **Lunch served** 1-4pm, **dinner served** 9pm-midnight, Mon-Sat. **Average** 3,500ptas. **Credit** MC, V.
The centrepiece of the menu at this carnivores' haven is the superb beef fillet, *lomo de buey*, done any way, at 5,000ptas a kilo. Also to be had are a dozen first-courses, two fish alternatives for the main course, and home-made desserts.
Air-conditioning.
Branch: Plaza de la Marina Española 1 (541 30 41).

La Catedral

C/Ayala 100 (576 05 28). Metro Goya/bus 7, 26, 61, 74. **Lunch served** 1.30-4.30pm, **dinner served** 8.30-11.30pm, daily. Closed Aug. **Average** 2,000ptas. **Credit** V.
A recently-revived 1930s neighbourhood restaurant with a

A hidden haunt for red pepper connoisseurs, the **Centro Riojano**. *See page 102.*

very relaxed, young feel for smart Salamanca. The imaginative daily set menu and its more elaborate Sunday-lunch version are particularly good value, and it also has great desserts. There are often long queues at lunchtime.
Air-conditioning.

El Gourmet del Palacio

C/García Luna 1-3 (519 12 90/416 71 88). Metro Cruz del Rayo/bus 1, 9, 29, 52, 73. **Meals served** 11am-1.30am Mon-Sat. **Average** 2,000ptas. **Credit** AmEx, DC, MC, V.
A splendid place to eat behind the **Auditorio Nacional** (*see chapter* **Music: Classical & Opera**). Its eclectic menu allows you to pick from around the regions, with such things as Canary Island *papas arrugadas* (new potatoes baked in salt, with a hot sauce), Galician soups and home-made *orujos* (grain spirit), and other gourmet goodies.
Air-conditioning. Wheelchair access.

Hylogui

C/Ventura de la Vega 3 (429 73 57). Metro Sevilla/bus 5, 9, 15, 20, 51, 52, 53. **Lunch served** 1-4.30pm daily. **Dinner served** 9pm-midnight Mon-Sat. Closed Aug. **Average** 2,500ptas. **Set menu** 1,700ptas. **Credit** AmEx, V.
Some say this long-established *casa de comidas* has gone downhill, but it's still a good central spot for straightforward cooking, with good-value vintage wines. The long menu – over 100 dishes – is built around carefully selected produce, from *mollejas* (sweetbreads) to Atlantic fish. The queue usually moves fast, and it's particularly good for Sunday lunch.
Air-conditioning.

La Playa

C/Magallanes 24 (446 84 76). Metro Quevedo/bus 16, 61 149. **Lunch served** 1-4.30pm daily. **Dinner served** 8.30pm-midnight Mon-Sat. Closed Aug. **Average** 2,500ptas. **No credit cards.**
A great old family restaurant in Chamberí serving home-style Spanish favourites such as *acelgas con patatas* (chard and potatoes), *albóndigas* (meatballs), *pimientos rellenos* (stuffed peppers), the odd more unusual dish such as *merluza a las angulas* (hake with elvers), and great home-made desserts. The emphasis is firmly on quality of product.
Air-conditioning. Wheelchair access.

De La Riva

C/Cochabamba 13 (458 89 54). Metro Colombia/bus 7 14, 16, 29, 51. **Lunch served** 1-6pm Mon-Fri. Closed Aug. **Average** 3,500ptas. **Credit** V.
Weekday lunch only – served till 5pm – is provided at this excellent, informal restaurant near the Bernabéu stadium, where executives and workers alike tuck in to *judías con liebre* (beans with hare), *arroz con almejas* (rice with clams), *pimientos con morcilla de Burgos* (red peppers with Burgos black pudding) and a huge range of other dishes. There's no menu, but dishes are suggested as they are prepared. This, and good food and wines, help keep the atmosphere buzzing.
Air-conditioning.

Fish & Seafood

Fish and shellfish dishes are also available in most restaurants, but those listed here all specialise in or only serve seafood. Fine seafood can also be found in many bars (*see chapter* **Tapas**).

O'Pazo

C/Reina Mercedes 20 (553 23 33). Metro Lima/bus 5, 43, 149, C. **Lunch served** 1-4pm, **dinner served** 8.30pm-midnight, Mon-Sat. Closed Aug. **Average** 5,000ptas. **Credit** MC, V.

A highly-regarded Galician restaurant offering finest-quality fish and seafood – *vieiras, caldo a la marinera* (fish and shellfish soup), hake, *cigalas* (crayfish), *besugo* and so on – much of it, again, flown in almost from the dockside. Inevitably high prices and its location in high-rise office land means that most of the diners are business people.
Air-conditioning. Wheelchair access.

Ribeira Do Miño
C/Santa Brígida 1 (521 98 54). Metro Tribunal/bus 3, 40, 149. **Lunch served** 1-4pm, **dinner served** 8pm-midnight, Tue-Sun. Closed Aug. **Average** 3,000ptas. **No credit cards.**
Extremely good-value, virtually undecorated Galician *marisquería*, hung with nets, in a Chueca sidestreet. A *Mariscada* – shellfish platter – for two is 3,400ptas. There are also a few, cheap fishless dishes, and good Ribeiro house wine.
Air-conditioning. Wheelchair access.

Taberna de Abajo
C/Limón 16 (547 54 29). Metro Noviciado, Plaza de España/bus 1, 2, 44, 133, 147, C. **Lunch served** 1.30-4.30pm, **dinner served** 8.30pm-1.30am, daily. Closed Aug. **Average** 2,500ptas. **No credit cards.**
A very simple bar-restaurant with only a couple of tables, and shellfish stacked up behind glass at the bar. The speciality is *carabineiros,* red prawns, beautifully cooked – mainly boiled or grilled *a la plancha* – with bread and wine to go with them.
Air-conditioning.

La Trainera
C/Lagasca 60 (576 80 35). Metro Serrano/bus 1, 9, 19, 51, 74. **Lunch served** 1-4pm, **dinner served** 8pm-midnight, Mon-Sat. Closed Aug.
Average 4,000ptas. **Credit** EC, MC, V.
Reportedly, this was Francis Bacon's favourite restaurant on his many trips to Madrid. It was set up by a wholesaler, and all the fish and shellfish is selected with an expert eye. Prices are unavoidably high, but the atmosphere is pleasantly unsmart.
Air-conditioning. Wheelchair access.

International

Indian & Oriental

Strange as it may seem, Japanese food, especially sushi and sashimi, is particularly good in Madrid, due to the quality of fish available in the markets.

Adrish
C/San Bernardino 1 (542 94 98/542 93 74). Metro Plaza de España/bus all routes to Plaza de España. **Lunch served** 1.30-4pm, **dinner served** 8.30pm-midnight, Tue-Sun. **Average** 2,500ptas. **Set menus** 1,200, 1,550ptas. **Credit** AmEx, DC, MC, V.
Not far from the Plaza de España, an Indian restaurant offering a menu that stretches beyond clichés. Chicken *chap* (a tandoori dish with almonds) and dried-fruit *kabli nan* are among the interesting dishes baked in the clay oven.
Air-conditioning. Wheelchair access.

Robata
C/de la Reina 31 (521 85 28). Metro Gran Via/bus all routes to Gran Via. **Lunch served** 1.30-4pm, **dinner served** 8.30-11pm, Mon, Wed-Sun. Closed Aug.
Average 3,500ptas. **Credit** AmEx, DC, MC, V.
A stylish, minimalistic designer Japanese restaurant with tatami rooms and sushi chefs at work behind an open bar. One-dish meals cost 1,500ptas. A cheaper but similar option is the neighbouring **Janatomo**.
Air-conditioning.

Italian

Palacio de Anglona
C/Segovia 13 (366 37 53). Metro La Latina/bus 31, 50, 65. **Meals served** 8pm-3am daily. **Average** 2,000ptas. **Credit** AmEx, MC, V.
A three-level bar and restaurant with vaguely-trendy décor, young staff and imaginative, light, modern pasta, pizza and other internationally-oriented dishes at very nice prices. It's a particular favourite with students and late-night eaters, and nearly always full till closing time.
Air-conditioning.

Latin American

Taquería La Calaca
C/de las Fuentes 3 (541 74 23). Metro Opera, Sol/bus all routes to Puerta del Sol. **Lunch served** 1-4pm daily. **Dinner served** 8pm-1am Mon-Thur, Sun; 8pm-3am Fri, Sat. **Average** 1,500ptas. **Credit** AmEx, DC, MC, V.
A dead-central Mexican café offering a dozen tequilas, various margaritas and specialities like *pollo borracho* (chicken stewed with chilli), tacos, tamales and quesadillas. There are only small, high tables, without proper seating.
Air-conditioning.

La Vaca Argentina
Paseo del Pintor Rosales 52 (559 66 05). Metro Argüelles/bus 21, 74. **Lunch served** 1-5pm, **dinner served** 9pm-midnight, daily. **Average** 3,500ptas. **Credit** AmEx, DC, MC, V.
A recently-opened Argentinian restaurant overlooking the Parque del Oeste, with outside tables in summer, serving great grilled steak (*churrasco*) and a few other Argentinian dishes, plus sticky-toffee *dulce de leche* to follow.
Air-conditioning. Tables outdoors June-Sept.

Zara
C/de las Infantas 5 (532 20 74). Metro Gran Via/bus 3, 40, 149. **Lunch served** 1-5pm, **dinner served** 8.30-11.30pm, Mon-Fri. Closed Aug. **Average** 2,000ptas. **Set menu** 1,100ptas. **Credit** AmEx, DC, MC, V.
Zara serves simple Cuban food and ace cocktails under a pseudo-bamboo roof. Forget the set menu and try the 'Typically Tropical' dishes such as *arroz a la cubana* (rice with tomato sauce and fried egg), banana omelette or *frijoles negros* (refried black beans). Very friendly service and budget prices mean that queues are long, especially at night.
Air-conditioning.

Moroccan

Al-Mounia
Paseo de Recoletos 5 (435 08 28). Metro Banco de España/bus all routes to Cibeles. **Lunch served** 1.30-3.30pm, **dinner served** 9pm-midnight, Tue-Sat. Closed Aug. **Average** 4,500ptas. **Credit** AmEx, MC, V.
Ornate tiled décor, fine service and high culinary standards make this a wonderful place to eat. Meals run from the house aperitifs through salads, delicious *pastilla* (pigeon pie) and couscous, to a trolley of Moroccan pastries and dried fruits.
Air-conditioning.

Northern Europe

Bellman
Hotel Suecia, C/Marqués de Casa Riera 4 (531 69 00). Metro Sevilla, Banco de España/bus all routes to C/Alcalá. **Lunch served** 1-4pm Mon-Fri. **Dinner served** 9pm-midnight Thur-Sat. Closed 15 June-15 Sept. **Average** 4,000ptas. **Credit** AmEx, DC, MC, V.

Eat yourself silly at the smörgåsbord table laid out in the restaurant of the **Hotel Suecia** (*see* chapter **Accommodation**) on Thursday, Friday and Saturday evenings. The choice of around 30 dishes includes ham with gooseberry sauce, smoked eel and marinated herrings cooked three different ways, plus salads and cakes. *Air-conditioning. Wheelchair access.*

Budget

More budget-range restaurants are listed in other sections. See particularly **La Freiduría de Gallinejas** (*under* **Traditional Madrileño**) and **Casa Mingo** (*under* **Around Spain: Asturias**), as well as the restaurants in *Comida Casera* (*under* **Around Spain**). Many other restaurants that are normally more expensive may also fit into this category at lunchtime, when they offer a set *menú del día*.

Belmar
C/Cabeza 12 (no phone). Metro Antón Martín, Tirso de Molina/bus 6, 26, 32, 57. **Meals served** 6.30am-1am Mon-Fri; 8am-1am Sat; 9am-1am Sun. **Average** 1,200ptas. **Set lunch** 900ptas. **No credit cards.**
A great neighbourhood bar-restaurant with half-a-dozen tables near Tirso de Molina, serving a set-menu and a selection of dishes from around the regions. If you cannot get a table, or don't want a full meal, they also do good tapas. *Air-conditioning.*

Cafetería del Museo del Prado
Museo del Prado, Paseo del Prado (429 65 37). Metro Atocha, Banco de España/bus 9, 14, 27, 37, 45. **Meals served** 9.30am-6pm Tue-Sat; 9.30am-1pm Sun. **Average** 1,200ptas. **No credit cards.**
If you're in or close to the Prado, the museum's own café is a good choice for lunch or a snack. A selection of over 20 salads supplements hot Spanish dishes such as *estofado de ternera*, paella, *sopa de fideos* (noodle soup) and so on. *Air-conditioning. Wheelchair access.*

El Parrondo
Gran Vía 13 (522 18 96). Metro Gran Vía/bus 1, 2, 74, 146. **Lunch served** 1-4.30pm Sun-Fri. **Average** 3,000ptas. **Set lunch** 1,200-2,000ptas. **No credit cards.**
Excellent-value lunchtime-only restaurant on the second floor (take the lift) of the army *Casino*, an officers' club – though run separately. The nineteenth-century dining room seats 400, and is rarely full. The set menus feature a good choice of dishes from around Spain, with very good fish. *Air-conditioning.*

Pizzería Mostropiero
C/San Vicente Ferrer 34 (no phone). Metro Tribunal, Noviciado/bus 3, 40, 147, 149. **Meals served** 8pm-1am Mon-Thur, Sun; 8pm-2.30am Fri, Sat. **Average** 1,200ptas. **No credit cards.**
A good, if cramped Argentinian pizzeria in Malasaña, decorated with political posters. The 20 or so pizzas come small (750ptas) or large (1,500ptas), and there are also pastries, *empanadas* (pies), quiches, and cheap wine.

Teruteru
C/Aduana 23 (522 68 58). Metro Sol, Gran Vía/bus all routes to Puerta del Sol. **Lunch served** 1-4pm, **dinner served** 8-11.30pm, Mon-Sat. **Average** 1,500ptas. **Set menu** 975ptas. **No credit cards.**
A fine-value Japanese noodle bar close to the Puerta del Sol, with a good but knock-down price set menu.

Tienda de Vinos
C/Augusto Figueroa 35 (521 70 12). Metro Chueca/bus 3, 40, 149. **Lunch served** 1-4.30pm Mon-Sat. **Dinner served** 8.30pm-midnight daily. Closed Aug. **Average** 1,500ptas. **No credit cards.**
A long-popular, regularly-full bar-restaurant in Chueca, known as *El Comunista* because of its role as a leftist meeting-point under the old régime, serving traditional standards such as *estofado de ternera* (beef stew) and grilled fish from a chalked-up menu. Service is famously deadpan (it's nothing personal), the food can be hit-and-miss, but a great atmosphere, décor that's a real piece of old Madrid and very friendly prices make up for it.

Vegetarian

Vegetarian restaurants are still few and far between in Madrid, and useful alternatives are Japanese places, rice restaurants, or pizzerias. Just about any bar-restaurant will serve tortilla and salad, but with regard to other dishes it's worth remembering that a lot of vegetable dishes will come sautéd with ham, and lentil and bean stews may well be made with a meat stock, so it's advisable to check when ordering.

Artemisa
C/Ventura de la Vega 4 (429 50 92). Metro Sevilla/bus 5, 9, 15, 20, 51, 52, 53. **Lunch served** 1.30-4pm daily. **Dinner served** 9pm-midnight Mon-Sat. **Average** 1,800ptas. **Set menu** 1,100ptas. **Credit** AmEx, DC, MC, V.
Always busy, perhaps because of its central location and bargain prices, although the dishes – organic gazpacho, vegetable curry or salads and pizzas– are not exciting. *Air-conditioning. Wheelchair access.*

La Galette
C/Conde de Aranda 11 (576 06 41). Metro Retiro/bus all routes to Puerta de Alcalá. **Lunch served** 2-4pm, **dinner served** 9pm-midnight, Mon-Sat. Closed Aug. **Average** 2,200ptas. **Credit** AmEx, DC, MC, V.
The most upmarket of Madrid's vegetarian eateries, with international dishes – often with oriental and Caribbean influences – and excellent Viennese-style cakes. There are also some meat and fish dishes for non-vegetarians. *Air-conditioning. Wheelchair access.*
Branch: C/Bárbara de Braganza 10 (319 31 48).

El Granero de Lavapiés
C/Argumosa 10 (467 76 11). Metro Lavapiés, Atocha/bus 27, C. **Lunch served** 1-4pm Sun-Fri. Closed Aug. **Average** 2,000ptas. **Set menu** 1,000ptas. **No credit cards.**
The favourite among local vegetarians for its simple, unfussy style, with an attractive tiled dining room. Food ranges from broccoli with carrot mayonnaise to *cardos con almendras* (cardoon, a type of edible thistle considered particularly healthy, with almonds).

El Restaurante Vegetariano
C/Marqués de Santa Ana 34 (532 09 27). Metro Noviciado, Tribunal/bus 3, 40, 147, 149. **Lunch served** 1.30-4pm Tue-Sun. **Dinner served** 9-11pm Tue-Sat. Closed Aug. **Average** 1,500ptas. **Set menu** 800ptas. **Credit** V.
The menu here changes every three months and features interesting vegetarian dishes such as roast Mediterranean vegetables with houmous and *sopa de pepinos* (cucumber soup). Its décor features plain pine tables and hanging plants. *Air-conditioning.*

Tapas

Gutsy meats, delicate canapés and superb seafood can all be sampled on a tour round Madrid's wonderful array of tapas bars.

From their humble Andalusian origins as a quick bite on a saucer provided to keep the dust off a glass of wine (the word *tapa* means lid), tapas have developed into a culinary genre all on their own, and spectacular arrays of dishes in glass bar cabinets are a part of every Spanish urban landscape. They've also become very much a Madrileño ritual, as journalist Pedro Soleras recounted in *El Pais*.

'The tapa, invented in an age less obsessed with productivity, is a trick for spinning out your drinks without getting drunk. It's thus of primordial interest to visitors. If you don't want to look like an outsider or yokel, avoid pointing with your fingers and instead ask for one of this or one of that, and so on.... And, above all, don't get scared when the waiter shouts: it's not at you, it's at the kitchen. If you want the people with you to hear what you are saying, shout as well. If you don't, it's suspicious. You shouldn't leave your olive stones on the plate either. Chuck them away.'

It's also part of the ritual to move from one place to another. According to one Madrid veteran, to *tapear* you should visit as many bars as there are stations of the cross in a church (14, for those without the benefit of a Catholic education), although not many people quite reach this goal every weekend. You have one or two dishes in each place, together with the appropriate drink, and then move on.

To make this possible it's naturally necessary for bars to be near to each other, and most of the city's best-known tapas-providers are clustered in identifiable areas. The bars listed here are also grouped by area, so you can work out your own routes on foot. Each area has a distinct character, but all are most lively from about midday to 3pm and 8-11pm, with peak activity on Friday evenings and Saturdays, and Sunday around the Rastro.

As they've spread around Spain, tapas have taken on regional colour. Many regions also have their speciality drinks to go with their tapas: rough cider (*sidra*), theatrically poured with the bottle above the head to separate out the sediment, in Asturian bars; cold dry *fino* sherry in Andaluz bars; and white Ribeiro wines, served in small bowls rather than glasses, in Galician seafood bars, although you can equally just have a beer in any of them.

Among Madrid's own tapas specialities are *patatas bravas* (deep-fried potato chunks in a pepper sauce), assorted offal – from pig's ear (*orejas*) and tripe (*callos*) to sweetbreads (*mollejas*) and

many other things –, snails in a hot sauce and, of course, the huge range of shellfish that arrives here daily from the coast. Madrileños also claim that their versions of standards such as *croquetas* or tortilla are the best in Spain, but then, they would.

One thing to remember is that, while tapas are a wonderful way of trying new tastes and dishes, they are now rarely given free with a drink and, indeed, have become quite an expensive way of eating. Once you start sampling, the cost can soon mount up. For more information on bar customs and other bars more suited to drinking, having coffee or a night out – but which also often serve tapas, since in Spain these divisions are never precise –, *see chapters* **Cafés & Bars** *and* **Nightlife**. For a listing of bars, restaurants, shops and other facilities by area, *see page 264* **Area Index**.

Villa y Corte

Originally the classic district for a tapas tour, but now quite tourist-oriented. There are still a few gems, if not many bargains. Also excellent outlets for seafood tapas in the area are the two branches of the **Casa Gallega** (*see chapter* **Restaurants**).

El Anciano Rey de los Vinos
C/de la Paz 4 (532 14 73). Metro Sol/bus all routes to Puerta del Sol. **Open** 1-4pm, 6-11pm, daily.
A historic old *taberna* near the Puerta del Sol famed for its wines, and also for an unusual speciality – *torrijas*, bread soaked in wine and spices, coated in sugar and deep fried. There also plenty of alternatives for those with less of a sweet tooth to stem the effects of the wine, such as fried *bacalao*, tripe and *albóndigas*, all at around 600ptas. *See also chapter* **Cafés & Bars**.

Asquiniña
Plaza de la Puerta Cerrada 3 (366 59 44). Metro Sol/bus 18, 23, 31, 50, 65. **Open** noon-midnight Mon-Fri; noon-4pm, 7pm-midnight, Sat, Sun.
A small bar with kitschy, grass-green plaster décor but good, classic Galician tapas such as *pulpo*, *lacón* and *pimientos de Padrón*. Prices average around 700ptas.

Café de Oriente
Plaza de Oriente 2 (547 15 64). Metro Opera/bus 3, 25, 33, 39. **Open** 8.30am-1.30am Mon-Thur, Sun; 8.30am-2.30am Fri, Sat.
A slightly self-conscious recreation of turn-of-the-century *belle époque* opulence, the smart Oriente also has rather pricey, sophisticated canapé-style tapas such as *tostas* with asparagus, and good chorizo and other cold meats. *See also chapter* **Cafés & Bars**.
Tables outdoors April-Sept.

THE ORIGINAL ROCK´N ROLL RESTAURANT

MADRID

**Restaurant & Merchandise Store
Open Daily**

Paseo de la Castellana, 2   Teléfono: 435 02 00
28048 MADRID   Fax: 431 84 83

LONDON   PARIS   BERLIN

Las Bravas, *for the definitive* patatas bravas. *See page 112.*

Casa Paco

Plaza de la Puerta Cerrada 11 (366 31 66). Metro Sol/bus 18, 23, 31, 50, 65. **Open** *1-3.45pm, 8.30-11.45pm, Mon-Sat.*
A classic old-town tavern with top-quality (if expensive) *Manchego* cheese and *jamón serrano.*

Los Cien Vinos

C/del Nuncio 16 (no phone). Metro La Latina, Sol/bus 18, 23, 31, 50, 65. **Open** *Sept-June* noon-4pm, 7pm-midnight, *June-Sept* 1-4pm, 8pm-midnight, daily.
There may or may not be 100 wines to chose from here, but this lovely, plain stone *taberna* certainly has a range that's not far from it, plus half a dozen small *pinchos* and the same number again of simple larger dishes, from gazpacho to veal stew (*estofado*).

El Pulpito

Plaza Mayor 10 (366 21 88). Metro Sol/bus all routes to Puerta del Sol. **Open** *9am-1am daily.*
A small, pleasant bar that's one of the least touristy on the

Ordering Tapas

There are three basic sizes of tapas portion: a *pincho* (more or less a mouthful), a *tapa* (a saucerful or so) and a *ración* (a small plateful). Some places sell *medio raciones*. Whatever the experts may say, if something isn't identifiable on the menu but you want to try it, just point. Bread – *pan* – will normally come automatically, but if not, you can always ask for it. Remember you usually pay up to 25 per cent more if you sit at a table rather than eat at the bar. Finally, as with other bar bills, you let a tapas bill mount up and pay it all together when you've finished, rather than when you order.

For other dishes most normally eaten as part of a full meal (but which may also appear as tapas), *see chapter* **Restaurants**.

Basics

Bocadillo sandwich in a roll; **Cazuelita** individual hot casserole; **Montados** canapé-style mixed tapas, often with a slice of bread topped with anything from cheese to shellfish; **Pincho/pinchito** small titbit on a toothpick, or mouthful-sized tapa; **Ración** a portion (small plateful), which you can order in halves; **Pulga** small filled roll; **Tabla** platter (of cheeses, cold meats); **Tosta** slice of toast with topping; **Una de gambas, chorizo, etc** one portion of prawns, chorizo, etc; **Por unidad** per item.

Carne, Aves y Embutidos (Meat, Poultry & Charcuterie)

Albóndigas meat balls; **Alitas de pollo** chicken wings; **Cecina** very dry cured beef; **Chistorra** Navarrese sausage with paprika; **Flamenquines** breadcrumbed ham and pork rolls; **Oreja (de cerdo)** pig's ear; **Mollejas** sweetbreads; **Pincho moruno** grilled meat brochette; **Riñones al Jerez** kidneys cooked in sherry; **San Jacobo** fried ham and cheese sandwich; **Sobresada** soft Mallorcan paprika

sausage; **Torrezno** grilled pork crackling; **Zarajo** grilled sheep's intestine on a stick.

Pescado y Mariscos (Fish & Shellfish)

Ahumados smoked fish; **Anchoas** salted conserved anchovies; **Anguilas** eels; **Angulas** elvers; **Berberechos** cockles; **Bienmesabe** marinated fried fish; **Boquerones en vinagre/fritos** pickled fresh anchovies; **Calamares en su tinta** squid cooked in their ink; **Carabineiros** red ocean prawns; **Centollo** spider crab; **Chanquete** tiny Mediterranean fish, served deep fried; **Cigalas** crayfish; **Chipirones en su tinta** small Atlantic squid in their ink; **Chopito** small cuttlefish; **Croqueta de bacalao** salt-cod croquette; **Fritura de pescado** flash-fried fish; **Gambas al ajillo** prawns fried with garlic; **Gambas en gabardina** prawns deep-fried in batter; **Huevas** fish roe; **Mojama** dried and salted tuna fish; **Navajas** razorfish; **Nécora** swimming crab; **Percebe** gooseneck barnacle; **Pulpo a feira/a la gallega** octopus with paprika and olive oil; **Quisquilla** shrimp; **Salpicón** cold chopped salad, often with shellfish; **Soldaditos de pavia** fried salt-cod strips; **Tigres** mussels filled with spicy tomato sauce and béchamel; **Zamburiñas** small scallops.

Vegetales (Vegetable Tapas)

Aceitunas, olivas (adobados, rellenos) olives (pickled, stuffed); **Almendras saladas** salted almonds; **Pan con tomate** bread rubbed with fresh tomato and olive oil; **Patatas (papas) bravas** or **a la brava** deep-fried potatoes with hot pepper sauce; **Perdiz de huerta** lettuce hearts; **Pimientos de Padrón** fried hot baby green peppers; **Queso en aceite** cheese in olive oil; **Setas** wild mushrooms.

Other Tapas

Caracoles snails; **Croquetas** potato croquettes (may be with chicken, ham, tuna, and so on); **Empanada** flat pies, usually with a tuna filling; **Empanadilla** small fried pasties, usually with a tomato and tuna filling; **Ensaladilla** Russian salad, usually with tuna; **Huevos rellenos** stuffed cold hard-boiled eggs; **Migas (con huevo frito)** fried breadcrumbs (with fried egg).

Another hectic lunchtime at **Casa Labra**.

Plaza Mayor. The *pulpo* isn't necessarily the best thing on the menu: try the *albóndigas* or *callos*.

La Torre del Oro
Plaza Mayor 26 (366 50 16). Metro Sol/bus all routes to Puerta del Sol. **Open** 8am-2am daily.
A little piece of Seville on one side of the Plaza Mayor, just a bit touristy, staffed by genuine Andaluz waiters who yell at each other and the punters with unflinching and manic glee. To complete the atmosphere there are Sevillano tiles and a mass of bullfighting accoutrements on the walls, and great *fino* sherry. The tapas are mostly fried seafood, and they have great prawns and *pescaditos* (whitebait) for around the 1,000ptas mark.
Tables outdoors Feb-Nov.

Sol & Gran Vía

Casa Labra
C/Tetuán 12 (531 00 81). Metro Sol/bus all routes to Puerta del Sol. **Open** 9.30am-3.30pm, 5.30-11pm, Mon-Sat; 1-4pm, 8.15-11pm, Sun.
Founded in 1860, this *taberna*-restaurant with traditional zinc bar was in 1879 the birthplace of the Spanish Socialist Party, as a plaque outside indicates (*see chapter* **History: The Restoration**). It's also known for its *soldaditos de pavía* (fried *bacalao* strips in batter) and great salt-cod *croquetas*. Because it's so busy at lunchtimes this is one of the few bars where you are asked to pay as you order.

Huertas & Santa Ana

The best-known and most fashionable place for Madrileños to *tapear*, probably because it has the biggest range, from elegant to tatty. Huertas proper connects well with another fine clutch of bars nearby in the streets running into the Puerta del Sol, which offer wonderful contrasts of old and new, popular and élite.

Las Bravas
Pasaje Matheu 5 (521 51 41). Metro Sol/bus all routes to Puerta del Sol. **Open** 12.30pm-4pm, 7.30pm-midnight, daily.
If you only eat one tapa, it has to be these *patatas bravas*. They claim to have invented – and patented – them here. As well as good they're very cheap, and filling. The bars also offer fine *pulpo* and *orejas*.
Tables outdoors June-Oct.
Branches: C/Espoz y Mina 13; C/Alvarez Gato 3.

Casa Alberto
C/Huertas 18 (429 93 56). Metro Antón Martín/bus 6, 26, 32, 57. **Open** noon-2am Tue-Sat; noon-4pm Sun.
Founded in 1827, Alberto's still retains its red-painted tavern façade from the last century, behind which you can choose from a fine range of freshly-made tapas – *caracoles*, *calamares*, prawns – and some larger dishes.

Casa de Pontevedra
C/Victoria 2 (522 06 18). Metro Sol/bus all routes to Puerta del Sol. **Open** 10.30am-4.30pm, 7.30pm-midnight, daily.
A bar that offers mainly Basque specialities, with three types of *bacalao*, *pimientos rellenos* (stuffed peppers), roast sardines and great Basque *txacoli* white wine.

La Dolores
Plaza de Jesús 4 (429 22 43). Metro Antón Martín/bus 6, 26, 32, 57. **Open** 11am-1am Mon-Thur, Sun; 11am-2am Fri, Sat.
Prices are high at this old, tiled bar, which consequently often attracts a slightly more affluent clientèle than many in the area, but the *montados* and other tapas are good, and there's a great selection of beers. It's hugely popular on weekend lunchtimes. *See also chapter* **Cafés & Bars**.

Garabatu
C/Echegaray 5 (no phone). Metro Sevilla/bus all routes to Puerta del Sol. **Open** 8.30am-midnight daily.
An Asturian bar-restaurant with great earthy tapas such as chorizo *a la sidra* (in cider) and nose-bending *Cabrales* cheese, and to go with it the necessary coarse Asturian cider.

El Lacón
C/Manuel Fernández y González 8 (429 60 42). Metro Sevilla, Sol/bus 6, 26, 32, 50, 57. **Open** noon-4pm, 8pm-1am, daily.
A down-to-earth Galician bar with excellent *pulpo, caldo gallego* (a heavy, meat-and-vegetable broth) and *empanadas.*

Lerranz
C/Echegaray 26 (429 12 06). Metro Sevilla/bus all routes to Puerta del Sol. **Open** 10.30am-2.30pm, 6.30-9.30pm, Mon-Fri; 10.30am-2.30pm Sat.
A hip tapas bar that began as an off-shoot of the **Cenador del Prado** (*see chapter* **Restaurants**), and which offers everything from onion rings and traditional country bread with a variety of toppings to *patatas rellenas* (stuffed potatoes) and other modern inventions. There's also a set lunch menu, for about 1,000ptas.

Lhardy
Carrera de San Jerónimo 8 (521 33 85). Metro Sevilla, Sol/bus all routes to Puerta del Sol. **Open** 10.30am-2.30pm, 6.30-9.30pm, Mon-Fri; 10.30am-2.30pm Sat.
The aristocrat of Madrid's tapas bars. Serve yourself to consommé from the silver samovar and their knock-out croquettes from the glass cabinets, or order *finos* and a hot pastry-boat with kidneys (*barquitos de riñones*) from the waiters. You pay as you leave, explaining what you've had to the person on the cash till. Taking tapas at Lhardy's is a much more reasonable way of getting a look at this local institution than by eating in the restaurant. *See also chapter* **Restaurants.**

La Toscana
C/Ventura de la Vega 22 (429 60 31). Metro Sevilla/bus all routes to Puerta del Sol. **Open** 8pm-midnight Mon; 1-4pm, 8pm-midnight, Tue-Sat.
Morcilla is a speciality at this typical Castilian bar, which has plenty of table space and *raciones* for around 1,000ptas. There are also good egg *revueltos* with different ingredients mixed in and nice salads.

La Trucha
C/Manuel Fernández y González 3 (429 58 33). Metro Sevilla, Sol/bus 6, 26, 32, 50, 57. **Open** 11.30am-4pm, 7.30pm-midnight, Mon-Sat.
A bar-restaurant that offers tasty *raciones,* and is invariably packed at peak times. There's a big range to look through, from smoked fish and *pescaditos* to marinated artichokes, all at around 1,000ptas a *ración.*

Bar Viña P
Plaza Santa Ana 3 (531 81 11). Metro Sol/bus 6, 26, 32, 50, 57. **Open** 1-5pm, 8pm-midnight, daily.
The bar to come to right on the Plaza Santa Ana for *montados, gambas al ajillo,* asparagus, stuffed mussels, *almejas* and many other tapas for about 1,000ptas a *ración.*

Lavapiés/Rastro/Atocha

The Rastro is busiest on a Sunday morning, which is the time to find a great atmosphere there – and crowds. The surrounding streets are full of bars, and as you wander around you'll find plenty of other places as well as the selection listed here. Excellent (and very well-priced) tapas are also available at **Belmar** (*see chapter* **Restaurants**).

El Brillante
Glorieta del Emperador Carlos V 8 (528 69 66). Metro Atocha/bus all routes to Atocha. **Open** 7am-midnight Mon-Thur, Sun; 7am-1am Fri, Sat.
On the edge of the Lavapiés area, this is one of a no-nonsense chain of café/bars with high-quality food at very reasonable prices. You can choose from a huge variety of fresh bread *bocadillos,* as well as tapas and hot meals. An ideal starting-off point for a night's carousing, it's always busy, especially in the early morning when it fills up both with recent arrivals from Atocha station and with revellers ending the night with hot chocolate and *churros.* There are also ready-to-go snacks for train travellers. There are several branches dotted around the city; for addresses, check the phone book.

Café Melo's
C/Ave Maria 44 (no phone). Metro Lavapiés/bus 6, 26, 32, 57. **Open** 9am-2am Mon-Sat. Closed Aug.
The thing to try at Melo's are their fat, delicious, fresh *croquetas, zapatillas* (sandwiches made with Galician country bread, cheese and ham) and *empanadas.*

Los Caracoles
Plaza Cascorro 15 (265 26 19). Metro La Latina/bus 17, 23, 35, 60. **Open** 10am-3.30pm, 6-11.30pm, daily.
Genial host Don Amadeo welcomes all who come to his bustling bar at the top of the Rastro, famous for its house speciality – snails, cooked up in a rich broth with chorizo sausage and paprika, a fast-disappearing local delicacy. If that doesn't appeal, there are plenty of other things to choose from. *See also chapter* **Cafés & Bars.**

Bar Castilla
C/Mesón de Paredes 24 (467 54 56). Metro Tirso de Molina/bus 6, 26, 32, 57. **Open** 9am-1.30am Mon-Fri, Sun.
On a Sunday morning, you have a choice of over 200 different *croquetas* (nine for 450ptas) at this little bar, with just six tables. It's also good for *chipirones en su tinta* (650ptas).

Cayetano
C/Encomienda 23 (527 77 07). Metro La Latina/bus 17, 23, 35, 60. **Open** 9.30am-3.30pm, 5.30pm-midnight, Mon, Wed-Sun.
Another good Rastro stop-off, this time for shellfish and wine. A sizeable portion of prawns in their shells will cost you about 1,300ptas.

La Mancha
C/Miguel Servet 13 (467 65 15). Metro Embajadores/bus all routes to Embajadores. **Open** noon-4pm, 7pm-midnight, Mon-Sat; noon-4pm Sun.
La Mancha combines the best of the old and the new. Wines come by the glass or bottle, and its fine tapas include farmhouse cheeses, quality ham and cold meats, and fish in *escabeche.* It's usually pretty lively.

La Taberna de Antonio Sánchez
C/Mesón de Paredes 13 (539 78 26). Metro Tirso de Molina/bus 6, 26, 32, 57. **Open** noon-4pm, 8pm-midnight, Mon-Sat; noon-4pm Sun.
Madrid's most historic *taberna,* founded by a bullfighter in 1830 and still more or less unchanged, with its classic zinc bar and mounted bulls' heads around the walls. Its fine tapas vary from *callos* to *morcilla* and smoked fish *montados.* Full meals are also available. *See also chapter* **Cafés & Bars.**

Malasaña & Chueca

Malasaña and the streets that run across towards Argüelles (*see below*) make up one of the best areas for good food and reasonable prices. Chueca, now more a night-dive centre, still has several old-fashioned restaurants, *tabernas* and excellent tapas bars.

No-one gets to sit down at **El Bocaíto**.

Batela

C/Silva 27 (522 14 42). Metro Callao/bus all routes to Plaza de Callao. **Open** *9am-2am daily.*
Batela, just off the Gran Vía, sports nautical décor and offers a wide range of good-value tapas. Oyster mushrooms and *bacalao al pil-pil* (salt cod, fried very hot in garlic) are both 800ptas. To drink there's excellent Basque *txacolí* wine.

El Bocaíto

C/Libertad 6 (532 12 19). Metro Chueca/bus 3, 40, 149. **Open** *1-4.30pm, 8.30pm-midnight, Mon-Fri; 8.30pm-midnight Sat.*
Madrileños rate this pricey tapas bar highly. Energetic, jokey waiters dish up *huevas* (fish roes), a variety of *revueltos*, pâtés, salads, pastries, mushroom kebabs and other unusual tapas. There are no seats, so it's not for leisurely eating.

Casa do Campañeiro

C/San Vicente Ferrer 44 (521 57 02). Metro Noviciado, Tribunal/bus 3, 40, 147, 149. **Open** *1.30pm-midnight Mon-Sat.*
A Galician bar with wonderful tiles on the wall and several dozen traditional tapas – *jamón, pimientos de Padrón*, shellfish, all costing 250-500ptas – and fine-quality Galician wines.

Santander

C/Augusto Figueroa 25 (522 49 10). Metro Chueca/bus 3, 40, 149. **Open** *10.15am-3.30pm, 7-10.30pm, Mon-Sat.*
Santander offers one of the largest assortments of tapas and canapés in Madrid, with around 100 to choose from, including *brandada* (salt-cod and potato purée), *empanadas*, stuffed mussels and a huge range of *montados*. They're also very well-priced, from 75ptas upwards each.

El Timón

C/General Castaños 13 (308 01 22). Metro Colón/bus all routes to Colón. **Open** *noon-4pm, 7pm-midnight, daily.*
Lawyers from the Palacio de Justicia across the street flock to this smart nautical-style bar with a great range of tapas, all of them excellent – from shellfish to a salad of *pimientos*. The average price is 800ptas, and *fino* is 200ptas.

Salamanca & the Retiro

Upmarket – and the prices reflect it – but there are some marvellous, long-established family bars, while the local clientèle demand high standards. Tapas here are often more sophisticated than the traditional earthy varieties common in the city centre. Particularly good for Galician tapas in the district is **O'Caldiño** (*see chapter* **Restaurants**).

El Aguilucho

C/Hermosilla 18 (575 60 40). Metro Serrano/bus 1, 9, 19, 21, 51, 53, 74. **Open** *9am-11pm Mon-Sat.*
First opened in 1875 but currently sporting the décor it acquired in a fifties' revamp, El Aguilucho sells quality shellfish – everything from *cangrejo* (crab) to *navajas* (razor-shells) and a fine *salpicón* (mixed shellfish salad) – at steep prices.

Alkalde

C/Jorge Juan 10 (576 33 59). Metro Serrano, Velázquez/bus 1, 9, 19, 51, 74. **Open** *1-4pm, 8.30pm-midnight, Mon-Fri; 1-4pm Sat.*
An old-fashioned Basque bar that's again quite expensive, but has good seating space. *Chistorra*, tortilla with red peppers, *morcilla, jamón, empanadillas*, and *chipirones en su tinta* are all on the menu.

Buen Provecho

C/Ibiza 35 (573 32 51). Metro Ibiza/bus 2, 26, 61, 63, C. **Open** *1pm-1am Mon-Fri; 8pm-1am Sat.*
A shop selling fine-quality produce on the east side of the Retiro, which also has a bar and just one table at which you can eat small stews, farmhouse cheeses and other tasty morsels. It's not cheap, but useful if you're in the area.

Casa Puebla

C/Príncipe de Vergara 6 (576 55 79). Metro Príncipe de Vergara/bus 15, 29, 52, 146. **Open** *10am-4pm, 6.30pm-midnight, Mon-Fri; 10am-4pm Sat.*
A tiled, family-owned *taberna* near the Retiro that's

remained resolutely unchanged for years, with great simple cooking (a particularly fine tortilla), a local clientèle and reasonable prices.

Hevia

C/Serrano 118 (561 46 87). Metro Núñez de Balboa, Avda de América/bus 9, 19, 51, 61. **Open** 9am-1.30am Mon-Sat.

A very upmarket, but buzzy, Salamanca tapas bar that uses excellent ingredients which they'll put together in pretty much whichever canapé-combination you want. The tapas are not cheap, and service by the white-jacketed waiters is great. The clientèle are usually as plush as the locale.
Tables outdoors May-Sept.

José Luis

C/Serrano 89 (563 09 58). Metro Núñez de Balboa, Rubén Darío/bus 1, 9, 19, 51, 74. **Open** noon-1am daily.

A classic, very smart Salamanca bar with cocktail-type tapas from a menu largely unchanged since the fifties (smoked salmon tartare, melted Brie and pâté, small steak canapés and many mixed *montados*), delicious cakes and a heavily yuppyish crowd. You help yourself to tapas and pay when you leave.
Tables outdoors May-Sept.
Branches: C/Serrano 91; Paseo de la Habana 4-6; C/San Francisco de Sales 14-16.

Jurucha

C/Ayala 19 (575 00 98). Metro Serrano, Velázquez/bus 1, 9, 19, 21, 53, 74. **Open** 7.30am-11pm Mon-Sat.

An unpretentious, efficient Basque bar dating from the 1920s, with a long barful of great croquettes, *montados* and hot and cold bites worthy of San Sebastián, the tapa-capital of the Basque Country. There's also a small dining room at the back.

Peláez

C/Lagasca 61 (575 87 24). Metro Núñez de Balboa/bus 1, 9, 19, 51, 74. **Open** 10am-midnight Mon-Sat.

A wonderful old bar, surprising to find in the middle of Salamanca, where Luis Peláez has been turning out creative tapas – *huevas*, *montados*, excellent *mojama* (dried tuna), smoked fish tortillas – for about 40 years. It's also very good value.

Other Areas

Argüelles

La Bilbaina

C/Marqués de Urquijo 27 (541 86 98). Metro Argüelles/bus 1, 21, 44, 133, C. **Open** noon-3.30pm, 7pm-midnight, Mon-Sat; noon-3.30pm Sun.

Though its speciality is shellfish, this bar also has plenty of other things from *chistorra* to *lomo* marinated in olive oil.

La Fortuna

Plaza de los Mostenses 3 (547 30 98). Metro Plaza de España/bus all routes to Plaza de España. **Open** 10am-midnight daily.

Visit this bar near the Plaza de España to sample fine wines (425ptas for a jug), fried *boquerones*, roast *chorizo* and bountiful supplies of other meaty tapas. The average price is 1,000ptas.

Mesón Los Toledanos

Travesía de Conde Duque 6 (no phone). Metro Ventura Rodríguez/bus 1, 2, 44, 133, C. **Open** 7am-11am Mon-Fri, Sun. Closed Aug.

This down-to-earth tapas bar near the Cuartel Conde-Duque offers a great spread of *chipirones*, *caracoles*, very hot chorizo, trout in *escabeche* and other earthy dishes.

Chamberí

Another area with a lively tapas-round of its own – C/Cardenal Cisneros and C/Hartzenbush are virtually lined with bars. There's nothing wildly original here, but the bars are reasonably priced and varied, attracting both locals and a lot of students.

El Aldeano

C/Cardenal Cisneros 33 (447 42 87). Metro Bilbao, Quevedo/bus 147, 149. **Open** 10am-5pm, 7pm-1.30am, daily.

An Asturian bar, with *chorizo*, *cangrejos* and *mollejas* (around 900ptas), and natural cider at 500ptas a bottle.

Bodegas La Ardosa

C/Santa Engracia 70 (446 58 94). Metro Iglesias/bus 3, 16, 61, 149. **Open** 10am-3.30pm, 6-10pm, daily.

Locals and buyers from the nearby market come in droves to this classic red-fronted *taberna*. It sells brilliant *patatas bravas*, good marinated sardines, shellfish and lots of fried things. There are no tables; tapas prices start at 220ptas.

La Giralda

C/Hartzenbusch 12-15 (445 17 43). Metro Bilbao/bus 21, 147, 149. **Open** 12.30-4pm, 8pm-midnight, Mon-Sat.

Tiles and forged metal decorate this Andalusian tavern whose offerings include fairly pricy *huevas*, *arroz con almejas* (rice with clams) and *rabo de toro* (bull's tail).

Rincón de Mondeñedo

C/Cardenal Cisneros 6 (446 17 43). Metro Bilbao/bus 21, 147, 149. **Open** 11am-midnight Mon-Sat.

A modern bar with a very decent range of tapas, among them wild mushrooms, fried *calamares* and grilled meat sold by weight.

Taberna 2

C/Sagasta 2 (532 21 43). Metro Bilbao/bus 21, 147, 149. **Open** 10.15am-3pm, 6pm-midnight, Mon-Sat.

An old Asturian-Galician wine bar (but with table-quality wine) with *montados* of *sobresada* (a soft, peppery Mallorcan sausage) for as little as 60ptas. Galician chorizo costs 200ptas and a pungent plate of *Cabrales* cheese is 800ptas.

Las Ventas

Los Timbales

C/Alcalá 227 (725 07 68). Metro Ventas/bus 12, 21, 38, 53, 106, 201. **Open** 7am-midnight daily.

A fine traditional tapas bar next to the bullring. It's an institution among Madrid's *aficionados*, and packed to bursting on bullfight days.

The homely **Los Caracoles**. *See page 113.*

Time out in Madrid

Cafés & Bars

Whether you want an ice cold beer, a delicate fino or to linger over a coffee, Madrid provides an enormous variety of places to choose from.

Madrid often seems to have more bars, cafés and other drinking holes than shops, restaurants or any other type of amenity. Wherever you are in the city, you never need walk more than a hundred yards or so to find food, drink and shelter from the summer heat or winter cold. The bar is Madrid's most universal social institution, and there is no better way to get a feel for the place and its people, their comings and goings, than by sitting in a neighbourhood bar or café, just watching or eavesdropping.

This being so, it's impossible for any brief list to be exhaustive. The selection listed here aims to give an idea of the best of Madrid bars, while concentrating on the central areas of the city. They are roughly divided up according to the main types of bars found here, but any division into categories is inevitably arbitrary. Virtually all of the places listed in this chapter serve food of some kind, and many are open very late. However, for other bars where the emphasis is more emphatically on food, but where, of course, you can still just have a drink, *see chapter* **Tapas**. For still more places that you would more likely visit later in a night-time tour of the city, *see chapter* **Nightlife**.

Many bars keep only roughly to their 'official' opening times, and those listed here should be taken only as guidelines, particularly for traditional bars. Most cafés and neighbourhood bars close around midnight, although on Fridays and Saturdays they often stay open until 1am or so. In the centre all bars tend to stay open later, and for those caught between nightspots they offer a cheap way to keep the alcohol and food intake up.

For a list of bars, restaurants, shops and other facilities in each area, *see page 264* **Area Index**.

Cafés

Many of the grand establishments that housed the café society of former times (*see chapter* **History: The Restoration**) have disappeared in the last fifty years, but those that remain – and more recent revivals – are still wonderful places for taking stock of the world.

Café del Círculo de Bellas Artes

C/Alcalá 42 (531 77 00). Metro Banco de España/bus 1, 2, 20, 51, 52, 74, 146, 150. **Open** 8am-2am daily.
A few years ago the **Círculo de Bellas Artes** (*see chapters* **Sightseeing**, **Art Galleries** *and* **Music: Classical**

The **Café Gijón** has seen them all in its time. See page 119.

Bar Hanging

The **Cervecería Alemana**. *See page 120.*

Etiquette.

The civilised tradition that you only pay when you are ready to leave is still the norm in bars in Spain, and rarely abused. Service, at the bar or at tables, is usually rapid and efficient. Spaniards generally respect queues, and you'll find it easy to get a waiter's ear with a brisk *oiga* (literally, 'hear me', a perfectly polite way of attracting someone's attention).

In busy bars people tend to get their drinks down quickly. Added to the fact that in the centre there are entire streets given over to bars, this means that at night people often move from place to place, have a drink and then move on. Settling in to one place is something more usually done in cafés, or in summer at outdoor *terrazas (see page 122)*.

Tipping is discretionary. Change is usually returned in a small dish, and regardless of the amount spent it's unusual to leave over 100ptas. Most people just leave a few coins.

One final point. Except in smartish bars, olive stones, toothpicks and other disposables are thrown on the floor, and when at the bar it is near-obligatory to wipe your mouth or hands regularly on the tissue-type napkins (*servilletas*), screw them up and then throw them on the floor as well.

Coffee & Tea

For breakfast, most people have a *café con leche*, a largish, milky coffee, which at that time of day comes in a cup. At later times it will often be smaller and served in a glass, and if you want a cup you should ask for a *taza grande*. A plain black espresso coffee is a *café solo*; the same with a dash of milk added is *un cortado*, while *un americano* is a *solo* diluted with twice the normal amount of water. With a shot of alcohol, a *solo* becomes a *carajillo*. If you simply ask for a *carajillo* it will normally be made with brandy (*un carajillo de coñac*), but you can also ask for a *carajillo de whisky, de ron* (rum), *de anis* (strong Spanish anisette) or anything else you fancy. Decaffeinated coffee is *descafeinado*. The quality of coffee in bars varies enormously.

Coffee tends to arrive at medium temperature, and if you want it really hot you should remind the waiter *que esté bien caliente, por favor*. In summer a great café alternative is *café con hielo*, iced coffee, usually with a slice of lemon.

Tea in bars is usually awful, as most have little idea how to prepare it. Very popular, however, are herb teas, *infusiones*, such as *menta* (mint) or *manzanilla* (camomile).

Beer

Wine may be more traditional in Spain, but in terms of quantity *cerveza* has overtaken it as the national drink. Draught beer (*de barril*) is served in *cañas*, a measure around ¼ litre (in bars people often just ask for *una caña, dos cañas*, and so on) in tall glasses called *tubos*, or in a *doble*, which is around ½ litre. Some places even serve *pintas*. Bottled beer is usually served in *tercios* (⅓ litre) or *botellines* (¼ litre).

Spain produces some good-quality beers. In Madrid, the best is Mahou, brewed here and still largely distributed only in the Madrid region. The brewery produces two basic varieties, green label and the stronger red label. A darker Mahou beer (*negra*) is also increasingly available. Other common local brands worth a try are Aguila and Cruzcampo. Quite a few bars now also stock imported beers, but they are a good deal more expensive than Spanish brands.

Wines, Spirits & Other Drinks

All bars have a sturdy cheap red (*tinto*) on offer, and usually a white (*blanco*) and rosé (*rosado*). A traditional but fast-disappearing drink is *tinto con sifón*, red with a splash of soda. If you fancy a better wine, then most bars listed here will have at least a decent Rioja, and probably *Cava*, Catalan sparkling wine. Good wines, however, are often expensive in bars that do not have wine as a speciality. Sherry is *jerez*. The type virtually always drunk in Spain is a dry *fino*, served very cold. A good fuller-bodied variety is *palo cortado*. Sweet sherries have traditionally been only for export.

Vermouth (*vermút*) with soda is still common in older bars, usually as an aperitif. If you're looking for a powerful after-dinner drink, try Galician *orujo*, a fiery spirit similar to grappa or schnapps, which comes plain (*blanco*) or *con hierbas*, with a luminous green colour. Other *digestivos* include *Patxarán*, a fruity anis-flavoured liqueur from Navarra, and the more Castilian *anis*, famously made in Chinchón (*see chapter* **Around Madrid**) and available dry (*seco*), or sweet (*dulce*). A favourite for non-alcohol drinkers is the Campari-like but booze-free *Bitter Kas*.

Food

At any time of day, you can always accompany your coffee or drink with something to eat. For breakfast, many places have traditional *churros* or *porras*, sweet deep-fried sticks of batter, or fresh pastries such as croissants, *napolitanas* (soft, glazed pastries filled with egg custard) *sobaos* (a buttery sponge from Santander) or *madalenas*, sponge cakes. To sustain up your ritual *caña*, even bars that do not have a particularly distinguished display of tapas offer such things as a *pinchito de tortilla*, a little piece of potato omelette, sometimes for free. For more on bar food, *see* chapter **Tapas**.

Tobacco

Probably a majority of people in Spain still regard a cigarette as an automatic accompaniment to a drink. In bars cigarettes (*cigarros*) are sold in machines. Spaniards differentiate between cigarettes of black tobacco (*tabaco negro*) and those of international-style light tobacco (*rubio*). If you want to pass for a native, try a Ducados or its stronger brother *Habana*, full-blooded black tobacco. Popular Spanish brands of *rubio* tobacco are Fortuna and Nobel. Marlboro, Camel and Winston are also popular, particularly light versions.

& Opera) decided to charge the nominal sum of 100ptas for non-members to use its elegant and spacious café overlooking the Calle Alcalá. It's well worth the money, if you want to sit and read or chat for a few hours among turn-of-the-century décor. The café also has tasty tapas and sandwiches. *Tables outdoors May-Oct.*

Café Comercial
Glorieta de Bilbao 7 (521 56 55). Metro Bilbao/bus 21, 40, 147, 149. **Open** 8am-1.30am Mon-Thur; 8am-2.30am Fri, Sat. Closed Aug.
An institution, overlooking the Glorieta de Bilbao for more than a century, the Comercial is the most famous meeting point in Madrid. With heavy wooden tables and leather-lined seats, its mirrored interior attracts all kinds of people, from huddled bunches of students and would-be literary types to elderly local residents who have been taking breakfast there since before the Civil War. Bring a newspaper, and settle in. *Tables outdoors May-Oct.*

Café Gijón
Paseo de Recoletos 21 (521 54 25). Metro Banco de España/bus all routes to Cibeles. **Open** 9am-2am daily.
Madrid's definitive literary café, opened in 1888. It maintains its literary connections with an annual short-story prize, and has tried to keep the *tertulia* tradition (*see chapter* **History: The Restoration**) alive with rather formalised gatherings of writers, film makers, bullfighters and so on. The food, however, is average-quality and overpriced, and service at the tables is less than attentive. Get a window seat if you can, or stand at the bar, which as well as the literati attracts an in-off-the-street crowd of concierges and office workers. Outside it has a pleasant if expensive terrace bar in summer. *Tables outdoors May-Oct.*

Cafe Isadora,
C/Divino Pastor 14 (445 71 74). Metro Bilbao/bus 21, 40, 147, 149. **Open** 3pm-1.30am daily.
Books and old prints line the walls, giving this Malasaña café a relaxed, literary feel. Opened in the late seventies, it has a black-and-white tiled interior and chunky, dark wood furniture. Worth examining is their collection of different kinds of *Patxarán* (*see p118* **Bar Hanging**), many individually-made.

Cafe Lion
C/Alcalá 57 (575 00 51). Metro Banco de España/bus all routes to Plaza de Cibeles. **Open** 9am-1.30am daily.
A must for lovers of faded splendour. The Lion's 1920s decor has been quietly going to seed for the last 30 years, despite its location opposite the post office just down from the Puerta de Alcalá. Like other cafés of the era it was once an important meeting place for artists and political activists, but sadly, the Lion has largely been left behind. As an authentic literary cafe, though, it gets our vote over the Gijón. *Tables outdoors May-Oct.*

Cafe Moderno
Plaza de las Comendadoras 1 (522 84 61). Metro Noviciado/bus 21, 147. **Open** 4pm-2am daily
Tucked away in a corner of a pleasant square and next to the seemingly abandoned convent of Santiago (which does, though, still house a community of nuns), the Moderno is fake art deco, but quietly elegant. It's a good place to meet up if you're going to outdoor concerts at the nearby **Centro Cultural Conde Duque** (*see chapter* **Madrid by Season**). *Tables outdoors May-Oct.*

Café de Oriente
Plaza de Oriente 2, (247 15 64). Metro Opera/bus 3, 25, 33, 39, 148. **Open** 8.30am-1.30am Mon-Thur, Sun; 8.30am-2.30am Fri, Sat.
Modern, but designed very much to recall an atmosphere of late-nineteenth-century elegance, the Oriente is also reassuringly expensive. In summer, its terrace offers a fine view

of the Palacio Real, even though buskers, flower-sellers and sundry hawkers can take the shine off things. The very comfortable interior is best, especially in winter, when the plush décor acts as an extra buffer against the cold outside. There is also a basement restaurant. *See also chapter* **Tapas**. *Tables Outdoors May-Oct.*

Café de Ruiz,
C/Ruiz 11 (446 12 32). Metro Bilbao/bus 21, 40, 147, 149. **Open** 3pm-3am daily.
An amiably old-fashioned feel makes this Malasaña café, a *Movida* meeting-point in its time, a pleasant spot to kill a few hours or to retreat from the night-time grunge. Fine coffee, milkshakes (*batidos*), cocktails such as *mojitos* (rum and lime) and even Havana cigars can all be mulled over while reading the papers or eavesdropping on the next table.

El Espejo
Paseo de Recoletos 31, (398 23 47). Metro Colón/bus all routes to Plaza de Colón. **Open** 9am-1.30am Mon-Thur; 9am-2.30am Fri-Sun.
Opened only in 1978, the Espejo set out to be the art nouveau bar Madrid never had, with positively Parisian 1900s décor. It has since spread into a terrace bar on Recoletos, with a splendid glass pavilion reminiscent of a giant Tiffany lamp. Fashionable and comfortable, it has excellent tapas at reasonable prices, particularly the *croquetas* and tortilla. *Tables outdoors May-Oct.*

Lisboa
C/Argensola 17 (no phone). Metro Alonso Martínez/bus 3, 7, 21, 40, 149. **Open** noon-1.30am Mon-Thur; 6pm-2.30am Fri-Sun.
Stylish bar in Chueca opened in 1992, with imported beers and spirits. Cool, quiet, and with a faithful clientèle, the Lisboa regularly hosts photography exhibitions and discussions. There are also books, art and postcards on sale.

As they say, **Viva Madrid**. *See page 121.*

La Mallorquina

Puerta del Sol 2 (no phone). Metro Sol/bus all routes to Puerta del Sol. **Open** 8.30am-9pm Mon-Sat.
La Mallorquina is a splendid slice of local life still going strong after 50 years. Downstairs it's a bustling pastry shop with a stand-up café serving baked-on-the-premises cakes and savouries. Above, there is a proper, table-service café regularly full of *señoras* chatting over excellent coffee and arguably the best *napolitanas* in the city.

Nuevo Café Barbieri

C/Ave María 45 (527 36 58). Metro Lavapiés/bus 6, 26, 32, 57. **Open** 3pm-2am Mon-Thur; noon-2am Fri-Sun.
After many years of shabby decline, in the late seventies the Barbieri was taken over by a cooperative who partly restored its nineteenth-century columned interior to its former glory. It still retains a certain seedy quality, despite attracting a largely young clientèle. Newspapers and magazines provided make it an excellent spot to while away an afternoon while exploring Lavapiés. *See also chapter* **Women's Madrid**.

Cervecerías & Cocktail Bars

El Anciano

C/Bailén 19 (559 53 32). Metro Opera/bus 3, 25, 33, 39, 148. **Open** 10am-3pm, 5-11pm, Mon, Tue, Thur-Sun.
Dating back to 1900s, this was originally a sister bar to **El Anciano Rey de los Vinos** (*see below* **Tabernas & Traditional Bars**). Kept much as it was fifty years ago, and extremely simple, it serves well-kept beer and wines and good tapas. Great for a drink after visiting the Palacio Real.

Balmoral

C/Hermosilla 10 (431 41 33). Metro Serrano/bus 1,9, 19, 21, 51, 74. **Open** 12.30-3pm, 7pm-2am, Mon-Sat.
The Balmoral keeps itself to itself, tucked away in the heart of wealthy Salamanca. However, behind its slightly daunting exterior you will find not only a bizarre recreation/mishmash of Scottish-English styles (tartan carpet, the *Monarch of the Glen* and hunting prints), but also a clientèle ranging from crusty older locals to bikers. There are excellent cocktails and impeccable service too, even if it is a bit expensive.

Bar Cock

C/de la Reina 16 (532 28 26). Metro Gran Vía/bus all routes to Gran Vía. **Open** 7pm-3am daily.
After about 1am, the most modish of the three cocktail bars – the others being **Del Diego** and **Chicote** (*see below*) – that form a tiny city-centre triangle. Its dark wood-panelled walls and high-beamed ceiling give it a subdued air, and it is perhaps the least atmospheric, but it can compete with the best in attracting the media, theatre and fashion crowd. The cocktails are suitably fine.

Casa Pueblo

C/León (no phone). Metro Antón Martín/bus 6, 26, 32, 57. **Open** 6pm-2am daily.
A perfect recreation of a turn-of-the-century bar/café, Casa Pueblo has been offering quietly formal but relaxed service to its regulars for the last 15 years. Excellent jazz and big band on tape, and at midnight a live pianist, make this one of the capital's most pleasant watering holes.

Cervecería Alemana

Plaza Santa Ana 6 (429 70 33). Metro Sol/bus 6, 26, 32, 50, 57, 150. **Open** 8am-11.30pm Mon, Wed-Sun.
Built in 1904 and based on a German bier keller, the Alemana still serves beer in steins, if you ask for it. Along with countless other visitors, Hemingway actually did drink here during his stays in Madrid, and the old place is still much as it was then. Although on the tourist trail, this is just as much a locals' bar, particularly on a Sunday morning when it offers tranquility and an ideal setting to browse over the paper.

Cervecería Santa Ana

Plaza Santa Ana 10 (429 43 56). Metro Sol/bus 6, 26, 32, 50, 57, 150. **Open** 10am-1pm daily.
Slightly overshadowed by the Alemana next door, the Santa Ana is plainer to look at but still offers good beer, including draught Guinness and Belgian bottled beers. There are no tables, and in the evenings places at the bar are highly sought-after. Good cheese, pâté and other tapas are on offer.

Cervecería Santa Bárbara

Plaza Santa Bárbara 8 (319 04 49). Metro Alonso Martínez/bus 3, 7, 21, 40, 149. **Open** 11am-11pm daily.
A popular meeting-place on the north side of the Chueca bar-and-nightlife area that on weekends is not so much bustling as positively packed out. There's well-kept draught beer to have with the bar's speciality tapas, prawns and oysters. They are very expensive, above all if you order at a table.

Chicote

Gran Vía 12 (532 67 37). Metro Gran Vía/bus all routes to Gran Vía. **Open** 11am-3am daily.
The doyen of Madrid cocktail bars, with the city's best example of 1930s interior design, and famous among many other things for never having closed throughout the Civil War. The seats are also original from the thirties – which means that, yes, you could actually be sitting where old Hemingway and the rest of the international press spent their days sheltering from the artillery shells flying down the Gran Vía. Since then, luminaries such as Grace Kelly, Ava Gardner and about every Spanish writer, actor or artist of the last sixty years have passed through too. The cocktail range is impressive, although you should expect to pay up to 1,000ptas for them. The waiters are gentlemen from another epoch. Grab one of the alcove tables and savour a treat to remember.

Del Diego

C/de la Reina 12 (523 31 06). Metro Gran Vía/bus all routes to Gran Vía. **Open** 6pm-3am daily.
Founded by former **Chicote** waiter Fernando del Diego, this bar has a younger ambience and a lighter style not associated with traditional *coctelerías*. Light-coloured wooden walls and bright lighting make for a convivial atmosphere. The cocktails are something else too. Ask for a *Diego*: vodka, kirsch, peach, lime and crushed ice.

De 1911

Plazuela San Ginés 5 (266 35 19). Metro Opera, Sol/bus all routes to Puerta del Sol. **Open** 12.30pm-2.30am daily.
Tucked away not far from Sol, the Plazuela San Ginés is a haven of tranquility. One of the nicest of its bars is this one, so named because it's been there since 1911. Inside, it's been finely refurbished with hand-painted tiles. It offers a selection of beers from around the world, along with Irish coffee.

Los Gabrieles

C/Echegaray 17 (429 62 61). Metro Sol, Sevilla/bus all routes to Puerta del Sol. **Open** 12.30pm-2.30am daily.
With an even more impressive tiling job than its near neighbour **Viva Madrid** (*see below*), Los Gabrieles is an institution. Until the seventies it was a brothel, run by gypsies, with rooms in the now-inaccessible cellar that saw them all come and go, so to speak. It then became a bar, and at the height of its popularity during the *Movida* years it attracted all the city's beautiful and famous. More recently it's tended to become a pick-up place for rich kids, and pricey with it.

Kairos

C/del Nuncio 19 (364 01 25). Metro Tirso de Molina/bus 17, 18, 23, 35. **Open** 8pm-3am daily.
Just off Calle Segovia is this well-designed, pleasant bar with a faithful local clientèle, fine cocktails and excellent coffee, wines and bottled beer. Despite its small size it has an upstairs balcony that's ideal for a relaxing coffee. *Tables outdoors May-Oct.*

Take the evening air at **Kairos**. *See page 120.*

Naturbier

Plaza Santa Ana 9 (429 39 18). Metro Sol/bus 6, 26, 32, 50, 57, 150. **Open** *11.30am-1am Mon-Thur; 11.30am-3am Fri-Sun.*
A neighbour to the Cervecerías **Alemana** and **Santa Ana** (*see above*), Naturbier's attraction is that it is one of the few places in Madrid which brews its own beer, following traditional German recipes. It's very popular with students and foreigners, but its brew is unlikely to find its way into a real-ale fan's roll of honour.

The Quiet Man

C/Valverde 44 (523 46 89). Metro Tribunal/bus 3, 40, 149. **Open** *1pm-2am Mon-Thur; 1pm-3am Fri-Sun.*
There are several 'Irish Pubs' around Madrid, but the Quiet Man, opened in 1992, has been the most successful. It's a fair recreation of a Dublin (or London Irish) pub, which can be disconcerting if you enter the place for the first time already under the influence. A favourite of the local British and Irish community, it boasts more than 44 different beers, although the one most requested is of course Guinness.

Reporter

C/Fúcar 6 (429 39 22). Metro Antón Martín/bus 6, 26, 32, 57. **Open** *6pm-1.30am Mon-Thur; 6pm-3.30am Fri-Sun.*
Splendid cocktails and fruit juices are a major attraction in this trendy cocktail-café near the Huertas fun trail, with low-volume cool jazz and occasional photographic exhibitions. At the back is a wonderful, ivy-shrouded garden terrace bar, and ideal spot for a summer drink that's been the centre of a long-running battle with the city authorities because of noise and its opening hours.
Tables Outdoors May-Oct.

Viva Madrid

C/Manuel Fernández y González 7 (no phone). Metro Sol/bus all routes to Puerta del Sol. **Open** *8pm-3am daily.*
One of Madrid's best known bars, a favourite with both visitors and residents. It's a little expensive, but the interior, with its vaulted ceiling, whirling fans, beams, and fabulous painted tiles of Madrid scenes dating back to the 1900s is worth it, and the atmosphere's great too. A classic place to start off the night in Madrid, and especially a crawl around Huertas and Santa Ana.

Tabernas & Traditional Bars

Styles come and go, but Madrid still has many traditional tiled *tabernas*, of a kind seen here when cafés or cocktails had scarcely been invented.

El Anciano Rey de los Vinos

C/de la Paz 4 (559 53 32). Metro Sol/bus all routes to Puerta del Sol. **Open** *10am-4pm, 6-11pm, Mon-Sat; closed Aug.*
Unchanged, and hopefully unchanging. The 'Old Man King of Wines' has a wonderful tiled interior, and excellent tapas to accompany the fine wines the bar is famous for. It's often full in the early evening, with crowds going to the Teatro Albéniz opposite. *See also chapter* **Tapas**.

Angel Sierra

Plaza de Chueca (531 01 26). Metro Chueca/bus 3, 40, 149. **Open** *11am-midnight daily.*
There was a time when Madrid was filled with *tabernas* such as this: tiled walls and a zinc bartop with overflowing sink for washing the glasses, stacked on wooden slats. It's featured in many a film or photo report, and the order to have is vermouth and a splash, with an anchovy and olive tapa.

La Ardosa

C/Colón 13 (531 68 35). Metro Tribunal/bus 3, 40, 149. **Open** *noon-3pm, 6pm-midnight, Mon-Thur; 6pm-1am Fri-Sun.*
A *taberna*, but with strong Irish links and one of the first bars in Madrid to serve Guinness. It also has a fine selection of other imported beers. The décor combines Spanish tiles and Goya with posters from Irish pubs. Check out the list of winners of its Guinness-drinking competitions.

El Cangrejero

C/Amaniel 25 (548 39 35). Metro Noviciado/bus 21, 147. **Open** *noon-11.30pm daily.*
Over 60 years old, the Cangrejero is very much a Madrileño secret, off the tourist trail near the Cuartel Conde Duque. The secret of its success is its superbly kept beer: served in the old style with a thick, frothy head and ice cold, and with mussels as a great accompaniment. No-nonsense formica tables and a comically gruff owner add to the charm.

A Table in the Shade

When the temperature rises, the natural thing to do is to sit and take a drink in the shade. In Madrid, this can become a little uncomfortable on July afternoons when the heat approaches 40°C, but at other times the weather is much more compliant. Madrid's balmy summer nights, especially, are the perfect excuse for lingering at one of the city's open-air *terraza* bars, which are generally open from May to October. Some new-style *terrazas*, particularly along the Castellana, are like open-air clubs, with the music and frenetic mingling one would expect. For these night *terrazas, see chapter* **Nightlife**. If on the other hand you are on the Castellana and feel more in need of a quiet chat amid elegant surroundings, then make for the **Hotel Castellana Inter-Continental** (*see chapter* **Accommodation**), which has a patio open to non-residents with fountain, plants, impeccable service and surprisingly reasonable prices.

The old quarter of the city, from Sol to the Calle Bailén, offers several opportunities for stop-offs during day-time sightseeing or nocturnal rambling. Heading west from a perhaps obligatory, but expensive, stop in the cafés of the **Plaza Mayor** you could take in the **Plaza Conde de Barajas**, a secluded square cut off to traffic and generally overlooked by the crowds nearby. From there, carry on down to Calle Segovia and the **Café del Nuncio** and **Café el Buen Gusto**, tucked amid the walls of the Palacio del Nuncio, one of Madrid's oldest buildings. Nearby too is **Kairos**, an attractive modern bar (*see page 120*). Moving down the hill of Calle Segovia there are some more good outdoor cafés in the Plaza de la Cruz Verde, particularly the **Café del Monaguillo**.

From there, a walk across C/Segovia and up the Calle de la Morería brings you to **Las Vistillas**, a great (and very popular) terrace bar

with views across the Casa de Campo all the way to the Guadarrama. Not far away along C/Bailén is the more expensive terrace of the **Café de Oriente** (*see page 119*), for views of the Palacio Real.

The **Retiro** and the **Casa de Campo** parks both contain many small bars with food, mainly around their lakes. If you have transport or fancy a walk, head deep into the Casa de Campo to Monte Garabitas, the park's highest point, where you'll find a secluded bar open until well after midnight in summer. East of the Casa de Campo at the other end of the cable car line, alongside the Parque del Oeste, there is also the tree-lined **Paseo del Pintor Rosales**, another favourite spot with many *terrazas* open by day and by night.

In the centre, the **Café Gijón**, **El Espejo** (*see page 119*) and **Teide** all have *terrazas* in the Paseo de Recoletos that maintain a dignified old-world charm and tend to attract an older crowd. For a very different, more grungy ambience head for the **Plaza Dos de Mayo** in Malasaña. Note, though, that wherever you are, in the same way that you pay extra if you are served at a table inside a bar, you will pay more again for sitting outside.

Café el Buen Gusto,

C/Nuncio 12 (366 09 06). Metro Tirso de Molina/bus 17, 18, 23, 35. **Open** 6pm-1.30am Mon-Thur; 6pm-2.30am Fri-Sun.

Cafe del Monaguillo

Plaza de la Cruz Verde 3 (541 29 41). Metro La Latina/bus 17, 31, 50, 65. **Open** 6pm-2am daily.

Cafe del Nuncio

C/Segovia 9 (366 08 53). Metro La Latina/bus 17, 31, 50, 65. **Open** 2pm-2.30am daily.

Las Vistillas

C/Bailén 14 (366 35 78). Metro Opera/bus 3, 25, 33, 39, 148. **Open** 3pm-2.30am daily.

Los Caracoles

Plaza Cascorro 18 (no phone). Metro La Latina/bus 17, 23, 31, 35, 50. **Open** 11am-4pm, 7-11pm, Mon, Thur-Sun; 11am-4pm Tue.
The great speciality tapa of this very friendly Rastro bar, hugely busy on Sunday lunchtimes, is snails, cooked in the traditional Madrileño style. To go with them and the other fine tapas available there's delicious ice cold beer, or cheerfully cheap red wine. *See also chapter* **Tapas**.

Casa Antonio

C/Latoneros 10 (366 63 36). Metro Tirso de Molina/bus 17, 18, 23, 35. **Open** noon-11.30pm daily.
It's said that this has been a bar since the building was put up 180 years ago, and the feel is certainly traditional, with

old bullfighting relics around the walls. Despite its closeness to the Plaza Mayor the clientèle is mostly local, with a fair few old boys disputing this or that. Again, there's a zinc bar top, sink, and rapidly-dispensed drinks, including a fine speciality Valdepeñas.

La Dolores

Plaza de Jesús 4 (429 22 43). Metro Antón Martín/bus 9, 10, 14, 27, 34. **Open** 11.30am-4pm, 7pm-midnight, daily.
Dating back to the twenties', the Dolores' is a bustling bar with a clientèle divided between the overspill from nearby Huertas at weekends and office workers who come in after lunch or work during the week. The beer is good and reasonably priced, but the tasty, tempting tapas are expensive.

El 21

*C/Toledo 21 (366 28 59). Metro Sol/bus all routes to
Puerta del Sol.* **Open** noon-4pm, 6pm-midnight, daily.
A perfect stop-off near the Rastro, the 21 and its marble coun-
tertop seem locked in a time warp. No sign identifies the bar
from the street, and most of the time it's filled with elderly
locals, although a young crowd arrives at night and weekends. The owner, a definite candidate for the hostess with
the mostest, receives all with unabashed hospitality.
Renovation work has been carried out lately, and it has often
been closed, but hopefully any changes will be slight.

Los Gatos

*Plaza de Jesús 2 (no phone). Metro Antón Martín/
bus 9, 10, 14, 27, 37, 45.* **Open** 11.30am-4pm, 7pm-
1.30am, daily.
Fortunately overlooked on most tourist trails despite its location at the bottom of Huertas, the veteran Los Gatos is a companion bar to its near-neighbour **La Dolores** (*see above*).
Popular with the bullfighting fraternity (among many others), it retains the feel of a local bar, offering great tapas and
well served, frothy beer at its pleasantly down-at-heel tables.

La Taberna de Antonio Sánchez

*C/Mesón de Paredes 13 (539 78 26). Metro Tirso de
Molina/bus 6, 26, 32, 57.* **Open** noon-4pm, 6pm-
midnight, Mon-Sat; noon-4pm Sun.
Dating back to 1830, and the best-preserved *taberna* in
Madrid. Its owners have all been involved in the world of
bullfighting, and it still holds informal discussions between
critics, *toreros* and *aficionados*. It has also been patronised
by writers and artists, among them the painter Ignacio
Zuloaga, who left a fine portrait of the original Antonio
Sánchez. Despite its fame, however, the place is still very
much a local establishment. The friendly owners are happy
to explain the bar's history, and there are also excellent tapas.
Nearby it had for years a similar competitor, the **Casa
Humanes** (C/Embajadores 80), known as the *taberna* where
during the 1870s King Alfonso XII finished off the night
whenever he slipped out of the palace to look for wild times
among the masses. This great bar has been closed for some
time for renovation, but should reopen at some point, and
may be worth checking out. *See also chapter* **Tapas.**

Tomás

*C/Aguila 21 (no phone). Metro La Latina, Puerta de
Toledo/bus 3, 18, 23, 41, 60, C.* **Open** noon-4pm, 7pm-
midnight, daily.
You will have to take your chances on the opening times at this
little bar, as the elderly owner now opens 'when he feels like
it'. The best bet is around midday or in the early evening.
However, when it's open, locals flock in, and if it is closed,
there's compensation at hand in the surrounding area of La
Latina, one of Madrid's classic working-class *barrios*.

La Venencia

*C/Echegaray 7 (429 73 13). Metro Sevilla, Sol/bus all
routes to Puerta del Sol.* **Open** 7pm-1.30am daily.
Cheerfully down at heel, the Venencia is worthy of a film set,
with peeling sherry posters from no-one knows when,
sherry barrels alongside the bar and walls and ceiling burnished into a rich gold by decades of tobacco smoke. It serves
nothing but sherry, from a dry *fino* to a robust *palo cortado*,
accompanied by olives or *mojama*, dry-cured tuna.

Vinos

*C/Calatrava 21 (no phone). Metro La Latina/Puerta de
Toledo/bus 3, 18, 23, 41, 50, 60, 148, C.* **Open** 10am-
4pm, 7pm-1am, daily.
'Vinos' is what you'll see outside, but this old-time bar is
known locally as Gerardo's. It's the place to be during **La
Paloma** in August (*see chapter* **Madrid by Season**), but
at other times it's still an essential part of this traditional
neighbourhood, serving excellent sausage, ham and cheese.

When you need something cool instead of alcoholic,
Spain also offers a variety of traditional summer
refreshers. Most unusual is *horchata*, a milky drink
made by crushing a root called a *chufa*. It has to be
drunk fresh, from a specialised shop, as it curdles
once made. The same places also offer *granizados*
– crushed ice with fresh lemon, orange or coffee.

Los Alpes

*C/Arcipreste de Hita 6 (no phone). Metro Moncloa/bus 1,
16, 44, 61, C.* **Open** 9am-11.30pm daily.
Tucked away in Moncloa is this unassuming ice cream par-
lour. As well as excellent ices it offers good *horchata* and
granizados, and is the only place left in Madrid selling the
traditional *agua cebada*, made from toasted barley and
spliced with lemon juice, and once drunk throughout Spain.

Bruin

*Paseo del Pintor Rosales 48, (541 59 21). Metro
Argüelles/bus 21, 74.* **Open** 10am-midnight daily.
One of Madrid's oldest and best-known ice-cream parlours,
ideally located near the **Teleférico** cable car (*see chapter*
Sightseeing). More than twenty different flavours, as well
as ice-cream cakes, *granizados* and *horchata*.
Tables outdoors May-Oct.

Café Viena

*C/Luisa Fernanda 23 (no phone). Metro Ventura
Rodríguez/bus 1, 2, 44, 74, 133, C.* **Open** 6pm-1.30am
Mon-Thur, Sun; 6pm-2.30am Fri, Sat.
This velvet-draped, gilt-covered café specialises in Irish and
similar coffees, hot chocolate and cakes. Another feature of
the café is its very popular Monday-night 'Lyrical' sessions,
when singers perform opera and *Zarzuela* favourites.

Embassy

*Paseo de la Castellana 12 (576 00 80). Metro Colón/bus
all routes to Plaza de Colón.* **Open** 9am-1.30am daily.
For a real cup of tea, this 1930s tea-room is the place to come.
Popular with the prosperous inhabitants of Salamanca, it has
dozens of teas, and even little diamond-shaped cucumber
sandwiches. For something stronger, there are also cocktails.

Oliveri

*Paseo de la Castellana 196 (359 77 19). Metro Colón/bus
all routes to Plaza de Colón.* **Open** 10am-1am daily.
When this café first opened in the sixties there were still sheep
grazing at the top end of the Castellana, and it was a favourite
stop-off for ice-creams on Sunday walks. Remarkably, it has
managed to survive while the surrounding spaces have filled
up with apartment and office blocks. With a front garden, it's
popular with locals by night and office workers during the day.
Tables outdoors.

Muñiz

*C/Calatrava 1 (no phone). Metro La Latina/Puerta de
Toledo/bus 3, 18, 23, 41, 148, C.* **Open** 9am-midnight
daily.
A corner bar/café in La Latina with very much a marketplace feel. It offers superb chocolate, good wines, *cava* and
vermouth and well-prepared, rapidly-served hot snacks.

Viena Capellanes

*C/Princesa 73 (543 10 10). Metro Argüelles,
Moncloa/bus 1, 21, 44, 74, 133.* **Open** 9am-1.30pm, 4.30-
9pm, Mon-Sat.
The Viena chain of cake and pastry shops is scattered
throughout Madrid, but this branch has counter and table
service for on-the-spot sampling of their delicious snacks and
coffee. For addresses of other branches, pick up a napkin.

Nightlife

Madrid after dark: it's a world of its own, varied, vibrant and vital.

After a bustling aperitif-and-tapa tour around the bars, a late and leisurely dinner and even a live show, you might think it was time to call it a day. Think again. It's 1am and the city centre streets are teeming. Welcome to Madrid – the night is about to begin and a bewildering array of choices faces the committed reveller.

Madrid's late-night renown was born in the late seventies, as Madrileños rediscovered their traditional flair for having a wild time and losing sleep at the slightest excuse, and the place exploded with energy. The *Movida* took off, marked by all-night fun, 5am traffic jams, a highly original style and an artistic whackiness embodied by Pedro Almodóvar and his coterie.

The quasi-subversive rawness that invigorated the capital in the early 1980s has gone, but Madrid remains a great night city, with highlife and lowlife sometimes just a street corner apart. The street here has an altogether different function compared to its utilitarian role in more northerly cities, especially when the weather is kind. It's the place where people meet up, watch each other, and patrol from bar to bar, *terraza* to *terraza,* with the odd break to grab a cab and move to another district or any places further afield.

WHERE YOU ARE

It is said – not many people know this – that there are more bars between Madrid's two main railway stations, Atocha and Chamartín, than in the whole of Belgium. But, since people naturally need to be able to get round a fair number in the same walk, night bars and other venues tend to be clustered together in fairly distinct areas.

For a loud, laid-back good time, head for the 'sex'n'drugs'n'rock'n'roll' streets of Malasaña. For something less black leather and more breezy, try Huertas, or the very studentish Argüelles. Chueca is in part an overspill from Malasaña, but is also the gay centre of Madrid, and in the north, around Calle Fernando VI, has an atmosphere not unlike Huertas. Salamanca, too, has it's own clutch of ritzy night time haunts, full of the young and very affluent. Madrid, though, is known more for the bizarre than the stylish, and the design bars that are Barcelona's trademark are not much to be seen.

There are also less easily-accessible places where after midnight you can bet on a horse, or combine a dance and a swim, before ending off the night with the traditional hot chocolate and *churros* at dawn.

Madrileños love the night. It's a different world, and whole areas of the city are busier at 4am than they ever are during the day. The number of places is endless, and bars and clubs open, close and come in and out of fashion all the time. Below is a select sample of what you will find as you make your way round.

Other venues that present live music, but where you can nearly always dance after the show, will be found in *chapter* **Music: Rock, Roots & Jazz.** For a list of bars, restaurants, shops and other facilities in each area, *see page 264* **Area Index.**

Night Bars

Agapo
C/Madera 22 (no phone). Metro Noviciado, Tribunal/bus 3, 40, 149, N16-18. **Open** 11pm-5am daily.
The pioneer of garage-punk in Madrid, now often given over to heavy metal. The décor is porn-dayglow-psychedelia, and in the eighties it saw concerts by bands that went on to greater things – or oblivion. Still authentic and hardcore.

The **BageLüs** babes. See page 128.

Avapies

C/Lavapiés 5 (no phone). Metro Lavapiés/bus 6, 26, 27, C, N12. **Open** 6pm-4am daily.
A large venue with a rarely-used stage in Lavapiés. Cuban-salsa parties (admission 500ptas, with rum, lemon and mint *mojito* included) are held on the last Friday of every month. Welcoming and lively, and the *mojitos* are a joy.

Café Soto Mesa

C/San Felipe Neri 4 (548 00 21). Metro Sol/bus all routes to Puerta del Sol. **Open** 9pm-3am Wed-Sun.
An elegant, small city centre venue that attracts a wealthy crowd, and offers (and has the acoustics for) a multiple range of entertainments from cabaret to flamenco and chamber music. Consciously smart, and maybe a bit snooty, it's still pleasant if you can handle the stiff prices (drinks from 1,000ptas). Shows are at 11pm and 1.30am.

La Coquette

C/de las Hileras 14 (no phone). Metro Opera/bus 3, 25, 33, 39, N13, N15. **Open** 8.30pm-2.30am daily.
Known popularly as the Blues Bar, that's just what it is – Madrid's only bar dedicated fully to blues. Swiss-Spanish owner Albert has gathered quite a record collection, and purists won't be disappointed. If you can ignore the snogging students and don't mind the wafts of hash smoke, you'll enjoy the well-intentioned if a bit ersatz Spanish harp wailing. *See also chapter* **Music: Classical & Opera**.

La Fídula

C/Huertas 57 (429 29 47). Metro Antón Martín/bus 6, 26, 32, 57, N8-12. **Open** 7pm-2.30am daily.
Amid a sea of rowdy rock bars stands this island of classical calm. In what was a nineteenth-century grocer's shop, La Fídula presents concerts of chamber music, at 11.30pm and again at 1am at weekends. Be punctual – the doors are closed while the musicians perform, and no talking is allowed during the concert. *See also chapter* **Music: Classical & Opera** *and* **Women's Madrid**.

Kik's Mode

C/Manuela Malasaña 22 (no phone). Metro Bilbao, San Bernardo/bus 21, 147, 149, N19. **Open** 9pm-4am daily.
A down-at-heel, cheerful reggae bar – the only one in Madrid –, popular with the African community and with young kids out for a wild time. A bit of a pick-up joint, but great music.

King Creole

C/San Vicente Ferrer 7 (no phone). Metro Tribunal/bus 3, 40, 149, N19. **Open** 8pm-3am daily.
American-decorated rock 'n' roll bar, which livens up at weekends when the rockabillies come in from the outer suburbs, all quiffs and sideburns or B-52-style lacquered hair and flowing dresses. When the music is good, it's fantastic – pure fifties.

Libertad 8

C/Libertad 8 (532 11 50). Metro Chueca/bus 3, 40, 149, N1, N19, N20. **Open** 5pm-2am daily.
A unique, homely tavern-style bar in a 120-year-old building with a great atmosphere. The slightly musty air enhances its intimate, leisurely feel, which heats up during the nightly 11.30pm cabaret or music show. In July and August things get too hot, although the ceiling fans help a little.

Mala Fama

C/del Barco 17 (no phone). Metro Gran Vía/bus all routes to Gran Vía. **Open** 11pm-3am daily.
A deeply shabby bikers' bar in the grottiest end of Malasaña with great rock'n'roll and a grizzled clientèle who sometimes need to be handled with care. The line of Harleys outside make it easy to find.

Montera 33

C/Montera 33 (523 03 61). Metro Gran Vía, Sol/bus all routes to Puerta del Sol. **Open** 11.30pm-5am Wed-Sat.
Walk down the stairs then through a series of what look like brick railway arches, and you're in one of Madrid's currently most fashionable disco bars. What was until 1993 the site of the Art Business Centre – with an exhibition space, cock-

Night-time Habits

Most good late-night places don't get going until around midnight, which leaves plenty of time for dinner or to meet up with people in tapas bars and cafés. Unless you make your way to one of the bigger venues on the edge of the city, you'll find that the liveliest nightlife areas – Huertas, Malasaña, Chueca, the big clubs around Calle Arenal – can easily be reached one from the other on foot. And this is what people do, because exploring and checking out several places in one night is a central part of the whole show. Madrileños are always terrified they might be missing a better bar up the road.

Madrid has much more of a bar than a club culture. You can dance more or less anywhere, but many nightspots are what are called *disco-bars*, smallish bars with a smaller dance floor usually at the back. They don't charge admission, but make it up on the drinks prices. A beer may cost from 500 to 1,000+ptas, and many punters go for *combinados*, spirit mixes such as a *gintonic* or a *cuba libre* (rum and coke), since they cost the same. Note that as there's no fixed measure in Spain most barmen will give you at least a half-glass full of spirit.

Around 2am is when the crowds begin to move on to larger, more club- or disco-like venues, although even then many will go to a few rather than settling in one. At busy times they usually do charge admission, commonly around 1,500ptas, and usually including a con-

sumición of one drink. Away from the largest venues, though, pricing policy is very inconsistent; a place may still be free or have different prices at different times, and, as everywhere, a good many people always blag their way in anyway. You never know your luck.

On weekend nights the movement on the main drags doesn't really start to thin out until after 4am. Closing times have been creeping earlier, however. The conservative city council, in power since 1991, takes a dim view of street life and has been steadily tightening the restrictions on bars. Many places that once closed at 5am now do so two hours earlier. Something else that has changed is the attitude to drugs. Since the eighties, hash smoking in particular had virtually been tolerated in Spain, but the legal position has now been altered once more and all public consumption of banned drugs is again illegal. In their own interests bar owners are often concerned to see that nobody contravenes this law on their premises.

As regards closing times, though, it's a hard one for the authorities to break long-established habits. At 5 or 6am is when those who are staying the course make for the 'After Hours' venues, often the most bouncing of the lot. Again, there are fewer than there once were, but still enough to provide a port in the storm. After that, the thing to do is to head for breakfast, for by that time there are plenty of cafés opening up for the day.

---

tail bar and audiovisual zone – is now a slightly tacky, cavernous dive in a very tacky street lined by prostitutes. It's very popular with gays, but open to all. It also has kudos, and draws serious dancers. *See chapter* **Gay Madrid**.

Torito

C/Pelayo 4 (532 77 99). Metro Chueca/bus 3, 40, 149, N1, N19, N20. **Open** 10pm-5am daily.
A favourite among non-Spaniards even though, or because, it plays only Spanish music, 90% of it flamenco. Wonderfully tacky, its walls cluttered with a bizarre mix of cuttings in dazzling montages that'll keep your eyes busy after a few drinks.

La Via Lactea

C/Velarde 18 (446 75 81). Metro Tribunal/bus 3, 40, 149, N19. **Open** 8pm-3am daily.
The doyen of Madrid's rock bars (established 1979), Malasaña's 'Milky Way' is lined with posters, cuttings and photographs covering 15 years of the history of rock. Of course, with hundreds of competitors now within a few minutes' walk, it's not what it was, but it was the first.

Villa Rosa

Plaza de Santa Ana 15 (521 36 89). Metro Sol/bus all routes to Puerta del Sol. **Open** 10pm-5am daily.
Years ago this venue right on the Plaza Santa Ana was a renowned flamenco club. Nowadays it's a very popular late

night dance bar, but it still has an exquisite arabesque tiled interior that's a real touch of old Seville – an Andaluz look for one of the most regularly-packed places in the Huertas area, attracting a fairly studentish crowd.

Clubs, Discos, Latin Music

For notes on prices, *see above* **Night-time Habits**.

Aire

C/Cea Bermúdez 8. (553 08 25). Metro Ríos Rosas, Quevedo/bus 2, 3, 12, 37, N19. **Open** 10pm-5am Thur-Sun. **Admission** *average* 1,500ptas incl. one drink.
A large two-level disco near the student heartland of Argüelles, with several bars and a touch of class. It's been around for a while, but is still a fun place that attracts some very pretty punters.

Aqualung

Paseo de la Ermita del Santo 40-48 (470 23 62). Metro Puerto de Toledo, then bus 17 or bus 25, 50, N13. **Open** 11pm-3am Mon-Thur; 11.30pm-5.30am Fri-Sun. **Admission** (except concerts) 800ptas incl. one drink.
Behind the tacky, brightly-lit pizza and hamburger stalls at the entrance to this indoor waterpark and leisure centre, the Aqualung concert hall-cum-disco is a delight. On different levels with several bars, the 2,000-capacity venue has the best

Terraza Society

During the day and early evening, *terrazas* are just regular pavement cafes. In the last few years, however, some *terrazas* have taken on a whole new nocturnal dimension. In the face of Madrid's obvious lack of a beachfront along which to take the air, they have transmogrified into its equivalent of beach bars and open-air discos, in the middle of the city and amid the traffic. Lately, some of those in the know claim that night *terrazas* have been taken over by a smart but dull bunch of wannabe-trendies, replacing the hip crowd that first started them up. The city council hate them too, because of noise and traffic problems, and fine them regularly for staying open too late (which is why many last just one season).

Even so, others start up again each summer, and there are always some that are acceptably groovy. From June onwards Madrid's indoor venues quieten down, and nightlife moves out still more onto the street. It's on balmy nights in July, after days of 40° C heat, that the *terrazas* really come into their own.

The magnet for *terraza*-lizards is the Castellana, which despite city hall crackdowns still boasts 15 to 20 *terrazas* between Atocha and the Plaza de Lima. The biggest concentration is around the junction with Calle Juan Bravo. Another *terraza* zone is the Paseo del Pintor Rosales, near the Parque del Oeste. But trendy *terrazas* come and go – every summer there are new ones in different parts of the city, while old favourites have disappeared.

Bavaro Beach

Paseo del Prado, next to Jardín Botánico (no phone). Metro Atocha/bus all routes to Atocha.
Open *May-Oct* 10am-3am daily.
The southern-most *terraza*, this is a sedate watering hole for Prado tourists in the day, but welcomes a much noisier crowd, with a fair few rich kids, after dark. It was set up by Quique, a guitarist from eighties' Madrid rock band Gabinete Caligari. Crazy party night is Wednesday.

Bolero

Paseo de la Castellana 33 (no phone). Metro Rubén Darío/bus 5, 14, 27, 45, 150, N1, N20. **Open** *May-Oct* 7pm-3am Mon-Fri; 7pm-4am Sat, Sun.
Perhaps the wildest of the bunch, with what seems like a party every other night. It's large and noisy, and when the so-called PR staff haven't arranged a record launch or a fashion show, then it's a *Miss Castellana* 'beauty' contest with drag queens more than welcome to enter.

Boulevard

Paseo de la Castellana 37 (435 54 32). Metro Rubén Darío/bus 5, 14, 27, 45, 150, N1, N20.
Open *May-Oct* noon-3am daily.
Close to the Bolero and even brasher – the kiosk-bar has a neon-lit triangular top. The ambience is true to the eighties' style of non-stop frivolous fun, especially on party night (Thursday). Attractions include disco music as loud as they can get away with, and lucky-number draws with prizes.

Terraza Bardem Torero

Jardines del Cabo Noval, Plaza de Oriente (no phone). Metro Opera/bus 25, 33, 39, 148, N15-18.
Open *May-Oct* noon-3am daily.
In a corner of the Plaza de Oriente facing the Palacio Real, this is further from the traffic than most *terrazas*. Surrounded by statues and trees, and with the palace looming 100 yards away, it makes for an agreeable setting. It was set up by actor Javier Bardem, pouting star of sex-soaked Bigas Luna movies such as *Golden Balls*, his director brother Carlos and the club **Torero** (*see p130*). 'Crazy parties' are put on from time to time, as in all the rest.

---

acoustics in town, and is now Madrid's leading mid-size live music venue. At other times there's still a good mix of music, and, when it get's too hot, you can take advantage of the pool. *See also chapter* **Music: Rock, Roots & Jazz**.

Archy

C/Marqués de Riscal 11 (308 31 62). Metro Rubén Darío/bus 5, 7, 27, 45, 150, N1, N20. **Open** 1pm-5am daily. **Admission** 900-1,200ptas incl. one drink. *Restaurant* **Open** 1pm-2.30am daily. **Average** 3,500ptas. **Credit** AmEx, MC, V.
A club/restaurant ultra-trendy with the media and fashion crowd in the eighties, and still home to a cool, international bunch. The small basement disco is pretty plain, but the post-modernish bars and restaurant upstairs have more character.

BageLüs

C/Maria de Molina 25 (561 61 00). Metro Avenida de América/bus 9, 12, 16, N1, N3, N4.
Open 24-hours daily. **Admission** normally free.
BageLüs is Spain's first and only 24-hour cultural and leisure space, opened in 1994 in an elegant former mansion first built in 1908. Options include a restaurant, bars, a *terraza* in summer, a record and bookshop and a traditional café, and there are plans to add a limousine hire service and an air-ticket sales point. It also host cabaret and a multi-varied programme of live music (classical, jazz, salsa flamenco, pop), on the third floor. It's maybe a bit too bright and breezy for its sophisticated intentions, but attracts both rich kids and their elders in large numbers.

Bocaccio

*C/Marqués de la Ensenada 16 (319 93 29). Metro
Colón/bus all routes to Plaza Colón.* **Open** 10.30pm-
4.30am Mon-Fri, Sun; 10.30pm-noon Sat.
Admission 1,000-2,000ptas incl. one drink.
A plush nightclub much frequented by older media glitterati,
young bankers and the like, with a crew of bouncers to make
sure that no undesirables enter. It's famous for its after-hours
sessions on Saturday nights.

Calentito

*C/Jacometrezo 15 (547 00 81). Metro Callao, Santo
Domingo/bus all routes to Plazo de Callao.* **Open** 8pm-
4am daily. **Admission** normally free.
Calentito offers salsa with both humour and sensuality.
Androgynous thinly-clad types dance on the bar, avoiding
the hanging plastic limbs that serve as decoration, and
attracting a more individual class of voyeur. The place
becomes one complete dance floor, and is excellent until the
sheer volume of people proves overwhelming.

Clamores

*C/Albuquerque 14 (445 79 38). Metro Bilbao,
Quevedo/bus 3, 37, 149, N19.* **Open** 8.30pm-3am daily.
Admission normally free.
This premier jazz club has spread its wings to include odd
nights of tango dancing and even karaoke. The largest jazz
stage in the city ensures a good-natured, knowledgeable jazz
crowd. Two other features – clients play ludo (yes, ludo) in the
early evening, and it claims to have Madrid's biggest selection of Cava. *See also chapter* **Music: Rock, Roots & Jazz.**

Fuego Fuego

*C/Costanilla de los Desamparados 21 (429 37 59). Metro
Antón Martin/bus 6, 26, 32, 57, N8-12.* **Open** 7pm-
3.30am Mon-Thur; 7pm-5am Fri-Sun.
Admission normally free.
A new, modest Caribbean dance club, opened in mid-1994,
where musical styles from the Dominican Republic such as
merengue, *bachata* and *perico ripiao* are the norm. A fine,
friendly place with potential, and one of the meeting places
for Madrid's Spanish-Caribbean population.

Joy Eslava

*C/Arenal 11 (366 37 33). Metro Opera, Sol/bus all routes
to Puerta del Sol.* **Open** 11pm-5.30am Mon-Thur; 7pm-
5am Fri-Sun. **Admission** 1,500ptas Mon-Thur, Sun;
2,000ptas Fri, Sat.
Now this *is* a disco. A star of the genre in Madrid, opened in
1981 in an 1850s theatre, and dead plush, with velvet everywhere. Trendy it is not, but swarms of smart, good-looking
fun-seekers with lots of gold jewellery keep it as popular as
ever. It keeps up with the times too – computerised laser
lights and the latest club sounds – and the original theatre
shell adds charm.

Keeper

*C/Juan Bravo 21 (562 23 79). Metro Núñez de
Balboa/bus 1, 9, 19, 51, 74.* **Open** 7pm-3am Mon-Fri,
Sun; 7pm-6am Sat. **Admission** *average* 1,500ptas incl.
one drink.
A three-floor multi-space with plenty of bars that's one of
the centrepieces of the Salamanca night-time round, usually
full of well-scrubbed young things with perfect skins. It also
sometimes hosts fairly big-name rock and pop concerts.
Along the same street there are plenty more similarly preppy
nightspots, such as the giant **Catedral** at number 35.

Morocco

*C/Marqués de Leganés 7 (531 31 77). Metro Callao,
Santo Domingo/bus all routes to Plaza de Callao.* **Open**
11pm-4am daily. **Admission** normally free.
Owned by *Movida*-megastar Olvido Alaska (*see below* **Stella**),
this stylishly tacky disco bar with mock leopardskin seats had

Youth takes to the streets.

a first burst at the height of fashion when opened in 1992. It's
gone off the boil a bit since, and the music could be much better. It sometimes hosts cool invite-only concerts by international acts launching new records in Spain, if you can get in.

Nairobi

*C/San Vicente Ferrer 17 (no phone). Metro Tribunal/bus
3, 40, 149, N19.* **Open** 11pm-5am daily.
Admission normally free.
Chic *and* kitsch. The African décor includes old Tarzan film
posters, tribal shields and spears. That's just on the walls,
and under the glass surface of the bar there's a gold mine of
maps, teeth, and an assortment of African junk. The music
is acid house, hip hop and acid jazz. One of its original owners was Almodóvar-actress Rossy de Palma, so initial success in the fashionability stakes was assured. It's still a
pretty special place, and fine for dancing if you can find
enough space to strut your stuff.

Pachá

*C/Barceló 11 (446 01 37). Metro Tribunal/bus 3, 40,
149, N19.* **Open** 10pm-5.30am Wed-Sun.
Admission 1,500ptas.
Possibly Madrid's classiest disco, forming in its different
way a double act with Joy Eslava as fixed points on the nocturnal round. A 1994 refurbishment – right down to the staff
and music policy – has kept it at the centre of attention, and
it continues to attract a crowd that's both large and fashionable. Reggae, soul and funk have replaced the banal
bakalao rave music that threatened the place's style. The
expensive cars outside give an idea of the clientèle. *See also
chapter* **Music: Rock, Roots & Jazz.**

Palacio de Gaviria

*C/Arenal 9 (526 60 69). Metro Sol/bus all routes to
Puerta del Sol.* **Open** 10pm-3am Mon-Thur; 10pm-5am
Fri-Sun. **Admission** 1,000ptas Mon-Thur, Sun;
1,500ptas Fri, Sat.
Something really different. An exquisite 1851 palace with
most of its grand fittings and ornate marble statues intact,
and a nightspot since 1991. At the top of the imposing staircase entrance there are 12 rambling rooms-cum-halls, most
with their own bars. It's a fantastic space, although the
divinely decadent look is sometimes let down by banal, run-
of-the-mill music. As well as being a relaxing drinking spot
it also hosts other things such as *bailes de salón* (pasadobles,
tangos, maybe even waltzes), Thursday to Saturday, and
cabaret on other nights.

Revólver Club

*C/Galileo 26 (448 01 43). Metro Argüelles, Quevedo/bus
16, 61, N18.* **Open** 10pm-5am Tue-Thur; midnight-7am
Fri-Sun. **Admission** 1,000-2,000ptas.
Leather-jacketed folk swarm around this large and murky
space. It has been the premier venue for hardcore in all its
forms, its dark walls brightened by dayglow scenes of sex

*The **Hipódromo** by night. See page 132.*

and urban crisis, but lately the music has moved on to include reggae, tex-mex, blues, zydeco – and flamenco, on Monday nights. There are live gigs most nights, and club sessions afterwards. The air-conditioning is lousy. *See also* chapters **Music: Rock, Roots & Jazz** *and* **Flamenco**.

Salsipuedes

C/Puebla 6 (522 84 17). Metro Gran Vía/bus all routes to Gran Vía. **Open** 11pm-6am daily.
Admission 1,000ptas incl. one drink.
Aka *El Palacio de la Salsa*, this great two-storey venue pioneered salsa in Madrid. There are live bands on some nights, but the place is heaving with cute salsa dancers at all hours.

Stella

C/Arlabán 7 (531 01 92).Metro Sevilla, Sol/bus all routes to Puerta del Sol. **Open** midnight-7am Tue-Sun.
Admission *average* 1,000ptas Tue-Thur, Sun;
1,000ptas Fri, Sat; incl. one drink.
One of the 'places to go' for a good while, and still for many the best dance club in town. Not tacky, not ritzy and not too trendy, just good house music (on Saturdays) and dancing. On other nights different musics are offered. Like **Morocco** (*see above*) it's owned by Olvido Alaska, erstwhile leader of Spain's number-1 punk combo Alaska y los Pegamoides, and so a godmother of the *Movida*. Hence it's a noted celebrity hang out. Also distinctive is the antique but still-functioning bowling alley on the bottom floor.

Teatriz

C/Hermosilla 15 (577 53 79). Metro Serrano/bus all routes to Plaza Colón.
Bar Open 9pm-3am daily. **Admission** normally free.
Restaurant Lunch served 1.30-4pm, **dinner served** 9pm-1am, daily. **Average** 4,000ptas. **Credit** AmEx, DC, V.
Madrid's only real design bar, one of the slickest joints in town, this Philippe Starck-designed former theatre reopened in 1990 is an aesthete's delight. Ultra-cool, if not positively cold. Each of three bars has a different style, and the restaurant is where the stalls once were, in front of the stage. The toilets are twenty-first century, and the dance floor – a tiny room with padded walls – must be the smallest in Madrid.

Teatro Kapital

C/Atocha 125 (420 29 06). Metro Atocha/bus all routes to Atocha. **Open** midnight-5am Wed-Sat.
Admission 2,500ptas.
A long-established shabby disco was converted in 1994 at vast expense into a wacky, seven-floor multi-space that now boasts the largest dance floor in central Madrid. It also has several different bars, all fitted out in suitably bizarre and decadent fashion, and immediately became a first-choice hang out for the city's most crucial night-owls. When the weather warms up there's an open *terraza* on the roof, too.

Torero

C/de la Cruz 26 (429 89 69). Metro Sevilla, Sol/bus all routes to Puerta del Sol. **Open** 10pm-6am daily.
Admission 1,200ptas incl one drink.
One of the more bouncing and imaginative disco bars, especially in the downstairs space. The mainstreamish music can be a bit insipid, but it still gets packed with good-looking boys and girls.

Windsor Gran Via

Plaza de Callao 4 (531 01 32). Metro Callao/bus all routes to Plaza de Callao. **Open** 7.15pm-6am Tue-Sun.
Admission 1,000ptas incl. one drink.
Old-style, tacky disco fun. It always attracts plenty of out-of-towners impressed by its gigantic advertising hoardings and who don't know where else to go, and for a high old time it's as good as anywhere. The music is naturally Top 40 fodder.

After Hours

Max

C/Aduana 21 (522 98 25). Metro Gran Vía, Sol/bus all routes to Puerta del Sol. **Open** 5am-10am Fri-Sun.
Admission *average* 2,000ptas incl one drink.
A fairly classy early-morning fun-spot. Admire the fake Roman statues, whose physiques are not unlike those of the doormen. Kids with a chemical bent come here to expend remaining energies. The music's nothing special, but the company is a curious mixture of the sleazy and the select.

Space of Sound

Estación de Chamartín (733 35 05). Metro Chamartín/bus 5, N20. **Open** 6am-noon Sat, Sun, public holidays. **Admission** 1,000ptas incl one drink.
A thumping club in the shopping centre on top of Chamartín station that as the sun comes up will keep serious clubbers going with a breakfast of mainly trance sounds.

Warhol's Club

C/Luchana 20 (593 04 19). Metro Bilbao/bus 3, 37, 40, 147, N19. **Open** 5am-10am Mon-Sat; 5am-noon Sun.
Admission *average* 1,200ptas incl. one drink.
A large bar that opens after most places have closed, and soon gets crowded. Music and drinking until so late it's early.

Xenon

Plaza de Callao 3 (531 97 94/521 25 06). Metro Callao/bus all routes to Plaza de Callao. **Open** 11pm-5am Thur; 6-10.30pm, midnight-7am, Fri-Sun.
Admission 1,500ptas.
The feathers and sequins at this former dance hall have given way to house, trance, garage and most other forms of underground music. The new owners want to bring back some of the eighties' freshness to Madrid, and so have provided an after-hours dance haven in the heart of the city, complete with sofas on the first floor.

Dance Halls

As a change from the usual grind, you can have a go at dancing cheek-to-cheek, including traditional Spanish favourites like the pasodoble, an Argentinian tango, or an athletic rumba. In some places, too, there'll be a live band. There aren't that many of Madrid's truly traditional dance halls left today, but in a vaguely decadent way this sort of dancing has long been trendy in Madrid, and several louche and entirely modern venues – among them **Clamores**, **Palacio de Gaviria**, **Swing** – stage what are called *bailes de salón*, in addition to

Macrodiscos & Bakalao

Bakalao – from, naturally enough, *bacalao*, salt cod – was the name given to Spain's own techno-rave scene when it started up in about 1992. Its big centre was around Valencia, and for a while the thing to do in Madrid was to drive off on a Friday night on the *ruta del bakalao*, the bakalao route, going from club to club all the way to Valencia and keeping going right up until the return to Madrid on Monday. This ecstasy- or booze-fuelled endurance test won it international fame, but also led to horror stories in the Spanish media and an eventual police crackdown, above all when roads began to be spattered with smashed cars driven by kids whose energy had failed them. As an alternative to the whole trip, there was also a mini-*bakalao* route around Madrid, based in a few city-centre venues and huge *macrodiscos* around the outskirts.

During 1994, *bakalao* fell from fashion in most city clubs. It and successor-trance sounds are still popular with the kids, though, and ravers who want to find it should head out to the city's

fringes, to giant disco-complexes where the hammer rhythms can't disturb anybody.

Costa Polvoranca

Avda Polvoranca, Polígono Industrial Urtinza, Alcorcón (643 27 20). Bus 513 from Estacion del Norte. **Open** approx 10pm-6am daily.
Easily the largest single concentration of discos and disco bars in the Madrid region, about 10 miles south-west of the city in the sixties suburb of Alcorcón. It was a light industrial estate, and the buildings are of the style you might expect. Up to 15,000 people gather here at weekends in search of fun. There are so many clubs – Sky, Tam-tam, Voltereta, La Cupula, Phobia and more – the list could be endless. Some DJs play bakalao, some heavy metal, and some just plain disco

Kilómetro Doce

Parque de Andalucia, Carretera de Burgos (N-I) km 12, Alcobendas (435 68 85). Bus 151, 152, 153, 154 from Plaza de Castilla. **Open** approx 9pm-6am daily.
Another open space in the outskirts, this time a few miles north in Alcobendas. A bit more comfy than the Polvoranca, with attractions that include discos, bars, an indoor lake, *terrazas*, a restaurant and, of course, corners for *bakalao*.

---

those listed below. Spanish people seem to learn their basic dance steps almost from birth, but there's no need to be an expert to take the floor.

A real fad of a few years ago was the vogue for dancing Andaluz *sevillanas*. There are still several *salas rocieras* around the city where you can try your feet at these and other southern styles. For these venues, *see chapter* **Dance**.

But
C/Barceló 11 (448 06 98). Metro Bilbao, Tribunal/bus 3, 40, 149, N19. **Open** 10pm-5am Tue-Sat; 7pm-3am Sun.
Admission 1,000ptas Tue-Fri, Sun; 1,200ptas Sat.
Madrid's only full-time dance hall, even though it doesn't have a live band. The pasodoble, tango, foxtrot, waltz, cha-cha-cha, mambo and merengue are all danced with flair and enthusiasm, and there are classes for beginners. It's right above **Pachá** (*see above*).

Long Play Boite
Plaza Vázquez de Mella 2 (531 01 11). Metro Gran Vía, Chueca/bus 3, 40, 149, N1, N19, N20. **Open** *dance hall* 11pm-5.30am Tue-Sun; *disco* midnight-9am daily.
Admission 1,000ptas incl. one drink.
Two places in one. Downstairs there's a disco that opens late and hots up after-hours. Upstairs is a genuine 1950s dance hall, small and intimate, offering only Hispanic dance music – pasodoble, rumba, sevillanas, salsa.

Tiber
C/Covarrubias 42 (446 00 36). Metro Alonso Martínez/bus 3, 7, 21, N19. **Open** 6-10.30pm Mon-Thur, Sat, Sun; 6pm-5am Fri. **Admission** 300ptas.
Old-fashioned in every sense, right down to the hours. As in days of yore an orchestra keeps the faithful happy, there are lucky-draw prizes and gentlemen even get an invitation to bring along a 'señorita' free the next time.

Cabaret & Cuplé

Undergoing a slight renaissance in Madrid recently has been cabaret, much of it comedy or magic, but also featuring *cuplé*, the classic Madrileño revue-style songs from before the Civil War.

Berlin Cabaret
Costanilla de San Pedro 11 (366 20 34). Metro La Latina/bus 3, 17, 31, 50, 65, N13, N14. **Open** 11pm-3am Mon-Thur; 11pm-4am Fri-Sun.
Admission normally free.
Traditional cabaret and modern comedy on a stage which is actually the access to an upper level via a spiral staircase. Faded red velvet seating accommodates the young, trendy professionals who can afford the expensive drinks.

Café del Foro
C/San Andres 38 (445 37 52). Metro Bilbao, Tribunal/bus 40, 147, 149, N19. **Open** 7pm-2am daily.
Admission normally free.
A veteran on the Malasaña scene, the Foro draws a fairly literary and student clientèle for its nightly shows featuring music and cabaret, followed by live salsa and merengue. It's a pretty bar, with an imitation star-lit sky above the stage area. *See also chapter* **Music: Rock Roots & Jazz**.

Candilejas
C/Bailen 16 (365 55 45). Metro La Latina, Puerta de Toledo/bus 3, 148, N13, N14. **Open** 7pm-3am Mon-Thur, 7pm-4am Fri-Sun. **Admission** 400ptas Thur, Sun; 600ptas Fri, Sat.
A marvellous bar based around old film posters and musical soundtracks – Candilejas is the Spanish title for Chaplin's film *Limelight*. From Thursday to Sunday, owners Ninetto and Absurdino perform funny, alternative-ish cabaret around midnight.

China Club

*C/Amor de Dios 13 (429 74 24). Metro Antón
Martín/bus 6, 26, 32, 57, N8-12.* **Open** 10.30pm-3am
daily. **Admission** *average* 1,000ptas incl one drink.
Cabaret acts start at 12.30am and usually tend to the outrageous, with drag shows a favourite. The place itself is distinctively post-modern – a dark, phosphorescent entrance
leads down a passage into the large, dimly-lit main area with
pipes and tubes running around the walls. After the show,
there's dancing to a variety of sounds.

Noches de Cuplé

*C/de la Palma 51 (532 71 15/657 03 94). Metro
Noviciado/bus 147, N19.* **Open** 9pm-3am Mon, Tue,
Thur-Sat. **Admission** *dinner & show* 5,300ptas; *drink &
show* 2,250ptas. **Credit** AmEx, V.
The queen of Madrid's old-time cabaret clubs. Olga Ramos,
now close to 80, has been reigning here for decades. Her performances of *cuplés* and *chotis* have inspired many younger
artists. The shows start at 11.15pm, or 11.45pm at weekends.

No se lo digas a nadie

*C/Ventura de la Vega 11 (429 75 25). Metro Sevilla,
Sol/bus all routes to Puerta del Sol.* **Open** 9pm-3am daily.
A feminist-run bar which a while ago abandoned its women-
only policy. Irreverent cabaret can be seen some nights, and
in the same downstairs space there's also dancing before and
after. Above, there's a bar and a feminist bookshop in a
beautiful ex-pharmacy. *See also chapter* **Women's Madrid**.

Making a Splash

When you're working up a sweat, it's only natural
to want to jump in a pool, and this too you can do
when some of Madrid's waterparks (*see chapter*
Children) reopen for the night. You can also try
twisting by the pool at **Aqualung** (*see above*).

Acuático de San Fernando de Henares

*Carretera de Barcelona (N-II) km15.5 (673 10 13). Bus
Continental Auto 281, 282, 284, 285 from Avda de
América/train Cercanías line C-2, C-7 to San Fernando.*
Open *June-Sept* 11pm-8am daily. **Admission** 1,100ptas
Mon-Fri; 1,500ptas Fri-Sun.
Make your way out to San Fernando and you'll find *terrazas,*
restaurants, live Spanish pop bands, giant discos and water
slides to boot, and all of them going all night.

Lagosur

*Autovía Madrid-Toledo (N401) km9 (686 57 11). Metro
Oporto, then bus 485/train Cercanías line C-5 to
Zarzaquemada.* **Open** *June-Sept* 11pm-8am daily.
Admission 950ptas Mon-Fri; 1,100ptas Sat, Sun.
Water, water everywhere. Amid the pools – even the wave
pool becomes an aqua disco at 4am – there are 19 bars, six
dance floors, the **Universal Sur** rock venue (*see chapter*
Music: Rock, Roots & Jazz) and *terrazas,* offering music
from karaoke to bakalao. Lagosur is about seven miles south
of the city, and has capacity for 20,000 people.

A Night at the Races

Hipódromo de la Zarzuela

*Carretera de La Coruña (N-VI) km7.8 (357 14 10). Free
bus service from Moncloa 10.30pm-1am, otherwise bus
601, 656, 657, 658, N61 from Moncloa/by car Carretera
de La Coruña to El Pardo.* **Open** *July-Sept* 6pm-3am
Fri, Sat. **Admission** 500ptas;
concert nights (average) 2,000ptas.
A spectacular and outrageous institution. From the end of
June to mid-September Madrid's racecourse becomes a major
night attraction. Races takes place between 10.30pm and

2am on Saturdays, and the track can be seen from any of the
terrazas and restaurants that fill the huge site. The crowd
that attends are multi-varied and of all ages, and you can of
course bet, at the official windows, although the racing is not
taken very seriously. Other attractions include bunjee-jump-
ing from a 60m-crane, archery, a bowling alley, bumper
bikes, virtual reality shows, video games and still more
discos and drinking areas. Live bands perform on Fridays,
and a house salsa group plays on Saturdays. For more regular racing, *see chapter* **Sport & Fitness**.

Casino

Casino Gran Madrid

*Carretera de La Coruña (N-VI) km28.3, Torrelodones
(856 11 00). Free bus from Plaza de España, Plaza Colón
4.30-11.30pm/by car Carretera de La Coruña to Las
Matas exit.* **Open** 5pm-4am Mon-Thur; 5pm-5am Fri, Sat,
public holidays. **Admission** 500ptas.
Madrid's only casino is a gambling oasis amid pine trees some
18 miles north-west of the city. It has two gaming rooms, as
well as a restaurant, four bars, a disco, and a convention hall.
To get in, you must be over 18 and show your passport. Men
must wear a jacket, and jeans and trainers are not allowed.

Late & Early Eating

As well as the places listed here, a favourite place
for late-night eating is the **Palacio de Anglona**,
open till 3am (*see chapter* **Restaurants**). More
bland but also handy are the many branches of
Bob's and **Vip's** multi-purpose store-restaurants,
which close at 3.30am (*see chapter* **Shopping**).

Cambalache

*C/San Lorenzo 5 (310 07 01). Metro Tribunal/bus 3, 40,
149, N19.* **Open** 8.30pm-5am.
Average 2,500ptas. **Credit** V.
Between Malasaña and Chueca, Cambalache offers
Argentinian food and tango dancing too from 9pm until 5am.
A little piece of Buenos Aires in Madrid.

La Carreta

*C/Barbieri 10 (532 70 42). Metro Chueca/bus 3, 40, 149,
N1, N19, N20.* **Open** 8.30pm-5am daily.
Average 3,500ptas. **Credit** AmEx, V.
One of many Argentine restaurants, but here the floor show
is more extensive. A dance floor allows customers to join the
tango fun, and the theme is gaucho, with wagon wheels, sad-
dles, riding boots and spurs. The restaurant is good, but if
you don't eat you pay 1,500ptas admission, with drink. The
show is from midnight to 4am, Thursday to Saturday.

Chocolatería San Ginés

*Pasadizo de San Ginés 5 (265 65 46). Metro Sol/bus all
routes to Puerta del Sol.* **Open** *Oct-May* 7pm-7am Tue-
Sun; *June-Sept* 10pm-7am Tue-Sun.
Bleary-eyed revellers have been rounding off the night with
churros – deep-fried sticks of sweet batter – dunked in thick
hot chocolate ever since it opened in 1894. Plenty of early-
morning cafés serve *churros y chocolate,* but San Ginés is the
last one dedicated to the custom. It's just off C/Arenal, behind
the **Joy Eslava**. It also serves alcohol all night, but between
4am and 7am the packed crowds will be busy a-dunking.

La Farfalla

*C/Santa María 17 (429 89 53). Metro Antón Martín/bus
6, 26, 32, 57, N8-12.* **Meals served** 8.30pm-6am daily.
Average 2,500ptas. **Credit** AmEx, V.
Less than palatial, this Argentine-run late-night restaurant
satisfies the munching needs of revellers in the Huertas bar
area. Good, basic, cheap, and with a boisterous atmosphere.

Shops & Services

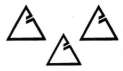

SHOPPING

IMPORTANT

When you make your purchases you pay a tax already included in the price.

By law you are entitled to claim back this tax, thus making your shopping more profitable. This applies only for residents outside the European Union.

In Madrid you will find a great number of quality shops offering the "Tax-free system".

TAX FREE
FOR TOURISTS
Europe Tax-free Shopping

In the shop you must ask the shop assistant for a "Tax-free cheque" which shows your tax refund amount.

When leaving, present your "tax-free cheque" at Banco Exterior at the airport and receive your refund in cash.

REMEMBER: DON'T LEAVE YOUR MONEY BEHIND!

Shopping

The shops and stalls of Madrid cover the gamut from high-fashion design outlets through great food stores and markets to the rambling bazaar of the Rastro.

In the late eighties Madrid enjoyed a massive consumer boom. This accelerated the arrival of some major changes with regard to traditional Spanish shopping habits. Today, more people than ever before shop at the hypermarkets around the M30 ring road. The influence of these giant retailers has been greatly resented by traditional small shopkeepers, who fear they will simply be swept aside.

Until quite recently a great many people did their food shopping almost daily, and mainly at small local shops and markets. For clothes, they went to the city centre. These local traders are now facing unprecedented competition. Nevertheless, central Madrid at least will surely retain its innumerable small, independent shops for a good while to come, for they cover an enormous and idiosyncratic range that the megastores cannot match, from high fashion to dirt cheap, stylish to tacky. The city's markets and food shops, too, offer a wonderful choice of delicacies and produce.

SHOPPING BY AREA

Madrid has more than one centre as far as shopping is concerned. The area around the Calle Preciados between Sol and Gran Via is still considered the heart of the city, but is rivalled by other shopping districts. Affluent Salamanca, particularly Calles Serrano, Velázquez, Goya and cross-streets in between, is the main area for expensive fashion and furnishings, although you will be surprised at how many bargains there are too.

Nearby is the Calle Almirante, just into the smart side of Chueca between Calle Barquillo and the Paseo de Recoletos, the main drag for designer fashion. Barquillo itself is known as *La Calle del Sonido* ('The Street of Sound'), with a string of hi-fi shops. To the north up the Castellana towards the AZCA development there is another, pretty bland shopping area, with branches of several major stores and, right at the top, **La Vaguada** shopping mall.

And, back in the centre, and as a complete alternative, there's the **Rastro**, Madrid's huge and time-honoured Sunday flea market (*see page 149*). The streets around the market are where you can find antiques and all manner of knick-knacks, even during the week. For a general listing of shops and other amenities by area, *see page 264* **Area Index**.

Out of Hours

The chains Bob's and Vip's are multi-purpose emporia offering a variety of things you might need in the middle of the night or on a Sunday afternoon – restaurants, cafés, (expensive) supermarkets, books, cosmetics, records, toys, newsstands. They have been hugely successful.

Bob's
Glorieta de Quevedo 9 (448 51 02). Metro Quevedo/bus 149. **Open** 8am-2am Mon-Fri; 9am-3.30am Sat, Sun. **Credit** AmEx, DC, MC, V.
English language books at bargain prices are among Bob's attractions.
Branches: C/Serrano 41; C/Miguel Angel 11.

7-11
C/Toledo 78. Metro Puerta de Toledo/bus 3, 17, 18, 35, 60 C. **Open** 24 hours daily. **Credit** V.
General stores for non-sleepers and those who have simply forgotten something. There are a great many 7-11 branches around Madrid, particularly at petrol stations.

Vip's
Gran Via 43 (559 64 57). Metro Callao, Santo Domingo/bus 1, 44, 74, 133. **Open** 9am-3.30am daily. **Credit** AmEx, DC, MC, V.
Vip's generally house a pizzeria, and also offer bargain books, including some in English, in their bookshop. They also have a large toy stock. Numerous branches around the city. *See also chapter* **Women's Madrid**.

One-Stop

El Corte Inglés
C/Preciados 3 (phone for all branches 556 23 00). Metro Sol/bus all routes to Puerta del Sol. **Open** 10am-9pm Mon-Sat. **Credit** AmEx, DC, MC, V.
This symbol of modern Spain is an institution, the most complete department store in the country. It's the place for trouble-free shopping: prices vary greatly, but service isn't bad and English-speaking staff and tax-free shopping for tourists are available. It also provides a range of handy services such as key-cutting and shoe repair,and the supermarket is a godsend on a Saturday afternoon when all other shops have closed until Monday. There's a special, separate toys-and-sports branch on the Castellana (*see below* **Children**).
Branches: C/Princesa 42; C/Goya 76; C/Raimundo Fernández Villaverde 79.

FNAC

C/Preciados 28 (595 61 00). Metro Callao/bus 44, 75, 133. **Open** 10am-10pm Mon-Sat.
Credit AmEx, DC, MC, V.
Not really a complete one-stop shop, but this huge French-owned emporium has certainly given the Madrid retail world a jolt by stocking an enormous range of books, CDs, videos, magazines, newspapers both Spanish and foreign, computers and software, most of them at discount prices and displayed in convenient and ultra-modern fashion. There is a reasonable stock of books in English and French, as well as a photo developing service and a tremendously successful ticket agency (*see chapter* **Services**).

Galerías Preciados

Plaza del Callao (phone for all branches 446 32 00). Metro Callao/bus 44, 75, 133, 149. **Open** 10am-9pm Mon-Sat. **Credit** AmEx, DC, MC, V.
Galerias has long been the main rival of El Corte Inglés, and has undergone a series of changes since passing into British hands a few years ago. It compares well for prices.
Branches: C/Goya 87; C/ Serrano 47; Centro Comercial La Vaguada.

Marks & Spencers

C/Serrano 52 (431 67 60). Metro Serrano/bus 1, 9, 19, 51, 74. **Open** 10am-8.30pm Mon-Sat. **Credit** V.
M&S has been going in Madrid for some time now – the local British community appreciate the goods, but it also sells increasingly to Spaniards too. The company also has a lingerie section in La Vaguada, and will soon be opening an additional site.

Shopping Malls

Centros Comerciales (shopping malls) are another innovation that took wing during Spain's eighties boom. Many are finding the going tough in the crisis-ridden 1990s.

Centro Comercial Arturo Soria Plaza

C/Arturo Soria 126 (759 76 32) Metro Arturo Soria/bus 11, 70, 120, 122. **Open** 10am-9pm Mon-Sat; 10am-3pm Sun.
A comprehensive mall, less frantic than La Vaguada, less exclusive than Galeria del Prado and quite relaxing if you don't mind piped Julio Iglesias. You'll find a supermarket, a florist's, men's, women's and kid's wear, software, gifts and a Body Shop as well as goodies to eat and drink.

Centro Comercial Madrid-2, La Vaguada

Avda Montforte de Lemos 36. Metro Barrio del Pilar/bus 83, 128, 132, 134. **Open** 10am-10pm; *leisure area only* 10am-3am, daily.
About 350 outlets, plus a floor totally turned over to leisure pursuits (cinemas, a disco, a bowling alley, and a mini fairground) make up this huge mall, Madrid's biggest.

Galería del Prado

Plaza de las Cortes 7(429 75 51). Metro Banco de España/bus 9, 14, 27, 34. **Open** 10am-9pm Mon-Sat.
Jewellery, gifts, fashion for all ages, leather, suede and fur can be found in this small shopping centre. It's situated in the basement of the Hotel Palace, and pretty exclusive.

El Jardín de Serrano

C/Goya 6-8 (577 00 12). Metro Serrano/bus 9, 19, 21, 51, 53. **Open** 10am-9pm Mon-Sat.
A small but ultra-chic mall in the heart of swish Salamanca that actually won a European shopping-mall design prize. The 20 or so shops mainly offer high-fasion clothes and accessories.

Mercado Puerta de Toledo

Ronda de Toledo 1 (366 72 00). Metro Puerta de Toledo/bus all routes to Puerta del Toledo. **Open** 11.30am-9pm Tue-Sat; 11.30am-3pm Sun.
This hopefully stylish and upmarket centre was opened in 1989 in a former fish market. However, it failed to catch on, and the whole complex is threatened with closure. It's perhaps worth a visit out of architectural and social interest. On one side of the building is **La Oca**, (*see below* **Design & Household**), which insists that it will remain open.

Antiques

There are various fascinating concentrations of antiques shops and *Almonedas* (auction houses, but which also sell in the normal fashion) either side of the **Rastro**. There are also some antiques galleries, and all the adjacent streets are worth investigating, with shops whose stock ranges from junk to real oddities. There are many antique shops too in the Huertas area, around Calle del Prado and Calle Lope de Vega.

The main area for (very) expensive, luxury antiques is in Salamanca. Streets such as Lagasca, Claudio Coello, Serrano, Velázquez and Jorge Juan contain around fifty prestigious antique shops.

Galerías Piquer

C/Ribera de Curtidores 29. Metro La Latina/bus 17, 18, 23, 35. **Open** 10am-8.30pm Mon-Sat; 10am-2.30pm Sun.
Twenty different antique shops in one space. Opening times may be different for the various shops.

Nuevas Galerías

C/Ribera de Curtidores 12. Metro La Latina/bus 17, 18, 23, 35. **Open** 10am-8.30pm Mon-Sat; 10am-2.30pm Sun.
There are 11 different antique shops in this arcade. Again, opening times may differ in the various shops.

Bookshops

The Madrid bookselling world has been thrown into a certain turmoil by the arrival of the **FNAC** (*see above* **One-Stop**). One of the centres of the more traditional book trade is the appropriately named **Calle de los Libreros** ('Booksellers' Street') just off Gran Vía, where there are many specialised shops stocking university text books. For travel book and map shops, *see chapter* **The Sierras**.

General

La Casa del Libro Espasa Calpe

Gran Via 29 (521 21 13). Metro Gran Via/bus all routes to Gran Via. **Open** 10am-8.30pm Mon-Sat.
Credit AmEx, DC, MC, V.
Madrid's most important and comprehensive bookshop, this five-storey monster has its own publishing house, and a good English section on the ground floor.

Crisol

C/Juan Bravo 38 (322 48 00). Metro Diego de León/bus 26, 29, 52, 61. **Open** 10am-10pm Mon-Sat.
Credit AmEx, DC, MC, V.
A bookshop with a bit of everything, and a good book-finding service. There are good English language, foreign press and record sections too. Five more branches around the city.

*If you must have everything under one roof, make your way to **La Vaguada**. See page 136.*

The Arts

Libros Argensola
C/Doctor Mata 2 (539 58 13). Metro Atocha/bus all routes to Atocha. **Open** 10am-2pm, 5-8pm, Mon-Fri; 10am-2pm Sat. **Credit** AmEx, DC, MC, V.
Argensola stocks a tremendous selection of art, photography, general and specialised books about the history of arts and handicrafts, many of them in English.

English-Language Bookshops

Booksellers
C/José Abascal 48 (442 79 59). Metro Ríos Rosas/bus 3, 12, 37, 149. **Open** 9.30am-2pm, 5-8pm, Mon-Fri; 10am-2pm Sat. **Credit** AmEx, DC, MC, V.
Booksellers has a good range of videos in English, and a wide choice of children's books. The staff are very helpful indeed.

Turner
C/Génova 3-5 (319 28 67). Metro Alonso Martínez/bus 21. **Open** 10am-8pm Mon-Fri; 10am-2pm Sat. **Credit** AmEx, V.
Madrid's foremost English bookshop. In its basement it has a wide selection of fiction, poetry and classics, as well as teaching materials and so on. There's also a noticeboard, if you're looking for a flatshare or to give English classes. The Spanish and French departments are on the floor above.

Second-Hand & Rare Books

Bookshops dealing in rare and antique books are mostly concentrated around Huertas. Listed below are just a couple of them. A great place to find

cheaper second-hand books is the **Cuesta de Moyano**, on the street that runs up to the Retiro alongside the Jardín Botánico, near Atocha. It contains a line of small wooden kiosks selling second-hand books, from rare editions to recent remainders. Some are open all week at different times, but they are busiest on Sunday mornings.

Librería Clío
C/León 18 (429 54 36). Metro Antón Martín/bus 6, 26, 32, 57. **Open** 10.30am-1.30pm, 5-8pm, Mon-Sat. **Credit** V.
Clío has old editions, ancient postcards and other treasures.

Librería del Prado
C/del Prado 5 (429 60 91). Metro Antón Martín/bus 6, 26, 32, 57. **Open** 10am-2pm, 5-8pm, Mon-Sat. **No credit cards**.
Many books in their stock are from the eighteenth and nineteenth centuries, as well as old manuscripts, postcards and the like. Prices are reasonable.

Children

Clothes

Children's clothes are very expensive in Spain. Adult fashion chains such as **Zara** (*see below* **Fashion**) also have imaginative children's lines.

Adams
C/Fuencarral 132 (593 00 37). Metro Bilbao, Quevedo/bus 147, 149. **Open** 10am-2.30pm, 4.30-8pm, Mon-Sat. **Credit** MC, V.

Crisol *offers an excellent choice of Spanish and foreign books. See page 136.*

Adams is a breath of fresh air on the kids' clothing scene – the stuff is sensible, practical but fun, and cheap.
Branches: Avda Felipe II 16; C/Bravo Murillo 109.

Chicco

C/Goya 109 (577 68 87). Metro Goya/bus 21, 30, 53, C. **Open** 10am-2.30pm, 4.30-8pm, Mon-Sat.
Credit AmEx, V.
Expensive, as you would expect from this Italian chain, but excellent for gadgets necessary to make your home child-safe.

Prenatal

C/Fuencarral 17 (521 64 24). Metro Gran Via/bus 3, 40, 149. **Open** 10am-1.45pm, 4.30-8pm, Mon-Sat.
Credit AmEx, DC, MC, V.
The range here runs from pregnancy wear until a child is about 8 years old. Prams and pushchairs, Moses baskets and cots, feeding bottles and toys are sold too. It's quality stuff, at a price. Branches throughout the city.

Toys

Bazar Mila

Gran Via 33 (531 87 28). Metro Gran Via, Callao/bus 46, 146, 149. **Open** 9.30am-8.30pm Mon-Sat.
Credit AmEx, DC, MC, V.
A traditional toy shop with a window stuffed with gigantic teddies and pandas, as well as train sets, modelling kits and dolls' houses. There's more inside, too.

El Corte Inglés

Paseo de la Castellana 85 (556 23 00). Metro Nuevos Ministerios/bus all routes to Paseo de la Castellana. **Open** 10am-9pm Mon-Sat. **Credit** AmEx, DC, MC, TC, V.
A specialised toys-and-sports branch of the Corte Inglés that's by far the largest toy shop in Madrid, this three-storey madhouse covers all needs.

Puck

C/Duque de Sesto 30 (575 07 43). Metro Goya, O'Donnell/bus 2, 15, 28, C. **Open** 4.30-8pm Mon; 10am-1.30pm, 4.30-8pm, Tue-Sat. **Credit** V.
The speciality here is wooden, educational toys and dolls houses for assembly at home.

Cosmetics & Perfumes

Perfumerías are to be found on just about every street in Madrid, and all the major department stores naturally carry a full range of cosmetic and beauty products. Here are a few that are a little more unusual.

O Boticàrio

C/Preciados 23 (522 89 90). Metro Sol, Callao/bus 44, 75, 133, 149. **Open** 10am-9.30pm Mon-Sat.
Credit MC, V.
Stockists of perfumes and natural cosmetics from Brazil that are based mainly on rain-forest plants from the Amazon.

Comercial Chinere

C/Pizarro 20 (522 89 61). Metro Noviciado/bus 147.
Open 10am-8pm Mon-Sat. **No credit cards.**
A small shop which specialises in beauty products (and some foodstuffs) from Africa and Latin America.

Manuel Riesgo

C/Desengaño 22 (531 19 56). Metro Gran Via/bus all routes to Gran Via. **Open** 9am-1.30pm, 4.30-7.30pm, Mon-Fri. **Credit** MC, V.
This incredible establishment offers around 25,000 products (pigments, essences, oils, waxes, colourings and so on) which can be used in the fields of beauty, pharmaceuticals or art.

Design & Household

Aldaba

*C/Belén 15 (308 38 33). Metro Chueca, Alonso
Martínez/bus 3, 7, 37, 40, 149.* **Open** 10.30am-2pm,
5.30-9pm, Mon-Sat. **Credit** AmEx, MC, V.
This roomy shop just on the trendy side of Chueca offers a
good selection of lamps, household items and ornaments.

BD Ediciones de Diseño

*C/Villanueva 5 (435 06 27). Metro Serrano, Retiro/bus 1,
9, 19, 51, 74.* **Open** 9.30am-1.30pm, 4.30-8pm, Mon-Fri;
10am-1.30pm Sat. **Credit** AmEx, DC, MC, V.
A high-style design shop much frequented by designers and
architects themselves, where you'll find the very latest in furniture and ornaments both by Spanish designers such as
Oscar Tusquets and by international colleagues such as the
Memphis group. Many designs are exclusive to the shop.
Wonderful to look at, correspondingly expensive.

Gastón y Daniela

*C/Velázquez 42 (435 24 21). Metro Velázquez/bus 1, 9,
19, 51, 74.* **Open** 10am-1.45pm, 4.30-8pm, Mon-Sat.
Credit AmEx, DC, V.
Possibly the best shop in Madrid for curtain material, cover-
ings and cloth. The shop in C/Hernani 68 has ends of lines
from the plusher shops in Salamanca.
Branches: C/Velázquez 47; C/Hernani 68.

La Oca

*Ronda de Toledo 1 (365 13 01). Metro Puerta de
Toledo/bus 41, 60, 148, C.* **Open**: 10am-2pm, 5-8.30pm
Mon-Sat; 11am-2.30pm Sun. **Credit** AmEx, MC, V.
This designer kitchen and household emporium next to the
Mercado Puerta de Toledo (*see above* **Shopping Malls**)
carries a substantial range of articles from the inevitable
Philippe Starke lemon squeezer through Alessi coffee pots
and original ashtrays to carpets, lamps, sofas and dining
tables. Great for browsing and for buying gifts.

Fashion
Medium Range

Blanco

*C/Mayor 14 (366 44 26). Metro Sol/bus all routes to
Puerta del Sol.* **Open** 10am-9pm Mon-Sat.
Credit AmEx, DC, MC, V.
A fun shop with daring styles in women's clothing, shoes,
belts and bags, at very accessible prices.
Branch: Centro Comercial La Vaguada.

Casandra

*C/Serrano 88 (577 16 71). Metro Nuñez de Balboa/bus 1,
9, 19, 51, 74.* **Open** 10am-2pm, 5-8.30pm, Mon-Sat.
Credit AmEx, DC, MC, V.
Casandra stocks Moschino, Calvin Kline, Armani, Gaultier
and a host of other international names in women's wear. It
also has a great but expensive kid's range, Casandra Junior.
Branch: Galería del Prado.

Ekseption

*C/Velázquez 28 (577 43 53).Metro Velázquez/bus 1,9,
19, 51, 74.* **Open** 10.30am-2.30pm, 5-9pm, Mon-Sat.
Credit AmEx, DC, JCB, MC, V.
Gaultier, Dolce & Gabanna, Sybilla are just some of the
names to be found in this imaginatively designed boutique.
Women's clothes only.
Branch: C/Claudio Coello 50.

Massimo Dutti

*C/Princesa 79 (543 74 22). Metro Moncloa,
Argüelles/bus 1, 44, 133, C.* **Open** 10am-2pm, 5-8.30pm,
Mon-Sat. **Credit** AmEx, DC, MC, V.

Despite the name, this isn't Italian – it's run by a young
Spaniard who began selling shirts all at one price, and now
sells a whole range of fashionable but good-value menswear.
Branches: C/Alberto Aguilera 37; C/Fuencarral 139;
C/Goya 73-75; C/Narváez 6; C/Velázquez 46; Paseo de la
Habana 40.

Springfield

*C/ Montera 7 (533 59 13). Metro Sol/bus all routes to
Puerta del Sol.* **Open** 10am-8.30pm Mon-Sat.
Credit MC, V.
A newcomer, this chain sells smartish casual wear for men
at reasonable prices, and offers good end-of-season bargains.
Branches: Gran Via 54; Fuencarral 107; Alcalá 309.

Zara

*C/Princesa 45 (541 09 02). Metro Argüelles/bus 1, 44,
133, C.* **Open** 10am-8pm Mon-Sat.
Credit AmEx, DC, MC, V.
Zara has over 100 branches all over Spain and abroad.
Whatever top designers produce each season, Zara copies at
a fraction of the price within a few weeks. Men, women and
small kids are all catered for. Check buttons, zips and seams
when buying.

Designer

Adolfo Domínguez

*C/Ortega y Gasset 4 (576 00 84). Metro Nuñez de
Balboa/bus 1, 9, 19, 51, 74.* **Open** 10am-2pm, 5-8pm,
Mon-Sat. **Credit** AmEx, DC, JCB, MC, V.
Adolfo Domínguez earned his fame by bending the rules and
dressing Spanish trendsters and politicians alike in simple,
comfortable and original clothes. His current lines are sober,
but very stylish.
Branch: C/Serrano 96.

Agatha Ruiz de la Prada

*C/Marqués de Riscal 8 (310 44 83). Metro Rubén Darío,
Alonso Martínez/bus 5, 7, 14, 27, 150.* **Open** 10am-2pm,
5-8pm, Mon-Fri; 10am-2pm Sat. **Credit** MC, V.
Agatha Ruiz manages to sell to the public the sort of wacky
couture that seems made only for the catwalk and those that
walk on it. Circus motifs have been a recent favourite.

Gianfranco Ferré

*C/Serrano 29 (575 70 12). Metro Serrano/bus 1, 9, 19,
51, 74.* **Open** 10.30am-2pm, 5-8.30pm, Mon-Fri; 10.30am-
2pm Sat. **Credit** AmEx, DC, V.
Baroque evening wear for women; stylish, elegant menswear.

Gianni Versace

*C/Ortega y Gasset 14 (577 37 88). Metro Nuñez de
Balboa/bus 1, 9, 19, 51, 74.* **Open** 10am-8pm Mon-Sat.
Credit AmEx, DC, JCB, MC, V.
The daring, immaculately-stubbled Versace refused to put
on a tie for a formal reception in Madrid, but now has a shop
here where the ties fetch upwards of 9,500ptas. Striking
designs for both sexes in an exquisitely sophisticated setting.

Giorgio Armani

*C/Ortega y Gasset 17 (576 10 36). Metro Núñez de
Balboa/bus 1, 9, 19, 51, 74.* **Open** 10am-2.30pm, 4-
8.30pm, Mon-Sat. **Credit** AmEx, DC, JCB, MC, V.
The Italian genius' impeccable style sold here, while
clothes for younger style-setters can be found at Emporio
Armani, Claudio Coello 77 (575 14 37).

Kenzo

*C/Ortega y Gasset 11 (577 36 45). Metro Nuñez de
Balboa/bus 1, 9, 19, 51, 74.* **Open** 10.15am-2pm, 5-
8.30pm, Mon-Sat. **Credit** AmEx, DC, JCB, MC, V.
Wild colours from the Japanese designer with an international outlook.

La Calle Almirante

During the eighties this street was colonised by fashion shops, becoming Madrid's most concentrated single 'fashion row'. The *efecto Almirante* also spread to other streets around it, such as Conde de Xiquena, Campoamor, Argensola and Orellana. The last few years haven't been too kind to the upper end of the fashion business – witness the number of empty shops and discount offers. Even so, a good many places are still there, and apparently thriving. Though a lot of the clothes on sale in the area are expensive, the shops are a lot more hip – and more relaxed – than in the rather stuffy high-fashion area of Salamanca

On Calle Almirante itself, **Ararat**, at no.10, and the adjacent kids' shop **Ararat Junior** offer sometimes a-little-off-the-wall fashions for teenagers and upwards. In the same building is **Berlin**, with clothes that are more sober than the sign above the window designed by Javier Mariscal. **Anvers**, at no.22, has very elegant women's clothes.

In Conde de Xiquena, at no.13, you can ponder the avant-garde, sometimes contorted but

beautifully crafted and elegant jewellery of **Joaquín Berao**. Around the corner, at Marqués de Monasterio 2, is the shop of **Lurdes Bergada**, a rising young Catalan designer.

Sybilla

C/Jorge Juan 12 (578 13 22). Metro Retiro, Serrano/bus 1, 9, 19, 51, 74. **Open** 10am-2pm, 4.30-8.30pm, Mon-Sat. **Credit** AmEx, JCB, MC, V.
Sybilla, known as the *maga* (sorceress) of Spanish design, was a celebrity-figure of the *Movida*. She's since moved the centre of her operations to Paris, but her Madrid shop still sells an exciting range of accessories, shoes and bags as well as clothes.

Second-Hand Clothes

There isn't much of a second-hand clothes culture in Spain – a great many people would be horrified at the thought of wearing somebody else's cast-offs. However, there are a few trendy-ish second-hand shops in Malasaña. Otherwise, try the **Rastro** on Sundays (*see page 149*), especially the Plaza General Vara del Rey.

Camaleón Usados

C/Arenal 8 (523 21 63). Metro Sol/bus all routes to Puerta del Sol. **Open** 10am-2.30pm, 4.30-8.30pm, Mon-Sat. **Credit** AmEx, MC, V.
A smartish classic clothes shop where you can find second-hand Levi's for around 2,900ptas, original American forties' baseball jackets and biker's jackets and jeans recycled into dresses. It also has new jeans and jackets too, at fairly standard prices.
Branch: C/Preciados 32.

Mercado de Colores

C/de la Palma 34 (no phone). Metro Noviciado/bus 147. **Open** 5.30-10pm Mon-Sat. **No credit cards**.

A large, laid-back second-hand Malasaña bazaar with all sorts of things from local ends-of-lines to imported American clothes, and very cheap. There's also a special pot-luck box with everything at 100ptas each, and a free condom with every purchase.

Lingerie & Underwear

Corsetería La Latina

C/Toledo 49 (365 46 22). Metro La Latina/bus 17, 18, 23, 35, 60. **Open** 9am-1.30pm, 5-8pm, Mon-Sat. **Credit** AmEx, DC, MC, V.
Foundation underwear for a race of giants. Corsets, bras, girdles and suspenders all in huge sizes. For many years people walking down the street have, despite themselves, been unable to resist pulling up in front of the window display in sheer amazement.

Cristina de Jos's

Galería del Prado, Plaza de las Cortes 7 (420 22 90). Metro Banco de España/bus 9, 14, 27, 34. **Open** 10am-9pm Mon-Sat. **Credit** AmEx, V.
Luxurious, feminine underwear, nightwear, bodies and so on, by Warner and Kissinger. Knickers cost from 2,000ptas, bras from 3,000ptas.

¡Oh, qué Luna!

C/Ayala 32 (431 37 25). Metro Velázquez/bus 1, 74. **Open** 10am-2pm, 5-8.30pm, Mon-Sat. **Credit** AmEx, DC, MC, V.
Very stylish, sexy underwear, nightwear and dressing gowns for men and women, as well as sheets and bedlinen.
Branch: Galería del Prado.

Shoes & Leather

A modern Madrid institution are the **Zapaterías de Muestrarios**, shoe shops that specialise in end-of-line footwear. Top-name shoes cost from 5,000ptas. There are about twenty of them, based around the Calle Augusto Figueroa in Chueca (Metro Chueca). Several expensive shoe shops can be found in Calle Almirante (*see above*).

Antigua Casa Crespo

C/Divino Pastor 29 (521 56 54). Metro San Bernardo/bus 21, 147. **Open** 9.30am-1.30pm, 4.30-8pm, Mon-Fri. **No credit cards.**
The most famous espadrille shop in Madrid, with every kind of traditional *alpargata* in a shop that is itself a museum piece.

Camper

Gran Vía 54 (547 53 23). Metro Gran Vía, Callao/bus all routes to GranVía. **Credit** AmEx, DC, MC, V
Camper shoes combine comfort with a rugged, chunky style. Shoes from 8,000ptas.
Branches: C/Ayala 13; C/Princesa 75.

Farrutx

C/Serrano 7 (576 94 93). Metro Serrano/bus 1, 9, 19, 51, 74. **Open** 10am-2pm, 5-8pm, Mon-Sat. **Credit** AmEx, DC, JCB, MC, V.
Among the best shoe stores in terms of elegance and quality, with prices starting at about 12,000ptas.

Los Guerrilleros

Puerta del Sol 5 (522 80 04). Metro Sol/bus all routes to Puerta del Sol. **Open** 9.30am-2pm, 5-8.30pm, Mon-Sat. **Credit** AmEx, MC, V.
A bargain-basement store that's known for its very silly sign (given their stock) 'Don't buy here, we're very expensive!'. Actually dead cheap, but sometimes momentarily stylish.
Branches: C/Montera 25; Plaza Lavapiés 5.

Loewe

C/Serrano 26 & 34 (578 39 21/577 60 56). Metro Serrano/bus 1, 9, 19, 51, 74. **Open** 9.30am-2pm, 4.30-8.30pm, Mon-Sat. **Credit** AmEx, DC, MC, V.
A world-famous Spanish leather goods company with superb-quality bags, suitcases and other accessories, as well as classic coats and jackets for men and women.

Food & Drink
Chocolates, Cakes & Sweets

Casa Mira

Carrera de San Jerónimo 30 (429 67 96). Metro Sol, Sevilla/bus all routes to Puerta del Sol. **Open** 10am-2pm, 5-9pm, Mon-Sat. **No credit cards.**
Going for almost 150 years now, Casa Mira is a specialist in *turrón* (a type of nougat, most commonly very hard, although there are different kinds) which is an inseparable part of a Spanish Christmas. Each December, the queues stretch way up the street. There is also a wide selection of chocolates, marzipan sweets, cakes and a few savouries, like *empanadas*.

Size conversion chart for clothes

Women's clothes									
British	8	10	12	14	16	•	•	•	•
American	6	8	10	12	14	•	•	•	•
Spanish	36	38	40	42	44	•	•	•	•
Women's shoes									
British	8	10	12	14	16	•	•	•	•
American	6	8	10	12	14	•	•	•	•
Spanish	36	38	40	42	44	•	•	•	•
Men's suits/overcoats									
British	38	40	42	44	46	•	•	•	•
American	38	40	42	44	46	•	•	•	•
Spanish	48	50/2	54	56	58/60	•	•	•	•
Men's shirts									
British	14	14.5	15	15.5	16	16.5	17	•	•
American	14	14.5	15	15.5	16	16.5	17	•	•
Spanish	35	36/7	38	39/40	41	42/3	44	•	•
Men's shoes									
British	8	9	10	11	12	•	•	•	•
American	9	10	11	12	13	•	•	•	•
Spanish	42	43	44	45	46	•	•	•	•
Children's shoes									
British	7	8	9	10	11	12	13	1	2
American	7.5	8.5	9.5	10.5	11.5	12.5	13.5	1.5	2.5
Spanish	24	25.5	27	28	29	30	32	33	34

Children's clothes
In all countries, size descriptions vary from make to make, but are usually done by age

*The **Almacén de Licores David Cabello**.*

Horno San Onfre

C/San Onofre 3 (532 90 60). Metro Gran Vía/bus all routes to Gran Vía. **Open** 9am-9pm Mon-Sat; 9am-8pm Sun. **Credit** V.
Not to be missed is this fine old establishment. Everything is baked on the premises, including all the seasonal cakes (*torrijas* at Easter, *turrones* at Christmas, *Roscón de Reyes* for 6 January). The *tarta de Santiago* (a traditional sponge cake) is excellent as are savouries such as *empanada Gallega*. There's also a branch, **Tahona San Onofre**, just around the corner at Calle Hortaleza 9, and another, the **Horno La Santiaguesa**, at C/Mayor 73. The latter shop is also a café.

El Madroño

C/Caravaca 10 (527 68 43). Metro Lavapiés/bus 26, 27, 32, 57. **Open** 10am-2pm, 6pm-midnight; Tue-Thur, Sun; 6pm-3am Fri, Sat. **No credit cards.**
Possibly the most original cake shop of all, this Lavapiés establishment serves its own liqueur, *Licor del Madroño* (a delicate, strawberry-ish invention which by all accounts the old man who started the business years ago stubbornly refused to sell the patent for) and a wide variety of cakes made from such unlikely ingredients as spinach or beetroot. **Branch**: C/ Espíritu Santo 30.

Olive Oil

Patrimonio Comunal Olivarero

C/Mejía Lequerica 1 (308 05 05). Metro Tribunal, Alonso Martínez/bus 3, 21, 37, 40, 149. **Open** 9.15am-1.30pm, 4.30-7.30pm, Mon-Fri; 10.15am-1.30pm Sat; closed August. **No credit cards.**
A vast range of olive oils from all over Spain, in quantities from ½ litre bottles up to 5-litre tins.

Regional Products

Méndez

C/Ayala 65 (402 43 78). Metro Lista/bus 26, 29, 52, 61. **Open** 9am-2.30pm, 5-8.30pm, Mon-Sat. **Credit** AmEx, V.
Specialists in products from the north of Spain, Asturias, Galicia, Cantabria and León. Goods include a range of cooked and cured meats, tinned products, fish in various states of curation, dried beans, wines and spirits.

Supermarkets

Madrid's booming new hypermarkets are almost all around the city's edge, and accessible only by car. If you're mobile and really need to stock up, look for any advertising for **Alcampo**, **Continente**, **Jumbo** or **Pryca**. There are several on or near the A2 road to Barajas airport and around the M30. Smaller, city-centre supermarkets can in any case cover most short-term convenience-shopping needs.

Expresso

C/Alcalá 137 (576 21 95). Metro Manuel Becerra/bus 12, 21, 53, 56, 106, C. **Open** 9.30am-2pm, 5-8pm Mon-Sat. **Credit** V.
A little more upmarket than other supermarkets in central Madrid, Expresso stocks a range of imported items such as German beers, French, Italian and other cheeses and English tea – at a price. There are many branches throughout the city

Simago

C/Valencia 2 (467 42 08). Metro Embajadores/bus 27, 34, 36, 41, 119, C. **Open** 9am-8.30pm Mon-Sat. **Credit** V.
This supermarket recalls a Woolworths' of a few years ago. The supermarket prices always has some excellent offers. Other sections offer kids' clothes, underwear and household goods. There are several branches around Madrid

Vegetarian & Health Foods

Autoservicio Ecológico

C/Huertas 5 (429 64 25). Metro Antón Martín/bus 6, 9, 26, 32, 57. **Open** 10am-2pm, 5-8pm, Mon-Fri; 10am-2pm Sat. **Credit** V.
A full range of wholefoods, cosmetics, cleaning materials and literature for the ecologically aware.

Central Vegetariana

C/de la Palma 15 (447 80 13). Metro Tribunal/bus 3, 40, 147, 149. **Open** 10am-2pm, 5-8pm, Mon-Fri; 10am-1.30pm Sat. **No credit cards.**
Organic food, herbal medicines, and natural cosmetics.

Wine & Drink/*Bodegas*

A *bodega*, literally a cellar, can be anything from an old tavern where you drink on the premises to a superbly-stocked wine and spirits shop.

Almacén de Licores David Cabello

C/Cervantes 6 (429 52 30). Metro Antón Martín/bus 6, 26, 32, 57. **Open** 10am-2.30pm, 5.15-8.30pm, Mon-Fri; 10am-2.30pm, 6.30-8pm, Sat. **No credit cards.**
This bodega wasn't designed with the comfort of the customer in mind – it's often hard to get in the door, such is the confusion of bottles overspilling from the shop, crates, red-nosed locals and assorted felines. Once over the threshold, the effort is worthwhile, however, as there's an incredible selection of wines (500 table wines) and spirits. Prices – chalked up on the wall outside – are reasonable.

Licorilandia

C/León 30 (429 12 57). Metro Antón Martín/bus 6, 26, 32, 57. **Open** 9.30am-2pm, 5-8.30pm, Mon-Fri; 9.30am-2pm Sat. **No credit cards.**
What began as a shop specialising in miniatures has now graduated to full-size bottles. The selection of cavas is particularly good, as are the vintage wines and spirits (especially the range of rums from Cuba, Nicaragua, Venezuela and Martinique).

A temple of tasty togs, **Ekseption**. See page 139.

Mariano Aguado

C/Echegaray 19 (429 60 88). Metro Sol,Sevilla/bus all routes to Puerta del Sol. **Open** 9.30am-2pm, 5.30-8.30pm, Mon-Fri; 9.30am-2pm Sat. **No credit cards**.

The name of this place is embossed only in the doorstep, and does not appear anywhere else. It's a slightly solemn establishment rather oriented to the serious wine connoisseur, and always has a few lesser-known but good quality wines from Rioja and Navarra, plus a good selection of whites from Rueda from 295ptas.

Mariano Madrueño

C/Postigo de San Martín 3 (521 19 55). Metro Callao/bus 44, 46, 133, 147. **Open** 9.30am-2pm, 5.30-8.30pm, Mon-Fri; 10.30am-2pm Sat. **Credit** V.

This fabulous bodega, complete with wrought iron columns and carved wooden shelves, will be celebrating its 100th birthday in 1995. The enormous selection of wines and spirits comes from all over Spain.

Gifts

El Arco de los Cuchilleros

Plaza Mayor 9, bajos (365 26 80). Metro Sol/bus all routes to Puerta del Sol. **Open** 11am-8pm Mon-Sat. **Credit** AmEx, MC, V.

An attractive small craft, jewellery, glass and gifts shop with an interesting selection of modern craft work. It also has a gallery space that hosts innovative exhibits by Spanish craft workers and designers. What's more, despite its being right in the arch of the same name on one side of the heavily-touristed Plaza Mayor, prices are very reasonable.

Azcart

C/Dr Drumen 7 (527 35 72). Metro Atocha/bus all routes to Atocha. **Open** 10am-2pm, 5-8.30pm, Mon-Sat. **Credit** AmEx, DC, MC, V.

Tasteful posters, designer knick-knacks and a small range of T-shirts.

Cerámica El Alfar

C/Claudo Coello 112 (411 35 87). Metro Núñez de Balboa/bus 9, 19, 51. **Open** 10am-2pm, 5-9pm, Mon-Sat. **Credit** AmEx, DC, MC, V.

Traditional ceramics and tiles from Talavera, Toledo, Sevilla and other regions of Spain. In addition to the comprehensive range of strictly traditional designs, the shop also stocks a variety of entirely modern work..

La Compañía de China y del Oriente

C/Conde de Aranda 14 (575 64 84). Metro Retiro/bus 19, 20, 28, 51, 146. **Open** 10am-2pm, 4.30-8pm, Mon-Sat. **Credit** AmEx, DC, V.

A large and fairly extensive store that's a favourite for last-minute gift-buying for anyone with exotic tastes: as well as oriental and middle eastern crafts, textiles, carpets, rugs and household accessories there is also a very large range of natural perfumes.

Items D'ho

C/Hermosilla 88 (576 12 10). Metro Goya/bus 21, 43, 53, 146. **Open** 10am-2pm, 5-8pm, Mon-Sat. **Credit** AmEx, DC, JCB, MC, V.

Up-to-date designer gifts and accessories, mainly for men but not exclusively, plus items for the house.

Branch: Mercado de la Puerta de Toledo.

SHOPPING

IMPORTANT

When you make your purchases you pay a tax already included in the price.

By law you are entitled to claim back this tax, thus making your shopping more profitable. This applies only for residents outside the European Union.

In Madrid you will find a great number of quality shops offering the "Tax-free system".

TAX FREE
FOR TOURISTS
Europe Tax-free Shopping

In the shop you must ask the shop assistant for a "Tax-free cheque" which shows your tax refund amount.

When leaving, present your "tax-free cheque" at Banco Exterior at the airport and receive your refund in cash.

REMEMBER: DON'T LEAVE YOUR MONEY BEHIND!

Hams, Cold Cuts & Cheeses

*The fine display at the **Museo del Jamón**.*

The range of names, sizes, shapes and prices of Spanish *embutidos* (a generic term for just about anything crammed into a skin and cured) and *fiambres* (cold meats) is amazing. There are also great variations in quality. The difference in price between *Jamón Serrano* (cured ham) at around 2,500ptas per kilo and *Jamón de Jabugo* at upwards of 8,000ptas stems from the fact that the latter comes from pigs fed on a diet of acorns and has been cured carefully and entirely naturally for at least a year, while a lot of cheaper *serrano* is produced very 'industrially'. More expensive still is *Jamón Ibérico* (the best is *pata negra*, 'black foot'), also acorn-fed but from the native Iberian breed of pig. These products have *denominaciones de origen* like fine wines; the same applies with the best types of chorizo and cured *lomo* (loin) – from 4,500ptas a kilo. Others to look out for are *chorizo cular*, less fatty than other types; *chorizo picante de jabugo*, seasoned with paprika; and *salchichón*, especially *a la pimienta*, smothered in black pepper. *Longaniza* is a hard, thin *embutido* the best of which is flavoured with herbs. Not of pork but equally worth trying are *mojama*, dry-cured tuna, and *cecina*, cured veal steak.

Then there are the blood sausage or black puddings, *morcilla* and the Catalan *butifarra negra*. *Morcilla de Burgos* comes stuffed with rice, whereas the thinner *morcilla de asturias* is just blood and a little fat. Both are great fried or stewed.

CHEESE/*QUESOS*

Spain is not famous for its cheeses, and yet can boast a tremendous variety of them, including some of very high quality. Asturias alone produces 28 types, while other northern regions, La Mancha and even the Balearics also offer a selection of cheeses ranging from soft and creamy to hard, crumbly or very strong. A few are made

with cow's milk, but most are sheep's or goats' milk cheeses. Here is a brief guide to the best.

Manchego
The 'standard' Spanish cheese, and as there is so much of it, quality varies hugely. It can be 'industrially' made or a craft-made product. It ranges from *tierno*, young and mild (or even *mantecoso*, buttery), to *añejo*, fully mature. Also a major difference is between *Manchego semi*, semi-soft and quite creamy, and *seco*, hard and dry. An *añejo seco* is pretty strong. Some Manchego is cured (*curado*) in oil for upwards of two years, and very tangy indeed. Normal prices go from 1,400ptas per kilo up to about 3,000ptas.

Burgos, Villalón, Requesón
All similar to cottage cheeses, and often eaten as dessert. They are relatively cheap.

Cabrales
A must for fans of really strong cheeses. From Asturias, made from a mixture of sheep's and goat's milk and matured in caves, It's creamy in texture and almost spicey in taste. A good one costs about 1,900ptas the kilo.

Idiazábal
Made from pure sheep's milk in the Basque Country, this cheese comes smoked and unsmoked. The smoked variety can be recommended. Upwards of 1,500ptas the kilo.

Mahón
A normally-mild, creamy cow's milk cheese from Menorca, although there are slightly stronger *añejo* versions. Pay about 1,500ptas for a decent one.

WHERE TO BUY
All markets have stands with a full range of meats and cheeses. In **La Cebada** market there is a particularly good cheese stand, no.20/21, **Magerit**. Otherwise, the shops listed below all have encyclopaedic selections of Spanish products.

Jamonería Ferpal
C/Arenal 7 (521 51 08). Metro Sol/bus all routes to Puerta del Sol. **Open** 9am-2.30pm, 5.30-8pm Mon-Sat. **Credit** MC, V.
Right in the centre of the city, and with as good a selection as you will find anywhere of *embutidos* and cheeses.

Museo del Jamón
Carrera de San Jerónimo 6 (521 03 46/531 57 21). Metro Sol/bus all routes to Puerta del Sol. **Open** 9am-midnight Mon-Sat; 10am-midnight Sun, public holidays. **Credit** MC, V.
The five branches of the 'Ham Museum' around the city centre are not the cheapest place to stock up on Spanish hams and cheeses, but surely the most spectacular. As well as buying to take home you can sample some of their exhaustive stock at the bar or in their giant restaurants.

El Palacio de los Quesos
C/Mayor 53 (548 16 23). Metro Sol/bus all routes to Puerta del Sol. **Open** 9am-2.30pm, 5.30-8.30pm Mon-Sat. **No credit cards.**
After the Museum of Ham, visit the Palace of Cheese. This fine old shop also has great wines and other delicacies.

The Market/El Mercado

The market is for those who want to shop for food the traditional way, who like hustle and bustle and are prepared to try out phrases like *'¿Quién da la vez?'* or *'¿Quién es el último?'* – both mean 'Who's the last in the queue?' – to avoid squabbles. There's always an astounding range of quality and prices. The assault on the senses comes from colourful displays of fruit and vegetables, wet fish stands, delicatessens piled high with odorous cheeses and all manner of pork products, and hawkers in the doorways with bags of garlic bulbs at 100ptas.

Some of the more interesting markets in Madrid include: **La Cebada** – ugly to look at, but among the most competitive price-wise. **La Paz** in Salamanca has the most varied selection in central Madrid. **Maravillas**, in Tetuán, is among the biggest of them all, with a near-unbeatable range of fresh fish. **San Miguel**, though very central, is more of interest for its architectural value.

Markets

Antón Martín *C/Santa Isabel 5. Metro Antón Martín/bus 6, 26, 32, 57.*

Suddenly, no-one knew whose turn it was.

La Cebada *Plaza de la Cebada. Metro La Latina/bus 17, 18, 23, 35, 60.*
Chamartín *C/Potosí. Metro Colombia/bus 7, 16, 29, 51.*
La Paz *C/Ayala 32. Metro Velázquez, Serrano/bus 1, 9, 19, 51, 74.*
Maravillas *C/Bravo Murillo 122. Metro Cuatro Caminos/bus 3, 45, 149.*
San Miguel *Plaza de San Miguel. Metro Sol/bus all routes to Puerta del Sol.*
Open 10am-2.30pm, 4.30-8.30pm, Mon-Fri; 10am-3pm Sat.

Quetzal

C/Mayor 13 (365 11 68). Metro Sol/bus all routes to Puerta del Sol. **Open** 10am-2.30pm, 4.30-9pm, Mon-Sat. **Credit** AmEx, DC, MC, V.
With the opening of this second branch in C/Mayor, Quetzal has become firmly established as Madrid's foremost purveyors of Guatemalan products and traditional textiles, as well as clothes and crafts from the rest of Central and South America.
Branch: C/López Silva 3.

Sargadelos

C/Zurbano 46 (310 48 30). Metro Rubén Darío/bus 5, 16, 40, 61, 147. **Open** 10am-1pm, 5.30-8pm, Mon-Sat. **Credit** AmEx, MC, V.
An interesting ceramics shop showcasing the work of young potters and ceramics designers from Galicia, mostly based in traditional styles but introducing many fresh touches. Much of the work on show is strikingly original.

Photographic

For fast-developing shops, *see chapter* **Services**.

Aquí

Plaza Santa Ana 1 (532 62 09). Metro Sevilla, Sol/bus all routes to Puerta del Sol. **Open** 10am-2pm, 5-8pm, Mon-Fri; 10am-2pm Sat. **Credit** AmEx, V.
Santa Ana is a professional centre selling films in bulk, renting equipment and so on, while the branches in Príncipe and Espoz y Mina are more geared to the enthusiast, and also have a good developing service.
Branches: C/ Espoz y Mina 11; C/Príncipe 6; twelve others round Madrid.

Fotocasión

C/Carlos Arniches 22 (467 64 91). Metro Puerta de Toledo, Embajadores/bus 41, 60, 148, C. **Open** 4.30-8.30pm Mon; 9am-2pm, 4.30-8.30pm, Tue-Fri; 9am-2pm Sat, Sun. **Credit** AmEx, DC, MC, V.
This marvellous treasure trove is a favourite amongst professional and amateur photographers and collectors of old cameras and photographic magazines. Owner José Luis Mur is a walking encyclopaedia on anything relating to cameras and films. He also invariably has great offers on spare parts, new equipment, second-hand cameras and just-past-the-date films and materials.

Records & Music

The **FNAC** (*see above* **One-Stop**) also houses a comprehensive record store.

El Flamenco Vive

C/Unión 4 (547 39 17). Metro Opera/bus 3, 23, 33, 39. **Open** 10.30am-2pm, 5-9pm, Mon-Sat. **Credit** MC, V.
Apart from a good selection of flamenco CD's and tapes this recently-opened shop offers books on the genre (some are in English). For those wishing to get properly kitted out it also has a stock of flamenco clothing and other paraphernalia.

Madrid Rock

Gran Vía 25 (523 26 52). Metro Gran Vía/bus all routes to Gran Vía. **Open** 10am-10pm Mon-Sat. **Credit** MC, V.
The biggest general record store in Madrid, with a very complete selection of all styles and classes of music. It often has good clear out offers. It also sells tickets for rock concerts (*see chapter* **Services**). There are several more branches around the city.

Ay Ay Ay

There's no getting away from it, Spain is a treasure trove of kitsch, from lurid 1960s postcards to plastic bulls with velveteen hair. They just keep on producing the stuff. However, in amongst it all it's possible to find fine examples of traditional craft work.

Almirante 23
C/Almirante 23 (308 12 02). Metro Chueca/bus 5, 14, 27, 37, 150. **Open** 11am-2pm, 4.30-9pm, Mon-Sat. **Credit** AmEx, MC, V.
Basically a living room, this wonderful tack and junk shop specialises in old postcards and prints.

Almoraima
Plaza Mayor 12 (365 42 89). Metro Sol/bus all routes to Puerta del Sol. **Open** 10.30am-2pm, 4-8pm, Mon-Sat. **Credit** AmEx, MC, V.
Traditional fans of all descriptions and for all tastes.

Caramelos Paco
C/Toledo 55 (365 42 58). Metro La Latina/bus 17, 18, 23, 35, 60. **Open** 9.30am-2pm, 5-8pm, Mon-Sat; 11am-3pm Sun. **No credit cards.**
All manner of boiled sweets are sold in this sugar palace including replicas of hams, sausages, figurines and giant lollipops. If you're worried about your teeth, just take a photo of the window display.

La Casa de las Escayolas
C/León 5 (429 48 50). Metro Antón Martín/bus 6, 26, 32, 57. **Open** 9.30am-2pm, 5-8.30pm, Mon-Sat. **Credit** V.
A shop dedicated to the plaster statue trade. Pick up your 60cm reproduction of Michelangelo's 'David', and paint him bright pink in the comfort of your own home. Nearby at no.19 is the very similar **Escayolas Inma**, its permanent rival.

Objetos de Arte Toledano
Paseo del Prado 10 (429 50 00). Metro Banco de España, Atocha/bus 9, 10, 14, 27, 34. **Open** 9.30am-8pm Mon-Sat. **Credit** AmEx, DC, JCB, MC, V.
This souvenir shop should be visited if you are going to the Prado – it has everything from flamenco dancing dolls to full-size suits of armour with swords, as well as porcelain by Lladró and pearls by Majorica. Across the way in the Paseo del Prado you can do the ultimate and get your own name on posters as a bullfighter or a flamenco singer.

Seseña
C/de la Cruz 23 (531 68 40). Metro Sol/bus all routes to Puerta del Sol. **Open** 10am-1.30pm, 4.30-8pm, Mon-Sat. **Credit** AmEx, DC, V.
A long-established business that's the only one left in the city specialising in traditional Madrileño capes. Ideal for the aspiring dandy. They're beautifully made, wonderfully warm, and expensive.

Manzana
C/Montera 4 (521 40 61). Metro Sol/bus all routes to Puerta del Sol. **Open** 10.30am-2pm, 5-8.30pm Mon-Fri; 10am-3pm Sat. **Credit** AmEx, DC, MC, V.
An excellent selection of Latin music (Salsa, Cumbias, Merengue.) as well as goodish jazz, blues and world music sections. Also, rare to find these days, a lot of stuff on vinyl. A Tarjeta del Cliente (shop card) earns you the right to a free record, cassette or CD after you've made ten purchases.

Musical Instruments

Spain has long been famous for craftsmanship in making musical instruments, particularly of course guitars. There are several more shops selling hand-made guitars and other instruments around the Huertas area.

Garrido Bailén
C/Bailén 19 (542 45 01).Metro Sol, Opera/bus 3, 148. **Open** 10am-1.30pm, 4.30-8.15pm, Mon-Fri; 10am-1.30pm Sat. **Credit** AmEx, V.
Possibly one of the best shops for musical instruments you will ever find anywhere. They stock everything from tiny ocarinas to Alpine horns, modern electronic keyboards and drum machines and every kind of traditional Spanish musical instrument.

Guitarrería F. Manzanero
C/Santa Ana 12 (266 00 47). Metro La Latina/bus 17, 18, 23, 35, 60. **Open** 10am-1.30pm, 5-8pm, Mon-Fri. **No credit cards.**
The very friendly Felix Manzanero has been making guitars for almost 45 years, some 30 of them in his own shop close to the Rastro. They can cost upwards of 20,000ptas for a straightforward classical guitar, 25,000ptas for a Flamenco one and up to half a million for a special commission. The shop also has a display of old and rare string instruments.

Manuel Contreras
C/Mayor 80 (Tel/fax 542 22 01). Metro Sol, Opera/bus 3, 148. **Open** 10am-2pm, 5-8.30pm Mon-Fri. **No credit cards.**
Similar prices to Felix Manzanero for standard guitars. A concert instrument will cost upwards of 175,000ptas.

Religious Articles

The area between Sol and Plaza Mayor is particularly strong on shops selling all things religious.

Sobrinas de Pérez
C/Postas 6 (521 19 54). Metro Sol/bus all routes to Puerta del Sol. **Open** 9.30am-1.30pm, 4.30-8pm Mon-Sat. **Credit** AmEx, DC, MC, V.
Since 1867 this small but crammed establishment has been selling model baby Jesuses, crucifixes, candles, prints, and bibles. The window display is fabulous.

Sports Goods

Deportes Chamberí
C/Eloy Gonzalo 28 (448 33 66). Metro Iglesia/bus 16, 61, 149. **Open** 10am-1.30pm, 4.30-8.30pm, Mon-Fri; 10am-2pm, 5-8.15pm, Sat. **Credit** AmEx, V.
One of the few sports shops in Madrid that covers practically all sports instead of specialising in one. Skis repaired and racquets restrung.

The Rastro

Thought to date back five centuries, the Rastro, Madrid's teeming flea market, is a must even if you're not much of a shopper, for the show that develops here every Sunday is something to be seen. Keen marketgoers arrive before the rush, say around 7am, when they can watch the stalls being set up. It really gets going about 9pm, and from 10am to 2pm it's shoulder-to-shoulder all the way down Calle Ribera de Curtidores. It's as much a mass hang-out point as a place to buy and sell, although most people try and look as if they're after something.

The Rastro is a rambling affair, and while it has traditionally been centred on Ribera de Curtidores its popularity means that it's spreading outwards all the time. Stalls sprawl down Ribera de Curtidores from the main square, the Plaza de Cascorro, which serves as a good meeting point. Those towards the top mainly offer clothes and cheap jewellery, but down the hill or in the surrounding streets you can buy anything from spare car parts to a TV remote control, from real and fake antiques to fifties furniture, from second-hand clothes to the latest in bondage gear. Clothes, camping equipment, books old and new, porno films and comics, religious relics, prints, paintings, birds, hippy paraphernalia and lots of plain junk are all bought and sold here. There are fewer second-hand goods than cheap, fairly new ones.

On Ribera de Curtidores there are mostly commercial goods, while streets to the right going down contain second-hand clothes, furniture and anything else you might want to buy, or not. Some parts have a reputation for fencing stolen goods. The Rastro is not a dangerous place, but care regarding pickpockets is very necessary. This is the one place in Madrid where they are most active, and you need to keep your wits about you. Don't look careless or carry open bags or a wallet in a back pocket, and be aware if somebody seems to be sticking too close behind you in the crowd.

Along the Rastro streets there are also permanent shops, such as the antiques galleries (*see page 136* **Antiques**), which are also open (and much more peaceful) during the week. Other shops worth checking out are **Marihuana** in Plaza del Cascorro, for all sorts of groovy stuff in black, **El Transformista**, Calle Mira el Río Baja 18, for fifties' designs and furniture, or **Mamoto**, across the street at no.13, for second-hand clothes.

Haggling is usually restricted to very expensive items, or extremely cheap stuff. By about 1pm, the crowds have become pretty immobile, and in summer it's also very hot. This is the time to repair to one of the district's many bars, which also do a booming trade every Sunday (*see chapter* **Tapas**).

El Rastro
C/Ribera de Curtidores. Metro La Latina, Puerta de Toledo/bus 17, 18, 23, 35, 60, 148, C. **Open** dawn-approx 2pm Sun, public holidays.

Deportes Legazpi
C/Ribera de Curtidores 8 & 11 (527 04 37). Metro La Latina/bus 17, 23, 35, 60. **Open** 10am-2pm, 5-8pm, Mon-Sat. **Credit** V.
A general sports shop on the Rastro that's especially hot on bargain prices for outdoor and mountain sports equipment. Tents, rucksacks, sleeping bags, camping stoves and skiing gear area all available at excellent prices.

Stamps & Coins

Stamp & Coin Market
Plaza Mayor. Metro Sol/bus all routes to Puerta del Sol. **Open** approx 9am-2pm Sun.
Every Sunday the Plaza Mayor is taken over by an avid mass of stamp and coin collectors buying, selling and eyeing the wares. It's also become quite a Sunday-morning attraction for anyone on a stroll about the city centre, whether or not they share a fascination with tarnished old pesetas, stamps of all nations and turn-of-the-century share certificates. The market has diversified too, and there are now traders selling old magazines, second-hand books, postcards, badges, old former-Soviet block military regalia, and other things. In short, just about anything collectable is there.

Stationery & Art Supplies

Carlin
C/Carretas 13 (522 90 96). Metro Sol/bus all routes to Puerta del Sol. **Open** 10am-2.30pm, 3.30-8.30pm, Mon-Sat. **Credit** MC, V.
A supermarket for all items of stationery for the office and personal use. Several branches elsewhere.

Macarrón
C/Jovellanos 2 (429 68 01) Metro Banco de España, Sevilla/bus all routes to Plaza de Cibeles. **Open** 9am-1.30pm, 4-7.30pm, Mon-Sat. **Credit** AmEx, DC, MC, V.
The official art materials supplier to the Círculo de Bellas Artes, patronised by Dalí and Picasso. Helpful, friendly staff.

Tobacco & Smoking

The oldest, biggest and best official *Estanco* (*see chapter* **Essential Information**) in Madrid is at Calle Alcalá 18, the **Expendeduría Nº 1 Santiago**, which has everything for the convinced smoker. Cigarettes are also sold in bars, in vending machines.

Services

The small repair shop round the corner rather than the city-wide chain still survives at the head of service culture here.

The service sector in Madrid, like so many things, is caught in flux between the traditional and the very modern. Traditionally, all over the city there were any number of small, specialist shops that would alter a jacket or fix your shoes. In addition, a crop of more modern service companies also sprang up during the eighties. Both sectors have been under pressure lately. Many new-style businesses, particularly pizza delivery companies, have closed with the recession. Hundreds of small traditional shops have folded too in the face of competition from consumer-friendly superstores. **El Corte Inglés** also offers many of the services listed below (travel agents, hairdressing, film processing, fax, opticians, key-cutting and so on) at any of its branches (*see chapter* **Shopping**).

Even so, in most *barrios* of Madrid there are still plenty of small (and sometimes unusual) shops struggling on, and you should find most basic services locally. In general, staff in shops are helpful. *Servicio a domicilio* means they deliver it, collect it or come to your house to repair it. *En el acto* means they do it while you wait. If you really can't find anybody to do what you need, it could be worth watching *Tele-empleo*, a nightly job-hunting programme on TeleMadrid which has a 'sell yourself' spot featuring a variety of offbeat services.

Car & Bike Hire

Car Hire

To hire a car in Spain you must be over 21 and have had a driving licence for over a year. You will also need a credit card, or have to leave a sizeable cash deposit. Check whether insurance, IVA (VAT) at 15 per cent and unlimited mileage are included in the price. It is always advisable to take out Collision Damage Waiver (CDW) and personal accident insurance on top of the basic cover.

Hire companies frequently offer good weekend deals. For more information on driving in and around Madrid, *see chapter* **Survival**.

Altai
Paseo de la Castellana 121 (555 10 10). Metro Lima, Nuevos Ministerios/bus 27, 40, 147, 150. **Open** 9am-2pm, 4-7pm, Mon-Fri. **Credit** AmEx, MC, V.
A small company offering cheap weekly hire (29,000ptas for a Fiat Uno). There's a discount for Visa payment.

Atesa
C/Infanta Mercedes 10 (571 32 94). Metro Estrecho/bus 3, 43, 149. **Open** 8.30am-1.30pm, 4-8pm, Mon-Fri; 9am-1pm Sat. **Credit** AmEx, DC, MC, V.
Spain's biggest national car hire company. Weekly rental from 39,000ptas; 15,500ptas for the weekend. Cars have radio cassettes and air-conditioning.
Branch: Barajas Airport (305 86 60).

Chóferes Privados
C/Cochabamba 5, bajo 2° (315 77 33). Metro Colombia/bus 7, 11, 16, 40, 51. **Open** 9am-2pm, 4-8pm, Mon-Fri. **Credit** AmEx, DC, MC, V.
Got a car? Can't drive, won't drive? These people, all professional drivers, will do it for you. From 2,000ptas per hour.

Europcar
C/General Yagüe 6 (556 15 00). Metro Cuzco, Lima/bus 5, 40, 149, 150. **Open** 8.30am-7.30pm Mon-Fri. **Credit** AmEx, DC, MC, V.
A Peugeot 205 or equivalent costs 18,700ptas for a weekend (Friday midday to Monday morning) and 45,500ptas a whole week, including VAT. The staff speak English.
Branches: Barajas Airport (305 44 20); Atocha station (530 01 69); Chamartín station (323 17 21); C/San Leonardo 8 (541 88 92); C/Orense 29 (555 99 30).

Cycles, Scooters & Motorbikes

For accompanied mountain-biking tours into the sierras around Madrid, *see chapter* **The Sierras**.

Motoalquiler
C/Conde-Duque 13 (542 06 57). Metro Noviciado/bus 2, 21. **Open** 8am-2pm, 5-8pm, Mon-Fri; 9am-1.30pm Sat. **Credit** AmEx, DC, MC, V.
Scooters (*vespinos*) and motorbikes (*motos*) for hire from 2,450ptas per day plus 15,000ptas deposit for a 50cc machine, to 7,500ptas per day and a 35,000ptas deposit for a Yamaha 250cc bike.

Jomark Ibérica
Casa de Campo (526 00 03). Metro Lago, Batán/bus 31, 33, 36, 39. **Open** 4-8.30pm Mon-Fri; 11am-9pm Sat, Sun. **No credit cards.**
Only *Bicicars* (four-wheelers with two seats side-by-side), for 700ptas per hour (half an hour, 400ptas). Ideal for a gentle pedal round the lake, but less suitable for the hilly terrain of this massive park.

Mountain Bike World
C/Uruguay 1 (458 29 20). Metro Colombia/bus 7, 11, 16, 40, 51, 52. **Open** 10am-2pm, 5-8.30pm, Mon-Fri; 10am-2pm Sat. **Credit** MC, V.
Half the price of Karacol (from 1,000ptas per day, with the same deposit and ID requirements) but not as central.

Sport Karacol
Paseo de las Delicias 53 (539 96 33). Metro Palos de la Frontera/bus 6, 45, 55. **Open** 10.30am-2pm, 5.30-8.30pm, Mon-Fri; 10.30am-2pm Sat. **Credit** AmEx, V.

Mountain bikes can be hired for 2,000ptas a day on production of a photocopied ID, plus 5,000ptas deposit. *See also chapter* **The Sierras**.
Branch: C/Montera 32 (532 90 73).

Clothes & Accessories

Cleaning & Repairs

Truly self-service *lavanderías* (laundrettes) are hard to find and, if you do find one, they are generally expensive. Even though the machines are automatic in most there will be an attendant, invariably a woman, who if you are a man will probably assume that you want her to do your washing for you, for a small extra charge. *Tintorerías* are officially dry-cleaners, but also offer all sorts of clothing care services (including repair) and will sometimes take in laundry by weight. Every neighbourhood has at least one.

Don Arreglo

C/Hermosilla 97 (435 77 83). Metro Goya/bus 21, 43, 53, 61. **Open** 10am-2pm, 5-8.30pm, Mon-Sat. **No credit cards**.
'Mr Fix It' for zips, rips and all kinds of alterations.

Don Planchón

C/Santa Feliciana 18 (445 73 28). Metro Iglesias/bus 3, 37, 40, 147. **Open** 9am-2pm, 3-9.30pm, Mon-Fri. **No credit cards**.
Your dirty laundry collected, washed, ironed and returned. From 200ptas per piece, minimum five pieces. **Telecamisa** *(535 15 53)* offers a similar service.

Lavomatique

C/de la Palma 4 (447 85 05). Metro Tribunal/bus 3, 40, 149. **Open** 9am-9pm daily. **No credit cards**.
A coin-operated, self-service laundrette in Malasaña. A basic wash costs 550ptas. Note that you must take your own washing powder.

Tinte Rapi-Seco

C/Gaztambide 35 (543 30 32). Metro Moncloa/bus 16, 44, 61, C. **Open** 8.30am-8pm Mon-Fri; 8.30am-2pm Sat. **No credit cards**.
A good dry cleaners with opening hours more convenient than most. There's a discount of 10% if you pay in advance.

Dress Hire & Party Wear

Cornejo

C/Magdalena 2 (530 55 55/539 16 46). Metro Tirso de Molina/bus 6, 26, 32, 57. **Open** 10am-2pm, 3-7pm, Mon-Fri. **No credit cards**.
Dress yourself up as Napoleon, a cossack or Cleopatra or find that gorilla suit you've always wanted at this historic costume-hire shop. Their stock is enormous and prices start from 6,000ptas for a weekend (Friday to Monday). Should you be swept away at the party they also hire out wedding dresses and formal attire. It's hugely busy at Carnival time. There are several similar (but smaller) shops along the same street, making it Madrid's veritable fancy-dress row.

Fiestas Paco

C/Toledo 55 (365 45 28). Metro La Latina/bus 17, 18, 23, 35, 60. **Open** 9.30am-2pm, 5-8pm, Mon-Sat; 11am-3pm Sun. **No credit cards**.
Organising a *fiesta*, or just going to one? Stock up on masks, disguises, decorations, tricks, jokes and goodies at this super-

A leisurely shoe-shine on the Gran Vía.

market of silliness. They can also put you in touch with clowns, magicians and other entertainers.

Gerardo

C/Príncipe de Vergara 25 (576 12 94). Metro Velázquez/bus 29, 52. **Open** 10am-1.30pm, 5-7.30pm, Mon-Fri; 10am-1.30pm Sat. **No credit cards**.
White tie and tails from 12,500ptas per day. Look a million dollars (in tuxedos, ties and trimmings) at a fraction of the price.

Menkes

C/Mesonero Romanos 14 (532 10 36). Metro Callao/bus 44, 75, 133, 146. **Open** 9.30am-2pm, 4.30-8.30pm, Mon-Sat. **Credit** AmEx, DC, MC, V.
Spanish regional costumes (*castizo* outfits) and fancy dress (Father Christmas, the Three Kings) for hire. Also available are made-to-measure flamenco dresses and shoes.

Embroidery

Carmelitas Descalzas de Aravaca

Carretera de Aravaca a Húmera km1.5 (307 1874). Bus Llorente 657 from Moncloa/train Cercanías line C-7 to Aravaca. **Open** 10.30am-1.30pm, 4-7pm, Mon-Fri; 10.30am-1pm Sat. Closed Easter Week. **No credit cards**.
Few things could be more in keeping with one traditional conception of Spain than having a favourite piece of clothing hand-embroidered by the Barefoot Carmelite nuns. You must take the article of clothing to the convent, where you can choose the kind of work you want done, and then pick it up in a few days. Designs, as one might expect, are rather traditional. Prices vary, but are very low for the quality of the work.

Shoeshine & Shoe Repairs

Shoeshine men still ply their trade along the Gran Vía and in the Puerta del Sol, at a normal rate of 400ptas a shine. For repairs, every market and most *barrio* streets have a shoe repairer – look out for signs saying *rápido* or *reparación de calzados*.

Márquez y González

C/Hermosilla 60 (531 82 73). Metro Goya/bus 21, 29, 52, 53. **Open** 9.30am-2pm, 4.30-8pm, Mon-Fri; 9.30am-2pm Sat. **Credit** AmEx, MC, V.
Artisan shoemakers and repairers.

Electrical Repairs

Abatel
C/Angosta de los Mancebos 8 (366 70 99). Metro La Latina/bus 31, 50, 60, 65. **Open** 9am-2pm, 4-7pm, Mon-Fri; 9am-noon Sat. **No credit cards.**
Specialists in video repair who fix stereos and other electrical goods too. There is no call-out charge and free estimates are given. If the number on your receipt matches that day's winning ONCE lottery ticket, they will give you 100,000ptas.

Florists

Unlike many cities Madrid does not have a central flower market. Gypsies set up stalls on street corners and outside Metro stations, where you can buy flowers and small plants relatively cheaply. One of the biggest and best is outside the Calle Génova exit of Alonso Martínez Metro. Note that cut flowers are quite expensive in Madrid.

Center Blumen
Centro Comercial de La Vaguada (739 20 28). Metro Barrio del Pilar/bus 83, 128, 132, 134. **Open** 10am-10pm daily. **No credit cards.**
Center Blumen offers the full works, from wreaths to red roses. There are several branches around the city.

Roses Only
C/Antonia Mercé 5 (576 18 18). Metro Goya/bus 15, 29, 30, 53, C. **Open** 10am-9pm Mon-Sat; 11.30am-2.30pm Sun. **Credit** V.
As the name says, nothing but roses, for 575ptas-2,850ptas a dozen, plus wrapping (175ptas) and delivery (875ptas).

Food Delivery

TelePaella
Glorieta de Miguel Rubiales 1 (459 20 10). Metro Estrecho/bus 43, 64, 127, 128. **Open** 10am-4pm, 8-11.30pm, Mon-Sat; 10am-4pm Sun. **No credit cards.**
The paella is freshly cooked, so delivery takes about an hour. From 2,750ptas for three to four people.

Telepescaíto
C/Caleruega 19 (767 05 13). Metro Chamartín/bus 7, 29, 49, 129, 150. **Open** noon-4pm, 7.30pm-midnight, daily. **Credit** MC, V.
Food delivery culture *a la Andaluza*. Flash-fried whitebait (900ptas) *pipirrana* (tuna salad) and other traditional Andalusian dishes brought to your door, with chilled *fino* as well. Minimum order 2,500ptas. Note too that they are based in north Madrid, a long way from the centre.

Telepizza
Glorieta de Santa Maria de la Cabeza (539 41 03). Metro Palos de la Frontera/bus 55, 59, 60. **Open** 1pm-midnight daily. **No credit cards.**
The idea's American, the food's Italian, but this is a peculiarly Spanish success story. Leo Fernández built an empire of 100 outlets in five years – he says the secret's in the dough.

¡Torti-ya!
C/Raimundo Fernández Villaverde 26 (553 53 14). Metro Cuatro Caminos/bus 42, 149, C. **Open** 12.30-5pm, 7.30pm-midnight, daily. **No credit cards.**
Several varieties of traditional Spanish potato omelette brought to your door on a brightly-liveried scooter.

Health & Beauty
Hairdressers

Alta Peluquería Vallejo
C/Santa Isabel 22 (527 44 48). Metro Antón Martín/bus 6, 26, 32, 57. **Open** 9am-2pm, 4.30-8pm, Mon-Fri; 9am-2pm Sat. **No credit cards.**
A traditional gentlemen's barber's. It's friendly, cheap (900ptas) and offers good basic cuts.

Jofer
C/Galileo 52, 6° (446 77 03). Metro Quevedo/bus 2, 16, 61. **Open** 9am-9pm Mon-Sat. **Credit** V.
Reasonably-priced unisex salons which also help beauty and sunbed treatments. At their training school supervised apprentices are let loose on your locks. You pay just 400ptas. There are several more branches around the city.
School: Taller de Peluqueros C/Madera 7 (531 01 69).

Tattoo
Travesía de Belén 3 (319 61 57). Metro Chueca/bus 3, 37, 40, 149. **Open** 1-9pm Mon-Fri; noon-4pm Sat. **Credit** MC, V.
A trendy place for groovy cuts. A wash and cut for women is about 3,500ptas; for men, 2,000ptas.

Opticians

General Optica
C/Velázquez 49 (575 21 95). Metro Velázquez/bus 1, 9, 19, 51, 74. **Open** 9.30am-2pm, 4.30-8pm, Mon-Fri; 10am-2pm, 5-8pm, Sat. **Credit** AmEx, MC, V.
All products come with a year's guarantee, and there are frequent special offers for students and pensioners.
Branches: C/Carmen 22 (521 00 65); C/Preciados 22 (522 21 21); C/Nenufar 8 (571 69 40); Avda Albufera 115 (437 60 55).

Ulloa Optico
C/Carmen 14 (521 74 74). Metro Sol/bus all routes to Puerta del Sol. **Open** 10am-2.30pm, 5-8.30pm, Mon-Fri; 10am-2.30pm Sat. **Credit** AmEx, DC, MC, V.
Traditional opticians offering all the usual services, including sunglasses with graduated lenses. They also fit hearing aids. No appointment necessary. There are 14 more branches throughout Madrid.

Tattooists

Mao & Cathy
C/San Vicente Ferrer 20 (594 49 56). Metro Noviciado, Tribunal/bus 3, 40, 147, 149. **Open** 11am-2pm, 3-7pm, Tue-Sat. **No credit cards.**
Choose from a catalogue of 5,000 designs or have your own made up, from 2,500ptas. Hygiene guaranteed.

Leather Goods & Watch Repairs

Arte de Relojes
Plaza de Santa Ana 10 (429 64 63). Metro Sevilla, Sol/bus all routes to Puerta del Sol. **Open** 9.30am-1.30pm, 4.30-8pm, Mon-Fri; 9.30am-1.30pm Sat. **No credit cards.**
Specialists in antique timepieces, as well as general repairs.

Restauraciones Peña
C/Ave María 8 (369 39 97). Metro Antón Martín/bus 6, 26, 32, 57. **Open** 9.30am-1.30pm, 4.30-8pm, Mon-Fri; 9.30am-1.30pm Sat. **No credit cards.**
All kinds of leather goods – bags, cases, clothes – repaired, cleaned or restored, quickly, cheerfully and with great skill.

Choose from over 5,000 designs at **Mao & Cathy**. *See page 152.*

Pharmacies

Farmacia a Domicilio

(575 53 75). **Open** *2-5pm, 8pm-9am, Mon-Fri; 24 hours Sat, Sun.* **No credit cards**.
Any product available in a chemist, from condoms to cough mixture, delivered to your door for a 500ptas charge plus the cost of the goods. The service operates whenever normal pharmacies are closed.

Photography, Photocopying, Fax

Most stationers (*papelerias*) or printers (*imprentas*) have fax and photocopying machines. There is a telephone and fax office on the ground floor of the **Telefónica** building at Gran Vía 30 (*see chapter* **Survival**). Specialist photocopy shops are the cheapest option, but larger Metro stations also have photocopiers. Copy shops are particularly common around the University area of Moncloa. For camera shops, *see chapter* **Shopping**.

Foto Sistema

Gran Vía 22 (521 20 63). Metro Plaza de España/bus all routes to Plaza de España. **Open** *9.30am-8pm Mon-Fri; 9.30am-2pm Sat.* **Credit** *AmEx, MC, V.*
A good-quality fastdeveloping service, with several more branches around central Madrid.

Reprografía C Moreno

C/Fernando el Católico 88 (543 41 61). Metro Moncloa/bus 16, 61. **Open** *9.15am-3pm, 4-8pm, Mon-Sat.* No credit cards.
A large specialist copy shop abel to do amplifications, colour copying and so on, and much used by students.

Picture Framing

In the Santa Ana and Huertas area look out for signs saying *marcos* or *molduras*. The area's also very good for antique shops and second-hand bookshops.

Salón Cano

Paseo del Prado 26 (420 05 20/420 16 77). Metro Antón Martín/bus 6, 9, 26. **Open** *10am-1.30pm, 5-8.30pm, Mon-Fri.* **No credit cards**.
Suppliers to the Prado museum across the road and royal households, and founded in 1905. *The* place, if you like your pictures in big fancy gold frames.

Ticket Agencies

Tickets are also sold in all branches of El Corte Inglés; *see chapter* **Shopping**.

FNAC

C/Preciados 28 (595 61 00). Metro Callao, Sol/bus all routes to Puerta del Sol. **Open** *10am-10pm Mon-Sat.* **Credit** *AmEx, DC, MC, V.*
The huge French-owned discount music and book superstore has a ticket desk in the stylish foyer selling theatre and concert tickets. They do not charge commission. *See also chapter* **Shopping**.

Madrid Rock

Gran Vía 25 (523 26 52). Metro Gran Vía/bus all routes to Gran Vía. **Open** *10am-10pm Mon-Sat.* **Credit** *MC, V.*
A record shop that's one of the main outlets for rock and pop concert tickets. There are several branches in the centre. *See also chapter* **Shopping**.

TEYCI

C/Goya 7 (576 45 32). Metro Serrano/bus 9, 19, 21, 51, 53. **Open** *10am-2pm, 4-8pm, Mon-Thur; 10am-8pm Fri-Sun.* **No credit cards**.
A traditional ticket agency that can obtain tickets for the theatre, opera, bullfights, football and most other events in Madrid, except rock gigs. They charge 2% commission.

Travel Agents

TIVE

C/Fernando el Católico 88 (543 02 08). Metro Moncloa/bus 16, 44, 61, C. **Open** *10am-2pm Mon-Fri; 9am-noon Sat.* **Credit** *MC, V.*
The official student and youth travel agency issues student and youth hostel cards, and has a range of discounts available on air, rail and coach tickets to anyone under 26, or to students up to the age of 30. There is also a branch inside the **Instituto de la Juventud** (*see chapter* **Students**).

Viajes Zeppelin

Plaza de Santa Domingo 2 (547 79 04). Metro Santo Domingo/bus 44, 133, 147. **Open** *9am-7.30pm Mon-Fri; 10am-1pm Sat.* **Credit** *MC, V.*
The best place for cheap European charter deals. It's very popular so don't be surprised if you have to queue, but service is fast and friendly.

Museo Nacional Centro de Arte Reina Sofía

C/ SANTA ISABEL 52. 28012 MADRID
TF: 91- 4675062 - 4675161   FAX: 91- 4673163

Galleries & Museums

Art Galleries

Madrid's art scene has been insular, but its spectacular galleries and public spaces are now open to an ever wider range of contemporary art.

The **Casa de América**.

Madrid is – despite an ongoing rivalry with Barcelona – regarded as the centre of the Spanish art scene. As part of the explosion of interest in contemporary culture of all sorts that accompanied Spain's political transition and Madrid's own *Movida* scene (*see chapter* **History: Dictatorship & Rebirth**), new galleries appeared all over the city centre at the beginning of the 1980s. Even some foreign gallerists, led by a belief that Spain suddenly represented a vast new market, opened up their own spectacular spaces here. They did not realise that Spanish art buyers were relatively new to the game, and generally only wanted to buy Spanish artists. To an extent they still do. Consequently, even though artists from all over Spain come to live and work in Madrid, so that there is plenty of good work around, a lot of Spanish art that is really only second-rate also gets

displayed here too. The situation has changed a little since recession hit Spain in 1993, causing many commercial galleries to close their doors, although a surprising number have survived.

One characteristic feature of the Madrid art scene is that most major galleries – both commercial and public – are run by women, known by local wags and many artists as *la mafia de las bragas* (the Knicker Mafia). A select group of women, among them Soledad Lorenzo, Juana de Aizpuru and the late Juana Mordó, have been the main movers and arbiters of taste in the city's developing art world, and wield their power knowingly.

ART SPACES & ART FAIRS

While the commercial gallery scene was expanding, so too was the public sector. The new democratic authorities – the central government and, above all, the Madrid regional and city authorities – were keen to open up new cultural spaces, making up for the complete neglect of such facilities under the Franco régime. First to make a mark were the wonderfully-restored cultural centres run by the city, such as the **Conde Duque**, in a vast eighteenth-century barracks, and the three halls in the **Retiro** park (*see chapter* **Sightseeing**), the **Casa de Vacas**, the **Palacio de Cristal** and the **Palacio de Velázquez**. In addition, many banks and savings banks, encouraged by Spanish laws on banking profits, have traditionally run cultural foundations, and they too have expanded their role in the art scene since the seventies. As a result, and despite cut-backs in city arts funding under the right-wing Partido Popular council (in power since 1991), Madrid now has art foundations, exhibition spaces and museums to challenge those in any other European cities.

The central government's major contribution has been the **Museo Nacional Centro de Arte Reina Sofía**, a superb gallery that hosts many excellent temporary travelling exhibitions that don't necessarily reach other European centres. On the other hand, permanent contemporary Spanish art collections in Madrid, including the one at the Reina Sofia, are not overly representative of the national scene.

The other highlight of the Madrid art scene is **ARCO** (*see page 161*), a vast art showcase-and-market held annually since 1981. A real success story, it is now one of Europe's main annual art fairs and a major cultural event in itself.

The best source of up-to-date information on what's on in both private and public galleries is the free monthly magazine *Guiarte*, available from the better galleries and (usually) all tourist offices. The *Guía del Ocio* and the main newspapers also have gallery listings as well as reviews *(see chapter* **Media***)*.

Public Galleries & Foundations

In addition to the venues listed here, temporary exhibitions are also frequently held in the city's major museums *(see chapter* **Museums***)*.

Casa de América
Palacio de Linares, Plaza de Cibeles (595 48 00). Metro Banco de España/bus all routes to Plaza de Cibeles. **Open** 11am-7pm Tue-Sat; 11am-2pm Sun. **Admission** free.
Housed in the Palacio de Linares, a former aristocratic residence dating from 1872, the Casa de América was opened in 1992 to showcase the visual arts of Latin America and promote friendship between these countries and Spain. As well as exhibitions of both known and young artists from Mexico, Cuba and elsewhere in Latin America, the Casa offers music and theatre performances, talks and other events and good print and video libraries. There's also an interesting bookshop and a fine café/restaurant with a relaxing garden. New Latin American art has an enthusiasm and energy often lacking in work from elsewhere, and is not to be missed.
Wheelchair access.

Centro Cultural Casa de Vacas
Parque del Retiro (409 58 19). Metro Retiro/bus all routes to Puerta de Alcalá. **Open** 10am-2pm, 5-9pm, daily. Closed Aug. **Admission** free.
The Casa de Vacas, idyllically situated in the Retiro next to the boating lake, resembles nothing so much as a kind of suburban Spanish dream house. It's run by the city and tends to house an unpredictable variety of shows, but it's worth looking in on if you are going round the park.

Centro Cultural Conde Duque
C/Conde Duque 11 (588 58 34). Metro Ventura Rodríguez, Noviciado/bus 1, 2, 21, 44, 133, C. **Open** 10am-2pm, 5.30-9pm, Mon-Sat; 10am-2pm Sun. **Admission** free.
The Cuartel Conde Duque, a magnificent eighteenth-century edifice built by Philip V's favoured architect, Pedro de Ribera, as a barracks for the Palace Guard, now functions as a multi-purpose exhibition space, concert venue and home for a variety of other services, all under the aegis of the city council. There are three big granite-walled galleries with three- to five-metre high ceilings, while the three massive patios are used to show sculpture. The centre stages about 12 exhibitions a year of Spanish and international artists, with both single artist and group shows. Future exhibition subjects will include Nordic Contemporary Art, Francisco San José, Dimitri Perdikidis and, in a more idiosyncratic retrospective, Carlos Sáenz de Tejada, the monumental, traditionalist painter who set the visual style of the Franco régime at its most militant during the 1940s.
Wheelchair access.

Centro Cultural de la Villa
Jardines del Descubrimiento, Plaza Colón (575 60 80). Metro Colón/bus all routes to Plaza Colón. **Open** 10am-9pm Tue-Sun. **Admission** free.
Go down the steps under the deafening but very refreshing water cascade in the Plaza Colón, below Columbus' monument, and you come to the city authorities' only purpose-

At the **Centro Cultural Conde-Duque**.

built cultural centre. It offers theatre, concerts, a café and a huge gallery where group shows of important Hispanic artists are staged. Unfortunately, these tend to be worthy, but bland. *See also chapter* **Theatre**.
Wheelchair access.

Círculo de Bellas Artes
C/Alcalá 42 (531 77 00). Metro Banco de España, Sevilla/bus all routes to C/Alcalá. **Open** 5-9pm Tue-Fri; 11am-2pm, 5-9pm, Sat; 11am-2pm Sun. **Admission** 100ptas.
This multi-functional cultural and social centre, housed in its own fine building since 1926, is in some ways comparable to the ICA in London or the Kitchen in New York, although it's older and much larger. It continues to play a major part in every area of the arts in Madrid. Apart from a theatre and concert hall, and a vast café where you can hang out all day should you wish, there are four impressive exhibition spaces that show work in all media. *See also chapters* **Sightseeing**, **Cafés & Bars** *and* **Music: Classical & Opera**.

Fundación Arte y Tecnología
C/Fuencarral 1 (531 29 70). Metro Gran Vía/bus all routes to Gran Vía. **Open** 10am-2pm, 5-8pm, Tue-Fri; 10am-2pm Sat, Sun. **Admission** free.
The mega-rich Spanish national telephone company, the *Telefónica*, uses this large space to show selections from its permanent collection of Spanish art, which includes work by Eduardo Chillida, Luis Fernández, Joan Miró, Picasso and Antoni Tàpies. A second gallery space hosts temporary exhibitions of artists from Spain and abroad.

Fundación Banco Central Hispano
C/Marqués de Villamagna 3 (558 25 70). Metro Rubén Darío/bus all routes to Castellana. **Open** 11am-2pm, 5-9pm, Tue-Sat; 11am-2.30pm Sun. **Admission** free.
The art foundation of the Banco Central Hispano has a collection of more than 800 works by Spanish artists, among them Broto, García Sevilla and Chillida. It also has a good gallery space for temporary shows of Spanish art.

A major contemporary art patron, the **Fundación Juan March**.

Fundación La Caixa

C/Serrano 60 (435 48 33). Metro Serrano/bus 1, 9, 19, 21, 53, 74. **Open** 11am-8.30pm Mon, Wed-Sat; 11am-2pm Sun. **Admission** free.

The Catalan savings bank *La Caixa* is the largest and richest in Spain, and its cultural foundation's branch in Madrid is famous for its high-quality exhibitions. They often focus on twentieth-century Spanish artistic movements, although international artists such as Takis, Cragg and Beuys have also been shown. Its ultra-clean gallery space makes a perfect backdrop for contemporary art.

Fundación Juan March

C/Castelló 77 (435 42 40). Metro Núñez de Balboa/bus 1, 29, 52, 74. **Open** *Sept-June* 10am-2pm, 5.30-9pm, Mon-Fri; 10am-2pm Sat, Sun. **Admission** free.

Set up in 1955 by Juan March, one of Spain's richest men, the Fundación March is today one of the most important private art foundations in Europe. Its current building was opened in 1975. Every year the foundation organises, sometimes in collaboration with other museums, galleries and private collectors, nearly 35 art exhibitions, which are regularly among the most interesting in Madrid. They are presented in the Fundación's own space here in the capital, as well as in other centres throughout Spain and abroad. Exhibitions include great Spanish or foreign artists such as Kandinsky, Picasso and Matisse, and group shows based on particular movements or schools, including photography and other media. The foundation's own collection contains over 1,300 works of art by some of the best contemporary Spanish artists, some of which are on permanent exhibit in the Madrid building. The Fundación March is also a major patron of music (*see chapter* **Music: Classical & Opera**). *Wheelchair access.*

Museo Nacional Centro de Arte Reina Sofía

C/Santa Isabel 52 (467 50 62). Metro Atocha/bus all routes to Atocha. **Open** 10am-9pm Mon, Wed-Sat; 10am-2.30pm Sun. **Admission** *Mon, Wed-Fri, 10am-2.30pm Sat* 400ptas; 200ptas students; free under-18s, over-65s. *2.30-9pm Sat, Sun* free.

The San Carlos Hospital, built between 1776 and 1781 by

Francesco Sabatini, was entirely refurbished during the eighties, and first opened as an exhibition hall in 1986. It was only following a second phase of building work that ended in 1990, though, that it was finally completed as the Centro de Arte Reina Sofía, which is undoubtedly the most impressive space in Madrid for displaying works of art. Despite the presence of the *Guernica*, the much-criticised permanent collection is not necessarily the main attraction – often more exciting are the major travelling exhibitions of international artists and important collections from around the world, which are shown on the lower floors of this vast building. At any given time there are always at least three significant, high-quality shows covering painting, sculpture, photography, prints and so on, making the Reina Sofía one of Europe's foremost exhibition venues for contemporary art. In addition, the building has a cinema, a good, large bookshop, a library, restaurant and café. For information on other aspects of the building and the permanent collection, *see chapters* **Sightseeing**, **Museums** *and* **Music: Classical & Opera**. *Wheelchair access.*

Palacio de Cristal

Parque del Retiro (574 66 14). Metro Retiro/bus all routes to Puerta de Alcalá. **Open** 11am-6pm Tue-Sun. **Admission** free.

Madrid's 'Crystal Palace', a typically-nineteenth-century glass-and-wrought iron structure overlooking a lake, is the largest of the three exhibition halls inside the Retiro. First built by architect Ricardo Velázquez to house an exhibition of 'Exotic Plants' in 1887, it was, like the nearby **Casa de Vacas** and **Palacio de Velázquez**, beautifully restored during the eighties, and now makes an attractive venue for large-scale exhibitions.

Palacio de Velázquez

Parque del Retiro (574 66 14). Metro Retiro/bus all routes to Puerta de Alcalá. **Open** 11am-6pm Tue-Sun. **Admission** free.

Built by Ricardo Velázquez for a Mining Exhibition in 1883, this fine brick and tile building surrounded by the trees of the Retiro is topped by large iron and glass vaults. The galleries are wonderfully airy, and it usually hosts very good touring shows.

Sala del Canal de Isabel II

*C/Santa Engracia 125 (445 10 09). Metro Ríos
Rosas/bus 3, 12, 37, 149.* **Open** 11am-2pm, 5-8.30pm,
Mon-Fri; 11am-2pm Sun. **Admission** free.

A water-tower, built in elaborate *neo-Mudéjar* style in 1907-
11 and considered one of the finest examples of industrial
architecture in Madrid, has been restored and imaginatively transformed into a unique exhibition space, specialising
in photography. Its shows are often world-class.

Commercial Galleries

As in other cities, galleries in Madrid have tended
to cluster together. Traditionally the major centre
of the up-market gallery trade has been in
Salamanca, above all on Calle Claudio Coello.
Several more galleries have also appeared just
across the Castellana around the Calle Génova and
in Chueca, although mostly in the classier part of
the district, close to the Calle Almirante. Most
recently a new crop of often more adventurous galleries has emerged further south towards Atocha,
close to the **Reina Sofía**.

Most private galleries are closed in August,
although a few sometimes decide to stay open.

Salamanca District

Anselmo Alvarez

*C/Conde de Aranda 4 (431 55 95). Metro Retiro/bus all
routes to Puerta de Alcalá.* **Open** 5-9pm Mon; 11am-2pm,
5-9pm, Tue-Fri; 11am-2pm Sat.

Anselmo Alvarez also owns the graphics gallery **Tórculo**
(*see below*), and many of the artists he favours there also
exhibit in this multi-storey space, only with painting and
sculpture. Frequently featured are Mati Klarwein, Miquel
Conde and Jorge Castillo.

Guillermo de Osma

*C/Claudio Coello 4, 1° (435 59 36). Metro Retiro/bus all
routes to Puerta de Alcalá.* **Open** 10am-2pm, 4.30-
8.30pm, Mon-Fri.

This influential gallery specialises in artists from the avant-
garde movements of 1910 to 1940. Two of its exhibitions –
of Barradas and Maruja Mallo – later transferred to major
state museums. It's an unusual and curious place, but one
which knows what it's doing.

Ignacio Várez

*C/Maldonado 4 (578 26 18). Metro Núñez de Balboa/bus
9, 19, 51.* **Open** 10am-2pm, 5-9pm, Tue-Sat.

This extravagant space opened in 1992, with the aim of promoting young Spanish artists, as well as the occasional foreigner. Covering two large floors, it's owned by one of the
newer generation of gallerists in Madrid, who shows artists
such as Iñigo Güell, Francisco Rossi, Miguel Zapata and
Carlos Márquez, and sells their work at realistic prices.
Wheelchair access.

Oliva Arauna

*C/Claudio Coello 19 (435 18 08). Metro Serrano, Retiro/bus
1, 9, 19, 51, 74.* **Open** 11am-2pm, 5-9pm, Tue-Sat.

This gallery started up in 1985, and its main areas of inter-
est are in sculpture and conceptual and minimal art. One of
Spain's best sculptors, Susana Solano, shows here; others
who have exhibited in the gallery include Fernando Sinaga,
Rosa Brun and a few foreign artists such as Per Barclay and
Marion Thieme. An interesting place.
Wheelchair access.

Sen

*C/Núñez de Balboa 37 (435 52 02). Metro Velázquez/bus
1, 74.* **Open** 11am-2pm, 5-9pm, Mon-Sat. Closed July.

The Sen gallery is dedicated to contemporary figurative art,
promoting the work of both new and established artists. It's
one of the galleries associated with slick, playful *Movida*
artists such as Ceesepe, but other names to watch out for are
Costus, Eduardo Sanz or the Barcelona-based comic-book
artist Nazario. Sen also produces editions of graphic art and
sculptures.

Tórculo

*C/Claudio Coello 17 (575 86 86). Metro Serrano,
Retiro/bus 1, 9, 19, 51, 74.* **Open** 10am-2pm, 5-9pm,
Mon-Fri; 10am-2pm Sat.

The Tórculo gallery, run by Anselmo Alvarez (*see above*)
has been going since 1979, putting on around 14 shows a
year. Most of the work shown consists of prints and original
works on paper, mainly by Spanish artists – look out for José

Ediciones Benveniste

Danish-born Dan Benveniste, a master cop-
perplate printer, came to Madrid in 1990 to
set up a print workshop. In the past he'd
worked with artists Jim Dine, A.R. Penk and
Keith Haring, and soon found that he was
highly sought after.

He recently moved to larger premises on
the first floor of an eighteenth-century convent, and decided to use part of the enormous
space as a gallery. He now holds four exhibitions a year, each running for two to three
months. They tend to feature foreign artists,
which in a city where the market is so geared
towards the home-grown is a brave move.
There is, though, a new generation of
Spaniards who are more open to outside influences, and Benveniste's first shows have
proved very successful.

The gallery is totally relaxed, with none of
the pomposity that pervades many other
Madrid art venues, and is definitely one of the
most exciting places to see art in the city.
Don't be surprised if you see ink-covered
artists rushing about during your visit, as
both workshop and gallery are on the same
floor. You can also ask to see prints of the
other artists that Benveniste has worked
with, and many are for sale. Among the
Spaniards are Miquel Conde, Damián Flores
and Pedro Castrortega, while non-Spanish
collaborators include Troels Wörsel, Peter
Neuchs, Alison Wilding and Kirsten Ortwed.

Ediciones Benveniste *C/Relatores 20, 1° (429
80 09). Metro Tirso de Molina/bus 6, 26, 32, 57.*
Open 11am-2pm, 5-9pm, Tue-Fri; 11am-2pm Sat.
Wheelchair access.

Hernández, Joaquín Capa and Lucio Muñoz. The gallery also organises a range of other cultural activities, including conferences, concerts, literary discussions and art workshops. *Wheelchair access.*

Chueca & C/Génova

Antonio Machón
C/Conde de Xiquena 8 (532 40 93). Metro Chueca/bus all routes to Recoletos. **Open** 11am-2pm, 5.30-9pm, Tue-Sat. Closed July.
Situated near the fashionable Calle Almirante shopping area, the Machón gallery mainly deals with renowned, older-generation artists such as Tàpies, Antonio Saura and Bonifacio, but also hosts exhibitions of younger contemporary Spanish artists.

Bárcena & Cía
C/Fernando VI 13 (319 60 31). Metro Alonso Martínez/bus 3, 7, 21, 37, 40, 149. **Open** 11.30am-2pm, 5-9pm, Tue-Sat.
This gallery specialises in young Spanish painters, and has been very successful since opening in 1991. Memorable shows have included Javier Riera, Alberto Reguera and Ana Cañavate.
Wheelchair access.

Elba Benítez
C/San Lorenzo 11 (308 04 68). Metro Tribunal/bus 3, 40, 149. **Open** 11am-2pm, 5.30-9pm, Tue-Sat. Closed July.
Located in the courtyard of a nineteenth-century mansion, this gallery opened in 1990 with the objective of introducing the work of major foreign artists to the Spanish audience – particularly those who had gained international acclaim but remained unknown in Spain. Another intention was to assist young Spanish artists who were beginning to gain popularity, but had not yet gained wide recognition. The fact that it has stuck to its brief makes it one of Madrid's more interesting galleries – it has definitely got guts. Artists to look out for are Jordi Teixidor, Michel Sauer, Ton Mars and Ignasi Aballi.

Elvira González
C/General Castaños 9 (319 59 00). Metro Colón/bus all routes to Plaza Colón. **Open** 10.30am-2pm, 5-9pm, Mon-Fri; 11am-2pm Sat.
Elvira González was very much part of **Theo** (*see below*) before setting up on her own. A true professional, she deals mostly in modern masters, among them Calder, Chillida, Léger and Picasso, although she also promotes some Spanish artists and is interested in minimalism and non-figurative painting. Every exhibition of living artists held here is complemented by a special print edition of the same artists' work, made to coincide with the show.

Estampa
C/Justiniano 6 (308 30 30). Metro Alonso Martínez, Colón/bus 3, 7, 21, 37. **Open** 11am-2pm, 5-9pm, Tue-Sat. Closed July.
A rather preciously-run gallery which gained its reputation by producing limited editions of small objects created by artists, and which also deals in print editions. Spanish artists such as Juan Hidalgo, Juan Bordes and Fernando Alamo are represented here.

Fúcares
C/Conde de Xiquena 12 (308 01 91). Metro Chueca/bus all routes to Recoletos. **Open** 11am-2pm, 5-9pm, Tue-Sat.
Norberto Dotor Pérez is a dedicated gallerist who likes to promote young Spanish artists. His exhibition programme aims to bring together the different generations of artists he represents, so you'll see relatively established local names such as Javier Baldeón and Ignacio Tovar along with the latest trends in the art world.

Galería Juana de Aizpuru
C/Barquillo 44 (310 55 61). Metro Chueca, Alonso Martínez/bus 3, 37, 40, 149. **Open** 10am-2pm, 5-9pm, Tue-Fri; 10am-2pm Sat.
Juana de Aizpuru, one of the powerful women who have dominated the modern Madrid gallery world, opened her first gallery in Seville in 1970, and this sister operation in Madrid in 1982. She has been a, if not the, driving force in the international promotion of Spanish art, and **ARCO**, the Madrid international art fair (*see p161*) arose out of one of her initiatives. Her life is devoted to art, and she's well known for her generosity – Aizpuru openings are famous for their lavish supplies of food and drink, and attract a mixture of established and lesser-known artists. In the large gallery space you'll see work by sculptor Eva Lootz, Luis Claramunt, Jiri Dokoupil, Sol LeWitt and many others.

Galería Soledad Lorenzo
C/Orfila 5 (308 28 87). Metro Colón, Alonso Martínez/bus 3, 7, 21. **Open** 11am-2pm, 5-9pm, Tue-Sat.
Soledad Lorenzo is the most professional gallery owner in Madrid. She's traditional and extremely powerful, and her stable is made up of established Spanish and foreign artists from Miquel Barceló and José Maria Sicilia to Julian Schnabel, Ross Blechner and Anish Kapoor. The gallery itself is quite beautiful, as well as being the most prestigious in the city.

Marlborough
C/Orfila 5 (319 14 14). Metro Colón, Alonso Martínez/bus 3, 7, 21. **Open** 11am-2pm, 5-9pm, Tue-Sat.
This is the Madrid branch of the Marlborough – the others are in London, New York and Tokyo. The gallery is in an extremely ugly building, but thanks to the American architect Richard Gluckman, who specialises in art spaces, it has a stunning interior. The Marlborough trades on its reputation for twentieth-century masters and should be ashamed of some of the artists it has taken on recently, even if it is catering to the nouveau riche.

Masha Prieto
Travesía de Belén 2 (319 53 71). Metro Chueca/bus 3, 37, 40, 149. **Open** 11am-2pm, 5-9pm, Tue-Sat.
A small space that tends to focus on the Spanish avant-garde. Surreal *Movida* photographer Ouka Lele shows here, as do Patricia Gadea and Angel Bofarull.

Moriarty
C/Almirante 5, 1° (531 43 65). Metro Chueca/bus all routes to Recoletos. **Open** 11am-2pm, 5-9pm, Tue-Sat. Closed July.
Founded by the dramatically-named Lola Moriarty in 1981, this gallery was a prime hang-out point and showcase for the artists on the *Movida* scene, the photographers, painters, designers, sculptors and other modish figures immortalised in the early films of Pedro Almodóvar. Sadly, many of the Movida figures have not survived, partly because of an excess of drugs and drink. However, you'll still find here names such as A. García Alix, Ouka Lele, Mireia Sentís, Guillermo Pérez Villalta and the Barcelona designer/artist Mariscal, and the gallery still puts on interesting and wacky shows.

Theo
C/Marqués de la Ensenada 2 (308 23 59). Metro Colón/bus all routes to Plaza Colón. **Open** 10.30am-2pm, 5-9pm, Tue-Sat.
This prestigious gallery opened in 1967 and has always focused on the key artists of the contemporary era. It gave special prominence to those Spanish artists who, for political or other reasons, lived outside the country, and put on the first-ever exhibition of Juan Gris in Spain. Without toeing any aesthetic line, Theo continues to present important twentieth-century figures from Spain and abroad. Miró,

ARCO

Madrid's ARCO, one of the most important contemporary art fairs in Europe, was started in 1981. It was the first fully-international event of this kind to take place in Spain, and over the years has gradually earned the respect of the international art brigade, above all during the late eighties when it expanded massively. State funding is not now as lavish as it was during Spain's boom years, but it is still a major annual event.

ARCO was formerly held in the Casa de Campo, but has now been transferred to the gleaming new **Feria de Madrid** trade fair site out towards the airport (*see chapter* **Business**). Each year it brings together about 140 galleries from Spain and all over the world showing twentieth-century, mostly contemporary, work. Recently a decision has been taken to spotlight a specific country each year – in 1994 Belgium, in 1995 the USA. Most countries, though, are represented by their top galleries, and it provides a great opportunity to see what is happening in the international art market.

ARCO is open both to professionals and to the general public, which has had the noticeable effect of boosting Spanish interest in contemporary art and its new forms of expression, and makes the atmosphere less formal than at some similar events elsewhere. This has not led to any compromise in quality, but it does mean that it's absolutely packed. The best time to go is between 2pm and 4pm, when locals will normally be lunching. It's also worth noting that all work is for sale. Check out what you are interested in, go back late on the final day and make an offer. Many galleries prefer to sell work cheaply than pack it up again for shipping back home. If you need to have anything shipped, ARCO has an official agent, **Transférex**, who will take charge of customs formalities, packing, shipping and the reclaim of IVA (Value-added tax) for non-EU residents, on a sliding scale of fees.

ARCO/Feria Internacional de Arte Contemporáneo *Parque Ferial Juan Carlos I (722 50 00/722 51 80/fax 722 58 01/telex 44025). Metro Arturo Soria, then bus 122.* **Dates:** *1995* 9-14 Feb. *1996* 8-13 Feb. *1997* 13-18 Feb. **Admission** 1,200ptas.

Tàpies, Picasso, Julio González, Chillida, Calder, Arp – you'll find the big names here. Opposite is **Theographic**, which specialises in works on paper. *Wheelchair access.*

Atocha/Around the Reina Sofía

Galería & Ediciones Ginkgo
C/Doctor Fourquet 8 (539 92 52). Metro Atocha/bus all routes to Atocha. **Open** 11am-2pm, 5.30-9pm, Tue-Sat.
A small upbeat gallery that regularly publishes graphics and reproductions of contemporary Spanish artists including Dis Berlin, Adolfo Schlosser and Eva Lootz. *Wheelchair access.*

Galería del Progreso
C/Magdalena 6, 1° (530 25 31). Metro Tirso de Molina/bus 6, 26, 32, 57. **Open** 11am-2pm, 5-9pm, Tue-Sat. Closed July.
One of the few real fringe galleries in Madrid, housed on the first floor of a wonderfully dilapidated eighteenth-century building. It tends to show first-time exhibiting artists who are trying to establish themselves and can be a bit over the top. Nonetheless, the city could well do with more spaces like this in its rather self-important art scene. Among artists on its roster are Pep Carrió, Quico Vidal and Mariano Otero.

Gamarra y Garrigues
C/Doctor Fourquet 10-12 (468 09 99). Metro Atocha/bus all routes to Atocha. **Open** 11am-9pm Tue-Fri; 11am-2pm Sat.
Carmen Gamarra and Isabel Garrigues' gallery moved to its present site in 1990. It is a spectacular space and perfectly located in the new gallery area near the Reina Sofía. It's mostly dedicated to Spanish artists such as Eduardo Arroyo, Miquel Navarro and the fine Catalan sculptor and installation artist Jaume Plensa. Its shows, though, are inconsistent, with more misses than hits.

Helga de Alvear
C/Doctor Fourquet 12 (468 05 06). Metro Atocha/bus all routes to Atocha. **Open** 11am-2pm, 5-9pm, Tue-Sat.
The parent of this gallery was opened by Juana Mordó, one of the original prime movers of the Madrid contemporary art scene, in 1964. It well earned its reputation as one of the foremost galleries in the city. Dedicated to promoting young artists, it launched Spain's *El Paso* group and others of the same generation – Lucio Muñoz, Mompo, Zobel and Julio López Hernández – and also introduced Botero, César, David Hockney and Kandinski to the Spanish market in the sixties, Robert Motherwell and Miquel Conde in the seventies, and A.R. Penk and Nam June Paik in the eighties. Mordó died several years ago, but the gallery continued under her deputy Helga de Alvear, who has now moved to a new site, one of the most spectacular galleries in Madrid, under her own name. Other artists it represents are the photographer Javier Vallhonrat and Bonifacio.

Elsewhere

Estiarte
C/Almagro 44 (308 15 70). Metro Rubén Darío/bus 7, 40, 147. **Open** 10.30am-2pm, 5-9pm, Mon-Fri; 10.30am-2pm Sat.
Estiarte specialises in the printing and sale of original graphic work, mostly prints and lithographs by contemporary artists. It represents many big names past and present – Miquel Barceló, Max Ernst, Calder, Chillida, Picasso, Piensa, José María Sicilia and Tàpies, to name but a few.

Museums

A near unrivalled feast of masterpieces – with a side order of the curious and the bizarre.

The **Prado**, the **Thyssen** and the **Reina Sofía**. Few cities can rival this formidable trio of museums, whatever reservations might have been made about the Reina Sofía. Madrid's acquisition of the Thyssen-Bornemisza in 1992 sealed its reputation as one of Europe's leading art capitals. Museum-going in Madrid could be confined just to these three, the city's so-called 'Golden Triangle', if you are only in the city for a short stay. However, there are also many surprises to be found in other, less well-known collections.

In painting, there are also great works by El Greco, Goya and Velázquez, and non-Spanish artists of the standing of Dürer, Constable or Titian, in the **Museo Cerralbo**, the **Real Academia de San Fernando**, the remarkable if strangely neglected **Museo Lázaro Galdiano** and the magnificent monastery of the **Descalzas Reales**. The **Museo Arqueológico Nacional** is one of the most varied collections of its kind, and even Madrid's main military museums, the **Museo del Ejército** and **Museo Naval**, while they leave one in no doubt about who won the Spanish Civil War, do also contain some rare historical artefacts alongside the more recent weaponry. In addition, Madrid has now finally recovered the **Museo de América**, an exhibition of relics from pre-Columbian America unequalled in Europe, after its seemingly endless renovation.

Standards of care and presentation in museums range from impeccable to scandalous. Also, some noteworthy museums are still undergoing long-term and long-drawn-out restoration work. The **Museo de Carruajes** (Carriage Museum) next to the **Palacio Real** (*see chapter* **Sightseeing**) is one such museum for which no opening date is in sight at time of writing.

There are also some museums, such as the **Acciona** interactive science museum and the **Museo de Cera** (Wax Museum), of particular interest to children. For these, *see chapter* **Children**.

TICKETS & TIMES

Until summer 1994 admission to the Spanish national museums (which includes most of the majors, except the **Thyssen**) was free for Spanish citizens, but charges had to be paid by all foreigners. This system has now been abolished follow-

ing complaints of discrimination from the European Union, and a standard adult entry charge introduced of 400ptas for all. However, there are still discounts for students, and admission is now free to everyone, Spanish or otherwise, under 18 or over 65 – something that is not appreciated by many foreign visitors, who assume they have to pay. It is also worth noting that admission to all the national museums is also free for everyone on Saturday afternoons and Sunday mornings, and that some less-frequented museums are still free at all times.

Most museums are shut on Mondays, with the exception of the Reina Sofía which closes on Tuesday. Many of the national museums offer volunteer guides free of charge, but they rarely speak English and are mostly used by local school groups. If you want a personal English-speaking guide you will almost certainly have to pay. Catalogues, brochures, postcards and so on are available at virtually all museums but, again, only the majors will always have copies in English. Similarly, most museum exhibits are labelled only in Spanish, with a few rare exceptions like the **Thyssen** and the **Museo Taurino**.

Fine Art & Decorative Arts

Museo Cerralbo
C/Ventura Rodríguez 17 (547 36 46). Metro Plaza de España/bus all routes to Plaza de España. **Open** 9.30am-2.30pm Tue-Sat; 10am-2pm Sun. Closed Aug & public holidays. **Admission** *Tue-Sat* 400ptas; 200ptas students; free under-18s, over-65s. *Sun* free.

This sumptuous, two-storey late-nineteenth-century mansion houses the personal collection of its former owner Enrique de Aguilera y Gamboa, the seventeenth Marqués de Cerralbo. A man of letters, reactionary politician and fanatical collector, he travelled extensively throughout Europe and Asia in pursuit of valuable pieces to add to his collection, which he left to the Spanish state when he died in 1922. One curious feature of the museum stems from the fact that in his will the Marqués stipulated that the collection should be displayed exactly as he had arranged it – which means in a way that no museum curator would contemplate today, with paintings hung in three levels up the walls. Of the paintings, the major highlight is El Greco's *The Ecstasy of Saint Francis of Assisi*, but there are also works by Zurbarán, Alonso Cano and other Spanish masters. The centrepiece of the ground floor of the house, presumably the domain of the Marqués' wife, is the lavishly-decorated ballroom. The upper level has a much more masculine air, and this is where you will find his astonishing collection of European and Japanese armour, weapons, watches, pipes, leatherbound books, clocks and many other things. A few pieces are labelled. Guided tours in Spanish are available but must be requested in advance.

Museo Lázaro Galdiano

C/Serrano 122 (561 60 84). Metro Avda de América, Núñez de Balboa/bus 9, 16, 19, 51, 61. **Open** 10am-2pm Tue-Sun. **Admission** 300ptas; free Spanish citizens.
This extraordinary and little-known private collection of 15,000 paintings and *objets d'art* is certainly impressive in size and scope. Like the **Museo Cerralbo** (*above*), it is housed in the former home of its founder, in this case financier José Lázaro Galdiano (1862-1947), who is said to have amassed his eclectic collection between the ages of 15 and 80. The monumental four-storey mansion and its gardens are a sight in themselves. Unfortunately, the care and presentation of the museum leave a great deal to be desired. In some rooms, lighting is limited to a chandelier, or comes only from the curved recesses of vaulted ceilings. Also, the present lack of air conditioning makes for an uncomfortable visit in the summer, although some improvements are now being made in this area. Amongst an abundance of religious gold and silverwork, ivory, jewellery, medals, fans and other decorative pieces, this highly personal collection, very unusually for Madrid, boasts some fine works by English painters. Gainsborough, Ramsay, Reynolds, Constable, and Sir Thomas Lawrence can be seen alongside Flemish, Spanish and other paintings from various periods. There is even a soulful portrait of *The Saviour* that is attributed to Leonardo de Vinci. A whole room is devoted almost exclusively to Goya, and you will spot a Rembrandt and a couple of Hieronymus Bosch paintings as well.
Wheelchair access.

Museo Nacional de Artes Decorativas

C/Montalbán 12 (532 64 99). Metro Banco de España, Retiro/bus all routes to Plaza de Cibeles. **Open** 9am-3pm Tue-Fri; 10am-2pm Sat, Sun, public holidays.
Admission *Tue-Sat* 400ptas; 200ptas students; free under-18s, over-65s. *Sun* free.
Founded in 1871 primarily for teaching purposes, the National Museum of Decorative Arts consists of *objets d'art*, furniture, tapestries and so on from all over Spain. Since 1932 it has been housed in a small palace overlooking the Retiro that was acquired from the estate of the Duchess of Santoña. The palace's three stories were expanded to the current five to house the state's increasing hoard. Of the 58 display rooms, the most prized is the tiled kitchen on the fifth floor, painstakingly transferred from an eighteenth-century Valencian palace. Its 1,604 painted tiles depict a typical domestic scene of that era, with a coterie of servants making tea for the lady of the house. The museum also contains a wealth of curious objects, including the graphically-shaped jewel cases from the 'Dauphin's Treasures', the rest of which are in the Prado (*see p164* **The Prado**), nineteenth-century dolls' houses, antique fans and an ornate sixteenth-century four-poster bedstead. Guided tours are available, usually in Spanish only, but must be requested in advance.
Library.

Museo de la Real Academia de Bellas Artes de San Fernando

C/Alcalá 13 (522 14 91). Metro Sol, Sevilla/bus all routes to Puerta del Sol. **Open** 9am-2.30pm Mon, Sat, Sun, public holidays; 9am-7pm Tue-Fri. **Admisssion** *Tue-Fri* 200ptas; *Mon, Sat, Sun* free.
Having just celebrated its two-hundredth anniversary in 1994, the San Fernando Royal Academy of Fine Arts can rightfully claim to be the oldest art institution in Madrid. Its eclectic display collection is partly made up of works donated by aspiring members to gain admission to the academy. It has several works by Goya, an important figure in the academy. There are two self-portraits, and a lesser-known

masterpiece, a portrait of his friend the playwright Moratín. Also look out for one of the academy's most prized possessions, Italian mannerist Giuseppe Arcimboldo's *Spring*, a playful portrait of a man made up entirely of flowers. It was one of a series on the four seasons painted for Ferdinand I of Austria in 1563. *Summer* and *Winter* are still in Vienna, but the whereabouts of *Autumn* is unknown. The academy also has a valuable collection of plans and drawings, such as those of Prado architect Juan de Villanueva, as well as an impressive collection of rare books. Outstanding is the second Latin edition of Dürer's Treatise on the *Proportions of the Human Body*. In the same building as the academy is the **Calcografía Nacional**, a collection and archive dedicated to engraving, fine printing and related topics, which has some of the original plates used for the etchings of Goya. *Guided tours. Wheelchair access.*

Museo Romántico

C/San Mateo 13 (448 10 45). Metro Tribunal/bus 3, 37, 40, 149. **Open** 9am-3pm Tue-Sat; 10am-2pm Sun, public holidays. **Admission** *Tue-Sat* 400ptas; 200ptas students; free under-18s, over-65s. *Sun* free.
This rather weather-beaten museum is undergoing a gradual restoration, and until it is fully refurbished will remain a fairly grimy reflection of nineteenth-century romanticism in Spain, although its very neglect does give it a rather ghostly nostalgic charm. The period is contemplated here through a collection of furniture, paintings, ornaments, memorabilia associated with various Spanish writers and so on. There are several interesting early pianos. The museum is another set up by a private collector, the Marqués de Vega-Inclán, and the house, from 1770, is of interest in itself. Gracing its chapel is the museum's most valuable painting, Goya's luminous *Saint Gregory the Great*, showing the saint weighed down by his robes as he sits hunched over a book with a quill pen. *Guided tours. Wheelchair access.*

At the **Museo Sorolla**. *See page 171.*

The Prado

Madrid's most celebrated attraction extends along the loveliest tree-lined boulevard in the city, the Paseo del Prado. The core of the museum, first opened in November 1819, is the Spanish royal art collection, supplemented by later purchases and works seized from religious houses following their dissolution in the 1830s. The royal collection itself reflects the shifting tastes and political alliances of Spain's kings of the sixteenth and seventeenth centuries. Naturally, there is a comprehensive selection of works by the Spanish court painters Diego de Velázquez and Francisco de Goya. Close ties with Italy, France and especially the southern, Catholic, Netherlands led to the presence of many superb works by Titian, Rubens and Hieronymus Bosch, among others.

Conversely, their choices caused some gaps in the collection. The monarchs' unfamiliarity with artists predating the High Renaissance is evident, and hostilities with England, Holland and other Protestant states also led to little representation of artists from these countries, although more recent acquisitions have made up for this to some extent.

Royal collecting began centuries before the museum was inaugurated, and in the 1500s Queen Isabella 'the Catholic' already possessed a large number of Flemish paintings. Under Charles V (1516-56) and Philip II (1556-98), Italian and Flemish painting still dominated the royal collections. Titian was favoured by both kings. Philip II's eclectic taste led him to purchase several paintings by Bosch, among them one of the Prado's most popular, the enigmatically surreal triptych *The Garden of Earthly Delights*, which Philip kept in his bedroom at El Escorial. The white face beneath a hat in the 'Hell' panel is believed to be Bosch's self-portrait.

Philip IV (1621-65) commissioned several works from Rubens. The latter was contemptuous of Spanish painters until he saw the work of the young Velázquez, who would serve Philip IV as court painter for nearly 40 years. Velázquez also supervised the acquisition of other works for Philip IV, who added to the collection nearly 2,000 paintings by Renaissance and seventeenth-century masters, including some by Van Dyck and others that had been in the collection of Charles I of England.

The 1734 fire that destroyed the old *Alcázar* or royal palace in Madrid took with it over 500 works of art. However, more were bought or commissioned to replace these losses. The first Bourbon King of Spain, Philip V (1700-46) brought with him one of the Prado's most extraordinary possessions, the *Tesoro del Delfín*, the 'Treasures of the Grand Dauphin'. The *Grand Dauphin*, eldest son of Louis XIV and father of Philip V of Spain, accumulated a massive art collection, part of which was left to Philip. The 'Treasure' consists mostly of sixteenth- and seventeenth-century Italian *objets d'art*, such as vases of rock crystal studded with semi-precious stones and fitted with gold and silver trimmings.

The last monarch to add significantly to the royal collection was Charles IV (1788-1808), the employer of Goya, possibly the least respectful court painter that ever lived. The neo-classical edifice by Juan de Villanueva that houses the Prado was originally built in the 1780s to be a science museum, and it was Spain's 'non-king', Joseph Bonaparte, who took the first steps towards using it to exhibit the royal pictures, in what he intended to call the *Museo Josefino*, after himself. Surprisingly, though, the restored Ferdinand VII, not a king known for any democratic impulses, continued with the idea, and so the Prado was inaugurated, as one of the world's first public art museums.

Highlights

The Prado contains such a high concentration of masterpieces that it is really impossible to do it justice in only one visit, or in just a brief survey. Also, its layout is quite confusing, although the free maps given out at the entrance do help. The main entrance is now the Puerta de Goya, at the north end, which brings you in via steps directly onto the first floor, where most of the major Spanish paintings are displayed.

In the distance, past galleries to the left that contain the Prado's major Italian paintings, including Titian's portraits of Charles V and Philip II, you can spot Velázquez' *Las Meninas*, often described as the greatest painting in the world, because of its complex interplay of perspectives and realities. Velázquez paints himself at the left of the picture, supposedly painting a portrait of the King and Queen, who can be seen bizarrely in a 'mirror' at the end of the room, but in whose place stands every spectator, watched for ever by Velázquez, the little Infanta Margarita and other figures in the painting.

In the great hall at the centre of this floor are the massive state portraits painted by Velázquez of Philip IV and his court, with their air of melancholic grandeur; also nearby is his wonderful *Surrender of Breda* (known in Spanish as *Las Lanzas*, 'The Lances'). There are also many religious paintings by El Greco, Zurbarán and other Spanish Golden Age masters.

Further on along the same floor, towards the south end of the museum, are the eighteenth-century Spanish paintings and the main rooms devoted to Goya. Every stage of his artistic career is superbly represented in the Prado: around 40 of the 60 light, carefree tapestry cartoons he designed for the royal palaces; his sarcastic portraits of the royal family and members of the aristocracy; and the renowned *Majas*. There are also his tremendous images of war, including the masterpiece *The Third Of May*, depicting the executions carried out by the French in Madrid in 1808.

Still more fascinating are the *Pinturas Negras* or 'Black Painting', the dark, turbulent images executed during his last years, exhibited on the floor below. Witchcraft, violence and historical drama are combined in an astonishing array of monstrous images, many originally painted on the walls of his home, the *Quinta del Sordo,* between 1819 and 1823. The Prado also has most of the drawings for his series of etchings from the same period, such as *Los Caprichos* or the *Desastres de la Guerra*, selections from which are regularly on view in the exhibition space on the ground floor.

Also on the ground floor are the museum's holdings of early-Spanish and Flemish and German paintings, with Bosch, Brueghel the Elder and Dürer. Elsewhere in the Prado, and often almost unnoticed, you can also find later acquisitions such as Botticelli's *Story of Nastagio degli Onesti* or Rembrandt's *Artemisia*.

The Prado has undergone major renovation in the last ten years that has vastly improved the standard of presentation of its pictures, although the museum's administration is frequently immersed in controversy. Most importantly, the original building can exhibit only about 1,500 of the Prado's 9,000 works of art at any one time. It is forever demanding more room in which to expand, and in 1994 several new rooms were opened within the museum in order to exhibit 19 long-unseen paintings by Rubens. Proposals have also been made for new space to be created underground, and/or for it to take over the building occupied by the **Museo del Ejército**, but as yet nothing has been resolved.

The Prado does have, however, a good temporary exhibition space, on the ground floor next to the Puerta de Goya, which is used to show selections from the museum holdings not on permanent view, such as the Goya etchings, as well as

hosting visiting exhibitions from other museums. There is also an unusually good cafeteria, by the south entrance (*see chapter* **Restaurants**). *See also chapter* **Sightseeing**.

Museo del Prado

Paseo del Prado (429 07 70/420 28 36/420 37 68). Metro Atocha, Banco de España/bus 9, 14, 27, 37, 45. **Open** 9am-7pm Tue-Sat; 9am-2pm Sun, public holidays. **Admission** *Tue-Fri, 9am-2.30pm Sat* 400ptas; 200ptas students; free under-18s, over-65s. *2.30-7pm Sat, Sun* free. *Book & souvenir shop. Wheelchair access.*

Casón del Buen Retiro

C/Felipe IV 13 (420 26 28). Metro Banco de España, Retiro/bus 9, 14, 27, 37, 45. **Open** 9.30am-7.15pm Tue-Sat; 9am-2.15pm Sun, public holidays. **Admission** included in Museo del Prado ticket.

A five-minute walk from the main Prado, this building now houses the museum's assembly of nineteenth-century Spanish art (if you visit the Prado and intend to carry on to the Casón, keep your ticket stub). It and the adjacent **Museo del Ejército** are also all that remain of Philip IV's Buen Retiro palace (*see chapter* **Madrid by Area**). Luca Giordano's ceiling fresco *The Order of the Golden Fleece* dominates the main salon, once Philip IV's ballroom. Eclectic is the best word for its paintings and sculptures, ranging from realist portraits to massive historical canvases. There are also many landscapes, and *Costumbrista* paintings depicting rural life and customs, to complement works by better-known Spanish painters of the era such as Joaquín Sorolla or Santiago Rusiñol. *Book & souvenir shop.*

The Sleep of Reason, *by Goya.*

The Reina Sofía

Still Life on a Wall, by Francisco Bores.

Two glass and steel lift-shafts stand out against the sombre façade of this building, which from 1781 until 1965 was the San Carlos hospital. Designed by British architect Ian Ritchie, the lifts provide uninterrupted dramatic views of Madrid while you ride up to any of its four exhibition floors. The rest of the centre is a little more low-key, but still a spectacular art space.

Madrid's national museum of modern art is housed in one of the largest buildings in the city, boasting all of 12,505 square metres of exhibition space, an area that in Europe is surpassed only by the Centre Pompidou in Paris. The initial conversion of the old hospital was carried out between 1981 and 1986, when Queen Sofía of Spain first opened the new facility named after her. It was initially only a temporary exhibition space, and more thoroughgoing renovation – with the addition of the lifts – continued until

1990, when it finally opened as a museum with a permanent collection.

The great jewel of the museum is unquestionably Picasso's *Guernica*, his impassioned denunciation of war and fascism that commemorates the 1937 destruction of the Basque town of Guernica by German bombers supporting the Francoist forces in the Spanish Civil War – although some art historians have seen it more in formal terms, as a reflection on the history of western painting, using elements seen in the work of the old masters. It has only been here, behind a bullet-proof glass panel on the second floor, since 1992, when it was transferred here from the **Casón del Buen Retiro** (*see p165* **The Prado**) amid great controversy. As is well known, Picasso refused to allow the painting to be exhibited in Spain during the Franco régime, and it was in 1981 that it was finally brought to Madrid from the Museum of Modern Art in New York. Picasso had intended that it should be housed in the Prado – of which the Casón was at least an annex – and his family have bitterly opposed the change of location, which, though, has successfully boosted the prestige of the Reina Sofía.

The rest of the permanent collection, however, the bulk of which came from the now-closed Museo Español de Arte Contemporáneo in the Ciudad Universitaria, has not escaped controversy. The most common criticism is that, while it does contain works by just about all the major Spanish artists of this century – Picasso, Dalí,

One of the images of the twentieth century: Guernica.

Miró, Juan Gris, Julio González, Tàpies and Antonio Saura are all here – the representation of individual artists is often patchy, with few major works. Complaints have also been made about the erratic coverage of foreign art.

In response, an active acquisitions policy has been adopted that is filling some of the gaps in the display of Spanish art and creating a growing collection of works by foreign artists as well. A number of works amassed over the previous three years were officially presented during 1994, including names such as Donald Judd, Anish Kapoor, Bruce Nauman, Tony Cragg, Rosemarie Trockel and Julian Schnabel. Picasso's *Figura* (1928) is another significant recent acquisition.

The collection, all on the second floor, has been arranged combining both chronological order and conceptual affinity. Thus, the first room is dominated by Picasso's *Woman in Blue* (1901), around which there are several paintings by other Spanish artists of the same period such as Nonell and Zuloaga, and María Blanchard's naive, symbolist art. It then continues on to Cubism, the avant-garde movements of the twenties and thirties, Surrealism and so on, before going on to the movements of mainly non-figurative artists who maintained the vigour of Spanish art after 1940.

Miró, the greatly influential Julio González and Dalí are accorded rooms of their own. Major paintings by the latter in the Reina Sofia include *The Great Masturbator* and *The Enigma of Hitler*. Several of the works by Miró in the museum are from the last years of his life, in the 1970s. In the next room are some striking works by leading exponents of constructivism and geometric abstraction – Oteiza, Palazuelo and Sempere.

A final series of rooms is labelled simply 'Proposals' toward a future permanent collection, rather than being arranged with any idea of chronological order. They are occupied by a myriad range of styles and artists, Spanish and foreign – among them foremost Spanish sculptor Eduardo Chillida, Tàpies, Tony Cragg, Susana Solano, Ellsworth Kelly, Barnett Newman, Lucio Fontana and Dan Flavin.

The giant size of the building, with its large and tranquil inner courtyard, is a great advantage for the exhibition of monumental pieces. Outside in this central garden Alexander Calder's beautiful 1974 mobile *Carmen* immediately commands your attention. Miro's *Lunar Bird* (1966) sculpture also graces this green area. Inside, long halls, high-vaulted ceilings and masses of windows lend an airy, spatial feel to the museum.

As well as housing its own permanent collection, the Reina Sofía also functions as a venue for many other activities, and has developed into a dynamic and highly popular cultural centre. In its role as a space for major temporary exhibitions in contemporary art it has won universal praise, and has become one of the most important art exhibition centres in Europe (*see chapter* **Art Galleries**). Recent shows have included major retrospectives on Lucian Freud, Joseph Beuys and Spanish Surrealism, and a presentation of work from the Hague Worldwide Video Festival.

It also acts as a base for Madrid's principal contemporary music centre, the **Centro para la Difusión de la Música Contemporánea** (*see chapter* **Music: Classical & Opera**), and has a library and archive of around 40,000 books, together with material on video, cassette, slides, CD and computer disk, all focussed on twentieth-century art and culture. There is also an excellent bookshop and a pleasant café. The energy with which it is run has been a major factor in its success, and the number of visitors has increased by a hundred thousand each year since it opened. *See also chapter* **Sightseeing**.

Museo Nacional Centro de Arte Reina Sofía

C/Santa Isabel 52 (467 50 62). Metro Atocha/bus all routes to Atocha. **Open** 10am-9pm Mon, Wed-Sat; 10am-2.30pm Sun. **Admission** *Mon, Wed-Sat, 10am-2.30pm Sat* 400ptas; 200ptas students; free under-18s, over-65s. *2.30-9pm Sat, Sun free. Book & souvenir shop. Library. Wheelchair access.*

Millet's Angelus, *as seen by Dalí.*

The Thyssen

Reclining Nymph, *by Lucas Cranach the Elder, from 1530-34.*

The third point of Madrid's Golden Triangle was completed with the official opening of the Thyssen-Bornemisza Museum on 10 October 1992. Widely regarded as the most important private collection in the world, it's just a stone's throw away from the Prado and the Reina Sofía, providing a very rich complement and contrast to their respective displays of art.

Madrid's acquisition of Baron Hans-Heinrich Thyssen-Bornemisza's invaluable collection against counter-bids from London and other cities was quite a coup. It originally came to Spain on a nine-and-a-half year loan, but later negotiations led to a purchase agreement for the 775 paintings being concluded in June 1993.

No doubt the Baron's fourth wife, Carmen *Tita* Cervera, a former Miss Spain, influenced his final decision. More pivotal, however, was Madrid's offer to house it in the Palacio de Villahermosa, an early nineteenth-century pile that was empty and available at the time. It had been converted into offices in the sixties, and so architect Rafael Moneo was able to give it an entirely new interior. This conversion, which cost over four billion pesetas (£21 million), is itself one of the most remarkable features of the museum. Terracotta-pink walls, skylights and marble flooring provide a luminous setting for the collection, and rarely is it possible to see old-master paintings so perfectly lit.

This inimitable collection was begun by the present Baron's father, who started acquiring old masters in the 1920s. On his death in 1947, however, his 525 paintings were dispersed among his heirs. His son Baron Hans-Heinrich has since set out to round the collection up once more, buying them back from his relatives, and has also taken up his father's vocation with a passion, buying old masters until the 1960s and then turning towards contemporary art. It was his desire to keep the collection together that led him to search for a larger home for his paintings, as his own Villa Favorita in Lugano in Switzerland could only accommodate about 300 pictures. Hence the attraction of the Villahermosa, although a part of the collection given to Spain, mostly early medieval works, is to be exhibited separately in the fourteenth-century Pedralbes Monastery in Barcelona.

THE COLLECTION

A visit to the Thyssen-Bornemisza affords an extraordinary lesson in the history of western art. You begin at the top, on the second floor, with the thirteenth century and the early Italians (exemplified by Duccio di Buoninsegna's *Christ and the Samaritan Woman*), and work your way downwards through all the major schools until you reach the ground floor and the likes of Roy Lichtenstein's *Woman in Bath*, or even the basement café and Renato Guttuso's 1976 *Caffè*

Greco. Alternately, head straight for a favourite period, guided by the free plan provided.

The Thyssen-Bornemisza effectively fills in the gaps you may find at the Prado or the Reina Sofía. Unlike either of the latter, it houses a significant selection of German Renaissance works, seventeenth-century Dutch painting, Impressionism, German Expressionism, Russian Constructivism, geometric abstraction and pop art.

Detractors have alleged that the Thyssen is no more than a ragbag, a catch-all collection of every kind of style put together without discrimination or eye to quality. However, one of its great attractions is that, while it is extraordinarily broad in scope, it is also very recognisably a personal collection directed by a distinctly individual taste, as seen in the wonderful room dedicated to early portraits, with works by Antonello da Messina and Joos van Cleve. Equally quirky is the section on early North American painting, including a *Presumed Portrait of George Washington's Cook* by Gilbert Stuart, and works by artists such as Bierstadt and Winslow Homer.

And the museum does have its share of masterpieces. Among the old masters, the works of Duccio, Van Eyck and Petrus Christus stand out. The museum's most reproduced painting is Domenico Ghirlandaio's exceptional, idealised *Portrait of Giovanna Tornabuoni*, in the portrait room.

Two rooms further on is Vittore Carpaccio's allegorical *Young Knight in a Landscape* (1510: *see chapter* **Sightseeing**) replete with symbols, and another of the gems of the collection. From among the masters of the Flemish School is the sublime *Annunciation* Diptych by Van Eyck, more a three-dimensional sculptural relief than a painting. The German Renaissance is best represented by Albrecht Dürer, whose *Jesus among the Doctors* portrays an idealised, almost effeminate Christ pressed upon by diabolical doctors.

From the later sixteenth-century and Baroque there are superb paintings such as Titian's evocative *St Jerome in the Wilderness* – one of the works in which his change in style to bolder, sweeping strokes and closer attention to chromatic harmonies is most evident – and Caravaggio's wonderfully powerful *Saint Catherine of Alexandria*. Also there are representative works by El Greco, Mattia Preti, Rubens and Jusepe Ribera.

The first floor, below, begins with several rooms of seventeenth-century Dutch painting. There follows the most remarkably varied section of the museum, with such things as an *Easter Morning* by Caspar David Friedrich, a Goya portrait of his friend *Asensio Juliá*, a great selection of French Impressionists, and even Constable's 1824 *The Lock* – though not jumbled together, but carefully ordered and arranged. The collection is generally very strong in German art, with several rooms of Expressionists and some great works by Kandinsky, Emil Nolde, Karl Hubbuch and Max Beckmann.

Also present, on the ground floor, are more familiar modern masters, such as Braque, Mondrian, Klee, Max Ernst and Picasso, in the shape of his 1911 *Man with a Clarinet* among other works. The last few rooms concentrate on the USA, with a fabulous Georgia O'Keeffe, *New York with Moon*, a *Hotel Room* by Edward Hopper and Robert Rauschenberg's *Express* from 1963, but also there are *Large Interior, Paddington* by Lucian Freud and an early David Hockney, *In Memoriam Cecchino Bracci*.

At once personal and eclectic, and also fun, the Thyssen-Bornemisza collection allows you to contemplate a range of work that it would otherwise be physically impossible to reach – that is, without unlimited time, travel privileges, and access to various private collections and museums. Before leaving, moreover, you have the opportunity to pay your respects to the giant, chocolate-box portraits of the Baron and *la Tita* themselves in the lobby, both significantly larger than the companion pictures of the King and Queen of Spain further along the same wall.

Museo Thyssen-Bornemisza

Palacio de Villahermosa, Paseo del Prado 8 (369 01 51/420 39 44). Metro Banco de España, Atocha/bus 9, 14, 27, 37, 45. **Open** 10am-7pm Tue-Sun.
Admission 600ptas; 350ptas students, under-18s, over-65s.
Book & souvenir shop. Wheelchair access.

Picasso's 1923 Harlequin with a Mirror.

Museo Sorolla

Paseo del General Martínez Campos 37 (310 15 84).
Metro Iglesia, Rubén Darío/bus 5, 7, 16, 40, 61, 147.
Open 10am-3pm Tue-Sun. **Admission** *Tue-Sat* 400ptas;
200ptas students; free under-18s, over-65s. *Sun* free.
This museum, the elegant former home of the Valencian artist
Joaquín Sorolla, is a must-see. Built in 1910, the mansion now
guards the legacy of Spain's foremost Impressionist painter,
who lived and worked here. A visit to the house starts at the
back, through a peaceful, Moorish-inspired garden. Skylights
are essential architectural elements in the home of an artist
most renowned for his iridescent, sun-drenched paintings.
His studio contains a curious Turkish bed, decrepit but still
in one piece, where he apparently used to take his siesta.
Around the room are his collections, ranging from exotic to
kitsch. Whereas the ground floor has been carefully preserved
to give the visitor a feel of Sorolla's life, the second floor has
been converted into a gallery, and its bright white walls and
curved ceilings contrast with the earthier look of the lower
floor. In his exquisite portrait of the singer Ráquel Méller, set
on an easel, her white dress shimmers with flecks of green,
violet, ochre and pink. Beside it is a picture of Sorolla's family, lying on a sea of deep green grass. The few men as subjects are usually portrayed toiling away, while women and
young boys are seen at play or rest. It's easy to dismiss
Sorolla, for his leisured subject matter, and for producing pictures that are incorrigibly like greeting cards – for which purpose they are often used, throughout the world – but few
people fail to find his world at least a little seductive, or to
admire his use of light.

The Monastery Museums

Real Monasterio de las Descalzas Reales

Plaza de las Descalzas 3 (522 06 97). Metro Callao,
Sol/bus all routes to Puerta del Sol. **Open** *guided tours*
only 9am-6pm Tue-Sat; 9am-3pm Sun, public holidays.
Admission 800ptas; 300ptas students,
under-18s, over-65s.
Those who chance upon this monastery-museum cannot
help feeling smug about such a find, for few expect to come
across such a treasure trove smack in the middle of one of
Madrid's busiest shopping areas, close to the Puerta del Sol
and almost next door to a branch of the Corte Inglés department store. The *Descalzas Reales* (literally, 'Barefoot
Royalty') is in fact a convent, founded in 1564 by the daughter of Charles V and sister of Philip II Joanna of Austria, and
today still occupied by an enclosed order of Franciscan nuns.
Founded with royal patronage, the Descalzas became the
preferred destination of the many widows, youngest daugh-
ters and other women of the royal family and high aristocracy of Spain who entered religious orders. It was for this
reason that it also came to acquire a quite extraordinary collection of works of art, given as bequests by the lofty novices'
families – paintings, sculptures, tapestries and religious
objets d'art. Equally lavish was the baroque decoration of
the building itself, with its grand painted staircase, frescoed
ceilings and 32 chapels, of which only some can be visited.
Various schools are represented among the monastery's
paintings, although the largest non-Spanish contingents are
Italian, with Titian, Luini, Angelo Narddi and Sebastian del
Piombo, and Flemish, with Brueghel (*The Adoration of the
Magi*), Joos Van Cleve and Rubens. The Descalzas Reales is
also an exceptional showcase for the best in Spanish religious baroque art, with important works by the sixteenth-
century artists Gaspar Becerra, Miguel Barroso and Luis de
Carvajal, while seventeenth-century Spanish art is best rep-

*The **Museo Municipal** occupies Pedro de
Ribera's 1722 hospice. See page 173.*

resented by Zurbarán, Claudio Coello, and Herrera Barnuevo.
From another epoch, there is even a tiny painting attributed
to Goya. The monastery was virtually closed to the public
for many years, and its restoration led to its being given the
Council of Europe museum prize in 1988. However, it can
only be visited on the obligatory guided tours, the guides for
which rarely speak English, although the wealth of things
to see can easily make up for this. Each tour lasts about 45
minutes. *See also chapter* **Sightseeing**.
Book & souvenir shop.

Real Monasterio de la Encarnación

Plaza de la Encarnación 1 (547 05 10). Metro Opera,
Santo Domingo/bus 25, 33, 39, 148. **Open** 10.30am-
12.30pm, 4-5.30pm, Wed, Sat; 10.30am-12.30pm Sun.
Admission *Sat, Sun* 350ptas; *Wed* free.
Now endowed by only 17 nuns, this convent-monastery was
once a *Casa de Tesoro* (treasury) connected to the nearby
Alcazar via a passageway. Of the original convent building
commissioned by Philip III and his wife Margaret of Austria
in 1616, however, all that remains is the façade, since much
of the rest was destroyed by fire in 1734. Though not as lavishly endowed as the **Descalzas Reales** (*above*), the
Encarnación still contains a great many pieces of seventeenth-century religious art, with several rooms replete with
fine paintings and sculpture from that time, the most impressive being Jusepe Ribera's shimmering chiaroscuro portrait
of *John the Baptist*. The Encarnación's most awesome room,
though, is the *reliquiario*, the relics room. In its glass case-
ments are displayed some 1,500 saintly relics, most of them
in extravagantly bejewelled copper, bronze, glass, gold and
silver reliquaries. Most are bone fragments and/or former
possessions of saints and martyrs. There is a femur or two,
draped in sashes and bedecked with jewels. This relics room
has been said to be the most important in the Catholic world,
besting even those in Rome, because of the high artistic value
of the reliquaries themselves, many of which are unique. On
the altar dominating the room is a prized relic of a charred,
burnt wooden Christ figurine, inside an ornate bronze and
glass case. Even more amazing is the solidified blood of San
Pantaleón, kept inside a glass orb. The blood reportedly
liquifies from midnight on the eve of his feast day (27 July)
until the stroke of midnight on the day itself, 28 July. The
wait for this to happen becomes a national news item each
year. *See also chapter* **Sightseeing**.

Archaeology & Anthropology

Museo Africano

C/Arturo Soria 101 (415 24 12). Metro Arturo Soria/bus
11, 70, 114, 115, 201. **Open** *guided tours only* 6.30pm
Thur; 11.30am Sun. Closed July-Sept. **Admission** free.
'Museum' is really too grand a term to describe this simply
displayed, albeit interesting, collection of African artefacts
that is chiefly intended to educate. It has been assembled
over the past 30 years by the Combonian Missionaries, a religious order founded by Italian priest Father Daniel Comboni.
Its most prized hoard is its collection of tribal masks, but it
also contains many unusual musical instruments to complement its knives, machetes, terracotta figures, gourds and
implements used in traditional magic. There is also a fine
collection of recordings of traditional African music.

Museo de América

Avda de los Reyes Católicos 6 (543 94 37). Metro
Moncloa/bus 1, 46, 82, 132, 133. **Open** 9.30am-3pm
Tue-Sat; 10am-2.30pm Sun. **Admission** *Tue-Sat*
400ptas; 200ptas students; free under-18s, over-65s.
Sun free.
The finest collection of pre-Columbian art and artefacts in
Europe was finally reopened in 1994, after a renovation last-
ing over 12 years. Just why it took so long has been a mat-
ter of considerable speculation. Its collection, though, is one

of the most intriguing in Madrid, combining articles that were brought back at the time of the Spanish Conquest with others that have been donated in more friendly vein by various Latin American countries, and later acquisitions. All the main pre-Columbian cultures are represented – among the highlights are Inca stone sculptures and funeral offerings from Peru, and some fascinating gold ornaments and finely modelled, comical and sometimes highly sexual figurines from Colombia that give a vivid impression of the lives of their makers. From Mexico there are Aztec obsidian masks, and a Mayan *Codex* or illustrated manuscript – like other pre-Columbian peoples, the Mayans had no written script – relating the story of the arrival of the Spaniards, and one of only a very few in existence. Another section is devoted to art produced in Spanish America during the three centuries between the Conquest and Independence, including the remarkable *Entry of the Viceroy Morcillo into Potosí* (1716) by the early Bolivian painter Melchor Pérez Holguín. Now exhibited for the first time is a large collection of gold and other objects from the galleons *Atocha* and *Margarita*, sunk off the Florida coast in the eighteenth century and only recovered in 1988. There is also a great collection of contemporary folk art from all the countries of the former Spanish empire, including the Philippines, with many wonderfully colourful things such as puppets and Mexican *piñatas* and Day-of-the-Dead paraphernalia.
Wheelchair access.

Museo Arqueológico Nacional

C/Serrano 13 (577 79 12). Metro Colón, Serrano/bus all routes to Plaza Colón. **Open** 9.30am-8.30pm Tue-Sat; 9.30am-2.30pm Sun. **Admission** *Tue-Fri, 9.30am-2.30pm Sat* 400ptas; 200ptas students; free under-18s, over-65s. *2.30-8.30pm Sat, Sun* free.

The archaeological museum is one of Madrid's oldest, set up in 1867, and traces the evolution of human cultures from prehistoric times right up to the fifteenth century. Its collection of artefacts includes finds from the Iberian, Celtic, Greek, Egyptian, Punic, Roman, Paleochristian, Visigothic and Moslem cultures. Remarkably, most of them came from excavations carried out within Spain, illustrating the extraordinary continuity and diversity of human settlement in the Iberian peninsula. Indeed, some of the most interesting relics come from the area around Madrid itself, such as the 4,000-year-old neolithic campaniform pottery bowls found south of the city at Ciempozuelos. If you wish to do the whole museum you should start your visit from the basement, which holds paleontological material including a selection of skulls, tombs and a mammoth's tusks still attached to its skull. The ground floor holds the museum's most famous possession, the Iberian sculpture the *Dama de Elche*, an enigmatic figure whose true gender is a mystery. Further up, the usual definition of archaeology is stretched somewhat to include very interesting exhibits on post-Roman Visigothic and Moslem Spain, with some wonderful ceramics and fine metalwork from Moorish Andalusia. In the front garden, steps lead underground to a reproduction of the renowned Altamira cave paintings in Cantabria. It is not very impressive, but since the actual caves have now been closed to visitors in order to preserve them from further deterioration this may be the best you can do. Items in the museum are labelled in Spanish only.

Museo Nacional de Antropología

C/Alfonso XII 68 (539 59 95/530 64 18). Metro Atocha/bus all routes to Atocha. **Open** 10am-7.30pm Tue-Sat; 10am-2pm Sun, public holidays. **Admission** *Tue-Fri, 10am-2.30pm Sat* 400ptas; 200ptas; free under-18s, over-65s. *2.30-7.30pm Sat, Sun* free.

It would be a shame to see this collection – previously called the Museum of Ethnology, and this is still the name on the building – transferred to the former Museum of Spanish Contemporary Art building, as has been suggested. Its present home is a stately three-storey edifice near the Retiro. The interior is structured around a grand open hall that allows a view of all levels, and each floor is devoted to a specific region or country. The first level has an extensive collection from the Philippines, a former Spanish colony, dominated by a six-metre long dugout canoe made from a single tree trunk. Among the museum's bizarre highlights are a late nineteenth-century Philippine helmet made from a spiky blowfish, shrunken human heads from Peru, and the skeleton of Don Agustín Luengo y Capilla, a resident of Extremadura who attracted scientific attention by being 2.25 metres (7'4") tall. Even more enticing is an emaciated tobacco leaf-skinned mummy, said to have once been in Charles III's Royal Library. The latter two are to be found in the annexe to the first level.

Bullfighting

Museo Taurino

Patio de Caballos, Plaza Monumental de las Ventas, C/Alcalá 237 (725 18 57). Metro Ventas/bus 12, 21, 53, 74, 146. **Open** 9.30am-2.30pm Tue-Fri; 10am-1pm Sun. **Admission** free.

Its prime location beside the stables in the Las Ventas bullring makes this rather austere museum easy to find – just let your nose lead you to it. If this fails, head towards the right side of the bullring entering from Calle Alcalá. It was renovated a few years ago, and only six bulls' heads remain from the original museum, which then seemed to be mostly a homage to the bull. The present museum celebrates more the man and the bullfight itself. It consists mainly of sculptures and portraits of famous matadors and *trajes de luces*,

From the **Museo Nacional de Antropología**.

suits of lights, including the pink and gold outfit worn by the legendary Manolete on the afternoon of his death in the ring in 1947. Among the eighteenth-century paintings is a portrait of *torero* Joaquín de Rodrigo said to be by Goya, although this is still under debate. More bullfight memorabilia completes the collection. This is one of the few museums with labels in both Spanish and English.

Literary & Historical

Casa-Museo de Lope de Vega

C/Cervantes 11 (429 92 16). Metro Antón Martín/bus 9, 14, 27, 37, 45. **Open** *guided tours only* 9.30am-3pm Mon-Fri; 10am-2pm Sat. **Admission** *Mon-Fri* 200ptas; free students, under-18s, over-65s. *Sat* free.
Spain's most prolific playwright and poet Félix Lope de Vega Carpio (1562-1635) spent the last 25 years of his life in this rather sombre three-storey house, oddly enough on a street now named after his rival Cervantes. The house is itself the most interesting thing to see, as the furnishing and ornaments, obtained from various sources, are approximations of Lope de Vega's inventory of his household rather than originals. Even the garden, though, contains the fruit trees and plants he detailed in his journals. If you are lucky, the guide you get on the compulsory guided tour will speak reasonable English, as nothing is labelled, although catalogues and brochures are available at the entrance. The tour begins at the tiny chapel on the second floor. Lope de Vega, whose tumultuous life had included numerous love affairs, scandals and service in the Spanish Armada, became a priest in 1614. His tiny alcove of a bedroom has a window that opens to the chapel so he could hear mass from his bed, as Philip II did at El Escorial. Curiously, just outside his alcove was the room where the women of the household met to sew and chat. It has no chairs, only a low platform with silk cushions propped round a brazier. In the children's bedroom on the top floor, you can see a quaint belt of amulets draping a small chair by a crib, of a type that were often given to children at that time to ward off the evil eye. The house also holds within it 1,500 antique books, all from the sixteenth and seventeenth centuries.

Museo de la Ciudad

C/Príncipe de Vergara 140 (588 65 99). Metro Cruz del Rayo/bus 1, 29, 52. **Open** 10am-2pm, 4-6pm, Tue-Fri; 10am-2pm Sat, Sun. **Admission** free.
Opened in 1992, in a brand-new building close to the **Auditorio Nacional** (*see chapter* **Music: Classical & Opera**), this museum seeks to show both Madrid's history and future projects in store for the city. The collection, though, is patchy, and the museum's historical material is distinctly inferior to that in the **Museo Municipal** (*below*). Informative but often heavy going are the exhibits on the development of all the different city services – the Metro, gas, water system and so on. More interesting than the permanent exhibits can be the temporary exhibitions on Madrid-related topics that it hosts regularly.

Museo del Ejército

C/Méndez Núñez 1 (522 89 77). Metro Banco de España, Retiro/bus 9, 14, 27, 37, 45. **Open** 10am-2pm Tue-Sun. **Admission** free.
This massive collection of military memorabilia, the Army Museum, may eventually be transferred elsewhere if the Prado has its way and succeeds in taking over this historic building (*see p164* **The Prado**). In the meantime, it is still easy to visit this surprisingly sumptuous collection, begun in 1803, which holds such historical treasures as *La Tizona*, supposedly the sword of the semi-legendary Castilian hero El Cid, and which, the story goes, he won in battle by slaying its owner King Bucar of Morocco. There is also a fragment of the cross planted by Columbus on his arrival in the New World. Toy soldier enthusiasts will be delighted with a whole room devoted to such miniatures. Even more curi-

ous is a room at the back that is dedicated to a handful of Spanish heroines. Here you can find a portrait of seamstress Manuela Malasaña, killed by French soldiers in Madrid in 1808 when she tried to defend herself with a pair of scissors (*see chapter* **History: Revolutions & Railways**), although the room is dominated by a rather soppy picture of the 'anonymous heroines' (soldiers' wives) by Nicolás Soria. Also, the building the museum occupies is one of the only remaining parts of the Buen Retiro palace (*see chapter* **Madrid by Area**), and its *Sala de los Reinos* ('Hall of the Kingdoms') retains most of its original decoration, some of it by Velázquez. The Army Museum is one of the few places in Madrid where these days you can still see a monument to General Franco.
Shop. Wheelchair access.

Museo Municipal

C/Fuencarral 78 (522 57 32/521 66 56). Metro Tribunal/bus 3, 37, 40, 149. **Open** 9.30am-8pm Tue-Fri; 10am-2pm Sat, Sun. Closed public holidays. **Admission** free.
The principal highlights of Madrid's municipal museum are its façade and exuberantly ornate entrance by Pedro de Ribera, considered to be among the finest examples of baroque architecture in Madrid and, inside, the impressive 1833 model of the city that occupies an entire room. The large building was first commissioned as a hospice, the *Hospicio de San Fernando*, and completed in 1722. The museum collection, inaugurated in 1929, traces the history of settlement in the area and the growth of Spain's capital from the prehistoric age to the nineteenth century, with many unusual maps, manuscripts, paintings and artefacts, among them the oldest comprehensive map of Madrid, by Pedro Teixeira (1656). There are also some noteworthy paintings, by Goya, Sorolla and Eugenio Lucas. In the hospice garden there is a pretty baroque fountain, the *Fuente de la Fama* ('Fountain of Fame'), also by Ribera.
Guided tours. Wheelchair access.

Museo Naval

Paseo del Prado 5 (379 52 99). Metro Banco de España/bus all routes to Plaza de Cibeles. **Open** 10.30am-1.30pm Tue-Sun. **Admission** free.
Judging from the baritone hum of voices heard in the high-ceilinged rooms of this recently-renovated museum, most visitors here are male. Amidst the sophisticated assortment of navigation instruments, muskets, guns and naval war paintings are spoils from the expeditions led by Columbus and similar mariners. Glass displays enclose primitive weapons, some of which, like the swords lined with sharks' teeth from the Gilbert Islands, promise greater damage than their western counterparts. The most impressive room is one dominated by a huge mural-map that traces the various routes taken by Spain's intrepid explorers. In front of it are two equally impressive giant globes, created by AP Coronelli in the late seventeenth century. The room also holds the museum's most valuable possession: the first known map of the Americas made by a European. Dating from 1500, the parchment paper drawing by royal cartographer Juan de la Cosa is believed to have been made for the Catholic monarchs, Ferdinand and Isabella.
Guided tours. Shop.

The Natural World

Museo de Ciencias Naturales

C/José Gutiérrez Abascal 2 (411 13 28). Metro República Argentina, Nuevos Ministerios/bus all routes to Castellana. **Open** 10am-6pm Tue-Fri; 10am-8pm Sat; 10am-2.30pm Sun, public holidays. **Admission** *Tue-Fri, 10am-2.30pm Sat* 400ptas; 250ptas under-18s, over-65s. *2.30-8pm Sat, Sun* free.
Don't confuse the street name with that of a larger street

The **Museo Arqueológico**. See page 172.

called José Abascal, which is actually just on the other side of the Castellana from this museum. The Museum of Natural Sciences is made up of two buildings, behind a sloped garden. The building to the north was only inaugurated in January 1994, and due to its newness has what is one of the more dynamic and interactive displays in Madrid. The history of the earth and of all living creatures is illustrated here via audiovisual presentations and some hands-on exhibits, in imaginative displays that make learning fun. The second building contains a simpler, more old-fashioned presentation of fossils, dinosaurs and geological exhibits. The two-level open exhibition area is dominated by the replica of a Diplodocus, surrounded by the real skeletons of a Glyptodon (giant armadillo), an *Elephas Antiquus* (mastodon) and other extinct animals. The most distinguished skeleton here, though, is that of the *Megatherium Americanum*, a bearlike creature from the pleistocene period unearthed in Luján, Argentina, in 1788.

Museo Geominero

C/Ríos Rosas 23 (349 57 00). Metro Ríos Rosas/bus 3, 12, 37, 45. **Open** 9am-2pm Mon-Sat. **Admission** free.
The most striking thing about this geological and mining museum is the splendid stained glass roof overhead – the best vantage point to see it is from beside the 450kg block of rose-coloured quartz in the centre of the vast hall. Surrounding it above are three narrow exhibition floors, reached by a precipitous spiral staircase. Fossils and minerals are set out in display cases dating from 1925, although the collection was actually begun in 1865. A separate section deals with the history of mining in Spain, but it is normally open only to school groups.

Stamps & Coins

Museo Casa de la Moneda

C/Doctor Esquerdo 36 (566 65 44). Metro O'Donnell/bus 2, 30, 71, C. **Open** 10am-2.30pm, 5-7.30pm, Tue-Fri; 10am-2.30pm Sat, Sun. **Admission** free.
Unless you're a coin collector, this museum will probably be of little interest, and some of the many display rooms are poorly lit, if not in virtual darkness. However, the size and scope of the collection, which was first begun in the eighteenth century, place it among the most important in the world. The history of coins is represented here in chrono-

logical order, and complemented by displays of seals, bank notes, engravings, rare books and medals.
Guided tours. Shop. Wheelchair access.

Museo Postal y de Telecomunicación

Palacio de Comunicaciones, C/Montalbán (521 60 00). Metro Banco de España/bus all routes to Plaza de Cibeles. **Open** 10am-1.30pm, 5-7pm, Mon-Fri. **Admission** free.
Stamp collectors should find this tiny museum interesting, as it contains a wealth of stamps from all over the world arranged by country and year. There are also exhibits relating to the history of the post office and telecommunications. They include some antique switchboards, telephones, postmasters' uniforms, seals, weighing machines and even lion's-head mailbox slots from the nineteenth century.
Library (open 9am-2pm Mon-Fri).

Transport

Museo del Aire

Carretera de Extremadura (N-V), km. 10.5 (509 16 90). Bus De Blas 511, 512, 513, 514, 518, 521, 522 from Estación del Norte/by car Alcorcón exit from Carretera de Extremadura/by train Cercanías line C-5 to Cuatro Vientos, then bus. **Open** 10am-2pm Tue-Sun. **Admission** 100ptas; free under-10s, over-65s.
Spain's recently-renovated air museum is housed on one side of the military airbase at Cuatro Vientos, on the south-west road out of Madrid, and is a suitably gung-ho collection of historic aircraft, models, uniforms, photographs and other relics from the Spanish and some foreign air forces. Some civil aircraft and artefacts are also included, including a 1930s Autogiro, an early form of the helicopter that was invented by the Spaniard La Cierva. The star attraction, though, is the De Havilland Dragon Rapide that was hired by Spanish aristocrats in England in order to fly Franco secretly from the Canaries to Spanish Morocco just before the Civil War in 1936.
Wheelchair access.

Museo Angel Nieto

Avda del Planetario 4 (468 02 24). Metro Méndez Alvaro/bus 102, 112, 148/train Cercanías line C-5 to Méndez Alvaro. **Open** Oct-May 10am-2pm, 4.30-7pm, Tue-Fri; 11.30am-2pm, Sat, Sun. *June-Sept* 11am-2pm, 5.30-8pm, Tue-Fri; 11.30am-2pm, 5.30-8pm, Sat, Sun. **Admission** 150ptas; 100ptas under-14s; 75ptas groups of ten or more.
In 1988 Madrid's city hall ceded this building, in the south of the city near the **Planetario** (*see chapter* **Children**), to sporting legend and local-boy-made-good Angel Nieto, 13-times world motorcycling champion in 50-250cc, to house his personal collection of memorabilia. Everything to do with his career is here – bikes, photos, trophies, press cuttings, helmets, gloves, and videos of him on the track. Could be fascinating and fun if you're a biker or a racing fan, although even then you might think Angel's ego is a tad overblown.
Wheelchair access.

Museo Nacional Ferroviario

Antigua estación de Madrid-Delicias, Paseo de las Delicias 61 (527 31 21). Metro Palos de la Frontera/bus 19, 45. **Open** 10am-5.30pm Tue-Fri; 10am-3pm Sat, Sun. **Admission** *Tue, Wed, Fri-Sun* 400ptas; 200ptas students; free under-18s, over-65s. *Thur* free.
Concealed behind the national railway offices is the elegant old station of Delicias, with ironwork by no less than Gustave Eiffel himself. Now disused, it houses the National Railway Museum, an evocative collection of old engines, impressive railway models and antique railway equipment and memorabilia. You can climb aboard, have a drink in an old restaurant car or watch historic film footage of Spanish railways, and it's a particularly good museum for kids.

Arts & Entertainment

Media

Between earnest papers, gossipy glossies and tabloid TV, Spain's media run to extremes.

The Press

At the first light of day, Madrid's hundreds of newspaper kiosks open their metal shutters and spread their colourful contents onto the city's pavements. They offer a vast array of magazines, newspapers and, in some cases, books, even though the percentage of Spaniards who actually buy a daily paper, about 10 per cent, is pretty small. Newspaper readership is, though, higher in the major cities.

Most newspapers are tabloid in size rather than outlook. What there is of sensationalist journalism, here called *la prensa amarilla* (yellow press), is pretty tame, certainly by British standards, and mostly confined to the gossip magazines, the *prensa del corazón* (literally, press of the heart). With the notable exception of *El Mundo*, more serious investigative journalism isn't a priority either. Instead, the general style is a rather humourless mix of political reports – featuring much verbatim-quoting of politicians – updates on the country's long-running corruption cases, strong local coverage, and the usual litany of traffic accidents, forest fires and freaky crimes. Extensive, often pretty erudite coverage of sports, arts and entertainments is another standard. No Spanish paper would feel complete, either, without its name columnists, given ample space in which to pontificate on matters of the day.

For the news-hungry, trips to Madrid's newspaper libraries, the **Hemeroteca Municipal** and **Hemeroteca Nacional**, which stock a wide range of the Spanish and international press, are recommended. For details *see chapter* **Students**.

Daily newspapers

ABC

Extraordinarily old-fashioned, archly conservative and staunchly monarchist, *ABC* might seem to be no more than a leftover from the Franco years, but is still the preferred reading of Madrid's most solidly established citizens. It takes some getting used to the curious format – the cover and first few pages are all photos, and the rest almost uninterrupted text, with line drawings – and the leaden style, famed for its *correctísimo* Spanish, but it does have a well-regarded arts supplement on Mondays.

Diario 16

D16 looks and reads like a more middle-of-the-road version of *El Mundo* (*see below*), to whom it lost its most prominent journalists a few years ago. No balls but plenty of bulls – full colour gore from the *corrida* is a speciality, and sports coverage in general is a strongpoint.

Información de Madrid

Launched in 1994, this is Madrid's only specifically local paper, with *barrio*-by-*barrio* round-ups taking precedence over national and international news. It has a bright, clean layout and comprehensive daily venue and events listings.

Marca, As

The most important – in Madrid – of the many titles devoted to the Spanish obsession with sport. *Marca*, in fact, is the second-best-selling daily. Football, basketball, cycling and the rest are all reported with statistical zeal and hysterical headlines, but most attention is naturally given to Madrid's major football clubs, Real and Atlético.

El Mundo

Fiercely critical of the González government, while not being pro anything in particular, this lively paper has been largely responsible for unearthing the recent corruption scandals, stories sometimes ignored by its rival *El País*. Which gives some credence to the claims of its crusading editor Pedro J. Ramírez, formerly with *Diario 16*, that *El Mundo* is to Spain what the *Washington Post* was to America in the seventies, although the august *Post* was perhaps never quite so cavalier about floating stories without full corroboration. Among the (too) many columnists, the acerbic if self-adoring Francisco Umbral stands out, and there's also good sports coverage. The weekend magazine is a triumph of style over content, but design students love the typefaces.

El País

Spain's biggest-selling paper is competent without ever being exciting, but it provides excellent international coverage, as well as an informative daily Madrid supplement. Founded in 1976 not long after Franco's death, it immediately established itself as required reading for the liberal middle classes, becoming as synonymous with democratic Spain as Felipe González. Indeed, after the Socialists came to power in 1982 its government-friendly reputation earned it the nickname *Boletín Oficial del Estado* (the real *Boletín* is the official gazette, in which all new laws are published), although it has become more critical of late. The Friday edition includes the arts and listings supplement *Tentaciones* (*see below*), and the Sunday edition, which comes with a glossy magazine, is good for job ads.

Ya

Spain's Catholic daily, another long-established survivor from the Franco era, is currently struggling to ride out industrial disputes and falling circulation.

Foreign Newspapers

Most of the big kiosks around Sol, Gran Vía, C/Alcalá and the Castellana have a decent selection of foreign newspapers the day after publication at the latest. The *International Herald Tribune* and many British daily papers arrive the same day.

Magazines

Ajoblanco

Arty, intellectual and ever-so-slightly alternative, *Ajoblanco* first began life in the wild post-Franco years as a hippy-anar-

chist journal, but is now far more sleek. It compensates for its know-it-all tone with regular contributions from some of Spain's best young writers.

Cambio 16, Tiempo, Panorama, Tribuna, Epoca, Interviú

These are all weekly current affairs magazines of varying persuasions. *Cambio 16*, the sister publication of *Diario 16*, has a bright, campaigning style, and its jokey covers sometimes conceal some good reporting. *Tiempo* and *Panorama* are in a more light-hearted vein, while *Tribuna* and *Epoca* lean towards politics and business. *Interviú* is a peculiar Spanish hybrid – for the most part a girly-and-celebs magazine more concerned with nudes than news, but which occasionally carries some hard-hitting if sensationalist reporting.

El Gran Musical

A redesign has done wonders for *EGM*, once a crooners' comic, but now a state-of-the-art monthly entertainment magazine with eye-catching graphics.

¡Hola!, Pronto, Diez Minutos, Semana

Aaaah! *La prensa del corazón*, 'the press of the heart', a quintessentially Spanish invention, which gives beautiful people the chance to show off their beautiful homes, babies, boy/girlfriends and weddings, and to explain to a waiting public how much better they are feeling after coming to terms with their recent childbirth, divorce, car smash or corruption trial. *¡Hola!*, the fairy godmother of the genre, started in 1944 and is still the one the others imitate. Its unchanging format has been successfully exported to Britain in the shape of the ineffable *Hello!*

Lookout

An English-language magazine that's a cut above the other publications aimed at the ex-pat market, with some well-written pieces on Iberian life. It also publishes a range of books on Spanish culture, countryside, cookery and law.

Listings Magazines

Guía del Ocio

A weekly pocket-sized 'leisure guide', published every Thursday, with comprehensive cinema, arts and entertainment listings. However, much of Madrid social life works by word of mouth, and there are sometimes events – or last-minute changes – on which it misses out.

Metrópoli

Free with *El Mundo* on Thursdays. It has exhaustive film listings, as well as reviews of new releases and the week's films on television.

Segundamano

Not a listings guide as such, but a recently-expanded small-ads magazine that comes out three times a week, on Mondays, Wednesdays and Fridays. This is the first stop for anyone in search of a flat. To bag the bargains, buy each edition and start calling as early as possible. Adverts are placed free at any of its many offices around the city.

Tentaciones

This arts and entertainments pull-out is free with *El País* on Fridays. Despite an apparent obsession with Hollywood faces and international pop stars, its features provide good in-depth analysis of current fashions, and it carries listings for Madrid and the Spanish provinces.

TV & Radio

Until the eighties Spain had only two, state-run television channels. Regional stations began to

open at the beginning of the decade, the first in Catalonia in 1983, but it is only since the broadcasting laws were liberalised and private channels made their appearance in 1989 that the *caja tonta*, the 'idiot box', has really started to live up to its name. Hollywood movies, three-hour *espectáculos* (variety shows), South American soaps (called *culebrones*, literally 'big snakes', because of their endlessly tortuous plots), home-produced 'reality shows', football and bullfighting clog the airwaves, as the networks battle for audiences and revenue. The amount of advertising makes you want to break the set, even on the state-owned channels, and is so excessive it actually breaks the law. Equally frustratingly, newspaper TV listings are often unreliable – programmes are regularly cancelled or delayed. Notwithstanding all this, the Spaniards are a nation of TV addicts.

For a saner take on life, turn on the radio. The medium is perfectly suited to Spaniards' love of a good argument, and talk radio is often entertaining, informative and educational. Commercial radio tends to be more music-based, with a relentless mix of DJ patter and ads. Few newspapers bother to print details of radio programmes, so channel-hopping is often the best means to find your way around the dial.

TV

TVE 1 (La Primera)

Professional, if a little predictable, this is the flagship channel of the state broadcaster RTVE, and manages to remain reasonably calm amid the excesses of its competitors. For 20 years it's been home to Spain's most famous TV export, the game show *Un, Dos, Tres* (shown in Britain as *3, 2, 1*).

TVE 2 (La Dos)

The wacky graphics give it away – this is the minority channel. Arts, documentaries, education, children's programmes and sport are all well represented. Every night after midnight classic films are shown in the original language, with Spanish subtitles.

Antena 3

Populist, but more serious than its rival Tele 5, Antena Tres recently overtook TVE 1 as the most-viewed channel, despite (or perhaps because of) the inordinate amount of trashy series in its schedules. For sanctimonious and unashamed-

The **Torrespaña** TV tower, centre of TVE.

ly, often hilariously biased 'news' and comment, there is nothing like José María Carrascal's late-night bulletin.

Tele 5

Colourful, commercial and crass – Tele 5 is a byword for tackiness. Media czar and, at time of writing, Italian Prime Minister Silvio Berlusconi was a major investor when the channel was set up, and it was with the programming style first seen on his channels in Italy that it barged its way into the ratings. In post-1992 Spain it has been felt that the public's taste for all this fluff might be waning, and the channel has declared an intention to become more serious, but there's been little evidence of this on screen. Gorgeous young pre-

senters, audience-participation shows and legions of bimbos fill up the gaps between second-rate films. The legendary, loveable, slightly loopy Carmen Sevilla, presenter of the nightly lottery draw, is a Spanish cultural icon.

Telemadrid

Like every other autonomous region, Madrid has its own TV station. Telemadrid is cheerful and upbeat, and great for local news and live league football on Saturday nights.

Canal Plus (Canal+)

This classy, stylish channel, normally available only to subscribers with a signal decoder, shows a healthy diet of high-quality films (uninterrupted by ads), sports exclusives and documentaries. The open-access, unscrambled output includes ABC World News, at 8.05am each morning, video chart shows in the afternoon, and on Monday night *El Día Después*, the best football programme on television.

National Radio

RNE-1 (88.2 FM)

The traditional café *tertulia* has found a natural home on the airwaves, and Radio Uno is where you'll hear plenty of intelligent chat. A more bouncy, sometimes slightly silly local talk station is **Onda Madrid** (101.3 FM).

RNE-2 (96.5 FM)

Classical music station – an oasis of calm. The newly-launched **Sinfo Radio** (104.3 FM) is similarly serene.

RNE-3 (93.2 FM)

Pop music channel which gets more alternative after dark. Rocky and ravey by turns, plus gig details.

RNE-5 (90.3 FM)

A rolling news station with full bulletins every hour.

So this is reality...

In your face and in your living room, 'reality television' is, like so much on Spanish TV, American in concept. However, Spanish broadcasters have adopted and refined it as their very own, and 'reality shows' now dominate the primetime schedules. Director Pedro Almodóvar has satirised the trend in his film *Kika*, featuring Victoria Abril as host of a show called 'The Worst of the Day'. The movie, though, was a commercial and critical flop on its home patch.

Examples of the reality genre are many and varied, but the basic premise is simple – where there are blood, sweat or tears there's a programme to be made. Their success has a lot to do with the Spanish concept of *morbo* – an intense curiousity about other people's lives, combined with an enthusiastic fascination for anything vaguely perverse.

¿Quién Sabe Dónde? ('Who Knows Where?', TVE 1), a missing persons programme, is the most popular show on television, and has escaped serious criticism because of its supposed public service element. Even so, it's not

above broadcasting live phone calls between distraught parents and runaway teenagers and exploiting the attendant emotional chaos to the full. Ambulance-chasing is taken to new extremes in *Emergencia* ('Emergency' Telemadrid), while old wounds are gleefully and graphically reopened in *Misterios sin Resolver* ('Unsolved Mysteries', Tele 5).

Perhaps the most comical is *La Máquina de la Verdad* ('The Truth Machine', Tele 5), in which minor celebrities at the centre of some scandal are grilled by a panel and then wired up to a lie detector. The most talked-about show, though, is *Lo que Necesitas es Amor* ('All You Need Is Love', Antena 3), a maudlin but highly addictive three-hour spectacular on Sunday nights based on the 'best part of breaking up is the making up' principle. Jilted Romeos and Juliets attempt to win back their loves on national TV, with ritual humiliation awaiting the rejected. The format has proved so successful that highlights are now repeated several nights a week, as the tears flow, and the ratings grow.

Bullfighting

Humans 6, Bulls 0, is the usual score at Las Ventas, but that's not really the point.

Probably the one thing most people in the world know about Spain is that there is bullfighting. It is the one activity that most sets the country apart and makes it unique, for good or ill. Foreigners have long been fascinated or repelled by it, and taken it as a symbol or a demonstration of the country's dark, exotic, mysterious nature.

It is, certainly, the extreme, dramatic spectacle so admired by Hemingway and other foreign writers; it can also be very vulgar, with lots of noise, raw humour and primary colours. Many Spaniards, for their part, are sick to death of this sort of stuff, and see bullfighting as a regrettable hangover from a Spain forever locked into a tedious stereotype, something they'd rather not be associated with.

And yet, bullfighting has been intertwined with the country's culture for centuries, and is something from which it cannot easily be disentangled. It is thought to have originated in the Bronze Age Minoan civilisation in Crete. In Castile and Andalusia the bull is an ever-present symbol in traditional folklore, and bullfights of varying degrees of formality have been held since at least the middle ages. Like sports that are an integral part of a nation's life such as cricket or baseball, only more so, it has inspired a great deal of literature, from press reports through endless technical analyses and nostalgic reminiscences of *toreros* of the past to one of the greatest works of modern Spanish poetry, García Lorca's *Llanto por Ignacio Sánchez Mejías*, an elegy for a bullfighter friend of the poet killed in the ring in 1934.

For many years it has been suggested that bullfighting is dying out. Not a bit of it. The 1990s has seen it more in vogue than ever, achieving massive gates. At the ring, you're likely to bump shoulders and rub knees with representatives from every strata of Madrileño society, from the beret-wearing old villager to fashion models and young business types with slicked-back hair and sharp suits. This revival in bullfighting is perhaps the most striking expression of modern Spaniards' interest in re-evaluating their roots.

One of the problems with bullfighting is in saying exactly what it is. It's not a sport, as there is no competition involved. It's more a ritual, with certain set requirements.

How it is viewed by those who have grown up with it or become addicted to it is naturally very

Take me back to the bullpark.

different from the way it's seen by those who simply find it revolting. One cultured *aficionado* has said that a *corrida* is a combination of *arte, ética y estética* – art (the skill the bullfighter needs), ethics (he must face up to the risk, and give the bull plenty of chance to catch him, and if he doesn't will not be asked back) and aesthetics (the grace in movement that wins the greatest praise from the hyper-critical crowd). To put it another way, a bullfight is the ultimate fulfilment of the old English sporting adage that it ain't the winning but the taking part. Barring occasional incidents, the outcome is highly predictable, but it is how it is achieved, with what degree of courage, skill, cunning and even elegance, that is all important. A long-established Spanish expression of admiration is to say that somebody did something *a la torera* – with no other resources than nerve, flair, style, and not a little cheek.

You can't beat a bit o' bully.

Of course, you could say that this is nothing but the sort of stuff more likely to come out of the end of a bull by the tail. But, over and above such considerations, what keeps most *aficionados*, and quite a few foreigners, coming back to the ring is that they find there's no other spectacle that gives them such a buzz, that's quite so gripping or even spine-chilling. For, in order for a *corrida* truly to be a demonstration of grace under pressure, there has to be a real element of danger for the bullfighter at every stage, no matter how formalised, and even corny, the event may appear.

THE CORRIDA

A bullfight is a complicated affair, and if you go to one it's advisable to have an idea of what you are going to see first. The main type of bullfight is the *corrida*, where the bull is confronted by a matador, a *torero*, on foot. Although its rules and rituals are now regarded almost as holy writ they only became established towards the end of the eighteenth century, when this relatively proletarian form of bullfighting first became dominant. The bullfights staged in the Plaza Mayor in imperial Madrid were mainly of the old aristocratic type, on horseback. Called *rejoneo*, this is still practised today, but though very skilled it is not regarded highly by hard-core *aficionados*.

Every aspect of the bullfight is determined by strict rules and time-honoured rituals, whether it's the opening parade or the role of the *Presidente* of the *corrida*, (in Madrid, usually a police inspector) who directs the different stages of the event by waving a series of different-coloured handkerchiefs. The *corrida* itself is rigidly divided into six 15-minute-long sections, with three *toreros* alternating and killing two bulls each.

And while the bullfight goes on, for two hours or more, the running commentaries from fans munching on their tortilla *bocadillos* while the wine is passed back and forth, the raucous abuse they yell at the *torero* or the bull-breeder's mother, the cries of the beer and whisky hawkers and the lively *pasodobles* from the resident brass band ensure a thoroughly festive spirit.

Fighting bulls, *toros bravos*, weigh between 500 and 600 kilos and are reared semi-wild on large ranches. They should have as little contact with a human on foot as possible before their entrance into the ring. At midday before the fight they can be seen in the *apartado* outside the ring, when they are put into individual pens where they stay for the rest of the afternoon. When finally released from his confinement into the ring, the animal's natural instinct is to charge and remove or kill all that moves before him. At this point the bull is too fast and strong for the bullfighter to be able to kill it in the strictly prescribed manner. It has to be weakened, and for the *torero* to get close enough he has to try to bring it under his control with the skill of his capework.

Each quarter-hour fight is divided into three sections called *tercios* (thirds). The first begins with the matador carrying out *pases* or movements with a large pink cape to test out the temperament, strength and speed of the animal. This can seem one of the simplest and most innocent parts of the *corrida*, as if the two were playing. It is actually extremely dangerous, for the bull still has all its strength, and the work of the bullfighter always looks much easier and more casual than it is.

Next, still during the first *tercio*, two lance-wielding *picadores* appear on heavily-padded horses, inciting the animal to charge and then stabbing it in its bulging neck muscle to force it to lower its head. This is one of the parts of the fight most condemned by those opposed to bullfighting. For *aficionados*, however, it's crucial in gauging the bull's bravery, on the basis of whether it returns to charge the *picador* and his horse despite having been spiked and felt pain.

The next *tercio* involves the *banderillas*, long, multi-coloured barbed sticks. The *torero* and his three assistants run towards or receive the charging bull, and then stab the *banderillas* into the back of its neck. This is perhaps the most spectacular part of the bullfight, and also one of the bloodiest.

Finally, in the last third, comes the *faena de muleta*, the bullfighter's period alone with the bull, when he demonstrates his artistry in dominating the beast by making it follow a smaller red cape, the *muleta*. The bull is now wounded and weakened, but for this same reason is much more unpredictable. This culminates, after the traditional dedication of the bull to someone in the crowd, in the kill, the one moment when the ring falls silent. A 'good' kill, in which the sword is plunged in through a two-square-inch area between the shoulder blades and into the heart with precision, causing the bull to drop in seconds, will be received rapturously by the crowd. In contrast, matadors will be booed and heckled deafeningly if the animal is seen to suffer through bungled attempts to get the sword in the right place.

More than in any other spectacle the crowd plays a vital part in bullfighting. They complain and criticise constantly. It is only through the crowd's insistent waving of white handkerchiefs that a *torero* is presented with the prized ear or, better still, the tail of the bull he has killed. Likewise, if it is considered that the bull has displayed remarkable courage, the crowd can demand he be pardoned and granted a regal life back on the ranch thereafter. If they think a bull is not up to scratch they can also insist it be taken away, with green handerkerchiefs.

If a good kill is far from guaranteed, a good bullfight is also hard to come by, although the first-time visitor need not worry so much about this as it takes some experience to distinguish a good from a bad one. For those involved, a truly good bullfight is as elusive as any masterpiece. They may cite the case of veteran *torero* Curro Romero, capable of demonstrating his superb artistry in a fleeting five minutes, and then spending several years floundering about the ring and running scared stiff from every bull he faces. Neither is the presence of top-ranking *toreros* of the moment such as Espartaco, Emilio Ponce, Joselito or Jesulín de Ubrique on the bill a guarantee either, although they are more likely to give better value for money.

Some critics put the lack of good fights down to other factors. Bullfighting today, even though it may seem from another age, is very much part of modern Spain, moving billions of pesetas each year. There is much talk of 'decaffeination', with star *toreros* accused of using their influence to get ranchers to breed weaker, more easily managed bulls, and stories of horn-shaving (to make the bulls shy from attacking the bullfighter) and all kinds of other devious practices. Of course, like all sports, bullfighting is never as good as it used to be, and many of the same complaints were probably made in the last century. Anyone wanting to discover more on the history of bullfighting should visit the **Museo Taurino**, alongside the bullring (*see chapter* **Museums**).

Going to the Toros

Madrid's **Las Ventas** bullring is the mecca for all practitioners of the art. *Corridas* are held every Sunday from March to October, at 7pm. In addition, during the **Feria de San Isidro**, from May into June, and the **Feria de Otoño**, beginning in late September, fights are held every day. San Isidro is also immediately preceded by another fair, the **Feria de la Comunidad**, which includes several *novilladas* for novice bullfighters. The way in which the ring is run is as traditional as bullfighting itself. Tickets go on sale only two days in advance. Similarly, it is difficult to get an idea much in advance of which *toreros* will be appearing on a given day.

Some ticket agencies sell tickets, with commission (*see chapter* **Services**), but the way most people acquire theirs is by queuing up outside the ring. There are many different grades of ticket – the main division is between the cheap *Sol* (sun) and *Sombra* (shade), although there are some intermediate seats that are *Sol y Sombra*. Naturally, sitting in *Sol*

in midsummer can be very uncomfortable, and it's worth paying the extra to be in the shade. The best seats, which are very expensive, are in *Sombra* near the front, the *barrera*. At Las Ventas you get a pretty good view from any point, but probably the best ratio of price to comfort is in *Sol y Sombra* about half way up. Wherever you sit and at whatever price, rent yourself a cushion as you go in, or else the cramped stone seats will give you pains for days afterwards. The cushions also come in handy for joining in as the crowd showers insults and other things on a bullfighter they disapprove of.

Plaza de Toros de Las Ventas

C/Alcalá 237 (726 48 00/356 22 00). Metro Ventas/bus 21, 38, 53, 106, 201. **Box office** *Mar-Oct* 10am-2pm, 5-8pm, daily. **Tickets** 1,000-12,000ptas. **No credit cards**.

Bull Fairs around Madrid

In addition to the fights at Las Ventas most of the villages and towns in the surrounding region also hold *corridas* every Sunday during the season; less prestigious, but just as passionate affairs. Many also hold bull fairs, with bullfights daily, during their annual fiestas. These small-town fairs often include an *encierro*, in which young bulls are run through the streets first thing in the morning, as in the most famous of such events, Pamplona's San Fermín. They are pretty manic, with a good deal of drink taken, and anyone wanting to try out the full Hemingway-esque experience should be prepared for a fair few bruises, and also keep in mind that an *encierro* always involves a very real risk.

One such fair, in **Valdemorillo** to the north east, offers the earliest bullfights of the year, in February, providing a rare opportunity to see a *corrida* in the freezing cold. Probably the most spectacular *encierro* near Madrid is in **San Sebastián de los Reyes**, almost a suburb of the city, at the end of August. The most prestigious fair is the one in **Colmenar Viejo**, also only just outside the city, which attracts some major bullfighting names. The most important local fairs are listed below. Dates may vary slightly each year; further information is available close to the date from the individual town halls.

Bull Fairs

Aranjuez *(information 891 74 42). For travel details, see chapter* **Around Madrid**. **Feria de San Fernando** end May; **Feria de Septiembre** Sept.
Chinchón *(information 894 00 87). For travel details, see chapter* **Around Madrid**. **Feria de Agosto** 11-17 Aug.
Colmenar Viejo *(information 845 00 53). Bus 721 from Plaza Castilla.* **Feria de Agosto** 27 Aug-5 Sept.
Galapagar *(information 858 00 51). Bus 631 from Moncloa/train Cercanías line C-8.* **Feria de Septiembre** Sept.
Manzanares el Real *(information 853 00 09). Bus 724 from Plaza Castilla.* **Feria de Agosto** 5-8 Aug.
San Sebastián de los Reyes *(information 652 62 00). Bus 152, 154 from Plaza Castilla.* **Feria de Agosto** 26 Aug-3 Sept.
Valdemorillo *(information 897 73 60). Bus 641, 642 from Moncloa.* **Feria** 2-5 Feb.

Dance

Although venues may be few, Madrid's dance scene can still offer a unique and remarkable range of styles.

Madrid's claim to be the dance capital of Spain, in the face of the customary rivalry from Barcelona, is based on its position as home to two national companies, the *Ballet Nacional de España*, specialists in Spanish Dance, and the *Compañía Nacional de Danza*. It can also point to the wide spectrum of dance styles that can be studied and seen here, from classical ballet through contemporary to serious flamenco. The city's festivals also bring in a wide range of foreign companies.

However, dance has long been the Cinderella of the Spanish arts. Several Madrid theatres offer dance programmes, but there is no dedicated house showing dance all year round. Most major performances come within the framework of festivals, the budgets for which occasionally run to commissioning or co-producing work.

Visitors looking for classical ballet performances will have to look hard, now that under glamorous and dynamic young director Nacho Duato what was the *Ballet Lírico* has transformed itself into the *Compañía Nacional de Danza*. Duato previously worked at the Nederlands Dans Theater under Jiri Kylian, and his fluid contemporary works are in a similar style to that of his mentor. The *Compañía Nacional* also performs works by Kylian himself, occasionally donning pointe shoes for works by William Forsythe. The company has a heavy touring schedule and usually only performs in Madrid two or three times a year, in the **Teatro de la Zarzuela** in December and the **Teatro de Madrid** in spring or summer.

The *Compañía de Victor Ullate*, built up by the ex-director of the *Ballet Nacional*, offers a more varied neoclassical repertoire, including some Balanchine and *Les Sylphides*, and can be seen in short seasons at the **Teatro de Madrid** or **Teatro Albéniz**. Otherwise, the only classical ballet to be seen is in the annual visits of the weary *Ballet de Cuba* or snippets performed in school shows and by small semi-professional companies.

Contemporary dance other than that favoured by the *Compañía Nacional* struggles gamely to establish itself too, with minimal funding and very few performance outlets. Few local companies apart from the lively *10 y 10* and the earnest *Provisional Danza* manage to continue from one year to the next – most contemporary dancers and choreographers survive on a flexible project basis, working with different groups at the same time.

The **Compañía Nacional de Danza**.

With such diverse activity it's hard to identify a local style, although many of Madrid's best contemporary dancers have come from the school and company of Carmen Senra. Work tends to be physically and emotionally energetic. Limón and Pina Bausch are major influences. Among the independents look out for solo performances by the outrageously entertaining María José Ribot, or work by Madrid-based choreographers such as Francesc Bravo, Denise Perdikidis, Debra Greenfield, Carl Paris, Teresa Nieto and Blanca Calvo.

Dance Venues

Other Madrid theatres also host occasional dance seasons. The **Teatro de la Zarzuela** (*see chapter* **Music: Classical & Opera**) in particular presents performances by the major Spanish and visiting international companies.

Centro Cultural de la Villa

Jardines del Descubrimiento, Plaza Colón (575 60 80).
Metro Colón/bus all routes to Plaza Colón. **Box office**
11am-1.30pm, 5-8pm, Tue-Sun. Closed Aug. **Tickets**
average 800ptas. **No credit cards.**
This middle-scale city-run auditorium programmes smaller
ballet companies, Spanish Dance and some contemporary
work. It's very comfortable, but sightlines from the sides are
poor. *See also chapters* **Art Galleries** *and* **Theatre.**

Sala Olimpia

Plaza de Lavapiés (527 46 22). Metro Lavapiés/bus 27, C.
Box office 5-9pm Tue-Sun. **Tickets** 1,500ptas Tue, Wed,
Fri-Sun; 850ptas Thur; 750ptas under-26s. **Credit** V.
As the *Centro Nacional de Nuevas Tendencias Escénicas*,
Madrid's official 'fringe' venue, this theatre has been the main
home of contemporary dance, hosting visiting companies, co-
producing work by local artists and mounting an annual festival, *Danza en Diciembre.* In 1994 it came under the control
of the *Centro Dramático Nacional* and its future commitment
to new dance is uncertain. *See also chapter* **Theatre.**

Teatro Albéniz

C/de la Paz 11 (531 83 11). Metro Sol/bus all routes to
Puerta del Sol. **Box office** 11.30am-1pm, 5.30-9pm, Tue-
Sun. **Tickets** *average* 1,000-3,500ptas. **Credit** V.
This theatre, the main venue for the **Festival de Otoño**, is
perhaps closest to the heart of the local dance community,
and scene of some of the most significant annual dance
events. The stage is a bit cramped for ballet, but good for
middle-scale work. *See also chapter* **Theatre.**

Teatro de Madrid

Avda de la Ilustración (730 49 22). Metro Barrio del
Pilar/bus 42, 83, 128, 132, 147. **Box office** noon-2pm,
5-8.30pm, Tue-Sun. **Tickets** *average* 2,000ptas; reduced
price groups, over-65s. **No credit cards.**
This beautiful modern theatre in the north of the city with
large stage and excellent sightlines seems tailor-made for
dance. Built by the city, it's now run by private program-
mers, but they are continuing the policy of featuring a variety of Spanish and international dance companies, including
a good deal of Spanish Dance. *See also chapter* **Theatre.**

Teatro Pradillo

C/Pradillo 12 (416 90 11). Metro Concha Espina/bus 9,
43, 52, 120. **Open** *box office* one hour before
performance, Thur-Sun only. Closed July, Aug. **Tickets**
average 1,500ptas. **Credit** DC, MC, V.
This intimate studio theatre nevertheless has a good space
for dance, and tends to programme small-scale experimental work of a more dance-theatre orientacion.

Events

See also chapter **Madrid by Season**: *the* **Veranos**
de la Villa *and above all the* **Festival de Otoño.**

Como hoy se baila

Information Centro Coreográfico La Ventilla (*see below*).
One of the most valuable activities of the **La Ventilla** centre is the organisation every few months of showcase performances of small-scale contemporary work by independent
choreographers, under the title 'How we dance now'. The studio is converted into a tiny theatre space.

Día Internacional de la Danza

Information Asociación de Profesionales de la Danza
(*see below*). **Dates** 28-30 April.
International Dance Day, 29 April, is celebrated with a Gala
at the **Teatro Albéniz** featuring just about every major or
rising figure in dance in Spain today. Increasingly popular,
the programme is now shown over three days.

Madrid en Danza

Information Comunidad de Madrid (580 25 75). **Dates**
May-June.
Held over three to four weeks, this festival originally featured
only contemporary work, but recently has included some ballet, and there are usually a few interesting foreign companies.
Main venues are the **Albéniz**, the **Sala Olimpia** and the
Pradillo, and related activities have included workshops and
video dance showings. Look out for the *Espacios Insólitos* project, a day of open-air work in unusual sites around Madrid
commissioned from local choreographers.

Certamen de Coreografía de Danza
Española y Flamenco

Information Producciones Maga (547 69 79). **Dates** July.
Held over three days in July at the **Albéniz**, this choreo-
graphic competition is a splendid opportunity to spot new
trends and talents in the somewhat traditional world of
Spanish Dance. Audiences are passionately partisan.

Certamen Coreográfico de Madrid

Information Paso a Dos (365 70 37). **Dates** mid-Sept.
This competition, held at the **Sala Olimpia**, is open to
Spanish contemporary and classical choreographers.

Classes & information

Asociación de Profesionales de la Danza

C/Carretas 14, 7°, A-4 (tel/fax 521 16 52). Metro Sol/bus
all routes to Puerta del Sol. **Open** 10am-6pm Mon, Wed,
Fri; 10am-3pm Tue, Thur.
Represents the interests of the dance community, publishes
the bi-monthly magazine *Por La Danza* and organises a wide
variety of courses and events. It's an invaluable source of
information, especially at adult and professional level.

Centro de Danza Karen Taft

C/Libertad 15 (522 84 40/532 13 73). Metro Chueca,
Banco de España/bus 3, 40, 149. **Open** 10am-2pm, 5-
8.30pm, Mon-Fri.
A range of classes in ballet and modern techniques. It's the
base for the Isabel Quintero school for Spanish Dance.

Estudio de Carmen Senra

C/Jorge Juan 127 (359 16 47). Metro Goya, O'Donnell/bus
29, 30, 43, 63, C. **Open** 10am-2pm, 5-9pm, Mon-Fri.
Madrid's most important studio for contemporary dance,
offering classes in a variety of styles, including jazz. There
are regular visits by interesting guest teachers.
Branch: C/Apolonio Morales 13-11 (401 10 72).

Estudios Amor de Dios

C/Fray Luis de León 13 (530 16 61). Metro
Embajadores/bus 27, 34, 36, 41, 119, C. **Open** 10am-
10pm Mon-Fri, 10am-3pm Sat.
Previously the nerve centre of Madrid's flamenco dance scene
was a crumbling basement studio in Calle Amor de Dios packed
with students eager to learn from prestigious artists and vibrat-
ing with stamping feet and castanets. Redevelopment forced
the dancers out, but after a public outcry alternative accommodation was found in a modern block off the Ronda de Atocha.
Twelve studios of varying sizes offer classes in all the Spanish
styles and techniques, or are available to rent by the hour.

Centro Coreográfico La Ventilla

C/Carmen Montoya 12 (314 70 68). Metro Ventilla/bus
42, 147. **Open** 9.30am-2pm, 5-10pm, Mon-Fri; 9.30am-
2pm Sat.
Set up by Carmen Werner, this simple space in Tetuán is the
shared rehearsal base of her own company *Provisional*
Danza and *10 y 10*, directed by Pedro Berdayes and Monica
Runde. The morning company contemporary class is open;
there are also regular ballet classes.

Spanish Dance

Spain is unique in Europe in possessing an entirely indigenous dance tradition that covers the range of sophistication from pure folk dance to highly studied and refined techniques. The differences in styles can be hard to distinguish for newcomers, but even so, devotees can dispute passionately whether this or that movement is within the never-quite-defined tradition.

Flamenco is only one of the four major categories. The others are *escuela bolera*, developed in the eighteenth century, using castanets, *danza folclórica*, regional folk dances from all over Spain, and *danza estilizada*, often called *Ballet Español* or Spanish Ballet, a theatricalised hybrid combining elements from all other styles, and usually to music by Spanish classical composers.

Spanish Dance styles (especially flamenco) have huge commercial success outside Spain – so much so that the foremost company of all, the polished and spectacular *Ballet Nacional de España*, spends most of its time touring and only performs in Madrid for a few weeks each year, usually in the **Festival de Otoño**. In Madrid, on the other hand, in spite of there being many companies, performers and teachers based here, there are few regular programmes, although some theatres do often host short seasons (*see page 182* **Dance Venues**). If you catch them, the *Ballet Nacional* have recently been pushing at the borders of Spanish Dance with highly imaginative productions.

TABLAOS & SALAS ROCIERAS

Where people are perhaps most likely to see Spanish Dance, though, is at a flamenco show, a *tablao*, which is also where flamenco artists high and low earn their bread and butter in between theatrical performances. There are several around Madrid, but those listed here are the ones where you are most likely to catch genuine, intense performances. As well as the show, you can dine or just have a drink; both are appallingly expensive, but if you stay to closing time you can get your money's worth of flamenco dance and music. The fun really starts about midnight, when most tourists go off to bed and the major artists appear; up till then you may get a kitsch Spanish Dance show or the enforced jollity of the *cuadro flamenco de la casa* (the regular musicians and dancers).

The venues listed here mainly feature flamenco dance. You can also often see fine dance performances outside of a *tablao* setting at flamenco music venues (*see chapter* **Flamenco**).

As well as watching a Spanish Dance show you can also join in, by making for a *sala rociera* or Andaluz dance club for a bout of *sevillanas* and the odd *rumba*. Atmosphere is guaranteed. Note, though, that Seville's elegant dance is complex. Dance schools offer courses, and as an introduction the 1992 Carlos Saura film *Sevillanas* contains definitive performances in an astonishing variety of styles.

Al Andalus

C/Capitán Haya 19 (556 14 39). Metro Lima/bus 5, 27, 40, 149. **Open** 10pm-6am Mon-Sat; show starts 11pm. **Admission** free.

With the obligatory *sala rociera* décor reminiscent of a *caseta* at the April fair in Seville, Al Andalus offers a brassy live show, but best of all is watching the mainly middle-aged public get on to the floor and throw themselves into passionate and idiosyncratic *sevillanas* until dawn. There's a minimum bar and tapas charge of 2,000ptas, Mon-Wed, and 3,000ptas, Thur-Sat.

Almonte

C/Juan Bravo 35 (562 13 63). Metro Diego de León/bus 26, 52, 56, 61, C. **Open** 9pm-6am. **Admission** free.

On two floors, this pretty *sala rociera*-disco rubs shoulders with upmarket clubs in Salamanca and is packed with trendsters letting their hair down. No live show, just pricey drinks and tapas and a lot of smouldering *sevillanas*.

Café de Chinitas

C/Torija 7 (547 15 02/1). Metro Santo Domingo/bus 44, 133, 147. **Open** 9pm-2am Mon-Sat; show starts 10.30pm. **Admission** *dinner & show* 8,000ptas; *drink & show* 3,900ptas. **Credit** AmEx, DC, MC, V.

With a plushy, nostalgic ambience evoking its nineteenth-century namesake, the recently renovated Café de Chinitas is Madrid's most luxurious *tablao*, with a good *cuadro* of 10 performers. The artists now change every month, in order to maintain the interest of a discerning local public.

Corral de la Morería

C/de la Morería 17 (365 84 46). Metro La Latina/bus 17, 23, 35, 60. **Open** 9pm-3am daily; show starts 10.45pm. **Admission** *dinner & show* 10,000; *drink & show* 3,800ptas. **Credit** AmEx, DC, MC, V.

Another of Madrid's more serious *tablaos*, smaller and more rustic in style. Apart from the *cuadro*, the show features two respected senior figures of the Madrid flamenco scene, El Camborio from Sunday to Wednesday, and Blanca del Rey on Thursdays, Fridays and Saturdays.

Zambra

C/Velázquez 8 (435 51 64). Metro Príncipe de Vergara/bus 1, 9, 19, 51, 74. **Open** 9pm-2am daily; show starts 10.15pm. **Admission** *dinner & show* 9,500ptas; *drink & show* 3,750ptas. **Credit** AmEx, DC, MC, V.

Less intimate and slightly larger, Zambra, in the **Hotel Wellington** (*see chapter* **Accommodation**) has a reputation for having a *cuadro* of pretty young girls. The show is directed by Cristóbal Reyes, one of an important family of flamenco dancers, so watch out for occasional seasons by some really exciting artists.

Film

Spain's mini-Hollywood closed down a good while ago, but its grand movie palaces keep the cinema-going tradition alive.

Spain has an illustrious film-making tradition of its own, but in recent years, like the rest of the world, it has felt the onslaught of adroitly marketed US movies, which now capture an average 80 per cent of the Spanish market. Local film production is only a fraction of what it was at its peak in the early 1960s, when the country was a major centre for international co-productions such as the Spaghetti westerns made near Almería. Interest in such collaborations faded when it ceased to make good economic sense for foreign film-makers to shoot here.

Spanish cinema has attracted a fair deal of international attention in the last few years to a great extent thanks to one director – Pedro Almodóvar. It was, though, his compatriot Fernando Trueba who nabbed a 1994 Foreign Language Oscar with his lush, romantic period comedy *Belle Epoque*. Both directors are partial to comedies, but their approaches couldn't be more different. Almodóvar taps into a dark, off-the-wall humour, while Trueba, who idolises traditional Hollywood, aims for something lighter and more conventional. Between them they epitomise the creative impulses driving Spanish film-making today. Almodóvar, who of late has sounded quite disillusioned with many aspects of Spanish life, has a highly individualistic style that makes it unlikely he will ever work with a major studio. The ambitious Trueba, on the other hand, is just taking off, and his latest project *Two Much* is an international production in English, with Antonio Banderas and Melanie Griffith.

For all these international successes, though, former industry staples such as the cheap comedies made for the Spanish domestic market have continued to fade in number. Nonetheless, a growing understanding between the industry and the Spanish authorities may in future provide a new impetus for film-making initiatives. A new studio complex just to the west of Madrid at Pozuelo, the *Ciudad de la Imagen*, was already open for business at the end of 1994, and if current plans come to fruition a film school should open here in 1996. Madrid's last such school closed down over 20 years ago.

MOVIEGOING IN MADRID

While film production might not be major league, movie-going is a serious business in Madrid. Massive cinemas still line the Gran Vía, and their

For classic movie palaces, the Gran Vía.

extraordinary publicity hoardings, hand-painted for each film, are one of the sights of the city. Some are divided into multiplexes, others still carry on in their original 1-2,000-seater form, and all of them attract capacity audiences on Sunday nights for the dubbed international blockbusters they mostly screen.

Most Spaniards still prefer to see foreign movies dubbed, but there has been a steady increase in the number of VO (*versión original*) houses that show films in their original language with Spanish subtitles. When a film is shown undubbed this is indicated by the letters VO in newspapers and on cinema publicity. Films are also always screened in VO at the official film theatre, the **Filmoteca**.

Newspapers and the *Guía del Ocio* (*see chapter* **Media**) are reliable sources of cinema schedules. The most popular screenings of the day are those at around 10pm. Several of the VO cinemas have additional late shows at weekends. Some cinemas

offer lower ticket prices for the first show in the afternoon, and many more have a special reduced-price *Dia del Espectador* (Filmgoer's Day), on Mondays or Wednesdays.

The Gran Vía Cinemas

Avenida
Gran Vía 37 (521 75 71). Metro Callao, Gran Vía/bus all routes to Gran Vía. **Box office** 3.30-10.30pm daily. **Tickets** 650ptas Mon, Tue, Thur-Sun; 400ptas Wed except public holidays.
This gleaming, Italian marble interior with its glittering chandeliers was a theatre in its first decade of existence, over 60 years ago. Its size (seating over 1,500), giant 70mm screen and Dolby sound make it ideal for blockbusters.

Callao
Plaza de Callao 3 (522 58 01). Metro Callao/bus all routes to Gran Vía. **Box office** 11am-1pm, 4.30-10.15pm, daily. **Tickets** 650ptas.
An established landmark, the façade of this twenties cinema looms over the Plaza Callao. It seats over 1,000, but recent refurbishment means it's comfortable and welcoming.

Gran Vía
Gran Vía 66 (570 66 33). Metro Plaza de España/bus all routes to Gran Vía, Plaza de España. **Box office** 4-10.30pm daily. **Tickets** 650ptas Mon, Tue, Thur-Sun; 400ptas Wed except public holidays.
Where to come for old-world elegance – the Gran Vía's sparkling splendour is set off by nearly a dozen chandeliers, some of Bohemian crystal. It still has just one, 1,000-seater auditorium, and there are no plans at the moment to convert it into a multiplex.

Lope de Vega
Gran Vía 55 (547 20 11). Metro Callao, Santo Domingo/bus all routes to Gran Vía. **Box office** 4-10.30pm daily. **Tickets** 650ptas Mon, Tue, Thur-Sun; 400ptas Wed except public holidays.
This massive cinema also started out as a theatre in the thirties. It sometimes hosts concerts by local divas and the like.

Palafox
C/Luchana 15 (446 18 87). Metro Bilbao/bus 3, 37, 40, 147. **Box office** 4.30-10.30pm daily. **Tickets** 650ptas.
A celebrated première held here was that of producer Samuel Bronston's *55 Days in Peking (see page 187)*, which drew such luminaries as Rita Hayworth, John Wayne, Claudio Cardinale and Tony Curtis – all in town to make *Circus World*.

Palacio de la Musica
Gran Vía 35 (521 62 09). Metro Callao/bus all routes to Gran Vía. **Box office** 4.30-10.30pm daily. **Tickets** 650ptas Mon, Tue, Thur-Sun; 400ptas Wed except public holidays.
A grand old cinema dating back to the thirties. Gilded balustrades and carved relief surfaces add to the opulence of this 2,000-seater former concert hall.

Palacio de la Prensa
Plaza de Callao 4 (521 99 00/522 73 94). Metro Callao/bus all routes to Gran Vía. **Box office** 4-10.30pm daily. **Tickets** 650ptas.
A massive forties cinema with nearly 2,000 seats, the Palacio has been transformed into a three-screen multiplex.

VO Cinemas

Alphaville
C/Martin de los Heros 14 (559 38 36). Metro Plaza de España, Ventura Rodríguez/bus 1, 2, 44, 74, 133, C. **Box office** 4-11pm Mon-Thur, Sun; 4pm-1am Fri, Sat. **Late shows** *begin* 12.30-1am Fri, Sat. **Tickets** 625ptas Tue-Sun; 400ptas Mon except public holidays.
Alphaville has established a loyal following of film enthusiasts since it opened in 1977. It's a four-screen multiplex with a basement cafeteria that was an important in-vogue meeting point in the cinema's heyday in the early eighties, when it was used for non-commercial screenings and performances by avant-garde theatre and musical acts. A screen in the café remains as a reminder of these efforts to create an alternative space within Madrid's conservative arts scene, and it's still occasionally used to support off-the-wall initiatives. Nowadays, though, people may be more likely to visit the café for the Italian chef's tasty Apfelstrudel.

Arlequin
C/San Bernardo 5 (547 31 73). Metro Santo Domingo/bus all routes to Gran Vía. **Box office** 4.30-10.15pm daily. **Tickets** 600ptas Tue-Sun; 400ptas Mon except public holidays.
This 400-seater screens a mix of mainstream and art-house fare, but easily wins the vote for least comfortable of the VO cinemas, and sound and projection quality aren't great either.

Bellas Artes
C/Marqués de Casa Riera 2 (522 50 92). Metro Banco de España/bus all routes to C/Alcalá. **Box office** 5.30-10.15pm daily. **Tickets** 625ptas Tue-Sun; 400ptas Mon except public holidays.
Originally a theatre, the Bellas Artes was converted into a cinema in 1937. In 1970 it pioneered the screening of mainstream and art-house foreign films in their original language, and started providing movie-goers with film notes. There is a cafeteria and film souvenir shop on the upper level. The Bellas Artes boasts Dolby sound and the latest projection equipment, but is probably the only cinema in Madrid where a vendor still walks up and down the aisles selling popcorn and drinks.

California
C/Andrés Mellado 53 (544 00 58). Metro Moncloa/bus 2, 16, 61, C. **Box office** 4-10.30pm daily. **Tickets** 600ptas Mon, Tue, Thur-Sun; 400ptas Wed except public holidays.
This 500-seat cinema near the University screens mainly commercial films. It also, though, encourages schools and students to use it for English-teaching purposes.

Ideal Multicines
C/Doctor Cortezo 6 (369 25 18). Metro Sol, Tirso de Molina/bus 6, 26, 32, 57. **Box office** 4-11pm Mon, Sun; 5.30-11pm Tue-Thur; 5.30pm-1am Fri; 4pm-1am Sat.

Late shows *begin* 12.30-1am Fri, Sat. **Tickets** 650ptas Tue-Sun; 450ptas Mon except public holidays.

An eight-screen multiplex that programmes a mix of Spanish films and box-office hits and art-house movies in VO, and attracts a varied crowd of locals and foreigners. It hosted the Madrid horror and fantasy film festival (Imagfic), before the event went bust in 1993.

Princesa

C/Princesa 3 (559 98 72). Metro Plaza de España/bus all routes to Plaza de España. **Box office** 4-11pm Mon-Thur, Sun; 4pm-1am Fri, Sat. **Late shows** 12.45am Fri, Sat. **Tickets** 650ptas; 400ptas students and over-65s, first show Mon-Fri.

The most recent addition to the Renoir chain (*see below*), this ultra-modern, six-screen multiplex offers a combination of Spanish films and foreign movies in VO. It's one of the most comfortable cinemas in Madrid, with plush seats, wide screens, and fine Dolby sound.

Renoir (Plaza de España)

C/Martín de los Heros 12 (559 57 60). Metro Plaza de España, Ventura Rodríguez/bus 1, 2, 44, 74, 133, C. **Box office** 4-11pm Mon-Thur, Sun; 4pm-1am Fri, Sat. **Late shows** *begin* 12.30-1am Fri, Sat. **Tickets** 650ptas; 400ptas students and over-65s, first show Mon-Fri.

The enterprising Renoir chain has three VO multiplex cinemas in Madrid and plans for more. The Plaza de España five-screen – the first of the chain – opened in 1986. It lays on film notes, and good late-night screenings.

Renoir (Cuatro Caminos)

C/Raimundo Fernández Villaverde 10 (534 00 77). Metro Cuatro Caminos/bus all routes to Cuatro Caminos. **Box office** 4-11pm Mon-Thur, Sun; 4pm-1am Fri, Sat. **Late shows** *begin* 12.30-1am Fri, Sat. **Tickets** 650ptas; 400ptas students and over-65s, first show Mon-Fri.

Another very comfortable Renoir VO multiplex, with tables, chairs and fold-down seats along the walls in the foyer for easy queuing. High ceilings also allow for larger screens. It shows a mix of commercial and art-house films.

Rosales

C/Quintana 22 (541 58 00). Metro Argüelles, Ventura Rodríguez/bus 1, 2, 44, 74, 133, C. **Box office** 4.15-

10.30pm daily. **Tickets** 600ptas Mon, Tue, Thur-Sun; 350ptas Wed and first show Mon-Fri.

The Rosales first opened in 1969, and now specialises in art-house films in VO. The 360-seat cinema sometimes stages theme weeks featuring directors or, for example, French or Italian cinema, and always gives out film notes.

The Filmoteca

Filmoteca Española (Cine Doré)

C/Santa Isabel 3 (369 11 25). Metro Antón Martín/bus 6, 26, 32, 57. **Open** *box office* 6.30-10.45pm, *bar-restaurant* 5pm-1am, Tue-Sun. **Tickets** 225ptas; 1,700ptas block ticket for 10 films.

Founded in 1953, Spain's official film theatre has recently expanded its role in restoring and preserving the heritage of Spanish cinema. Films are also screened regularly in the old Cine Doré in Lavapiés, with foreign films always undubbed. In summer, films are shown outside in the rooftop bar, and there is also a cinema bookshop. As a member of the International Federation of Film Archives, it has access to the archives of other member-countries to feed its series on classic directors, genres or the cinema of different countries. The Filmoteca's own collection of 20,000 titles was transferred in 1994 to the *Ciudad de la Imagen* (*see introduction*).

Open Air Cinema

Cine de Verano

Screenings *July-Sept* from 10.15pm daily. **Tickets** 400ptas; 250ptas over-65s; free under-7s.

As part of the city's **Veranos de la Villa** festival (*see chapter* **Madrid by Season**) films are shown in an open-air venue, with a double bill nightly through the summer. Most of the films screened are fairly mainstream, but more unusual fare is also included, and some films are shown in VO. In previous years the giant screen has been set up in the Retiro, or in front of Las Ventas bullring. In summer 1994, though, the venue was moved to the Parque de la Bombilla, down by the river on the Paseo de la Florida. It isn't possible to say where the location will be in coming years, but local papers or the *Guía del Ocio* (*see chapter* **Media**) will have details.

Bronston's Lost Empire

Before he went bankrupt in 1966, producer Samuel Bronston operated his own little off-shoot of Hollywood in Spain. His tumultuous romance with the country began in 1959 with the production of *Captain Jones* directed by John Farrow, whose daughter Mia was placed in a Madrid convent school for a spell. Characteristic Bronston productions were widescreen epics such as Nicholas Ray's *55 Days in Peking* and *King of Kings*, and Anthony Mann's great *El Cid* and *The Fall of the Roman Empire*. Exteriors were shot all over Spain, but other scenes were filmed in the sprawling Bronston Studios near Chamartín station in Madrid.

Appropriately, *The Fall of the Roman Empire* presaged the collapse of Bronston's own empire.

Financial mismanagement and a series of box-office flops finally did for his mini-Hollywood. Henry Hathaway's 1964 *Circus World* (aka *The Magnificent Showman*) dealt the final blow, despite a stellar cast led by John Wayne and Rita Hayworth.

The 30,000-square metre Bronston studios were sold off piecemeal, in part to state broadcaster RTVE. Now known as the Estudios Luis Buñuel, this section has a 2,200-square metre sound stage that's one of the largest in Europe and mainly used for game shows and other TV productions. Bronston himself didn't end his days in Spain, but shortly after he died in January 1994 his ashes were flown here, in keeping with his final wishes.

Music: Classical & Opera

Classical music has made great strides in Madrid in the last few years, despite post-1992 cutbacks.

Madrid composer Luis de Pablo once wrote that the city's music scene was improving thanks to the aeroplane, since local music lovers could now get a flight out to hear what they were missing at home. Spanish composers have long lamented the marginal position of serious music within the country's culture as a whole, but today only the hyper-critical would agree with this damning indictment. Central Europe it is not, but concert-goers in Madrid can still delight in top-class music.

Spain's rapid economic growth during the eighties was the background to a blossoming in the classical scene. Madrid now has, for example, three major orchestras (*see below*). It was, though, the construction of the **Auditorio Nacional** (*see below*) in 1988 at a cost of 2,500 million pesetas (about £12.5 million) which was fundamental in reviving the city's musical fortunes and galvanising interest.

Opera in Madrid has fared less well. The principal opera house, the **Teatro Real**, was closed for thorough renovation in 1987, but this much-needed refurbishment has developed into an endless saga, and completion dates are regularly revised. The latest one is October 1995, although conventional wisdom suggests that it could be even later. In the meantime the opera company has been installed in the **Teatro de la Zarzuela** (*see below*), previously devoted only to ballet and Spanish light opera (*see page 191* **Zarzuela**).

In 1992 Madrid had its moment as 'European City of Culture'. Optimistic souls believed this would herald the city's establishment on the international stage, but really it was more of a curtain call for a city for which the economic bubble had burst. In 1993 Spain was plunged into a recession which brought a drop in grants, sponsorship, commissions and audiences. Since then music has been subject to the law of an economic jungle in which only the strongest ensembles may survive. Particularly sad are the problems affecting contemporary music, after all the efforts made in the last decade had brought greater recognition and the creation of new institutions and ensembles.

Tickets

Concert tickets in Madrid are reasonably priced and relatively easy to obtain. Some state-funded theatres, among them the **Auditorio Nacional** and the **Teatro de la Zarzuela**, have a computerised joint ticketing system which makes it possible to buy tickets for all these venues at any one of them (*see also chapter* **Theatre**). There can be problems getting tickets for the large-scale weekend performances at the **Auditorio Nacional**, which give upper-class madrileños a chance to rattle their jewellery. In many cases most tickets for these concerts are only available to subscribers with season tickets for a specific concert series. Season tickets do bring significant reductions, and are recommended for those planning longer stays. To see opera, while it lacks a permanent home, it's necessary to book well in advance. Ticket agencies (*see chapter* **Services**) will usually be able to get opera and concert seats for you, but charge commission. Touts are an undesirable last resort.

Concert seasons are packed into the October to June period. During the summer months, and August in particular, many music venues virtually close down, and regular concerts are at a premium. It is possible to hear music at this time, though, at open-air performances as part of the city's festivals, and the summer is also the main season for *zarzuela* (*see below* **Festivals & Free Music** *and* **Zarzuela**).

Orchestras & Ensembles

Grupo Círculo

Founded in 1983, and based at the **Círculo de Bellas Artes** (*see below* **Venues**), the group has as musical director José Luis Temes, one of Madrid's contemporary leading lights. The very survival of this twelve-strong ensemble testifies to its members' determination and sense of inspiration. They divide their energies between performances (over a hundred premières so far) and recording (21 CDs) of Spanish contemporary music, featuring works by composers of international renown such as Cristóbal Halffter and Luis de Pablo, and by younger and lesser-known names.

Orquesta Nacional de España & Coro Nacional de España

The ONE has been the flagship of Spanish classical music over the last half-century. The triple obligations of attracting public attention, creating basic repertoires and simultaneously enlarging them into new areas have often been too much for it to bear. Its history mirrors that of the country as a whole. Initially founded in 1938 in Barcelona, then capital of the Spanish Republic, it was officially re-created two years later in Madrid after the Nationalist victory. Recently it has been marked by internal strife. Musicians, whose role is complicated by their position as state employees, went on strike in 1993 for the first time in the organisation's history, and the most recent musical director, the Italian Aldo Ceccato,

*The Minsk Opera orchestra at the Centro Cultural Conde-Duque. See **Festivals** page 190.*

left in June 1994 after a three-year tenure predicting a bleak future for the orchestra. For the immediate future there is to be a series of guest musical directors, hardly a satisfactory arrangement. At the same time, the National Choir also saw the departure of its director, Adolfo Gutiérrez Viejo. Orchestra and choir now have an excellent permanent home in the **Auditorio Nacional** (*see below* **Venues**), but recession-enforced cutbacks in state grants seem destined to exacerbate their relative disarray.

Orquesta y Coro de RTVE

Born out of the need to perform classical music for broadcasting, the excellent Spanish Radio and Television Orchestra initially began concert performances in summer tours of Spanish cities as an initiative of Franco's Ministry of Information and Tourism. Instrumental in its origins was Ernesto Halffter, commonly regarded as one of the finest Spanish composers of this century, and uncle of Cristóbal Halffter, one of Spain's foremost composers today. The orchestra made its début on 27 May 1965 at the **Teatro de la Zarzuela** (*see below* **Venues**). Since then it has made some magnificent recordings of Spanish works, and a particularly successful *Antología de la Zarzuela*. It moved into its new home at the **Teatro Monumental** (*see below* **Venues**) in 1988, and two years later the Romanian Sergiu Comissiona took charge. The varied repertoire covers romantic classics, Spanish works and contemporary music.

Orquesta Sinfónica de Madrid

Unencumbered by extra-musical problems, this orchestra was awarded the Madrid music prize in 1993. Founded ninety years previously, its most famous musical director, the violinist Enrique Fernández Arbos, was appointed in 1905 and stayed for thirty years. He composed the pre-war period so much that the orchestra became known as the *Arbos*, and his retirement shortly before the Civil War poignantly represented both a musical and political watershed. Despite several attempts to revive the orchestra's fortunes, it was not until 1981 that it fully recovered from the disintegration caused by the war. That year saw its controversial appointment as resident orchestra at the **Teatro de la Zarzuela** (*see below* **Venues**), a move opposed by Madrid's two other major orchestras. However, it has completely justified the vote of confidence. A pioneer in its field, it no longer has a musical director but an artistic committee, an arrangement that so far has proved highly successful.

Trio Mompou

Based in Madrid, and so-named as a tribute to the late Catalan composer and master pianist Frederic Mompou, this contemporary chamber ensemble is highly regarded at home and abroad. Mompou himself once remarked on the 'quality and exquisite musicality of their performances', and their repertoire comprises over a hundred works by almost every Spanish composer of this century. Highly recommended.

Venues

Auditorio Nacional de Música

C/Príncipe de Vergara, 146 (337 01 00). Metro Cruz del Rayo/bus 1, 29, 52. **Open** *box office* 5-7pm Mon; 10am-5pm Thur, Fri; 11am-1pm Sat. **Main season** Oct-June. **Tickets** *ONE concerts* 700ptas-3,900ptas. **Credit** AmEx, DC, MC, V.

The inauguration of this ugly building in 1988 put Madrid on the itineraries of the most important international conductors, soloists and orchestras, attracted by a new symphony hall rivalling the Berlin Philharmonie and Amsterdam Concertgebouw in capacity (2,000-plus in the main hall). The home of the troubled **Orquesta Nacional de España** and its associated choir, it has, despite outward appearances, symphonic and chamber music halls that are light, comfortable venues with excellent acoustics. Most concert activity revolves around a series of regular annual seasons or concert series, run in parallel. The centrepiece season features the Orquesta Nacional de España with international guest conductors and soloists, and runs from October to June, usually on Fridays and Saturdays. The same programmes are also performed by the ONE at 11.30am on Sundays, tickets for which go on sale just one hour in advance. Concerts are also presented under the heading *Grandes Autores e Intérpretes de la Música*, featuring guest international orchestras, ensembles and soloists, and a third season is *Ibermúsica*, centred on Spanish music. In addition, there are organ recitals on occasional Tuesdays from October to June, also featuring international names. In the 692-seat chamber hall the season *Cámara y Polifonía* – 'Chamber and Polyphony' – is the main event; 20 concerts are held on Tuesdays and Thursdays from October to June. Chamber works receive less attention from Madrid music-goers, so tickets are never a problem.

Círculo de Bellas Artes

C/Marqués de Riera 2 (531 77 00). Metro Banco de España, Sevilla/bus all routes to C/Alcalá. **Main season** Sept-June. **Tickets** prices vary according to concert.

Funded jointly by state and private institutions and yet perpetually on the brink of financial ruin, the Círculo is a Madrid landmark: architecturally because of the beauty and history of its building; socially because of its great café and wild, fancy-dress carnival ball; and culturally because of its contribution to the capital's artistic life. It is also one of the city's most important contemporary music centres, acting as a base for the **Grupo Círculo** and hosting concerts organised by the **Centro para la Difusión de la Música Contemporánea** *(see below* **Institutions)** and international touring groups. *See also chapters* **Sightseeing, Cafés & Bars** *and* **Art Galleries.**

Teatro Monumental

C/Atocha 65 (581 77 19). Metro Antón Martín/bus 6, 26, 32, 57. **Open** *box office* 11am-2pm, 5-7pm, daily. **Main season** Oct-May. **Tickets** 900ptas-1,900ptas; nine-concert season tickets 6,300ptas-15,300ptas. **No credit cards.**

Lacking the facilities of the **Auditorio Nacional** or the charm of the **Teatro de la Zarzuela**, the main function of this theatre is to record concerts by the **RTVE** Orchestra and Choir for broadcasting. It's a reasonably-priced venue which offers orchestral concerts, opera and *zarzuela*, and opens its doors to the public for general rehearsals free of charge on Thursday mornings. It has a good contemporary music season *Música del Siglo XX*, from October to April.

Teatro Real

Plaza de Isabel II. Metro Opera/bus 3, 25, 33, 39.
Once renovation is finally completed, Madrid's opera house is supposedly due to reopen during 1995 with *Don Giovanni*.

Teatro de la Zarzuela

C/Jovellanos 4 (429 82 25). Metro Sevilla/bus all routes to C/Alcalá. **Open** *box office* noon-6pm daily (noon-8pm, performance days).* **Main season** Jan-July. **Tickets** 1,900ptas-11,550ptas. **Credit** AmEx, DC, MC, V.

A theatre with a chequered history, designed along the lines of Milan's Scala, this beautiful building was opened in 1856, in an attempt to boost the prestige of *Zarzuela*. It was ravaged by fire in 1909, but later rebuilt. It was not until 1956, though, when it was purchased by Spain's Writers' Union that its fortunes received a boost. Callas sang here in 1958, and an annual opera festival began in 1964. It was taken over by the state in 1970 and declared a national monument in 1994. It has been Madrid's official opera house since the closure of the **Teatro Real** in 1987, and devotes seven months per year to opera, as well as fulfilling its obligations to ballet and *Zarzuela*. Under current director Antoni Ros-Marbà, the opera company has staged some much-praised productions, notably of *Don Giovanni* and *Eugene Onegin*.

Institutions

Asociación Filarmónica de Madrid

Avda de América 4 (726 50 50). Metro Avda de América/bus 12, 29, 52, 72, 114, 115, C.
Run by the indomitable Tola de Urbueta, the association now organises two concerts per month for its 1,700 members at the **Auditorio Nacional** *(see above* **Venues).** Recent programmes have featured Barbara Hendricks, Kiri Te Kanawa, and the Vienna Philharmonic. Tickets are available to non-members, but at a higher price.

Centro para la Difusión de la Música Contemporánea

Centro de Arte Reina Sofía, C/Santa Isabel 52 (467 50 62). Metro Atocha/bus all routes to Atocha. **Main season** Oct-May.

This innovative music centre has been based since 1987 in the **Reina Sofía** *(see chapters* **Sightseeing, Art Galleries** *and* **Museums),** although it was started in 1983. In its early stages the pressure of battling against musical conservatism nearly finished off its valiant founder, composer Luis de Pablo, who left after only two years. However, it is thanks to his work that the centre is now firmly established as the city's main focus for contemporary music, under his successor composer Tomás Marco. It gives 30 or so commissions annually to Spanish and foreign composers alike, which are then premièred at two or three concerts each month, held on Wednesday evenings in the chamber hall of the **Auditorio Nacional** and on Sunday mornings in the **Círculo de Bellas Artes** *(see above* **Venues).**

Fundación Juan March

C/Castelló 77 (435 42 40). Metro Núñez de Balboa/bus 1, 29, 52, 74. **Main season** Oct-June.

The Fundación March, a major player in many areas of the arts in Spain *(see also chapter* **Art Galleries),** has provided financial support for musical creation and research since its foundation in 1955. In 1975 it opened its own centre in Madrid, and some 350 composers, musicians and conductors have benefitted from its support. The small concert hall is in constant use, and its free Saturday concerts, featuring a variety of styles and genres, are recommended. The Foundation also organises concerts for young people; publishes books on music; and has an extensive Spanish Contemporary Music Library. Access to the library is free, provided you have your passport with you and can give a reason for wishing to consult it (such as study).

Festivals & Free Music

The main festivals in Madrid that feature classical music are the **Veranos de la Villa,** the **Festival de Otoño** and, of course, the **Festival Mozart** *(see chapter* **Madrid By Season).** Some of the events in the Veranos de la Villa festival are usually free.

In addition, Madrid offers music fans many other opportunities to see free concerts. A varied programme with an emphasis on baroque works is presented in the historic **Academia de Bellas Artes de San Fernando** *(see chapter* **Museums)** and free, open-air concerts are regularly held in many of Madrid's city-funded cultural centres, such as the **Centro Cultural Conde Duque** *(see chapters* **Madrid by Area** *and* **Art Galleries).** For information, consult tourist offices or the *010* information phoneline *(see chapter* **Essential Information).** Also, there are bars for most occasions in Madrid, and some host good music. The smart **Café Viena** *(see chapter* **Cafés & Bars),** near the Plaza de España, has sessions every Monday night where opera and *Zarzuela* singers perform for an enthusiastic public.

La Fídula

C/Huertas 57 (429 29 47). Metro Antón Martín/bus 6, 26, 32, 57. **Open** 7pm-2.30am daily.

La Fídula, right in the heart of the Huertas bar district, presents concerts, usually of chamber music, on most nights of the week from September to June, and at weekends in summer. The performers are mostly music students, but are often extremely good, and it's also very pleasant just as a bar. *See also chapters* **Nightlife** *and* **Women's Madrid.**

Zarzuela

Madrid is the home of *Zarzuela*, Spain's very own form of light opera. Its distant origins are in the Golden Age, in the entertainments staged for King Philip IV at the hunting lodge of La Zarzuela outside Madrid. Real *Zarzuela* in its recognisable, commercial, form, however, developed from the 1830s onwards. It is comparable to the contemporary German *singspiel* or Viennese operetta, but with a distinctively Spanish musical idiom.

At the end of the last century *Zarzuelas* dominated the world of entertainment in Madrid, and there were often ten different productions playing in the city at the same time. Their plots dealt not with great themes or heroic figures, but instead offered very identifiable, usually comic, sometimes slightly bawdy scenes of local life. *Zarzuelas* played a great part in establishing the *castizo* mythology of working-class Madrid (*see chapter* **Madrid by Season**), with stories of romances between flat-capped *chulos* and flashing-eyed, razor-tongued *chulapas* in flowered shawls. The world of *Zarzuela* also became part of this mythology itself, since singers like the baritone Emilio Mesejo or the soprano La Pastora entered the jet set of the era, and it was the height of fashion for young aristocrats to have *las tiples*, the girls of the *Zarzuela* chorus, as lovers.

The *Zarzuela* repertoire is huge, and includes some fine, soaring, sometimes subtle music. Barbieri's *Jugar con Fuego*, Tomás Bretón's *La Verbena de la Paloma*, Pablo Sorozábal's *La del Manojo de Rosas*, Ruperto Chapí's *La Revoltosa* and Lorente and Serrano's *La Dolorosa* are some of the classics. New *Zarzuelas* were produced right up until the 1930s, and it was only the Civil War and its aftermath, with the body-blows they dealt to Madrid's traditional culture, that saw a final decline in the genre's popularity.

In more recent years *Zarzuela* has struggled against the contempt of many serious music lovers, and the accusation that it is opera's poor relation. It has also often been dismissed as just plain corny and kitsch. Nevertheless, it is one of Spain's, and above all Madrid's, most distinctive cultural forms, and it retains a keen following, and there is considerable official interest in ensuring it survives. One of its most enthusiastic supporters is Plácido Domingo, himself the son of *Zarzuela* singers, who has successfully recorded collections of *Zarzuela* songs.

WHERE TO SEE IT

Madrid's *Zarzuela* season is in summer, between June and September. Both the **Auditorio Nacional** and the **Teatro de la Zarzuela** (*see* **Venues**) stage one production each year, which are highlights in the musical calendar. Three other venues also stage *Zarzuelas* every summer – the **Centro Cultural de la Villa**, the **Teatro Albéniz** and the **Teatro de Madrid** (for all, *see chapter* **Theatre**). One of the most popular ways in which to catch a *Zarzuela* production, though, is in the traditional, open-air setting of **La Corrala**. *Zarzuela* buffs may also hear it sung in a handful of bars throughout the city.

La Corrala

C/Tribulete 12 & C/Sombrerete 13 (no phone). Metro Lavapiés/bus 27, 60, 148, C. **Season** late-July-Aug. **Performances** 9.30pm daily. **Tickets** 1,800ptas. **No credit cards.**
This 1882 building is the best surviving example of the traditional corridor-tenements that were once found throughout working-class Madrid, and which formed the backdrop to many a popular *Zarzuela*. Since its restoration in 1979 it has been used to stage *Zarzuela*, effectively in a real-life setting. One production is presented each year – usually one of the classics of the genre – with performances nightly during the short, month-and-a-half season. This event has become a fixture of the Madrid summer scene, and to cap the nostalgic atmosphere some of the audience turn up in genuine 1890s *castizo* costume. *See also chapter* **Madrid by Area**.

Mr. Sellers

C/Alberto Alcocer 7 (350 64 79). Metro Cuzco/bus 5, 11, 27, 40, 150. **Open** 7.30pm-2.30am Mon-Sat.
In this plush but otherwise fairly featureless bar in the bland heart of the business district, after 1am on Fridays and Saturdays, customers are regularly treated to impromptu appearances by Guadalupe Sánchez, probably the most important *Zarzuela* soprano in Madrid today.

Music: Rock, Roots & Jazz

Welcome to the city where the rock scene can be luke warm, but the jazz is hot and the salsa and merengue are steaming.

If the Mayor of Madrid, José María Alvarez del Manzano, had been Mayor of New Orleans, jazz would never have been invented, complained one letter writer to a newspaper while bemoaning the closure of a concert venue for alleged 'clandestine performances' – that is, without its license completely in order. This is perhaps a bit of an exaggeration, but the conservative city council he has presided over since 1991 hasn't done live music many favours. In contrast to the early-eighties Socialist administration led by the late and much-lamented Enrique Tierno Galván, who were happy to be seen as godfathers of the *Movida*, they have cut the budget of the annual **San Isidro** festival (*see chapter* **Madrid by Season**) by two thirds and adopted a policy of clamping down on clubs and other venues for the slightest irregularity.

Needless to say, this has done nothing for the progress of the local music scene. The mainstream Spanish pop world is pretty derivative, as a quick look at the top 40 will show. International supergroups and Eurodisco dominate. Despite being the home of the guitar, Spain does not have a great tradition of innovation in rock and pop music, and many bands cheerfully trundle along more or less copying long-running foreign models.

Nevertheless, there are, of course, exceptions. Spanish pop performers have access to a range of influences in their own language – flamenco, salsa, all the other Latin American styles – that means they can sometimes be more distinctive and original than those in, for example, most other Mediterranean countries. Los Ronaldos (funky pop), Los Rodriguez (witty Argentinian/Spanish band), Celtas Cortos (tuneful eight-piece Gaelic thrashers), Héroes de Silencio (goth rock) and Rosario (daughter of Lola Flores *(see below)*, but herself performing an imaginative pop/flamenco/salsa crossover) are some who have made names for themselves in the last few years. Previously, the *Movida*, Madrid's eighties' new wave, spawned a good many – but not many good – groups with names like Kaka de Lux ('luxury shit') and Radio Futura. The most exciting and innovative music being made in Spain at the moment is the fusion of

flamenco with blues, jazz, and even reggae, known as New Flamenco (*see chapter* **Flamenco**).

Some say that the current low-key state of Madrid's music scene is due to a kind of post-*Movida* cultural hangover. But there is a more general public apathy about live music, and it's often seen as a pleasant distraction rather than the main attraction in an evening's entertainment. Curiously, of all the musical forms, jazz is perhaps the best represented and one of the best supported. There are several very good jazz cafés, many of which double as small venues, and the annual **Festival Internacional de Jazz** attracts top names. Madrid is also a great place to hear live salsa and other Latin music, with several good resident bands and regular visits by stars and new acts from Colombia, Cuba and elsewhere.

Aside from these various musics, another form that's always still going strong – it'll never go away – is *la canción española*, traditional Spanish popular music, the vaguely-flamenco-ish sound you'll hear thumping out of many a neighbourhood bar. It's never been greatly appreciated by showbiz fans outside the country. Which might be an omission, as it forms part of a complete world of entertainment, and on a good day grand divas like Rocío Jurado or Lola Flores can make Shirley Bassey look like a wilting violet. An essential part of the experience is to get a copy of *¡Hola!* or *Lecturas* to follow the storm-tossed lives of the stars. Good places to see them in person in Madrid are the **Teatro La Latina** (*see chapter* **Theatre**) and the **Parque de Atracciones** in summer.

VENUES & CONCERTS

Due in part to the efforts of the city council and partly to a long-standing insufficiency, Madrid suffers from a lack of rehearsal space and of good medium-sized venues. Places in the city centre tend to be small or dingy, while the bigger concert halls are often a fair distance from the rest of the nightlife. **Universal Sur**, for example, is out in the industrial periphery in Leganés. Big stadium concerts take place at Atlético Madrid's home the

*The samba's always hot at the **Oba-Oba**. See page 196.*

Vicente Calderón or the **Palacio de los Deportes** (*see chapter* **Sport & Fitness**). The bullring, **Las Ventas**, also makes a great outdoor venue (*see chapters* **Madrid by Season** *and* **Bullfighting**).

During the *Movida* years Malasaña was the most happening *barrio* for live music, and for the most part it still is, with a fair number of smaller venues. Entrance to these places is often free or, if not, no more than a few hundred pesetas including a *consumición*, or free drink. Likewise, most jazz venues don't charge entry, but they do reckon on making their money at the bar: you can expect drinks to cost two or three times what they would elsewhere. Many venues combine live gigs with dance sessions. Similarly – since strict boundaries are not found anywhere in Madrid bar-and-nightlife – many of the venues in *chapter* **Nightlife** may sometimes host live music.

Lots of gigs are sponsored by radio stations like Cadena Ser or Onda Cero, in which case you can usually buy tickets from their reception desks. Other ticket outlets are listed in *chapter* **Services**. For details of concerts coming up, check flyposters, the listings pages in local papers – especially their entertainment supplements – and the *Guía del Ocio* (*see chapter* **Media**). A free monthly music magazine, *Todas Las Novedades*, which you should find in many of the places listed below and a few bars besides, also carries comprehensive listings.

Rock Venues

Al'Laboratorio
C/Colón,14 (532 54 27). Metro Tribunal/bus 3, 40, 149. **Open** 9pm-3am Tue-Thur, 10pm-5am Fri-Sun. **Admission** 500ptas.
Country & Western décor combines with pop music at this lively, if dingy, two-floor local. You won't find any big names here on Thursday, Friday and Saturday nights, but Al'Lab declares 'a passion for music' and encourages young groups, organising 'battle of the bands' style contests.

Aqualung
Paseo de la Ermita del Santo 40-48 (470 23 62). Metro Puerta de Toledo, Marqués de Vadillo/bus 17, 25, 50. **Open** 11pm-3am Mon-Thur, 11.30pm-5.30am Fri-Sun. **Admission** *average* 1,000-3,000ptas.
This water-park pleasuredome, part of the giant La Ermita leisure complex, becomes a 2,000-capacity club and music venue by night. It has several bars, excellent acoustics, and is also now the city's main medium-sized venue for British and US groups on tour. Paul Weller, Arrested Development, Chris Rea and Iggy Pop are some of the recent visitors. At other times, there's plenty of recorded music to dance to. *See also chapter* **Nightlife**.

La Coquette
C/de las Hileras 14 (no phone). Metro Opera/bus 3, 25, 33, 39. **Open** 8.30pm-2.30am daily. **Admission** normally free.
A brick-lined cellar where old-school blues bands play from Tuesday to Thursday. Quality musicians are attracted by the cosy, smoky atmosphere. *See also chapter* **Nightlife**.

Maravillas
C/San Vicente Ferrer 33 (522 19 01). Metro Tribunal/bus 3, 40, 149. **Open** 8pm-5am Wed, Thur, Sun; 10.30pm-5am Fri, Sat. **Admission** 300-1,000ptas.

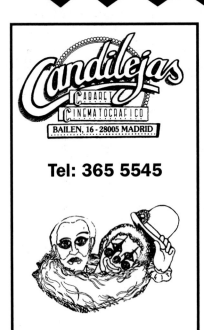

This recently-reopened 'alternative pop' club in the heart of Malasaña also functions as much needed rehearsal space. New bands often get their first chance to play live here, and there are concerts nearly every night.

Pachá
C/Barceló 11 (446 01 37). Metro Tribunal/bus 3, 40, 149. **Open** 10pm-5.30am Wed-Sun. **Admission** *average* 1,000-3,000ptas.
This ritzy disco in a thirties' theatre only puts on the occasional concert, but when it does it's usually a one-off gig from someone good, most recently Björk. It's better known as a club for Madrid's young and beautiful. *See also chapter* **Nightlife**.

Revólver Club
C/Galileo 26 (594 27 05/448 01 43). Metro Quevedo/bus 2, 16, 61. **Open** 10pm-5am Tue-Thur; midnight-7am Fri-Sun. **Admission** *average* 2,000ptas.
This large 1000-capacity venue, probably Madrid's best known, brings in a young, enthusiastic crowd. The acoustics aren't so pretty, which is a shame because it's a great place to see foreign groups (Charlatans, The Fall) who are not so well known in Spain, or homegrown acts on their way up. It's also a big hit as a club, and its Monday-night Flamenco sessions have played a major part in broadening the music's appeal. *See also chapters* **Nightlife** *and* **Flamenco**.

Riviera
Puente de Segovia (no phone). Bus 25, 31, 33, 36, 39, 65, 138, C. **Open** 10pm-6am Thur-Sun. **Admission** *average* 2,000ptas.
A disco next to the Manzanares, Riviera is at its liveliest in the summer when it throngs with models, actors and Madrid celebs like Pedro Almodóvar. From time to time, suitably hip acts like the Brand New Heavies make an appearance. Nice place, shame about the door policy.

Siroco
C/San Dimas 3 (593 30 70/ 532 13 57). Metro Noviciado/bus 147. **Open** 9.30pm-3am Tue-Thur; 10pm-6am Fri-Sun. **Admission** normally free.
An unpretentious little place with a bar upstairs and disco in the basement that plays Latin jazz most Fridays and soul on Saturdays. During the week you're just as likely to hear jangly guitar bands and a variety of other new local performers onstage. *See also chapter* **Nightlife**.

El Sol
C/Jardines 3 (532 64 90). Metro Gran Vía/bus all routes to Gran Vía. **Open** 11.30pm-5am Mon-Sat. **Admission** *average* 700ptas Mon-Thur; 900ptas Fri, Sat.
One of the melting pots of the *Movida* in the 1980s now serves up interesting international acts and up and coming local talent at fanzine-sponsored nights. It's slightly tatty – in a nice way – and open very late.

Swing
C/San Vicente Ferrer 23 (531 31 13). Metro Tribunal/bus 3, 40, 149. **Open** 10pm-5am daily. **Admission** 800ptas incl. one drink.
A popular dance venue with a highly eclectic music policy which now hosts live music sessions almost nightly, featuring anything from blues and Spanish pop to cabaret and *canción española*, albeit in a slightly trendy version.

Universal Sur
Autovía Madrid-Toledo (N401) km9 (686 57 11). Bus Metro Oporto, then bus 485/train Cercanías line C-5 to Zarzaquemada. **Open** 9pm-5am daily. **Admission** *average* 2,000ptas.
Part of the giant **Parquesur** leisure and waterpark complex in Leganés, with 19 bars (count them!) and six dancefloors. One of Madrid's largest rock venues, it now doesn't hold as many gigs as it used to, having lost out a little to **Aqualung**.

Jazz

Café Central
Plaza del Angel 10 (468 08 44). Metro Sol/bus all routes to Puerta del Sol. **Open** noon-1.30am Mon-Thur; noon-2.30am Fri-Sun. **Admission** *concerts only* 700ptas.
This beautiful high-ceilinged café/bar just off the Plaza Santa Ana was a mirror shop until its conversion 12 years ago. Since then it has built itself a reputation as Madrid's best jazz venue – and the eighth best in Europe according to *Wire* magazine. International and Spanish performers (George Adams, Don Pullen, Jorge Pardo, Tete Montoliu) play in a relaxed atmosphere. Note for cheapskates: if you turn up at about 12.15am you usually catch the end of the set for free.

Café Populart
C/Huertas 22 (529 84 07). Metro Antón Martín/bus 6, 26, 32, 57. **Open** 8pm-2am daily. **Admission** normally free.
Just around the corner from the Central, this former pottery shop puts on groups playing a range of music from jazz and blues to salsa and sometimes reggae. There are two sets nightly, at 10.30pm and 1am, and the atmosphere's nicely relaxed and friendly.

Clamores
C/Albuquerque 14 (445 79 38). Metro Bilbao, Quevedo/bus 3, 37, 149. **Open** 8.30pm-3am daily. **Admission** normally free.
Clamores, in Chamberi, is larger than most Madrid jazz clubs and can be lacking in atmosphere. It does, though, offer nightly variations on a roughly jazz theme – from Latin to Dixie, with tango and a few other things thrown in. *See also chapter* **Nightlife**.

Colegio Mayor San Juan Evangelista
C/Gregorio del Amo 4 (534 22 00). Metro Metropolitano/bus 132, C. **Concerts** Oct-June 10.30pm Sat. **Admission** *average* 1,500ptas.
The music club in this student residence (entirely open to, and long popular with, non-students) in the middle of the Ciudad Universitaria has over many years established a reputation as one of Madrid's most discriminating jazz venues, regularly attracting high-quality American and other names. It also presents concerts of classical and world music, and particularly Flamenco.

Free Jazz
Plaza de la Morería 4 (364 18 88). Metro La Latina/bus 31, 50, 60, 65. **Open** 8pm-3am daily. **Admission** free.
A relaxed piano bar with live jam sessions. If you're 'in the mood' and you can play a bit, they'll let you join in.

Segundo Jazz
C/Comandante Zorita 8 (554 94 37). Metro Nuevos Ministerios, Lima/bus 42, 43, 149, C. **Open** 7pm-3.30am daily; *performances* midnight Mon-Sat. **Admission** free.
There's jazz on Mondays and Tuesdays, Brazilian music on Wednesdays and Thursdays, and the resident band plays on Fridays and Saturdays.

Latin

Café del Foro
C/San Andrés 38 (445 37 52). Metro Bilbao, Tribunal/bus 40, 147, 149. **Open** 7pm-2am daily. **Admission** free.
This cabaret club, located in an old shopping arcade in Malasaña, is just the right side of cutesy, with an imitation star-lit sky painted above the stage. Magicians, hypnotists and comedians appear on Sunday and Monday nights, then it's salsa and merengue the rest of the week..

Café del Mercado

Ronda de Toledo 1 (365 37 86). Metro Puerta de Toledo/bus 1, 41, 60, 148, C. **Open** 11pm-4am daily. **Admission** free.

The café is sited in the failed **Mercado Puerta de Toledo** development, an attempt to create a swish modernist shopping complex in a former fish market (*see chapter* **Shopping**), but is unaffected by its neighbours' problems. It lays on one of the most varied and interesting menus of Latin music in the city – merengue, salsa, bolero and chachachá. Like a lot of the best places, it doesn't get going until after midnight.

Fénix

C/Magdalena 21 (no phone). Metro Antón Martín/bus 6, 26, 32, 57. **Open** 10pm-2am daily. **Admission** free.

A lively little bar that is heaving by the small hours. Friday and Saturday nights feature short impromptu performances by singers and percussionists. Feeling hot, hot, hot? You will: there's no air conditioning so a man with a mop soaks up the sweat as it drips off the ceiling.

Oba-Oba

C/Jacometrezo 4 (531 06 40). Metro Callao, Santo Domingo/bus all routes to Plaza de Callao. **Open** 10pm-5am daily. **Admission** 800ptas incl. one drink.

This friendly, thumping Brazilian bar pumps out the samba until the sun comes up, with the music live and recorded most nights of the week, and is packed with a good-time crowd from about 1am onwards. Let your feet do your talking; it's too loud for conversation and too small for sitting down..

La Taberna Encantada

C/Salitre 2 (528 52 38). Metro Lavapiés/bus 9, 27, 86, C. **Open** 7pm-2am Tue-Sun; *performances* 11pm Fri, Sat; 9pm Sun. **Admission** free.

A huge ceramic mural outside lets you know you've found your way to this low-key, roomy bar, where everything you could want from South American music of all sorts through African to sefardi, the delicate and beautiful music of the Spanish Jews, is on offer. Nice food, too.

La Tolderia

C/Canos Viejos 3 (366 41 72). Metro La Latina/bus 31, 50, 65. **Open** 11pm-3.30am Tue-Sun. **Admission** free.

Latin American folk – not dance – music from throughout the continent is performed for a serious but appreciative audience. On most nights there are three acts, between about 12.30 and 3am. Not a place to let your hair down, and not cheap either: there's no admission charge, but drinks cost 1,500ptas.

Outdoor Venues

In summer, Madrid comes alive after dark and out of doors. Balmy evenings, generous festival programmes and some original and often inspired locations make this just about the best time of year to enjoy live music. As well as those listed here, the wide, open courtyards of the **Centro Cultural Conde-Duque** make great performance spaces for contemporary music from Van Morrison to New Flamenco, usually as part of the **Veranos de la Villa** festival (*see chapter* **Madrid by Season**).

Celtibaria

Parque Tierno Galván (541 75 61). Metro Méndez Alvaro/bus 148/train Cercanías line C-5 to Méndez Alvaro. **Admission** *when charged* 1,200ptas; 1,000ptas in advance.

Celtibaria is a shallow amphitheatre in the Tierno Galván park that is ideal for the open-air concerts held in July and August as part of the **Veranos de la Villa** festival. The emphasis is on Celtic and similar music.

The stage at the **Parque de Atracciones***.*

Hipódromo de La Zarzuela

Carretera de la Coruña (N-VI) km7.8 (307 01 40). Bus 601, 656, 657, 658, N61 from Moncloa/by car Carretera de La Coruña to El Pardo exit. **Open** *June-Sept* 6pm-3am Fri, Sat. **Admission** free; *concerts* 2,000ptas Fri.

Madrid's racecourse was big enough to hold Jean-Michel Jarre's lasers and muzak extravaganza (only a freak summer storm forced its cancellation). During summer bars are set up in the paddock, and there are weekend 'megadiscos' and regular concerts by the best-known Spanish groups. *See also chapters* **Nightlife** *and* **Sport & Fitness**.

Muralla Arabe

Cuesta de la Vega (no phone). Metro Opera/bus 3, 31, 50, 65, 148. **Concerts** July-Aug. **Admission** 2,000-3,000ptas.

This last remnant of Madrid's Moorish past, with the flood-lit Almudena above it, forms a spectacular backdrop for some great world music and jazz concerts during July and August, again as part of the **Veranos de la Villa**. The programmes cover a truly world-wide range of music.

Parque de Atracciones

Casa de Campo (463 29 00/463 64 33). Metro Batán/bus 33, 36, 39, 65. **Open** *Sept-June* noon-11pm Mon-Fri, Sun; noon-1am Sat; *July, Aug* noon-11pm Mon-Thur, Sun; noon-3am Fri, Sat. **Admission** 350ptas.

All the fun of the fair and spectacular sunsets to boot. Summer gigs by Spanish family favourites and well-known local rock bands are usually free. The rides cost, though. *See also chapter* **Children**.

Festivals

As well as the **Veranos de la Villa** and other art festivals, a good many of Madrid's annual events also feature good live music. **San Isidro**, despite budget limitations, still includes a large-scale music programme, presented in the Casa de Campo, with some major international rock acts. On the bill in the last few years have been Bob Geldof and Texas. The **May Day** celebrations and the **Fiestas del Partido Comunista** in September are a good opportunity to see a range of local bands.

Festival Internacional de Jazz

Information: *Colectivo Promociones Jazz (373 93 61).* **Dates** Nov.

In November, when other cities are beginning to feel the cold, Madrid is blowing hot. The Jazz Festival, which comes at the end of the general **Festival de Otoño** (*see chapter* **Madrid by Season**), is growing in stature and rightly so. In addition to the usual venues, classical theatres and auditoria get in on the act and open their doors to respected jazz musicians from the world over.

Flamenco

Though anchored in ancient traditions, flamenco music has lately been moving down exciting new paths.

Flamenco is Spain's most distinctive art form, one of the things, like bullfighting, that makes the country's culture so unique. It is also something that has been widely misunderstood and caricatured, both at home and abroad.

The swirling dresses, furious footwork and clattering castanets often served up to unwary tourists at hefty prices are no more than a sad parody of the real thing. Many Spaniards, too, have seen flamenco music and dance mainly as part of a hackneyed, kitschy and uncreative folkloric culture that they would rather get away from, above all under Franco when decaffeinated flamenco was an integral part of the régime's self-promotion campaigns. Even after the end of the Dictatorship, flamenco, associated with the poor south and timeless tradition, still seemed out of step with the new Spain's rush to prosperity and infatuation with all things *Europeo* and modern. And since the strongholds of the music were still very much among Spain's ever-unassimilated

Gypsy communities, a degree of racism also played its part.

Flamenco's prestige and fortunes sagged, and ten years ago in Madrid there were almost no venues regularly featuring quality live flamenco. Happily, this trend has been turned around in recent years. A major factor has been a remarkable coincidence of new and imaginative talent – above all the amazing guitarist Paco de Lucía and the singer Camarón de la Isla, one of the most extraordinary voices of this century, whose death at only 41 in 1992 was a national catastrophe. They helped vindicate the music's finest traditions while continually breaking new ground, and attracting entirely new audiences to flamenco. New venues opened their doors in Madrid, spearheading a flamenco resurgence. Today, the music is positively fashionable, concerts are well attended and young people are showing up in ever-larger numbers.

Most flamenco venues today feature both traditional performers, who have never been away whatever the current popularity level of the music, and what's called *nuevo flamenco*, New Flamenco. This has developed out of the innovations of Paco de Lucía and Camarón and the subsequent experiments of many young musicians, often themselves from traditional Gypsy families – where they absorbed the music with their mothers' milk – but also open to a whole range of other musical influences. New Flamenco artists are prepared to blend traditional styles with blues, pop, jazz, rock, folk, salsa, Latin American styles and Arab music, and experiment with such unflamenco-like instruments as saxophones and the electric bass. Far from becoming bland, though, much of New Flamenco still has an unmistakable Gypsy edge.

The flamenco world has a deep sense of tradition, and *aficionados* can argue endlessly over whether this kind of fusion represents a real advance for the music, or simply its dilution – even though there has always been a very vague line between flamenco and Spanish popular music in general, and many artists have long been happy to flit around between both. Another point at issue is how far flamenco can ever be open to *payos* (the Spanish Gypsy word for all non-Gypsies). The results of *nuevo flamenco* are certainly uneven, but no one can deny that this opening up of flamenco

CAFE DE CHINITAS

RESTAURANT
TABLAO FLAMENCO

THE BEST FLAMENCO SHOW IN MADRID

7, Torija St.
(Metro Sto. Domingo)
Tels. 559 51 35 - 547 15 02/01

can produce highly original, fresh and dynamic sounds. Talent and enthusiasm are there in abundance, making it by far the most exciting music being produced in Spain today.

THE TRADITION
The origins of flamenco can be traced back more than 500 years in southern Spain to the folk songs of Arab Andalusia. The late-medieval Gypsy immigration into Spain was, of course, the major factor in the development of the music, but it also combines elements of Indian chants, Spanish-Jewish folk music and other Middle Eastern, oriental and Latin American musical traditions and religious influences.

The essence of flamenco is the *cante jondo* or 'deep song': a voice, a guitar, a story to tell, and an audience to share in the telling. The guitar and singing are often accompanied by dancing, although good *cante* can always stand on its own. Guitar (always acoustic) and singer (the *cantaor* or *cantaora*) establish a taut communication, based on subtle rhythmic improvisation within the contours of the different styles, called *palos*. There are a great many of them, all richly inter-related, and differentiated by their intricate rhythmic patterns, chord structures, lyrical content and regional origin – *alegrías, bulerías, siguiriyas, soleares, tarantos, tientos, malagueñas, tangos* and *fandangos* are only the best-known. The audience plays a crucial part in the success of each performance. More than silence, what is demanded is rapt surrender to the artists' travails. Side-performers and the audience can accompany the more rhythmically intense *palos* with intricate hand-clapping and shouts of *¡olé!*, though this is probably better left to the well-initiated.

The emotional repertory is far-ranging: from tender desperation to joyful celebration, a miner's lament, songs that speak of love, of solitude, of despair, of dire foreboding. Even the most ecstatic of *alegrías*, though, seems never to break away completely from the deep sense of pain and anguish that marks all *cante jondo*. Nor is the stark tragedy of a *siguiriya*'s deathly brooding ever without some element of cathartic relief.

Raw and honest, flamenco is an audacious music, full of risks and improvisation. Singers rely on plaintive wails, stifled sobs and throaty murmurs to recount tales of personal or collective tribulation. In its most inspired moments, when what *aficionados* call the *duende* – an untranslatable word roughly meaning 'spirit' or 'enchantment' – possesses performer and listener alike, the effect can be stunning; a primal emotion, an atavistic river of tears, seems to flow through the artists. Commanding performers can envelop the most varied of audiences with a sense of common humanity and shared fate.

STARS & RISING NAMES
As a result of the flamenco resurgence Madrid, rather than anywhere in the south, is now the best place in Spain to hear good flamenco. A sample, and only that, of some of the individual names to watch out for in the more traditional field are José Menese, Carmen Linares, Aurora Vargas, José Mercé, Mariana Cornejo, Maite Martín, Chano Lobato, María Vargas, Fernanda de Utrera, Agujetas, Rancapino, and Chaquetón, among the singers. Leading guitarists are Paco de Lucía, Tomatito, Juan Habichuela, Gerardo Núñez, Rafael Riqueni and Enrique de Melchor.

Divisions between traditional and New Flamenco are never as precise as some people make out, and many musicians, like Paco de Lucía and Tomatito, work freely between both camps. Best-known of the New Flamenco groups is Ketama, who combine flamenco with jazz, rock and, latterly, salsa. The best flamenco/rock fusion has been the group Pata Negra, recently reformed by leader Rafael Amador. Other acts to look out for are the jazz/flamenco mix of Jorge Pardo, the experiments with flamenco and reggae of La Barbería del Sur (most-detested group of all for flamenco traditionalists), and singers Lole y Manuel, Enrique Morente, El Potito and El Lebrijano.

Venues
The flamenco venues listed here all mainly feature music and singing, although dancers may also sometimes appear. For details of other venues where the main attraction is dance (although, again, good musicians may well play there), *see chapter* **Dance**. For anyone new to flamenco probably the easiest introduction to the scene will be the Monday night sessions at **Revólver**. A more traditional type of venue are the *peñas*, private flamenco clubs – although this does not mean they are necessarily closed to casual visitors, or unwelcoming. There are a few around Madrid, but most are in the outer suburbs (the areas with the largest Gypsy communities), and **Chaquetón** is much the most central and accessible. In addition to these regular venues, it's worth looking out for flamenco nights in theatres and other music venues, or in outdoor locations in summer. The **Colegio San Juan Evangelista** music club (*see chapter* **Music: Rock, Roots & Jazz**) is one particular venue that schedules major flamenco shows at least five or six times a year.

Current concert listings can be found in local papers and the *Guía del Ocio* (*see chapter* **Media**). Note that, as spontaneity is part of the essence of flamenco, timekeeping is very imprecise, and opening and performance times listed here should be taken as guidelines only.

Candela

C/del Olmo, corner of C/Olivar (no phone). Metro Tirso de Molina, Antón Martín/bus 6, 26, 32, 57. **Open** 9pm-3am daily.

Although it does not actually programme live music, this bar is a cornerstone of the Madrid flamenco scene, simply because all flamenco artists seem to go there in their off hours. Consequently, it tends not to fill up before 2am, and often keeps going long after the official closing time. The after-hours jam sessions in the grotto-like cellar are legendary. Unfortunately, they tend to be by 'invitation' only, but if you are lucky enough to get asked in the results are likely to be memorable. Also, Candela is a good contact point for meeting guitarists willing to give private lessons. Spain sometimes seems to be as well stocked in exceptional guitarists as it is in olive trees, and the vagaries of the music business being what they are, it is not too difficult to find one willing to teach you flamenco guitar at a reasonable price.

Casa Patas

C/Cañizares 10 (369 04 96/369 15 74). Metro Tirso de Molina, Antón Martín/bus 6, 26, 32, 57. **Open** 9pm-5am daily. **Performances** midnight Thur-Sat; *May only* midnight Tue-Sat. **Admission** 1,500-2,500ptas.

One of the pioneers of the recent flamenco upswing, Casa Patas is a fairly comfortable bar-restaurant with a club space at the back where flamenco shows are staged on Thursdays, Fridays and Saturdays for most of the year, and most nights of the week during Madrid's main fiesta month in May. It's another favourite meeting point for Madrid's 'flamenco family', and dancers as well as musicians often feature in the shows. Patas regularly programmes some of the best traditional flamenco singers and dancers in Madrid, along with groups active in *nuevo flamenco*. Good, if a bit expensive, tapas are available in the bar.

Peña Flamenca Chaquetón

C/Canarias 39 (no phone). Metro Palos de la Frontera/bus 6, 19, 45, 47, 55. **Performances** *Sept-June* 11.30pm Fri. **Admission** 800-1,500ptas.

A *peña*, one of the small, non-profit-making clubs where *aficionados* stage flamenco recitals for their own delectation in a warm, intimate setting, evocative of the music's community roots. Chaquetón is the dean of Madrid *peñas*, a citadel of flamenco orthodoxy and highly respected among performers. Despite its small size, it manages to line up some of the best flamenco artists in the country. Do not be scared off by the 'members only' (*solo socios*) sign on the door; flamenco lovers of all kinds are welcome, although we certainly would not recommend showing up with a tour bus. Also, do not go expecting food, tapas, comfortable seating or colourful surroundings. With only a bare selection of drinks, no waiters, and poor ventilation, it is not for the comfort-seeker, the tobacco-weary or the casual listener. But more often than not, it is the best bet in Madrid for hearing pure *cante jondo* at its finest in the warm company of genuine *aficionados*.

Revólver Club

C/Galileo 26 (564 27 05/448 01 43). Metro Quevedo/bus 2, 16, 61. **Flamenco performances** 11pm Mon. **Admission** average 2,000ptas.

When the giant Revólver, mainly a rock venue, first began to schedule flamenco once one night a week in its *Lunes del Flamenco* ('Flamenco Mondays') it was seen as an eccentric gamble, but it has proved hugely successful. The programmes are put together by the indefatigable Juan Verdú, who also runs **Sala Caracol** and the Madrid flamenco festival and edits Spain's best flamenco magazine, *La Caña*. Every Monday night punks, heavy-metal fans and music followers of all sorts come together with traditional flamenco fans to see some of the biggest names in flamenco music, including, curiously enough, some of the more elderly, ortho-

dox stalwarts. The locale is large and raucous, with almost no seating, and the crowd noise can sometimes interfere with the music, but the colourful mix of people, sparky atmosphere and strong line-up of artists makes it a definite must, and one of the best means of appreciating the sheer range of modern flamenco. Note that flamenco sessions are not held on some Mondays between July and September, and it's always advisable to check the local press before going. *See also chapters* **Nightlife** *and* **Music: Rock, Roots & Jazz.**

Sala Caracol

C/Bernardino Obregón 18 (530 80 55/530 91 76). Metro Embajadores/bus all routes to Embajadores. **Open** 11pm-3am daily. Closed July, Aug. **Performances** 11pm-midnight Thur-Sat. **Admission** 1,500-2,500ptas.

Named after the great *cantaor* from Seville, Manuel Ortega Juárez, known to all as *Manolo Caracol* ('Manolo the Snail'), this restaurant-nightclub was partly modelled on Casa Patas, although it generally caters to a rather more upmarket crowd. Caracol offers flamenco recitals two or three nights a week, with a programme that mixes traditional flamenco acts with more experimental initiatives such as flamenco theatre, or a recent series dedicated to the links between the flamenco and bullfighting worlds. *Nuevo flamenco* figures also get regular billing. It's usually essential to book.

La Soleá

C/Cava Baja 27 (no phone). Metro La Latina/bus 17, 18, 23, 35, 60. **Open** 8.30pm-2am Mon-Sat.

This tiny bar, nestling in the middle of Madrid's best-known traditional restaurant area, has a house guitarist who is willing to accompany anyone wishing to test their luck in the art of flamenco singing. Anything can happen (and usually does if you visit often enough): you may be treated to a stirring recital by an outstanding artist who happens to come by, or an inspired amateur, or you may have to suffer through some direly inept droning. The only sure thing is the friendly, good-natured atmosphere amid which it all takes place.

Festivals

Madrid has three regular flamenco festivals, the **Festival Flamenco de Madrid**, in the Teatro Alcalá Palace at the end of January, the **Cita Flamenca**, in the Teatro Monumental in March or April, and the **Homenaje al Taranto** festival in the Colegio San Juan Evangelista in May. All consist of two or three nights of non-stop performances. For venue details, *see chapters* **Madrid by Season**, **Music: Classical & Opera** *and* **Music: Rock, Roots & Jazz.** There is also a major flamenco festival just outside Madrid in **Alcorcón**, in early September. In accordance with flamenco tradition, it's very difficult to get precise dates or details for any of these events much in advance, and the only way to be sure of catching them is to look out for posters and check with tourist offices and the local press closer to the time.

A slate of good flamenco concerts is also included in the various city-sponsored festivals, particularly **San Isidro** and **Los Veranos de la Villa** (*see chapter* **Madrid by Season**), often in open-air venues, and sometimes for free. Spain's most important purely-flamenco festival, though, is the **Bienal** in Seville; the next one takes place in early September 1996. For information, contact Seville (95) 421 83 83.

Sport & Fitness

Watch the superstars, work up a sweat or cool off with a swim at Madrid's great range of sports facilities.

Catching rays at the **Piscinas de la Casa de Campo**. See page 205.

In the last few years Spaniards, as fond of a grumble as anyone, have had to come to terms with the fact that their sportsmen and women have been very successful. The feats of Arantxa Sánchez, Conchita Martínez and Sergi Bruguera in tennis, iron man Miguel Induraín in cycling and Carlos Saínz in rally driving, not to mention the 22 Olympic medals – 13 gold – won in the 1992 games in Barcelona, represent an unprecendented level of achievement. In the sport most people most care about, football, success has not been so outstanding, but performances have still been respectable.

All this success has increased interest in taking part in sport in a country where spectator sports have always been followed with a passion, and more people do so than ever before. In central Madrid demand for sporting facilities outstrips supply, but there are still sufficient venues for visitors not to have any problems taking some exercise while they're here.

For information on sports that can be sampled in the mountains and countryside around Madrid, see chapter **Trips Out of Town**.

Spectator Sports

For football, see page 203 **Life & Death**.

Athletics

Sports authorities in Spain have been keen to demonstrate that their 1992 successes would not be a swallow of just one summer. Hence the huge investment in the stadium in Canillejas, on the eastern side of Madrid. Indoor athletics event are also held in the **Palacio de Deportes** (see below **Basketball**), in particular the *Trofeo Memorial Cagigal* international meeting each February.

Estadio de la Comunidad de Madrid
Avda de Arcentales (580 81 80). Metro Las Musas/bus 48, 109.
This strikingly-designed new athletics stadium, inaugurated in September 1994, has world-class facilities and capacity for 20,000 spectators. A meeting featuring many international names, the *Reunión Internacional Comunidad de Madrid*, is to be held annually in the first weekend in September, and it is hoped that it will host a European Championships within the near future. There is also an indoor hall and a range of ancillary services. It is also known

as the *Estadio de Canillejas* or the *Estadio Olímpico de Madrid*, and the city council hopes to use it as a base to bid for the Olympics of 2008.

Maratón Popular de Madrid
Information (521 79 83). **Date** late-April-May.
Madrid's marathon is more of a fun run than an outing for serious runners, and very popular. It's usually held on a Sunday in late April or early May, and finishes in the Retiro.

Basketball

A booming sport in Spain, particularly among teenagers, and second only to football. Madrid has two teams that play at the top of the Spanish league and in European competitions, **Estudiantes** and **Real Madrid** (a division of the football club). Both play at the **Palacio de Deportes**, which is also used for many other indoor sports.

Palacio de Deportes de la Comunidad de Madrid
Avda Felipe II (401 91 00). Metro Goya/bus 2, 15, 29, 63, C. **Open** *ticket office* 11am-2pm, 5-8pm, daily. **Tickets** 1,000-2,000ptas. **No credit cards.**
The season usually runs from September to early May, but really hots up in April with the league play-offs, when one of the Madrid teams almost inevitably clashes with one of their great rivals from the Barcelona area.
Clubs *Estudiantes* (562 40 22); *Real Madrid* (344 00 52).

Horse Racing

Hipódromo de La Zarzuela
Carretera de La Coruña (N-VI), km. 7.8 (307 01 40). Bus 601, 656, 657, 658, N61 from Moncloa/by car Carretera de La Coruña to El Pardo exit. **Open** *Feb-June, Sept-Dec* after 2pm Sun. *July-Sept* 10pm-2.30am Sat. **Admission** *June-Sept* 700ptas; *April-June, Oct-Nov* 300ptas. **No credit cards.**
Madrid's racecourse – one of only a very few in Spain – hosts two major flat racing meetings each year, the Spanish Derby in June and the *Memorial Duque de Toledo* meeting in November. Betting is entirely on-track, at the official tote. Its summer night-time sessions are also an important point on Madrid's nightlife round (*see chapter* **Nightlife**).

Motor Sport

Circuito del Jarama
Carretera de Burgos (N-I) km. 28,7, San Sebastián de los Reyes (657 08 75). Bus 171, 190-196/by car Carretera de Burgos to Fuente El Fresno.
This track formerly hosted the Spanish Grand Prix, but in 1992 this moved to the Catalunya circuit near Barcelona. Its calender of events is therefore a bit diminished but you can still see the *Ducados Open* international motorcycle race meeting on the first weekend in June and the European Truck Racing Championship in early October.

Other Events

Chess The *Torneo Magistral* tournament, category 16 in the international ratings, is held annually in May or June, and provides an opportunity to see Kasparov, Short and other masters in action. **Information** Federación Madrileña de Ajedrez (522 35 66).
Cycling *La Vuelta de España* (The Tour of Spain) makes its way around the country during September, and ends on the third weekend of the month in Madrid with a last stage of five laps of the Castellana, between Plaza Castilla

and the Estadio Bernabéu.
Golf The *Open de España* (Spanish Open) is held in late April or May at the **Club de Campo** (*see below* **Active Sports**).
Tennis The most important tournament during the year is the *Torneo Villa de Madrid* at the **Club de Tenis de Chamartín**, C/Federico Salmón 2 (345 25 00) in April or May, which regularly attracts major international names.

Sports Centres/*Polideportivos*

Madrid boasts 45 city-run *Polideportivos* or Sports Centres. At any of them you can pick up a map and a guide to what facilities are available at each municipal centre. Some offer a lavish range of activities, others are just a gym and little else. All have the same basic entrance fees, but there are often extra charges for some facilities. The most central place to get a leaflet is **La Chopera** centre in the Retiro.

Instituto Municipal de Deportes
Palacete de la Casa de Campo, Puente del Rey (463 55 63). Metro Norte/bus 25, 33, 39, 138, C. **Open** 8am-3pm Mon-Fri.
The central administration for all the city sports facilities will provide additional information on request.

Polideportivo de la Chopera
Parque del Retiro (420 11 54). Metro Atocha/bus 19. **Open** 8.30am-9.30pm daily. **Admission** 425ptas; 200ptas under-14s; 100ptas over-65s.
A gym, basketball, five-a-side football and tennis courts.

Estadio de Vallehermoso
C/Juan Vigón 10 (534 77 23). Metro Ríos Rosas/bus 2, 12, 44. **Open** 11am-8pm daily. **Admission** Mon-Fri 375ptas; Sat, Sun, public holidays 425ptas. **No credit cards.**
This athletics stadium and multi-purpose sports centre is run by the Comunidad de Madrid, and has an indoor sports hall, gym, a football pitch and an open-air swimming pool.

Parque Deportivo La Ermita
C/Sepúlveda 3-5 (470 01 11). Metro Puerta del Angel (open during 1995)/bus 17, 25, 500. **Open** 10am-11pm Mon-Fri; 10am-9pm Sat; 10am-3pm Sun. **Admission** *tennis* 900ptas per hour; *squash* 785ptas per ½ hour; *swimming pool* 1,500ptas per day Mon-Fri; 1,300ptas per day Sat, Sun. **No credit cards.**
This enormous private sports centre caters for just about every need, and no membership is needed. As well as racquet courts and an open-air pool, it has a gym and weights room and indoor sports halls. The centre also offers a range of sports tuition, particularly for children, with multi-sport programmes and activities outside the city during summer.

Billiards & Pool/*Billares*

Club Academia de Billar Guarner
Paseo de las Delicias 31, 6° (528 55 94). Metro Palos de la Frontera/bus 6, 16, 27, 45, C. **Open** 5.30pm-2am Mon-Thur; 5.30pm-3am Fri, Sat; 5.30pm-1am Sun.
Tables 800ptas per hour. **No credit cards.**
This 'academy' offers two-week courses in Spanish billiards, otherwise known as *carambola*. There are nine pool tables, one full-size snooker table – one of very few in Madrid – and two *carambola* tables. It's a little different from the usual smoke-filled pool hall, with sofas, armchairs and even a TV.

Life & Death

In its time, Spanish football has been a vehicle for all kinds of political tensions, and the number-one collective escape mechanism, for men at least. It has more competition in the national consciousness today, but nevertheless, in terms of passionate involvement, hot air expended over Monday-morning coffees and quantity of newsprint devoted to its ups and downs, *el fútbol* is still at the head of the pack.

Spanish football is often a very hierarchical affair. Only eight clubs have ever won the League, and each season the big question tends to be which of the two giants, Real Madrid and Barcelona, will carry off the title. Even so, the big boys don't always have things their own way – upstart Deportivo de La Coruña came within a penalty of knocking Barcelona off their perch in 1994 – and Spanish football can also be very exciting. Players like Michel, Guardiola, Guerrero, Caminero and many others could hold down a first team place at any club in the world. Hooliganism exists, but not so much as to spoil a marvellous spectacle.

Real Madrid present themselves as immensely grand. The only club to have won the European Cup six times (although the last time this happened in 1966), they have also won 25 League championships and 17 Spanish Cups. Real regularly draw 80,000 fans to the Bernabéu Stadium, and have space for 25,000 more. However, they've not had much to cheer about recently after a brilliant patch in the late eighties, the heyday of home-grown stars Michel and Butragueño. Expensive attempts at rebuilding by regal but sharp-tongued chairman Ramón Mendoza have proved fruitless, and in 1994 a new coach, Argentinian ex-Madrid star Jorge Valdano, was brought in as man with a mission to bring back the glory days of Di Stéfano and Puskas. To help him he has foreign stars Michael Laudrup and Argentinian Fernando Redondo.

Atlético Madrid, *El Atleti*, also have a fine record – eight League titles, eight Spanish Cups, and one European Cup. Traditionally a more working-class club, since 1987 they have been under the chairmanship of controversial (to put it mildly) construction magnate and Mayor of Marbella Jesús Gil, who has managed to see off 17 (and counting) coaches and countless quality players at fantastic expense without achieving the desired results, to the despair of the club's *incondicionales*. The *Colchoneros* (mattress-men, because of their striped shirts) do have the versatile Caminero, arguably the best Spanish player at present. Following the '94 World Cup, ex-Colombian national manager Pacho Maturana was also enticed to swap the pressures of the Medellín and Calí cartels for meetings with Sr. Gil every week, although whether he'll regret it is another question.

Football in Madrid doesn't end with the giants. Vallecas has its very own team, **Rayo Vallecano**. The West Ham of Spanish football, Rayo regularly pop in and out of the First Division. There are also two other Second-Division teams in the southern industrial suburbs, the battling **Leganés**, often saved from dropping another division by heroic finishes each season, and the once-bankrupt **Getafe**, with a young, home-produced team. The local derbies between these clubs are passionate affairs.

Times & the season

Matches are usually held at 5pm on Sundays during the September-May season, although they are increasingly held on Saturday evenings (at 8.30pm) as well, and the big clubs often have midweek cup or European games. As well as from the clubs, tickets are also available from ticket agencies (*see chapter* **Services**), but with commission.

Atlético de Madrid

Estadio Vicente Calderón, Paseo de la Virgen del Puerto 67 (366 47 07). Metro Pirámides/bus 17, 18, 23, 35. **Ticket office** 5-8pm daily; 11am-2pm, 5-8pm, two days before each match. **Tickets** 2,000-7,000ptas. **No credit cards.**
Atlético's stadium on the banks of the Manzanares has room for 60,000, but is often more animated than the Bernabéu. With a basic 2,000ptas ticket you get a decent view from the upper stands behind either goal.

Rayo Vallecano

Nuevo Estadio de Vallecas, Avda de la Albufera 132 (478 22 53). Metro Portazgo/bus 54, 57, 103, 140. **Ticket office** 5.30-8.30pm Mon-Fri. **Tickets** 1,500-3,500ptas. **No credit cards.**
With a capacity for 20,000, this is the stadium where Rayo's loyal followers ponder whether their team will ever manage to stay in the first division more than a few seasons.

Real Madrid

Estadio Santiago Bernabéu, C/Concha Espina (350 06 00). Metro Lima/bus 7, 14, 43, 120, 150. **Ticket office** 6-9pm daily; 11am-1pm, 6-9pm, two days before each match. **Tickets** 2,000-8,000ptas. **No credit cards.**
This magnificent stadium, recently enlarged, is often used for cup finals and internationals. Avoid the south end, the Fondo Sur, main base of Real's small neo-fascist hooligan element. As the stadium is so huge, any ticket for less than 4,000ptas will get you only a very poor view. *See also chapter* **Sightseeing**.

Recreativos Cortezo

C/Doctor Cortezo 15 (369 46 74). Metro Tirso de Molina/bus 6, 26, 32, 57. **Open** *9.30am-midnight daily.* **Tables** 800ptas per hour. **No credit cards.**
If you want the time-honoured billiard-hall atmosphere, this one is very traditional, with only Spanish *carambola* tables.

Bowling/*Boleras*

Bowling Azca

Paseo de la Castellana 77 (555 03 79). Metro Nuevos Ministerios/bus 5, 14, 27, 40, 149, 150. **Open** 11am-midnight daily. **Games** 450ptas Mon-Thur; 575ptas Fri-Sun; reduced prices for second and subsequent games.
Although it's in the heart of the business district this well-equipped 16-lane bowling alley has a relaxed atmosphere and attracts a varied public.

Canoeing/*Remo*

Lago Casa de Campo

Casa de Campo (464 46 10). Metro Lago/bus 33. **Open** 8am-8pm daily.
The lake in the Casa de Campo, where you can just hire a boat (*see chapter* **Sightseeing**), is also used by two canoe clubs, *Alberche* and *Ciencias*. Both offer weekly courses and canoes for experienced canoeists. Just turn up in the evening, or call Luis Ruiz, president of *Ciencias* (816 22 36).

Cricket

There is indeed a Madrid Cricket Club (the MCC, of course), which plays regularly from May to October (except for August), almost always against other ex-pat teams. Call Owen Thompson, the Captain, for more information (314 22 68).

Golf

Golf clubs around Madrid tend to be fairly exclusive, and expensive for non-members.

Club de Campo Villa de Madrid

Carretera de Castilla, km. 3 (357 21 32). Metro Moncloa, then bus 84. **Open** 9am-8pm daily. **Rates** Mon-Fri 1,565ptas club entry, plus 5,390ptas course fee. Sat, Sun 3,130ptas club entry, plus 10,240ptas course fee. **No credit cards.**
The best-equipped course in the Madrid area, with 36 holes and a driving range, and so very expensive. Rental of clubs costs an additional 2,100ptas. The lavishly-equipped club also offers squash, tennis, clay pigeon and range shooting, hockey pitches, polo, horse riding and a swimming pool.

Real Automóvil Club de España (RACE)

Carretera de Burgos (N-I) km. 25, San Sebastián de los Reyes (657 08 75). Bus 171, 190-196/by car Carretera de Burgos to Fuente El Fresno. **Open** 9am-9pm Mon-Fri; 9am-10.30pm Sat, Sun. **Rates** club and course 5,000ptas. **No credit cards.**
The Spanish auto club (*see chapter* **Survival**) has a golf and country club that is a little less expensive than some. There is also a good swimming pool. It is near the **Circuito de Jarama** race track (*see above* **Motor Racing**).

Gyms & Fitness Centres

Some hotels have agreements with private health clubs for guests to use their facilities. Check this when you sign in at your hotel.

Bodhidharma

C/Moratines 18 (517 28 16). Metro Embajadores/bus all routes to Embajadores. **Open** 8am-11pm Mon-Fri. **Rates** 9,000ptas per month, 22,000ptas per three months; *weekly temporary membership* 2,300ptas.
A well-equipped mixed health club with sauna, weights, exercise machines and aerobics and martial arts classes.

Tablas

C/General Pardiñas 45 (575 85 55). Metro Lista, Núñez de Balboa/1, 29, 52, 74. **Open** 9am-10pm Mon-Fri. **Rates** *average* 6,000ptas per month; *non-members* 1,100ptas aerobics class, 800ptas use of weights room, sauna etc.
A women-only health club with aerobics classes and a range of other facilities. Membership rates vary according to the facilities you use.

Votre Ligne

C/Serrano 27 (576 40 00). Metro Serrano/1, 9, 19, 51, 74. **Open** 8.30am-9.30pm Mon-Fri; hours variable Sat, Sun. **Rates** *annual membership* 26,600ptas; *daily rates* vary according to facility.
A lush women-only facility where Madrid's bodies beautiful go to make sure things stay that way. As well as a gym and aerobics classes it offers weights machines, a sauna, jacuzzis, a pool, massage, beauticians and several other services. There is an associated club for men, **El Presidente**. Both frequently offer special rates for non-members in summer.
Branches: Votre Ligne Plaza del Conde del Valle Suchil 17-19 (446 90 15). Metro San Bernardo/bus 21.
El Presidente (men only) C/Profesor Waksman 3 (458 67 59). Metro Cuzco/bus 5, 27, 40, 147, 149.

Horse Riding/*Hípica*

For information on facilities for riding in the mountains around Madrid, *see chapter* **Trips Out of Town**.

Escuela de Equitación Soto de Viñuelas

Carretera de Colmenar Viejo, km. 21 (803 22 66). Bus 712, 713, 723 from Plaza Castilla/by car Carretera de Colmenar Viejo to Soto de Viñuelas turn-off/train Cercanías line C-1 to Tres Cantos. **Open** 9am-1pm, 6-10pm, daily. **Rates** *lessons from* 8,400ptas five-class initiation course. **Credit** V.
A school north of Madrid that offers beginners' and more advanced courses for all ages from six years old upwards. Membership is not required, and they have very good horses. Trekking is not available.

Club Hípico El Trébol

Camino de Húmera, Casa de Campo (518 10 66). Metro Campamento/bus 65, 815, H. **Open** 10am-1pm, 5-9pm, Tue-Sun. **Rates** 20,000ptas ten-ride voucher. **No credit cards.**
On the western edge of the Casa de Campo, this club-cum-school offers more possibilities than just lessons. The 20,000ptas *bono* gives you the option of ten rides or ten classes depending on your level, and outings into the Casa de Campo accompanied by an instructor can be arranged.

Jogging & Running/*Footing*

There is a set jogging route in the **Retiro**, with recommended exercises marked at stops along the way, although you can easily go whichever way you want. More rural is the **Casa de Campo**, an excellent place to jog because the air quality is better. In summer, the time to go is first thing in the morning (certainly before 9am), as the freshness and contrast to the heat later in the day is wonderful. If you like longish straight runs, try the **Parque del Oeste**. Anyone interested in running in the marathon (*see above* **Spectator Sports**) should call the organisers (521 79 83).

Roller Skating/*Patinaje*

Rolling Disco.

Estación de Chamartín (315 30 00). Metro Chamartín/bus 5. **Open** 4.30-10.30pm Tue-Thur; 4.30-11.45pm Fri; 11am-2pm, 4.30-11.45pm, Sat, Sun. **Rates** *Tue-Thur* 700ptas inc. skate rental, 500ptas with your own skates; *Fri* 800ptas, 575ptas; *Sat, Sun* 900ptas, 650ptas. **No credit cards.**

On the second floor of the large, blank-looking shopping centre built over Chamartín station, this venue is what it says – a roller disco. It's inevitably full of kids and teenagers, but it's still a fun place.

Squash

Alama Squash

C/Ferrer del Río 15 (361 44 59/60). Metro Diego de León/bus 1, 12, 43, C. **Open** 10am-11pm Mon-Fri; 10am-2.30pm Sat. **Rates** *non-members* 1,200ptas per session; 8,000ptas ten sessions. **No credit cards.**

As well as squash courts this club has a gym and organises a series of out-of-town activities such as white-water rafting, skiing and pony-trekking.

Eridan

C/Embajadores 150 (473 21 00). Metro Legazpi/bus 19, 45. **Open** 8am-11pm Mon-Fri. **Rates** 1,000ptas per day; 250ptas ½ hour. **No credit cards.**

A straightforward, and cheap, squash club with six courts and a small sauna and bar-café.

Swimming Pools/*Piscinas*

A city hundreds of miles from the nearest beach and with summer temperatures reaching 40° C is naturally well equipped with swimming pools. There are also several water parks around Madrid which are fun for kids, and also sometimes nighttime attractions (*see chapters* **Nightlife** *and* **Children**).

City-run Open-Air Pools

Open *Casa de Campo* 1 May-mid-Sept, *other pools* 15 May-mid-Sept 10.30am-8pm daily. **Admission** 425ptas; 200ptas under-14s; 100ptas over-65s; 6,250ptas voucher for 20 admissions. **No credit cards.**

The best – and most popular – of the public pools are the ones in the Casa de Campo, where there is an indoor pool, (closed July-Aug) and three open-air pools: olympic standard, a children's pool and one intermediate-size. Like the other city pools it is attractively equipped and landscaped, with several cafés. Topless sunbathing is allowed, and there is an informal gay area. The pools get very crowded at weekends, but are more relaxed during the week. In addition to the other municipal pools listed below there are several more, mostly around the outskirts. Leaflets available at city sports centres (*see above*) have details. Note that the city council has been considering privatising the municipal pools, in which case the common price system would probably be dropped.

Piscinas de la Casa de Campo Avda del Angel (463 00 50). Metro Lago/bus 33.
Barrio del Pilar C/Montforte de Lemos (314 79 43). Metro Barrio del Pilar, Begoña/bus 83, 128, 132.
Concepción C/Jose del Hierro (403 90 20). Metro Concepción, Quintana/bus 21, 48, 146
Moratalaz C/Valdebernardo (772 71 21). Metro Pavones/bus 8, 32, 71.

City-run Indoor Pools

Open 8.30am-8pm daily. Closed Aug. **Admission** 425ptas; 200ptas under-14s; 100ptas over-65s; 6,250ptas voucher for 20 admissions. **No credit cards.**

The city also has several indoor pools, most of them open all year except for August (hours for some pools may vary). Full information is available from sports centres (*see above*). Chamartín is Olympic-standard, and the pool with the best facilities; La Latina is the only city pool in central Madrid.

Chamartín Plaza del Perú (350 12 23). Metro Pio XII/bus 7, 16, 29, 150.
La Latina Plaza de la Cebada 1 (365 80 31). Metro La Latina/bus 17, 18, 23, 35, 60.

Hotel Emperador

Gran Via 53 (547 28 00). Metro Gran Via/bus all routes to Gran Via. **Open** *July-mid-Sept* 11am-9pm daily. **Admission** *11am-3pm* 1,500ptas; *3-9pm* 1,000ptas. **Credit** DC, MC, V.

One of the most spectacular pools in Madrid is the one that stands on the roof of the **Emperador** hotel (*see chapter* **Accommodation**), which is also open to non-residents. Also on the roof terrace there is a café-restaurant, and both have great views over central Madrid.

Hotel Eurobuilding

C/Padre Damián 23 (345 45 00). Metro Cuzco/bus 150. **Open** noon-8am daily. **Admission** 3,500ptas. **Credit** AmEx, DC, JCB, MC, TC, V.

This business person's castle has excellent indoor and outdoor pools which are both open to non-residents, but very expensive. *See also chapter* **Accommodation**.

Piscina Club Stella

C/Arturo Soria 231 (359 16 32). Metro Arturo Soria/bus 7, 70, 87. **Open** 11am-8pm daily. **Admission** *Mon-Fri* 800ptas; *Sat, Sun* 900ptas; *public holidays* 1,000ptas. *Children 3-7 years* 475ptas. *Block tickets* 10,200ptas 15 admissions; 19,200ptas 30 admissions. **No credit cards.**

An attractive private swimming club that's also open to non-members.

Tennis/*Tenis*

Many city and private sports centres (*see above*) have clay or tarmac tennis courts for hire. At municipal *Polideportivos*, court hire costs 600ptas per hour. The larger clubs such as the **Chamartín**, where professional tournaments are held (*see* **Spectator Sports**), are entirely members-only.

Disabled Sports Facilities

The city sports institute is currently adapting all its *Polideportivos* to allow full access to disabled users but this programme will not be completed for some time. Most of the indoor swimming pools have been adapted, while most of the outdoor pools already have ramps and will also be given full-access changing-rooms in the near future.

Theatre

Fine productions of the classics, a knockabout fringe and multi-national festivals are just three of the features of Madrid's thriving theatre scene.

Spain's theatrical tradition is long and broad. Within it, you can pick from the great Golden Age dramatists Lope de Vega, Tirso de Molina and Calderón de la Barca, Romantics such as Zorrilla, turn-of-the-century realists or the poetic dramas of Federico García Lorca. Works of every era are regularly produced in Madrid.

Theatre in Madrid has suffered from the absence of a true national theatre company with an adequate permanent base. The nearest things to it are the *Centro Dramático Nacional*, based at the **Teatro María Guerrero**, and the *Compañia Nacional de Teatro Clásico*, dedicated to maintaining the heritage of classic Spanish drama, at the **Teatro de la Comedia**. Even so, the city's theatre scene has still made great strides in the last twenty years, in quality and the number of venues and productions. Good contemporary mainstream playwrights are not so much in evidence, but there is a sharp and enterprising fringe scene.

Commercial theatre also does good business in Madrid. Apart from Spanish plays, mainstream theatre programmes feature modern classics by Eugene O'Neill or Arthur Miller, or recent hits by Neil Simon, Willy Russell and so on. Madrid has also been added to the international musical circuit – the **Nuevo Apolo** was renovated expressly to accommodate a two-year run of *Les Miserables*, and productions of *Phantom of the Opera* and *Cats* are looming on the horizon.

THEATRES, SEASONS & TICKETS

The **María Guerrero**, the **Comedia** and the **Teatro Español** are the most prestigious theatres in Madrid. Of fringe venues, the most interesting shows are usually found at the **Sala Triángulo** and the **Alfil**.

The main theatre season runs from mid-September to June, but many theatres have summer programmes that continue through July, and theatre productions, some open-air, also feature in the **Veranos de la Villa** festival (*see chapter* **Madrid by Season**). Two great bonuses for theatre-fans come at the beginning and end of the main season, when the city hosts its two theatre festivals, the **Festival de Otoño** and the **Festival Internacional de Teatro** (*see below* **Festivals**).

All theatres are closed on Mondays. Details of what's on at any time will be found in the *Guía del*

Ocio and local papers (*see chapter* **Media**). It's also a good idea to check street posters for events not covered in the press. Performance times and prices at each theatre may vary considerably between productions. The best way to get tickets is simply at the box office at each theatre, although most theatres will take reservations by phone. Booking agencies, apart from the **FNAC**, charge substantial commission (*see chapter* **Services**). The state theatres the **Sala Olimpia**, the **Comedia**, the **María Guerrero** and the **Auditorio Nacional** and **Teatro de la Zarzuela** (*see chapter* **Music: Classical & Opera**) have a joint ticketing system through which tickets for all these venues can be bought at any one of them.

Several of the smaller venues stage children's shows at weekends. For specialised children's theatres, *see chapter* **Children**.

Main Theatres

Centro Cultural Galileo

C/Fernando el Católico 35 (593 22 30/593 22 00). Metro Quevedo/bus 16, 61. **Box office** 8am-1pm daily. Closed July, Aug. **Tickets** *average* 100-500ptas. **No credit cards.**
A former municipal undertakers', converted into a cultural centre that puts together imaginative theatre programmes usually featuring smallish groups for very short runs. It's well worth checking to see what they have on offer.

Centro Cultural de la Villa

Jardines del Descubrimiento, Plaza Colón (575 60 80). Metro Colón/bus all routes to Plaza Colón. **Box office** 11am-1.30pm, 5-8pm, Tue-Sun. Closed Aug. **Tickets** *average* 800ptas. **No credit cards.**
One of the more spectacular venues, under the waterfalls in the Plaza de Colón. The smaller of its two halls is used for concerts and children's theatre, and the larger for quality popular theatre, and zarzuela in summer (*see chapter* **Music: Classical & Opera**). It is super-comfortable. *See also chapters* **Art Galleries** *and* **Dance**.

Cuarta Pared

C/Ercilla 17 (517 23 17). Metro Embajadores/bus 27, 60, 148, C. **Box office** one hour before performance. **Tickets** 900ptas. **No credit cards.**
A reasonably-sized (capacity 170) fringe venue that presents a range of quality productions as well as housing theatre workshops, courses and children's shows.

El Montacargas

C/Antillón 19 (526 11 73). Metro (opening during 1995) Puerta del Angel/bus 31, 33, 39, 138. **Box office** one hour before performance. **Tickets** 800ptas.

No credit cards.
Recently opened, this sparky cultural association hosts children's shows (Sundays at 6pm), *café-teatro* (cabaret) and all sorts of workshops and other activities as well as its theatre programme, which is suitably unpredictable.

Sala Mirador

C/Doctor Fourquet 31 (539 57 67). Metro Atocha or Lavapiés/bus 6, 26, 27, 32, 57, 60, C. **Box office** one hour before performance. **Tickets** prices vary according to company. **No credit cards.**
Worth visiting for the unique entrance alone: an old-fashioned Madrid patio. Productions are very varied, and include dance and children's shows.

Sala Olimpia

Plaza de Lavapiés (527 46 22). Metro Lavapiés/bus 27, C. **Box office** 5-9pm Tue-Sun. **Tickets** 1,500ptas Tue, Wed, Fri-Sun; 850ptas Thur; 750ptas under-26s. **Credit** V.
Until 1994 this theatre had the subtitle *Centro Nacional de Nuevas Tendencias Escénicas* and was the official venue for avant-garde (or similar) work in all the performing arts: theatre, cabaret, dance, and modern opera. It has since become part of the *Centro Dramático Nacional*, and future programming is uncertain. *See also chapter* **Dance.**

Sala Triángulo

C/Zurita 20 (530 68 91). Metro Lavapiés/bus 27, C. **Box office** half hour before performance. **Tickets** 300-1,500ptas. **No credit cards.**
One of the best fringe venues, it has hosted about every theatrical movement at some point, and is a good showcase for new writing and young actors. It's the main base for the 'alternative' elements in the theatre festivals (*see below* **Festivals**) and also has children's shows, and *café-teatro* in the bar.

Teatro Albéniz

C/de la Paz 11 (531 83 11). Metro Sol/bus all routes to Puerta del Sol. **Box office** 11.30am-1pm, 5.30-9pm Tue-Sun. **Tickets** *average* 1,000-3,500ptas. **Credit** V.
Run by the Comunidad de Madrid, this theatre stages a wide variety of quality drama, and is also the main venue for major, prestige productions in the **Festival de Otoño.** It also hosts opera and dance performances. *See also chapter* **Dance.**

Teatro Alfil

C/del Pez 10 (521 42 96). Metro Noviciado/bus 147. **Box office** 7pm-midnight Tue-Sat; 4-10pm Sun. **Tickets** *average* 1,000ptas; reduced late students, under-26s, over-65s, unemployed. **No credit cards.**
The Alfil has survived various attempts to close it down, but after some renovation its future seems more assured. The programming, sometimes with two or three shows a night, promises to be 'risky' and tends to the wacky, but is often good as well as fun. There's also a bar, and it hosts kid's shows and flamenco and other music gigs at different times.

Teatro Bellas Artes

C/Marqués de Casa Riera 2 (532 44 37/8). Metro Bancode España, Sevilla/bus all routes to C/Alcalá. **Box office** 11.30am-1.30pm, 5-7pm, Mon, Tue, Thur-Sun. Closed June-Sept. **Tickets** prices vary according to company. **No credit cards.**
Part of the **Círculo de Bellas Artes** (*see chapters* **Sightseeing, Art Galleries** *and* **Music: Classical & Opera**), but run independently. It's particularly notable for revivals of twentieth-century Spanish classics, in solid, well-performed productions.

Teatro de Cámara

C/San Cosme y San Damián 3 (527 09 54). Metro Antón

Martín, Lavapiés/bus 6, 26, 32, 57. **Box office** half hour before performance. **Tickets** 500-1,200ptas. **No credit cards.**
An independent theatre that specialises in Russian drama, with Chekhov a mainstay, but also regularly features classical Spanish works.

Teatro de la Comedia

C/Príncipe 14 (521 49 31). Metro Sol, Sevilla/bus 6, 26, 32, 50, 57. **Box office** 11.30am-1.30pm, 5-9pm, Tue-Sun. Closed Aug. **Tickets** *average* 500-2,000ptas. **Credit** V.
For classical Spanish theatre there is no better. Under director Adolfo Marsillach the *Compañia Nacional de Teatro Clásico* has continuously raised its standards to become one of the best-respected and most vital Spanish companies. There are usually three productions a year, playing alternately for a month each. Occasional productions of French or English drama of similar epochs are staged as well as the Spanish Golden Age classics, and it sometimes hosts foreign companies with touring productions. A must.

Teatro Español

C/Príncipe 25 (429 62 97). Metro Sol, Sevilla/bus 6, 26, 32, 50, 57. **Box office** 11.30am-1.30pm, 5-8pm, Tue-Sun. **Tickets** 200-1,800ptas. **No credit cards.**
This site has housed a theatre ever since 1583, when the Corral del Príncipe, in which many of Lope de Vega's works were premièred, opened its doors. The current theatre, which replaced it in 1745, is the most beautiful theatre in Madrid. It now presents mainly twentieth-century Spanish drama and international classics: Shakespeare, Molière and so on.

Teatro Estudio de Madrid

C/Cabeza 14 (539 64 67). Metro Tirso de Molina/bus 6, 26, 32, 57. **Box office** half hour before performance. **Tickets** 900ptas. **No credit cards.**
A truly tiny (capacity under 40) fringe theatre that makes a suitably intense venue for solo shows or two handers.

Teatro La Latina

Plaza de la Cebada (365 28 35). Metro La Latina/bus 17, 18, 23, 35, 60. **Box office** 11am-1.30pm, 5-8pm, Tue-Sun. Closed July, Aug. **Tickets** *average* 2,000ptas; reduced price over-65s. **No credit cards.**
A giant revue theatre that's the place to come to catch up on kitsch stalwarts of the Spanish popular entertainment scene such as Lola Flores and family, or maybe Manolo Escobar, the original perpetrator of *Y Viva España*, plus revivals of thirties' Madrileño comedies.

Teatro de Madrid

Avda de la Ilustración (730 49 22). Metro Barrio del Pilar/bus 42, 83, 128, 132, 147. **Box office** noon-2pm, 5-8.30pm, Tue-Sun. **Tickets** *average* 2,000ptas; reduced prices groups, over-65's. **No credit cards.**
The newest theatre in Madrid, built by the city council far from the centre in the Barrio del Pilar, but with lavish facilities. It presents a mixture of ballet, Spanish dance and drama. *See also chapter* **Dance.**

Teatro María Guerrero

C/Tamayo y Baus 4 (319 47 69). Metro Colón/bus all routes to Plaza Colón. **Box office** 11.30am-1pm, 5-8pm, Tue-Sun. Closed June-Sept. **Tickets** 800-2,200ptas. **Credit** V.
The base for Spain's *Centro Dramático Nacional*, which presents international and more contemporary Spanish drama in high-quality productions with the best performers Spain can offer. The 1885 theatre has a beautiful interior.

Teatro Nuevo Apolo

Plaza Tirso de Molina 1 (429 36 95/429 52 38). Metro Tirso de Molina/bus 6, 26, 32, 57. **Box office** 11.30am-1.30pm, 5-8pm, Tue-Sun. **Tickets** *average* 2,000ptas. **No credit cards.**

Especially renovated for *Les Misérables*, and so now Madrid's venue for big musicals.

Teatro Príncipe Gran Vía

C/Tres Cruces 10 (523 13 69). Metro Gran Vía/bus all routes to Gran Vía. **Box office** 11.30am-1.30pm, 6-8pm, Tue-Sun. **Tickets** 600-2,200ptas; reduced price Tue, first show Sun. **No credit cards.**
A theatre with very unpredictable standards. You can just as easily find a fine touring production of Calderón, or the most appalling rubbish.

Festivals

The **Festival International de Teatro**, usually in April and May, and the **Festival de Otoño** (Autumn Festival), from September to November, are both held in a wide range of venues around the city, although the Autumn Festival is centred on the **Teatro Albéniz**. Both tend to feature young or little known companies from Spain and around the world rather than any major names, and provide a chance to see a multi-varied range of theatre, from Chinese opera one night to the most obscure Polish fringe group the next. Part of the Festival de Otoño is an international festival of 'Alternative Theatre' (the *Muestra Internacional de Teatro Alternativa*) centred on the **Sala Triángulo**, which in recent editions has featured about 80 different groups or performers. Naturally, with so many productions, what you get in either festival can be a matter of pot luck, but you can often make great finds. For further details, *see chapter* **Madrid by Season**.

Theatres from another age

Imagine being able to go to the original Globe Theatre to see *As You Like It* and you will have a rough idea of what the **Corral de Comedias** in Almagro, about a two-and-a-half hour drive south of Madrid, is like. Unique in Europe, it is a completely intact early-seventeenth-century *Corral* theatre, with one open patio surrounded by more exclusive covered galleries, of the type for which the Spanish Golden Age dramas were written.

It was restored in 1950, and now hosts an annual theatre festival in July and early August, featuring Spanish classics and other works from similar eras – Shakespeare, Molière, Goldoni – performed by the *Compañía Nacional de Teatro Clásico*, other Spanish groups and sometimes visiting foreign companies. Simultaneously, performances are also staged in churches and other venues around the town. As a setting for a comedy by Lope de Vega, for example, the *Corral* is unsurpassable, and an evening spent here, whether in the stalls open to the skies or in the galleries, is an unforgettable experience. Almagro itself is a beautiful little town, ideal for a relatively tourist-free weekend away from Madrid.

Less spectacular but equally fascinating is the **Real Coliseo de Carlos III**, a small eighteenth-century theatre built for King Charles III just north of the monstrous monastery at El Escorial (*see chapter* **Trips Out of Town**). It too is used as an occasional venue for classic drama, opera and chamber concerts, and there are few better ways to round off a day's footslogging than by seeing a performance in this beautifully-proportioned, exquisitely decorated theatre. Tourist offices in Madrid should have information on forthcoming programmes (*see chapter* **Essential Information**).

Corral de Comedias de Almagro

Information *(Festival season only 926/88 22 00).* **Getting there** *By bus* AISA from Estación Sur de Autobuses, 2 buses daily; *by car* N-IV south, at Puerto Lápice turn onto N420 for Almagro (190km). **Where to stay** Anyone wanting to make a real weekend of it should stay at the **Parador de Almagro**, Ronda de San Francisco (926/86 01 00), which occupies an old Franciscan monastery, and is not as expensive as one might think (about 11,000ptas per double room). A cheaper alternative is **Don Diego**, C/Ejido de Calatrava 1 (926/86 12 87).

Real Coliseo de Carlos III

C/Floridablanca 20, San Lorenzo de El Escorial (890 44 11). **Getting there** *see chapter* **Trips Out of Town**.

*On stage at the **Corral de Almagro**.*

In Focus

Business

Business in Madrid is a surprising mixture of old and new practices.

To do business in Madrid, it's useful to have a guide to the possible pitfalls.

Doing business in Spain must at some point involve coming to – and to terms with – Madrid. Its only real commercial rival is Barcelona, but the presence of the central government tends to make Madrid more convenient for foreign firms. Madrid is one of the most open and tolerant of European capitals, and an attractive place to work and do business.

Madrid now has a burgeoning expatriate business community. With the rest of the country it experienced an unprecedented economic boom after Spain joined the EU in 1986, and even after recession set in in 1992 the business scene has remained vibrant, despite some gloomy rhetoric from the big guns of finance and industry.

Spain's position in the European Union means that it is advisable for anyone doing business here to be familiar with EU legislation and the intricacies of the single market. Foreign operators should also investigate the loans and grants for different sectors of the economy that are available through the EU, as well as the possibilities for aid directly from the Spanish state, as they are an important means of softening the impact of Spanish tax.

Also, many of the European directives remain to be implemented, and the Spanish State has its ways of doing things irrespective of whatever proposals might be forthcoming from Brussels.

Anyone intending to do steady business here needs to know the ins and outs of the many Spanish legal and bureaucratic mazes, and particularly the requirements for certification and approval (*homologación*) of projects and qualifications. Chances are, you'll need to adjust to a slower schedule for payments from clients, a denser style of bureaucracy and a more tax-laden and expensive structure of overhead costs.

Flair, daring and charm can go a long way in Madrid. Contacts remain a key factor, and who you know often counts for more than what you know. For this reason, it is highly advisable to take advantage of professional consultants and agents familiar with the local scene when initiating business here. Spaniards themselves make use of intermediaries such as the universal *Gestoría* (*see below*), above all in their contacts with bureaucracy, much more than would be usual in Anglo-Saxon countries.

Institutions & Information

An essential first stop is the commercial section of the relevant embassy (*see chapter* **Survival**), as they provide information, advisory and library services, and can also initiate business contacts.

Chambers of Commerce

Invaluable sources of legal and business information, particularly on EU or state grants and loans.

Cámara de Comercio
e Industria de Madrid

Plaza de Independencia 1 (538 35 00/fax 538 37 19/18).
Metro Retiro/bus all routes to Puerta de Alcalá.
Open 8am-3pm Mon-Fri.
The Madrid Chamber's services are primarily oriented towards local business, but they also provide a range of information services for foreign investors, particularly if they may be exporting from Spain.

Consejo Supremo de las
Cámaras de Comercio de España

Claudio Coello 19 (575 34 00/fax 435 42 55). Metro Retiro, Serrano/bus 1, 9, 19, 51.
Open 8am-2.30pm, 4-6.30pm, Mon-Fri.
The joint body for all the local Spanish chambers.

Other Official Institutions

Banco de España

C/Alcalá 50 (338 50 00). Metro Banco de España/bus all routes to Cibeles. **Open** 8am-3pm Mon-Fri.
The bank's English-language CD-Rom database on economics, finance and business may be used by the public. The Research and Publications Departments also have economic and financial information available in English.

CEOE (Spanish Employers
Confederation)/CEPYME (Spanish
Small Business Confederation)

C/Diego de León 50 (563 96 41/fax 562 80 23). Metro Diego de León/bus 29, 52, 61, C. **Open** 8.30am-2pm, 3.30-6.30pm, Mon-Thur; 8.30am-3pm Fri.

Communidad Autónoma de Madrid
(Autonomous Community of Madrid)

Dirección General de Turismo, C/Duque de Medinaceli 2 (580 23 17). Metro Banco de España/bus 9, 14, 27, 34.
Open 9am-2pm Mon-Fri.

European Commission Office

C/Serrano 41 (435 17 00). Metro Serrano/bus 1, 9, 19, 51, 74. **Open** 9.30am-1pm, 3-6pm, Mon-Fri.

Instituto Español de Comercio Exterior
(Spanish Institute for Foreign Trade)

Paseo de la Castellana 14 (431 12 40/349 61 00/fax 431 61 28). Metro Colón/bus all routes to Plaza de Colón.
Open 9am-2pm Mon-Fri.
ICEX, the state trade organisation, helps small- and medium-sized businesses that export goods and services from Spain. It provides a wide range of information, along with access to data bases and personal consulting services. Enquiries should be directed to the *Servicio de Información* (General Information Service).

Stock Market

Bolsa de Madrid
(Madrid Stock Exchange)

Plaza de la Lealtad 1 (589 26 00/fax 589 14 17/special investor assistance service number 589 11 84). Metro Banco de España/bus 9, 14, 27, 37, 45.
Open 10am-2pm Mon-Fri.
Madrid's stock exchange occupies a distinguished nineteenth-century building opposite the Ritz hotel. *See also chapter* **Sightseeing**.

Comisión Nacional del Mercado de
Valores (Spanish National Securities &
Exchange Commission)

Paseo de la Castellana 19 (585 15 00/fax 319 33 73).
Metro Colón/bus all routes to Plaza de Colón.
Open 9.30am-2pm, 4.30-6pm, Mon-Fri.

Associations, Clubs & Contacts

The American Club

Edificio España, Gran Vía 88, Grupo 5, 9°-3 (547 78 02/547 78 04/fax 559 66 91). Metro Plaza de España/bus all routes to Plaza de España. **Open** 10am-2pm, 3-6pm, Mon-Fri.
An excellent meeting point for American businessmen, professionals, diplomats and their guests. Membership (individuals 15,000ptas a year, plus a joining fee of 3,000ptas) is open to individuals and companies of all nationalities.

English Yellow Pages

C/Victor de la Serna 32, 3°B (phone & fax 345 49 72).
Metro Colombia/bus 52. **Open** 4-9pm Mon-Fri.
An annual handbook of English-speaking services in Madrid, Barcelona and a number of other European cities. It's on sale in Madrid in English-language bookshops (*see chapter* **Shopping: Bookshops**) and at some newsstands.

Network

C/Doce de Octubre 13, 7° B (504 35 01/fax 504 35 01).
Metro Sainz de Baranda/bus 26, 61, 63, C. **Open** 9am-2pm Mon-Fri.
A professional women's networking and contact group founded by British women.

Press & Publications

The main Spanish business publications are *Cinco Días* and *Expansión*, both weekly. *Segundamano* is essential for anyone wanting to place general classified ads, while *Mercado de Trabajo*, published every Friday, concentrates on job ads. Of the local English-language magazines, *Lookout* is useful for placing ads and small-ads of all types; *Guidepost*, a weekly published through the American Club, has good summaries of Spanish business news, and a handy classified ad section. *See also chapter* **Media**.

Banking

Central branches of the major banks generally have some English-speaking staff. Non-residents from non-EU countries are subject to certain banking restrictions. Listed here are central branches of a few of the many options; for everyday banking needs, *see chapter* **Essential Information**.

Banco Bilbao Vizcaya (BBV)

Paseo de la Castellana 81 (374 80 00). Metro Nuevos Ministerios/bus 5, 27, 42, 150, C.
Open 8.30am-2pm Mon-Fri.

Banco Exterior de España (Argentaria)

Carrera de San Jerónimo 36 (537 70 00). Metro Sevilla/bus 9, 14, 27, 37, 45.
Open 8.30am-2pm Mon-Fri; 8.30am-12.30pm Sat.
Specialising in foreign transactions, the Banco Exterior offers efficient service and discounts on foreign exchange commissions for account holders.

*The grand **Stock Exchange**. See page 211.*

Fashion Week), both in February, and the **Semana Internacional del Habitat** interior design fair, in April. The IFEMA trade fair institute also runs the conference and exhibition site in the Casa de Campo, the **Feria del Campo**, Avda de Portugal (463 63 34/fax 470 21 54).

Palacio de Exposiciones y Congresos

Paseo de la Castellana 99 (337 81 22/fax 597 10 94). Metro Lima/bus 27, 40, 43, 147, 149, 150.
A longer-established conference venue, completed in 1980, with a dramatic Miró frieze across the front of the building. It's in the heart of the business district, with easy access to the city centre and main shopping areas. It has been used for several major international conferences. There are conference rooms, auditoriums and galleries of all sizes, and security, catering and many other ancillary services are available.

Business Services

Accountants & Consultants

The following firms do business mainly, although not exclusively, with larger business concerns. For individuals or small businesses it may be more appropriate to contact the kind of smaller consultancies listed below under *Gestorías*.

Arthur Andersen

C/Raimundo Fernández Villaverde 65 (597 00 00/fax 556 64 69). Metro Nuevos Ministerios/bus 5, 42, C.
Open 8am-9pm Mon-Fri.

Genesis Corporation

Paseo de la Castellana 53, 4º izq (442 67 33/fax 441 60 99). Metro Rubén Darío/bus 5, 27, 45, 150.
Open 9am-3pm Mon-Fri.
Consultants on appropriate techniques for entering the marketplace or investing in Spain and other EU countries.

Merrill Lynch

Paseo de la Castellana 31, 7º (319 70 12/fax 310 26 19). Metro Colón/bus all routes to Plaza de Colón.
Open 9.30am-2pm, 3.30-7pm, Mon-Fri.

Price Waterhouse

Paseo de General Martínez Campos 41 (308 03 75). Metro Rubén Darío/bus all routes to Castellana.
Open 9am-6pm Mon-Fri.
Branch: Paseo de la Castellana 43 (308 35 00).

SIRECOX

Paseo de la Castellana 95 (556 07 25/597 02 44). Metro Lima, Nuevos Ministerios/bus 5, 27, 40, 147, 149, 150.
Open 9am-2pm, 4-7pm, Mon-Fri.
A partially state-owned foreign trade company specialising in developing import and export strategies custom-designed to meet a client's needs.

Legal Services

The firms listed below offer commercial legal advice and representation in Spanish and English.

Bufete José Maraio Armero, Abogados

C/Velázquez 21, 4º (431 31 00/fax 431 85 76). Metro Velázquez/bus 1, 9, 19, 51, 74.
Open 9am-2pm, 4.30-7.30pm, Mon-Fri.

Ruiz-Gallardón y Muñiz, Abogados

C/Serrano Anguita 10 (446 70 81/fax 445 16 00). Metro Alonso Martínez/bus 7, 21.
Open 9.30am-2.30pm, 5-7.30pm, Mon-Fri.

Barclays Bank

Plaza de Colón 1 (336 10 00). Metro Colón/bus all routes to Plaza de Colón. **Open** *June-Sept* 8.30am-2.30pm Mon-Fri; *Oct-May* 8.30am-2.30pm Mon-Fri; 8.30am-1pm Sat.

Citibank

C/José Ortega y Gasset 29 (538 41 00/fax 538 41 18). Metro Lista, Núñez de Balboa/bus 1, 29, 52, 74.
Open 9am-7pm Mon-Fri.

Conference Venues & Services

Oficina de Congresos de Madrid (Madrid Convention Bureau)

C/Mayor 69 (588 29 00/fax 588 29 30). Metro Sol/bus 3.
Open *mid-Sept-June* 8am-3pm, 4-6pm, Mon-Thur; 8am-3pm Fri. *July-mid-Sept* 8.30am-2.30pm Mon-Fri.
An office set up by the city council to provide assistance for companies, institutions or individuals wishing to hold a conference or similar event in Madrid, and to facilitate contacts between them and all the local sites and service companies.

IFEMA/Feria de Madrid

Parque Ferial Juan Carlos I (722 50 00/722 51 80/fax 722 58 01/telex 44025). Metro Arturo Soria, then bus 122. **Open** 8am-10pm Mon-Fri.
Madrid's lavish, state-of-the-art trade fair centre, on the north-east side of the city not far from the airport, was opened in 1991. It consists of eight main pavilions, a 600-seater auditorium and many smaller facilities, all with excellent, high-technology services, and boasts 12 restaurants and 7,500 parking spaces. By the entrance to the park is the **Palacio Municipal de Congresos**, a 2,000-capacity conference hall. The site hosts a stream of events of different sizes throughout the year. Some of the most important are the **ARCO** art fair (*see chapter* **Art Galleries**) and the **Semana Internacional de la Moda** (International

Gestorías – administrative services

The *gestoría* is a distinctly Spanish institution, one of the main functions of which is to take away the weight of dealing with the many levels of local bureaucracy by doing it for you. They essentially combine the functions of notary, lawyer, book-keeper and business consultant. Most Spaniards and foreign residents employ a *gestor* at some point, be it for filing income tax or arranging an application for a driver's licence. English is spoken at the *gestorías* listed below.

Gestoría Calvo Canga
Plaza Tirso de Molina 12, 2° (369 34 99/369 35 03/fax 369 31 15). Metro Tirso de Molina/bus 6, 26, 32, 57.
Open 9am-2pm, 5-8pm, Mon-Fri.
A traditional *gestoría* dealing in labour law, tax, accountancy, immigration and residency issues.

Suadellum Consultants
Gran Vía 86, Grupo 6, 22°, Office 4 (541 60 58/fax 541 60 58). Metro Plaza de España/bus all routes to Plaza de España. **Open** 9.30am-1.30pm, 4.30-7.30pm, Mon-Fri.
Commercial legal services and representation, accountancy, payroll and tax advice and general consultancy services for companies and individuals.

Syncordia, SL
C/Arturo Soria 187, Office 2, Sótano 1 (519 43 92/fax 519 65 66). Metro Arturo Soria/bus 11, 70, 120, 201.
Open 9am-3pm Mon-Fri.
Small business consultants offering accounting, payroll, and other advisory services.

Translation & Conference Services

A feature of Madrid translation agencies is that many also provide conference and seminar services.

Isbell/Metzner
Costanilla de San Andres 12, 1° (tel/fax 365 71 97). Metro La Latina/bus 3, 31, 35, 60.
Open 9am-8pm Mon-Fri. **No credit cards**.
Organises seminars and conferences, and provides consultancy services for foreigners developing a specific business or cultural project in Spain.

SIASA
Paseo de la Habana 134 (457 4891/fax 458 10 88). Metro Lima, Colombia/bus 14, 40.
Open 9am-2pm, 4-7pm, Mon-Fri. **No credit cards**.
Simultaneous translation, attendant equipment rental and the organisation of business conferences.

Courier Services

The following services offer same-day delivery services within Madrid and next-day deliveries to other Spanish and international destinations. For fax services, *see chapter* **Services**. For information on post and telephones, *see chapter* **Survival**.

RUM
C/Galileo 91 (535 38 16). Metro Quevedo/bus 2, 12.
Open 9am-8pm Mon-Fri. **No credit cards**.
An efficient local courier company. Pickups and deliveries can be made by bike or van. A 1kg package for delivery by bike within Madrid costs 440ptas. for non-account customers.

SEUR
Phonelines for collection & delivery *(For Madrid & Spain 778 26 14/International 329 45 00).*
Open 9am-7pm Mon-Fri.
Paseo de la Castellana 95 (556 72 07/general information 902 10 10 10). Metro Nuevos Ministerios/bus 5, 27, 42, 150, C. **Open** 10am-3pm, 5-8.30pm, Mon-Fri. **No credit cards**.
The largest Spanish courier company. Same-day deliveries in Madrid of up to a kilo cost 957ptas, the rate rising to 981pts for up to 2kg and 1,050pts for packages of up to 3kg. Express national and international services also available.

UPS (United Parcel Service)
Centro de Transportes de Madrid (Madrid Transport Centre), Carretera de Villaverde, km 3.5 (507 08 88).
Bus 88. **Open** 8am-7pm Mon-Fri. **No credit cards**.
Rapid courier, messenger and transport services for deliveries in Madrid, across Spain, and internationally.

Office Services
Equipment Hire

Data-Rent
C/Maldonado 5 (411 78 12). Metro Núñez de Balboa/bus 9, 19, 29, 52, 61. **Open** 9am-2pm, 4-7pm, Mon-Fri.
Credit MC, V.
IBM-compatible computers for rent on a daily, weekly or monthly basis. Fees range from 18,000ptas to 35,000ptas a day for computers. Laser printers are also available.

Micro Rent
C/General Yagüe 10, 1°B (597 32 82). Metro Cuzco/bus 5, 14, 27, 40, 140. **Open** *Sept-June* 9am-6pm, *July, Aug* 8am-3pm, Mon-Fri. **No credit cards**.
A wide range of office equipment is available, including Apple and IBM computers (from 10,000ptas to 40,000ptas a week), printers, fax machines, overhead projectors and so on.

Housing & Office Space
American Service Organization
Gran Vía 88, Edificio España, Grupo 2, 5° (548 01 07/fax 542 60 46). Metro Plaza de España/bus all routes to Plaza de España. **Open** 9am-2pm, 4-6.30pm, Mon-Fri.
No credit cards.
Apartments, offices, industrial sites, for rent or purchase.

Regus
Paseo de la Castellana 93, 4° (555 87 72/fax 555 99 57). Metro Nuevos Ministerios/bus all routes to Castellana. **Open** 9am-7pm Mon-Fri. **Credit** AmEx, V.
A fully-equipped business centre with offices from 80,000ptas to 250,000ptas a month. Administrative and secretarial services are available on request.

Removal & Relocation Services
Goldman & Laurent
C/de las Norias 75, Majadahonda (634 25 32/fax 634 24 68). Bus 561, 567, 626, 651-4 from Moncloa/train Cercanías line C-7 to Majadahonda. **Open** 9am-3pm Mon-Fri. **No credit cards**.
Relocation consultants who locate residential or office space.

SIT Transportes International, SA
Gran Vía 66 (541 94 94/541 5151/fax 559 85 10). Metro Plaza de España/bus all routes to Plaza de España. **Open** 8am-5.30pm Mon-Fri. **No credit cards**.
International household goods movers providing door-to-door service anywhere in the world.

Children

Keeping kids happy in Madrid means adjusting to a different rhythm of life.

Spaniards love children, and Madrileños are no exception. If you travel around the city with kids they will attract jovial remarks from taxi drivers, courteous attention from waiters, handfuls of sweets from shop assistants and admiring comments from old ladies. Family ties are still strong. From birth children are absorbed into a wide social circle spanning the generations, with innumerable cousins and older relatives. They take part in outdoor social life, the evening *paseo* and long, leisurely sessions in cafés and restaurants.

Services specifically for children, on the other hand, can seem curiously lacking; facilities or attractions are often outdated and crumbling. The common assumption seems to have been that families would provide for kids' needs themselves.

The dramatic fall in Spain's birthrate has probably contributed to making modernisation and innovation in this area seem less of a priority. A great many families nowadays have only one child, in part because housing space is so tight. At the same time, however, the enormous social changes that have pushed and pulled at the traditional family structure over the last forty years – most of all, rapid urbanisation and the incorporation of women into the work force – have created a need for alternative facilities that has not yet been resolved, despite the growth in *Guarderías* or nurseries (*see below* **Childcare & Babysitting**).

If you are coming to Madrid with children it is vital to take into account a very different timetable. Forget seven o'clock bedtimes and prepare to go with the flow; children here stay up late. It's quite normal to see whole families out at midnight, or going round the **Parque de Atracciones** at two in the morning. In the summer heat this timetable makes perfect sense. By far the most pleasant time for children to be out playing is the late evening.

Combining this with the requirements of a long school day (most Spanish schools run from 9am until at least 5pm) is eased by very long summer holidays from mid-June to mid-September. The rest of the year school hours make for earlier bedtimes, but generally Spanish children always tend to stay up later than their British or American counterparts. Even small children don't get to bed much before 10pm.

Sightseeing

Given that most kids can only take so much great art palaces often wear them out, although of the 'Big Three' the **Reina Sofía** is perhaps the one most likely to have exhibits that engage young imaginations, particularly in its temporary exhibitions. Of the other major sights, the **Palacio Real** impresses most children with its sheer size and opulence. Highlights are the enormous chandeliers, and the collection of clocks. The armoury also has elaborate suits of armour, including some for dogs and horses. The **Faro** ('lighthouse') observation tower in Moncloa is also fun, offering a ride in a glass lift and an impressive panorama of the city. For details of all three, *see* chapter **Sightseeing**.

Tren de la Fresa (Strawberry Train)
Estación de Atocha (527 31 21). Metro Atocha RENFE/bus all routes to Atocha. **Open** *May-Sept Sat, Sun, public holidays;* depart from Atocha 10am. **Price** (return ticket) 2,300ptas; 1,500ptas 2-12s, over 65s.
Recreate a favourite outing of Madrileños of 100 years ago, travelling by steam train to Aranjuez to enjoy its palaces, gardens and the fresh produce of its riverside orchards, notably the strawberries (*fresas*) for which the town is famous. The historic engine and coaches depart from Atocha at 10am and roll south at a leisurely pace, returning late in the afternoon; the ticket includes entry to Aranjuez's delightful palaces and gardens. Hostesses on the train don period costume and travellers can sample Aranjuez strawberries. It's very popular in May and June, but you can book tickets in advance at travel agents, Renfe offices or the **Museo Nacional Ferroviario** (*see chapter* **Museums**). For further information on Aranjuez, *see* chapter **Around Madrid**.

Museums & Exhibits

Among its museums and galleries Madrid can count a few more obviously of interest to children. Very few have information available in English.

Acciona – Museo Interactivo de la Ciencia
C/Pintor Murillo, Parque de Andalucia, Alcobendas (661 39 09). Bus Interbus 151, 152, 153, 154 from Plaza Castilla. **Open** 10am-6pm daily. Closed Aug. **Admission** 600ptas; 400ptas under-12s, over-65s.
Although some way out of town in the northern suburb of Alcobendas this recently-opened science museum is proving very popular and has had some attractive temporary exhibitions. Hands-on, fun exhibits demonstrate principles of chemistry, optics and so on. There is also a special room for small children with imaginative, interactive learning games.

Acuárium de Madrid

*C/Maestro Vitoria 8 (531 81 72). Metro Callao, Sol/bus
all routes to Puerta del Sol.* **Open** 11am-2pm, 5-9pm,
daily. **Admission** 500ptas; 300ptas under-8s.
On the ground floor this bizarre privately-run establishment
is a pet shop, specialising in tropical fish. The basement
levels, meanwhile, are given over to a fascinating collection
of fish, reptiles and spiders.

Museo de Cera (Wax Museum)

*Paseo de Recoletos 41 (308 08 25/319 26 49). Metro
Colón/bus all routes to Plaza Colón.* **Open** 10am-2pm, 4-
8.30pm, daily. **Admission** 750ptas; 500ptas 4-18s.
Tacky and not cheap, but popular. A mixed bag of scenes
from serious historical figures to a motley collection of current celebrities (mainly Spanish) with the inevitable horrible
crimes and gory 'Tortures of the Inquisition'. Some are life-
like, others (Mrs Thatcher and Hillary Clinton) laughably
grotesque. It's not well labelled, so it's necessary to buy the
glossy colour guide to make sense of the first section.

Planetario

*Parque Tierno Galván (467 38 98). Metro Méndez
Alvaro/bus 148/train Cercanías line C-5 to Méndez
Alvaro.* **Shows** 5.30pm, 6.45pm, Tue-Fri; 11.30am,
12.45pm, 5.30pm, 6.45pm, 8pm Sat, Sun, public holidays.
Admission 375ptas; 200ptas 2-14s, over-65s.
Madrid's planetarium is in the Tierno Galván park south of
Atocha, a new park created during the eighties. The display
is very modern but in Spanish only, and even kids who do
know the language often find it too long, wordy and dull.
The nice playground outside could be its best feature.

Parks & Gardens

Since most Madrileños live in flats all public open
spaces are made great use of, and even the tiniest
square has a few shady trees, benches and a children's play area. However, most swings, slides and
climbing frames are in poor condition, set on stony
ground and unsuitable for small children except
under eagle-eyed supervision. Some attempt at
improvement has been made recently in the centre,
particularly in the Paseo del Prado and Plaza de
Oriente, but the best-choice play area is by the
Plaza de Independencia entrance to the **Retiro**.
This wooden complex with slides, chain ladders,
and chutes is immensely popular, and so best
avoided at peak hours – after school and on
Sunday mornings.

Another ride that kids enjoy is the **Teleférico**
cable-car between the Casa de Campo and the
Parque del Oeste. For details of this and more
information on all of Madrid's parks, *see chapter*
Sightseeing.

Campo del Moro

*Paseo Virgen del Puerto (542 00 59). Metro Norte/bus
25, 33, 39, 46, 75, 138, C.* **Open** *Oct-April* 10am-6pm
Mon-Sat; 9am-6pm Sun, public holidays. *May-Sept* 10am-
8pm Mon-Sat; 9am-8pm Sun, public holidays.
These beautiful gardens, formerly part of the **Palacio Real**,
can only be entered from the Paseo Virgen del Puerto.
Perhaps for this reason they are usually empty, and so provide a shady, tranquil place to go with small children. The
entrance affords a fairytale vista of the palace, and is also
frequented by masses of cats. The park's museum of royal
carriages is likely to be closed for restoration for some years.

Casa de Campo

Metro Lago, Batán/bus 33, 41, 75.
Locals tend to cluster along the southern edge of this enormous area of rough parkland, site of major children's attractions such as the **Parque de Atracciones** and the **Zoo** (*see
below*). There's also the boating lake with numerous cafés,
the swimming pools (*see chapter* **Sport & Fitness**) and a
stand for hiring bicycles to accommodate the whole family
(*see chapter* **Services**). This is only a short walk from the
Teleférico. In the opposite direction you leave crowds and
cars behind for rolling land that's ideal for walking, jogging
or mountain biking, and you may even come across sheep
grazing. Best for picnics in spring when the wild flowers are
out – in summer it's too hot, and the grass is dry and spiky.

Parque del Oeste

Metro Moncloa, Norte/bus 21, 46, 74, 82, 132, 133, C.
Sloping down towards the Manzanares, this is a beautiful
shady park. For children its major attraction is as the starting point of the **Teleférico** cable car. End the round trip
with an ice-cream at **Bruin** or in summer join other families
for an evening stroll along Pintor Rosales and refreshment
at one of the many *terrazas* (*see chapter* **Cafés & Bars**).

Parque del Retiro

Metro Retiro, Ibiza, Atocha/bus all routes to Retiro.
Open *Oct-April* 6.30am-10.30pm, *May-Sept*
6.30am-11pm, daily.
Madrid's best-loved park has many attractions for children,
most of all the boating lake. Around it you'll also find street
performers, puppet shows, fortune tellers and picturesque
waffle vendors. There are shady open-air cafés and tame red
squirrels, and sports facilities in the south-west corner. In
summer watch out for band concerts and weekend performances in the outdoor puppet theatre (*see below* **Theatre**).

Outings

As well as the traditional zoo and funfair, in the
last few years Madrid has acquired a new answer
to its summer heat in the shape of water parks with
all sorts of water-based theme rides. Most rides are
best suited to older kids, but the parks usually
have special sections for smaller children. For conventional pools, *see chapter* **Sport & Fitness**.

Acuático de San Fernando de Henares

*Carretera de Barcelona (N-II) km15.5 (673 10 13). Bus
Continental Auto 281, 282, 284, 285 from Avda de
América/train Cercanías Line C-2, C-7 to San Fernando.*
Open 11am-8pm, daily. **Admission** *Mon-Fri* 1,100ptas; 850ptas under-14s; *Sat,
Sun, public holidays* 1,500ptas; 1,100ptas under-14s.
Half-day entry 850ptas Mon-Fri; 1,200ptas Sat, Sun,
public holidays. **Credit** V.
The oldest of Madrid's waterparks, in San Fernando de
Henares, near the airport. Smaller than its competitors, it's
still pretty big and busy, with giant water slides, a large
lake/main pool, cafés, restaurants and, an added attraction,
later all-night disco sessions so that teens and upwards can
go back for a dance and a dip. Also a special small-kids pool.

AquaPalace

*Paseo de la Ermita del Santo 48 (526 17 79). Metro
Puerta de Toledo, Marqués de Vadillo/bus 17, 25, 50.*
Open *indoors* 11am-8pm daily; *outdoors* 11am-8pm
daily May-Sept only. **Admission** *Mon-Fri* 900ptas;
650ptas under-14s; *Sat, Sun* 1,100ptas; 800ptas under 14s.
Credit V.
A very attractive partly-indoor waterpark that's the most
central and accessible of the ones around Madrid. There are

At the **Acuático de San Fernando**.

indoor and outdoor pools with slides, twisters, wave machines, an 'Adventure Lake' and other fun things. Not as brash and hectic as the other parks, it's the only one open all year. The indoor section is kept at 30°C in winter. There's also a good pool for tiny children, jacuzzis, and a nice café.

Aquópolis

Villanueva de la Cañada, Carretera de La Coruña (N-VI) km25 (815 69 11/815 69 86). Bus Autoperiferia 581 from Estación Sur. Open June-Sept noon-7pm Mon-Fri; 11am-7pm Sat, Sun, public holidays. Admission Mon-Fri 1,500ptas; 1,000ptas under-14s; Sat, Sun, public holidays 1,700ptas; 1,100ptas under-14s.
Credit AmEx, MC, V.
A giant complex towards El Escorial, one of the largest water parks in Europe. The usual adventure lakes, wave machines and water slides – only bigger. There are plenty of places to buy food, but you can also take your own food in for a picnic.

Baby West

Paseo de la Ermita del Santo 48 (526 01 78). Metro Puerta de Toledo, Marqués de Vadillo/bus 17, 25, 50. Open 6-11pm Mon-Fri; noon-midnight Sat; noon-10pm Sun. Admission free; rides 125ptas each.
A special children's funfair, like Aquapalace part of the La Ermita leisure complex, offering Wild West theme rides as well as trampolines and a play pool with giant plastic balls.

Lagosur/Parquesur

Autovía Madrid-Toledo (N401) km9 (686 70 00). Metro Oporto, then bus 485/train Cercanías line C-5 to Zarzaquemada. Open June-Sept 11am-8pm, 11pm-5am,

daily **Admission** *Lagosur: Mon-Fri* 950ptas; 700ptas under-14s; *Sat* 1,100ptas; 700 under-14s; *Sun, public holidays* 1,400ptas; 800 under-14s. *Parquesur:* free; 800ptas block ticket for all rides. **No credit cards.**
Another huge complex, with a funfair and other attractions as well as the Lagosur waterpark. It also has **Universal Sur,** a disco and music venue *(see chapter* **Music: Rock, Roots & Jazz).** All the usual attractions, and a small-kids area and pool. It's another one that reopens for (very) noisy night-time fun *(see chapter* **Nightlife).**

Parque de Atracciones

Casa de Campo (463 29 00/463 64 33). Metro Batán/bus 33, 36, 39, 65. **Open** *Sept-June* noon-11pm Mon-Fri, Sun; noon-1am Sat; *July, Aug* noon-11pm Mon-Thur, Sun; noon-3am Fri, Sat. **Admission** 350ptas; *Bono superdiversión* 1,500ptas; 800ptas under-7s.
No credit cards.
A perennial favourite, this rambling funfair offers over 40 rides ranging from the gentlest merry-go-round to the stomach-churning Top Spin. There's also an open-air auditorium offering concerts by popular artists and pop bands three times a week, and twice-nightly cavalcades, at 9pm and 11.45pm. The best ticket to get is the *Bono Superdiversión* for an all-in price (a transfer stuck on your hand gives you access to unlimited rides). It's packed after dark in summer, and you may have to queue, but the Flume Ride is worth it.

Zoo de la Casa de Campo

Casa de Campo (711 99 50). Metro Batán/bus 33, 36, 39, 65. **Open** 10am-9.30pm daily. **Admission** 1,240ptas; 895ptas under-8s. **No credit cards.**
This attractive zoo contains over 2,000 animals covering 150 species of mammal and 100 species of bird, including 29 endangered ones. Its star is *Chulín* the giant panda, born at the zoo in 1982. Other highlights are a parrot show and the dolphinarium, with morning and afternoon performances. There is a special children's section and a train ride. Plenty of snack bars are dotted about the zoo as well.

Theatre

Many fringe theatres such as **El Montacargas** and **Cuarta Pared** put on children's shows on weekends. They are, naturally, in Spanish, but look out for shows by Anna Maria Speight, a local English actress who has created a bilingual show to help children learning English. Spanish children's programming includes puppet shows in the **Centro Cultural de la Villa** and *El Gato con Botas (Puss in Boots)* at the **Teatro Español** during the Christmas season. *See also chapter* **Theatre.**

Sala San Pol

Plaza San Pol de Mar 1 (541 90 89/547 94 22). Metro Norte/bus 75, 46. **Performances** 6pm Sat, Sun, public holidays; Closed July-Sept. **Tickets** 700ptas. **No credit cards.**
Madrid's official children's theatre, home to the theatre company *La Bicicleta*. Productions are lavish, but a bit verbose.

Teatro Municipal de Títeres del Retiro

Parque del Retiro (409 02 17). Metro Retiro/bus all routes to Retiro. **Performances** 1pm Sat, Sun; *Titirilandia July-Sept only* 7pm Thur-Sat; 7pm, 8.30pm, Sun. **Admission** free.
This open-air puppet theatre in the Retiro offers free shows every weekend throughout the year. During summer, as part of the **Veranos de la Villa** festival *(see chapter* **Madrid by Season)** it offers extra shows in the *Titirilandia* festival, featuring puppet companies from around the world.

Star of Madrid **Zoo**, *Chulín. See page 216.*

Events & Fiestas

Many events in Madrid's calendar of *fiestas* and festivals include activities for children. Christmas, as one might expect, is particularly full of possibilities. The traditional Spanish Christmas decoration is the *Belén* or nativity scene. Watch out for the annual *Exposición de Belenes* mounted by the **Museo Municipal** in December. If you feel inspired to create your own, the Christmas fair in Plaza Mayor is where you can buy the necessary terracotta figures in all sizes and prices, as well as Christmas trees, decorations and all sorts of jokes.

Spanish children leave out a shoe to receive their presents from the Three Kings on the night of 5 January. On **Reyes**, the next day, the Kings' arrival is celebrated with a lavish procession from their helicopter landing point in the Retiro along Calle Alcalá to Sol and Plaza Mayor. Crowds are huge. During **Carnaval** in February many special children's carnivals are organised around the city: they're great opportunities for dressing up.

There are also plenty of entertainments and events for kids in **San Isidro** and, on a smaller scale, at the summer **Verbenas**. For programme information, check with tourist offices. For more information on festivals and fiestas in Madrid, *see* chapter **Madrid by Season**.

Eating Out

Spanish children are accustomed to eating out from an early age, and consequently you can take a child almost anywhere. Because of this, though, very few places offer special children's menus. If you can't find any Spanish food that kids will accept, international hamburger and pizza chains are an obvious resort, and easy to find. For smaller children (there is a height limit) the **McDonald's** in the **Centro Comercial La Vaguada** shopping mall has an excellent open-air play complex with play pool, rope ladder, tunnels and slide. The local shop/restaurant chains **Vip's** and **Bob's** are also handy, offering quick service and a range of meals or snacks outside normal Spanish meal times (*see* chapter **Shopping**).

Childcare & Babysitters

Official school education in Spain does not begin until the age of six, but many children start pre-school at three. For working mothers childcare normally means granny or a nursery (*Guardería*). Some are run by the city or institutions such as savings banks, while others are private. They are aimed at mothers in full-time employment, and offer daily care for children from as young as three months. If you are to be in Madrid for a while it's worth making a habit of going to the nearest playground late mornings or after school hours. This is the best way for you and your child to make friends and contacts, and to get recommendations on babysitters or local *Guarderías*.

Many hotels provide babysitting services. Alternately, contact **Nenos**. English-speaking babysitters also sometimes advertise in *Lookout* (*see chapter* **Media**).

La Casa de la Abuela

C/Condes de Torreanaz 11 (574 30 94). Metro O'Donnell/bus 2, 30, 56, 71, C. **Open** 24 hours daily. **Credit** AmEx, DC, MC, V.
Not far from the Retiro, this is a 'children's hotel' where you can leave a child for any length of time from a few hours to several weeks. It's bright and modern, and children are looked after and entertained by fully-trained staff. Prices vary considerably depending on requirements.

Centro Infantil Nenos

C/Uruguay 21 (416 98 22). Metro Colombia/bus 16, 29, 40, 51, 52. **Open** *supervision* 10am-1.30pm, 4- 9pm, daily. **Credit** V.
Nenos is one of several recent initiatives that respond to the need of Spanish families for a reliable place to leave their children while both parents are working, shopping or whatever. It has an indoor play area (with bouncy castles and pools with plastic balls) and a range of related services, as well as a bar for parents. You can leave your child under experienced supervision. Payment is by the hour and works out cheaper if you buy a *bono* or season ticket for ten hours. The atmosphere is pleasant, and it's used a lot by resident English-speakers. Nenos also offers a list of reliable babysitters, including some English-speaking ones.

Dinopeppino

C/Mártires de Alcalá 4 (559 61 21). Metro Ventura Rodríguez/bus 1, 2, 21, 44, C. **Open** *supervision* 4- 8.30pm Mon-Fri; 11.30am-8.30pm Sat, Sun, public holidays; Closed July, Aug. **No credit cards.**
Offers a similar drop-off service to Nenos but with a more limited timetable. It does not have a babysitting service.

St George's Church

British Embassy Church of Saint George, C/Hermosilla 43 (576 51 09). Metro Serrano/bus 1, 9, 19, 51, 74.
A meeting point for Madrid's extensive English-speaking community. A playgroup meets on Wednesdays and Fridays at 10am. Also a good place to arrange babysitting.

Gay Madrid

Madrid's thriving gay scene has created its own place in city life, summer and winter.

Madrid's gay scene burst into life, like so many things in the city, with the explosion of energy associated with the *Movida* at the end of the seventies. Indeed, since many central *Movida* figures and no less than Pedro Almodóvar himself are gay, the gay community could be said to have been one of the most important elements in the whole thing. As Madrid after dark offered a rapidly increasing number of choices, the general growth in the number of clubs, bars and discos was matched by a similar boom in gay venues. And so, despite the fact that the scene hasn't been going for very long, there is a fair number of places to choose from.

Chueca is the heart of gay Madrid and the place where you'll find most gay night-spots, although there are a few other venues dotted about the city. The gay community's move into Chueca has played a major part in reviving the atmosphere of the area, which a few years ago had more of a reputation as a run-down district with serious drugs and crime problems.

The genteel **Café Figueroa**.

The style of the gay social round is pretty similar to the general pattern of Madrid nightlife (*see* chapter **Nightlife**). The *marcha* – untranslatable, but roughly meaning energy, activity, movement – really begins when many other Europeans are already calling it a night, and people hop from bar to bar and bar to club through the night. Gays perhaps even more than other Madrileños are great lovers of going to as many places as possible in one night. Hence, it's much easier if places are close together, although people are not averse to hopping in a car to check out somewhere else away from the main round, which is why there are often traffic snarl-ups at 4am. With such an emphasis on bar-hopping, the scene can be pretty cruisey. However, in the last few years a more varied range of gay bars and clubs has opened up, making it easier to find different, more relaxed atmospheres when you want to.

DISCRIMINATION, OR THE LACK OF IT

Spain may still be associated in the minds of many people outside the country with a very traditional, repressive Catholicism, but in fact the atmosphere of most of the country today, especially regarding sexual behaviour, is extremely liberal. Most modern Spaniards are very uncensorious, at least in practice – as in France or Italy, the general attitude is 'each to his own'. Towards gays, a common reaction among the non-gay public is more curious than disapproving. As in other countries, well-known gays are very prominent in the media and arts worlds, and flamboyant drag stars, while not quite the national obsession they are in Italy, are still fairly integrated in mainstream entertainment.

Along with other Mediterranean countries, Spain has no tradition of legal discrimination against gay people either, except for during the Franco Dictatorship. On a street level, gay men may still come across a few throwbacks who are rigidly intolerant, and potentially violent, towards them, but they are a fairly rare exception. How people might react to a gay person within their own family is, as everywhere, a more complicated question, but the general attitude of Spaniards towards the thriving, growing gay movement is one of acceptance. This public attitude has allowed the Madrid gay scene to develop with an open, relaxed and easy style.

The magazine *Mensual* is the best local guide to all aspects of gay life in Madrid and to gay bars, clubs and discos. It's published monthly and is available from most city-centre newsstands. For the lesbian scene in Madrid, *see chapter* **Women's Madrid**. For a list of bars, restaurants, shops and other facilities in each area, *see page* 264 **Area Index**.

Bars & Clubs

Despite increasing restrictions imposed by the Madrid city council Spain as a whole still has very lax legislation on where and when drinks may be served, and the size they should be. The closing times of many bars have been moving earlier, towards 3am, but there are still plenty of gay venues open later. Equally, drink measures are determined only by the eye of the barman and are usually pretty large – if you get on well with him you'll usually get more too.

Below we list some of Madrid's most popular gay venues, but more are opening and closing all the time, and it's always a good idea to check the magazine *Mensual* – or indeed just look around Chueca – for the new arrivals. Some of the places listed here are simply bars, while others are *discobares* with a dance floor, but no admission charge. For more information on night-time habits in general in Madrid, as well as some more clubs, *see chapter* **Nightlife**.

Black & White
C/Libertad 34 (531 11 41). Metro Chueca/bus 3, 40, 149. **Open** 8pm-5am daily.
Transformed from its former incarnation as a rent boy pick-up joint, this club has now become very popular with a different crowd. From Monday 'till Friday it hosts colourful drag shows, as well as the best strip-tease acts in town, and there are theme parties too on some nights. The disco downstairs attracts all types and ages. Drinks are reasonably priced.

Bajo Cuerda
C/Benito Pérez Galdós 8 (523 19 01). Metro Chueca/bus 3, 40, 149. **Open** 8.30pm-3am daily.
A small, intimate drinking bar patronised mainly by an older clientèle. Again, drink prices are user-friendly.

Café Figueroa
C/Augusto Figueroa 17 (521 16 73). Metro Chueca/bus 3, 40, 149. **Open** 5pm-2am daily.
The only gay venue in Madrid that's also an old-style, traditional café, ideal for chatting with friends over coffee, reading the papers or practising your Spanish with the friendly waiters. There's a pool table upstairs, and it's long been a favourite place to start off on a night on the town. Women are welcome too.

Summer Cruising

Like other aspects of Madrid life, the gay scene changes greatly with the summer heat. As the days become less and less conducive to staying amid the city streets and more and more suited to taking it easy in the sun, gay Madrileños spend their spare time in the parks, swimming-pools and café *terrazas*, and gays flock to the city from all around Spain to take full advantage of the situation. Some of the most popular areas to hang out in are the **Casa de Campo**, the **Retiro** and the **Parque del Oeste**.

The Casa de Campo is one of the prime sites for gay encounters. As well as its zoo, amusement park and exhibition centre, it offers the most important swimming pool in town, right opposite the Lago Metro station. There are three different swimming pools, but it's easy to spot the one where the gay crowd gathers. Gays in Madrid, since the city is so far from the coast and a real beach, like to spend the summer days sunbathing at swimming pools or in parks, in order to cultivate a tan to show off in the clubs (unfortunately, the more tanned you are, the more success you'll have). For full information on the Casa de Campo swimming pool, *see chapter* **Sport & Fitness**.

There is another recognised gay cruising spot much further into the Casa de Campo, near the end of the **Teleférico** cable-car line from the Parque del Oeste (*see chapter* **Sightseeing**). The main meeting-point is to the right coming out of the Teleférico station. A word of warning is necessary here. The Casa de Campo is a huge, rambling park, and some way from the city centre, and this is one place where gays have occasionally been attacked. To be totally safe, when you go to areas of the park away from the main attractions, go with friends.

Madrid's main park, the Retiro, may be much smaller than the Casa de Campo, but still offers lots to do, and is a good place for encounters. There are fortune-tellers alongside the lake, and a great number of cultural events taking place. As for cruising, the main area is next to La Chopera sports centre – where you can play tennis or football, or do some bodybuilding. The Retiro is safer than the Casa de Campo, but it's still a large area and you should exercise vigilance. The Parque del Oeste, meanwhile, is perhaps the prettiest of Madrid's parks, and just a great place in which to while away an afternoon. For general information on all parks, *see chapter* **Sightseeing**.

Café Galdós

C/Benito Pérez Galdós 1 (532 12 86). Metro Chueca/bus 3, 40, 149. **Open** 7pm-1am daily.
Another excellent meeting point. This new café attracts a young, gossipy crowd, which gathers here in the early evening before moving on to other clubs and bars in the area.

Leather Bar

C/ Pelayo 42 (308 14 62). Metro Chueca/bus 3, 40 ,149. **Open** 8pm-3am daily.
Despite the name this popular club doesn't cater for a leather crowd, but it is very cruisey. There's a bar and a dance floor downstairs, connected by a maze of stairways, as well as a darkroom. Drinks are cheap.

Montera 33

C/Montera 33 (523 03 61). Metro Sol, Gran Vía/bus all routes to Puerta del Sol. **Open** 8pm-4.30am daily.
Not wholly a gay bar but nevertheless still recognised as one of the latest additions to Madrid's gay scene. Three cellar bars with a boisterous atmosphere (especially at weekends) attract a young, trendy crowd. It's fun, and women are welcome. The music varies but it can be excellent, although drinks are pricey. *See also chapter* **Nightlife**.

Rick's

C/Clavel 8 (no phone). Metro Gran Vía/bus 1, 3, 40, 44, 149. **Open** 10pm-5am daily.
A stylish Casablanca-themed bar that's considered the best in town. The punters are young, good-looking and friendly, the up-to-the-minute music is truly excellent, and women are more than welcome. Saturday nights can be highly recommended. There's a quiet area at the back.

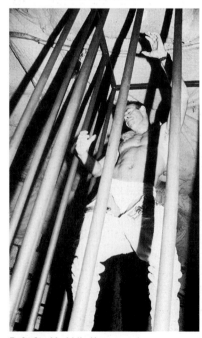

Refugio: *Madrid's Heaven.*

Rimmel

C/Luis de Góngora 2 (525 55 90). Metro Chueca/bus 3, 40, 149. **Open** 8pm-3am.
Small and a little seedy but always busy, this place is noted for two gigantic screens showing MTV clips and porno films. There's a darkroom too.

Troyans

C/ Pelayo 4 (521 73 51). Metro Chueca/bus 3, 40, 149. **Open** 9.30pm-3am Mon-Thur, Sun; 9.30pm-4am Fri, Sat.
The only bar in Madrid that hosts private leather parties, on the first Thursday of every month. Other features include cages, poppers and a darkroom. Not recommended for the shy and retiring, and strictly men-only.

Discos

Ales

C/Veneras 2 (548 20 22). Metro Santo Domingo/bus 44, 133, 147. **Open** midnight-6am daily. **Admission** 1,200-1,500ptas incl one drink.
Although its day as Madrid's busiest and most popular gay disco is over, Ales still attracts a cosmopolitan crowd of all ages. There are bars (with good food) and dance floors on three levels, plus a darkroom. There's rave music on the lower level, while upstairs you can camp it up dancing *sevillanas*, and on Sundays it also offers cabaret. It's normally best between 3am and 5am.

Cruising

C/Benito Pérez Galdós 5 (521 51 43). Metro Chueca/bus 3, 40, 149. **Open** midnight-6am daily. **Admission** 1,200-1,500ptas incl one drink.
Busiest at the weekends this aptly-named men-only, slightly shabby disco is popular with all ages. Attractions include bars on two levels, darkrooms and a video room.

Refugio

C/Doctor Cortezo 1 (308 14 62). Metro Tirso de Molina/bus 6, 26, 32, 57. **Open** midnight-5am daily. **Admission** 1,200-1,500ptas incl one drink.
Madrid's answer to London's Heaven or new York's Sound Factory – recently opened, this fresh, spacious club is one of the liveliest gay venues in town. A wacky range of theme parties are held during the week. Drinks, however, are a bit expensive. Note that another of its original features is that it's actually some way from Chueca.

Strong Centre

C/Trujillos 7 (548 20 22). Metro Santo Domingo/bus 44, 133, 147. **Open** midnight-6am daily. **Admission** 1,200-1,500ptas with a drink.
With the same owner as **Ales**, this club is big and racy – the darkroom takes up most of the club. It's popular with a young crowd, and a bit expensive.

Saunas

Comendadoras

Plaza de Comendadoras 9 (532 88 92). Metro Noviciado, San Bernardo/bus 21, 147. **Open** 24 hours daily. **Admission** 1,500ptas; 1,000ptas under-24s.
Considered the best sauna in town, Comendadoras has a friendly and relaxing environment.

Príncipe

C/Príncipe 15 (429 39 49). Metro Sevilla, Sol/bus all routes to Puerta del Sol. **Open** 3pm-midnight Mon-Thur, Sun; 3pm-2am Fri, Sat. **Admission** 1,250ptas; ten-bath ticket 8,000ptas.
A welcoming and popular venue just off the Plaza Santa Ana.

*People often go to **Rimmel** to keep up with the latest movies. See page 220.*

Bookshops

Berkana

C/La Palma39 (532 13 93). Metro Noviciado/bus 40, 147, 149. **Open** 10.30am-2.30pm, 4-8pm, Mon-Fri; noon-2pm, 5.30-8.30pm, Sat. **Credit** V.

Madrid's only specifically-gay bookshop is run by a lesbian, Mili Hernández, but caters equally to men and women and serves as a handy meeting and information point for the whole of the gay community. Among its extensive stock there's a good range of English and other foreign-language books, and the staff are very helpful. They also have a varied stock of gadgets and knick-knacks. *See also chapter* **Women's Madrid**.

Contacts & Information

Club Gay Service

(542 30 41). **Open** 10am-2pm, 5-8.30pm, Mon-Fri.
A contacts, introductions and information service.

COGAM (Coordinadora Gay de Madrid)

C/Carretas 12 (522 45 17/522 00 70). Metro Sol/bus all routes to Puerta del Sol. **Open** 5-9pm daily.
An umbrella organisation that campaigns on gay-rights issues and also offers health information, a library and a variety of meetings, discussions and social activities. *See also chapter* **Women's Madrid**.

Gay Inform

(523 00 70). **Open** 5-9pm Mon-Fri.
An information phoneline with details of future events on the gay scene in Madrid, and which also provides health advice and information. Some of the volunteer staff speak English, but you may have to ring back to catch them.

La Radical Gay

C/Hortaleza 19, 1º, 28004 Madrid; PO. Box 8294, 28080 Madrid (no phone). Metro Gran Vía, Chueca/bus 1, 3, 40, 74, 149.
As the name indicates, the most radical of the gay campaigning organisations in Madrid.

AIDS (SIDA)

Spain has had one of the highest AIDS rates in Europe, much of it related to the country's serious hard drugs problem rather than to sex. Even so, gay organisations have still played a major part in promoting AIDS awareness and organising effective prevention campaigns. The same groups have also given a great deal of support to gay hard drugusers. Thanks to this swift reaction the incidence of AIDS among the gay community, while still obviously a problem, has partly been contained. There is now a higher percentage of new Sida cases among heterosexuals than homosexuals.

A further demonstration of Spanish tolerance is the willingness of gay organisations to help with information or the distribution of condoms to interested parties, gay or straight. This has, as one might expect, encountered the opposition of the Catholic church, which has in turn sparked off a further counter-campaign organised by gay associations, other radical groups and the Gay magazine *Mensual*. Gay Christians were urged publicly to resign from the Church, and about 15,000 did so – one of the most significant signs that homosexuals from all over the country are now fighting for their rights.

For more information on all forms of healthcare, *see chapter* **Survival**.

Comité Anti-SIDA de Madrid

C/del Barco 10 (531 10 19). Metro Gran Vía/bus all routes to Gran Vía. **Open** 10am-2pm, 4-8pm, Mon-Fri.
The main local AIDS campaigning and support organisation, and the place to go for support and advice on HIV and AIDS. It's run by volunteers who may not necessarily speak English, but will normally be able to find somebody who can.

Students

Essential pointers that will help you get organised in the educational jungle.

There are over 250,000 students in Madrid, studying every kind of subject. One thing they have in common is a feeling of discontent about the state of public education. In 1993 Madrid's Universidad Complutense, the largest university in Spain, was like others throughout the country the scene of student riots and demonstrations which succeeded in dissuading the government from a planned rise in enrolment fees. The normal cost of college education has therefore stayed relatively low, but many students feel that, given what they get in return, nobody could justify it being any higher. The Spanish government pumps large amounts of money into the public universities, but even so the quality of facilities and teaching remains poor.

The main cause for concern among both students and teachers is overcrowding. Traditionally in Spain, as in many other European countries, admission to university has been available by right to everyone who has completed secondary school and a series of exams. Consequently, as secondary education has improved, student numbers in higher education have grown. Overcrowding in the classes leads to a lack of personal contact between teachers and students, and a general loss of interest on both sides. Attendance levels are notoriously low, and drop-out rates high.

One official response to overcrowding has been to introduce entrance requirements in terms of exam grades for those faculties and courses in highest demand (the same requirements do not, though, apply for foreign students). Because of this, many Spanish students are now turned away from their first-preference courses and obliged to enrol in subjects that have very little or nothing to do with their interests, or ultimate ambitions. This, naturally enough, only further increases their dissatisfaction.

DEGREES & ENROLMENT

In the Spanish system, as it existed until recently, admission to different faculties was only restricted according to the type of *Selectividad* examination (arts- or science-based) taken at the end of secondary school. Most university courses last for a minimum of five years, running from October to June. The normal degree awarded upon completing university studies is the *Licenciatura*, although there are some specific subjects for which only three years study is required, leading to a *Diplomatura*.

The Spanish state universities are, however, currently in the process of adopting a pan-European system of credits, qualifications and semesters. The new scheme is gradually being implemented, and posing many problems for students who have been caught astride the transition. For students from abroad the new system will, once it is complete, alleviate the never-ending process of convalidation of foreign degrees. Foreign students who are not citizens of a European Union country will need a visa to study in Spain.

Information & Agencies

Instituto de la Juventud

C/Ortega y Gasset 71 (347 77 00). Metro Lista/bus 1, 26, 61, 74. **Open** 9am-2pm, 4-6pm, Mon-Fri.
This official youth information centre issues International Student (ISIC), youth hostel (IYHF) and youth travel (FYTO) cards. The Institute also provides free information on courses, educational exchanges and a wide range of activities involving students and youth in general, as well as advice services. Due to problems with short-term lettings the accommodation service can only assist people intending to be resident in Madrid for at least two years, but there is a noticeboard where you can look for flat shares. There is also a branch of the student travel service, **TIVE** (*see chapter* **Services**), which is open only in the mornings.

Universities, Public & Private

Public

Madrid did not have a university of its own until the last century, but has made up for this lack with massive expansion in the last fifty years. Today the Madrid University District consists of five main campuses and several other centres scattered throughout the city, the suburbs and the surrounding province. Only the largest are listed here.

Universidad de Alcalá de Henares

Plaza San Diego, Alcalá de Henares, 28071 Madrid (889 04 00). Train Cercanías lines C-2, C-7. **Open** *Rectorado (administration)* 9am-2pm Mon-Fri.
The university dominates the historic town of Alcalá de Henares, 31km (19 miles) east of Madrid. Known to the Romans as *Complutum*, it was a major centre of learning when Madrid was still only one of several potential Spanish capitals, and is also famous as the birthplace of Cervantes. A college was established in the town by King Sancho IV of Castile in 1293, but it was Queen Isabella's mentor Cardinal Cisneros who founded the university, in 1498. It was the most important of the many colleges founded by him, and a focus of humanist thought, theology and the study of languages throughout the sixteenth century. It was transferred to

The Rectorado, **Universidad de Alcalá.**

Madrid in 1836 to provide the capital with an institution of higher education, but the University of Alcalá was reopened in 1977, since when it has expanded rapidly. Its faculties now spread throughout the town and its outskirts, although the administration is again housed in the original Renaissance-style building. Since Alcalá is a small city, there is naturally less to do than in Madrid, but student life there in many ways has more of an identity than in the capital. *See also* chapter **Trips Out of Town.**

Universidad Autónoma de Madrid
Ciudad Universitaria de Cantoblanco (397 51 00). Carretera de Colmenar Viejo (M607), km 15. Bus 714 from Plaza Castilla/train Cercanías line C-1 to Cantoblanco Univerisdad. **Open** *Rectorado (administration) 9am-2pm, 4-6pm, Mon-Fri.*
Located in the northern outskirts, the Autónoma is easily accessible by train from Atocha or Chamartín. Founded in 1968, it now has 32,000 students. This young institution was the first to bring a breath of fresh air into Madrid's university world, introducing changes in course structures that have resulted in more practical, less drawn-out degree courses. Today, despite its newness, it can compete in prestige as a teaching institution with the Complutense (*below*).

Universidad Complutense
C/Isaac Peral, Ciudad Universitaria (394 12 71/394 33 89). Metro Metropolitano, Ciudad Universitaria/bus A, B, D, F, G, H, I, 62. **Open** *Rectorado (administration) 9am-2pm Mon-Fri.*
The name of Madrid's main university derives from the Roman name for Alcalá de Henares, its original home. When it first moved to Madrid in 1836, the university was housed in the old Jesuit Novitiate on Calle San Bernardo, which proved entirely inadequate as the institution expanded. The *Ciudad Universitaria Complutense,* one of the largest building projects in Madrid this century, was opened in 1928 by King Alfonso XIII. The initial project was still incomplete when it became a major battlefield during the Civil War (*see* chapter **History: Republic & Civil War**) and was severely damaged. However, it was quickly rebuilt by the Franco regime, and expanded into the sprawling, monotonous total-

itarian-style compound we know today. The Complutense is by far the largest campus in Madrid, with 130,000 students, of which 2,600 are from abroad. It offers interesting summer seminars and language courses for foreigners (*see below* **Learning Spanish**).

Private

There are several private teaching institutions in Madrid, with fees that range from 600,000 to one million pesetas per year.

European University
C/Darro 15 (564 49 04). Metro Lima/bus 7, 14, 43, 150. **Open** *administration 8.30am-7.30pm Mon-Fri.*
The Madrid college of a business school with branches in 15 other European cities to which students can transfer if they wish to continue their studies there. A four-year Bachelor's in Business Administration and a one-year MBA are the main courses. The first two years of the BBA can be taken in English or Spanish; the second two years and the MBA are taught only in English. There are around 100 students each year, about half of whom are from outside Spain.

Instituto de Empresa de Madrid
C/Maria de Molina 15 (562 25 60). Metro Avda. de América/bus 12, 29, 52, 73, 114. **Open** *administration 10am-2pm, 4-8pm, Mon-Fri.*
Founded in 1973, this is one of the most prestigious private schools for post-graduate studies in business, commercial law and economics, including the International MBA. The institute has 1,100 students.

Schiller International University
C/Rodríguez San Pedro 10 (446 23 49). Metro San Bernardo/bus 2, 21. **Open** *administration 9.30am-6.30pm Mon-Fri.*
The only foreign university with full international accreditation operating in Madrid, which offers a four-year degree programme specialising in international business, marketing, economics and international relations. A two-year International MBA degree is also available. The Schiller has ten campuses around Europe and the US, and a completely multi-national student body.

Universidad Pontificia Comillas
C/Alberto Aguilera 23 (542 28 00). Metro San Bernardo, Argüelles/bus 2, 21. **Open** *administration 9am-2pm, 4-6pm, Mon-Fri.*
The Comillas, founded in Santander in 1890 by Pope Leo XIII, is one of the most prestigious (and expensive) Catholic teaching institutions in Spain. It specialises in theology, but its degrees in social work, computer science, economics, law and languages are also highly regarded. There are 10,000 students, around 300 of whom are foreigners. The Comillas also offers summer courses in international relations, law and business.

University of Saint Louis, Missouri in Madrid
C/Olivos 21 (554 58 50). Metro Metropolitano, Guzmán el Bueno/bus 2, 44, 132, C, F. **Open** *administration 9am-2pm, 4-6pm, Mon-Fri*
This university offers US degrees in both arts and science subjects. The study programmes begin in Madrid, and degrees are then completed at the University of Saint Louis itself. There are 600 places.

Learning Spanish

A great many foreigners study Spanish in Madrid and the surrounding towns. As well as the specialised language schools, the state universities also offer a range of courses in Spanish language and culture, at much more accessible prices.

Servicio Central de Cursos de Español

C/Trafalgar 32, 1° D, 28010 Madrid (593 19 49/fax 445 69 60). Metro Iglesia/bus 3, 37. **Open** *Mid-Sept-June* 10am-2pm, 4-7pm, *July-mid-Sept* 9am-3pm, Mon-Fri.

A short cut around the difficulties of making contact with colleges in Spain from outside the country is provided by this English-speaking private agency, which provides information on language courses in both private schools and state universities and colleges throughout Spain, and will also handle the formalities of registration. Information is provided free, but if you then register for a course through them there is a charge of 10,000ptas on top of the college's fees. For an additional 25,000ptas they will arrange accommodation in private homes. Most of their business is conducted by mail or fax, and they prefer people wanting to use the service to phone first before visiting the office.

College Courses

Conditions for foreign students on language courses at the state universities are generally much better than those suffered by many Spanish students, although overcrowding still sometimes occurs. Several of these courses can be taken by students from universities and colleges in other European Union countries as part of the EU's Erasmus Programme, for which discretionary grants are available. Applications for Erasmus courses must be made through the student's home university, which should have full information about the programme.

Universidad Complutense

Address for information *Secretaría de Cursos para Extranjeros, Facultad de Filosofía y Letras, Edificio A, Universidad Complutense, Ciudad Universitaria, 28040 Madrid (394 53 25).* **Open** *administration* 9am-2pm, 4-6pm, Mon-Fri.

The Philology Faculty offers a variety of courses for foreign students. Some run for a full academic year, but there are also summer courses. The programmes for higher-level students include Spanish grammar, linguistics, literature and culture. Alternately, if you are starting from scratch or are at more of an intermediate level in language, you can take an intensive course in 'Spanish for foreign students'. These courses usually run for two or three weeks, at a cost of 50,000-70,000ptas. Accommodation is not provided. Spanish courses for foreigners are also offered during the college year, but not in summer, at the **Universidad de Alcalá de Henares** (*see above* **Universities: Public**).

Universidad Autónoma de Madrid

Address for information *Servicio de Idiomas, Universidad Autónoma de Madrid, Pabellón A, Ciudad Universitaria de Cantoblanco, 28049 Madrid (397 46 33).*

The language programmes at the Autónoma are very similar to those offered by the Complutense, with all-year and summer courses, although fees are slightly lower.

Language Schools

Berlitz

Gran Vía 80 (541 61 03). Metro Plaza de España/bus all routes to Plaza de España. **Open** 10am-2pm, 5-8pm, Mon-Fri.

Berlitz offers a variety of Spanish courses at different levels, with super-intensive, intensive and year-long courses.

Escuela Oficial de Idiomas

C/Jesús Maestro (533 58 05). Metro Ríos Rosas/bus 2, 12, 44. **Open** *Sept-June* 10am-1pm, 4-7pm, Mon-Fri.

This government-run institution offers courses in a wide variety of languages, including Spanish for foreigners, during the academic year, but runs no summer courses. Admission is problematic, because the fees here are far lower than at the private schools, and demand is very high. If you plan to stay in Madrid long enough, it might be worth camping out by the school the night before registration, and putting up with the incredible queues. To be admitted you must first apply in early June (pre-enrolment); if you pass this first hurdle, final registration takes place in early September.

Inlingua

C/Arenal 24 (541 32 46). Metro Sol, Opera/bus all routes to Puerta del Sol. **Open** 9am-5.30pm Mon-Fri.

At this centrally-located school you can join a Spanish class any time you like, as some intensive courses run on a weekly basis. You can also find courses that run all year long, as well as summer intensives lasting one month. The only drawback is that this flexibility is reflected in prices that are significantly higher than those of most other private language schools.

International House

C/Zurbano 8 (310 13 14). Metro Alonso Martínez/bus 3, 7, 21. **Open** 8.30am-8.30pm Mon-Fri.

Alongside courses in several other languages, this well-known school offers a wide range of possibilities for those eager to learn Spanish, at all levels and throughout the year. As well as their regular courses they also have particularly cheap short courses where the teachers are themselves students studying for the IH Spanish Teachers' diploma.

Linguarama

C/Orense 34 (555 04 85). Metro Nuevos Ministerios/bus 5, 42, 149, C. **Open** 8am-8pm Mon-Fri.

Linguarama offers Spanish classes on an individual, one-to-one basis, or in groups of no more than five. Prices range from high to even higher, starting at 21,000ptas for a two-week, semi-intensive group class.

Libraries

There is a considerable number of libraries in Madrid, large and small – for a complete list, check the local yellow pages under *Bibliotecas*. Most of them will only ask you to show your passport in order to be admitted. The university libraries can only be used by registered students.

Strangely enough, there are no specialised student bookshops in the Ciudad Universitaria. For second-hand books, Calle Libreros and Cuesta de Moyano are the places to go (*see chapter* **Shopping**).

Ateneo Científico y Literario de Madrid

C/del Prado 21 (429 17 56). Metro Sevilla, Antón Martín/bus 9. **Open** 9am-1am Mon-Fri; 9am-10pm Sat, Sun.

A literary, scientific and philosophical club founded in 1820 (but with a considerable ability for self-rejuvenation), Madrid's Ateneo has been a focal point in the cultural life of the city at many times during its history as a meeting-place for artists, writers and politicians. It also has the second-largest and most valuable library in the country, which has the added advantage of being open when other libraries are closed. If you are planning to stay in Madrid long enough, it will definitely be of interest, if rather expensive, to become a member of the Ateneo. Membership is currently 15,000ptas per year. As well as being able to use the library, members also have free access to cultural events, seminars, talks and many other activities. To join, you will need the signature of two other members of the Ateneo. *See also chapters* **History: The Restoration** *and* **Madrid by Area**.

Biblioteca Nacional
Paseo de Recoletos 20 (575 29 57). Metro Colón/bus all routes to Plaza Colón. **Open** 9am-9pm Mon-Fri; 9am-2pm Sat.
The library, located in a magnificent building next to the **Museo Arqueológico Nacional** (*see chapter* **Museums**), has many historic manuscripts and early editions on permanent display. You will only be allowed to consult the library and take out books on loan if you are carrying out research work and have accreditation from a university or similar institution. *See also chapter* **Sightseeing**.

Biblioteca Pedro Salinas
Glorieta de la Puerta de Toledo. Metro Puerta de Toledo/bus all routes to Puerta de Toledo. **Open** 8.30am-8.45pm Mon-Fri.
In spite of its recent creation, this general reference library holds a large and varied stock of books, and is the most attractive and convenient of Madrid's newly-created public libraries. Books can be taken out on loan by any registered member.

Hemeroteca Municipal
C/Conde Duque 9–11 (588 57 71). Metro Noviciado/Ventura Rodríguez/bus 2, 21, 44, 74, 133, C. **Open** 9am-8pm Mon-Fri; 9am-2pm Sat. Closed Aug.
The city newspaper library, founded in 1918, is one of several institutions now housed in the beautifully-restored **Cuartel Conde-Duque** (*see chapters* **Madrid by Area** *and* **Art Galleries**). It has an exhaustive stock of the press published in Madrid, and many titles from the rest of Spain and further afield. To be admitted you will need a researchers' card, for which you need to provide a photocopy of your passport and two passport-size photos.

Hemeroteca Nacional
C/Magdalena 10 (468 54 99). Metro Tirso de Molina/bus bus 6, 26, 32, 57. **Open** 9am-2pm, 4-9pm, Mon-Fri; 9am-8pm Sat.
The national newspaper library holds collections of virtually every periodical published in Spain over the last 150 years, as well as a comprehensive daily stock of the modern Spanish press and a wide choice of foreign publications. Facilities have recently been thoroughly modernised, and there are no restrictions on access.

The **Biblioteca Nacional**.

Washington Irving Library
C/Marqués de Villamagna 4 (435 69 22). Metro Rubén Darío/bus 5, 45, 27, 150. **Open** 2-6pm Mon-Fri. Closed 15 Aug-1 Sept.
A small English-language library founded in 1970 and run by the US Embassy. Books can be taken out on loan by members, and registration is free of charge.

Student Life
Accommodation

There is no well-defined student district in Madrid, but students do tend to gather around Moncloa, due to its closeness to the Complutense. Even though housing is not particularly cheap here, many of the students who do not still live with their families share large flats in Moncloa. A cheaper but convenient option are the districts around Cuatro Caminos and Tetuán. It's not difficult to find a flat in Madrid if you look at the right time, such as in early-to-mid September before the academic year begins. Depending on the area a room in a flat shared with two others should cost about 30,000 to 50,000ptas a month. The best places to look for flatshares are the noticeboards around the university campuses and at the **Instituto de la Juventud** (*see above* **Information & Agencies**), and in the small-ads magazine *Segundamano* (*see chapter* **Media**). If you use *Segundamano*, be sure to buy it and begin calling by 8am on the day of publication, as flats go very fast.

Another alternative for students with more to spend are the various student residences or *Colegios Mayores*, mostly located near the Ciudad Universitaria. Prices range from 60,000 to 100,000ptas a month, but often include facilities such as full board, laundry and so on. Most *Colegios Mayores* are segregated between men and women. For information on student residences, inquire at the Rectorado at the Complutense.

Socialising

Similarly, there is no one specific district where students generally hang out, although the most-frequented areas are Moncloa, Malasaña and Huertas (*see chapter* **Madrid by Area**). A comprehensive run-through of the bars and restaurants of Madrid, even limited to places commonly used by students, could easily be a guide in itself. Among the perennial student favourites, though, mainly because of their cheapness and friendly atmosphere, are the **Café Comercial** in Bilbao, for chatting or writing up your notes, and, to eat, **Casa Mingo** and the **Palacio de Anglona**. For these and other amenable venues, and notes on bar-crawling habits, *see chapters* **Restaurants**, **Tapas**, **Cafés & Bars** *and* **Nightlife**.

Women's Madrid

Women's rights have improved immensely in recent years, but attitudes often lag behind.

Spanish women, 51 per cent of the population, have come a long way since they were first given the vote by the Republic in 1932. In 1937, during the Civil War, the Republican side in the conflict had one of the first woman ministers in Europe in the shape of the anarchist Federica Montseny, who died in 1993 in exile in Toulouse. After the death of Franco in 1975 the reinstatement of democracy was followed by a series of legal measures oriented towards ending institutionalised discrimination against women. In December 1978, the new Constitution proclaimed the equality of men and women to be one of the main principles of Spain's new judicial order.

Divorce was made legal – after having been tacitly recognised for years, in the form of permanent separation – in 1981, and in 1988 after a long struggle abortion was finally authorised, although only in very specific cases. During the eighties, too, women were officially allowed entry into a whole range of formerly male professions, including the police and the armed forces.

AND NOW...

The number of single-parent families has been increasing rapidly in Spain. Nevertheless, on the whole the nuclear family structure still prevails, and in many households the burden of domestic chores and childcare continues to fall entirely on women, regardless of whether or not they work outside the home.

Women's rights have continued slowly to improve. During 1994 the proceedings of the Spanish Parliament were dominated for months by a heated debate over the complete legalisation of abortion. At time of writing, it seems almost certain that in spite of the protests of anti-abortion groups, Spanish women will soon effectively have the choice of termination without having to travel abroad. Several other issues are still pending. Another question entirely is the gulf that often exists between the various legal rights established in the last fifteen years and what actually happens in practice, particularly regarding discrimination in the workplace.

Spanish women began to celebrate International Women's Day (8 March) for the first time at the end of the seventies. Although in some countries this event is regarded as a second version of Mother's Day, while in others it's virtually ignored, in Spain it has maintained its original political character, since, despite all the improvements, important changes are still to be won. Around 8 March an extensive, week-long programme of events is organised (*see chapter* **Madrid by Season**). Its main theme in 1994 was the encouragement of women's participation in the political arena.

Helplines

There is a helpline for women run by the Ministry of Social Affairs on line *900 19 10 10*. This is a freephone number that operates 24 hours a day. It provides victims of violence with back-up and legal support, and offers free counselling services and legal advice on almost any topic associated with women. For less urgent matters or information, call their direct number *580 36 51* 9am-2pm Mon-Fri. Some staff speak English.

Centro de Acogida de Urgencia para Mujeres del Ayuntamiento

C/O'Donnell 42. (409 20 65). Metro O'Donnell/bus 2, 28, 71. **Open** 24 hours daily.
A city-run women's refuge that provides temporary accommodation for women in emergencies or in cases of domestic violence.

Organisations & Centres

Organisations

Centro de la Mujer

C/Barquillo 44, 1° izq. (319 36 89). Metro Chueca/3, 40, 149. **Open** 4-8pm Mon-Fri; *library* 4-8pm Thur, Fri.
This small women's centre – it occupies one flat – is the meeting point for a wide variety of women's organisations. Feminist and lesbian associations, as well as other groups that are more conventionally political or whose activities are mainly cultural all equally use it as a base. Each group holds periodic meetings and lectures. The Centre receives a subsidy from the Instituto de la Mujer (*see below*), but is basically independent. For more information on their activities, give them a ring.

Dirección General de la Mujer de la Comunidad de Madrid

C/Conde de Peñalver 63 (580 47 00). Metro Lista/bus 26, 61. **Open** 9am-2pm Mon-Fri
One of the branches of the Instituto de la Mujer (*see below*), operating exclusively in Madrid. In its very large and well-equipped centre it offers all sorts of counselling, legal advice and other services to women, as well as information on professional training courses and business and employment opportunities for women, all free of charge. They also produce their own publications.

Instituto de la Mujer

C/Almagro 36 (319 67 25/347 80 00). Metro Alonso Martínez/Rubén Darío/bus 7. **Open** 9am-2pm Mon-Fri.
This government organisation was created in 1988 as a branch of the Ministry of Social Affairs, and acts as an umbrella organisation coordinating and promoting the activities of its various member bodies. Its objective is to promote equality between the sexes as well as a higher involvement of Spanish women in social, economic, political and cultural life. The Institute has its own documentation centre (*C/Caracas 21/347 80 46*; open 9am-2pm Mon-Fri), with reports, videos, information guides, directories (Spanish and international), and all sorts of publications related to women. Some are in languages other than Spanish. The Institute also publishes the magazine *Mujeres* (*see below*).

Publications

The most important non-commercial publication is *Mujeres*. Published by the Instituto de la Mujer, this newsletter covers a wide variety of topics affecting the position of women nationally and internationally. It's available at the Instituto, free of charge. *8 de Marzo* is published by the Dirección General de la Mujer, and features comparative studies, articles of social and cultural interest, and information on the latest programmes undertaken by the Comunidad de Madrid to promote women in work. It's available at any of the organisations mentioned above.

Bookshops

Librería de Mujeres

C/San Cristóbal 17 (521 70 43). Metro Sol/bus all routes to Puerta del Sol. **Open** 10am-2pm, 4-8pm, daily.
Credit V.
The only bookshop entirely for women in Madrid, which has its own publishing house, *Horas y Horas*. There is a very small selection of books in English. The shop has a particularly good stock of Spanish non-sexist children's books.

EU citizens are entitled to health care at local health centres (Centros de Salud) of the Spanish national health service provided they have an E111 form. Any medical treatment (including gynaecology and family planning) requires an appointment with the general physician, who will then re-direct you to a specialist for treatment. This procedure can be time-consuming, and it may be best to go private, at least for gynaecological treatment. For more information on all health services, *see chapter* **Survival**.

One other tip – tampons are expensive in Spain, so it's worth bringing a batch with you.

Clínica Duratón

C/Colegiata 4, 1° izq (429 77 69/429 75 52). Metro Tirso de Molina. **Open** 9.30am-1.30pm, 4.30-8.30pm, Mon-Fri.
A family-planning centre run exclusively by female doctors and assistants. A complete gynaecological check-up costs from 10,000 ptas.

Espacio de Salud entre Nosotras

Avda Alfonso XIII, 114 (519 56 78). Metro Colombia/bus 14, 150. **Open** 10am-1pm Mon-Fri.
A non-profit-making feminist medical association run by doctors and health workers. They offer free advice, counselling, and group-therapy treatment for women coping with depression, menopause, sexual abuse, abortion, and other problems.

There are no entirely women-only bars or restaurants in Madrid, but listed below are a few good places where women alone can relax and feel perfectly comfortable.

Cafés & Bars

La Fídula

C/Huertas 57 (429 29 47). Metro Antón Martín/bus 6, 26, 32, 57. **Open** 7pm-2.30am daily.
Apart from good coffee, this elegant and very comfortable classical music café has a wide selection of cocktails, an appropriate choice of sweet or salty snacks and a special atmosphere. Mostly-young musicians play chamber music at 11.30pm every day, and again at 1am on weekends. *See also chapters* **Nightlife** *and* **Music: Classical & Opera**.

No se lo digas a nadie

C/Ventura de la Vega 11 (429 75 25). Metro Sevilla, Sol/bus all routes to Puerta del Sol. **Open** 9pm-3am daily.
'Don't tell anyone about it' is the name, but then, we just did. Founded by a feminist collective several years ago this bar was initially women-only, but changed its stance a few years ago in favour of an 'open doors' policy. It still attracts a higher proportion of women than many places, and there's a small feminist bookshop at street level. Downstairs there's a disco, which also hosts cabaret nights. *See also chapter* **Nightlife**.

Nuevo Café Barbieri

C/Ave María 45 (527 36 58). Metro Lavapiés/bus 6, 26, 32, 57. **Open** 3pm-2am Mon-Thur; noon-2am Fri, Sun.
A beautiful nineteenth-century baroque-style café near the Plaza de Lavapiés in the heart of old Madrid, with an unusual but relaxed atmosphere. It gets busier in the evenings, naturally, when it's often full of chattering groups, but it's always cosy and friendly even if you're on your own. *See also chapter* **Cafés & Bars.**

Restaurants

CityVip's

C/Princesa 5 (559 48 00) Metro Ventura Rodríguez/bus all routes to Plaza de España. **Open** 9am-1.30am Mon-Thur, Sun; 9am-3am Fri, Sat. **Average** 1,500ptas.
Credit AmEx, DC, MC, V.
There are many VIP's store/restaurants in the city, but none quite like this one, divided into different 'countries'. Walk through the international buffet for the speciality of the day, or have an American hamburger in China or a spaghetti bolognese in Mexico. Like other Vip's it's a little bland, but relaxing, and the comfortable atmosphere is matched by fair prices. It's also handy for the **Renoir** original-language cinemas *(see chapter* **Film**). *See also chapter* **Shopping.**
Air-conditioning.

Da Nicola

Plaza de los Mostenses 12 (542 25 74). Metro Santo Domingo/44, 133, 147. **Lunch served** 1-4pm, **dinner served** 9-midnight, daily. **Average** 1,200ptas. **Credit** V.
At weekends this is a very popular and reasonably priced family restaurant; during the week Da Nicola caters mainly for business folk, although prices remain good. The menu is composed mainly of Italian dishes, although there are some Spanish ones too. The excellent carpaccio and the salads can be recommended.
Air-conditioning.

El Restaurante Vegetariano

C/Marqués de Santa Ana 34 (532 09 27). Metro Noviciado, Tribunal/bus 3, 40, 147, 149. **Lunch served** 1.30-4pm Tue-Sun. **Dinner served** 9-11pm Tue-Sat. Closed Aug. **Average** 1,500ptas. **Credit** V.
A homely little restaurant run by very friendly male staff. As well as the menu being vegetarian all the produce used and wines are organically grown. It's quite small, so it's often worth booking. *See also chapter* **Restaurants.**

Lesbian Madrid

According to the gay umbrella organisation COGAM there are over 400,000 male and female homosexuals in Madrid, in a city of 4 million people. Lesbians tend to be less open about their sexuality than their male counterparts, probably for fear of social rejection. With only a handful of specifically lesbian bars or clubs, the lesbian scene is naturally less self-sufficient than those in many other European cities.

It's only quite recently that the lesbian movement has created its own committees and organisations. Overt social discrimination is mostly overcome, but many lesbians consider this less an achievement on their part than the result of an empty, passive tolerance on the part of society. Attention has lately turned to civil rights issues, and especially the demand that gay couples should enjoy the same legal and social benefits as heterosexual couples. A draft bill has already been submitted to the Ministry of Social Affairs, and is pending approval. *See also chapter* **Gay Madrid.**

Safety

Madrid is as safe/unsafe for women as most other big cities. There are certain areas where you must be particularly careful at night, such as the Plaza de España, Sol and along the Gran Vía. Obviously, too, you should also try to avoid all parks at night. On the other hand, many women notice that on weekend nights especially the number of people about in the main nightlife areas *(see chapter* **Nightlife**) creates a sense of security and makes assaults unlikely. During the day, you should always mind your handbag, as it's an easy prey for *chorizos* (pickpockets and muggers). Keep your bag closed.

If you're fair-skinned, light-haired and travelling alone it's quite possible that you'll be approached by men. Spanish men have a penchant for women who fit this description, and some find it difficult to imagine the idea of a woman travelling alone for the pleasure of it. Many Spanish men like to flirt, so if you're seen alone at a bar or café, it's probable that someone will make some kind of remark to you, although it should be said that nowadays this is much less likely in Spain than in, for example, Italy or Greece. In the great majority of cases this kind of attention is brief or at worst tedious rather than threatening.

In the sixties, when mass tourism first burst in upon Spain, the local film industry made umpteen inane comedies showing how Manolo from the *pueblo* arrived in Benidorm to find a string of blonde *Suecas* (Swedes) waiting for his earthy charm. This attitude is considered utterly embarrassing by a great many Spaniards today, but nevertheless given the degree of encouragement it received it's not surprising if there are still a few such people about. Should any such attention become so persistent as to be disturbing shout assertively *¡Lárgate!* ('Get lost') or *¡Déjame!* ('Leave me alone', literally just 'leave me'), especially in a public place where it will cause maximum embarrassment.

The **Berkana** bookshop is a handy meeting point for lesbians and gay men.

Information & Organisations

Berkana

C/de la Palma 39 (532 13 93). Metro Noviciado/bus 3, 40, 147, 149. **Open** 10.30am-2.30pm, 4-8pm, Mon-Fri; noon-2pm, 5.30-8.30pm, Sat. **Credit** V.

The only gay bookshop in the city, unusually run by a lesbian, Mili Hernández. It's an important meeting point for the gay community, and caters to both men and women. The stock is pretty impressive, with a good selection of books in English, French and some other languages as well as Spanish, and if you can't see what you want, they'll order it for you. As well as books they have many other gadgets, postcards, posters, picture books, condoms for fingers, pendants, earrings and other accoutrements. *See also chapter* **Gay Madrid**.

COGAM (Coordinadora Gay de Madrid)

C/Carretas 12 (522 45 17/522 00 70). Metro Sol/bus all routes to Puerta del Sol. **Open** 5-9pm daily.

This campaigning group, made up of volunteer lesbians and gay men, was responsible for the draft bill on civil rights for homosexual couples. Apart from legal involvement (which includes a free counselling service), COGAM has a health section, a library and a social club that organises a whole range of activities, and also hosts discussion groups, meetings and conferences. Their bi-monthly magazine, *¿Entiendes?*, is available at many newsstands around the centre of Madrid.

CRECUL (Comité Reivindicativo Cultural de Lesbianas)

C/Barquillo 44, 1º izq (319 36 89). Metro Chueca/bus 3, 40, 149. **Open** *information* 8.30-10.30pm Thur, Fri.

Although its name suggests a campaigning organisation, CRECUL is probably more active as a social focus for local lesbians. It holds meetings at the **Centro de la Mujer** in the Calle Barquillo (*see above*) every Friday, starting at 8.30pm. Ring for further information.

Gay Inform

(523 00 70). **Open** 5-9pm daily.

This information phoneline for gay men and women has news of upcoming events on the gay scene in and around Madrid, and can also provide health and other general information. Some of the volunteers speak English, to varying degrees.

Bars, Restaurants & Discos

Ambient

C/San Mateo 21 (no phone). Metro Alonso Martínez/bus 3, 21, 40, 149. **Open** 9pm-5am Tue-Sun.

A relaxed, comfortable bar-pizzeria with nice music, yellow-ochre décor and good pizzas. There's no dance floor, but it occasionally throws parties. There's also a billiard table, and a notice board that's useful for making contacts and finding out about any events coming up.

Medea

C/de la Cabeza 33 (369 29 97). Metro Antón Martín/6, 26, 32, 57. **Open** 11pm-4am Tue-Sun. **Admission** 1,000ptas incl. one drink.

Very loud, dark and thumping, this is the largest lesbian disco in Madrid. It's popular most of all with younger lesbians, with a lot of leather on view, but there's also a fairly wide mix. Men are admitted if accompanied. It also has a pool table, and there are cabaret nights fairly regularly.

La Rosa

C/Tetuán 27 (531 01 85). Metro Sol/bus all routes to Puerta del Sol. **Open** 9pm-3am Wed-Sun. **Admission** 1,000ptas incl. one drink.

A disco that's a little quieter and attracts a slightly older crowd than Medea, although it's still not sedate. It's also a bit more plush-looking. Again, it's open to accompanied men, and a fair few gay men go there. There are cabaret shows every Thursday.

Are you missing something?

Your complete guide to the capital

*ƒ*5 from newsagents

Trips Out of Town

Getting Started

Before you leave Madrid, make sure you're on the right track.

By Bus

Most of the private companies that run inter-city coach services to and from Madrid operate from the **Estación Sur de Autobuses**, C/Canarias 17 (Metro Palos de la Frontera). A single phone line (468 42 00) is supposed to handle all enquiries but it's invariably engaged. It's better to look for the individual company in the Yellow Pages under *Autocares*: ads show the routes, as well as numbers for schedules and reservations. At the station itself there is a computer information system to tell you which companies serve which destinations.

Slightly confusingly most bus services to places within the Comunidad de Madrid and to some nearby towns such as **Alcalá de Henares**, **Chinchón**, **Cuenca**, **El Escorial** and **Segovia** do not use the bus station but run from the separate companies' own depots. Full details are available from tourist offices and, for services within the Comunidad, on map 4 of the series published by the Consorcio de Transportes. Some of the most important are listed below. Local tour companies also operate highly-programmed one-day coach excursions to most of the following destinations. For details, *see chapter* **Sightseeing**.

To Avila (94km): Automóviles Avila *Estación Sur, Window 5 (530 30 92).* One bus daily at 8.30am, arrives 10am. Return at 5.35pm (6.20pm Sun, public holidays). Extra buses on Fridays and days before holidays.
To Chinchón (45km): La Veloz *Avda del Mediterraneo, 19 (409 76 02). Metro Conde de Casal/bus 14, 32, 63, 145.* Departures on the hour 7am-9pm. Last return at 9.30pm.
To Cuenca (165km): Auto-Res *C/Fernandez Shaw, 1 (551 72 00). Metro Conde de Casal/bus 14, 32, 63, 145.* Eight buses daily 6.35am-8pm. Last return at 8pm.
To El Escorial (50km): Autocares Herranz *C/Fernández de los Rios, corner C/Isaac Peral (543 36 45). Metro Moncloa/bus all routes to Moncloa.* Departures every ½-hour, with extra service at peak periods, 7.15am-10pm (7.15am-11pm Sun, public holidays). Last return at 9pm (10pm Sun, public holidays).
To Segovia (90km): La Sepulvedana *Paseo de la Florida 11 (530 48 00). Metro Norte/bus all routes to Estación del Norte.* 11 buses daily 6.30am-10.15pm.
To Salamanca (215km): Auto-Res (*see above*) 12 buses daily Mon-Sat; eight buses Sun, public holidays.
To Toledo (70km): Empresa Galeano Continental *Estación Sur, window 12 (527 29 61).* Departures every ½-hour from 6.30am. Last return at 7.30pm.

By Car

The infamous six roads, numbered in Roman numerals N-I to N-VI, that are the driver's sole nor-

mal way out of Madrid can all be reached from the M-30 ring road (or the outlying M-40, if/when it is completed in 1996). For **El Escorial**, **Segovia**, **Avila** and **Salamanca**, take the N-VI north west, the Carretera de la Coruña. For the **Sepúlveda** area, the N-I (Carretera de Burgos) is the main road. For **Guadalajara** and **Sigüenza**, take the N-II Barcelona road, and for **Cuenca** and **Chinchón**, the N-III towards Valencia. The N-401 to **Toledo** can be reached from the M-30 or the N-IV.

Driving around Madrid can be an appalling experience at times when the whole city decides to go somewhere. On some weekends there are bottlenecks as far as Talavera de la Reina, 120km out on the N-V. For safety and/or your sanity's sake avoid leaving the city on Friday evenings. The real teeth-grinder is the return trip on Sundays: dead in the water from mid-afternoon 'till well past midnight. Immense backups and a record crop of accidents are also dismally predictable on long weekends and at the beginning and end of August.

By Train

Alcalá, **Aranjuez**, **El Escorial** and many towns towards the Guadarrama are on the *Cercanías* local rail network. At the main RENFE (Spanish railways) stations *Cercanías* platforms are signposted separately. Services to other destinations leave from the main-line stations, **Chamartín** and **Atocha**, although many trains also stop in between them at the Nuevos Ministerios and Recoletos *Cercanías* stations. Some towns, especially those on *Cercanías* lines, have frequent rail services; for others, particularly **Segovia**, buses are quicker and more frequent. For more information on rail services, *see chapter* **Getting Around**.

To Avila: 11 trains daily from Chamartin or Atocha 6.40am-7.10pm. Last return at 10.14pm.
To Aranjuez: *Cercanías* line C-3 from Atocha, 14 trains daily. On summer Saturdays, there is a special steam trainservice, *El Tren de la Fresa* (*see chapters* **Children** *and* **Around Madrid**).
To Cuenca: Six trains daily from Atocha 6am-8pm. Last return at 8pm. Journey time about three hours.
To El Escorial: *Cercanías* line C-8a, 18 trains from all stations 5.45am-11.35pm. Last return at 10.17pm.
To Salamanca: Four trains daily from Chamartin 9.30am-7.15pm. Last return at 9.20pm. Journey time 3½ hours. All Salamanca-bound trains pass through Avila, so the two can be combined in one longish overnighter.

Around Madrid

No visit to Madrid is complete without a foray into the surrounding towns, to see architectural wonders or sample finger-licking Castilian cuisine.

Due to Madrid's curious history as a capital, catapulted from obscurity by one man's decision, the city is more recent and less historic – and often less spectacular, simply to look at – than virtually all the towns around it. Ancient cities such as Segovia and Toledo offer a range of unique atmospheres and superb buildings from across the centuries that hectic, hucksterish Madrid can only envy.

If you feel like staying over in one of the outlying towns, Castile is very well supplied with **Paradores**, part of the state-run chain of hotels mostly established in historic buildings. All are very comfortable, many are in fabulous locations, and some are much cheaper than you might expect, at about 10,000ptas for a double room.

Alcalá de Henares

Some 31 kilometres east of Madrid along the N-II Barcelona road lies Alcalá de Henares. Although its name is Arabic in origin (*Al-khala Nahar* was the name the Moors gave their city-fort located here), excavations have shown that this privileged site on the banks of the Henares River has been home to homo sapiens since paleolithic times. Carthaginians, Romans and Visigoths had all settled here before the Moors arrived.

Now a fairly industrial city of 50,000 inhabitants, Alcalá once rivalled Madrid in cultural importance thanks to its university, founded in 1498 by Cardinal Cisneros, Queen Isabella's confessor and mentor and the most influential head the Spanish church ever had. The Universidad Complutense (*Complutum* was the Roman name for the city) was one of the most important in Europe, and the focal point of city life. In any given year up to 12,000 students would fill its benches. One of its greatest achievements was the Polyglot Bible commissioned by Cisneros, a colossal work of scholarship with the text in a range of languages. Cervantes was also born here, in 1547. When the university was moved to Madrid in 1836 the city entered into a decline that was only reversed in the 1960s. It now has a new University, opened in 1977 in an attempt to restore Alcalá's importance and bring back the ambience that made it special for over three centuries.

The effort seems to be paying off, and Alcalá is

Avila's *extraordinary walls. See page 235.*

a lively, interesting place to spend an afternoon and evening. Although many of its religious buildings were destroyed in the Civil War, some are still worth visiting. One, the heavily-reconstructed sixteenth-century **San Justo**, stands on the legendary site where the town's two child saints, San Justo and San Pastor, were supposedly murdered.

However, the **University** buildings and adjacent **Colegios Mayores** are the most popular sights for tourists. Built around three gardens, the University is justly famous for its striking Renaissance façade. The Colegios Mayores, built in the early years of the university as student residences, now house picturesque hotels, restaurants and schools.

After 7pm, the pedestrianised **Calle Mayor** fills with locals taking their evening stroll. Its ancient houses and porticoed passageways conserve the air of times past. On one side of the street is the **Casa Natal de Cervantes**, a reconstruction of the actual house in which the author of *El Quijote* was born. Next door is the **Hospital de Antequera**, a public hospital opened in 1493. Don't miss its typical Castilian patio courtyard, at the back. The **Capilla de San Ildefonso**, which houses the impressive marble tomb of Cisneros (although not his remains) is also of note, as is the fifteenth-century **Capilla de Oidar**. Now used for temporary exhibitions, it contains an exact reproduction, pieced together with the same stones, of the Roman font in which Miguel de Cervantes is said to have been baptised. If you have time, the neo-classical **Casa Consistorial** (Town Hall) is also worth a visit. Inside is a copy of the Polyglot Bible and Cervantes's birth certificate, not to mention various rare editions of *El Quijote*.

Information

Getting there: *by bus* Continental Auto 223 from Avda de América; *by car* N-II/A2, 25 minutes; *by train* Cercanías lines C-2, C-7; at least five trains per hour 5.30am-11pm..
Tourist Office: *Callejón Santa María, 1 (889 2694)*.
Where to eat: Hostería del Estudiante *C/Los Colegios 3 (888 03 30)*. Traditional Castilian food in a fascinating setting, a Golden Age students' hostel; **Reinosa** *C/Goya, 1 (889 00 42)*. A good second choice.
Where to stay: El Bedel *Plaza de San Diego 6 (889 37 00)*. In the centre of the city, but quiet.

El Escorial

Take it as you will: Philip's folly, the forbidding barracks of fanaticism, a megalomaniac's monument to himself. Foreigners have never thought much of this immense monastery-mausoleum, dreamt up by the same King who gave us the Invincible Armada. Any number of writers have seen it virtually as the Inquisition raised in stone. But, if you visit with an open mind, it's hard not to conclude that this is one of the most extraordinary structures ever built by man.

The statistics are staggering: 16 inner courtyards, 1,200 doors, 2,675 windows, 15 miles of passageways and 86 staircases. Its architects Juan Bautista de Toledo and Juan de Herrera built it on a rectangular pattern to represent the gridiron on which the martyr Saint Laurence roasted to death. What makes it so imposing is the hugeness and coldness of all that Guadarrama granite and the frugality with ornamentation that seems so un-Spanish.

Philip II, dour, devout and shy, required a resting place for his father where a community of monks could pray for the eternal repose of his lineage. He also needed somewhere to go to commune privately with God the Father – the two father figures were more than a little mixed up in his mind. Hence, he chose to combine a palace, monastery and royal tomb in one. All but two Spanish sovereigns and their consorts (with one exception, only heir-bearing queens were admitted) lie in the polished jasper, gold and marble mausoleum under the altar of the enormous basilica.

Philip's austerely-furnished private apartments are next to the altar, with a *jalousie* window so he needn't miss Mass when bedridden. Otherwise, he amused himself with his art collection, including a huge El Greco as well as works by Hieronymus Bosch, Titian and the Flemish masters. He could also browse under the colourful barrel-vaulted ceiling of the magnificent library, whose 50,000 volumes are said to rival the Vatican's holdings.

After the Spanish Habsburgs inbred themselves to extinction, their Bourbon successors did not make much use of the Escorial, except for that hunting-mad cuckold, Charles IV. His suite of apartments has recently been closed off to visitors and nobody wants to say for how long – a shame, since they have superb tapestries based on cartoons by Goya and his contemporaries. His father Charles III also added, not far from the monastery, but in complete contrast, the dainty little theatre the **Real Coliseo** (*see chapter* **Theatre**).

The monastery is in the town of **San Lorenzo de El Escorial**, a 2km walk (or bus ride) uphill from the train station, which is located in **El Escorial** proper. The latter town is often overrun by a cult who believe that the Virgin Mary appears on the first Saturday of every month and conveys messages of divine insipidity through her new spokesperson on earth, a 63-year old former char.

For suggested walks in the mountains around El Escorial, *see chapter* **The Sierras**.

Information

Getting there: *by bus* Herranz 661, 664 from Moncloa; *by car* N-VI to Guadarrama, then M600; *by train* Cercanías line C-8a.
Monasterio de San Lorenzo de El Escorial: Open *Apr-Sept* 10am-6pm, *Oct-Mar* 10am-5pm, Tue-Sun.
Admission 500ptas; free Wed for EU citizens.
Where to eat: El Regadero Real *C/del Rey 41 (890 45 13/890 45 47)*. *Closed Mon, Oct-May*. Chef Iñaki Oyárbide learnt his trade at Madrid's celebrated Zalacain, owned by his father. Similar Navarrese-Basque cooking is perceptible in the fish dishes, but Iñaki's starters (with intriguing variations on beans and pulses) and meats (stews and roasts) are firmly anchored in Old Castile.
Fonda Genara *Plaza de las Animas (890 43 57/890 33 30)*. You enter from a concealed street-level arcade. The upstairs dining room is adorned with period furnishings, old playbills and photos from the Real Coliseo.

El Valle de los Caídos

The 'Valley of the Fallen', Franco's vast monument to the dead on his own side in the Spanish Civil War, is 17km from San Lorenzo, back towards Madrid on the Guadarrama road. Opinions differ as to whether Franco had already decided to himself that this should be his own final resting place when he had chain gangs of Republican prisoners labour for a decade to quarry this giant tomb out

Walt Disney eat your heart out: the Alcázar at **Segovia**. *See page 237.*

of the rock. Quite a number died in the process.

Any Republicans thus admitted to the tomb can hardly be pleased at the company they are forced to keep: Franco on the one side and José Antonio Primo de Rivera, the rich boy founder of the Falange, on the other. Nor can they be delighted at finding themselves stuck for eternity in a basilica laden with gargantuan examples of that unadulterated kitsch so dear to the totalitarian mindset, topped by a 500-foot high stone cross, visible for 50km, whose only real purpose is to remind the world of Franco's place in history. The whole thing is so bizarre you can almost forget to dislike it. **El Valle de los Caídos: Open** 10am-6pm Tue-Sun.

Avila

The highest, the coldest corner of Old Castile, capital of a threadbare province consisting of seven parts mountain to one part tufted rock. If not for the medieval walls which make it lovely to look at, who would come to Avila? The saintly among us, presumably, for the city is also famous for the dour piety of its inhabitants.

Had Avila ever known real prosperity we probably would have lost the walls. It hasn't, and there they are, a perfectly preserved mile and a half of them, complete with 22 watchtowers and nine gates, still containing most of the town within them. If you approach from the small modern section, walk straight through and out at the northern end for the superb view from the Salamanca road. The walls can be climbed in one spot only, from the gardens of the **Parador** (*see below*).

The medieval city is stately and elegant, not least the stark, fortified **Cathedral** embedded in the walls. There's no mistaking its twelfth century origins, although the main portal is full-blown Gothic. Another stylistic hybrid, the **Basilica de San Vicente**, rivals the Cathedral in size and grandeur. In contrast, outside the walls is the pure Romanesque church of **San Andrés** and the palatial sixteenth-century **Santo Tomás** monastery, wherein lie the bones of the son Ferdinand and Isabella had hoped would succeed them.

Avila was settled by the knights who had a hand in chucking out the Moors in 1089, the year before work began on the walls, so noble palaces are plentiful. The city is most famous, however, as the home of Saint Teresa, greatest of Spanish mystics, and also a reformer, administrator, brilliant writer and self-assured woman of the Renaissance. Kitschy souvenirs apart, she is remembered with a little exhibit in an annexe to the **San Juan Bautista** church, with manuscripts and relics, including a couple of knuckle bones – but not the mummified arm which Franco kept at his bedside. As any Spaniard can tell you, this is because it made such a wonderful backscratcher.

Information

Getting there: *by bus* Automóviles Avila from Estación Sur; *by car* N-VI to Guadarrama, then A6 (motorway, toll road) and N110; *by train* from Chamartin.
Tourist Office: *Plaza de la Catedral, 4 (920 21 13 87).*
Where to eat: Mesón del Rastro *Plaza del Rastro 1 (920/21 12 18).* The usual Castilian fare plus beef and veal from the Amberes valley, stewed kid and stewed beans. Reliable. **El Molino de la Losa** *Bajada de la Losa 12 (920/20 21 22/21 11 02).* A simulacrum of a seventeenth-century grain mill, on the Salamanca road, on the far bank of the Adaja river. Great if the weather

The monthly magazine that tells you what's happening in Amsterdam.

Time Out
Amsterdam

Available throughout Holland and
at selected newsagents across London.

allows you to sit outside, especially at night when the walls are lit up, and they know how to grill a superior slab of steak. House wine (an exceptional '82 vintage from a mediocre growing zone, Toro) is a bargain.

Where to stay: Palacio de Valderrábanos *Plaza de la Catedral 9 (920/21 10 23)*; **Parador Raimundo de Borgoña** *C/Marqués de Canales 2 (920/21 13 40)*; **Hosteria de Bracamonte** *C/Bracamonte 6 (920 25 12 80)*. Three converted Renaissance palaces, all lavishly endowed with antique furnishings and atmosphere. The smallest, Bracamonte, had the best interior decorator, while the Parador restaurant is one of the select minority deserving a visit in its own right.

Segovia

There is life after dark in Segovia and ways of making a living that do not depend on hustling tourists. It's only slightly less monumentally endowed than Toledo, but has a sense of being a real place instead of a cultural theme park.

The Roman **Aqueduct** comes first, since all approaches to the old city, high on a bluff over the diminished Eresma river, bring you within a few feet of its double-decker span. The unsightly struts and braces around some of its 163 arches were put up just recently, when the whole thing seemed about to collapse due to car exhaust fumes. It was probably built early in the second century AD – no date was recorded by Roman contemporaries. As is evident, the rough-hewn blocks mesh perfectly without benefit of mortar. Generations of guidebooks have dutifully reported that it still carries water, but it hasn't done so for years.

Steps ascend the wall where the Roman span splices into the hilltop, or you can spiral up either of the streets that channel traffic up and down. Buttresses flying brazenly, the **Cathedral** stands to the left of the arcaded Plaza Mayor. It looks like a graceful piece of Gothic, but was actually built in this anachronistic style to replace a predecessor destroyed during the *Comunero* rising of 1521.

Second only to eating yourself silly, the attraction of Segovia is in wandering the narrow streets between the **Plaza Mayor** and the **Alcázar**, especially those on the outer ramparts with views over the vast dry plains of Castile. From the northeastern flank, you can just make out a Romanesque gem, the **Vera Cruz** church, built by the Templars with loot from the Crusades. It's a long walk out there, but well worth a close-up look.

Within the old town, **San Esteban** church is easy to spot because of its striking belltower and segment of cloister. A dozen more churches and convents from the twelfth-sixteenth centuries are likewise within reach. **San Millán** is first-rate Romanesque, with an elaborate carved wooden ceiling, but is often overlooked. As for secular buildings, the **Casa de los Picos**, with waffle-iron studs on its façade, is found amidst the downhill shopping streets south of the Cathedral.

The **Alcázar** juts out where the angles of the city's rocky plinth form a sharp natural prow, its ramparts forming an acute angle over the abyss into which a negligent nursemaid once dropped a fourteenth century heir to the throne of Castile. Its crenellated towers and turrets give it its flamboyantly un-Spanish fairy tale look – a model for all the castles drawn by the Disney organisation – but the attractive bits weren't added until the mid-nineteenth century. The Army (which owns the place) only recently got round to filling its chambers with a rather haphazard selection of weaponry, armour, tapestries and works of art so paying visitors would have something to see.

So much for the scenery. What hordes of cityfolk come to Segovia to do on a weekend, though, is to eat. The city is the capital of Castilian cuisine, and roasts of lamb and suckling pig are the star dishes for Sunday lunch in Segovia's traditional *Mesones*, their walls covered with photos of distinguished former clients. It used to be that Segovia had the best piglets and the surrounding towns – Torrecaballeros, Pedraza and especially Sepúlveda – saw to the lambs, because that's where they grazed. Insatiable demand on the part of daytrippers from Madrid has rendered that particular generalisation obsolete, and also impacted a little on the quality of the cooking at weekends.

Spaniards like their meat crisp on the outside, excruciatingly tender but well-done within (no pink lamb, ever). The best Segovia piglets are *lechones*, nurtured with the milk of barley-fed mothers, and no more than 21 days old when they go into a brick baker's oven. The late Cándido originated the stunt whereby the pork is sliced with the edge of a plate to show how tender it is.

Lamb is also eaten young, and sometimes suckled by two ewes to produce a superior quality meat. As a rule, a good quarter lamb serving two is cooked cavity-side up in a dry earthenware dish rotated according to a secret ritual. Some roasters baste their lamb with pork drippings but eschew herbs, garlic or salt so as not to interfere with the flavour of the smoke from ilex, oak and other fragrant woods. Don't expect *any* vegetables to eat with it; that would be to insult the meat.

If you have a car and have managed to digest your lunch you might want to continue north-east along the N110 to **Pedraza**, a classically beautiful medieval town with castle and arcaded main square that's much favoured by wealthy Madrileños as a weekend retreat.

Information

Getting there: *by bus* La Sepulvedana from Paseo de la Florida 11; *by car* N-VI to Guadarrama, then A6 (motorway, toll road) and N603; alternately, take Puerto de Navacerrada road from Guadarrama (mountain road with many curves); *by train* from Chamartin, very slow. **Tourist Office**: *Plaza Mayor, 10 (921 43 03 28)*. **Where to eat: Cándido** *Plaza Azoguejo 5 (921/45 59 11)*. Where Orson Welles wolfed down a roast piggy entire and called out for more. Touristy and overblown,

Completed 1493, the magnificent Cathedral in **Toledo**. *See page 240.*

the cooking is no better and no worse than elsewhere, only more expensive. Go for the pork, not the lamb. If you can't stand the sight of another roast, try the trout. They have exclusive rights to the catch from one particular stream. **Mesón del Duque** *C/Cervantes 12 (921/43 05 37)*. Castilian cooking with a tendency to fanciness. Only quarter-lambs served. Everyone gets a cholesterol-dissolving slug of brandy on the house. **Restaurante José María** *Cronista Lecea 11 (921/43 44 84)*. Consistently good all round; the best roast lamb in town and the *cochinillo* (suckling pig) is in a dead-heat draw with Cándido's. The house wine, an earthy Ribera del Duero red, is exactly right, as are the prices. **Where to stay: Los Linajes** *C/Dr Velasco 9 (921/43 17 12)*. In a thirteenth-century palace on a steep street edging the knoll: beamed ceilings, antiques in the rooms, cosy bar in the cellar, and a lush patio.

La Granja & Ríofrío

Eleven kilometres from Segovia, back towards Madrid on the N601, lies the royal demesne of **La Granja de San Ildefonso**, the former hunting estate where Philip V ordered a scaled-down version of the palace where he had spent his childhood, Versailles, to remind him of home. His wife Isabella Farnese, equally out of place in Madrid, added many Italianate touches.

The King liked gardens, even though he was told that a French garden would never take in the harsh sierra. And classical statuary by the hundredweight, arranged around splashing fountains. He imported trees and plants from his dominions to 'improve' the mountain pine groves – see the giant California sequoia towering outside the chapel, in semi-tropical company. Nature runs

ahead of the current maintenance budget, which gives the gardens an appealing unkempt edge. Nymphs and goddesses cavort at every shaded corner, but nowadays normally without cascades of spray around them, because of the drought.

The palace itself is notable for its collection of cut-glass chandeliers and for one entire wing displaying some of the choice Spanish and Flemish tapestries chosen from the five linear miles of wall hangings purportedly from the royal collections.

Information

Getting there: by bus from Segovia, or from Madrid, with La Sepulvedana from Paseo de la Florida 11; *by car* N-VI to Collado Villalba, then N601.
La Granja de San Ildefonso: (912/47 00 19): *Palace* **Open** 10am-1.30pm, 3-5pm, Tue-Sat; 10am-2pm Sun, public holidays. **Admission** 350ptas; free Wed for EU citizens. *Gardens* 10am-6pm (8pm in summer) daily. *Fountains* 5.30pm in summer. **Admission** 175ptas. **Where to eat: Restaurante Zaca** *C/Embajadores 6 (921/47 00 87)*. Closed 1-15 Oct. Opens only for lunch, and it's essential to book. Zacarías Peinador and his wife Doña Antonia Cornejo, who has presided in the kitchen since 1940, call it 'home-style' cooking: chunky casseroles, braised beef tongue and more in that line. No roasts, and incredibly generous portions.

Ríofrío

The palace of Riofrio has cause to feel slighted; despite their proximity, the day is just not long enough to see La Granja and move on to this pure-Italian residence, built for Philip V's widow Isabella Farnese in 1754. She built it smack in the middle of the best deer-hunting country near Madrid, so later sovereigns also came to this beau-

The Bourbons' pleasure palace, **Aranjuez**. *See page 240.*

tiful estate to blast away to their hearts' content.

There is a hunting museum in one wing of the palace, but many might be less than enchanted by hundreds of antlered skulls. You can also see the chambers where a heartbroken King Alfonso XII nursed his grief after Mercedes, his bride of a few months, died while still in her teens.

Getting there: Palace is south-west of Segovia, on a side road between the N110 and N603.

Palacio de Ríofrío *(912/47 53 50, ext 309)*: **Open** 10am-1.30pm, 3-5pm, Mon, Wed-Sat; 10am-2pm Sun, public holidays. **Admission** 350ptas; free Wed for EU citizens.

Toledo

It would be fair to say that Toledo is one of the most seen but least understood cities in the world. Almost every day of the year, thousands of tourists fill its streets, making getting around by car almost impossible. Although impressed by the magnificence of it all, these same visitors usually fail to see behind the Imperial City's austere red-brick façade and tourist shops to catch a glimpse of the human side of this crossroads of history.

Toledo, just 70 kilometres south of Madrid (and 35km down the Tagus from Aranjuez), bears little relation to its late-coming neighbours. Madrid did not even exist when Toledo was capital of Visigothic Spain (567-711 AD). Aranjuez was a sleepy village until the Royal Court decided it was a nice place to spend spring in the 1560s. Toledo has been Moslem, Jewish and very Christian, all at the same time. In fact, the fruitful cohabitation

of the three great monotheistic religions in Toledo during the last 300 years of the first millennium AD is often considered unique in the Western world. It was a centre for the *Mozárabes*, Christians who lived under Moslem rule with a semi-arabicised liturgy, and later *Mudéjares*, Moslems who did the reverse after the Christian conquest. It is no exaggeration to say that this rugged mountain ringed by the *Tajo* River holds a key to understanding the Spanish mind.

Which is why it is a shame that most visitors spend only half a day snapping photos, flashing past the El Grecos and haggling over local handicrafts before hopping back on the bus for Madrid. Toledo and its labyrinth of steep, cobbled streets and alleys is magical at dawn or dusk, when the summer's heat lessens and shadows evoke the ghosts of its past. Or under the light Castilian autumn and winter rain. Or when the fragrances of spring suddenly, unexpectedly invade the city one fine April day after four months of winter. At night, when the tourists have gone back to Madrid and the metal grates have come down over shop windows, Toledo's streets brim with Toledanos – yes, people actually live here – enjoying their jewel of a city. Gates and doors, locked tight during the day, swing open, revealing children skipping and women sitting gossiping as they knit. The smell of dinner wafts out of sixteenth-century windows, filling narrow alleys.

Beyond its human side, all of Toledo is an architectural delight, and there is too much to be seen in a day. If you can't spend a night or two at one of its hotels or the **Parador**, this one-day itinerary will give you a taste of this national treasure.

The starting point of any visit must be the **Puerta de Bisagra** (eleventh century), the only Moorish gate remaining in the sun-washed city walls. Before entering, however, visit the museum of the **Fundación Duque de Lerma** on the street behind you as you face the city, just past the Tourist Office. The museum is housed in the Hospital de Tavera, built in 1541. Inside are a chapel containing Cardinal Tavera's tomb, with its elegant funerary-marble statue, Renaissance courtyards and an interesting collection of works by Tintoretto, Zurbarán and, of course, El Greco, just the first you will see in his adopted hometown.

After visiting the museum, enter the city through the Puerta de la Bisagra (really two gates, the Moorish one and one dating from 1550). Walk uphill through the Puerta del Sol, past a ninth-century Mosque, now called **Cristo de la Luz** (normally locked). This leads to the heart of the city, the **Plaza de Zocodover**, a triangular square lined with pleasant cafés and filled with welcome shadey trees, buskers and sundry things for sale. Off the square to the right rises the **Alcázar**, the enormous fort that towers over the city (the museum inside, devoted mainly to the 1936 siege by the Republicans and the heroic Francoist defence, can be skipped if you're in a rush). Nearby is the magnificent Renaissance **Hospital de Santa Cruz**. Its main interior courtyard and staircase are very fine, and the museum inside contains a large collection of works by El Greco and Ribera.

Next, walk down the **Calle del Comercio**, the main street leading off Plaza de Zocodover, to the **Cathedral**. Completed one year after Columbus discovered America, work on it had actually begun 200 years earlier, and a Christian church is said to have been founded here during the first century AD by Saint Eugene, first Bishop of Toledo. Outside, a 91-metre-high tower, flying buttresses and enormous doors catch the eye. Inside, the dark, cavernous space is divided into five naves supported by 88 columns. There are 750 stained-glass windows from the fifteenth and sixteenth centuries. The sacristy (*Sacristía*) houses a spate of fine paintings, while the Treasury (*Tesoro*) holds many remarkable tombs. In the Cathedral sanctuary is a beautifully carved altarpiece on the story of Christ (1504). The choir, however, is perhaps the most outstanding feature of the Cathedral. Around the bottom are scenes of battles against the infidels, painted just three years after the conquest of Granada. The middle tiers show Biblical scenes, and the genealogy of Christ is depicted around the top. Also unforgettable is the *Transparente*, painted by Narciso Tomé and his sons in 1732. It is considered one of the most important of all Baroque conceits, with a magnificently evocative opening

in the roof through which sunlight streams down over swarming cherubs and billowing clouds.

After lunching on regional specialties such as venison, partridge *a la Toledana* or pickled quail, some more sights (mercifully) downhill from the cathedral can be taken in. The first is the medieval church of **Santo Tomé**, with a beautiful *Mudéjar* tower. In the back is a room housing El Greco's oversize masterpiece, *The Burial of Count Orgaz*. The **Casa de El Greco**, on the other side of the small square, is a reconstruction of a Toledo home of the time. This area was once the *Judería*, the Jewish area of the city; close by is the 1366 **Sinagoga del Tránsito**, one of the finest of all works of Jewish-*Mudéjar* architecture, and recently restored. Inside is an interesting museum of Sephardic Jewish culture. On the same street is the **Sinagoga de Santísima María la Blanca**, a Christian church for centuries but now also restored. Finally, the Gothic convent of **San Juan de los Reyes**, further up Calle de los Reyes Católicos and built for Ferdinand and Isabella, should also not be missed.

Information

Getting there: *by bus* Galeano Continental from Estación Sur; *by car* N401; *by train* from Atocha, several trains each hour.
Tourist Office: *Puerta Bisagra (925/22 08 43)*.
Where to eat: **Asador Adolfo** *C/Granada, 6 (925/22 73 21)*; **Venta de Aires** *Circo Romano 25 (925/22 05 45)*. Both serve fine traditional Toledano food.
Where to stay: **Parador Conde de Orgaz** *Paseo de los Cigarrales (925/22 18 50)*. On a hill across the river from the town, with superb views, and lavishly appointed. **Carlos V** *Plaza Horno de los Bizcochos 1 (925/22 21 00)*. A simpler but pleasant alternative.

Aranjuez & Chinchón

Just 45 kilometres south of Madrid, Aranjuez is an oasis in the arid plains of central Spain. Famous for its Royal Palace, asparagus and giant strawberries, it is situated in a wide valley formed by the Jarama and Tajo (Tagus) Rivers. The area has been inhabited since prehistoric times, and has seen Romans and Moors come and go. Aranjuez reached its greatest splendour, however, between the seventeenth and nineteenth centuries, when its palace served as the official spring residence of the Kings and Queens of Spain and their Court.

The Baroque/Classical **Real Palacio** and its gardens have dominated town life for centuries. When the Court came to town in the spring, the village's population of 6,000 increased four-fold. First built for Philip II in the 1560s, the palace was greatly enlarged in the 1770s by Charles III, who had Francesco Sabatini add a further two wings. Despite all this architectural fiddling the palace is surprisingly harmonious. Inside are lavish salons (the Throne Room, the Dress Museum, and the quite extraordinary Porcelain Room) filled with

Sept 10am-7pm, *Sept-April* 10am-6pm, Tue-Sun.
Admission *Palace (guided tours only)* 600ptas; 200ptas students, under-14s, over-65s. *Casita del Labrador & Casa del Marino (guided tours only)* 600ptas; 200ptas students, under-14s, over-65s. All free Wed for EU citizens. *Gardens* free.
Where to eat: La Alegría de la Huerta *Carretera de Madrid 4 (891 29 38).* **Casa Pablo** *C/Almibar 42 (891 14 51).*

Chinchón

A short distance east of Aranjuez and some 45 kilometres out of Madrid lies Chinchón, one of the most picturesque towns in the province. It's a popular weekend get-away for Madrilenos, who fill its typical *Mesones* for lunch and dinner, despite their rather shaky price-quality ratio.

Winters are cold in this part of Castile, and Chinchón is known for its *Anis*, an aniseed spirit especially popular with Spanish workers for getting their motors running on frosty mornings. The place is most famous, though, for its impressive town square, the **Plaza Mayor**. The Plaza, an oft-photographed and unforgettable setting for bullfights during the local fiestas in June and late August, is a natural amphitheatre ringed by three-storey, wooden balcony-lined houses that are centuries old. The whole is overlooked by the impressive façade of the town church, originally the Chapel of the Counts of Chinchón.

Mesones abound in this town of less than 5,000 inhabitants. Prices, menu and quality are similar in all of them, and only the décor and settings change. Several more popular ones have tables out on balconies overlooking the Plaza Mayor. Others have dining rooms lined with *tinajas*, the baked-clay casks formerly used for storing wine, or feature impressive wine cellars (*bodegas*, or *cuevas* as they are called in Chinchón) where you can sip a glass of red wine 10 metres underground.

A good place to sample Anis is at the splendid **Parador**, situated in what used to be a convent. Even teetotallers (and non-hotel guests) will enjoy a walk through its beautiful Moorish-style gardens graced with pomegranates, roses and hidden fountains. The ruins of a medieval castle, last burned by Napoleon's troops and more recently used as an Anis distillery, can be seen (from the outside) on a hill to the west of town.

The Plaza Mayor, **Chinchón.**

priceless treasures. The gardens that inspired Rodrigo's *Concierto de Aranjuez* lie between the palace and the Tagus, and are wonderful places for a stroll. Some sections (the **Jardín de la Isla**, the **Jardín del Príncipe**) were first laid out in the sixteenth century. A 15-year restoration programme has done wonders to return vegetation and fountains to their original splendour.

The **Casita del Labrador** is also well worth a visit. In the middle of the gardens, this Rococo fancy was built in 1803 as an indulgence for silly King Charles IV. Inside are beautiful painted ceilings, tapestry-lined walls, and porcelain and marble floors, some embedded with Roman mosaics brought from Mérida in Extremadura.

Information

Getting there: *by bus* ALSA from Estación Sur; *by car* N-IV; *by train* Cercanías line C-3 from Atocha. For a special treat, especially for families with children, the steam powered Strawberry Train (*Tren de la Fresa*) covers the 45 kilometres at a leisurely pace on summer weekends and holidays (*see chapter* **Children**).
Tourist Office: *(889 26 94).*
Real Palacio de Aranjuez: *(891 07 40).* Open *April-*

Information

Getting there: *by bus* La Veloz 337 from Conde de Casal. Services hourly 6am-9pm, journey time 50 minutes. *by car* N-III or N-IV, then N300.
Where to eat: Mesón La Cerca *C/Cerca 9 (893 55 65);* **Mesón Cuevas del Murcielago** *C/Quiñones, 29 (no phone);* **Mesón Cuevas de Vino** *C/Benito Hortelano 13 (894 02 85);* **Mesón de la Virreina** *Plaza Mayor 28 (894 00 15);* **Venta del Reyes** *Ronda de Mediodia 18 (894 00 37).* Café-bar with gardens that's open every day, but has meals only on weekends.
Where to stay: Parador Nacional de Turismo *C/Generalisimo 1 (894 08 36).*

The Sierras

When the city heat gets too much, within an hour of Madrid you can ski, ride, hang-glide or just walk among fabulous mountain scenery.

There's fun to be had in them thar hills: the **Sierra de Guadarrama**.

When a change is needed from sightseeing, ingesting the local fare or partying, the mountain ranges within a short distance of Madrid offer a perfect alternative, with superb scenery and any number of walks that range from gentle country strolls to routes suited to serious mountaineers. It's also possible to try out a whole variety of outdoor sports (*see page 244* **Out & About**).

All the commonsense rules that apply to mountain walking apply in the sierras. It's advisable to carry a compass and local maps, and to know how to use them. Many of the routes can be tackled in summer in trainers, but light walking boots with good ankle support are a much better option. Summer temperatures are high and the sunlight intense, so high-protection-factor suncream, sunglasses and a sunhat are indispensable. In winter temperatures drop well below freezing and there

can be dangerous icy patches and heavy snowfalls. Only experienced, fully-equipped walkers should attempt the higher walks in winter. Also, the weather in mountain areas is notoriously changeable: check the forecast before you go.

Buy food and water in Madrid or in villages before your walk. Water is scarce for much of the year, so you'll need to carry an adequate supply.

Organised Walking Excursions

Azimut

C/Jardines 3-4, 7° (521 42 84). Metro Gran Via, Sol/bus all routes to Puerta del Sol. **Open** 5-9pm Mon-Fri. **No credit cards**.

A group that organises one- and two-day walking tours many weekends of the year. One-day trips are mostly to the Guadarrama and other mountains within a 60km radius of Madrid. Prices include tour guide, route information, transport, board, lodging and insurance. *Tertulias* are held on Thursday evenings to welcome new walkers to the group.

Haciendo Huella

C/Juan de Dios 9 (542 61 94). Metro Noviciado/bus 147. **Open** 9.30am-3pm, 4-7.30pm, Mon-Fri. **No credit cards**.
The most professional agency of its kind, which organises one-, two-day and longer group walking tours almost every weekend of the year. Again, one-day tours are mostly to the Guadarrama; Gredos normally features in longer trips. Prices include guide, transport, board and lodging (half-pension) and insurance. Routes are well researched and planned and suitable for anyone in reasonable health. Meetings are held every Tuesday to welcome new walkers to the group.

Spain Step By Step

C/Rio Ulla, 24, 3°C (377 47 36). Metro Pueblo Nuevo/bus 38, 109, 201. **Open** 8.30am-6.30pm Mon-Fri (answerphone 6.30pm-8.30am). **No credit cards**.
An English-speaking company offering tailor-made walking tours all over Spain through the year for small accompanied groups, on demand only. Prices include full planning and organisation, private transport, board and lodging, English guide, information on routes, fauna, flora and other points of interest, insurance and any other details requested.

Maps & Information

Phoebe

C/Fernández de los Rios 95 (549 31 07). Metro Moncloa/bus 1, 16, 44, 61, C. **Open** 9.30am-2pm, 4.30-8pm, Mon-Fri. **Credit** V.
For maps and travel guides to Spain.

La Tienda Verde

C/Maudes 23 & 38 (535 38 10/534 32 57/533 07 91). Metro Cuatro Caminos/bus all routes to Cuatro Caminos. **Open** 9.30am-2pm, 4.30-8pm, Mon-Sat. **Credit** A, AmEx, DC, V.
The best general travelbook and map shops in Madrid.

Sierra de Guadarrama

The Sierra de Guadarrama, sometimes just called the Sierra de Madrid, is part of Spain's mountainous central cordillera. It runs from El Escorial in the south-west to Somosierra in the north-east, separating the two Castilian *mesetas*. The Guadarrama has long been appreciated for its abundance of natural springs and the wealth of game inhabiting its extensive forests. Many Madrileños have second homes in the villages of the Sierra, and many others regularly flee the 50km there to enjoy walking, climbing, skiing and a host of other activities away from the big city. Listed here is a selection of some of the best of the many walks possible in the area.

El Escorial

The best place from which to see the monastery of El Escorial (*see chapter* **Around Madrid**), is *La Silla de Felipe II* (Philip II's Chair), a rocky promontory from which the King watched the progress of his great edifice. The same vantage point also provides a splendid view of leafy oak forests and *dehesas*, pastureland with scattered trees. With your back to the main façade of the monastery, head for the Puerto de la Cruz Verde and take the track that traverses the oak woods

at Las Herrerías. Cross the M-505, and immediately get onto the asphalted track that climbs to La Silla. Once you get to the Ermita de la Virgen de Gracia follow the red-and-white striped markings of the GR10 long-distance footpath. This path is intended to run from Valencia to Lisbon, but its condition varies greatly in different areas. The walk to La Silla and back is about 2½ hours long, along easy, shaded tracks.
If you have six or seven hours to spare, you can follow the classic *Cumbres Escurialenses* route. It is typically walked on 10th August, the day of the patron saint, San Lorenzo of El Escorial. Continue north from La Silla to the Collado de Entrecabezas (1,180m, and the only place to pick up drinking water along the way); then follow the run of the spur north and east to the peak of Abantos (1,754m), before dropping down east to El Escorial directly from the Puerto de Malagón. The path is clear, but the walk takes you over five peaks, and therefore involves some effort. For transport and other details on El Escorial, *see chapter* **Around Madrid**.

Puerto de Guadarrama

Walk 2km up the N-VI from Tablada train station (itself 3km from the pass) to km56 and take the well-marked forestry track to the Peña del Arcipreste de Hita (1,527m), a rocky crag declared a 'natural monument' in honour of Juan Ruiz, Archpriest of Hita and author of the *Libro del Buen Amor*, a bawdy fourteenth-century classic. The route takes about three hours, passes Scots pines bent into fantastic shapes by the wind and allows you to orientate yourself with respect to some of the most important villages of the Sierra, Cercedilla, Los Molinos and Guadarrama. The forestry track drops steadily to the station at Los Molinos (1,045m).

Information

Getting there: *by car* N-VI to Puerto de Guadarrama (55km); *by train* from Atocha to Tablada, on Segovia line. **Getting back:** *by bus* Larrea 683 from Los Molinos to Moncloa; *by car* M995 from Los Molinos to N-VI; *by train* **Cercanías** line C-8b from Los Molinos.
Where to eat: Casa Longinos *Puerto de Guadarrama (852 0557).* A restaurant right on the Guadarrama pass.

Cercedilla & Valle de la Fuenfría

From the main station in Cercedilla, follow the M966 to Las Dehesas, until you reach the Casa Cirilo Restaurant. Take the *Calzada Romana* or Roman road (first century AD) towards the Puerto de la Fuenfría (1,796m), past two fine Roman bridges at El Descalzo and Enmedio. The road, well and poorly conserved by turns, climbs several steep slopes to the Puerto itself, three hours' walk away. The oldest pass in the Sierra, it's an important junction of paths. Walk back down the Carretera de La República, the track heading south, to return to Cercedilla station in another two hours.
La Mujer Muerta (The Dead Woman) is the Sierra's most famous silhouette and overlooks La Acebeda, clothed in beautiful pine forests. You can walk it in nine hours or so, although the walk is complicated by having to follow narrow paths and cross spectacular scree slopes. Walk the *Calzada Romana* to the Puerto de la Fuenfria and then head north and west towards the Collado del Montón de Trigo, ascending to the west to La Pinareja (2,193m), the 'head', to finish at the Puerto de Pasapán (1,843m), the 'feet'. On the north side, drop down to the San Rafael-Segovia road (N603) and at km81, turn off to Navas de Riofrio-La Losa station.

Information

Getting there: *by bus* Larrea 684 from Moncloa to Cercedilla; *by car* N-VI to Guadarrama, M622 to Cercedilla, M966 to Puerto de La Fuenfria (56km); *by train* **Cercanías** line C-8b to Cercedilla. **Getting back:** *by car* from km81 on N603 to San Rafael, then N-VI; *by train* Navas de Riofrio-La Losa (Segovia line) to Atocha.

Out & About

For facilities within the city, *see chapter* **Sport & Fitness**.

Air Sports

Federación Aérea Madrileña
Office: *C/Barquillo 19 (521 60 70).*
An umbrella organisation with information on all paragliding, parachuting, ultra-light and flying clubs around Madrid.

Global Aviation Services
Gran Via 55, 7°G (542 71 96/71 32). Metro Gran Via/bus all routes to Gran Via.
Open 9am-6pm Mon-Fri.
Half-hour Sunday morning helicopter excursions, taking in Valmayor reservoir, El Escorial and the Guadarrama. At time of writing the service was being reorganised, and future flights may run from Cuatro Vientos, in south Madrid, or Villanueva del Pardillo, near Las Rozas. The cost is about 12,000 ptas per person. Also helicopter flights to order.

Nueva Aviación
Paseo de la Habana 23, bajos (563 12 74/908 815 035). Metro Lima/bus bus 14, 43, 120, 150.
Open 10am-6pm Mon-Fri.
Balloon excursions lasting two hours, also departing from Villanueva del Pardillo. Prices start at 18,000ptas, including breakfast and a glass of cava. Also para-gliding courses from 35,000ptas including insurance, instruction and equipment hire, or ten-day flying courses (from 65,000ptas).

Fishing & Shooting

Licencias de Caza y Pesca, Dirección General del Medio Ambiente
C/Jorge Juan 39 (435 51 21). Metro Príncipe de Vergara/bus 1, 9, 19, 51, 74.
Open 9.30am-2pm Mon-Fri.
Fishing and shooting licences are issued on the spot. You need to pay the licence fee (about 1,100ptas) into the issuing authority's bank account, details of which are provided, and show the bank payment slip as proof that you have paid, together with your passport. For a shooting permit

you will also need a passport-size photograph, a firearms licence and civil liability insurance (which you can also buy on the spot for 2,100ptas).

Horse Riding

Federación Madrileña de Hípica
C/Alcántara 49, 1°c (319 16 52). Metro Diego de León/bus 1, 74, C.
Open 11am-1.30pm, 6-9pm, Mon-Fri.
The official federation has information on all riding clubs in and around Madrid and an inscription service for those wishing to participate in competitions.

Centro Ecuestre La Espuela
La Adrada, Valle del Tietar (920/867 03 87). Bus Doalid from Estación Sur/by car N-III, then C-501.
Open 9am-9pm Mon-Fri; 11am-2pm, 4.30-9pm, Sat, Sun. **No credit cards**.
If you're looking for a mountain idyll, try trekking around the Sierra de Gredos. Owner Luis Recio speaks some English and offers a weekend in a wooden cabin with at least four hours riding each day and full board for 12,500ptas per person. Riding classes and other leisure facilities including a pool and mountain bikes are also provided.

Los Jarales
Morata de Tajuña (504 07 54). By bus 337, 338 from Conde de Casal/by car N-III, then C300 to km32. **Open** 10.30am-9pm Sat, Sun. **No credit cards**.
Riding school for adults and children offering weekend classes, and trekking on demand for small groups. Courses start at 15,000ptas. Price includes lessons only and insurance. Trekking package includes insurance and trek-leader only, but can be extended to include lunch and other extras if required. Morata de Tajuña is in the countryside south of Madrid, near Chinchón.

Los Palomas
Club Hípico, Carretera de Colmenar Viejo km28.9 (908 728 795/803 31 76). By bus 721, 724, 725, 726 from Plaza de Castilla/by car Carretera de Colmenar Viejo.
Open 10am-2pm, 5-8pm, Tue-Sun. **No credit cards**.
Offers riding courses for all levels, and accompanied one-day to one-week trekking excursions in the Sierra de Madrid.

Mountaineering & Climbing

Club Alpino Español
C/Mayor 6 (532 76 94/522 79 51). Metro Sol/bus all routes to Puerta del Sol.
Open 10.30am-1.30pm Mon-Fri.
Offers climbing courses and organises walking, climbing and mountaineering excursions in the region and throughout Spain, for members only.

Escuela Madrileña de Alta Montaña
C/Apodaca 16, 1° (593 80 74). Metro Tribunal/bus 3, 40, 149. **Open** 10.30am-2pm, 6-9pm, Mon-Thur; 10.30am-2pm Fri.
Offers practical and theoretical climbing and mountaineering classes throughout the year for groups and individuals. Membership of the **Federación Madrileña de**

Montañismo, based at the same office, costs 5,000ptas a year and includes accident insurance, discounts for courses and use of mountain refuges, access to library facilities, discounts on equipment in various sports shops and other benefits. It can also suggest which of the climbing and walking clubs around Madrid to join depending on where you are staying and your walking and mountaineering experience.

Mountain biking

Bicibus

Puerta del Sol 14, 2° (522 45 01). Metro Sol/bus all routes to Puerta del Sol. **Open** 9.30am-1.30pm, 4.30-8pm, Mon-Fri. **Credit** AmEx, MC, V.

Organise one, two-day and longer excursions for small groups throughout the year. Prices for one-day trips start at 3,000ptas and include tour leader, accident insurance, transport and back-up vehicle. Prices for two days start at 7,500ptas and include accommodation and breakfast. One-day trips are mainly to the Guadarrama, longer trips go further afield. Also bike hire in Madrid: 500ptas for one day; 1,500ptas for a weekend.

Bicimanía

C/Jaen 8 (554 25 96). Metro Alvarado/bus 3, 42, 64, 127, 128. **Open** 10.30am-1.30pm, 5-8pm, Mon-Fri. **Credit** AmEx, V.

Organised group excursions throughout the year. Prices start at 1,000ptas, and include tour leader and a snack only.

Sport Karakol

Paseo de las Delicias 53 (539 96 33). Metro Palos de la Frontera/bus 6, 45, 55. **Open** 10.30am-2pm, 5.30-8.30pm, Mon-Fri; 10.30am-2pm Sat. **Credit** AmEx, V.

A large cycle hire shop that organises group excursions throughout the year. Prices start at 6,000ptas and include bike hire, tour leader, accident insurance, transport and back-up vehicle, plus half-board and lodging on longer trips. *See also chapter* **Services**.
Branch: C/Montera 32 (532 90 73).

Skiing

Federación Madrileña de Deportes de Invierno

C/Ayala 44, 2° (549 37 30). Metro Velázquez/bus 1, 74. **Open** 10.30am-1.30pm, 5-8pm, Mon-Fri.

Provides information and leaflets on all Spanish ski resorts. Also offer membership and associated facilities, including insurance to skiiers wishing to compete in local competitions.

ATUDEM Phoneline

(350 20 20).
Recorded information on snow conditions at ski resorts.

Ski resorts

Getting there: **La Pinilla** *by car* N-I to km104, N110 to Cerezo de Arriba, N112 to La Pinilla. **Puerto de Navacerrada**, **Valcotos** and **Valdesquí** *by bus* Larrea 691 from Paseo de la Florida; *by car* N-VI to Collado-Villalba, N601 to Puerto de Navacerrada, M604 to Valcotos, turn right for Valdesquí; *by train* Cercanías line C-8b to Cercedilla, then line C-9 to Navacerrada and Cotos.
La Pinilla *(921/55 03 04)*: 1 telecabin, 3 chairlifts, 8 button lifts; runs: 2 green, 5 blue, 8 red, 1 black; 15km of runs; snow cannons (7½kms); lift passes cost 2,000ptas (half-day) or 3,000ptas.

Puerto de Navacerrada *(852 14 35)*: 5 chairlifts, 3 button lifts; runs: 3 green, 8 blue, 2 red, 2 black; 9km of runs; snow cannons (1½kms); lift passes cost 1,500ptas (half-day) or 2,700ptas.
Valcotos *(435 15 48)*: 2 chairlifts, 5 button lifts; runs: 2 green, 2 blue, 3 red; 5km of runs; lift passes cost 1,300ptas (half-day) or 3,000ptas.
Valdesquí *(852 04 16)*: 3 chairlifts, 7 button lifts; runs: 10 green, 11 blue, 2 red; 18km of runs; lift passes cost 1,400ptas (half-day) or 3,200ptas.

Valcotos has the prettiest setting, and Valdesqui usually has the best snow of the four resorts. There is hotel accommodation only at Puerto de Navacerrada. The lifts get very crowded on Friday afternoons and weekends. These ski stations offer very limited skiing only and are of little interest to intermediate or more advanced skiiers looking for long, testing descents. They are ideal for day trips out of Madrid though, and the pleasure of swinging up the mountainside on a chairlift with the city away to the south is undeniable.

Water Sports

Popular – probably too popular – places for swimming and other water sports around Madrid are the reservoirs along the Alberche river. *See page 246* **Sierra de Gredos**.

Federación Madrileña de Vela

C/Cañaveral 69 (315 04 25). Metro Plaza de Castilla/bus all routes to Plaza Castilla. **Open** 10.30am-1.30pm, 5-8pm, Mon-Fri.

Provides general information on the sailing year and local clubs to join. Membership is obligatory for anyone who wishes to sail competitively in regattas and competitions in the region.

Escuela de Vela Valmayor

Embalse de Valmayor, Carretera de El Escorial a Galapagar, Colmenarejo (725 74 97). Bus Herranz 661 from Moncloa/by car N-VI then Galapagar exit. **Open** 5-8pm Mon-Fri; 5-9pm Sat, Sun. **No credit cards**.

Weekend sailing and windsurfing courses on a reservoir near El Escorial. Teaching, equipment hire and insurance are included, but you have to get yourself there and back.

Miño

C/Conde-Duque 18 (542 11 42). Metro Noviciado/bus 2, 21, 147. **Open** 10.30am-1.30pm, 5-8.30pm, Mon-Fri. **No credit cards**.

Kayak courses and kayak and rafting excursions organised for small groups throughout the year. Prices quoted include an excursion-leader/qualified teacher, equipment hire and insurance. Transport, board and lodging can also be arranged on request, with supplements. White-water trips mainly go to Gredos or to the Upper Tagus in Guadalajara, but trips are run to a great many rivers in the region, including the Durantón gorge (*see chapter* **Further Afield**). More quiet-water activities are also organised in various locations around Madrid.

Sport Natura

C/Martínez Corrochano 18 (501 34 34). Metro Pacífico/bus 8, 10, 24, 37, 56. **Open** 9am-2pm, 4-7pm, Mon-Fri. **No credit cards**.

Windsurfing, sailing, paragliding, caving and rafting classes and group trips are organised throughout the year, mostly in Gredos. Basic prices include teaching, equipment hire and insurance, but not transport and board and lodging.

Puerto de Navacerrada

Los Siete Picos (2,187m) is a magnificent walk along one of the main ridges of the Sierra. The walk along the seven granitic peaks runs west from the Puerto de Navacerrada and looks out over the pine forests of Valsaín, home to much of the area's most characteristic wildlife. You can walk up under the *Telégrafo* (ski) chairlift and skirt the peaks, consisting of huge rocky boulders, following the path until you reach the saddle between the fifth and sixth peaks; once there, dip down and south towards Camorritos. The walk is easy and takes about four hours.

La Cuerda Larga (the Long Cord) runs from the Puerto de Navacerrada to the Puerto de la Morcuera (1,800m), for the most part above 2,000m. There are panoramic views to the south to La Pedriza and its ever-present colony of watchful griffon vultures, and over the pine forests in the Valle de Lozoya to the north. Walk east from Puerto de Navacerrada, past the television masts on Bola del Mundo all the way to La Morcuera. Get down to Miraflores de La Sierra by following the M611 for two km. The whole walk takes seven hours, and the path is clear enough, although hard-going over stretches. Drinking water is very scarce in summer.

Information

Getting there: *by bus* Larrea 691 from Moncloa; *by car* N-VI to Collado Villalba, then M601 to Puerto de Navacerrada (57km); *by train Cercanías* line C-8b to Cercedilla, then line C-9 to Puerto de Navacerrada. **Getting back:** *by bus* from Miraflores de la Sierra, Colmenarejo 725; *by car* from Camorritos, M-966 to Cercedilla, M-600 to Guadarrama, then N-VI; *by train* from Camorritos *Cercanías* line C-9 to Cercedilla, then C-8b, from Miraflores de la Sierra (Burgos line) to Chamartín.

Puerto del Paular de los Cotos

The highest peak in the Sierra de Guadarrama, Peñalara (2,430m), and its cirque and lakes are the only visible vestiges of glacial action. It is easy enough to get to the top in about 2½ hours from the Puerto del Paular de los Cotos, although the climb is quite steep. The complete walk round the cirque can be accomplished in about 6½ hours; the path is tricky only because it is so rocky. Walk up under the Zabala chairlift (or take the lift, if you prefer), pass the Dos Hermanas and continue to the summit, from where you can see right to the southernmost point of the Sierra and north to Lozoya. Walk down to the north past the Risco Claveles, the Laguna de Los Pájaros and the Laguna Grande until you regain the Puerto de Cotos (1,830m).

El Palero, linking the Puerto de Cotos and the Monasterio del Paular (1,159m), is one of the historic paths of the Sierra and predates the construction of all the existing roads. The path is now part of the GR10 (*see above* **El Escorial**) and so is marked in red and white. Set off 500m below the Casa Marcelino (a favourite café of mountaineers and skiiers) by following the La Umbria stream to the M604, only some 800m from the Monastery. Cross the leafy pine forests, refuge of the last roe deer in the Sierra, at the head of the Lozoya valley, and enjoy the numerous streams and springs, all of which drain the Peñalara massif.

Information

Getting there: *by bus* Larrea 691 from Paseo de la Florida; *by car* N-VI to Collado-Villalba, M601 to Puerto de Navacerrada, then M-604 to Puerto de los Cotos. (64km); *by train Cercanías* line C-8b to Cercedilla, then line C-9 to Cotos. **Getting back:** *by bus* from Rascafria La Castellana 194 to Plaza de España; *by car* M611 Rascafria to Soto del Real, M609 to Colmenar Viejo, M607 to Madrid.

Manzanares El Real & La Pedriza

La Pedriza is a particularly wild region, formed almost exclusively of scattered and stacked granitic rock. It surrounds the upper stretches of the Manzanares, which is still clean and fine for swimming at this level. Its inaccessible crags are home to the biggest griffon vulture colony of the Sierra, and are protected as part of the *Parque Regional de la Cuenca Alta del Manzanares*.

The area's outstanding landmark is El Yelmo (1,716m), a dome-shaped rock, visible from the castle of Manzanares El Real. Leave the Plaza Mayor in Manzanares El Real, and head for the river without crossing it. Take the road towards El Tranco just before the bridge and get onto the path behind the small bars. Follow it for three hours to the foot of El Yelmo. You'll need to scramble 10 metres up a wide, easy chimney to get right to the top. The return walk to Manzanares takes about 1½ hours, along a well-marked but boulder-strewn path.

Information

Getting there: *by bus* Colmenarejo 724 from Plaza Castilla to Manzanares El Real; *by car* M607 to Colmenar Viejo, M609 towards Soto del Real, M862 and M-608 to Manzanares El Real (53km)
Where to eat: Casa Marcelino *El Tranco*.

Rascafría

The ancient path linking the Monasterio de El Paular (1,159m) and the palace of **La Granja** (*see chapter* **Around Madrid**), two of the most interesting monuments in the Sierra, runs through Rascafria. Walk west out of the village of Rascafria, past the new schools, and cross the dense oak stands, watching out for wild boar. Climb up to the Puerto del Reventón (2,034m), cross it, and continue downhill on the Segovia side of the Sierra until you reach Scots pines again and the gardens of La Granja. The paths are poorly marked, but the walk is easy. The whole walk takes about five hours.

Information

Getting there: *by bus* La Castellana 194 from Plaza Castilla; *by car* M607 Madrid to Colmenar Viejo, M609 to Soto del Real, M-611 to Rascafria (80km). **Getting back:** *see chapter* **Around Madrid: La Granja & Riofrío**.
Where to eat: Casa Hilaria *Valsaín*.

Sierra de Gredos

The craggy peaks and lush valleys of the Sierra de Gredos – the part of Spain's central cordillera straddling southern Avila – were little known until two decades ago. When roads brought them within an hour's drive from Madrid, though, they were turned into a playground. Now walkers, climbers, campers, mountain-bikers, hang-gliders, fishermen, hunters, swimmers, skiers and city-dwellers simply in search of peace flock in all year round.

Where and how you go will depend on the time of year: in summer, the reservoirs are packed with Madrileños swimming or windsurfing, while above them you can sleep in high mountain refuges or in the open air; in winter, roads into the mountains may be blocked by snow. All year round, too, there is a marked difference in temperatures between the cooler northern and the southern slopes. Locals consider May and June the ideal months.

From Madrid, there are fast approaches from the north (N-VI/A6 and N110) or the south (N-V), or you can cut in through more attractive country roads from El Escorial (*see chapter* **Around Madrid**). There are also buses from Avila. You should spend at least two days in the sierra to make the visit worthwhile, given that the journey from Madrid is about three hours.

The sierra runs, roughly speaking, from the River Alberche in the east to the Aravalle valley in the west (in some guides, the Béjar mountains are also included, as a westerly extension). Within this, it divides naturally into three sections.

In the eastern triangle between **San Martín de Valdeiglesias**, Cebreros and the pass at the **Puerto del Pico**, the land climbs from the mild, leafy Valle del Tietar through bare hills to the first real peaks at the Puerto. Here, a dramatically steep stretch of Roman road drops into the picturesque valley of **Mombeltrán**, with a medieval castle, sixteenth century church and surrounding villages. Two other nearby sights are the mysterious stone **Guisando** bulls, of Roman or Celtiberian origin (near San Martín) and the spectacular stalactites and rock formations of the **Cuevas del Aguila** (at Ramacastañas). Other stop-offs could be the reservoirs of **San Juan** (often very crowded), or, further up the valley, **Burguillo**, prettier and marginally less hectic. There's also the small wine-making town of **Cebreros**.

The heart of the sierra is the massif centred on the **Pico Almanzor**, protected as royal hunting lands (the Coto Real) – a forerunner of today's nature reserve – since 1905. Serious climbing is concentrated around the **Galayar**, a series of spectacular rock needles. For less serious climbers (and walkers), paths lead into the mountains, especially to the spectacular Circo, from both the north and south. Here you find ibex, or mountain goats, gambling around in the peaks, with eagles, vultures and kites circling overhead.

The main bases here are, to the south, **Arenas de San Pedro**, which bulges with tourists at peak times, and 18km further west, **Candeleda**, less picturesque but also less crowded. From either town there are lots of walking possibilities. The northern points of access are the quieter, cooler villages along the River Tormes, such as **Hoyos del Espino**, from which a road cuts right into the mountains. This valley, with its cattle pasture and pine forests along the stony river-bed, is the main area for horse-riding and fishing.

The western flank of the mountains is dominated by the **Tormantos** mountains and, in particular, the **Covacha** peak. To the south runs the valley of **La Vera**, with a string of pretty, half-timbered villages known in Spain for their tobacco-growing and paprika-making. In the autumn, strings of dried peppers hang off the rickety wooden balconies. Attractive spots are Jarandilla, Pasarón, Losar and Cuacos de Yuste, above which stands the monastery of **Yuste**, where Charles V retired from the world to die. It's a humble monument, but as rewarding as the grander model his son Philip II built at El Escorial.

On the north side of these westerly mountains is **El Barco de Avila**, with a fourteenth century church, the castle of **Valdecorneja** (open weekends only) and its Monday morning cattle and food market. However, since El Barco is most famous for the quality of its dried beans (*judías*), many locals come here simply to tuck in at one of the many restaurants.

There are plenty of other possibilities, too, depending on your interests. A short drive to the west is **Hervas**, a marvellously preserved hill village with a Jewish quarter; or the medieval city of **Plasencia**, on the River Jerte, which has a superb double cathedral. At **El Raso**, near Candeleda, there's also a walled Celtic fortress. For wild-flower and forest lovers, the pine woods at **Hoyocasero** and chestnut woods in **El Tiemblo** – both in the easterly section – are unmissable.

Whatever your interests, to make the most of a visit to the region, you need a good map and a detailed guidebook, since local roads are confusing and information for visitors is thin on the ground. To date all such guides are in Spanish only. Especially useful is *Anaya's Ecoguía*, by Rafael Serra, with detailed itineraries for walks. One warning: the sierra can be impossibly crowded at peak weekends and holidays, and it's much better to go mid-week.

Information

Getting there: *by bus* Alvarez 551 from Estación Sur to San Martin de Valdeiglesias, Cebreros and El Tiemblo/Burguillo; more services from Avila; *by car* (main route) N-V to Alcorcón, then C501.

Where to stay and eat:

Mombeltrán: Hostal Albuquerque *Parque de la Soledad (920/38 60 32).* Atmospheric family hostal in the centre of the town, with rooms for 4,000ptas, and an excellent base for the valley. Good basic cooking.

Navarredonda: Parador de Gredos *(920/34 80 48).* The first-ever Parador, a grey stone hunting lodge in a pine forest, opened in 1928 by Alfonso XIII. Good cooking but formal atmosphere. Rooms about 10,000ptas.

Navacepeda de Tormes: Hostal Capra Hispánica *(920/34 81 87).* An informal small hostal, with bar and dining room, and rooms for 5,000ptas. Excellent alternative to the parador.

El Barco de Avila: Hotel Manila *(920 341 222).* Best base for the west. Also organises riding, walking, mountain biking and so on, and has a campsite. **Casa Gamo** *Plaza Campillo 12 (920/34 00 85).* Of the town's clutch of restaurants offering good home cooking and the local beans as a speciality, this is reliable.

Losar de la Vera: Carlos V *C/Extremadura 45 (927/57 06 36).* Excellent Castilian cooking and mountain views.

Jarandilla de la Vera: Parador Carlos V *(927/56 01 17).* Rooms overlook the beautiful Renaissance courtyard of this former castle of the counts of Oropesa. Doubles cost about 10,000ptas.

Further Afield

Take a little more time to explore the countryside and ancient villages of Castile, or shoot down to Seville on a high-tech puffer.

Day trips may be enough – if often pretty rushed – to take a look at some of the famous towns near Madrid, but the city is also surrounded by many more historic towns, a little further away, that are much better appreciated with a stopover. There is, too, the Castilian countryside, still remote and often apparently timeless, with extraordinary scenery and villages that can combine Roman, Moorish and the Baroque in one stretch of wall.

Sepúlveda, Riaza, the Durantón

Immediately north of the Puerto de Somosierra the Castilian plains open up into the flat expanse of the *meseta*, with historic towns and villages dotted around against a patchwork of wheat-fields and rusty-red soil, beneath towering, concave skies. The best jumping-off points for exploring are **Riaza** and **Ayllón**, 1½ hours drive north of Madrid.

At the hub of both small towns are porticoed Castilian plazas. Riaza's is round and houses several restaurants, a baker and butcher. On the hill above is the Ermita de Hontanares, with magnificent views over five provinces. This is a great spot for a picnic, or even sleeping out in summer.

Ayllón has little to visit, but you can stroll round its well-preserved old centre entered through a Gothic archway. The façades of the **Palacio de Contreras**, its churches, convents and private houses all date from between the fifteenth and the seventeenth centuries. You also get a fine view from the town's medieval watch-tower on the ridge above, where vultures wheel in the skies.

The best-known town in the region is **Sepúlveda**, a gem of early Romanesque architecture perched on a spur above dramatic river gorges. A good starting point is the church of **Santiago**, near the main plaza, now converted into an information centre (open 10am-2pm, 4-7pm). It gives a rundown on the famous eleventh-century *fuero*, or municipal charter, kept in the town hall, as well as the town's history and its half-dozen main churches. Most are open only during mass, but **Nuestra Señora Virgen de la Peña**, perched over the gorge at the end of town, is always open, and well worth seeing.

From here you can enter the **Hoces de Durantón**, a natural park with lovely walking areas, eagles, superb Romanesque churches at

Durantón, the picturesquely sited **San Frutós** and truly magnificent gorge landscapes. The local information centre has guides and other details.

Less well-known but equally worth visiting is **Tiermes**, sometimes called the Spanish Pompeii, half an hour's drive north-east from Ayllón. This spectacularly-sited Celtiberian and Roman settlement, built into an outcrop overlooking a plain, has been inhabited for 40 centuries. It has dramatic gateways carved into the rock, two-storey cave-flats, a running water system in the cliff face, a Celtic necropolis, the ruins of a Roman fortress, taverns, a forum and Romanesque hermitage. Much remains to be excavated. Next to it is a good museum and excellent bar-restaurant, the Venta de Tiermes.

There are other possibilities too. **Maderuelo**, piled on top of a hill, is reached by taking the C114 north-west from Ayllón (you can then go on across country to Sepulveda). Perched above the Linares de Arroyo reservoir, it has a fine small church which retains the imprint of an earlier Mosque, and Baroque plasterwork against the *Mudéjar* brick. Fine craftsmen work here – to order and at a price – in leather and wood.

Another option is to take the C114 east from Ayllón through old *meseta* landscape and crumbling villages. The first, **Santibáñez**, huddled close to the river, is full of character. Further on, at **Campisábalos**, is the church of San Bartolomé, a small masterpiece of pure Romanesque (ask the Sacristan for the key). You can link up from there with Tiermes via a dirt-track, or continue on the C114 to reach Atienza and Siguenza (*see below*).

Information

Getting there: It is very difficult to explore this area without your own transport. *By bus* Continental Auto from C/Alenza 20 (Metro Cuatro Caminos: tel 533 04 00) to Riaza (two buses daily); more services from Segovia. *By car* N-I to Cerezo de Abajo, then N110 to Riaza and Ayllón or C112 to Sepúlveda.

Where to stay and eat:

Ayllón: Hostal-Restaurante Vellosillo *Avda Reconquista (911/55 30 62)*. Basic hostal, can be noisy, with a good-value restaurant. Double room 3,500ptas.

Montejo de Tiermes: La Venta de Tiermes *(908/43 80 57)*. An excellent inn with wood-grilled lamb and rabbit, plus some more modern and slightly more sophisticated dishes such as marinated salmon. Open daily July-early Sept; Sat, Sun only rest of the year.

Riaza: Hotel-Restaurante La Trucha *Plaza Mayor (no phone)*. Castilian country cooking – wood-roasts, *sopa castellana* – in a large, old dining room. A double room costs 8,000ptas. *(Continues p250)*

The spectacular gorges of **Durantón**.

The Plaza Mayor in the Romanesque town of **Sepúlveda**. See page 248.

Sepúlveda: Hotel-Restaurante El Panadero *C/Conde de Sepúlveda 4 (911/54 05 20)*. Friendly but traditionally smart restaurant, with bar below and rooms above. Highly recommended. Double rooms about 8,000ptas.
Restaurante-Bar Cristobal *C/Conde de Sepúlveda 8 (911/54 01 00)*. Sepúlveda's classic restaurant for roast *cordero lechal* (lamb), with all the trimmings.

Sigüenza, Atienza & Medinaceli

An hour and a half's journey east of Madrid, the medieval hill-town of **Sigüenza** offers a glimpse of Spanish country life little affected by tourism or industrial development. The rosy-brick old town, dominated by its massive castle-palace – built by the medieval bishops who governed the surrounding territories, and now heavily restored as a Parador hotel – spills down to the main plaza. Here you find the small but magnificent **Cathedral**, a compendium of twelfth- to fifteenth-century architectural styles. You can simply wander round, or pay to visit the famous *Tomb of the Doncel*, a remarkably beautiful effigy of a young noble who died at the gates of Granada. Highlights of the cathedral include the Renaissance barrel-ceiling of the sacristy, the Gothic *Casa del Doncel* and the cloister and wonderful retable of *Santa Lébrida*, showing eight twin sisters.

Diagonally opposite, next to a gossipy café, is the **Museo de Arte Antiguo**, which keeps a surprising hoard of treasures plucked from the region's village churches. Further down the main street, Calle José de Villaviciosa, you'll find small-town shops (good sausage meats in the butcher's). Elsewhere in the maze of hilly streets is **Santa María**, topped by storks' nests, the church of the **Ursulinas** and, at the bottom of the hill, the Hostal del Doncel for lunch.

With a car you can further explore the surrounding countryside. At **Atienza**, a pleasant half hour's drive north-west along the C114 through sunflower and wheat fields, past the Río Salado – literally River Salty – and salt-pans which brought wealth in medieval times, the old walls of the castle rise up sheer above the town from a rocky pimple. It gives splendid views up and down the valley and over the roofs and half-dozen medieval churches of the town below. Its double plazas, both with wonderful wooden carving under the eaves and arcades, are separated by a medieval gateway.

It's the salt-deposits which are supposed to make the valley's lamb so good, and in Atienza you can find good wood-roast lamb in various places. One suggestion, less pretentious than others, is the Fonda Molinero, which also serves local *jamón serrano*, partridges in *escabeche* and bean stew. From here, the shortest route back to Madrid is via Jadraque on the C101.

Alternatively, you can take the winding country road SO 133 to nearby **Medinaceli**, a windswept hilltop town that's so monumental, and so unlived in, that it looks like a film set. Its castle was once the centre of the northern defence line of Moslem Spain, from where orders were dispatched to, among other places, Madrid. The Roman arch, mosaics, Plaza Mayor and Colegiata are the main things to visit in the town, although it's as pleasant just to wander. Also, 20 minutes' drive away, is a fossil museum, the **Museo de Paleontología**, announced by a wonderful life-size elephant in a wheat field.

Information

Getting there: *by bus* Continental Auto from C/Alenza 20 (Metro Cuatro Caminos: tel 533 04 00) to Sigüenza; *by car* N-II, then C204 to Sigüenza (130km); *by train* from Chamartín to Sigüenza (Zaragoza line).
Where to stay and eat:
Atienza: Fonda Molinero *C/Héctor Vázquez 11 (911/39 90 17)*. Excellent traditional wood-roast lamb.
Medinaceli: Hostería El Mirador *(975/32 62 64)*. Modern hostal, with wonderful views.
Sigüenza: Hostal el Doncel *Paseo de la Alameda (911/39 00 01/39 10 90)*. Good value, traditional cooking, an easy walk from the railway station.
Parador-Castillo de Sigüenza *Plaza del Castillo (911/39 01 00)*. The bishops' palace, recently converted into a Parador, luxurious and peaceful, with old furnishings and magnificent views.

Guadalajara & the Alcarría

Arriaca to the Romans, this city was called *Wad-ilh-hajra*, or 'River of Stones' by the Moors, a name later hispanicised as Guadalajara. Conquered by the Christians in 1185, it achieved its greatest splendour during the sixteenth and seventeenth centuries, thanks to the Mendoza family. One of them financed the construction of the city's most important monument, the Gothic-*Mudéjar* **Palacio del Infantado**. Its *Patio de los Leones* and façade are outstanding.

Guadalajara also has several churches of historic and architectural interest. The thirteenth-century church of **Santa María** is the oldest. **San Ginés** contains the tombs of many members of the Mendoza family, and **San Nicolás** is famous for its Baroque altar. The church of **Santiago** (fourteenth century), on the other hand, is a magnificent example of the Gothic-*Mudéjar* architectural style.

Several towns and villages in the surrounding region, known as the **Alcarría**, make pleasant day-trips from Madrid if you have a car. The Alcarría is a rugged, formerly very isolated region of low mountains and valleys brought to the attention of the rest of Spain by Camilo José Cela in his book *Viaje a la Alcarría* ('Journey to the Alcarría'). Apart from Siguenza and Atienza (*see above*), **Pastrana** (85km from Madrid, 45km from Guadalajara) is one of its highlights. Reached by a good road off the N-II, this historic town is nonetheless now home to only a few thousand people. It was an important Roman city, and in the seventeenth century still had a population of almost 20,000. The best way to enjoy Pastrana is to walk through its winding, cobblestoned streets and admire the old, grey-stone houses of the village. The **Colegiata** museum is also worth a visit, and there are some good restaurants too.

Information

Getting there: *by bus* Continental Auto from C/Alenza 20 (Metro Cuatro Caminos: tel 533 04 00) to Guadalajara; local services run from there to Pastrana; *by car* N-II to Guadalajara (56km); then N320 and C200 for Pastrana; *by train* from Chamartín to Guadalajara (Zaragoza line).
Tourist Office: *Plaza Mayor 7, Guadalajara (949/22 06 98)*.
Where to eat: Casa Victor *C/Bardales 6, Guadalajara (949/21 22 47)*. Good-quality traditional Castilian fare.

Cuenca

The time for Cuenca is mid-autumn, when fallen birch leaves carpet the steep-sided ravine of the River Huécar that made the city an impregnable fortress. Perched on the steel footbridge across the gorge you get a classic juxtaposition of nature and human artifice, the latter in the shape of the spectacular *Casas Colgadas*, or hanging houses, crammed together at the top of a sheer cliff.

Who hung them is an open question, although in one form or another they date back to the sixteenth century. The glassed-in balconies artfully cantilevered over the abyss weren't thought of until 1927, though. One of them is a restaurant, while the other houses the **Museo de Arte Abstracto Español**. This rates as a work of art in itself, its lathe and timber innards transformed into the ideal setting for works by the pioneers of Spanish abstraction who gravitated to Cuenca in the 1950s, notably Tàpies, Chillida, Saura, Torner and Fernando Zóbel, whose own collection formed the nucleus of this model small museum.

Chillida in his most ponderous public mode reappears in the shadow of the Moorish-built **Mangana** tower. The **Cathedral** is also rather odd: it's the only Anglo-Norman structure in Spain. But Cuenca itself is the monument not to be missed, totalling much more than the sum of its museums and monuments, convents and churches: an up-and-down, walking-around delight. Unfortunately, its charms are well-publicised, and Cuenca has the good and bad fortune to be often overrun by day-tripping Spanish families, especially on long weekends and during Easter Week, when an international festival of religious music is held in the purpose-built auditorium.

The area due north and west of Cuenca is one of Spain's most prolific in those colours and contrasts which nature occasionally combines in just the right proportions to make for something truly picturesque. Known as the **Serranía de Cuenca**, it has been coming under increasing assault by heedless humans recently, but still seems to be holding its own, unlike too many less fortunate Spanish regions.

A car is essential to get to the **Ciudad Encantada**, a stretch of bizarre landscape so called because of the profuse sculptures in soft stone that have been created by centuries of wind and water erosion. It's past Villalba on the CU921 north-east towards Tragacete, and you climb steeply up a narrow cliffside road jutting over the Río Cuervo, which generates most of Cuenca's power and hatches most of its trout.

The destination of choice for a long day's journey out of Cuenca is the **Nacimiento del Rio Cuervo** (its source), a scenic spot near Tragacete where water trickles out of dozens of cracks and grottoes in a moss-draped rock face to form a

miniature cataract. There are wooden footbridges over the marshy part, and two restaurants and a picnic area nearby. For more scenic driving, instead of doubling back, keep going north and circle down again, keeping a sharp eye out for loggers' flatbeds, through mountains densely forested with Scotch pine, holm oak, willow and juniper. Here they had the good sense to set up the **El Hosquillo** game reserve, home to a handful of Spain's all-but-extinct indigenous brown bears, although you'll be very lucky if you see one.

Information

Getting there: by bus Auto-Res from Conde de Casal; by car N-III to Tarancón, then N400 (165km); by train from Atocha (Valencia line).
Tourist Office: *C/Dalmacio García Izarra 8, 1° (969/17 88 00)*.
Where to eat: **Mesón Casas Colgadas** *C/Canónigos (969/22 35 09)*. Closed Tue evening. The owner and many dishes on the menu in this three-tiered dining room in one of the *Casas Colgadas* are the same as at the Figón de Pedro down in the new town, but the fare is slightly fancier, mainly in the game dishes, to match the exalted setting. Quite expensive.
Where to stay: **Parador de Cuenca** *Hoz del Huécar (969/23 23 20)*. Spain's newest Parador is lodged in the long-neglected San Pedro monastery on the far side of the Huécar gorge. More comfortably and tastefully done-up than some 1960s Paradores, but it lacks a lived-in feeling. The view is priceless, but it's a tad expensive. **Posada de San José** *C/Julián Romero 4 (969/21 13 00)*. Overlooking the Huécar gorge, this complex of seventeenth-century houses, one of which belonged to Velázquez' son-in-law, was restored in 1954 by its Canadian owner. There are 25 no-frills but immaculate whitewashed rooms. It was recently given an extensive, long-overdue renovation. Book at least several weeks in advance for weekends. Most rooms are without a private bath, and fairly cheap.

Salamanca

Being home to the third-oldest university in Europe (after Bologna and Paris) has paid off for Salamanca to a degree that other monumentally-lush but comparatively lifeless cities might well envy. Coffee shops or cathedrals (yes, it has two), art galleries or architecture, blues from the basement or Baroque in the basilica, make it obvious all that burnished bronze stonework is pulsing with vitality as well as pervaded by history.

The porticoes of the spacious, stunning **Plaza Mayor**, long cited as Spain's grandest, admit a plethora of people coming and going, or stopping to natter: even the prostitutes congregate under the same archway they did almost as soon as this high Baroque showpiece designed by José de Churriguera was finished in 1753.

The old **University** building draws crowds risking terminal eyestrain trying to spot the one incongruous detail on the incredibly elaborate facade bearing the medallioned effigies of Ferdinand and Isabella. The trick is to pick out the

A vision of old Castile, the ancient town of **Sigüenza**. *See page 250.*

frog squatting on a skull amidst all the detail work of griffons, coats of arms, dragons, recognisable plant and flower species, popes and cardinals.

You have to pay for a glimpse of the carved wooden staircase, showing men and women making love and playing ball. The treasures of the library are protected by a sixteenth-century wrought iron gate and housed in Baroque bookcases by Churriguera. Opposite, the patios of the *Escuelas Menores* house administrative offices and a gallery for itinerant exhibitions.

The original **Cathedral**, an eminent example of late Romanesque reduced in the ranks to a mere parish church, is attached to and dwarfed by its flamboyantly Gothic successor, most of which was completed by 1577. The older one has a fifteenth-century altarpiece with some beautiful narrative imagery recapping the life of Christ, while the new one boasts fine ornamentation around the portals.

We could hardly list, let alone describe, Salamanca's surfeit of outstanding religious buildings, covering the gamut from Romanesque through Gothic, Renaissance and various Baroque subcategories. But they're never overwhelming. One is dedicated to Saint Thomas à Becket, consecrated within a few years of his canonisation.

The shell-studded exterior of the **Casa de las Conchas** attests to its original owner's prominence in the Order of Santiago, but in some ways is more interesting on the inside, where the original sixteenth-century layout is preserved. Getting into the city takes you across the Tormes river by way of the still solid **Roman bridge**. At least 15 of its arches date from the reign of Vespasian.

Information

As you might expect, Salamanca is loaded with tapa bars and student drinking hangouts. Try **La Covachuela**, at Portales de San Antonio 24 (northwest of the Plaza Mayor) which claims to be the tiniest bar in Spain, for stewed pig's jowls and ears washed down with local wine. Salamanca province is also one of Spain's great ham and chorizo heavens, but note that cured specialities from acorn-fed, free-ranging Ibérico piggies do not come cheap, even here.
Getting there: *by bus* Auto-Res from Conde de Casal; *by car* N-VI/A6 to Avila turn (N110), then N501 (215km); *by train* from Chamartin.
Where to eat: **El Mesón** *Plaza del Poeta Iglesias 10 (923/21 72 22)*. Considered the most reliable of three restaurants located on different angles of the same plaza, all specialising in classic Castilian cooking.
Restaurante Félix *Pozo Amarillo 6 (923/21 72 81)*. A bit distant from the student scene, but a favourite with the budget-minded.
Where to stay: **Gran Hotel** *Plaza del Poeta Iglesias 3 (923/21 35 00)*. Looks like a piano warehouse from the outside, but after a deluxe overhaul it's now quite posh and comfy – and inexpensive. So close to the Plaza Mayor you'll be eternally grateful for the double glazing. **Hotel Don Juan** *C/Quintana, 6 (923/26 14 73)*. Behind the emblazoned stone façade the rooms are all tiny, but immaculate and quiet; they cost about 9,000ptas.

The AVE to Córdoba & Seville

The AVE, Spain's high speed train, was one of the most controversial (and expensive) projects undertaken around Seville's Expo '92 mega-event. Opinions still fly about whether it was all worth it, but, thanks to this ultra-modern, 300kph Franco-German-Spanish creation the wonders of Córdoba and Seville are now just one hour 40 minutes and 2½ hours respectively from Madrid. Moreover, in an effort to get the line to pay its way by generating more business RENFE (Spanish Railways) keep fares down and offer many special deals, so that a return ticket to Seville can cost as little as 10,000ptas off-peak. Twelve trains leave the lavishly-refurbished **Atocha** station every day (information 534 05 05).

RENFE will also now refund the price of your ticket if the AVE is more than five minutes late at any destination. They are actually playing it quite safe: only one out of every 200 AVE trains has ever arrived more than three minutes behind schedule. Consequently, lunching at an outdoor café in Andalusia and sipping on a few *finos* before heading back north to Madrid is no longer a pipe dream.

Córdoba

After passing through the rugged olive- and oak-strewn Sierra Morena, the AVE descends into the valley of the Guadalquivir and pulls into Córdoba's new train station. Córdoba, largest city in the world around the year 1000, and capital of Moslem Spain, is now a rather provincial place of some 200,000 inhabitants. Still, its *Andalus* character makes a nice change from the hustle and bustle of Madrid.

Córdoba is not without relics of its former splendour, including a **Roman bridge** and some spectacular Arab mills. Greatest by far, though, is the eighth-century **Mosque**, one of the supreme works of Islamic architecture, that dominates the centre of the city. For an idea of its enormity, consider that inside, in addition to 850 onyx, marble and granite columns reflecting light below its delicately-carved cedar ceiling, is a grotesque Christian cathedral, crudely implanted in 1523.

The first half of May is the best time to visit Córdoba. As well as the fine weather, Cordobeses celebrate their *Festival de los Patios*, potting even more geraniums than usual and opening up their wonderful courtyards for visitors, and neighbours, to admire.

Information

Tourist Offices: *C/Torrijos 10 (957/47 12 35); Plaza Judah Levi (957/29 07 40)*.
Where to eat: **Almudaina** *Campo Santos Mártires 1 (957/47 43 42)*. A good, medium-priced choice. **El Caballo Rojo** *C/Cardenal Herrero 28 (957/47 53 75)*. One of Andalusia's finest, with the best of local cuisine. **Where to stay**: **Albucasis** *C/Buen Pastor 11 (957/47 86 25)*. **Meliá Córdoba** *C/Jardines de la Victoria (957/29 80 66)*.

Seville

As the on-board movie comes to an end, the AVE arrives in Seville, Spain's fourth-largest city and the capital of Andalusia. With its orange-blossom and jasmine-scented air and bougainvillea climbing up and around pitch-black painted grillwork over the windows of white-washed houses, this is truly one of the most beautiful cities in the world. A walk around its famous **Santa Cruz** district is a heady experience at any time of the year.

Obviously, there is no dearth of sights to see. The **Cathedral** is the world's largest Gothic structure, the third-largest church in Europe after Saint Peter's in Rome and Saint Paul's in London. It is best known, though, for its emblematic tower, the **Giralda**, the only surviving part of the thirteenth-century Mosque previously on this site, and a twin of the Koutoubia tower built by the same Almohad dynasty in Marrakesh. Not far away on the banks of the Guadalquivir sits the **Torre de Oro** (the Gold Tower), also built by Seville's last Moslem rulers. It is so named not for its colour but because the gold and silver brought from the Americas was stored there. The **Real Alcázar**, a fourteenth-century *Mudéjar* palace with tiled courtyards and jasmine-scented gardens, is perhaps the most beautiful example of the architecture developed by Moslem craftsmen working under Christian overlords.

Seville has been greatly marked by major exhibitions. The Plaza de España, in the peaceful Parque María Luisa, was built for the Spanish-American Exhibition of 1929. Much more recently, Expo '92 has left Seville with motorways, modernistic bridges and a pavilion-populated island that no one seems to know quite what to do with, the *Cartuja*. Plans to use it as a state-of-the-art industrial park with adjacent theme park (*Cartuja '93*) have failed to arouse more than local interest.

The most popular times to visit the city are during its renowned *Semana Santa* (Holy Week) and *Feria de Abril* (April Fair) celebrations. Hotel rooms must be booked far in advance, even though Seville has a hotel glut following the Expo. The religious fervour exhibited during the Easter processions is unrivalled in Western Europe. The April Fair, on the other hand, draws thousands of Sevillanos with their horses and carriages, not to mention visitors, to tents and wooden *casetas* mounted just outside the city for a non-stop week of sherry-sipping, dancing, bullfights and general merry-making.

Information

Tourist Office: *Avda Constitución 9 (95/422 14 04); Plaza de las Delicias (95/423 44 55)*.
Where to eat: **El Corral del Agua** *Callejón del Agua 6 (95/422 48 41)*. **San Marco** *C/Cuna 6 (95/421 2440)*. **Where to stay**: **Hotel Internacional** *C/Aguilas 17 (95/421 32 07)*. An attractive small hotel with charming Andaluz patios, and double rooms for about 11,000ptas. **La Rábida** *C/Castelar 24 (95/422 09 60)*. Also in a traditional Andaluz house, with doubles for about 9,000ptas.

Survival

Survival

So you've lost your passport, you need to park your car, and you can't find a pharmacy that's open. Just read on...

Bureaucracy/Living/Working

With unemployment running at over 20 per cent locally, jobs for foreigners are not easy to come by. Your best chances of finding work will be in English teaching and/or translation. It is very advisable to have a relevant teaching qualification, preferably the full RSA Diploma. If you get work in a school it will initially usually be on only a nine-month contract. That said, there is always private work available; the going rate for classes is from 1,500 to 3,000ptas an hour. To get your first classes, try putting up ads on the notice-boards at the **British Institute**, C/Almagro 5 (337 35 75), and in the **Turner** bookshop (*see chapter* **Shopping**).

If you do stay and work here there are various bureaucratic hurdles you will need to negotiate. If you come to work for a company having been contracted in your country of origin, any paperwork should be dealt with by your employer, who should also organise your Social Security number and contributions.

Residency & related paperwork

EU citizens working for a Company/*Cuenta Ajena*

Paperwork has become at least a little easier in recent years for EU citizens working in Spain. Work permits as such no longer exist, but you do have to become a resident to work legally. To do so you will need a contract or a firm offer of work (which can be for only three hours a week and with no stipulated duration, although there is no guarantee that this will be sufficient), and an application form, which is obtained from the special police station that deals with foreigners' affairs, the **Comisaría de Extranjería** (*see below*). The Comisaría will also require two photocopies of the information pages of your passport and three photographs. Keep photocopies yourself of all documents submitted. You may also be asked, arbitrarily, for a medical certificate and/or proof of sufficient funds. You will normally be given a Type A residency permit, valid for 12 months and not automatically renewable. This ties you to the company, the region and the business sector for which you have registered and, technically, you must leave the country on its expiry. Should you then reapply successfully at that time, you will be issued a Type C permit, which lasts for five years and is renewable.

EU citizens working freelance/*Cuenta Própia*

If you want officially to work freelance, as a *trabajador autónomo/a* or *trabajador por cuenta própia*, you must first

obtain a *Número de Identificación Fiscal* (tax code), which as a foreigner will be the same as your *Número de Identificación de Extranjero*. This can be obtained from the Comisaría de Extranjería (*see below*) or your local Tax Office (*Delegación de Hacienda*), the address of which will be in the phone book. Once you have a number, you can open a bank account, request a telephone line and so on. The next stop is also in the Tax Office: at the *Actividades Económicas* desk fill in form 845, specifying which sector (*Enseñanza*, for teaching) you wish to work in, and form 036, the *Declaración Censal*, and keep copies of both. This done, you then visit your local Social Security office (*Delegación de Seguridad Social*) and say you want the *alta como autónomo*. You can choose in which Social Security contribution band you want to pay. It is very expensive, and you should choose the lowest band (currently up to 28,000ptas per month), as you get few rights as a freelancer, and it's not worth paying more. As well as handing in these forms at this office you should also deposit copies of them back at the Tax Office. You will then have a Social Security number, and in future will be obliged to make annual tax declarations. Once you have your initial documentation you can apply for a *Cuenta Própia* residency permit at the Comisaría de Extranjería, with the same information (passport, proof of earnings, etc) as for the employee *Cuenta Ajena* permit (*see above*).

Non-EU citizens

First-time applicants need a special visa, for which you must apply at the nearest Spanish Consulate in your home country, although you can start the ball rolling in Spain if you don't mind making at least one trip back home. The basic documents needed are a contract or firm offer of work from a registered Spanish company, a medical certificate and a certificate of good conduct from your local police force. You must present these with various passport-style photos and translated copies of any relevant qualifications to the Consulate, who will pass them on to the Labour Ministry in Madrid. If they approve them the Consulate will then issue your special visa (this can take six months). If you apply to work freelance or to start you own business the procedures are slightly different and you will also be asked for proof of income. Once back in Spain the procedures for applying for your residency permit are similar to those for European citizens (*see above*).

Comisaría de Extranjería

C/Los Madrazo 9 (521 93 50). Metro Banco de España/bus all routes to Plaza de Cibeles. **Open** 9am-2pm Mon-Fri.

Legal Help

Legal advice on employment law, contracts and so on can be obtained through the English department of the trade union organisation *Comisiones Obreras* (CCOO), at C/Lope de Vega 38 (536 51 00). Ask for Steve Marsh. If you have been working and have reason to believe that your employer has not been paying your Social Security contributions (*cotizaciones*) go to your nearest Social Security office, show your SS number and ask for a *vida laboral* (contributions record). If no contributions have been paid, you can report your company.

Renting a Flat

It's relatively easy to find vacant flats in Madrid on reasonable terms, as post-1992 the property situation in the city has become more of a renter's market. The best local paper for property ads is often *Ya* (look under *Alquileres*); otherwise, just look for signs headed *se alquila* in an apartment-block doorways. The fundamental element in determining your rights and obligations as a tenant is the individual rental contract (*contrato de alquiler*) signed by you and the landlord. They vary a great deal, and before signing it's very important to be clear about the exact conditions in your contract, particularly regarding responsibility for repairs.

Contracts of over 12 months' duration are subject to an annual rental increase of not more than the official inflation rate, the *IPC* (*Índice de Precios al Consumo*, retail price index, published regularly in the press), although in the current climate landlords are keen to keep good tenants and may be willing to waive the first year's increase, or make other concessions. Note that for residents rents paid are tax deductible, provided you have all the necessary receipts. For more information on flat-sharing, *see chapter* **Students**.

Communications

For fax bureaux, *see chapter* **Services**. For courier and messenger services, *see chapter* **Business**.

Post

The **Palacio de Comunicaciones** is the main centre for all postal services. If, though, you only want to buy normal-rate stamps for postcards or letters it is much easier to do so in any *estanco* or tobacco shop (*see chapter* **Essential Information**).

Palacio de Comunicaciones
Plaza de Cibeles (536 01 10). Metro Banco de España/bus all routes to Plaza de Cibeles. **Open** 8am-10pm Mon-Fri; 8.30am-10pm Sat.
In the magnificent central post office all the different postal services are available at separate windows around the main hall: parcel post, telegrams, telex and so on. Faxes can also be sent and received at all post offices, but their rates are very expensive, and it's better to use private fax bureaux. There is also an information desk, near the main entrance. Note that within the general opening times not all the services are available at all times. Letters sent Poste Restante (General Delivery) to Madrid should be addressed to *Lista de Correos, 28000 Madrid, Spain*. To collect them go to window 18 at the Palacio de Comunicaciones, with your passport. If you need to send a letter by express post, say you want to send it *urgente*. *See also chapter* **Sightseeing**.
Other centrally-located post offices (open 8am-2pm Mon-Fri): El Corte Inglés, C/Preciados. Metro Sol/bus all routes to Sol.
C/Hermosilla 103. Metro Goya/bus 21, 26, 43, 53, 61.
C/Mejía Lequerica 7. Metro Alonso Martínez/bus 3, 37, 40, 149.
C/Sebastián Elcano 7. Metro Embajadores/bus 27, 60, 148.

Postal Rates & Post Boxes
Letters and postcards weighing up to 20gm cost 18ptas within Madrid, 29ptas to the rest of Spain, 55ptas to EU countries, 65ptas to the rest of Europe, 95ptas to the US and Canada and 150ptas to Asia and Australasia. Cards and letters to other European countries generally arrive in three to four days, and to North America in about a week. Aerogrammes (*Aerogramas*) cost 70ptas for all destinations. Normal post boxes are yellow, with two horizontal red stripes. There are also a few special red post boxes for urgent mail, with hourly collections.

Emergencies

The following emergency services are on call 24 hours daily. For information on the different police forces, *see* **Police & Security**.
Ambulance/*Ambulancia* *(061/522 22 22/092).*
Fire Service/*Bomberos* *(080).*
Municipal Police/*Policía Municipal* *(092).*
National Police/*Policía Nacional* *(091).*
Guardia Civil *(062/533 11 00).*
Poisoning cases/*Instituto Nacional de Toxicología* *(562 04 20).*

EMERGENCY REPAIRS
These lines are all open 24 hours daily. Which of the two local electricity companies you need to call will be indicated on your electricity meter.
Electricity Unión Fenosa *(594 49 94)*; Iberdrola *(508 64 44/5/6).*
Butane Gas/*Butano* *(348 66 00).*
Gas/*Gas Ciudad* *(589 65 55).*
Water/*Canal de Isabel II* *(593 35 19).*

Telephones

The Spanish national phone company (*Telefónica*) is a much-reviled local institution. Charges are high, particularly for international calls. It is cheaper to call after 10pm and before 8am, Monday to Saturday, and all day on Sundays.

Phone Numbers
In the last few years many Madrid numbers beginning with a *2* have been changed to begin with a *5*. If you are ever given a phone number starting with a *2* and cannot get through, try redialling substituting a *5* as the first digit.

Public Phone Boxes
In older-model phones, you insert the coins into a slot or aperture at the top of the phone before dialling, and then the coins will begin to drop when the call is answered. For a local call (minimum 13ptas) you will need to insert three *duros* (five peseta coins) and you will not get change if you put in a 25 or 50ptas coin. Increasingly common are more modern phones that accept coins, phonecards and credit cards, and also have a digital display with instructions in four languages including English. They will also give you credit to make further calls without having to reinsert your money, and are much more likely to work properly than the old-style call phones. Phonecards cost 1,000 or 2,000 ptas and can be bought at post offices or in *estancos*. In addition, most bars and cafés have a telephone for public use. They usually accept 5 and 25ptas coins, but in some bars they are set to take only 25ptas, an illegal but not-uncommon practice.

International & Long-distance Calls
To make an international call from any phone, dial 07, wait for a loud continuous tone and then dial the country code: **Australia** 61; **Canada** 1; **Irish Republic** 353; **New Zealand** 64; **United Kingdom** 44; **USA** 1, followed by the area code (omitting the first zero in UK codes) and individual number. To call Madrid from abroad, dial the international code (010 in the UK), then 34 for Spain and 1 for Madrid. If you are calling a Madrid number from somewhere else within Spain the area code is 91.

Gran Vía 30. Metro Gran Vía/bus all routes to Gran Vía.
Open 9am-midnight Mon-Sat; noon-midnight Sun, public holidays. **Credit** AmEx, MC, V.

At the *Telefónica* phone centres (*Locutorios*) you are allotted a booth and pay at the counter when you have finished all your calls, thus avoiding the need for pocketloads of change.
Other offices: Paseo de Recoletos 41. **Open** 9am-midnight Mon-Sat; noon-midnight Sun, public holidays. Palacio de Comunicaciones, Plaza de Cibeles. **Open** 8am-midnight Mon-Fri; 8am-10pm Sun, public holidays.

Operator services

All services are normally in Spanish only.
National directory enquiries 003
International directory enquiries 025
International operator *Europe & North Africa* 008; *Rest of World* 005
Telephone breakdowns 002
Telegrams 522 20 00
Time 093
Weather information 094
Alarm calls 096
Once the message has finished (when it starts repeating itself), key in the number you are calling from followed by the time at which you wish to be woken, in four figures, ie. 0830 if you want to be called at 8.30am.
General information 098
A local information service provided by Telefónica, with information particularly on duty pharmacies in Madrid. Otherwise, it is generally less reliable than the 010 line (*see chapter* **Essential Information**).

Disabled travellers

Madrid is not yet a city where disabled people, especially wheelchair users, can get around very freely. Public transport facilities are limited to accessible buses in use on a few routes, although they may be more widespread in future, and a special taxi service (*see chapter* **Getting Around**). The main railway stations, Atocha and Chamartín, however, are fully accessible to wheelchairs. Proposals have also been made to provide some access to the Metro system, but when they will be put into effect is another question.

There is no general guide to accessibility in the city. Access with lifts or ramps for wheelchair users is already provided at the city's major museums. Recent legislation also requires all public buildings in Madrid to be made fully accessible by 2003, although in practice the law is likely to be more demanding with new rather than existing buildings. Thanks to the **ONCE** (Spain's powerful lottery-funded organisation for the blind) more has been done on behalf of blind and partially-sighted people. Most street crossings in the centre have identifiable, knobbled paving and low kerbs.

COMFM

C/Eugenio Salazar 2 (413 74 41). Metro Prosperidad/bus 16, 29, 52. **Open** 8am-3pm Mon-Fri.
The *Coordinadora de Minusválidos Físicos de Madrid*, the umbrella organisation for disability groups in the city, which acts as a campaigning organisation and collects up-to-date information on changes in access and other facilities.

Driving in Madrid

Driving in Madrid may be a little wilder than you are used to. With a million and a quarter cars in the city's streets, jams are frequent, and so too is horn-punching and an assortment of aggressive maneouvres to get ahead. Serious accidents, though, are less common than slow-speed bumps.

In Madrid itself driving is rarely the most convenient way of getting anywhere. A car is a great asset, though, for trips outside the city (*see chapter* **Trips Out of Town**). If you do drive in or around Madrid, some points to bear in mind are listed below. For information on car and motorcycle hire, *see chapter* **Services**.

• You can drive in Spain with a valid license from most other countries, but it is useful also to have an international driving license, available in Britain from the AA and RAC.
• Keep your driving license, vehicle documents and insurance Green Card with you at all times.
• It is obligatory to wear seat belts at all times in cities as well as on main highways, and to carry a warning triangle in your car.
• Children under 14 may not travel in the front of a car.
• Speeding fines imposed on motorways (*autopistas*) and other main highways, policed by the Guardia Civil, are payable on the spot.
• Do not leave anything of value, including a car radio, in your car, and do not leave bags or coats in view on the seats. Take all of your luggage into your hotel when you park your car.
• In general drivers go as fast as they can irrespective of the speed limit. At traffic lights at least two cars will follow through on the amber light as it changes between green and red. Do not therefore stop sharply when you see a light begin to change, as the car behind will not be expecting this and could easily run into your back.
• When oncoming drivers flash their lights at you this means that they will *not* slow down (contrary to British practice). On main highways, the flashing of lights is usually a helpful warning that there is a speed trap up ahead.

Spanish Residents

If you become resident in Spain you must exchange your foreign licence for a Spanish one. The best way to do so is through the **RACE** (*see below*), which will take care of all the paperwork for you for about 13,000ptas. EU and US citizens do not need to take another driving test on exchanging their licences, but citizens of other countries may have to.

Breakdown Services

If you are taking a car to Spain it is advisable to join a motoring organisation such as the AA or RAC in Britain, or the AAA in the US. They have reciprocal arrangements with the local equivalent, the **RACE**, which is by far the most convenient source of assistance for drivers in distress, even for non-members. If you need more than emergency repairs, main dealers for most makes of car will be found in the local yellow pages under *Automóviles*.

RACE (Real Automóvil Club de España)

C/José Abascal 10 (593 33 33/freephone 900 11 22 22/traffic information 742 12 13). Metro Ríos Rosas/bus 3, 12, 37, 149. **Open** *Phonelines* 24 hours daily. *Office Sept-May* 9am-7pm Mon-Fri; *June-Sept* 8.30am-2.30pm Mon-Fri.

The RACE has English-speaking staff and will send immediate assistance if you have a breakdown. If you are outside Madrid, you should call the emergency freephone number, but you will be referred on to another local number. Repairs are carried out on the spot where possible; if not, your vehicle will be towed to the nearest suitable garage. Members of foreign affiliated organisations are not charged for call outs, but non-members must pay 6,900ptas for the basic breakdown service. The RACE also provides a range of other services for foreign drivers at low prices, and for free or at preferential rates for members of affiliated organisations

Forum Autorepairs

Nave 44, C/Sierra Albarracín 3, Polígono Industrial San Fernando de Henares (677 79 25). By car Autopista de Barcelona (A2) to Polígono de Torrejón exit/by train Cercanías lines C-2, C-7 to San Fernando de Henares. **Open** 9am-6pm Mon-Fri. **No credit cards.**

This English-speaking general repair garage is run by former US Air Force mechanics from the US base at Torrejón, who stayed on when it closed down. Current rates are approximately 3,500ptas per hour for labour, plus parts. It's located in an industrial estate in San Fernando de Henares, not far east of Barajas airport on the Barcelona road.

Parking

Parking is never easy in central Madrid. Tickets are given out frequently by the Municipal Police, although Madrileños commonly never pay them. Be careful though not to park in front of doorways with the sign *Vado Permanente*, indicating an entry with 24-hour right of access. Parking is banned in most major streets in the centre, but in most sidestreets the **ORA** pay-and-display parking system applies.

ORA

The ORA (*Operación Regulación Aparcamiento*) is a relatively complicated system, but its main features are: within the central ORA zone (roughly between Moncloa, C/José Abascal, C/Doctor Esquerdo and Atocha), residents park for free if they have an annual sticker. From 9am to 8pm (9am to 3pm in August) non-residents can also park here with an ORA card, valid for a period from 1/2-hour to a maximum of two hours. The cards can be bought from *estancos* or newsstands, cost 40-160ptas and should be displayed behind the windscreen. All streets within this zone that do not have an additional restriction signposted are ORA parking areas. In other zones time allowances are slightly more generous.

Car Parks

Central Car Parks *Plaza de las Cortes, Plaza Santa Ana, C/Sevilla, Plaza Jacinto Benavente, Plaza Mayor, C/Descalzas Reales, C/Tudescos, Plaza de España.* **Open** 24 hours daily. **Rates** 210ptas first hour; 190ptas second hour; 185ptas per hour for each hour after that; 1,880ptas 24 hours.

The 28 municipal underground *parkings* are indicated by a white 'P' on blue sign, with another to indicate if spaces are available: *Lleno* means full; *Libre* means there are spaces. You are especially recommended to use a car park if you are driving a car with foreign plates.

Towing Away & Car Pounds

(345 00 50). **Main Pounds:** *Plaza del Carmen. Metro Sol/bus all routes to Puerta del Sol.*
Avda de Alfonso XIII 135. Metro Colombia/bus 7, 40, 52.
If your car seems to have been towed away by the Municipal Police call the central number (open 24 hours) and quote your car number plate to be told which of the car pounds your vehicle has gone to. Staff do not normally speak English. It will cost 18,530ptas to recover your vehicle, plus 175ptas per hour, timed from the moment it was towed away.

Petrol

Most petrol stations (*Gasolineras*) now have unleaded fuel (*sin plomo*) as well as regular (*super*). Diesel fuel is *gas-oil*.

24-hour petrol stations

Atocha: Repsol junction of Avda Ciudad de Barcelona and Paseo de Infanta Isabel, next to Atocha station. **Credit** AmEx, MC, V.
Campsa Paseo de Santa María de la Cabeza 18, on southward exit from Glorieta del Emperador Carlos V. **Credit** AmEx, MC, V.
Both these stations also have 24-hour shops on site.
Avenida de América: Repsol Avda de América 80, near junction with C/Arturo Soria. **Credit** AmEx, MC, V.
Cuatro Caminos: Carva C/Ríos Rosas 1, junction with C/Bravo Murillo. **Credit** AmEx, MC, V.

Embassies & Consulates

For a full list of embassies in Madrid look in the local phone book under *Embajadas*. Outside the office hours listed all the embassies have answerphones which will give you an emergency contact number. For more information on what to do if you lose a passport, *see below* **Police & Security**.

American Embassy

C/Serrano 75 (577 40 00). Metro Rubén Darío/bus all routes to Castellana. **Open** 9am-12.30pm, 3-5pm, Mon-Fri.

Australian Embassy

Paseo de la Castellana 143 (579 04 28). Metro Plaza de Castilla/bus 5, 47, 147. **Open** 10am-1pm Mon-Fri.

British Embassy

Embassy *C/Fernando el Santo 16 (319 02 00/8). Metro Alonso Martínez/bus 3, 7, 21.* **Open** 9am-1.30pm, 3-6pm, Mon-Fri.
Consulate *C/Marqués de la Ensenada 16 (308 52 01/recorded passport information 410 29 44/310 29 44). Metro Colón/bus all routes to Plaza Colón.* **Open** 8am-2.30pm, *visa section only* 8am-noon, Mon-Fri.

Canadian Embassy

C/Núñez de Balboa 75 (431 43 00). Metro Núñez de Balboa/bus 1, 29, 52, 74. **Open** 9am-12.30pm Mon-Fri.

Irish Embassy

C/Claudio Coello 73 (576 35 00). Metro Serrano/bus 1, 74. **Open** 10am-2pm Mon-Fri.
Telephone calls are answered until 5pm.

New Zealand Embassy

Plaza de la Lealtad 2 (523 02 26). Metro Banco de España/bus 9, 14, 27, 37, 45. **Open** 9am-1.30pm, 2.30-5.30pm, Mon-Fri.

Health

All visitors can obtain emergency health care through the Spanish national health service, the *Seguridad Social*. EU citizens are entitled to basic medical attention for free if they have an E111 form, although if you can get an E111 sent or faxed within four days you are still exempt from charges. Many medicines will be charged for. In non-emergency situations short-term visitors will find that it is usually quicker and more convenient if possible to use private travel insurance rather than the E111 and the state system. Similarly, non-EU nationals with private medical insurance can also make use of state health services on a paying basis, but other than in emergencies it will be simpler to use a private clinic.

If you become a Spanish resident and contribute to the *Seguridad Social* you will be allocated a doctor and a local health clinic within the state system (*see above* **Bureaucracy/Living/Working**).

Emergencies/Hospitals

In a medical emergency the best thing to do is to go to the Casualty (*Urgencias*) department of any of the major hospitals. All are open 24 hours daily. If you are in the central area, go to the **Clínico** or the **Gregorio Marañon**.

Ciudad Sanitaria La Paz

Paseo de la Castellana 261 (358 28 31). Metro Begoña/bus all routes to Ciudad Sanitaria.
The largest city hospital, in the north of the city near Plaza Castilla.

Hospital Clínico San Carlos

Plaza Cristo Rey (449 25 00/544 15 00). Metro Moncloa/bus 1, 12, 44, C, N18.
Enter from C/Isaac Peral, just off the Plaza de Cristo Rey.

Hospital General Gregorio Marañón

C/Dr Esquerdo 46 (586 80 00). Metro Ibiza, O'Donnell/bus 2, 15, 26, 61, N7.
The *Urgencias* entrance is in C/Ibiza.

Hospital Ramón y Cajal

Carretera de Colmenar Viejo, km. 9 (336 80 00). Bus 135/by train Cercanías lines C-7, C-8 to Ramón y Cajal.
Also in the north of the city. The *Cercanías* station is actually in the hospital complex.

Emergency First-Aid Centres (*Casas de Socorro*)

If you have no E111, no private insurance policy and are not within the Spanish Social Security system you will still be attended at the Gregorio Marañón (*see above* **Hospitals**). Alternatively, go to a *Casa de Socorro*, where you will receive first aid and if necessary be sent to a hospital. All are open 24 hours daily.
Central area *C/Navas de Tolosa 10 (532 23 64). Metro Callao/bus all routes to Plaza de Callao.*
Retiro/Atocha area *C/Gobernador 39 (420 03 56). Metro Antón Martín, Atocha/bus 14, 27, 37, 45, N8-N12.*
Tetuán area *C/Bravo Murillo 357 (279 12 23). Metro Plaza de Castilla/bus 42, N20.*

Ambulances & Taxis

If it's impossible to get to a hospital or clinic, the ambulances of the Seguridad Social (061), the Red Cross or *Cruz Roja* (522 22 22) or the Municipal SAMUR service (via the Municipal Police, 092 are all free. Another alternative is to take a taxi – Madrid's taxi drivers are often brilliant in an emergency, forcing their way through the traffic blowing horns and waving handkerchiefs.

Private Health Care

Unidad Médica Angloamericana

C/Conde de Aranda 1 (435 18 23). Metro Retiro/bus all routes to Plaza de la Independencia. **Open** *Sept-July* 9am-

8.30pm Mon-Fri; 10am-1pm Sat. *August* 10am-5pm Mon-Fri; 10am-1pm Sat. Closed public holidays.
This British-American out-patients' clinic has bilingual staff, who will make house calls as well as seeing patients at the clinic. It has a complete range of medical services, including gynaecology and dentistry. The basic price of a first consultation is 13,000ptas, with subsequent visits 12,000ptas. Other charges vary.

Pharmacies

Pharmacies, *farmacias*, are signalled by large green, usually flashing, crosses, and are plentiful in central Madrid. They are normally open 9.30am to 2pm, 5 to 8pm, Monday to Saturday. At all other times a duty rota operates. Every pharmacy has a list of the *farmacias de guardia* (duty pharmacies) for that day posted outside the door, with the nearest ones highlighted. Duty pharmacies for the whole city are also listed in local newspapers, and information is available on the *010* and *098* phonelines (recorded message, in Spanish only, between 9.30pm and 8.30am). Note that at night duty pharmacies often appear to be closed, and it's necessary to knock on the shutters to be served.

Dentists

See also above **Private Health Care**

Clínica Dental Cisne

C/Magallanes 18 (446 32 21). Metro Quevedo/bus 16, 37, 61, 149. **Open** 10am-1.30pm, 3-8pm, Mon-Fri; 11am-1.30pm Sat. **No credit cards.**
Consultations are free; fillings or cleaning cost 4,000ptas. The dentists speak English, and there is a 24-hour emergency service. Note that dentistry is not covered by the E111 form.

AIDS/HIV

Centro Dermatológico de la Comunidad

C/Sandoval 7 (445 23 28). Metro San Bernardo/bus 21, 147, 149. **Open** 9am-noon Mon-Fri.
An official clinic that carries out free, confidential HIV tests.

Comité Anti-SIDA

C/del Barco 10 (530 10 19). Metro Gran Vía/bus all routes to Gran Vía. **Open** 10am-2pm, 4-8pm, Mon-Fri.
The best organisation to go to for support and advice about HIV and AIDS. The volunteers don't generally speak English, but efforts will be made to do so.

Contraception & Abortion

Condoms (*profilácticos* or *condones*) and other forms of contraception are generally, but not always, available at pharmacies. A very few pharmacies still refuse to stock them on religious grounds. At time of writing, abortion is only legally permitted up to twelve weeks and on three grounds: rape, if the mother's life is endangered, or if the foetus is seriously malformed. However, new legislation is currently in preparation.

Dator Médica

C/Hermano Gárate 4 (571 27 00/). Metro Tetuán/bus 3, 42, 149. **Open** 9am-9pm Mon-Fri.
A specialised gynaecological clinic with English-speaking staff, and authorised to carry out terminations.

Dr. Eduardo López de la Osa González

C/Tormes 11 (562 13 77). Metro Lima/bus 7, 14, 43, 51. **Open** 5-8.30pm Mon-Thur. Closed Aug.
An English-speaking gynaecologist.

Jolly coppers on parade. See **Police & Security** *page 262.*

Complementary Medicine

Instituto de Medicina Natural

*Plaza de la Independencia 4 (576 26 49). Metro
Retiro/bus all routes to Plaza de la Independencia.* **Open**
8.30am-2pm, 5-8pm, Mon-Fri; 8.30am-2pm Sat.
This centre provides acupuncture, homeopathy and other
forms of complementary medicine. There are some English-
speaking practitioners on the staff.

Helplines

Alcoholics Anonymous

*C/Juan Bravo 40bis, 2° (341 82 82). Metro Núñez de
Balboa/bus 9, 19, 29, 51, 52.* **Open** *phoneline*
24 hours daily.
The English-speaking AA group in Madrid has meetings
daily. Phone for more details.

Red Cross Centres
(Centros de la Cruz Roja)

*C/Fúcar 8 (429 19 60). Metro Antón Martín/bus 6, 26,
32, 57.* **Open** 8.30am-3pm Mon-Fri.
*C/Eduardo Marquina 33 (569 47 39). Metro Marqués de
Vadillo/bus 23, 55, 60.* **Open** 8am-9.30pm Mon-Fri.
The two Red Cross Centres offer counselling and help on a
variety of problems, including drug-related ones. There are
sometimes English-speakers available.

English-Speaking Helpline

(559 13 93). **Open** 7-11pm Mon-Fri.
You can call the helpline if you need to talk to someone in
complete confidence about anything, or want practical information about Madrid and Spain.

Gambling Addiction

*C/Hermanos García Noblejas 49 (327 06 04). Metro García
Noblejas/4, 28, 28, 70.* **Open** 10am-1pm, 6-8pm, Mon-Fri;
10am-1pm Sat.

The *Amajer* organisation offers help and advice, and some
of their volunteers speak English. An answerphone is in
operation whenever the office is closed.

Teléfono de la Esperanza

*C/Francos Rodriguez 51, chalet 44 (459 00 50). Metro
Estrecho/bus 44, 132.* **Open** *phoneline* 24 hours daily.
A privately-funded local helpline that caters for a wide range
of needs, from psychiatric to legal. English is sometimes spoken, but it's not guaranteed.

Lost Property

Airport & Rail stations

If you lose something land-side of check-in at **Barajas
Airport**, report the loss immediately to the *Aviación Civil*
office in the relevant terminal. You can also call 393 60 00,
ext 1010. If you think you have mislaid anything on the
RENFE railway network, look for the *Atención al Viajero*
desk or *Jefe de Estación* office at the nearest main station to
where your property has gone astray. To get information by
phone on lost property at main rail stations call their general information numbers and ask for *Objetos Perdidos*.

Buses

EMT *C/Alcántara 24-26 (401 31 00). Metro Lista/bus 1,
74.* **Open** 8am-2pm Mon-Fri.
Anything you have lost on a city bus may eventually arrive
here. Ask for *Objetos Perdidos*.

Metro/Taxis/
Municipal Lost Property Office

Negociado de Objetos Perdidos *Plaza de Legazpi 7
(588 43 46). Metro Legazpi/bus 6, 18, 19, 45, 148.*
Open 9am-2pm Mon-Fri.
The Municipal Lost Property office primarily receives articles found on the Metro or in taxis around the city, but if you
are lucky something you have lost in the street may also be
handed in and turn up here.

Police & Security

Like most other European countries Spain has several police forces. In Madrid the most important are the local *Policía Municipal*, in navy and pale blue, and the *Policía Nacional*, in black and white uniforms. Each force has its own set of responsibilities, although at times they overlap. The *Municipales* are principally concerned with traffic and parking problems and various local regulations. The force with primary responsibility for dealing with crime are the *Nacionales*. The *Guardia Civil*, in military green, are responsible for policing inter-city highways, for customs posts, and for guarding many government buildings.

If you are robbed or attacked you should report the incident as soon as possible at the nearest *Policía Nacional* station (*Comisaría*). For police emergency phone numbers, *see page 257* **Emergencies**.

Jefatura Superior de Policía

C/Leganitos 19 (541 71 60). Metro Santo Domingo/bus all routes to Gran Vía.
The *Policía Nacional* headquarters for Madrid, centrally located near the Plaza de España. If you report a crime you will be asked to make an official statement (*Denuncia*), which will be typed out for you. It is unlikely that anything you have lost will be recovered, but you will need the *Denuncia* to make an insurance claim. A very few officers speak English. Some other police stations in the city centre are listed below. All these *Comisarías* are open 24 hours daily.
Centro C/de la Luna 29 (521 12 36). Metro Noviciado/bus all routes to Gran Vía.
Retiro C/Huertas 76 (429 09 94). Metro Antón Martín/bus 6, 26, 32, 57.
Chamberí C/Rafael Calvo 33 (319 55 00). Metro Iglesia/bus 3, 40, 147, 149.

Lost Passports

The loss or theft of a passport must be reported immediately to the nearest *Comisaría*, and also to your national Consulate (*see above* **Embassies & Consulates**). If you lose your passport over a weekend and have to travel on the Saturday or Sunday your embassy will charge for having to open the office specially and issue you with an emergency passport. The Spanish authorities and most airlines are often prepared to let you out of the country even without this document if you do not look suspicious and have other documents with you, including the police *Denuncia* confirming the loss of your passport, but in such cases it's advisable to be at the airport in plenty of time, and be suitably prepared.

Public Toilets

Public toilets are not common in Madrid. There are clean toilets with an attendant in the Retiro, at the north end of the boating lake, and also good toilet facilities at Atocha and Chamartín stations and in the central boulevard of the Paseo del Prado. Also on the Paseo del Prado and outside the main post office in the Plaza de Cibeles there are some modern, pay-on-entry cubicles that cost 25ptas. Apart from that, you are best advised to pop into a bar or café if in need. Major stores and fast-food restaurants are also useful stand-bys.

Religious Services

Anglican & Protestant

British Embassy Church (Saint George's)
C/Hermosilla 43 (576 51 09). Metro Serrano/bus 1, 9, 19, 51, 74. **Services** 10.30am Fri; 8.30am, 10am, 11.15am, Sun.
Saint George's attracts a multi-cultural congregation.
Community Church
Colegio El Porvenir, C/Bravo Murillo 85 (858 55 57). Metro Cuatro Caminos/bus all routes to Cuatro Caminos. **Services** 10am Sun.
An international, multi-racial congregation, with a children's Sunday School.

Catholic Mass in English

Capilla de Nuestra Señora de la Merced
Avda Alfonso XIII 165 (533 20 32/554 28 60). Metro Colombia. **English mass** 10.30am Sun.
Father Sullivant gives Mass in English, followed by coffee and Sunday Schools for children and adults. There's also a party every St Patrick's Day.

Jewish

Sinagoga de Madrid
C/Balmes 3 (445 98 43). Metro Iglesia/bus 3, 5, 16, 61. **Prayers** 8am, 8pm most days; 7.30pm Fri; 9.15am Sat.
Between July and September there are no evening services.

Moslem

Centro Cultural Islámico de Madrid
C/Salvador de Madariaga 4 (326 26 10). Metro Barrio de la Concepción/bus 53, 74. **Open** *Cultural Centre* 9am-4pm Mon-Fri.
Known as the 'Mosque of the M-30' because of its dramatic appearance looming beside the Madrid ring road, the city's Saudi-financed mosque, built during the eighties, is one of the largest Islamic centres in Europe. Prayers are held in Arabic five times a day. In addition, there is a bookshop, restaurant, school, gym, exhibition space and social centre.

The **Centro Cultural Islámico.**

Further Reading

History, Politics, Culture

Braudel, Fernand: *The Mediterranean and the Mediterranean World in the Age of Philip II* (two vols., Fontana 1986-87). A huge and multi-faceted study of society, economics and culture at the height of Spain's Golden Age. There is also a one-volume edition, *The Mediterranean* (Harper Collins 1992).
Elliott, JH: *Imperial Spain, 1469-1716* (Penguin, 1990). The standard history.
Elms, Robert: *Spain* (Heinemann, 1992). Modern Spain is given the official stamp of grooviness.
Fletcher, RA: *Moorish Spain* (Weidenfeld & Nicholson, 1992). A varied account of a too-little-known period in European history.
Fraser, Ronald: *Blood of Spain* (Pimlico, 1992). An oral history of the Spanish Civil War and the tensions that preceded it, the most vivid and human account of Spain's great crisis.
Lalaguna, Juan: *A Traveller's History of Spain* (Windrush, 1994). A handy introduction.
Gibson, Ian: *Fire in the Blood* (BBC, 1992). An idiosyncratic vision of modern Spain by the biographer of Lorca.
Gilmour, David: *Cities of Spain* (Pimlico, 1994). With an informative, impressionistic chapter on Madrid.
Hooper, John: *The New Spaniards* (Penguin, 1995). An entirely new edition of the best survey of post-1975 Spain.
Jacobs, Michael: *Between Hopes and Memories: A Spanish Journey* (Picador, 1994). A quirky account of a voyage through modern Spain in its year of glory, 1992.
Preston, Paul: *Franco* (Harper Collins, 1993; paperback, 1995). A massive and exhaustive biography.
Preston, Paul: *The Spanish Civil War* (Weidenfeld & Nicholson, 1990). A good concise account.
Shubert, Adrian: *A Social History of Modern Spain* (Unwin Hyman, 1990). A little heavy, but comprehensive.
Thomas, Hugh, ed: *Madrid, A Traveller's Companion* (Constable, 1988). A great anthology of writings on Madrid from the Middle Ages to the 1930s, by authors as varied as Casanova, Pérez Galdós and the Duke of Wellington.

Art & Architecture

Brown, Jonathan: *Velázquez: Painter and Courtier* (Yale, 1988). The most comprehensive study in English.
Elliott, JH, and Brown, Jonathan: *A Palace for a King: The Buen Retiro and the Court of Philip IV* (Yale, 1986). A vivid reconstruction by historians of both art and politics of the life, culture and spectacle of the Habsburg Court and the grandest of Madrid's palaces.
Gassier, Pierre: *Goya, A Witness of His Times* (Alpine Fine Arts, 1986). A thorough biography and study.
Goya, Francisco de: *Disasters of War, Disparates, or the Proverbs; Los Caprichos* (Dover Publications, 1968, 1969 and 1970). Good-value reproductions of Goya's three most remarkable series of etchings.

Jacobs, Michael: *Madrid: Architecture, History, Art* (George Philip, 1992). A lively and detailed survey of the city by one of the best current foreign writers on Spain.
Mitchell, Angus: *Spain: Interiors, Gardens, Architecture, Landscape* (Thames & Hudson, 1992). Lavishly illustrated.

Literature

Almodóvar, Pedro: *Patty Diphusa Stories and Other Writings* (Faber, 1992). Frothy, instantly-disposable, but full of the sparky, sexy atmosphere of eighties' Madrid.
Cela, Camilo José: *The Hive* (Sceptre, 1992). Nobel-prizewinner Cela's sardonic masterpiece on Madrid in the aftermath of the Civil War, with hundreds of characters centred on a group of do-nothing writers sheltering literally and metaphorically around a café table.
Cela, Camilo José: *Journey to the Alcarria* (Granta, 1990). A vivid account of rural Guadalajara between traditional isolation and modernisation.
Cervantes, Miguel de: *Don Quixote* (Penguin, 1970). The classic portrait of Golden-Century Spain, although he only actually visits Madrid very briefly.
Cervantes, Miguel de: *Exemplary Stories* (Penguin, 1972). A collection of Cervantes' shorter pieces.
Montero, Rosa: *The Delta Function* (University of Nebraska, 1991). One of the most perceptive novels on Spanish women today.
Múñoz Molina, Antonio: *Prince of Shadows* (Quartet, 1993). A psychological thriller based on the legacy of the recent past in modern Madrid.
Pérez de Ayala, Ramón: *Honeymoon, Bittermoon* (Quartet, 1990). Two short novels from 1923 by one of the most prolific of pre-Civil War Madrileño writers.
Pérez Galdós, Benito: *Fortunata and Jacinta* (Penguin, 1988). The masterwork of Spain's greatest nineteenth-century novelist, a story of love and class of immense depth set in 1860s Madrid.
Pérez Reverte, Arturo: *The Flanders Road* (Collins-Harvill, 1994). A complex novel of intrigue set in the Madrid art world by the most lauded of the current crop of young Spanish writers.
Quevedo, Francisco de, and anon: *Two Spanish Picaresque Novels* (Penguin, 1969). The anonymously-authored *Lazarillo de Tormes* and Quevedo's 1626 *El Buscón* (translated as 'The Swindler'), an earthy, cynical masterpiece, the second-greatest work of classical Spanish prose and an essential text on the climate of the 'Golden Century'. Also a great deal shorter than *Quijote*.

Food & Drink

Boyle, Christine, and Nawrat, Chris: *Spain and Portugal* (Carbery Traveller's Food and Wine Guides, 1994). A pocket-sized handbook and glossary.
Cases, Penelope: *Food and Wines of Spain* (Penguin, 1988). A good general guide.

Area Index

See chapter **Madrid by Area** *for information on each district.*

Villa y Corte

ACCOMMODATION: Hostal Riesco, p24; Hostal Valencia, p24; Posada del Dragón, p24.

CAFES, BARS, TAPAS & NIGHTSPOTS: El Anciano Rey de los Vinos, p109, p121; Asquiniña, p109; Café de Oriente, p109, p119; Casa Paco, p109; Los Cien Vinos, p111; El Pulpito, p111; La Torre del Oro, p112; El Anciano, p120; De 1911, p120; Kairos, p120; Café el Buen Gusto, p122; Café del Monaguillo, p122; Café del Nuncio, p122; Las Vistillas, p122; Casa Antonio, p122; Terraza Bardem Torero, p128; Berlin Cabaret, p131; Candilejas, p131; Corral de la Morería, p184; Free Jazz, p195; La Tolderia, p196; Muralla Arabe, p196; La Soleá, p200.

RESTAURANTS: Casa Santa Cruz, p97; Botin, p99; Casa Lucio, p100; Casa Maxi, p100; Posada de la Villa, p100; Viuda de Vacas, p100; Gure-Etxea, p102; La Taberna del Alabardero, p102; Casa Ciriaco, p103; Mesón Prada a Tope, p103; El Tormo, p103; Casa Gallega, p103; Can Punyetes, p105; Palacio de Anglona, p106; Taquería La Calaca, p106.

SHOPPING: *fashion* Blanco, p139; *food & drink* Jamonería Ferpal, p145; El Palacio de los Quesos, p145; *gifts* El Arco de las Cuchilleros, p143; Quetzal, p147; Almoraima, p148; *markets* San Miguel, p147; stamp & coin market, p149; *musical instruments* Garrido Bailén, p148; Manuel Contreras, p148; *records & music* El Flamenco Vive, p147; *religious articles* Sobrinas de Pérez, p148; *stationery* Carlin, p149.

SIGHTSEEING: Plaza Mayor, p33, Plaza de Oriente, p33; Muralla Arabe, p36; San Nicolás de los Servitas, p37; San Pedro el Viejo, p37; San Andrés & Capilla de San Isidro, p37; Catedral de San Isidro, p37; Plaza de la Villa, p37; Puente de Segovia, p39; Basílica de San Francisco el Grande, p39; Palacio Real, p39; Catedral de Nuestra Señora de la Almudena, p43; Campo del Moro, p44, p215; Jardines de las Vistillas, p45.

Sol & Gran Vía

ACCOMMODATION: Hotel Arosa, p20; Hotel Carlos V, p20; Hotel Emperador, p20.

CAFES, BARS, TAPAS & NIGHTSPOTS: Casa Labra, p112; Café del Circulo de Bellas Artes, p117; La Mallorquina, p120; Bar Cock, p120; Chicote, p120; Del Diego, p120; La Coquette, p126, p193; Montera 33, p126, p220; Calentito, p129; Joy Eslava, p129; Morocco, p129; Palacio de Gaviria, p129; Windsor Gran Via, p130; Max, p130; Xenon, p130; Chocolatería San Ginés, p132; Café de Chinitas, p184; El Sol, p195; Oba-Oba, p196; Ales, p220; Strong Centre, p220; La Rosa, p229.

MUSEUMS & EXHIBITION SPACES: Circulo de Bellas Artes, p157, p190; Fundación Arte y Tecnología,

p157; Museo de la Real Academia de Bellas Artes, p163; Acuárium de Madrid, p215.

RESTAURANTS: La Bola Taberna, p99; La Cocina de Rosa, p102; Robata, p106; El Parrondo, p107; Teruteru, p107.

SHOPPING: *bookshops* FNAC, p136; La Casa del Libro Espasa Calpe, p136; *children* Bazar Mila, p138; *cosmetics* O Boticàrio, p138; Manuel Riesgo, p138; *department stores* El Corte Inglés, p135; Galerías Preciados, p137; *fashion* Springfield, p139; *food & drink* Mariano Madrueño, p143; *out-of-hours shopping* Vip's, p135; *record & music* FNAC, p136; Madrid Rock, p147; Manzana, p148; *shoes & leather* Camper, p141; Los Guerrilleros, p141; *tobacco* Expendeduría No. 1 Santiago, p149.

SIGHTSEEING: Plaza de España p33; Puerta del Sol, p33; Real Monasterio de las Descalzas Reales, p39, p171; Real Monasterio de la Encarnación, p39; p171; Círculo de Bellas Artes, p43.

Huertas & Santa Ana

ACCOMMODATION: Hotel Palace, p17; Hotel Villa Real, p18; Gran Hotel Reina Victoria, p18; Hotel Asturias, p20; Hotel Inglés, p20; Hotel Mora, p22; Hotel Santander, p22; Hotel Suecia, p23; Hostal Armesto, p23; Hostal Cervantes, p23; Hostal Delvi, p23; Hostal Filo, p23; Hostal Olga, p23; Hostal-Residencia Coruña, p23; Hostal-Residencia Sud-Americana, p24; Hostal Villamáñez, p24; Pensión Jaén, p24.

CAFES, BARS, TAPAS & NIGHTSPOTS: Las Bravas, p112; Casa Alberto, p112; Casa de Pontevedra, p112; La Dolores, p112, p122; Garabatu, p112; El Lacón, p113; Lerranz, p113; Lhardy, p98, p113; La Toscana, p113; La Trucha, p113; Bar Viña P, p113; Casa Pueblo, p120; Cervecería Alemana, p120; Cervecería Santa Ana, p120; Los Gabrieles, p120; Naturbier, p121; Reporter, p121; Viva Madrid, p121; Los Gatos, p123; La Venencia, p123; Café Soto Mesa, p126; La Fidula, p126, p190, p227; Villa Rosa; p127; Bavaro Beach, p128; Fuego Fuego, p129; Stella, p130; Teatro Kapital, p130; Torero, p130; China Club, p132; No se lo digas a nadie, p132, p227; Café Central, p195; Café Populart, p195; Fénix, p196.

MUSEUMS & EXHIBITION SPACES: Museo Thyssen-Bornemisza, p35, p168; Casa-Museo de Lope de Vega, p173.

RESTAURANTS: El Cenador del Prado, p98; Lhardy, p98, p113; El Caldero, p103; Paradis Madrid, p105; Hylogui, p105; Bellman, p106; Artemisa, p107; La Farfalla, p132.

SHOPPING: *art supplies* Macarrón, p149; *bookshops* Librería Clio, p137; Librería del Prado, p137; *fashion* Cristina de Jos, p140; *food & drink* Casa Mira, p141; Autoservicio Ecológico, p142; Almacén de Licores David Cabello, p142; Licorilandia, p142; Mariano Aguado, p143; Museo del Jamón, p145; *gifts* La Casa de las Escayolas, p148; Objetos de Arte Toledano, p148; Seseña, p148; *photographic* Aqui, p147; *shopping malls* Galería del Prado, p136.

SIGHTSEEING: Paseo del Prado p31; Banco de España, p43; Congreso de los Diputados, p43.

Lavapiés, the Rastro, Atocha

CAFES, BARS, TAPAS & NIGHTSPOTS: El Brillante, p113; Café Melo's, p113; Los Caracoles, p113, p122; Bar Castilla, p113; Cayetano, p113; La Mancha, p113; La Taberna de Antonio Sánchez, p113, p123; Nuevo Café Barbieri, p120, p228; El 21, p123; Tomás, p123; Vinos, p123; Muñiz, p123; Avapiés, p126; Café del Mercado, p196; La Taberna Encantada, p196; Candela, p200; Casa Patas, p200; Refugio, p220; Medea, p229.

MUSEUMS & EXHIBITION SPACES: Museo Nacional Centro de Arte Reina Sofía, p35, p158, p166, p190.

RESTAURANTS: La Freiduría de Gallinejas, p100; Malacatín, p100; Asador Frontón I, p102; Belmar, p107; El Granero de Lavapiés, p107.

SHOPPING: *antiques* Galerías Piquer, p136; Nuevas Galerías, p136; *bookshops* Libros Argensola, p137; *design & household* La Oca, p139; *fashion* Corsetería La Latina, p140; *food & drink* El Madroño, p142; *gifts* Azcart, p143; Caramelos Paco, p148; *markets* Antón Martín, p147; La Cebada, p147; the Rastro, p149; *musical instruments* Guitarrería F Manzanero, p148; *out-of-hours shopping* 7-11, p135; *photographic* Fotocasión, p147; *shopping malls* Mercado Puerta de Toledo, p136; *sports goods* Deportes Legazpi, p149; *supermarkets* Simago, p142.

SIGHTSEEING: Puerta de Toledo, p43; Estación de Atocha, p44.

Malasaña & Chueca

ACCOMMODATION: Hostal-Residencia Senegal, p20; Hotel Monaco, pp21-22; Hostal-Residencia Gloria, p23.

CAFES, BARS, TAPAS & NIGHTSPOTS: Batela, p114; El Bocaito, p114; Casa do Campañeiro, p114; Santander, p114; El Timón, p114; Café Comercial, p119; Café Gijón, p119; Café Isadora, p119; El Espejo, p119; Lisboa, p119; Cervecería Santa Bárbara, p120; The Quiet Man, p121; Angel Sierra, p121; La Ardosa, p121; Agapo, p125; Kik's Mode, p126; King Creole, p126; Libertad 8, p126; Mala Fama, p126; Torito, p127; La Via Lactea, p127; Bocaccio, p129; Nairobi, p129; Pachá, p129, p195; Salsipuedes, p130; Warhol's Club, p130; But, p131; Long Play Boite, p131; Café del Foro, p131, p195; Noches de Cuplé, p132; Al'Laboratorio, p193; Maravillas, p193; Siroco, p195; Swing, p195; Black & White, p219; Bajo Cuerda, p219; Café Figueroa, p219; Café Galdós, p220;

Leather Bar, p220; Rick's, p220; Rimmel, p220; Troyans, p220; Cruising, p220; Ambient, p229.

MUSEUMS & EXHIBITION SPACES: Museo Romántico, p163; Museo Municipal, p173; Museo de Cera, p215.

RESTAURANTS: La Gastroteca de Stéphane y Arturo, p98; Salvador, p100; Fuente la Xana, p101; El Puchero, p103; Ribeira do Miño, p106; Zara, p106; Al-Mounia, p106; Pizzería Mostropiero, p107; Tienda de Vinos, p107; El Restaurante Vegetariano, p107, p228; Cambalache, p132; La Carreta, p132.

SHOPPING: *accessories & jewellery* Joaquín Berao, p140; *bookshops* Turner, p137; Berkana, p221, 229; *children* Prenatal, p138; *cosmetics* Comercial Chinere, p138; *design & household* Aldaba, p139; *fashion* Ararat, p140; Berlin, p140; Anvers, p140; Lurdes Bergada, p140; *food & drink* Horno San Onofre, p142; Patrimonio Comunal Olivarero, p142; Central Vegetariana, p142; *gifts* Almirante 23, p148; *second-hand clothes* Camaleón Usados, p140; Mercado de Colores, p140; *shoes & leather* Antigua Casa Crespo, p141.

SIGHTSEEING: Paseo del Prado p31; Plaza de Cibeles p33; Palacio Longoria p44.

Salamanca & the Retiro

ACCOMMODATION: Hotel Castellana Inter-Continental, p17; Hotel Ritz, p18; Hotel Villa Magna, p18; Hotel Wellington, p18; Hotel Los Galgos Sol, p19; Hotel Alcalá, p20; Hotel Pintor, p22; Hotel Serrano, p22; Hostal Retiro/Hostal Narváez, p24; Apartamentos Juan Bravo, p25.

CAFES, BARS, TAPAS & NIGHTSPOTS: El Aguilucho, p114; Alkalde, p114; Buen Provecho, p114; Casa Puebla, p114; Hevia, p115; José Luis, p115; Jurucha, p115; Peláez, p115; Café Lion, p119; Café de Ruiz, p119; Balmoral, p120; Embassy, p123; Bolero, p128; Boulevard, p128; Archy, p128; Keeper, p129; Teatriz, p130; Almonte, p184; Zambra, p184.

MUSEUMS & EXHIBITION SPACES: Museo del Prado, p35, p164; Casa de América, p157; Centro Cultural Casa de Vacas, p157; Centro Cultural de la Villa, p157; Fundación Banco Central Hispano, p157; Fundación La Caixa, p158; Fundación Juan March, p158, p190; Palacio de Cristal, p158; Palacio de Velázquez, p158; Museo Lázaro Galdiano, p163; Museo Nacional de Artes Decorativas, p163; Museo Arqueológico Nacional, p172; Museo Nacional de Antropología, p172; Museo del Ejército, p173; Museo Naval, p173; Museo Casa de la Moneda, p174; Museo Postal y de Telecomunicación, p174.

RESTAURANTS: Viridiana, p98; Zalacaín, p99; Taberna de Daniela, p100; La Giralda, p100; El Rabo de Toro, p101; Casa Baltasar, p101; Casa Portal, p101; Centro Riojano, p102; O'Caldiño, p103; St James, p105; El Buey, p105; La Catedral, p105; La Trainera, p106; Cafetería del Museo del Prado, p107; La Galette, p107.

SHOPPING: *bookshops* Crisol, p136; *children* Chicco, p138; Puck, p138; *design & household* BD Ediciones de Diseño, p139; Gastón y Daniela, p139; *department stores* Marks & Spencers, p136; *fashion* Casandra, p139; Ekseption, p139; Adolfo Domínguez, p139; Gianfranco Ferré, p139; Gianni Versace, p139; Giorgio Armani, p139; Kenzo, p139; Sybilla, p140; ¡Oh, qué Luna!, p140; *food & drink* Méndez, p142; *gifts* Cerámica El Alfar, p143; La Compañía de China y del Oriente, p143; Items D'ho, p143; *markets* La Paz, p147; *shoes & leather* Farrutx, p141;

Loewe, p141; *shopping malls* El Jardín de Serrano, p136; *supermarkets* Expresso, p142.

SIGHTSEEING: San Jerónimo el Real, p37; Parque del Retiro, p41, p215; Observatorio Astronómico, p41; Puerta de Alcalá, p43; Bolsa de Comercio de Madrid, p43; Palacio de Comunicaciones, p43; Jardín Botánico, p45.

Moncloa, Argüelles, C. de Campo

ACCOMMODATION: Hotel Tirol, p23; Albergue Juvenil Casa de Campo, p25; Albergue Juvenil Santa Cruz de Marcenado, p25.

CAFES, BARS, TAPAS & NIGHTSPOTS: La Bilbaína, p115; La Fortuna, p115; Mesón Los Toledanos, p115; Café Moderno, p119; El Cangrejero, p121; Los Alpes, p123; Bruin, p123; Café Viena, p123; Viena Capellanes, p123; Aire, p127; Revólver Club, p129, p195, p200; Colegio Mayor San Juan Evangelista, p195; Parque de Atracciones, p196, p216.

MUSEUMS & EXHIBITION SPACES: Centro Cultural Conde-Duque, p157; Museo Cerralbo, p162; Museo de América, p171.

RESTAURANTS: La Taberna de Liria, p98; Casa Mingo, p101; Taberna de Abajo, p106; Adrish, p106; La Vaca Argentina, p106; CityVip's, p228; Da Nicola, p228.

SHOPPING: *bookshops* Phoebe, p243; *fashion* Massimo Dutti, p139; Zara, p139.

SIGHTSEEING: Ermita de San Antonio de la Florida, p39; Casa de Campo, p44, p215; Parque del Oeste, p45, p215; Faro de Madrid, p45; Teleférico de Madrid, p46; Parque de Atracciones, p196, p216; Zoo de la Casa de Campo, p216.

Chamberí

ACCOMMODATION: Hotel Santo Mauro, p18; Gran Hotel Conde Duque, p18; Hotel Zurbano, p19; Galiano Residencia, p20; Hotel Trafalgar, p23.

CAFES, BARS, TAPAS & NIGHTSPOTS: El Aldeano, p115; Bodegas La Ardosa, p115; La Giralda, p115; Rincón de Mondeñedo, p115; Taberna 2, p115; Clamores, p129, p195; Tiber, p131.

MUSEUMS & EXHIBITION SPACES: Museo Sorolla, p171.

RESTAURANTS: Balear, p103; La Playa, p105.

SHOPPING: *bookshops* Booksellers, p137; *children* Adams, p137; *fashion* Agatha Ruiz de la Prada, p139; *gifts* Sargadelos, p147; *out-of-hours shopping* Bob's, p135; *sports goods* Deportes Chamberí, p148.

Tetuán & the North

ACCOMMODATION: Hotel Cuzco, p19; Hotel Eurobuilding, p19; Apartamentos Plaza Basilica, p25.

CAFES, BARS, TAPAS & NIGHTSPOTS: Oliveri, p123; BageLüs, p128; Space of Sound, p130; Al Andalus, p184; Mr Sellers, p191; Segundo Jazz, p195.

MUSEUMS & EXHIBITION SPACES: Sala del Canal de Isabel II, p159; Museo de la Ciudad, p173; Museo de

Ciencias Naturales, p173; Museo Geominero, p174.

RESTAURANTS: Cabo Mayor, p97; El Olivo, p98; Las Cumbres, p100; Las Batuecas, p105; El Gourmet del Palacio, p105; De la Riva, p105; O'Pazo, p105.

SHOPPING: *bookshops* La Tienda Verde, p243; *children* El Corte Inglés, p138; *markets* Chamartín, p147; Maravillas, p147; *shopping malls* Centro Comercial Madrid-2, La Vaguada, p136.

SIGHTSEEING: Nuevos Ministerios, p43; Estadio Santiago Bernabéu, p44; Urbanización AZCA, p44; Museo de Escultura al Aire Libre, p45.

The Southern Suburbs

CAFES, BARS, TAPAS & NIGHTSPOTS: Costa Polvoranca, p131; Lagosur, p132; Universal Sur, p195.

MUSEUMS & EXHIBITION SPACES: Museo del Aire, p174; Museo Angel Nieto, p174; Museo Nacional Ferroviario, p174.

SIGHTSEEING: Puente de Toledo, p43; Planetario, p215.

The Northern Suburbs

ACCOMMODATION: Camping Osuna, p25.

CAFES, BARS, TAPAS & NIGHTSPOTS: Kilómetro Doce, p131.

MUSEUMS & EXHIBITION SPACES: Acciona – Museo Interactivo de la Ciencia, p214.

SHOPPING: *shopping malls* Centro Comercial Arturo Soria Plaza, p136.

SIGHTSEEING: Capricho de la Alameda de Osuna, p44; Parque Juan Carlos I, p45.

Index

Madrid Guide
Advertiser's Index
Please refer to the relevant sections for addresses/telephone numbers

Time Out Maps

TimeOut | City Guides

The essential guides to the world's most exciting cities

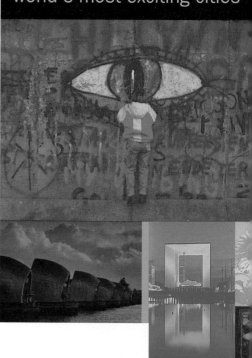

Amsterdam Berlin London Madrid New York Paris Prague Rome

Available from February 1996

Budapest & San Francisco